OECD ECONOMIC OUTLOOK

76

DECEMBER 2004

OECD

ORGANISATION FOR ECONOMIC CO-OPERATION AND DEVELOPMENT

The Organisation for Economic Co-operation and Development (OECD)

was set up under a Convention, signed in Paris on 14 December 1960, which provides that the OECD shall promote policies designed:

- *To achieve the highest sustainable economic growth and employment and a rising standard of living in member countries while maintaining financial stability, and thus to contribute to the development of the world economy.*
- *To contribute to sound economic expansion in member as well as non-member countries in the process of economic development.*
- *To contribute to the expansion of world trade on a multilateral, non-discriminatory basis in accordance with international obligations.*

The original member countries of the OECD are: Austria, Belgium, Canada, Denmark, France, Germany, Greece, Iceland, Ireland, Italy, Luxembourg, the Netherlands, Norway, Portugal, Spain, Sweden, Switzerland, Turkey, the United Kingdom and the United States. The following countries became members subsequently through accession at the dates indicated hereafter: Japan (28 April 1964), Finland (28 January 1969), Australia (7 June 1971), New Zealand (29 May 1973), Mexico (18 May 1994), the Czech Republic (21 December 1995), Hungary (7 May 1996), Poland (22 November 1996), Korea (12 December 1996) and Slovak Republic (14th December 2000). The Commission of the European Communities takes part in the work of the OECD (Article 13 of the OECD Convention).

The French version of the *OECD Economic Outlook* is entitled *Perspectives économiques de l'OCDE.*

The *OECD Economic Outlook* is published on the responsibility of the Secretary-General of the OECD. The assessments given of countries' prospects do not necessarily correspond to those of the national authorities concerned. The OECD is the source of statistical material contained in tables and figures, except where other sources are explicitly cited.

TABLE OF CONTENTS

Boxes

Tables

Figures

Conventional signs

$	US dollar	.	Decimal point
¥	Japanese yen	I, II	Calendar half-years
£	Pound sterling	Q1, Q4	Calendar quarters
€	Euro	Billion	Thousand million
mbd	Million barrels per day	Trillion	Thousand billion
. .	Data not available	s.a.a.r.	Seasonally adjusted at annual rates
0	Nil or negligible	n.s.a.	Not seasonally adjusted
–	Irrelevant		

Summary of projections

	2004	2005	2006	2004	2005				2006		Fourth quarter		
				Q4	Q1	Q2	Q3	Q4	Q1	Q2	2004	2005	2006
							Per cent						
Real GDP growth													
United States	4.4	3.3	3.6	3.5	3.1	3.2	3.4	3.5	3.6	3.7	3.8	3.3	3.6
Japan	4.0	2.1	2.3	2.8	2.3	2.5	2.5	2.5	2.2	2.1	2.6	2.4	2.1
Euro area	1.8	1.9	2.5	1.7	1.9	2.1	2.5	2.5	2.5	2.5	1.9	2.3	2.5
Total OECD	3.6	2.9	3.1	2.9	2.9	3.0	3.2	3.2	3.1	3.1	3.1	3.1	3.1
Inflation													
United States	2.0	1.8	1.7	1.5	2.1	1.7	1.7	1.7	1.9	1.6	2.2	1.8	1.7
Japan	-2.3	-1.3	-0.3	-1.6	-1.5	-1.2	-1.0	-0.6	0.0	0.1	-1.6	-1.1	0.2
Euro area	1.9	1.7	1.8	1.4	1.9	1.9	1.7	1.7	1.8	1.8	1.7	1.8	1.8
Total OECD	1.8	1.7	1.7	1.4	1.8	1.5	1.7	1.8	1.8	1.6	1.9	1.7	1.7
Unemployment rate													
United States	5.5	5.3	5.1	5.4	5.4	5.4	5.3	5.3	5.2	5.2	5.4	5.3	5.0
Japan	4.8	4.5	4.2	4.8	4.7	4.6	4.5	4.4	4.3	4.2	4.8	4.4	4.0
Euro area	8.8	8.6	8.3	8.8	8.7	8.7	8.6	8.6	8.4	8.4	8.8	8.6	8.2
Total OECD	6.6	6.5	6.3	6.5	6.5	6.5	6.5	6.4	6.4	6.3	6.5	6.4	6.2
World trade growth	9.5	9.0	9.5	8.4	8.7	8.9	9.3	9.4	9.7	9.7	9.4	9.1	9.6
Current account balance													
United States	-5.7	-6.2	-6.4										
Japan	3.5	3.5	3.7										
Euro area	0.7	0.6	0.9										
Total OECD	-1.2	-1.4	-1.3										
Cyclically-adjusted fiscal balance													
United States	-4.2	-4.0	-4.2										
Japan	-6.3	-6.4	-6.6										
Euro area	-2.1	-1.8	-1.8										
Total OECD	-3.4	-3.3	-3.3										
Short-term interest rate													
United States	1.5	2.8	3.8	2.1	2.5	2.7	3.0	3.2	3.5	3.7	2.1	3.2	4.2
Japan	0.0	0.0	0.4	0.0	0.0	0.0	0.0	0.0	0.2	0.2	0.0	0.0	0.5
Euro area	2.1	2.1	2.7	2.1	2.1	2.1	2.1	2.1	2.3	2.5	2.1	2.1	3.0

Note: Real GDP growth, inflation (measured by the increase in the GDP deflator) and world trade growth (the arithmetic average of world merchandise import and export volumes) are seasonally and working-day-adjusted annual rates. The "fourth quarter" columns are expressed in year-on-year growth rates where appropriate and in levels otherwise. The unemployment rate is in per cent of the labour force while the current account balance is in per cent of GDP. The cyclically-adjusted fiscal balance is in per cent of potential GDP. Interest rates are for the United States: 3-month eurodollar deposit; Japan: 3-month certificate of deposits; euro area: 3-month interbank rate.

Assumptions underlying the projections include:

- no change in actual and announced fiscal policies;
- unchanged exchange rates as from 5 November 2004; in particular 1$ = 105.70 yen and 0.771 euros;

The cut-off date for other information used in the compilation of the projections is 18 November 2004.

Source: OECD Economic Outlook 76 database.

EDITORIAL: REGAINING MOMENTUM DESPITE OIL TURBULENCE

Since the 2001 slowdown, the world economy has moved in fits and starts and economists as well as the general public are now longing for a smooth and sustained recovery, undisturbed by chronic geopolitical risks or abrupt gyrations in oil prices and financial markets.

Although economic fortunes have been contrasting over the past few quarters, with the United States forging ahead, East Asia slowing but from a rapid pace, and Continental Europe plodding along, households seem to have been lacking confidence OECD-wide. This pervasive sense of uncertainty has proved somewhat contagious since after a year of record growth in world trade, business confidence has fallen back to just above the historical average in the United States and Europe, dashing hopes that GDP would keep growing above trend over the next few months.

Compared to cautiously upbeat assessments that could be made even two months ago, this turnaround has been a source of disappointment. It has been prompted in large part by a surge in oil prices that has depressed real incomes as well as confidence in the OECD countries. There are nonetheless good reasons to believe that despite recent oil price turbulence, the world economy will regain momentum in a not-too-distant future. Supported by strong balance sheets and high profits, the recovery of business investment should continue in North America and start in earnest in Europe, while consumer spending will benefit from the recent retreat of oil prices to less onerous levels, in a context where job creation is progressively strengthening and monetary conditions remain very accommodative. All in all, there are still some good grounds to expect OECD economies to grow again above trend in the course of 2005 and 2006.

From a geographical perspective, the momentum of this recovery will benefit from continued Asian dynamism, in China, where activity accelerated in the third quarter, following a desirable slowdown during the first half of the year, and Japan, which staged a noticeable comeback based on a renewed export drive, broadening into a recovery of investment, employment and finally consumption, before marking a pause over the past few months. The strength of this recovery will also be enhanced by positive developments in North America. But it remains to be seen whether Continental Europe will play a strong supportive role through a marked upswing of final domestic demand.

On the latter issue, this *Outlook* takes a reasoned but positive bet on Europe. It tables on a significant pick-up of final domestic demand in the euro area in 2005-06, while world trade and OECD output would not accelerate over the period. Continental Europe, and more specifically, Germany, would thus have to find enough of an autonomous momentum to achieve a higher relative growth path. For this scenario to materialise, a modicum of stability in oil prices and exchange rates is required, which would allow a traditionally weakly resilient euro area to start catching up with the fast growing economies of the OECD.

A strong appreciation of the euro, in a context of worsening external imbalances, or further rises in oil prices, may thus bear disproportionately on Continental Europe, where growth is still over-reliant on exports and high oil prices do not find their counterpart in high output growth and energy demand.

However, Europe might not be at such a disadvantage, compared with the rest of the OECD, in coping with higher oil prices. Should an additional oil shock hit, the OECD countries, including euro area members, would be less vulnerable than in the past. First, dependence on oil, expressed as a share of GDP, has been halved since the 1970s, leading to a much lower income burden than in the past for households and businesses alike. Also, and more importantly, inflation expectations are now low and well anchored, so that rising oil prices have only impacted so far on headline inflation while nominal wages and core inflation barely budged. It would thus be very surprising if OECD countries were to suffer again, as they did in the 1970s, from a nightmarish situation where wages and prices are spiralling out of control and central banks are forced to switch into severe "tightening mode".

Nonetheless, when it comes to the impact of oil price shifts, economic agents' perceptions and economists' received wisdom do not seem to coincide. While estimates derived from econometric models signal a rather modest impact on output and inflation, oil price fluctuations take centre stage in the public debate and strongly influence economic confidence.

In this context, it was natural to devote a special chapter of this *Outlook* to the economics of oil. To better understand why oil matters, it is necessary to go beyond the short run. In a world where people are more "forward-looking", uncertainty about future oil prospects may have more of an impact on the current economic situation than, say, month-to-month changes in market prices.

Here OECD expertise suggests that recent oil prices were certainly well above long-term equilibrium levels, even allowing for strong market power on the part of the OPEC cartel. There are still important resources available on the supply side, especially among OPEC producers to match increasing demand for oil, and the efficiency of existing facilities could be significantly improved. Furthermore, alternative sources of energy may already become profitable at current prices.

This does not mean, however, that oil prices will quickly fall back to the low levels which prevailed three or four years ago. First, the fall may not be rapid in a context where strong geopolitical uncertainty and high price volatility inhibit investment in new oil facilities. Second, looking past the current situation, oil prices will retreat somewhat but are likely to remain higher than during the 1990s.

In this world of durably more expensive oil, demand emanating from dynamic emerging economies will play a strong role in shaping future prices. The importance of emerging economies stems not only from their increasing contribution to world growth but also and more importantly from the fact that for a given increase in activity their demand for oil is far larger than the OECD average. Indeed, future oil prices will crucially depend on further progress in energy conservation in emerging economies as well as the United States.

Prudent management of non-renewable natural resources is not the only issue that matters for the long-run sustainability of OECD societies. Putting public finances in order is also of vital importance for the well-being of future generations. In line with previous editorials, it bears repeating that, given existing budgetary plans, most of the largest OECD countries will see no substantial progress in bringing down structural deficits. This is regrettable in a context where pension and health care reforms are generating painful debate, and thus progressing with difficulty.

It might be hoped, of course, that prudent private agents would react to public profligacy by stepping up their own saving efforts and there certainly is evidence pointing in this direction. This is indeed the message delivered by the special chapter devoted in this *Economic Outlook* to the long-term impact of fiscal policies. But, as a general rule, private saving does not fully offset public dissaving and this precautionary reaction may be contingent on national and historical circumstances. It is, for instance, hardly discernible in the case of the United States.

At the end of the day, the role of fiscal policy is not to add to the financial pressures arising from ageing populations. It is rather to relieve them, and thus take advantage of the ongoing recovery to finally implement gradual but far-reaching retrenchment.

25 November 2004

Jean-Philippe Cotis
Chief Economist

I. GENERAL ASSESSMENT OF THE MACROECONOMIC SITUATION

Overview: an expansion facing headwinds

High oil prices have slowed but not derailed the global expansion

The global expansion has slowed as the effects of the sharp increases in oil prices have set in. The deceleration has been particularly marked in Japan and, outside the OECD, in China. It has been less pronounced but still tangible in the United States. In Europe, higher energy prices and weak confidence in some countries are reining in a recovery that had strengthened beyond expectations early in the year. In most OECD countries, headline inflation has been pushed up, but core inflation and wage demands have remained subdued – a tribute to the credibility built up by central banks since the oil shocks of the 1970s. Provided oil prices do not rise further, the global expansion should regain momentum in the course of 2005, following a period of milder growth, and much of the residual economic slack should be worked off by late 2006 (Table I.1). If as assumed second-round effects are contained, headline inflation should ease back. Unemployment should resume its decline once the bulk of the oil shock is absorbed, but would on average remain above its structural level.

Uncertainties and tensions have increased

Over the near term, the risks surrounding this projection are dominated by oil price uncertainty. While there is some evidence that oil prices have overshot, they could stay high or even rise. If so, their detrimental impact on activity, inflation

Table I.1. **The expansion continues**

OECD area, unless noted otherwise

	Average 1992-2001	2002	2003	2004	2005	2006	2004 q4	2005 q4	2006 q4
	Per cent								
Real GDP growth[a]	2.7	1.6	2.2	3.6	2.9	3.1	3.1	3.1	3.1
United States	3.4	1.9	3.0	4.4	3.3	3.6	3.8	3.3	3.6
Japan	1.2	-0.3	2.5	4.0	2.1	2.3	2.6	2.4	2.1
Euro area	2.0	0.9	0.6	1.8	1.9	2.5	1.9	2.3	2.5
Output gap[b]	-0.8	-1.4	-1.7	-0.8	-0.6	-0.2			
Unemployment rate[c]	6.8	6.7	6.9	6.6	6.5	6.3	6.5	6.4	6.2
Inflation[d]	3.9	2.6	2.0	1.8	1.7	1.7	1.9	1.7	1.7
Fiscal balance[e]	-2.5	-3.2	-3.7	-3.5	-3.2	-3.2			

a) Year-on-year increase; last three columns show the increase over a year earlier.
b) Per cent of potential GDP.
c) Per cent of labour force.
d) GDP deflator. Year-on-year increase; last three columns show the increase over a year earlier.
e) Per cent of GDP.
Source: OECD Economic Outlook 76 database.

and unemployment might exceed what is suggested by standard model-based simulations. Fiscal and external imbalances continue to be sources of potential tension. They need not lead to any disruptions in the near term but could push up long-term interest rates and will in any event require adjustments if they are to unwind benignly over the longer run. One specific risk relates to the possibility of a large fall in house prices, and hence lower consumption, where they are too richly valued, though the fact that housing prices have started to weaken in some countries can be seen as a natural counterpart to the resilience of the housing market as monetary policy eased in response to the downturn. On the bright side, however, and provided oil prices evolve favourably, strengthened business balance sheets and profits make it possible that corporate fixed investment would exceed expectations, following several lean years.

Monetary stimulus can be withdrawn gradually…

The impulse to growth from monetary stimulus is fading as policies in most OECD countries start reverting to a more neutral stance. The first-round price increases stemming from the oil shock did not call for interest rate hikes and indeed central banks have not invoked them to tighten their policy stance. However, over the next two years, shrinking economic slack and exceptionally cheap money will require a progressive withdrawal of central bank stimulus, albeit conditional on how swiftly the oil shock's adverse impact on activity is overcome. Accordingly, the US and UK monetary authorities, as well as those in several smaller economies, have already started to raise rates. Their counterparts in the euro area and Japan – who for the moment still have reasons to wait and see – are expected to follow suit with a substantial lag.

… but fiscal consolidation should not be put off

On the fiscal side, as noted above, the urgency to act is more general: in many OECD countries, deficits are large and persistent, whilst debt ratios are rising. With the pressures exerted by ageing populations either starting to be felt or approaching rapidly, the consolidation of public finances ought to be stepped up.

Higher oil prices exert a drag on the global expansion

Oil prices have risen substantially…

Crude oil prices have risen rapidly, from around $32 for Brent at the time of the previous *OECD Economic Outlook* to $50 in mid-October, although they eased back to around $42 in mid-November.[1] Measured in constant prices, the increase has been more limited than the oil shocks of the 1970s (Figure I.1). Moreover, OECD countries' dependence on oil, measured by the quantity of oil used per unit of real GDP, has almost halved since the 1970s, so the real income and terms-of-trade effects for most of them are smaller. At the same time, the easing of long-term interest rates indicates that inflation expectations are more firmly anchored than in the past, as the oil shock occurs in a context of low and stable core inflation. Nevertheless, higher oil prices and the associated uncertainty are contributing to the deceleration of activity observed in United States, Japan and a number of other countries in the course of 2004, and are impeding the euro area recovery (Figure I.2).

1. Over the past year, the price of West Texas Intermediate crude on average exceeded the price of Brent by some $2½. During the past two years, oil prices have consistently exceeded the upper bound of the $22-28 band set as a target by the Organisation of Petroleum Exporting Countries (OPEC) in 2000.

Figure I.1. **Oil prices have soared**

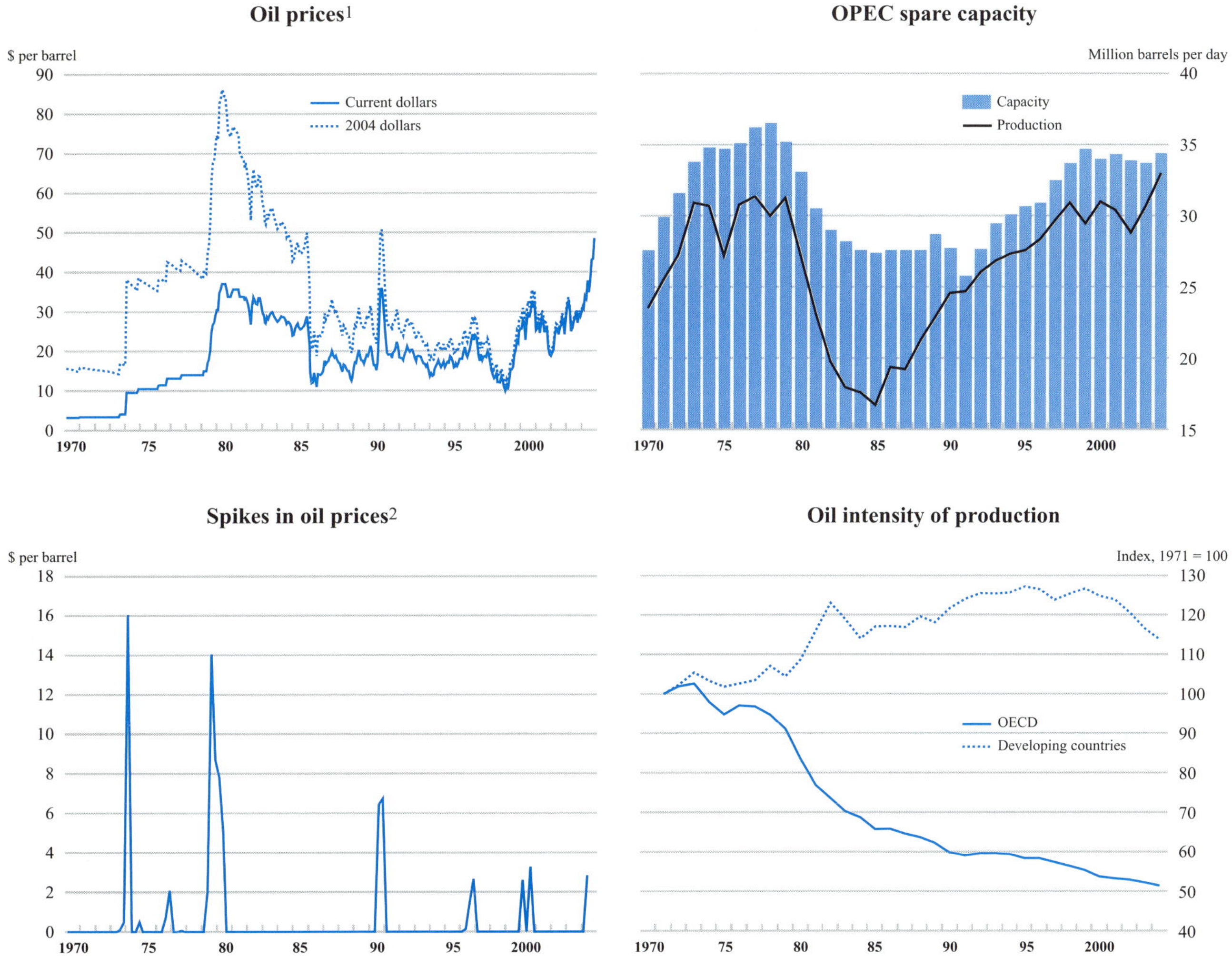

1. Brent crude oil from May 1987 on. Earlier data are OECD estimates for crude oil of the same quality as Brent. In real terms, deflated by US consumer price index.
2. Difference between latest quarterly average spot price of Brent crude and highest quarterly average over the preceding three years, in real terms.
Source: OECD Economic Outlook 76 database and International Energy Agency.

Figure I.2. **The expansion has lost some momentum**

Real GDP, percentage change from previous period

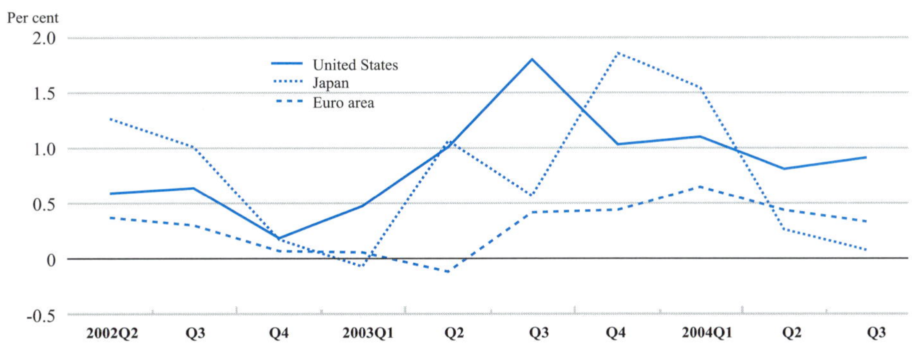

Source: OECD Economic Outlook 76 database.

... with growth slowing somewhat in the United States...

In the United States, growth fell back to around its potential rate in the second quarter but regained momentum in the third. Fixed business investment was buoyant, but household consumption of non-durables was dented by soaring energy prices. The US recovery has eventually become more job-intensive (Figure I.3), but it remains historically lean in that respect. The unemployment rate, which by October 2004 stood at 5½ per cent of the labour force, is lower than at the same stage of previous cycles but still distinctly above its structural level and the participation rate has declined.

... and held back in the euro area...

In the euro area, growth surprised on the upside in the first quarter of 2004 but subsequently slowed, whilst unused capacity remains distinctly higher than across the Atlantic. Growth has been pulled mainly by external demand. Household

Figure I.3. **Labour markets perform unevenly**

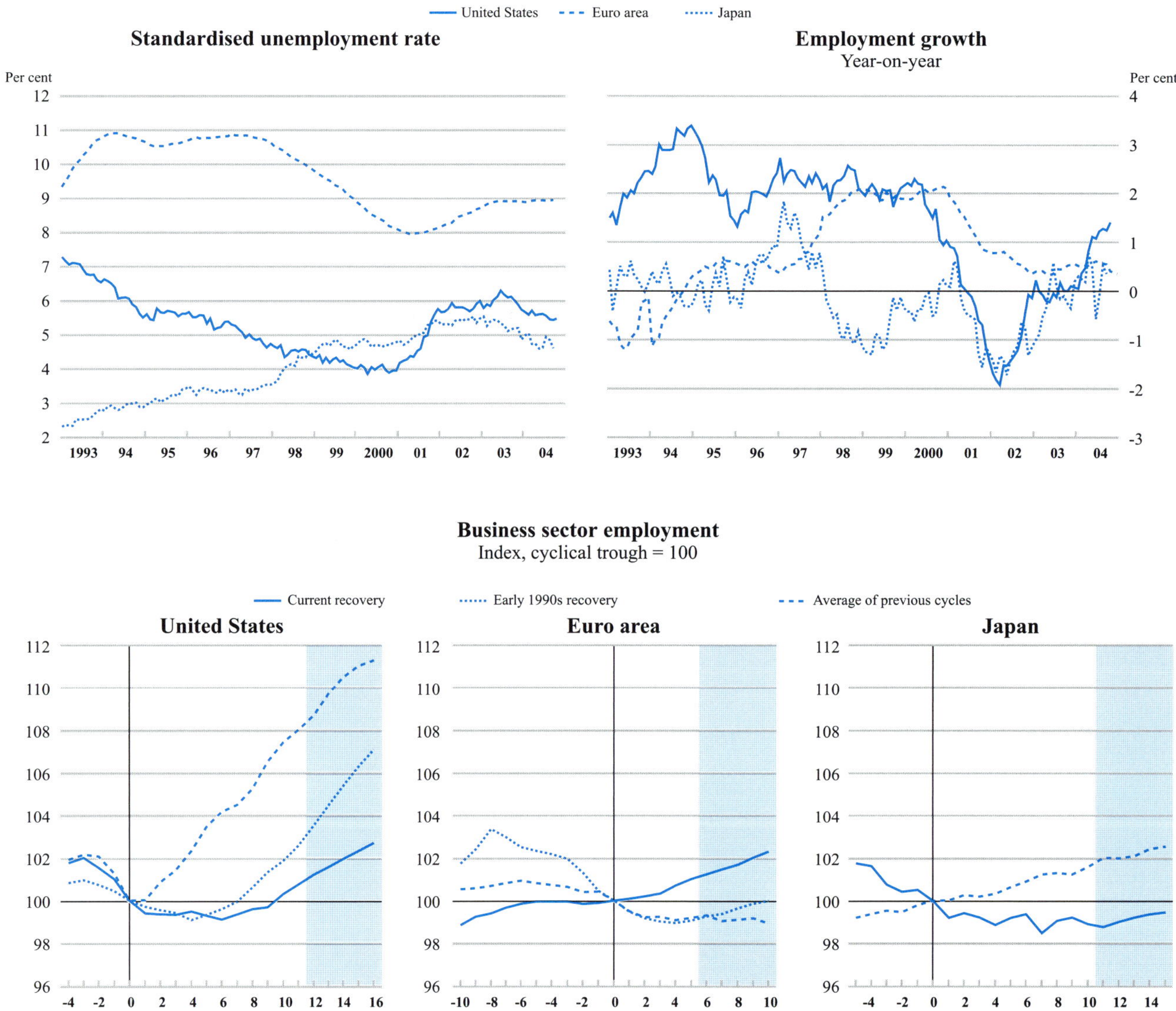

Note: A cyclical trough is usually defined as a trough in the level of real GDP. For the United States the NBER chronology is used. The average of previous cycles includes major cycles from the 1960s to the 1980s (late 1970s to 1990s for Japan). The last cyclical trough is 2001Q4 for the United States, 2002Q1 for Japan and 2003Q2 for the euro area. The shaded area shows the projection period for the current cycle.

Source: OECD Economic Outlook 76 database.

consumption has remained lacklustre, reflecting mediocre employment and income growth, with unemployment having drifted up to close to 9 per cent of the labour force. Thus far, business investment has also failed to take off in earnest, despite a brief spurt in late 2003. In sum, the recovery has not yet become self-sustained.

... where, however, developments diverge

Within the euro area, some countries have tended to show more domestic strength than others, and some have benefited more than others from the buoyancy of foreign demand.[2] Among the larger countries, France and Spain have stood out in 2004 with final domestic demand contributing most to real GDP growth, whereas in Germany it has been very weak (Figure I.4). There, the recovery was almost exclusively pulled by exports. In Italy, the persistent deterioration in export performance has been a drag on the recovery. In the smaller euro area countries – although not in the Netherlands – domestic demand growth has been fairly robust.

In many other countries, growth has firmed up

Elsewhere in Europe and North America, growth has remained vigorous or picked up despite higher energy prices. This is the case in many smaller OECD economies, including in the new members of the European Union and in Turkey. OECD (Mexico and Norway) and non-OECD net energy exporters have received a boost from rising oil and gas prices. In the United Kingdom, however, activity has recently slowed, albeit following a remarkably resilient performance in the course of the global downturn.

In Japan, activity has decelerated markedly,...

In Japan, growth has weakened, following a couple of very strong quarters around the turn of the year.[3] The deceleration was led by business fixed investment, which in the third quarter was held back by an unusually high number of typhoons. Exports also lost some of their momentum, partly reflecting a slowdown in Chinese demand. Consumption, however, held up well, supported by incipient job creation, even if most of the new hires have thus far been in the form of non-permanent contracts, which has contributed to putting downward pressure on average worker compensation and thereby on aggregate household income.

Figure I.4. **Recovery in Germany and Italy has relied more on exports**

Contributions to growth of real total aggregate demand in 2004, percentage points

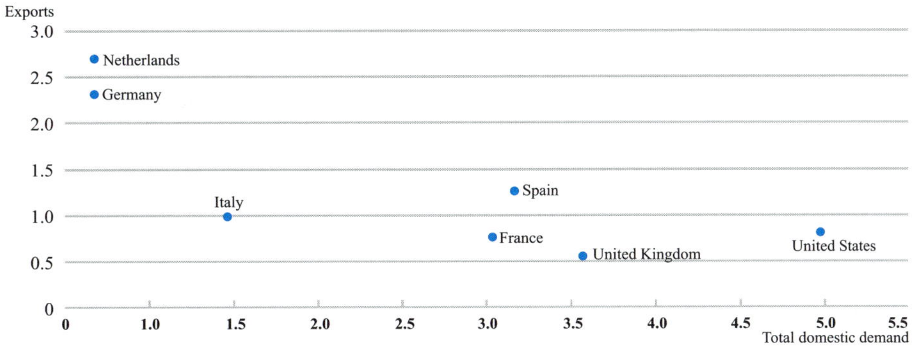

Note: Contributions are calculated in terms of total aggregate demand defined as total domestic demand plus exports.
Source: OECD Economic Outlook 76 database.

2. For further analysis of the underlying factors, see Hoeller, P., C. Giorno and C. de la Maisonneuve, "One money, one cycle? Making monetary union a smoother ride", *OECD Economics Department Working Papers*, No. 401, 2004.
3. The Japanese national accounts are to undergo a comprehensive revision in December 2004, with a switch to chain-linking. This will substantially affect the profile of real GDP (and of the GDP deflator) going back all the way to 1994.

... paralleling a slowdown in China

Meanwhile, in non-OECD Asia activity slowed markedly. In China, following monetary and administrative measures to address overheating symptoms and reflecting the adverse impact of higher oil prices,[4] credit growth slowed and investment decelerated. Growth in Latin America gathered speed, however, on the back of maintained robust export performance and helped by terms-of-trade gains.

Core inflation remains subdued in the United States...

So far, core inflation has generally remained rather subdued, even though energy price increases have pushed up headline inflation (Figure I.5). This decoupling reflects both the extent of cyclical slack and continuing competition and productivity gains in internationally open sectors. The very limited size of the second-round effects observed to date is also a result of greater central bank credibility than in past cycles. In the United States, the buffer provided by a combination of healthy profit margins and spare capacity has helped limit the pass-through of rising energy and commodity prices into core consumer prices. Wage inflation has been moderate, although non-wage labour costs – especially on account of health benefits – have continued to outpace wages. Inflation expectations appear much better anchored than in previous episodes.

... and did not increase significantly in the euro area

In the euro area, inflation expectations have remained low and well-anchored, with various core inflation measures hovering somewhat below the 2 per cent mark. This benign response to the inflationary consequences of an oil shock stands in stark contrast with the rigidity and persistence displayed in the past by euro area inflation, which failed to decline as the output gap was widening.[5] A number of temporary factors contributed to this persistence in the recent past, including higher-than-expected energy and unprocessed food prices as well as rises in indirect taxes (in particular on tobacco) and administered prices (notably in the health care sector). The stubbornness of inflation was also due to the fact that while labour costs decelerated, so did labour productivity, so that notwithstanding far greater slack, unit labour costs rose more rapidly than in the United States. However, more fundamentally, the extent of slack present in the euro area economy was probably more limited than estimated earlier, implying less downward pressure on inflation. Indeed, the recent re-estimation of output gaps for OECD countries – which is reflected in this *OECD Economic Outlook* – suggests that this may well be the case for most euro area members.

In Japan, deflation persists

In Japan, deflation lingers on, even according to the headline consumer price measure, which directly incorporates the effect of higher energy prices, but most strikingly as measured by the GDP deflator (which, however, suffers from downward bias).[6] As a result, nominal GDP has expanded by no more than 1½ per cent over the first ten quarters of the recovery and still stands about 4 per cent below its 1997 peak. In addition, land prices have continued to decline rapidly for the thirteenth year in a row. For inflation and inflation expectations to rise and durably stay positive, a sustained positive output gap may be required.[7]

4. The first-round impact of higher oil prices on Chinese real GDP growth is estimated to be far more severe than in past oil shock episodes and possibly as much as five times larger than in the OECD area as a whole, reflecting in particular China's much greater, and increasing, dependence on oil.
5. As a result, euro area inflation was typically underpredicted by Phillips-curve equations, as documented in *OECD Economic Outlook* No. 74, Table I.3.
6. The bias is partly due to the fact that the GDP deflator is a Paasche index based on fixed 1995 weights, in a context where the relative price of information technology goods falls rapidly, see Koga, M., "Why is the rate of decline in the GDP deflator so large?", Bank of Japan, *Economic Commentary*, No. 2003-02, 2003.
7. The flatness of the Phillips curve in Japan is documented by Mourougane, A. and H. Ibaragi, "Is there a change in the trade-off between output and inflation at low or stable inflation rates? Some evidence in the case of Japan", *OECD Economics Department Working Papers*, No. 379, 2004.

Figure I.5. **Core inflation generally remains subdued**

Year-on-year percentage change

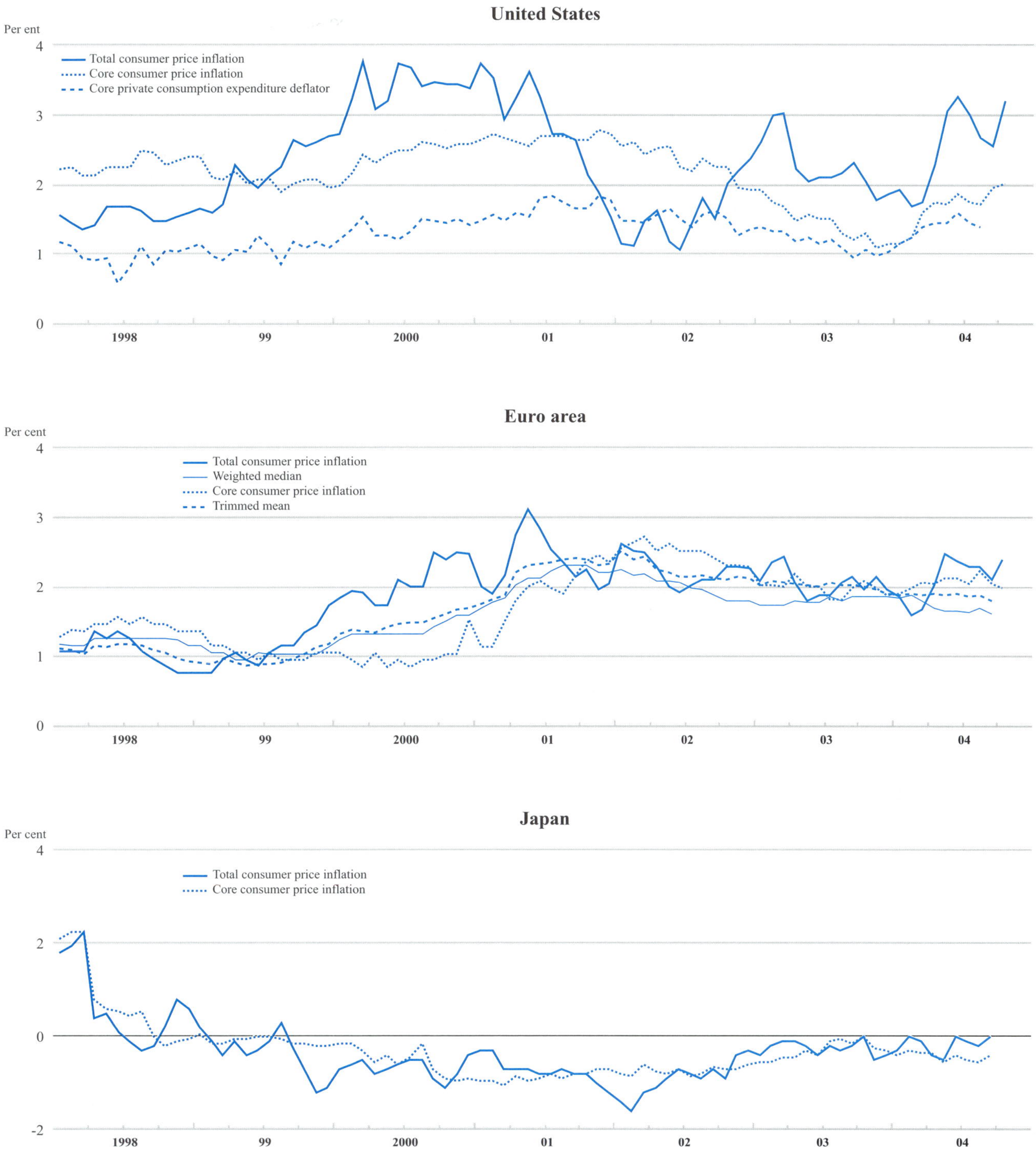

Note: Harmonised index of consumer prices (HICP) for the euro area. Core is measured as total less food and energy. The weighted median and the trimmed mean inflation are both calculated from the monthly price changes of individual HICP components (at the 3-digit level). The weighted median price increase for each month is the value such that HICP components for a cumulative weight of 50 per cent have a higher or equal monthly increase and the remaining 50 per cent a lower or equal one. The bilateral 15 per cent trimmed mean is calculated by first taking the items that in each month have the highest and the lowest price changes, for a total 15 per cent (in weight terms) on each side, and assigning them a zero weight; then, after re-normalising the weights to sum to 1, a weighted mean is calculated from the remaining items. In each case, year-on-year inflation rates are obtained by compounding the aggregate monthly rates.

Source: OECD, *Main Economic Indicators,* US Bureau of Economic Analysis and Statistical Office of the European Communities (Eurostat).

Prospects to 2006: overcoming the oil shock

The expansion should regain momentum in 2005

The adverse effects of the oil price shock are currently working their way through. However, provided oil prices do not rise above their assumed path, the expansion should firm during 2005, with the OECD-wide output gap closing towards late 2006. At the same time, headline inflation should slow somewhat in the course of the projection period, as the first-round impact of the shock fades and on the presumption that second-round effects remain limited. Unemployment will stay relatively high and international imbalances are set to worsen.

Some of the near-term indicators suggest weakening momentum

Confidence indicators…

Partly reflecting the oil price shock and the related uncertainty, business confidence has softened in the United States since early 2004, albeit from high levels (Figure I.6). In the euro area at large and Japan, it has improved, although it does not much exceed long-run averages. Moreover, in the case of the euro area, more favourable perceptions of current conditions are accompanied by some scaling down of expectations regarding future prospects. Consumers are generally less upbeat than firms although their confidence slightly exceeds long-run averages in Japan. In the euro area, confidence has slowly strengthened but remains sub-par, especially in Germany, where household sentiment has barely improved in recent quarters.

… order books…

Order books remain above average in the United States, despite a significant decline since April, led by weakening export orders. In contrast, strengthening export order books have underpinned a continued improvement in euro area orders in recent quarters, and these are now also above average.

… and indices of the high-tech cycle…

Growth in the high-tech sector seems to be peaking, at least as gauged by the semi-conductor billings for manufacturers headquartered in North America or by the so-called Tech-pulse index (Figure I.7). This is a factor underlying the deceleration

Figure I.6. **Confidence is fragile**

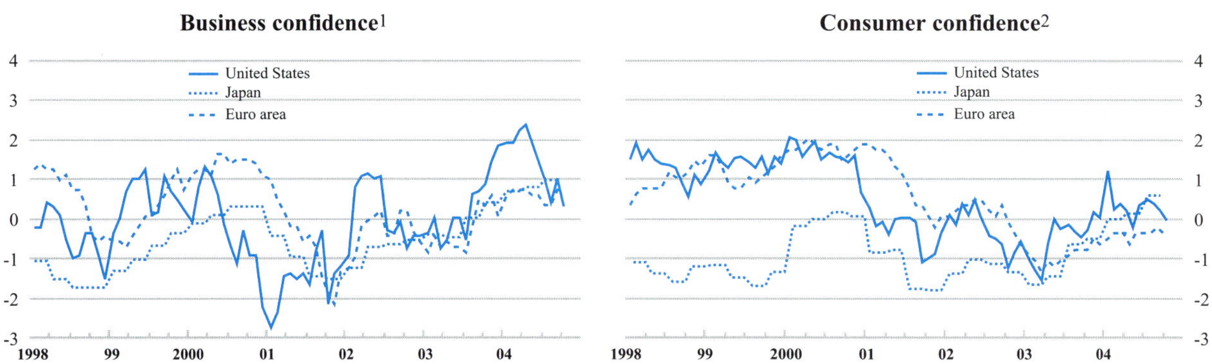

Note: All series have been normalised at the average for the period starting in 1985 and are presented in units of standard deviation. Monthly data, seasonally adjusted except Japan (quarterly, s.a.).

1. Business surveys for manufacturing: current production tendency for the United States, and future production tendency for Japan and the euro area.
2. Consumer confidence: composite indicators.

Source: OECD, *Main Economic Indicators*.

Figure I.7. **High-tech sector activity is decelerating**

12-month growth rate, in current dollar prices

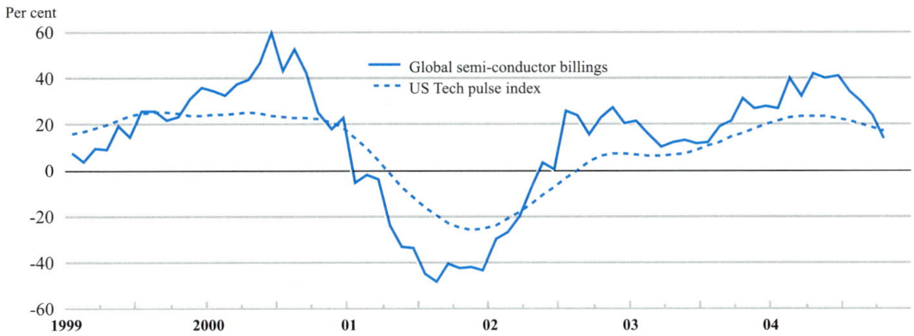

Source: Federal Reserve Bank of New York and the Semiconductor Industry Association.

of trade in Asia. It is also visible in the slowdown of Finland's information-technology exports. Insofar as the fortunes of the high tech sector constitute a leading indicator of the overall cycle,[8] this would be consistent with only limited closing of the output gap over the next few quarters.

... point to continuing growth in the near term

The OECD's indicator-based models, which incorporate most of the information contained in the above leading indicators as well as that embodied in a number of other high-frequency data, suggest that over the near term, the recovery should remain at or revert to a pace close to potential in the larger OECD economies (Table I.2).

Table I.2. **Near-term estimates point to continued growth**

Real GDP growth, per cent, quarter-on-quarter [a]

	Outcomes			Estimates[b]	
	2004 Q1	2004 Q2	2004 Q3	2004Q4	2005Q1
United States	1.1	0.8	0.9	0.9 (± 0.4)	0.8 (± 0.6)
Japan	1.6	0.3	0.1	0.7 (± 0.5)	0.6 (± 0.7)
Euro area	0.7	0.5	0.3	0.5 (± 0.3)	0.6 (± 0.4)
Germany	0.4	0.4	0.1	0.3 (± 0.5)	0.4 (± 0.6)
France	0.7	0.6	0.1	0.8 (± 0.4)	0.6 (± 0.5)
Italy	0.5	0.4	0.4	0.5 (± 0.4)	0.5 (± 0.4)
United Kingdom	0.7	0.9	0.4	0.6 (± 0.3)	0.8 (± 0.3)
6 largest OECD economies	1.0	0.6	0.5	0.7 (± 0.3)	0.7 (± 0.4)

a) Based on GDP releases and high-frequency indicators published by 19 November 2004. Seasonally and in some cases also working-day adjusted. Aggregation for the six largest OECD economies uses 2000 purchasing-power-parity weights.
b) These estimates are indicative of near-term GDP developments but do not necessarily coincide with the OECD projections. The one-standard-error range associated with the estimates is indicated in parentheses. Typically, OECD projections lie within that range.
Source : OECD Economic Outlook 76 database and OECD estimates.

8. Evidence supporting this hypothesis for the US economy is provided by Hobijn, B., K. Stiroh and A. Antoniades, "Taking the pulse of the tech sector: a coincident index of high-tech activity", Federal Reserve Bank of New York, *Current Issues in Economics and Finance*, Vol. 9, No. 10, 2003.

Growth and inflation differentials will narrow

Policy stimulus is set to fade

The forces behind the expansion are shifting. Overall, the macroeconomic policy stance, while still very accommodative, is becoming less so. Limited fiscal stimulus is being injected in 2004, and some tightening is in the pipeline for 2005 (Box I.1). Over the projection period, the monetary stance is set for some normalisation – the more so where output gaps are closing. Financial market forces partly work in the same direction, with equity prices having moved sideways or even weakened since the beginning of 2004. On the other hand, long-term benchmark interest

Box I.1. Policy and other assumptions underlying the central projections[1]

Fiscal policy assumptions are based as closely as possible on legislated tax and spending provisions (current policies or "current services"). Where policy changes have been announced but not legislated, they are incorporated if it is deemed clear that they will be implemented in a shape close to that announced. For the present projections, the implications are as follows:

- For the United States, the projection incorporates the defence appropriations for fiscal year (FY) 2005 enacted in August 2004 and anticipates a further $30 billion budget request in FY 2005 for military operations and reconstruction in Iraq and Afghanistan; thereafter funding requirements for these operations are assumed to decline. The projection also embodies the extension of the personal income tax provisions originally scheduled to expire at the end of 2004 and of the temporary indexation of the alternative minimum tax, as well as the American Jobs Creation Act passed in October 2004.
- For Japan, the projection takes into account the 2004 pension reform, which increases contributions by individuals and employers in every year from FY 2004 to FY 2017, as well as the recent broadening of the direct and indirect tax bases. No supplementary budgets are assumed to be implemented over the projection period.
- In the European Union, the projection for Germany takes into account the cuts in income taxes, subsidies and tax expenditures scheduled to take effect in 2005. For France, it is assumed that public employment and health care outlays are held in check. For Italy, it is assumed that the caps on public spending announced in the 2005 draft budget will be broadly adhered to in 2005-06. For the United Kingdom, the projection rests on the premise that the government's nominal expenditure plans are broadly realised, but that the elasticity of revenue will be somewhat weaker than budgeted.

Policy-controlled interest rates are set in line with the stated objectives of the relevant monetary authorities with respect to inflation and activity:

- In the United States, the federal funds target rate, which since mid-2004 has been raised in 25 basis point steps from 1 to 2 per cent, is assumed to increase gradually towards its neutral level (see Box I.4), and to reach 4 per cent towards the end of the projection period.
- In the euro area, the main refinancing rate, which has remained unchanged at 2 per cent since it was cut by ½ percentage point in June 2003, is assumed to start rising in early 2006, moving back to 3 per cent by the end of the projection period, against the background of persistent economic slack. Policy rates have already been raised by 125 basis points in the United Kingdom over the past year, and a further 100 basis point increase is built into the projection.
- In Japan, short-term interest rates are assumed to remain close to zero through the end of 2005 and to inch up in 2006, to ½ per cent by end-year, as consumer price deflation ends.

The projections assume unchanged exchange rates from those prevailing on 5 November 2004, at one US dollar equals ¥ 105.7 and € 0.771. For Turkey, the exchange rate is assumed to depreciate in line with the projected inflation differential *vis-à-vis* the United States.

As a working hypothesis, the price of Brent crude is assumed to decline linearly from $47 per barrel in late 2004 to $44 at the end of 2006. This is in line with the assumption underpinning the OECD's medium-run baseline scenario that the price of oil will gradually revert towards its long-term equilibrium level, as risk premia and other temporary factors abate. The posited decline is also broadly consistent with what recent far futures quotes have suggested.[2] Commodity price inflation is assumed to begin easing in the course of the projection period.

The cut-off date for information used in the projections is 18 November 2004.

1. Details of assumptions for individual countries are provided in Chapter II.
2. See Chapter IV, "Oil price developments: drivers, economic consequences and policy responses".

rates have eased significantly since the second quarter of 2004, while corporate bond spreads have remained quite narrow, although this partly denotes more subdued animal spirits. Recent exchange rate movements are helping growth and external adjustment in the United States but cutting into the contribution of the external sector to the expansion in the euro area and Canada.

US growth will continue to be led by business investment…

In the United States, the output gap is projected to close over the projection period, with job creation picking up but the employment rate remaining some 3 percentage points below the peak of the late 1990s. Firms have taken advantage of the prolonged spell of historically low interest rates to strengthen their balance sheets and enjoy ample profits.[9] This should allow for robust business spending, despite the expiration of temporary tax incentives favouring investment,[10] and make for increased hiring. Residential investment is projected to stabilise, as long-term interest rates rise. Household consumption will no longer be boosted by tax refunds and declining mortgage payments, and will therefore be more dependent on employment growth. Given that the household saving ratio is already low by historical standards, and on the premise that equity and housing wealth will not rise faster than income, consumption is unlikely to receive a fillip from a further decline in the propensity to save. The external sector is projected to become less of a drag on GDP growth as export volumes continue to expand rapidly and imports decelerate somewhat. Productivity gains, having recently declined markedly, should settle around rates closer to long-run averages and core inflation should remain muted.

… whilst in the euro area domestic demand will gradually strengthen

In the euro area as well, the expansion will be restrained by higher oil prices in the short run. But beyond that the recovery should broaden. For the area as a whole, final domestic demand should accelerate, with real GDP growth in Germany and the Netherlands gradually catching up. The conditions are favourable for business investment to pick up, given improved profitability, low real long-term interest rates and the restructuring of corporate balance sheets (although this has not proceeded as far as in the United States). Overall, the output gap is projected to narrow in 2005-06, but not fast enough for it to close. In the course of the upturn, hiring is projected to pick up only slowly, with the acceleration in output translating more into productivity gains and rising hours worked than job creation. Indeed, the resilience of employment during the slowdown – compared with both earlier slowdowns in the euro area and labour market behaviour elsewhere – may have reflected greater labour hoarding and reductions in hours worked per employee, as well as public subsidisation of certain types of jobs. Accordingly, the unemployment rate is not expected to decline substantially before 2006. For the euro area as a whole, wage moderation should be an enduring feature, but the structural competitiveness problems facing Italy in export markets are expected to persist (Figure I.8). Inflation should ease, as the energy price shock falls out and on the assumption that food price, indirect tax and other shocks witnessed in the recent past do not recur.

9. US non-financial corporations have brought down their debt-to-asset ratio to its lowest level in two decades, whilst lengthening the average maturity of their debt. Moreover, firms with floating-rate debt have used interest-rate derivatives to reduce their interest rate exposure, see Covitz, D. and S. Sharpe, "Which firms use interest rate derivatives to hedge? An analysis of debt structure and derivative positions at nonfinancial corporations", Federal Reserve Board, *mimeo*, September 2004.
10. The partial-expensing provision expiring at the end of 2004 provides an incentive to firms to invest in new capital goods. However, evidence relating to the quantitative effect of this tax measure is not clear-cut. If its impact is limited, its removal may not slow investment much.

Box I.2. Has there been a lasting shift in Japanese consumer behaviour?

The saving rate has been falling. The household saving rate in Japan, which has traditionally been among the highest in the OECD area,[1] declined sharply throughout the 1990s. By 2002 the net household saving rate stood at around 5 per cent of GDP and somewhat below the median for OECD countries.[2] The declining saving rate has supported consumption through the current expansion. While it is difficult to forecast how the saving rates will evolve, several forces influencing saving and consumption tend to suggest that the risk of a backup in household saving may be limited.

Population ageing is pushing the household saving rate down. The rapid ageing of the population is one important factor pushing down saving rates. Consistent with the life-cycle hypothesis, as the elderly enter retirement they begin to dissave. Due to the fall in the fertility rate, the cohort of workers entering the peak saving ages is too small to offset the decline in aggregate saving rate driven by the rising share of the elderly in the population. Expected demographic trends would suggest that there will be continued downward pressure on the household saving rate.[3]

Labour market developments are less negative. Full-time employment has fallen by over 5 million since the mid-1990s while part-time employment has risen by almost 4 million and now accounts for over 27 per cent of total employment. These changes on the labour market have allowed firms to reduce unit labour costs and, by driving down the labour share, have put downward pressure on disposable income growth, while also acting as an incentive to increase precautionary saving. This influence may now be abating. For full-time employees, labour market developments in 2004 point to a stabilisation, with posts expected to remain constant for the first time since the beginning of the decade. Insofar as this reduces employment uncertainty and increases consumer confidence, it will encourage households to reduce their precautionary savings.[4] The confidence of those currently on short-term contracts may also benefit from a continuing contraction in labour supply.

The corporate recovery is increasing retained profits and creates positive wealth effects. The decade of the 1990s was one of negative wealth effects from declining equity and land prices, which would, *ceteris paribus*, have acted to push the saving rate up. Now, as company profits rise, household consumption expenditure may be spurred by more positive – or less negative – wealth effects. However, equities have a small weight in Japanese household portfolios, which remain dominated by land and, to a lesser extent, housing wealth. So far, land and house prices have continued to decline, thereby offsetting the wealth effect stemming from households' financial assets.

Real interest rates are falling and deflation is abating. The impact on household saving of the deflation and high real long-term interest rates that prevailed during the 1990s is ambiguous. On the one hand, high real rates and the anticipation of lower prices would have created incentives to defer consumption. But the spending power of savers would have increased via positive "real balance" effects: the purchasing power of money balances rises with deflation, so that households can save less and still attain a given level of future consumption. These positive wealth effects would have offset the negative effects of falling equity and land prices. As deflation ends, the situation will reverse, to a degree dependent on how household portfolios adapt.

Fiscal consolidation would reduce upward pressure on private saving. Government debt as a share of GDP increased substantially over the 1990s and the anticipation of higher future taxes due to this trend would have acted, other things being equal, to push up the private saving rate. The social security system has recently experienced its first current deficits and there is, indeed, evidence of younger cohorts saving earlier and at higher rates than their predecessors, related to fears about income adequacy on retirement and scepticism over the financial sustainability of the public pension system.[5] However, if the government sticks to or accelerates its announced commitment to move gradually towards budget balance over the next decade, the perception of households' that the course of public finances is unsustainable may lessen, reducing the perceived need to save.[6]

1. For a retrospective review of factors advanced to explain the "high" Japanese saving rate, see Horioka, C., "Are the Japanese unique? An analysis of consumption and saving in Japan", Osaka University, *mimeo*, 2004.
2. More recent evidence from flow-of-funds statistics suggests that the household saving rate fell further until the end of 2003.
3. Kozu, T, Y. Sato, and M. Inada, "Demographic changes in Japan and their macroeconomic effects", *Bank of Japan Working Papers*, No. 04-E-6, 2004.
4. See Doi, T., "Precautionary saving and employment risk during the 1990s", *PRI Discussion Paper Series* No.04A-03, Ministry of Finance, 2004, who points to evidence that some households increased precautionary saving in response to uncertainty resulting from labour market adjustments.
5. According to survey evidence, 70 per cent of respondents were in favour of drastic reform to the national pension scheme (*http://globalag.igc.org/pension/world/2004/drastic.htm*). On the saving rates of different cohorts, see Ishikawa, T., "Has the saving behaviour of Japanese households changed? Distinguishing facts from fallacies", *NLI Research*, 2004.
6. See Chapter V, "Saving behaviour and the effectiveness of fiscal policy".

Box I.2. Has there been a lasting shift in Japanese consumer behaviour? *(cont.)*

In sum, the ongoing effects of population ageing will maintain downward pressure on household saving at a time labour market developments, wealth and fiscal consolidation effects are also beginning to move in a direction that reduces the risk of a backup in household saving. The end of deflation could in principle curb the incentives for households to save, but the net impact of lower real interest rates and lower real balance effects is uncertain.

A variety of forces influence household saving

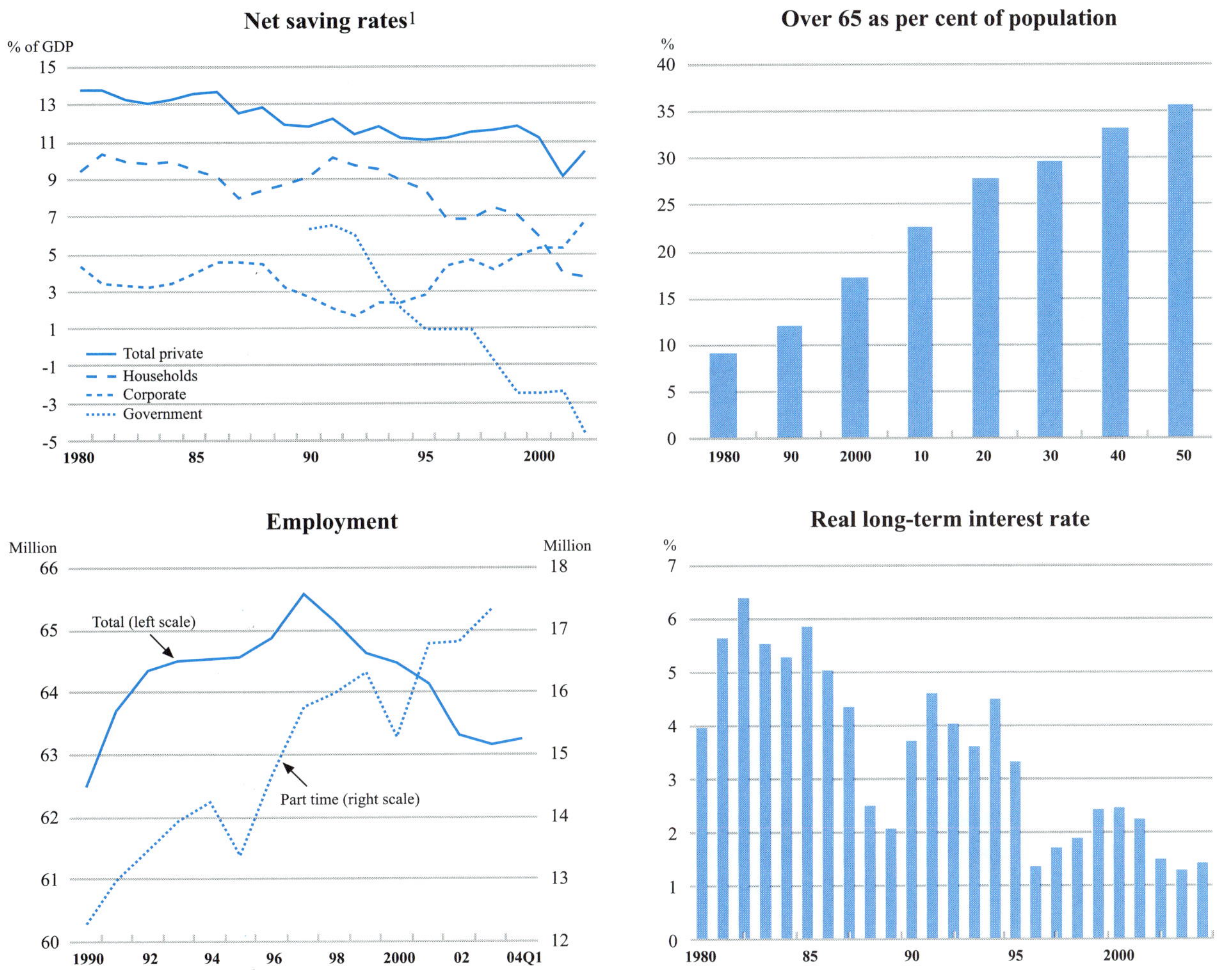

1. Net of consumption of fixed capital.

Source: OECD *Annual National Acounts*, 1970-2002; Statistics Bureau, Ministry of Internal Affairs and Communications, *Statistical Handbook of Japan*, 2004; *OECD Labour Force Statistics*, October 2004; OECD Economic Outlook 76 database.

Figure I.8. **Export performance is diverging among the larger euro area economies**

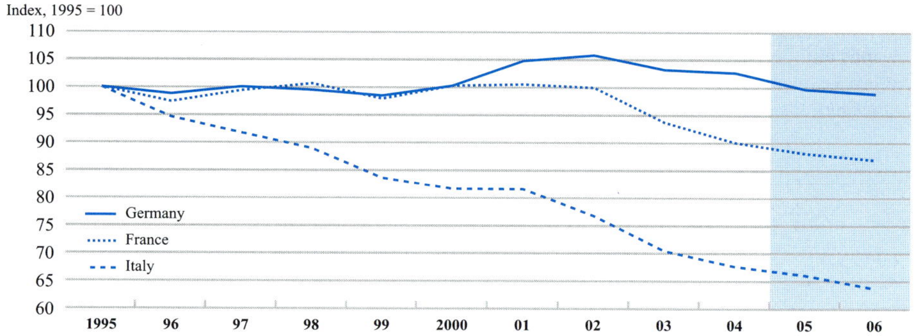

Note: Export performance is an index of exports relative to weighted import demand of trading partners. It is based on national accounts data for trade of goods and services.
Source: OECD Economic Outlook 76 database.

In Japan, the expansion is set to continue

In Japan, growth should settle at a rate somewhat above potential. As firms have restored profit margins, the expansion should be supported by business investment, whilst the role of exports should diminish. Indeed, foreign demand, notably from China, has slowed and, as noted, the high-tech cycle seems to have peaked. The household saving rate is projected to stabilise (Box I.2), but consumer spending will be sustained by employment creation and fading wage deflation. Consumer price inflation should turn marginally positive in the course of the projection period, as unemployment gradually declines towards its estimated structural rate.

Non-OECD countries should see sustained growth…

The impulse to global growth from the non-OECD area should continue to be significant. In China, the projection for the next two years remains one of sustained real GDP growth, even if most risks seem to be on the downside.[11] In Russia, growth is projected to moderate, in line with a slower expansion of the oil sector and notwithstanding considerable terms-of-trade gains. In Brazil, where exports have led the recovery so far, domestic demand is strengthening so that growth is becoming more broadly based.

… and world trade will continue to expand rapidly

Following a slowdown in the course of 2004 – especially in Dynamic Asia and China – world trade is projected to expand by around 9 per cent in 2005 and to maintain this pace in 2006 (Table I.3), which would be distinctly above the long-run average. With a lag of a few quarters, a significant portion of the extra oil revenues enjoyed by oil exporters should be spent on imports from OECD countries: Turkey should benefit most in terms of export market growth, with a 2½ percentage point gain, whilst Australia, France, Greece, Italy and the United Kingdom would all record a gain of over one percentage point. As discussed below, trade and current account imbalances are projected to persist or worsen.

11. See Chapter III, "Developments in selected non-member economies".

Table I.3. **World trade growth should be sustained**

	2003	2004	2005	2006
	Percentage change over previous period			
Goods and services trade volume				
World trade[a]	5.1	9.5	9.0	9.5
of which: OECD	3.0	8.4	7.7	8.1
NAFTA	2.5	9.6	8.3	8.0
OECD Asia-Pacific	8.7	13.6	9.0	9.9
OECD Europe	1.8	6.4	7.0	7.6
Non-OECD Asia	12.2	14.0	12.9	13.8
Other non-OECD	7.9	9.5	10.5	11.2
OECD exports	2.4	8.3	7.8	8.5
OECD imports	3.6	8.4	7.6	7.7
Trade prices[b]				
OECD exports	11.5	8.4	4.7	0.9
OECD imports	10.6	8.6	5.3	1.0
Non-OECD exports	6.1	10.0	6.6	2.1
Non-OECD imports	6.6	8.0	4.9	2.6
Current account balances	Per cent of GDP			
United States	-4.8	-5.7	-6.2	-6.4
Japan	3.1	3.5	3.5	3.7
Euro area	0.4	0.7	0.6	0.9
OECD	-1.1	-1.2	-1.4	-1.3
	$ billion			
United States	-531	-669	-761	-825
Japan	135	164	168	184
Euro area	32	67	61	96
OECD	-338	-395	-483	-482
Non-OECD	250	308	361	316
World	-88	-87	-122	-166

Note: Regional aggregates include intra-regional trade.
a) Growth rates of the arithmetic average of import volumes and export volumes.
b) Average unit values in dollars.
Source: OECD Economic Outlook 76 database.

In the near term, risks are dominated by oil price uncertainty

Oil price uncertainty casts a shadow over the projections

The single most prominent uncertainty surrounding the above projections pertains to the oil price. Others include those on the geopolitical front and concerning the emergence of protectionist tensions, which would complicate Doha Round negotiations. Some of the downside risks highlighted in earlier editions of the *OECD Economic Outlook* have become more acute, notably as house prices have begun to stall. Where house price rises have been related to speculation, the adjustments may still have further to go than posited in the projection. Other risks have not crystallised, but nor have they disappeared, in particular those related to a possible backup in long-term interest rates or to a hard landing of the Chinese economy. On the upside, there is a possibility that the balance sheet purge associated with the latest global slowdown has set the stage for a more forceful investment performance than projected.

Oil prices may surprise either way

The oil price could fall back significantly, consistent with the fact that spot oil prices appear to have been boosted by a number of short-run factors (Box I.3), but it could also turn out to be higher and more persistent than expected. The low

Box I.3. Have oil prices overshot?

Will higher oil prices persist? Oil price volatility has increased gradually over the past decade and in this context substantial spikes to the oil price are not particularly unusual. Over the same period, the persistence of oil price shocks has diminished, though *ex ante* it is difficult to determine whether an oil price shock is permanent or transitory. In this context, with oil prices in 2004 reaching levels that have not been seen since the oil price shocks in the 1970s and early 1980s, the question arises whether oil prices will remain this high or revert towards their longer-term trend.

Short-term futures reflect temporary risk premia and speculation. With respect to the short-term futures price, the oil market has been in almost continuous strong backwardation since 1999, the spot price being significantly higher than the six-month futures price. This is an unusually long period and suggests that current uncertainties are adding a large risk premium to the spot price. During 2004, fears over the security of supply have surfaced with regularity. Indeed, risk premia have risen with fears of supply disruptions arising from the sabotage of Iraq's oil export infrastructure, attacks on oil workers in Saudi Arabia, the uncertainty over the future of the Russian oil company Yukos (which accounts for almost 2 per cent of world production), and threats of supply disruptions in Nigeria and Venezuela. The impact of speculation on oil prices is harder to quantify, but may also account for some of the volatility.

Industry stocks have been low. With strong demand and supply tight, even small perturbations to the oil market can induce substantial price movements. In such a volatile market, industry participants have higher desired levels of inventories, and require a larger spot price increase, relative to the forward price, to release stocks to the market. This is the case at the moment. Oil industry stocks, having trended downwards over the 1990s, have been low in relation to demand and have reduced the flexibility of supply, but the demand for stocks has built up over the year, putting pressure on the oil price.[1]

Demand for oil has been stronger than anticipated. As uncertainty dissipates, the oil price will fall. However, some influences appear likely to be long-lasting. Over the first half of 2004, strong demand contributed to the strengthening of oil prices. The composition of oil demand in early 2004 reflected stronger than anticipated output growth in dynamic Asian economies, and particularly China. The dynamic Asian economies and China accounted for almost one half of the additional demand, with outturns somewhat higher than industry projections made at the beginning of the year. Pressures from the demand side are likely to continue, though if high prices persist the higher long-term price elasticity of demand will lead to lower demand in the future.

Low investment means production capacity is tight. Spare capacity in OPEC countries – principally in Saudi Arabia – has been reduced over the course of the year. As a result, it is estimated that spare capacity in OPEC countries has narrowed to around 1 million barrels per day.[2] At the same time, there has been little spare capacity available outside the OPEC producers to respond to surges in demand. More recently, in the context of expectations of rising oil prices, investment in exploration and development in non-OPEC countries has picked up relative to activity in the 1990s. But lead times in bringing additional supply to market mean that such investment does little to alleviate pressure in the short run, implying a comparatively inelastic short-run elasticity of supply. In short, without the increased development of OPEC producers' substantial reserves, supply is likely to remain tight for some time to come.

1. During the course of 2004 stocks attained levels that are similar for the same time of year in comparison with the recent past. But strong backwardation persisted over this period and created incentives to run down stocks. In this light, a "normal" level of stocks is likely to be higher than comparison with the recent past would suggest. Other temporary influences on stock levels include the impact of the hurricane season, which by reducing offshore production and delaying shipments to the United States reduced stock levels.
2. As recently as 2002, OPEC spare capacity exceeded 6 million barrels per day.

short-term elasticity of demand implies that supply disruptions reducing daily output by no more than one or two million barrels could lead to substantially higher oil prices.[12] The actual size of a possible further adverse oil price shock would, however, depend on its source, oil reserves being relatively concentrated geographically. Standard simulations using the OECD's Interlink model allow a rough quantification of the first-round demand-side effects of an oil price shock of the current magnitude, and the impact of policy responses, based on average behaviour during past episodes. Under the assumption that nominal interest rates are unaffected, they suggest that a

12. For further details, including simulations of the macroeconomic impact of oil price shocks, see Chapter IV, "Oil price developments: drivers, economic consequences and policy responses".

Box I.3. Have oil prices overshot? *(cont.)*

Far futures prices have risen. While price projections for a volatile market are very uncertain, and near-futures prices are poor predictors of the future spot price, several indicators point to expectations that as the influence of short-term factors abates, oil prices will be permanently higher. Far futures prices (six to seven years out) have risen, whereas, throughout the 1990s, prices for the longest available futures remained very stable at around $20 per barrel. Moreover, oil company analysts have raised their longer-term price expectations by around $5 per barrel since the beginning of the decade. Equity investors' valuations of oil company assets have also apparently risen, in line with expectations of higher oil prices.[3] Taken together, these factors suggest that, though prices will fall from current levels as the impact of short-term factors dissipates, some elements behind the recent rise will have a longer-lasting impact.[4] Most importantly, the longer-run elasticity of demand and supply for oil is higher than the short-run elasticity.

Crude oil spot and far futures prices

West Texas intermediate (WTI), current dollars, and three-month moving average

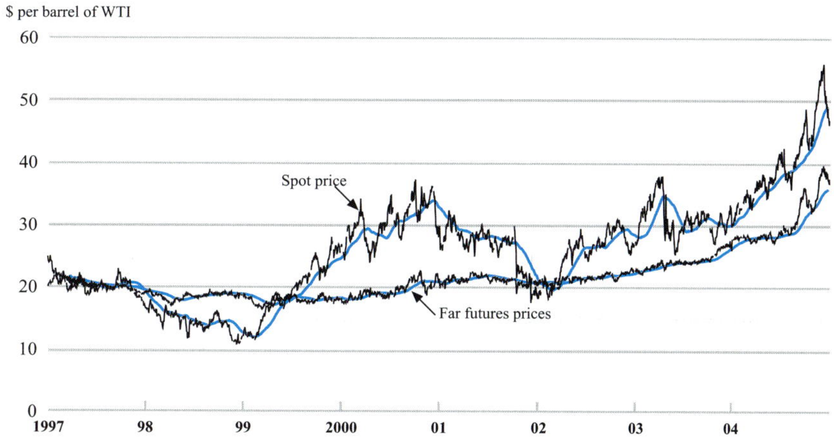

Source: Datastream.

3. See, for example, Randall & Dewey, *Global Acquisitions Review*, Third Quarter, 2004.
4. See Chapter IV, "Oil price developments: drivers, economic consequences and policy responses".

sustained $15 increase in oil prices – from the middle of the range targeted by OPEC in the past to $40 – subtracts some 0.2 percentage point from OECD-wide real GDP growth in the first full year. They also point to a concomitant rise in consumer price inflation of a slightly greater magnitude. Such simulations do not capture possible negative longer-run supply-side effects stemming from a lower return on capital, or the non-linearities which come into play in the event of a large price shock having an impact on confidence.[13]

13. In particular, ready reckoners tend to mask possible asymmetries, insofar as a $10 oil price increase may have stronger effects on output and inflation -- in absolute terms -- than a $10 decrease.

Figure I.9. **Investment has been picking up slowly in some countries**

Business sector investment, index, cyclical trough = 100

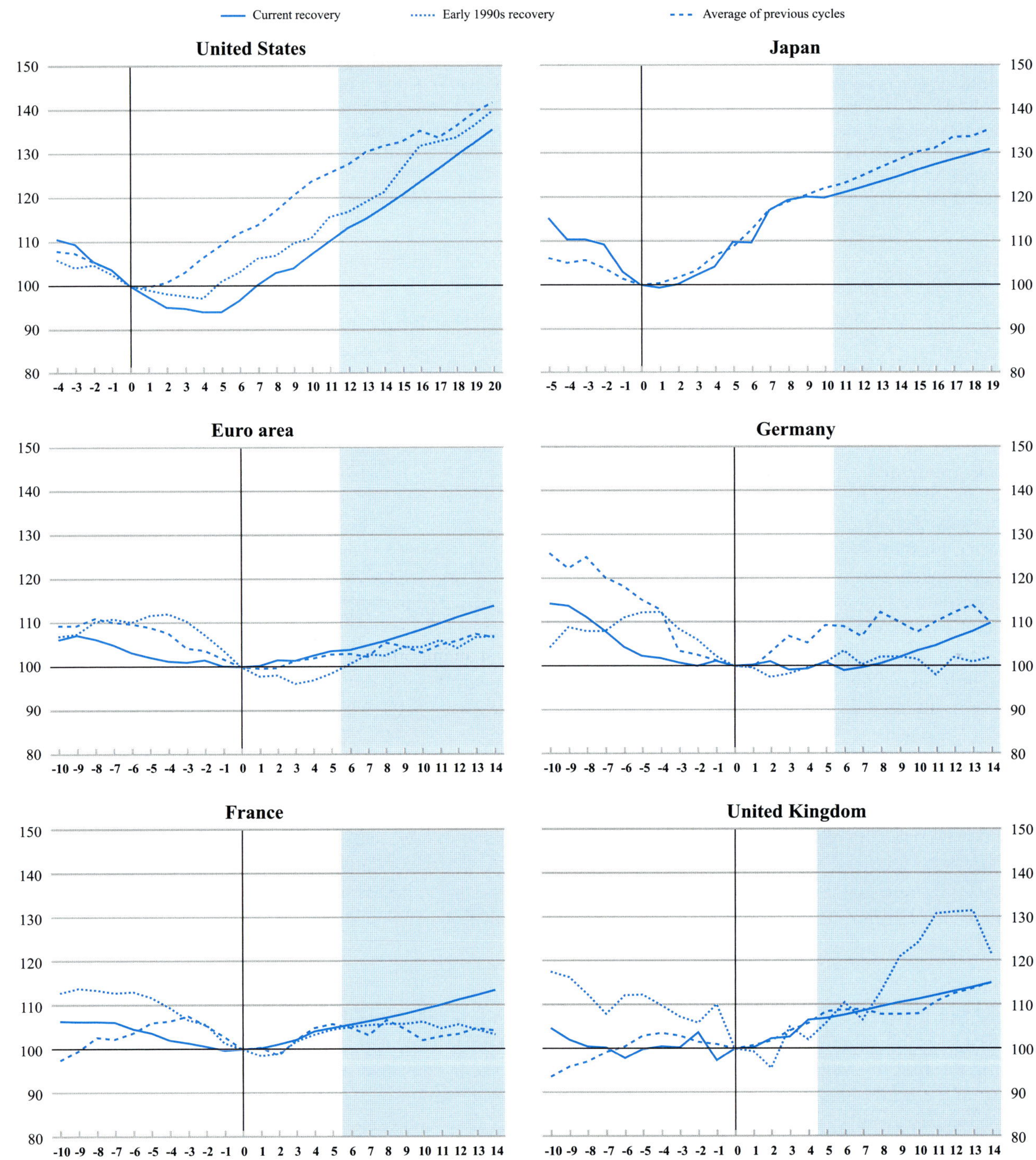

Note: A cyclical through is usually defined as a trough in the level of real GDP. For the United States the NBER chronology is used. For the United Kingdom, the last cyclical trough reflects a minimum in the output gap. The average of previous cycles includes major cycles from the 1960s to the 1980s (late 1970s to 1990s for Japan). The last cyclical trough is 2001Q4 for the United States, 2002Q1 for Japan and 2003Q2 for the European countries. The shaded area shows the projection period for the current cycle.

Source: OECD Economic Outlook 76 database.

Investment could be stronger than expected…

So far, investment has performed differently from past cycles, but not uniformly so. In the United States and Germany, it has been slower to pick up than usual, unlike in Japan, the United Kingdom and other members of the euro area (Figure I.9). Provided oil prices evolve favourably, there is an upside risk that flush corporate balance sheets and profits in the United States and several other large OECD economies may translate into stronger investment and hiring than in the projection, not least in view of the very large slump in investment during this downturn but also considering possible increases in scrapping rates related to a larger proportion of high-tech equipment. The upside risk to investment would be all the more significant if long-term interest rates were to remain below their assumed path, or if equity prices were to bounce back.

… but long-term interest rates could back up more abruptly than foreseen

However, long-term benchmark interest rates are currently very low, possibly reflecting some flight to safety, which makes for a rather flat yield curve at this stage of the cycle. At the same time, spreads on corporate bonds are far below recent historical averages. Hence, there is a risk of a more abrupt rise in interest rates than foreseen in the projection.[14] This risk is aggravated by a backdrop of persistent, large fiscal imbalances, insofar as they may not have been fully priced in.

Rapid house price inflation may have ended in several countries

In recent years, many countries have seen house prices far outpace consumer prices (Figure I.10). The associated wealth gains have helped to support household spending, especially where institutional arrangements are conducive to housing equity withdrawal in one form or another.[15] In a number of cases – notably Australia, Ireland, New Zealand, Spain and the United Kingdom – real estate prices have reached very high levels compared with rents or incomes and house prices seem, in fact, to have peaked in several of these countries. To the extent that this is a response to moderate monetary tightening, it may be seen as the counterpart to the resilience generated by the housing market during the cyclical downturn. Yet, even if they may not decline in absolute terms, more stable house prices imply that an important driver of household spending is no longer operative, or much less potently so, creating a drag on growth, as evidenced in the Netherlands and, most recently, in the United Kingdom.[16] Concerns have mounted regarding the risk of an abrupt housing market slowdown, in a context where house price rises may have been driven by speculative behaviour, especially where households have taken on considerable debt.

A hard landing in China would mostly, but not only, affect Asia

The importance of the Chinese economy for OECD countries, particularly via trade channels, has rapidly increased over time. In 2002-03, growth in Chinese imports accounted for one-fifth of export market growth in the United States, one-quarter to one-third in Japan and Australia and two-fifths in Korea.[17] While this

14. For further discussion, see Sløk, T. and M. Kennedy, "Factors driving risk premia", *OECD Economics Department Working Papers*, No. 385, 2004.
15. See Catte, P., N. Girouard, R. Price and C. André, "The contribution of housing markets to cyclical resilience", *OECD Economic Studies*, No. 38, 2004/1. Only part of withdrawn equity, however, is consumed in the near term: *e.g.* households selling a property without purchasing another one and those who trade down are more likely to pay off debt or save the proceeds than to spend them (see Benito, A. and J. Power, "Housing equity and consumption: insights from the Survey of English Housing", *Bank of England Quarterly Bulletin*, Vol. 44, No. 3).
16. It has been estimated that housing equity withdrawal has contributed about 1 percentage point to Dutch real GDP growth both in 1999 and in 2000, but that as equity withdrawal subsequently halved, its contribution turned negative, subtracting ½ percentage point from real GDP growth both in 2001 and in 2002, and exerting a further drag in 2003 ("Financial behaviour of Dutch households", De Nederlandsche Bank, *Quarterly Bulletin*, September 2003). The potential negative contribution of a slowdown in house price inflation in the United Kingdom is quantified in the latest *OECD Economic Survey of the United Kingdom*, Paris, 2004.
17. The impact on the market growth facing producers in the major European economies was smaller, at around one-tenth, as they tend to trade less heavily with China, with Germany nonetheless relatively more exposed.

Figure I.10. **Real house prices may be peaking in some countries**

Nominal price deflated by the overall consumer price index

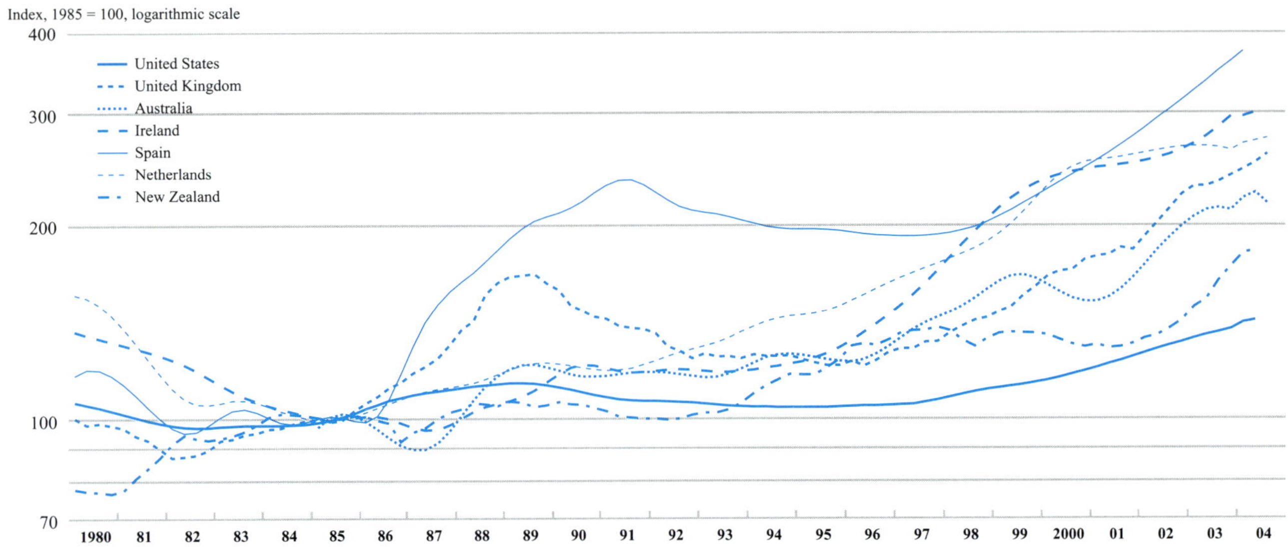

Source: Australian Commonwealth Bank Housing Industry Association; Bank of Spain; Irish Department of the Environment; UK Office of the Deputy Prime Minister; US Office of Federal Housing Enterprise Oversight; Reserve Bank of New Zealand; OECD, *Main Economic Indicators.*

proportion is declining somewhat, reflecting a pick-up in trade in other parts of the world, China's contribution to world trade growth is likely to remain well above its global export share. Thus, in the event of a hard landing in China – possibly precipitated by a more abrupt than foreseen end to over-investment or by higher oil prices (given China's greater dependence on oil) – the associated slowdown in imports would noticeably affect the export market growth of OECD economies. The direct impact would depend not only on the extent to which they trade with China, but also on the importance of external trade for the overall economy. More open economies may be more affected than others, even if they trade less heavily with China. For example, the drag on Canadian GDP of weaker growth in Chinese imports in 2004-05 would be approximately double that on US GDP, even though China accounts for a larger proportion of US exports. At the same time, an abrupt deceleration in China would reduce demand pressures in energy and raw materials markets, which would entail terms-of-trade gains for many OECD countries.

External imbalances will get larger

Sizeable external imbalances are projected to persist in a number of OECD countries, most notably in the United States, where the current account deficit is set to worsen from 4¾ per cent of GDP in 2003 to 6¼ per cent by 2006, with as its main domestic saving/investment counterpart persistent public dissaving (Figure I.11). In stock terms, non-residents are estimated to currently own some $10.5 trillion in US assets, implying that shifts in the US dollar exchange rate could have sizeable effects on balance sheets abroad. In net terms, US foreign liabilities, which at end-2003 amounted to 23.5 per cent of GDP, are projected to double by the end of the decade assuming unchanged policies and exchange rates.[18] Current account deficits of this

18. See Brook, A-M., F. Sédillot and P. Ollivaud, "Channels for narrowing the US current account deficit and implications for other economies", *Economics Department Working Papers*, No. 390, 2004.

Figure I.11. **The US current account has entered uncharted territory**

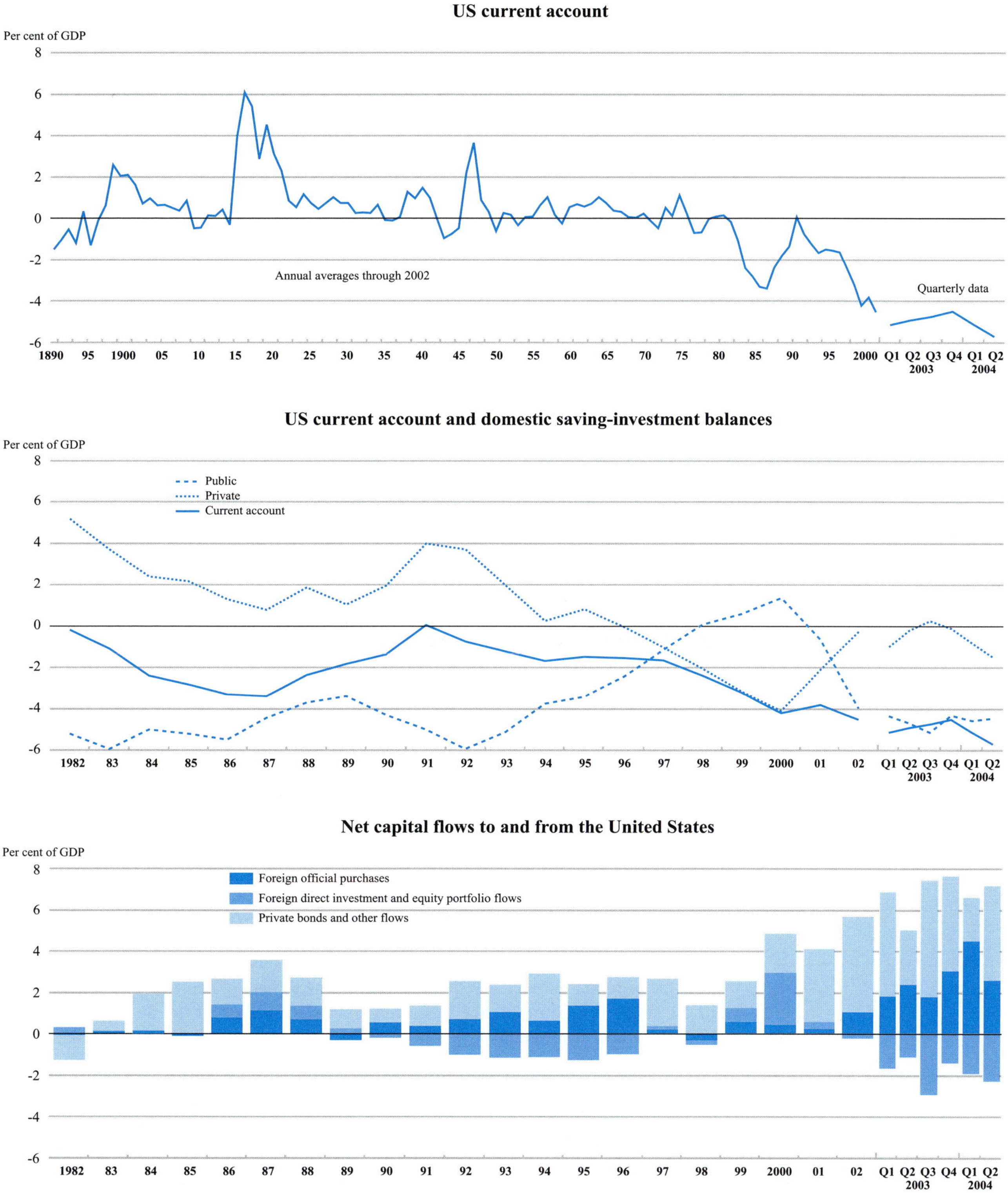

Source: US Bureau of Economic Analysis; Bureau of the Census: *Historical Statistics of the United States*, Washington DC, 1975.

order of magnitude can be sustained for some time. A case in point is Australia, where the current account gap has averaged 4½ per cent of GDP over the past two decades. However, Australia's economy is only one twentieth as large, so that the share of claims on Australia in foreign investors' portfolios is bound to remain modest. Moreover, the domestic counterpart has been private investment rather than government dissaving. While the US external deficit was mostly financed by direct and portfolio equity investment in 2000, it's funding has shifted towards purchases of bonds issued by the government or government-sponsored agencies, with a sizeable share of these purchases emanating from central banks, mostly in Asia. How long such a configuration can endure cannot be predicted, but debt accumulation at the current pace cannot continue indefinitely. When it ceases, this could well involve potentially disruptive downward pressure on the dollar and upward pressure on bond yields.

At what pace should macro stimulus be removed?

Macroeconomic policy stimulus should be withdrawn gradually

While, as noted, the impulse to growth from fiscal and monetary policies is diminishing, the macroeconomic policy stance remains quite loose in most OECD countries. As the recovery broadens, the degree of policy accommodation needs to be reduced gradually, not just to avoid procyclical stimuli but also, on the fiscal side, to address increasingly pressing medium-run challenges. However, while a movement towards a more neutral interest rate setting is projected, on current fiscal plans little consolidation is set to take place over the next two years (Figure I.12).

Monetary policy: returning to neutrality

Central banks have started to raise interest rates…

Most OECD central banks loosened the monetary policy stance following the onset of the latest cyclical slowdown. As a result, ample liquidity was created, and real interest rates were maintained at low levels for quite some time (Figure I.13). This helped support the recovery in the face of geopolitical and other headwinds. However, in order for the resulting liquidity not to fuel an unwelcome upsurge in inflation over the medium run, a gradual withdrawal of stimulus is called for, albeit with different timing and speed across regions, taking into account continuing headwinds, not least those stemming from oil prices. In general, the pace at which interest rates should be normalised need not be influenced by the first-round impact of energy price increases on headline inflation, insofar as longer-run inflation expectations have remained well-anchored around central banks' desired levels. The move toward a more neutral stance has already started in the United States, the United Kingdom and some smaller economies (*e.g.* Canada, New Zealand, Poland and Switzerland) where slack, if any, is limited and/or some inflationary pressures are surfacing. In contrast, the need to steer interest rates upwards is less urgent in the euro area and Japan.

… in the United States and the United Kingdom…

Since the previous *OECD Economic Outlook*, the US Federal Reserve has raised its key policy rate four times, in steps of 25 basis points each, to 2 per cent. Even so, both nominal and real interest rates remain very low in historical perspective. In a context where the output gap is shrinking and unit labour costs are picking up, further increases are warranted to bring rates closer to a neutral position

Figure I.12. **Monetary stimulus is being withdrawn at an uneven pace and fiscal adjustment is wanting**

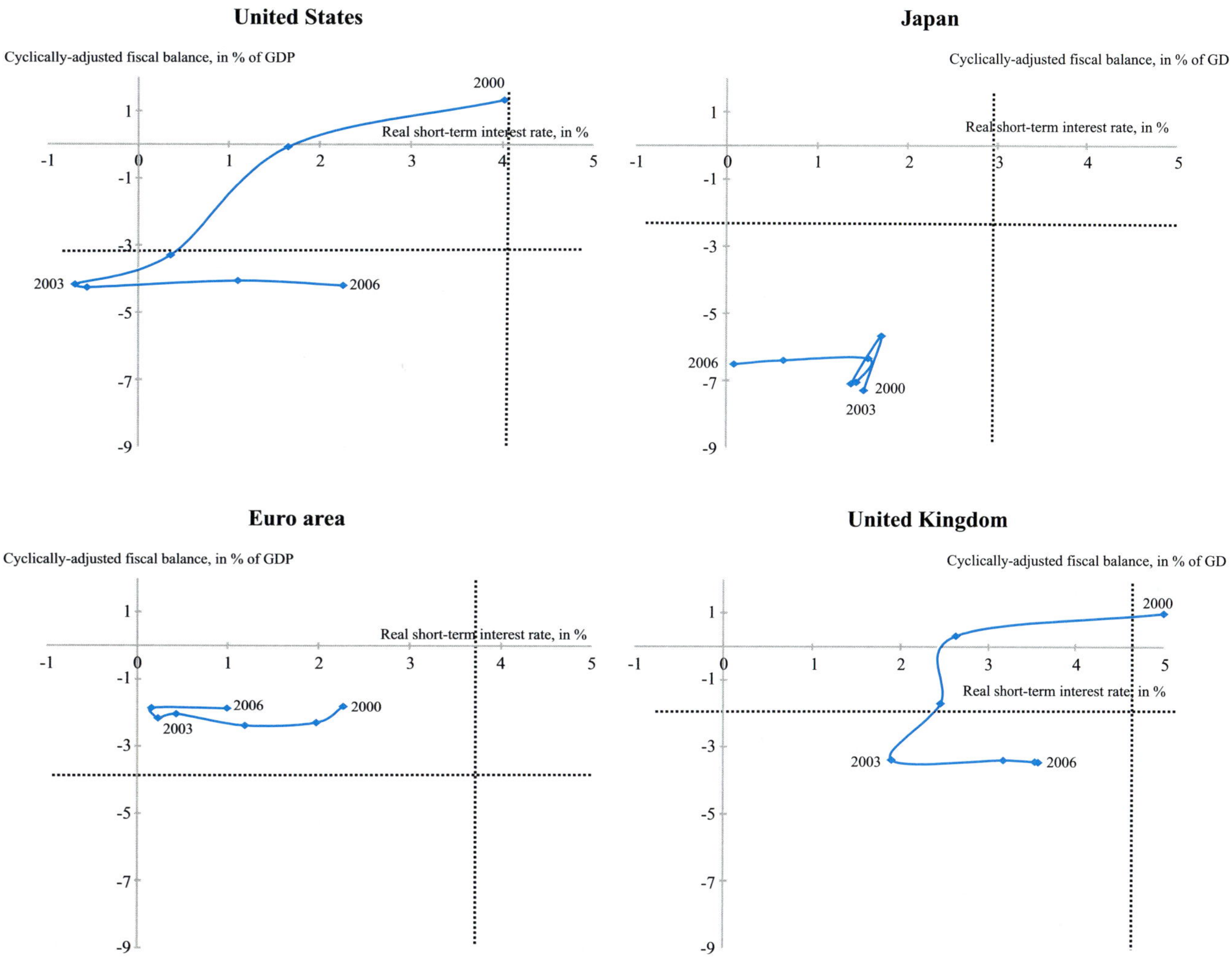

Note : In each panel, the dotted lines represent the 1980-2000 averages for short-term real interest rates and the cyclically-adjusted fiscal balance.
Source: OECD Economic Outlook 76 database.

(Box I.4). As corporate balance sheets have been consolidated substantially in recent years, and given comfortable profit levels, firms should be able to withstand the normalisation of interest rates with relatively little stress (see Appendix). Policy rates have also continued to be raised in small increments in the United Kingdom, but to a much higher level of 4¾ per cent, in a context where the output gap is turning positive. The tightening of the monetary stance, which started a year ago, has contributed to the slowing of house price inflation, but credit to households remains buoyant. In all likelihood, the policy rate is nearing neutrality and with consumer price inflation still surprisingly subdued, only limited further interest hikes seem warranted.

... but interest rates remain on hold in the euro area...

In contrast, the key policy rate has remained on hold in the euro area since June 2003, at 2 per cent. Over the same period, however, monetary conditions – as measured by the weighted average of real short-term interest rates and the real effective exchange rate – have tightened somewhat. For reasons discussed above, headline inflation has exceeded the Eurosystem's 2 per cent threshold almost unin-

Box I.4. Where does the "neutral" interest rate lie?

The "neutral" rate is an important conceptual benchmark. As policy-controlled interest rates start to move up from very low levels, the question arises of where their "equilibrium", "natural" or "neutral" level may lie. In its contemporary form, this concept refers to the interest rate consistent with output at potential and stable inflation. It plays a key role in some models of central banks' reaction function, such as the so-called Taylor rule, or when computing indicators of future inflationary pressures such as the real interest rate gap, understood as the difference between the observed and the neutral rate.[1] Below, the term "neutral rate" will be used as short-hand for the neutral short-term real interest rate.

Long-term averages and univariate estimates of the neutral rate can be misleading. Empirically, the neutral rate has been derived in a variety of ways. The simplest approaches are univariate and capture it as some long-run average of observed values (possibly with a greater weight on recent observations), or run a filter through the real interest rate data to obtain it as a relatively smooth trend – for example a Hodrick-Prescott (HP) filter. Such approaches do not incorporate the interactions between interest rates on the one hand and inflation and output on the other, and can therefore be misleading. They may make sense when applied over periods when actual output and inflation are fairly stable. But they do not adjust fast enough when output or inflation vary significantly. This was the case, for example, during the late 1960s and much of the 1970s, when inflation took off in many OECD countries, strongly suggesting that average real short-term interest rates were in fact well below neutral. Similarly, univariate filters mistake a large portion of the disinflationary policy action of the late 1970s and early 1980s for an upward shift in the neutral rate.

Kalman-filter estimates of the US neutral real short-term interest rate

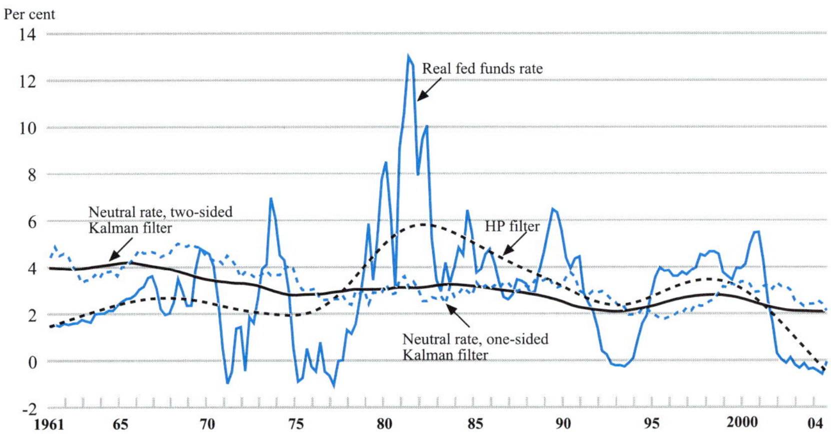

Source: Update of Laubach and Williams (2003), see footnote 2 in this box.

1. See Neiss, K. and E. Nelson, "The real interest rate gap as an inflation indicator", *Macroeconomic Dynamics*, Vol. 7, No. 2, 2003.

terruptedly since 2000, although not by much on average.[19] Yet, against the background of substantial residual slack in the economy, both headline and core inflation should ease over the next two years, suggesting that over the next few quarters, a wait-and-see posture may remain appropriate.

19. The Eurosystem focuses on medium-run inflation developments rather than on transient ups and downs, and since the launch of the euro annual headline inflation for the harmonised index of consumer prices has averaged exactly 2.0 per cent.

Box I.4. Where does the "neutral" interest rate lie? *(cont.)*

Multivariate estimates are more informative. Approaches designed to avoid this drawback therefore simultaneously take into account the interest rate, inflation and output. One such approach uses a technique called the Kalman filter to adjust the estimated neutral rate for deviations between predicted and actual GDP. For instance, if actual GDP exceeds predicted GDP, part of the unexpected strength in economic activity is attributed to a more stimulative monetary policy, and hence the estimate of the neutral rate is raised proportionately.[2] In the US case, the Kalman-filter methodology applied on four decades of data suggests that since the 1960s the neutral short-term interest rate has fluctuated between 2 and 5 per cent, and that in the third quarter of 2004 it stood at 2.1 per cent.

The neutral rate varies over time, across countries and across models. Studies on the euro area suggest that since the mid-1990s, the neutral rate has come down, to around 2¾ per cent by 2000 and to about 1½ to 2 per cent by the Spring of 2002.[3] For Canada, the neutral rate has been estimated at 1¼ to 2 per cent in late 2002.[4] For New Zealand, a comparison between 14 different models of the neutral rate shows that while in all cases it declined during the 1990s, the estimates as of early 2003 ranged from 3¼ to 4¼ per cent.[5] Lastly, Kalman-filter estimates for Poland put the neutral rate at around 4 per cent in 2003, down somewhat from its average level in earlier years, but clearly above euro area levels.[6]

Lack of precision makes it difficult to make the neutral rate operational. The above examples illustrate that considerable uncertainty surrounds any estimate of the neutral rate. For policy purposes, this drawback is worsened by the fact that future data can substantially alter the estimate of today's level of the neutral rate, as evidenced when comparing the estimate based on the full sample (two-sided filter), as above, with the one based on past data (one-sided filter), which makes use of observations only through the date at which the neutral rate is estimated.[7] For example, based on past data only, the neutral rate in the United States was estimated to exceed 3 per cent until mid-2002. When taking into account the subsequent moderate recovery, notwithstanding a real funds rate of around zero, the most recent neutral rate estimate is reduced to just above 2 per cent, and the neutral rate estimate for 2001-02 is revised to about the same level. An additional, though less severe, problem is that the end-period data entering the estimation are at times subject to substantial revisions. Like other unobservable macroeconomic variables, the neutral rate, while informative, should be used with caution in policy making.[8]

2. For a more rigorous exposition, see Laubach, T. and J. Williams, "Measuring the natural rate of interest", *Review of Economics and Statistics*, Vol. 85, No. 4, 2003. The real interest they use is an *ex ante* one, with inflation expectations proxied by a forecast of the four-quarter-ahead percentage change in the price index for personal consumption expenditures excluding food and energy, generated through a univariate autoregressive process.
3. See Giammarioli, N. and N. Valla, "The natural real rate of interest in the euro area", *ECB Working Paper*, No. 233, 2003, which is based on a stochastic dynamic general equilibrium model and ends in 2000, and Crespo-Cuaresma, J., E. Gnan and D. Ritzberger-Gruenwald, "Searching for the natural rate of interest: a euro-area perspective", *Empirica*, Vol. 31, No. 2-3, 2004, which is based on a multivariate unobserved component model and runs through the spring of 2002.
4. See Lam, J.-P. and G. Tkacz, "Estimating policy-neutral interest rates for Canada using a dynamic stochastic general-equilibrium framework", *Bank of Canada Working Paper*, No. 2004-9, 2004.
5. See Basdevant, O., N. Björksten and Ö. Karagedikli, "Estimating a time varying neutral real interest rate for New Zealand", *Reserve Bank of New Zealand Discussion Papers*, No. 2004/01, 2004. The fact that the neutral rate seems to be higher in New Zealand than in the aforementioned OECD economies may reflect greater GDP and exchange rate volatility, lower liquidity of the debt denominated in New Zealand dollars and/or a high net foreign debt ratio.
6. See Brzoza-Brzezina, M., "The information content of the natural rate of interest: the case of Poland", *mimeo*, 2004.
7. The one-sided estimate is not exclusively based on past information, as the model parameters are estimated using the entire sample. Nonetheless, given that these parameters are fairly stable over large parts of the sample, the one-sided estimate is a good approximation of what the neutral rate estimate would have been at that time, abstracting from later data revisions.
8. See Clark, T. and S. Kozicki, "Estimating equilibrium real interest rates in real time", *Federal Reserve Bank of Kansas City Research Working Papers*, No. 04-08, 2004.

... and in Japan

Monetary policy has also remained on hold for quite some time in Japan. The latest increase in the targeted level of bank current accounts at the Bank of Japan took place in January 2004. Interventions on the foreign exchange market, which were conducted on a massive scale until March 2004, have since ceased, and base money has decelerated strongly. At the same time, the process of contraction in bank lending, which started seven years ago, has continued, despite encouraging progress in reducing the stock of non-performing loans, through ongoing disposals and via a slowdown in the generation of new bad loans.[20] In the near term, with consumer price inflation still in negative territory, a continuation of the zero interest rate policy

Figure I.13. **Real interest rates remain relatively low**

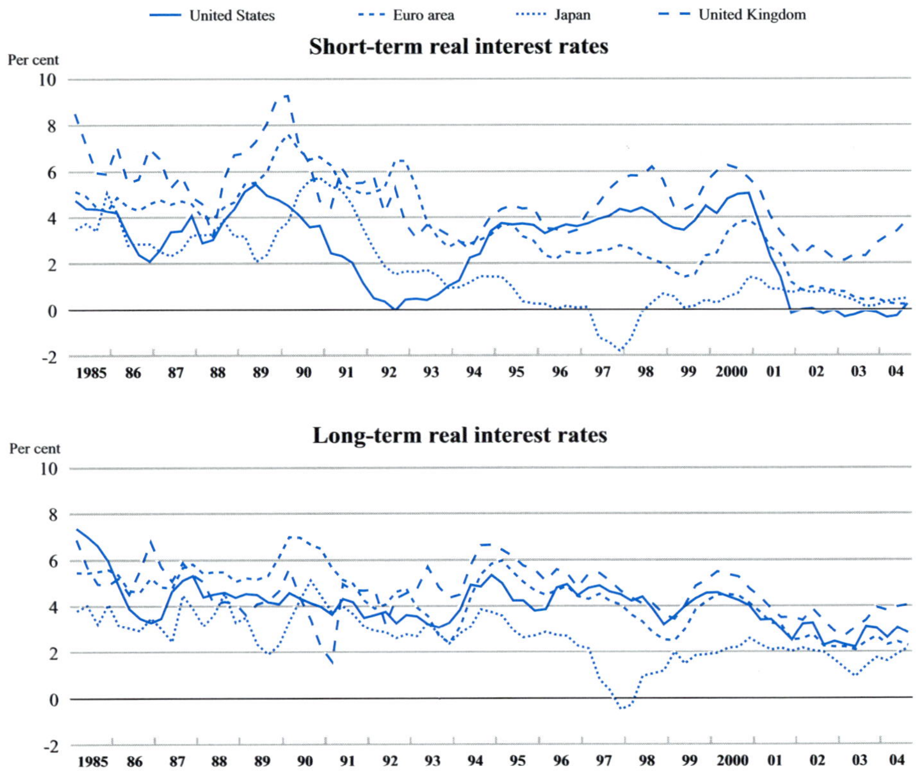

Note: Short-term refers to 3-month money market rates and long-term to 10-year government bond yields. Real interest rates have been deflated using the core inflation index (harmonised index for the euro area and the United Kingdom).
Source: OECD Economic Outlook 76 database.

is in order. While there is no evident need for further quantitative easing, the normalisation of interest rates should not start before inflation turns clearly positive.

Fiscal policy: speeding up consolidation

Fiscal adjustment should not be deferred any longer

Several OECD countries – including the United States, Canada, France and the United Kingdom – have enjoyed higher-than-projected revenue growth thus far in 2004. But at the same time, spending also continues to rise rapidly, in these as well as in a number of other OECD countries. More disquietingly, underlying fiscal positions generally are not improving and scant adjustment is in the pipeline (Table I.4) even though, as has been documented in earlier editions of the *OECD Economic Outlook*, fiscal positions are in many cases unsustainable. The momentous challenges lying ahead are admittedly acknowledged in virtually all OECD countries and are prompting a number of longer-run pension and health care reforms, but these need to gather pace (Box I.5).

20. Other signs of structural adjustment in the financial sector include the significant unwinding of cross-shareholdings amongst the big banks, which has halved since the late 1990s (see Nippon Life Insurance Research Institute, *Fiscal 2003 cross-shareholding survey*, September 2004). In addition, the Bank of Japan has recently announced that it would no longer purchase bank shares.

Table I.4. **Fiscal deficits are large and persistent**

	2002	2003	2004	2005	2006
	Per cent of GDP / Potential GDP				
United States					
Actual balance	-3.8	-4.6	-4.4	-4.1	-4.2
Cyclically-adjusted balance	-3.2	-4.1	-4.2	-4.0	-4.2
Cyclically-adjusted primary balance	-1.2	-2.3	-2.5	-2.1	-2.0
Japan[a]					
Actual balance	-7.9	-7.7	-6.5	-6.4	-6.3
Cyclically-adjusted balance	-6.8	-6.8	-6.3	-6.4	-6.6
Cyclically-adjusted primary balance	-5.4	-5.4	-4.8	-4.7	-4.5
Euro area					
Actual balance	-2.4	-2.8	-2.9	-2.6	-2.4
Cyclically-adjusted balance	-2.4	-2.0	-2.1	-1.8	-1.8
Cyclically-adjusted primary balance	0.9	1.0	0.8	1.1	1.1
OECD[b]					
Actual balance	-3.2	-3.7	-3.5	-3.2	-3.2
Cyclically-adjusted balance	-3.1	-3.4	-3.4	-3.3	-3.3
Cyclically-adjusted primary balance	-0.9	-1.4	-1.4	-1.2	-1.1

Note: Actual balances are in per cent of nominal GDP. Cyclically-adjusted balances are in per cent of potential GDP. The primary cyclically-adjusted balance is the cyclically-adjusted balance less net debt interest payments.

a) Includes deferred tax payments on postal saving accounts amounting to 0.1 per cent of GDP in 2002.

b) Total OECD figures for the actual balance exclude Mexico and Turkey and those for the cyclically-adjusted balance further exclude the Czech Republic, Hungary, Korea, Luxembourg, Poland, the Slovak Republic and Switzerland.

Source: OECD Economic Outlook 76 database.

Fiscal consolidation will require new measures in the United States…

In the United States, tax receipts as a share of GDP essentially stopped falling this year, mainly thanks to buoyant corporate profits. With the end of the 2004 tax refunds, the expiration of accelerated depreciation allowances and the slowing of federal government purchases, the fiscal stance – as measured by the change in the primary cyclically-adjusted balance – is shifting from slightly expansionary to moderately restrictive. However, revenues are not set to improve endogenously as much as they did during the second half of the 1990s, in a context of buoyant financial market conditions and growth. At the same time, spending commitments – whether or not already explicitly built into budgets – are growing rapidly. Among the larger uncertainties are the fate of the sunset clauses associated with the tax cuts implemented in recent years and the extent to which the alternative minimum tax (AMT), which if left unchanged will affect a growing proportion of taxpayers, will be indexed or otherwise altered.[21] On the spending side, formal budget plans assume restraint, but discretionary spending has tended to systematically overshoot programmed amounts. An additional uncertainty relates to the evolution of military spending.

… as well as in Europe…

In Europe, the 2004 headline general government deficit is set to approach or exceed 3 per cent of GDP in eleven of the 19 European Union (EU) countries that are OECD members. In the euro area, half of the countries are in this situation. Moreover, in some cases, the magnitude of the fiscal gap has been understated in the

21. The AMT is intended to limit taxpayers' ability to use certain tax breaks (it essentially boils down to adding back some of the latter into adjusted gross income). Estimates prepared by the Congressional Budget Office suggest that indexing the AMT for inflation would cost about ½ per cent of GDP each year.

Box I.5. Where do public pension reforms stand?

How sustainable are public pension systems? Over recent years, the progress across the OECD area in putting public pension systems on a sustainable basis has been mixed, with some countries still facing considerable increases in pension expenditure. Even after reforms, estimates point to spending increases of at least 2 per cent of GDP up to 2050 for half of the countries listed. An inability to address pension challenges in a timely manner risks increasing the scale of adjustment to benefit levels and contribution rates when they are eventually put in place. Moreover, long lead times are required to enable individuals to adapt their behaviour in response to alterations in pension system rules, so that actions to ensure the sustainability of public pensions have become increasingly urgent.

Ensuring pressure from ageing is minimised. Those countries where the projected increase in outlays is greatest (given current demographic projections) generally operate defined-benefit systems. Where defined-benefit public pension systems appear to be financially sustainable, a salient feature is that an earnings-related defined-benefit pension is not the only pension vehicle. In these cases, a share of retirement income will be derived from other pensions and also personal saving (for example, private pension saving is mandated in Australia and Hungary and encouraged in some other countries). With this type of pension system structure, the impact of ageing is a smaller threat to public finances in these countries. This is nonetheless contingent on the political sustainability of pensioner income declining relative to median income if insufficient supplementary pension income is available on retirement. An additional means of reducing pressure from ageing is through closing pathways to early retirement, as they can represent a considerable fiscal cost.

The notional defined-contribution pension is an alternative approach to achieving sustainability and a relatively recent innovation. This system determines benefit levels on the basis of contributions but uses a "revaluation factor" that mimics investment returns and allows for life expectancy at the point of retirement. The explicit consideration of life expectancy on retirement adds robustness to the public pension system by reducing pressure on public finances arising from increasing longevity. Linking the benefit level to life expectancy on retirement can allow individuals greater choice of retirement age, though this attribute is present in other types of pension systems which build in actuarially fair adjustments to benefit levels for early or later retirement. As life expectancy increases, individuals may need to remain in employment longer to attain their targeted replacement rates.

Parametric reforms can gradually reduce fiscal costs. The countries with less sustainable defined-benefit pensions largely rely on pay-as-you-go systems. There, incremental change through reforms of parameters such as benefit levels or contribution rates has reduced the projected burden somewhat, though further reforms will be necessary in most cases. Some of the recent reforms have indexed benefits payments to prices or to total wage bill growth rather than to per capita wage growth so as to cap the ratio of pension costs to wages. A second element is scheduled rises in contribution rates over time, running the attendant risk of weighing on GDP growth.

Pre-financing and paying down debt can ease the burden. While pension-system reforms are essential for containing ageing pressures, reducing government net debt can also assist governments in meeting the challenges arising from ageing. For example, Canada is pre-funding its second tier pension in a separate off-budget account. While other countries have adopted policies that nominally finance pension liabilities (or reduce national debt), significant and often rapid deteriorations of fiscal positions, such as in Japan over the 1990s and in the United States more recently, highlight the vulnerability of this strategy, especially in the absence of forward-looking fiscal rules.[1]

Governments need to consider the implicit liabilities associated with private pension provision. Ultimately reforms need to ensure that individuals on retirement will have adequate financial resources and, in this context, governments are increasingly looking to boosting private pension saving. If, however, pensioner income relative to median income falls to politically unacceptable levels, governments may be unable to resist pressure to guarantee income adequacy. A particular risk has arisen with respect to corporate pension plans, where large funding gaps emerged as tumbling stock prices eroded pension fund assets, highlighting the importance of ensuring adequate funding.[2] Government policy aimed at buttressing private pension provision needs to be carefully designed so as to avoid creating adverse incentives (such as pension fund insurance giving rise to underfunding) and imposing unnecessary regulatory burdens on private pension providers. A sound prudential framework is essential for encouraging effective private pension saving.

1. See "Fiscal sustainability: the contribution of fiscal rules", *OECD Economic Outlook*, No. 72, 2002 for a review of fiscal rules being used in OECD countries.
2. See Box I.4 in *OECD Economic Outlook*, No. 74, 2003 for a discussion of funding gaps in corporate pensions.

Box I.5. Where do public pension reforms stand? *(cont.)*

Reforms of retirement income systems in selected OECD countries[a]

	Date of last major reform	Gross replacement rate of mandatory pensions in 2003	National estimate of public pension spending increase Per cent of GDP 2000 to 2050	Public pension benefit	Mandatory private regime	Last major reforms: Changed level of defined benefits	Last major reforms: Increased contribution rates	Actuarial adjustment (earliest possible age) Per cent per annum[b]
Poland[c]	1999	70	-8.1	Notional defined contribution	Yes	Abolished	No	6.3
United Kingdom	2003	48	0.2	Defined benefit	No	No	No	10.4
Italy[d]	2004	70	0.1	Notional defined contribution	No	Abolished	No	7.7
Japan[e]	2004	53	0.7	Defined benefit, nominally funded	No	Reduced	Yes	12.0
Sweden[f]	1998	76	1.5	Notional defined contribution	Quasi	Abolished	No	6.2
Australia	1992	52	1.6	Defined benefit	Yes	No	No	9.4
Luxembourg	2002	71	1.9	Defined benefit	No	Increased	Yes	
United States	1983	45	2.0	Defined benefit, nominally funded	No		No	5.8
Canada	1997	56	2.2	Defined benefit, prefunded	No	No	No	6.0
France[g]	2003	71	2.7	Defined benefit	No	Reduced	Yes	5.0
Belgium[h]	2000	60	3.1	Defined benefit, debt repayment	No	Reduced	No	0.0
Hungary[i]	1998	85	3.4	Defined benefit	Yes	Reduced	No	0.0
Germany	2001	46	4.1	Defined benefit	No	Reduced	Yes	6.0
Czech Republic	1995	45	4.7	Defined benefit	No	Reduced	No	6.0
Korea	1988	71	5	Defined benefit, nominally funded	No	No	No	5.0
Greece	1992	53	10.0	Defined benefit	No	Increased	Yes	0.0

a) The coverage of pension spending is less homogeneous across countries than over time.
b) The actuarial adjustment is a change in the benefit level to take account of the pension contributions made and life expectancy upon retirement.
c) Assumes 2 per cent growth in the revaluation factor. The drop in projected pension outlays reflects a major shift away from the pay-as-you-go pillar, but the current national estimate far exceeds earlier OECD estimates and may overstate the extent of the foreseeable decline.
d) For people retiring after 2010. In 2004, the Italian parliament passed a framework law allowing the government to introduce implementing legislation to reduce the fiscal burden of pensions, including reforms to encourage later retirement and to augment the main pension with a supplementary pension.
e) The end-point of the projection is 2025 instead of 2050.
f) Assumes a revaluation factor of 1.6 per cent.
g) The end-point of the projection is 2040 instead of 2050.
h) Regime for private sector employees. The end-point of the projection is 2030 instead of 2050.
i) Excluding pensions financed by the Health Insurance Fund.
Source: National submissions in the 2003-04 stability or convergence programmes for EU countries (except Greece); Canadian Office of the Superintendent of Financial Institutions; US Congressional Budget Office; Japanese Ministry of Finance; forthcoming OECD Survey of Greece; Korea Development Institute; OECD, *Sustainable Development in OECD Countries: Getting the Policies Right*, Paris, forthcoming.

headline budgetary statistics.[22] The ongoing deterioration is especially striking in Greece. Against this backdrop of serious slippages, new tax reductions are to be implemented in 2005 in several countries, although in some the cuts are offset by spending measures or revenue-raising initiatives. It is important indeed that any cuts in tax rates be financed by base broadening and/or by spending measures, so that cyclically-adjusted deficits are put on a firm downward path in the coming years, with the pace of improvement necessary to enhance credibility probably being at least ½ percentage point of GDP per annum, in line with what has been an official objective for some time. In addition, any tax windfalls, such as witnessed in France during 2004, ought to be used primarily for deficit reduction. Efforts are also being deployed in a number of euro area countries, both *ex ante* and during budget execution, to restrain public spending, but overruns keep reoccurring, not least in areas such as health care. Fundamental reforms in a number of these areas are called for, rather than repeated stop-gap measures.

... where some of the rules are being rewritten

Sound and enforceable fiscal rules can contribute to fiscal discipline and help preserve or restore public finance sustainability, but they cannot substitute for such fundamental public spending reform. In Europe, the Stability and Growth Pact probably limited the deterioration in fiscal positions during the downturn, but it eventually proved far less binding than originally intended. An amended interpretation of the Pact has recently been proposed by the European Commission. It introduces extra flexibility by offering a looser definition of the "exceptional circumstances" under which the deficit can exceed 3 per cent of GDP without triggering disciplinary action. It also allows more leeway in deciding on the speed at which a deficit that is deemed excessive should be reduced, by explicitly taking into account the level of public debt and its dynamics. Furthermore, in line with earlier understandings, one-off measures are to be identified and controlled for more systematically. Finally, the intention is to strengthen incentives to exercise fiscal restraint during cyclical upturns. Overall, if not supported by binding mechanisms, continued reliance on peer pressure to enforce fiscal objectives would call for much greater self-discipline than mustered to date.

Fiscal efforts need to be more ambitious in Japan

In Japan, the general government deficit is projected to decline in calendar year 2004, to 6½ per cent of GDP, with gross public debt reaching 164 per cent of GDP. The effects of higher-than-projected growth and continued cuts in public investment (Figure I.14) are being partly offset by increased old-age-related spending, coupled with lower revenues due to reduced tax rates and reverse "bracket creep", as deflation pushes taxpayers into lower brackets. For fiscal year 2005, reductions in public investment and non-priority discretionary spending are planned, alongside social security reform, so that virtually no increase in general-purpose spending would be allowed. Further out, pension contributions will continue to rise over the coming decade following the passage of the reform bill. But rising debt-servicing costs, as interest rates move towards normalisation and debt continues to accumulate, will work in the opposite direction. More ambitious efforts – possibly in the form of a higher value-added tax rate – will be needed for the government to reach its goal of a

22. Compared with the March 2004 notification to Eurostat, the Greek deficit for 2003 has been revised up by almost 3 percentage points, to 4.6 per cent of GDP, with large upward revisions for earlier years as well. At the same time, the 2003 public debt ratio has been revised up by 7½ percentage points, to 110 per cent of GDP. In several other European countries, various measures embellish the reported fiscal balance and/or debt without a commensurate improvement in underlying positions, see Koen, V. and P. van den Noord, "Fiscal gimmickry in Europe: One-off measures and creative accounting", *OECD Economics Department Working Papers*, forthcoming.

Figure I.14. **Public investment shrinks but social benefit outlays rise**

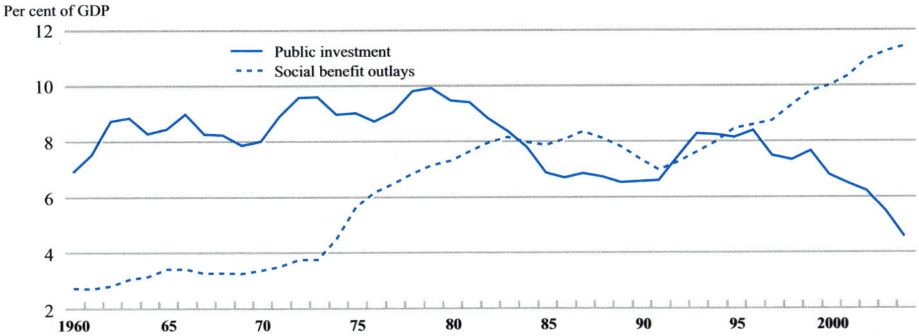

Source: OECD Economic Outlook 76 database.

primary surplus by the early 2010s. Public-sector reform can also help, and in this regard the steps recently announced to overhaul and prepare Japan Post for privatisation are encouraging, although it will be important to ensure that in the process the entity's monopoly power and state-sponsored privileges be duly curtailed.

Appendix: Corporate sector exposure to a rise in interest rates

As the recovery matures, interest rates might be expected to revert to more neutral levels, although timing and pace are very likely to differ across countries. How various economies will be affected depends *inter alia* on the resilience of their respective corporate sectors to interest rate hikes, as well as the latter's magnitude. Where firms tend to have higher debt loads and/or more limited financial resources to meet growing interest-rate obligations, the corporate sector is more likely to experience stress as monetary policy is tightened. This risk can be assessed by examining corporate balance sheet information drawn from the Worldscope database for the United States, Japan, Germany and the United Kingdom (Table I.5).[23] In this context, both economy-wide average indebtedness indicators and their distribution across firms are relevant.

It may be particularly instructive to compare the current situation with 1993, as it was also a year preceding a major policy tightening cycle. Compared with a decade ago, average debt-to-equity ratios have declined in the United States and especially Japan, where they had reached unparalleled levels in the early 1990s. In contrast, debt/equity ratios have increased in Germany – even if the trend appears to have reversed since 2001 – and even more so in the United Kingdom, where they have increased sharply in recent years.[24]

Turning to the distribution of debt loads across firms, the share of the US and of the UK corporate sector – whether based on equity-market capitalisation or employment – that is highly indebted and thus most exposed to an increase in inte-rest rates, had declined significantly by 2003. By contrast, in Japan and Germany, the proportion of heavily leveraged firms had risen.

Table I.5. **Debt-to-equity ratios**

In per cent

	United States		Japan		Germany		United Kingdom	
	1993[b]	2003	1993[b]	2003[c]	1993[b]	2003[c]	1993[b]	2003
Mean debt/equity ratio[a]	112	83	200	109	95	131	69	101
Share of market capitalisation represented by firms with high debt/equity ratios[a]	24	19	26	36	18	38	40	30
Share of employment represented by firms with high debt/equity ratios[a]	25	16	21	31	23	27	29	13
Memorandum item:								
Aggregate debt/equity ratio[e]	53	49	188	139	125	154	37	39

a) Debt/equity ratios for individual firms are weighted by their share in total market capitalisation and then aggregated to derive the economy-wide mean debt/equity ratio shown here.
b) Data for 1993 include all non-financial firms listed on the stock exchange in 1993 (*i.e.* firms that were delisted since then and no longer in business are also included).
c) For 215 Japanese and 68 German firms, 2003 data are not available and 2002 data have been used, but this should not significantly affect the results.
d) High debt/equity ratios are those that are at least one standard deviation above the mean.
e) From flow-of-funds statistics. For Germany debt as a percentage of gross value added is shown.
Source: Datastream and Deutsche Bundesbank.

23. Worldscope is maintained by Datastream and includes all major non-financial corporations listed on the stock exchanges of the said four countries, accounting for about a fifth of employment in the non-financial sector as a whole and a large fraction of market capitalisation.
24. The accounting perspective in the Worldscope database is conceptually different from the approach in the flow-of-funds statistics, where the market value rather than the book value of equity is used.

Vulnerability to interest rate increases also has to be gauged in the light of firms' ability to service their debt following the resultant shock to their cash flow (Table I.6). One relevant indicator is the ratio of current assets to current liabilities, or the "current ratio".[25] Another is the share of short-term in total debt: as interest rates back up, firms more dependent on short-term debt will face a quicker debt roll-over at the new, higher interest rates.[26] For the analysis here, firms are said to be in the "vulnerable zone" if their current ratio is under 1.5 when their debt/equity ratio exceeds 100 per cent or when their share of short-term debt exceeds 30 per cent.[27]

Table I.6. **Share of firms in the vulnerable zone**

In 2003, in per cent

	Based on market capitalisation	**Based on employment**
United States		
Debt/equity ratio > 100 per cent	27	19
Share of short-term debt > 30 per cent	16	11
Japan		
Debt/equity ratio > 100 per cent	46	37
Share of short-term debt > 30 per cent	41	59
Germany		
Debt/equity ratio > 100 per cent	36	54
Share of short-term debt > 30 per cent	22	45
United Kingdom		
Debt/equity ratio > 100 per cent	40	29
Share of short-term debt > 30 per cent	30	13

Source: Datastream.

In 2003, a lower proportion of US firms combined high overall indebtedness or a high share of short-term debt with a low liquid asset coverage of short-term liabilities compared with their Japanese, German and UK counterparts. However, on current projections, US firms are likely to face larger increases in interest rates.

25. Current assets consist of cash and other assets that could reasonably be expected to be liquidated, sold or consumed within one year. Current liabilities represent debt or other obligations that a company expects to meet within one year.
26. It should be borne in mind, however, that a portion of long-term debt carries a variable interest rate.
27. The 100 per cent benchmark for the debt/equity ratio is chosen to facilitate cross-country comparisons. The results are similar if the respective 2003 country means are used. As to the current ratio, the business finance literature suggests a threshold of 1.5 to 2.0. The 30 per cent benchmark for the short-term debt share is between the means for US and UK firms, the means for Japan and Germany being closer to 50 per cent.

II. DEVELOPMENTS IN INDIVIDUAL OECD COUNTRIES

United States

The expansion has lost some momentum, in part as a consequence of the energy price increases. These have already held back real disposable income gains and, with household savings near zero, are likely to weigh on consumption. Core inflation, which rose earlier in the year, has since fallen back towards the lower end of the desirable range. Productivity has decelerated towards trend growth, but profit margins remain high, supporting future investment. The economy is expected to keep growing above potential. However, further sustained increases in energy prices, weakness in the labour market, or a sharper than projected rise in long-term interest rates pose downside risks.

Although some stimulus has been removed, monetary policy remains supportive. Future tightening can afford to be gradual, as higher energy prices are restraining activity more than boosting inflation expectations. Government finances have improved more than expected, but faster revenue growth has been partly offset by higher spending, especially on defence and homeland security. Projected deficits thus remain large, underlining the need to adjust tax and spending levels to rein in the debt accumulation and prepare for impending demographic pressures. This might also lessen the record external imbalance.

Output growth is being buffeted by headwinds…

Real GDP growth picked up moderately in the third quarter, having slowed noticeably in the second quarter to about its potential rate. The swings in growth have largely been driven by household consumption, as steep increases in consumer energy prices reduced real income earlier in the year. Long-term interest rates have lately reversed most of last spring's increases, suggesting less robust growth expectations, but in the meantime supporting further growth in residential construction. The long decline in non-residential structures investment seems to have ended, and spending on equipment and software has continued its rapid expansions. Net exports have once more subtracted substantially from GDP growth, and the current account deficit has widened sharply.

United States

The labour market has only recently gained strength

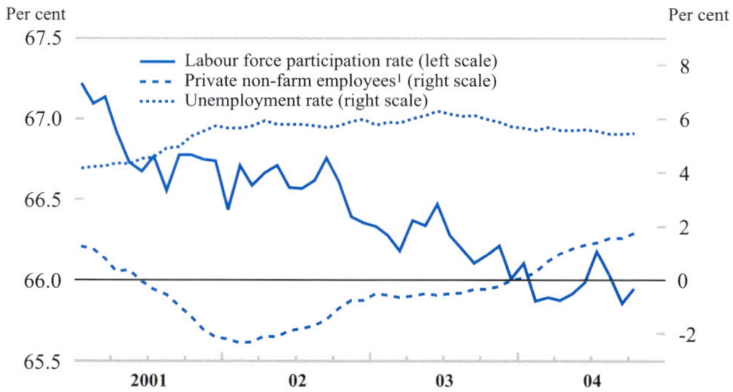

Energy prices have had little effect on core inflation[1]

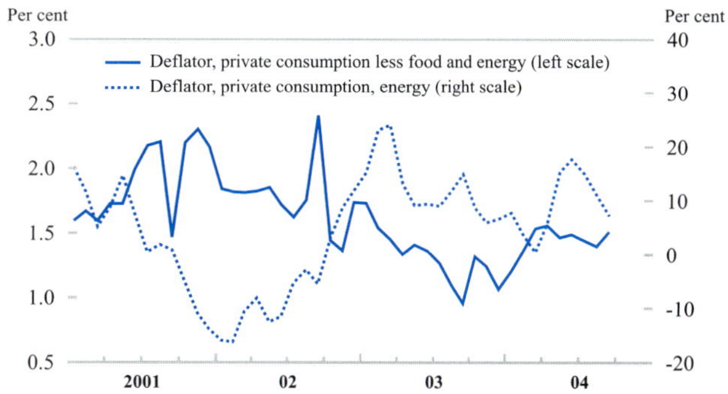

1. Year-on-year changes.
Source: Department of Labor and Bureau of Economic Analysis.

United States: **Employment, income and inflation**

Percentage changes from previous period

	2002	2003	2004	2005	2006
Employment[a]	-1.2	0.0	1.0	1.5	1.5
Unemployment rate[b]	5.8	6.0	5.5	5.3	5.1
Employment cost index	3.8	4.0	3.9	4.1	4.2
Compensation per employee[c]	3.0	3.7	4.1	4.0	4.1
Labour productivity[c]	3.7	3.4	3.7	2.0	2.2
Unit labour cost[c]	-0.6	0.3	0.4	2.0	1.9
GDP deflator	1.7	1.8	2.0	1.8	1.7
Consumer price index	1.6	2.3	2.6	2.4	2.1
Private consumption deflator	1.4	1.9	2.1	1.8	1.6
Real household disposable income	3.1	2.3	2.9	2.9	4.0

a) Whole economy, for further details see *OECD Economic Outlook* Sources and Methods, (*http://www.oecd.org/eco/sources-and-methods*).
b) As a percentage of labour force.
c) In the business sector.
Source: OECD Economic Outlook 76 database.

... while support from policies is diminishing...

The withdrawal of monetary stimulus has been under way since the middle of the year, but the current levels of real short- and long-term interest rates remain very low, with the real federal funds rate having just edged above zero. Federal fiscal policy is still supporting economic activity, although less so than until earlier in the year. Federal government purchases continue to grow rapidly, and the personal income tax provisions of the Jobs and Growth Tax Relief Reconciliation Act of 2003, originally scheduled to expire at the end of 2004, have been extended. Nonetheless, income tax payments in 2005 will be higher in part because the larger-than-normal refunds in 2004, due to the Act's retroactive nature, will not recur.

... and employment has only recently gained strength

Although over much of the past half year the household and payroll surveys have given conflicting signals, most recently both point to a pick-up in employment growth. Nevertheless, the marginal declines in the unemployment rate have mostly reflected continued weakness in labour force participation. The 2003 divergence of product and labour market developments is diminishing, with productivity decelerating from its previous extraordinary pace towards rates closer to trend. Combined with slightly

United States

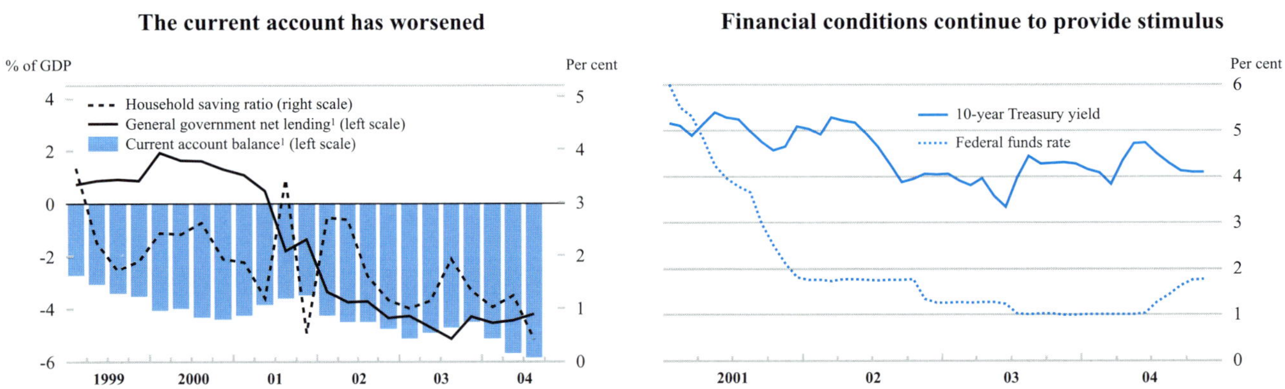

1. Figures for the third quarter of 2004 are estimates.
Source: Board of Governors of the Federal Reserve System; Bureau of Economic Analysis; OECD Economic Outlook 76 database.

United States: **Financial indicators**

	2002	2003	2004	2005	2006
Household saving ratio[a]	2.0	1.4	0.8	0.5	1.2
General government financial balance[b]	-3.8	-4.6	-4.4	-4.1	-4.2
Current account balance[b]	-4.5	-4.8	-5.7	-6.2	-6.4
Short-term interest rate[c]	1.8	1.2	1.5	2.8	3.8
Long-term interest rate[d]	4.6	4.0	4.3	4.7	5.3

a) As a percentage of disposable income.
b) As a percentage of GDP.
c) 3-month euro-dollar.
d) 10-year government bonds.
Source: OECD Economic Outlook 76 database.

faster wage growth, the productivity deceleration implies that declines in unit labour costs have ceased, but the pick-up to date has been marginal. Hence, with profit margins at historically high levels and still supportive financial conditions, the outlook for business investment remains favourable. Despite recent increases in energy and other commodity prices, inflationary pressures outside of these categories remain muted.

Withdrawal of monetary stimulus should gradually continue

Healthy profit margins and modest unit labour cost increases mean that there is unlikely to be immediate upward pressure on core inflation. Moreover, rising energy prices have so far not boosted inflation expectations and wage demands. As their second-round effects seem likely to remain modest, monetary policy can afford to focus on cushioning their adverse effects on economic activity. Resource utilisation is nonetheless projected to rise, especially in 2006, and thus the move toward a more neutral policy stance is projected to continue, though probably at a more gradual pace than in recent months. Long-term rates are also likely to rise as margins of slack diminish.

The fiscal deficit needs to be reduced over the medium term

Despite recent improvements in revenues, the structural budget deficit is projected to remain large, primarily at the federal level. On the spending side, the projection incorporates the defence appropriations for fiscal year (FY) 2005 and anticipates a fur-

United States: **Demand and output**

	2001	2002	2003	2004	2005	2006
	Current prices billion $	Percentage changes, volume				
Private consumption	7 055.1	3.1	3.3	3.6	3.1	3.1
Government consumption	1 501.6	4.0	2.9	1.8	1.6	1.2
Gross fixed investment	1 970.0	-3.1	4.5	8.9	5.8	5.9
Public	324.0	6.0	2.1	3.4	2.1	2.5
Residential	469.3	4.8	8.8	9.8	0.6	0.4
Non-residential	1 176.8	-8.9	3.3	10.2	9.9	9.8
Final domestic demand	10 526.8	2.1	3.4	4.3	3.3	3.4
Stockbuilding[a]	- 31.8	0.4	-0.1	0.5	0.1	0.1
Total domestic demand	10 495.0	2.5	3.3	4.7	3.4	3.5
Exports of goods and services	1 032.8	-2.3	1.9	8.9	9.2	10.0
Imports of goods and services	1 399.9	3.4	4.4	10.1	7.7	7.3
Net exports[a]	- 367.0	-0.7	-0.5	-0.6	-0.3	-0.1
GDP at market prices	10 128.0	1.9	3.0	4.4	3.3	3.6

Note: National accounts are based on official chain-linked data. This introduces a discrepancy in the identity between real demand components and GDP. For further details see *OECD Economic Outlook* Sources and Methods, *(http://www.oecd.org/eco/sources-and-methods).*
a) Contributions to changes in real GDP (percentage of real GDP in previous year), actual amount in the first column.
Source: OECD Economic Outlook 76 database.

United States: **External indicators**

	2002	2003	2004	2005	2006
			$ billion		
Goods and services exports	1 005.0	1 046.2	1 180.5	1 324	1 477
Goods and services imports	1 429.9	1 544.3	1 788.2	2 006	2 192
Foreign balance	- 424.9	- 498.1	- 607.8	- 681	- 716
Invisibles, net	- 49.1	- 32.6	- 61.3	- 80	- 110
Current account balance	- 473.9	- 530.7	- 669.0	- 761	- 825
			Percentage changes		
Goods and services export volumes	- 2.3	1.9	8.9	9.2	10.0
Goods and services import volumes	3.4	4.4	10.1	7.7	7.3
Export performance [a]	- 4.4	- 2.0	- 0.8	- 0.1	0.7
Terms of trade	0.9	- 1.2	- 1.5	- 1.4	- 0.5

a) Ratio between export volume and export market of total goods and services.
Source: OECD Economic Outlook 76 database.

ther budget request in FY 2005 for military operations and reconstruction in Iraq and Afghanistan. Growth in federal purchases of goods and services, which reached 8 per cent in FY 2004, is expected to halve by FY 2006. On the tax side, the projections embody the recent extension of the expiring personal income tax provisions and assume that the current limited relief from the Alternative Minimum Tax will be maintained. After increasing by 4 per cent in FY 2004, federal revenues are projected to rise by nearly 8 per cent in both FY 2005 and 2006. Nonetheless, the federal deficit is projected only to edge down to just above 3½ per cent of GDP. Revenues of state and local governments have recently improved, but their budgetary pressures are projected to ease only gradually, with their net borrowing declining only slightly below the FY 2004 level of ¾ per cent of GDP. The general government deficit is thus projected to remain above 4 per cent of GDP in cyclically-adjusted terms.

Output is projected to accelerate again…

After a temporary lull for the next few quarters during the absorption of the energy price shock, annualised GDP growth should exceed its potential rate of about 3¼ per cent. Consumption expenditures are projected to grow more slowly until mid-2005, due to higher energy prices and tax payments, before picking up moderately in response to accelerating real income. Business fixed investment is expected to advance rapidly, although the expiration of the partial expensing provisions at the end of 2004 is likely to reduce the growth of spending on equipment in early 2005. Residential investment, on the other hand, could weaken noticeably as the rise in long-term interest rates progresses and little pent-up demand remains, before increasing again in 2006 as the stock adjustment wanes. The rise in worldwide demand will probably limit the drag from net exports on GDP growth. Nonetheless, the momentum from consumption and investment should push real GDP growth back above 3½ per cent in 2006 even as federal purchases decelerate after the latest round of spending increases has run its course.

… but there are substantial risks around this projection

There are substantial risks to the outlook. If heightened uncertainty about future demand were to lead firms to continued caution in hiring, consumption could decelerate more than currently projected, slowing the pace of the expansion. Continued high federal budget and rising current-account deficits increase the risk of a larger rise in long-term interest rates than projected. On the other hand, growth may pick up to a greater extent and resource slack diminish more rapidly than projected, for example, if past energy price increases restrain demand less than projected or if investors' risk appetites continue to improve.

Japan

The economic expansion remains on track, though at a more moderate pace as a result of a slowdown in export growth. The resilience of domestic demand, reflecting the increased profitability of the corporate sector and employment gains, should help sustain growth at an annual rate of around 2¼ per cent through 2005 and 2006. The expansion, the strongest since the 1980s, is expected to bring an end to deflation, as measured by the consumer price index, in the course of 2005.

The Bank of Japan's policy of quantitative easing and zero interest rates should continue until inflation is sufficiently high to make the risk of renewed deflation negligible. A detailed and credible consolidation plan to achieve the government's goal of a primary budget surplus by the early 2010s is necessary for confidence in fiscal sustainability. Further progress in reforming the banking sector is important to sustain the recovery and should be accompanied by an acceleration of a broad structural reform programme to increase productivity.

While slowing in the second half of 2004, the expansion continues…

After accelerating to 5¼ per cent in the first half of 2004 (seasonally-adjusted annual rate), the fastest since 1990, output growth is slowing in the second half of the year. One factor has been a moderation of export growth, reflecting in part weaker demand from China, which has accounted for more than a third of Japan's export growth during this expansion. As for domestic demand, recent trends in machinery orders and retail sales also suggest slower growth. As a result, industrial production was essentially flat in the third quarter of the 2004. While growth has reached a plateau, this reflects the normalisation of an exceptionally strong recovery rather than the start of a downturn. Indeed, employment continues to rise, boosting consumer sentiment and sustaining private consumption. Moreover, the latest survey of the corporate sector reports rising confidence among both large and small firms.

… despite deflation and declines in land prices, wages and bank lending

Despite strong growth of 4 per cent in 2004, lingering problems from the decade of economic stagnation act as a drag on economic growth. In particular, deflation, as measured by the year-on-year change in the core consumer price index (excluding energy and food products), picked up to 0.4 per cent in the first half of 2004, indicating that deflation has become entrenched after five years. The deflator for GDP also declined at a faster pace, although this may reflect statistical problems. Land prices continue to fall on a nationwide basis despite a rebound in some central districts of Tokyo. Wages are also declining, as firms cut costs by hiring non-regular

Japan

Profits have recovered
Profit to sales ratios

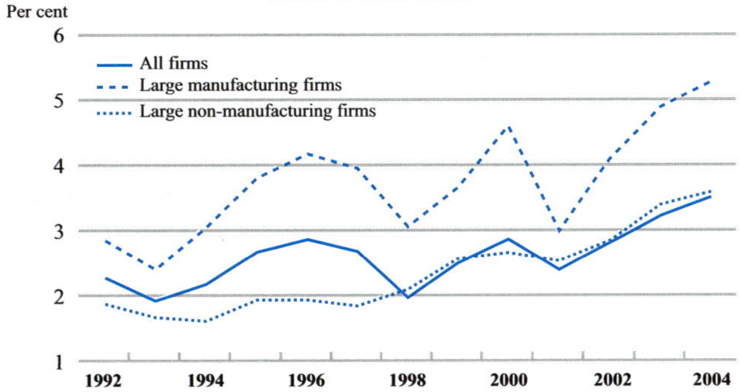

Earnings are still falling due to more part-timers
Year-on-year per cent change

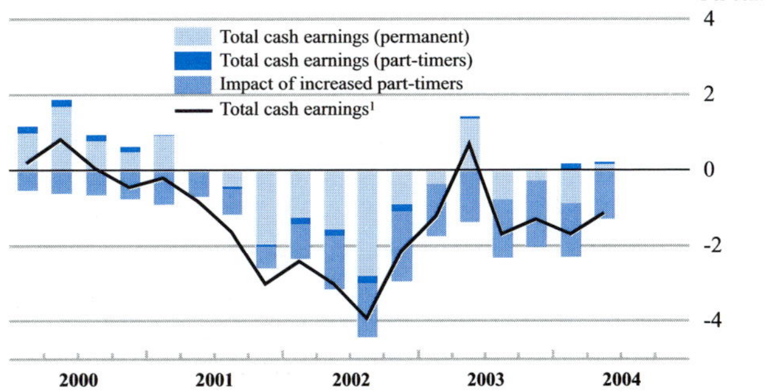

1. All workers, bonus inclusive.
Source: Ministry of Finance and Cabinet Office.

Japan: Employment, income and inflation

Percentage changes from previous period

	2002	2003	2004	2005	2006
Employment	-1.3	-0.2	0.3	0.2	0.3
Unemployment rate[a]	5.4	5.3	4.8	4.5	4.2
Compensation of employees	-2.9	-0.9	-0.1	0.4	0.9
Unit labour cost	-2.6	-3.2	-3.9	-1.7	-1.3
Household disposable income	-0.5	-0.3	0.1	1.0	2.0
GDP deflator	-1.2	-2.5	-2.3	-1.3	-0.3
Consumer price index	-0.9	-0.3	-0.1	0.1	0.6
Private consumption deflator	-1.3	-1.4	-1.5	-0.6	0.3

a) As a percentage of labour force.
Source: OECD Economic Outlook 76 database.

workers, whose hourly earnings are substantially less than regular workers. Non-regular workers now account for more than a quarter of employees. Finally, bank loans continue to fall, though at a slower rate. This modest improvement in credit trends may reflect stronger loan demand from the business sector, but it is also due to an improvement in the health of the banking sector. The major banks have cut non-performing loans to 5.2 per cent of total lending, in line with the government's goal of reducing such loans from 8.4 per cent of total lending in March 2002 to between 4 and 5 per cent by March 2005. Moreover, the banks recorded ordinary profits in 2003 for the first time since 1992.

The impact of monetary easing is hindered by banking-sector problems

The contraction of bank lending has limited the effectiveness of the quantitative easing policy adopted by the Bank of Japan in 2001. The target range for current account balances at the central bank has been left unchanged since January 2004, while short-term interest rates remain at zero. This policy has expanded the monetary base by 60 per cent over the past three years, although the pace of growth has slowed recently. Quantitative easing has also helped to keep long-term interest rates relatively low at around 160 basis points. The Bank of Japan has promised to maintain

Japan

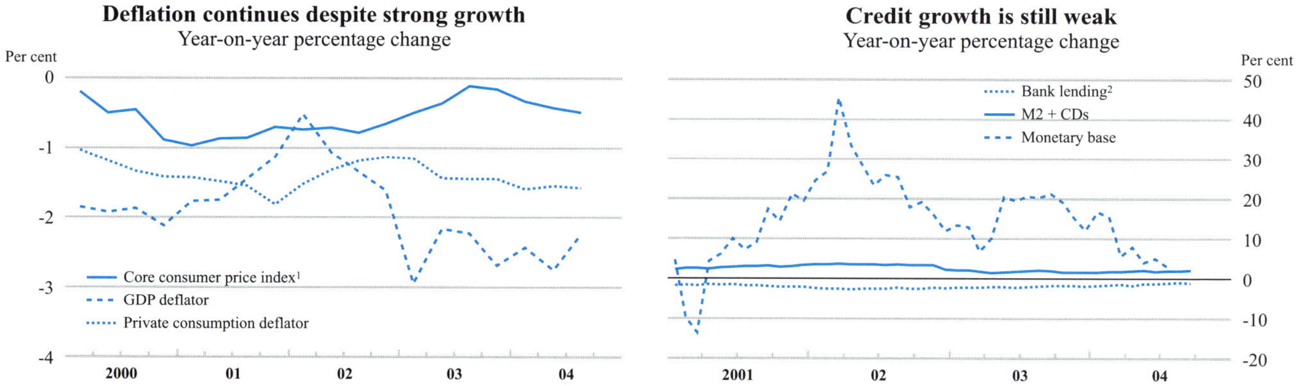

1. Includes publicly regulated prices which rose significantly in 2003.
2. Excluding loan write-offs and related items and securitisation of loans, and adjusting for exchange rate changes.
Source: Bank of Japan.

Japan: **Financial indicators**

	2002	2003	2004	2005	2006
Household saving ratio[a]	6.4	6.3	5.1	5.0	5.0
General government financial balance [b]	-7.9	-7.7	-6.5	-6.4	-6.3
Current account balance[b]	2.8	3.1	3.5	3.5	3.7
Short-term interest rate[c]	0.1	0.0	0.0	0.0	0.4
Long-term interest rate[d]	1.3	1.1	1.5	1.8	2.5

a) As a percentage of disposable income.
b) As a percentage of GDP.
c) 3-month CDs.
d) 10-year government bonds.
Source: OECD Economic Outlook 76 database.

its current policy stance at least until the change in the core consumer price index is zero or above and the Monetary Policy Board projects it to be positive in the future.

The fiscal policy stance is slightly contractionary in 2004

The strength of the expansion has reduced the government's primary budget deficit from 6¼ per cent of GDP in 2003 – the largest in the OECD area – to an estimated 5 per cent this year. However, significant further consolidation is not imminent on present policies. On the revenue side, the government will raise the pension contribution rate and take several steps to expand the personal income tax base in 2005, though the overall impact is likely to be very small. Expenditures, meanwhile, are to be limited in line with the government's medium-term objective of holding outlays to 38 per cent of GDP. This is to be accomplished through cuts in public works and discretionary spending that offset most of the mandatory increases in social security spending and interest payments. But on balance, the fiscal stance in 2005 is projected to be broadly neutral, with the primary budget deficit falling only slightly to 4¾ per cent. Gross government debt is projected to rise further, reaching a record 170 per cent of GDP.

Japan: **Demand and output**

	2001	2002	2003	2004	2005	2006
	Current prices trillion ¥	Percentage changes, volume (1995 prices)				
Private consumption	286.0	1.0	0.8	3.4	2.2	1.7
Government consumption	86.4	2.4	1.0	1.9	2.1	2.0
Gross fixed investment	130.3	-6.1	3.2	2.8	1.2	2.2
Public[a]	32.6	-4.4	-10.8	-15.7	-7.4	-4.0
Residential	19.0	-4.2	-0.8	2.0	1.0	-0.2
Non-residential	78.6	-7.2	9.6	9.0	3.4	4.0
Final domestic demand	502.7	-0.7	1.4	3.0	1.9	1.9
Stockbuilding [b]	0.0	-0.2	0.3	0.2	0.0	0.0
Total domestic demand	502.7	-1.0	1.8	3.2	1.9	1.9
Exports of goods and services	52.6	8.0	10.1	14.4	7.4	8.0
Imports of goods and services	49.4	1.9	5.0	9.9	7.1	6.9
Net exports [b]	3.2	0.7	0.7	0.9	0.3	0.4
GDP at market prices	505.8	-0.3	2.5	4.0	2.1	2.3

a) Including public corporations.
b) Contributions to changes in real GDP (percentage of real GDP in previous year), actual amount in the first column.
Source: OECD Economic Outlook 76 database.

Japan: **External indicators**

	2002	2003	2004	2005	2006
			$ billion		
Goods and services exports	446.6	508.8	609.2	674	731
Goods and services imports	395.3	439.7	522.5	590	639
Foreign balance	51.3	69.1	86.7	84	92
Invisibles, net	60.4	66.2	77.7	84	92
Current account balance	111.7	135.3	164.5	168	184
			Percentage changes		
Goods and services export volumes	8.0	10.1	14.4	7.4	8.0
Goods and services import volumes	1.9	5.0	9.9	7.1	6.9
Export performance [a]	2.7	3.5	2.8	- 2.2	- 2.3
Terms of trade	0.2	- 2.4	- 3.1	- 2.3	- 0.9

a) Ratio between export volume and export market of total goods and services.
Source: OECD Economic Outlook 76 database.

The expansion is expected to continue through 2006

Despite the headwinds of continued falls in bank lending and land prices, the expansion is projected to continue through 2006 at an annual rate of about 2¼ per cent. Further gains in employment and a stabilisation in nominal wages should be sufficient to support private consumption growth, even if the declining trend in the saving rate comes to an end. High levels of profits in the business sector, combined with the improved health of the banking sector, should sustain business investment, though at a slower pace. In addition, the contribution from external demand is likely to remain positive, although somewhat smaller. There is considerable uncertainty as to the timing of the end of deflation, giving that price changes appear not to be very sensitive to demand conditions. Nevertheless, with the economy projected to continue growing at a rate above potential and the output gap closing, deflation is projected to end in 2005. However, there are a number of risks, both external and domestic, to a sustained expansion. A slowdown in world trade would weaken the upturn, as would a significant appreciation of the yen. There is also a risk that the downward trend in wages could continue, thereby slowing private consumption, while the steady increase of public debt into uncharted territory could raise the risk premium.

Euro area

The recovery is facing headwinds because of higher oil prices and a recent renewed appreciation of the euro. Even so, spurred by still robust world trade, GDP should accelerate from a growth rate of just below 2 per cent in 2004 to 2½ per cent in 2006. This would not suffice, however, to fully absorb the economic slack and the unemployment rate would remain high at about 8½ per cent. Inflation is expected to recede once the impact of the oil price hike peters out. Monetary policy should be kept easy as long as the medium-term inflation outlook remains favourable.

The closer integration that monetary union was seen as bringing has not yet translated into any visible strengthening of trend growth or increased dynamism. The structural reform agenda, required to move the euro area economy towards the ambitious targets set by the Lisbon summit in 2000, needs to be reinvigorated. Greater dynamism would also help in achieving fiscal consolidation and thereby make fiscal policy more consistent with the requirements stemming from ageing populations.

The recovery has lost momentum

Growth accelerated in the first half of this year, but recent indicators suggest that momentum is stalling. The recovery from the 2001-03 downturn has thus remained unspectacular so far, with GDP growing by around 2 per cent at annualised rates since mid-2003. The upturn has been led by a strong pickup in world trade. But domestic demand has lagged. In 2004, consumption growth was buoyant early on but progressively lost steam and investment has remained sluggish throughout. As usual at this stage of the recovery, increased activity has led to a cyclical rebound in labour productivity so that employment has hardly picked up. The unemployment rate stabilised at around 9 per cent in 2004, a percentage point above its early-2001 low. Spurred by soaring oil and administered prices, inflation has moved about half a percentage point beyond the 2 per cent mark while core inflation remained relatively stable at a level consistent with the price stability objective of the European Central Bank (ECB).

Household confidence remains fragile

Weak labour market conditions, uncertainties over structural reforms, soft earnings prospects and the oil price hike have prevented any brisk recovery in household sentiment. As a result household savings have remained high and have even been rising in Germany. These upward saving pressures have contributed to largely offset the economic stimulus provided by the world recovery.

Euro area

The recovery has been helped by foreign trade
Year-on-year percentage change[1]

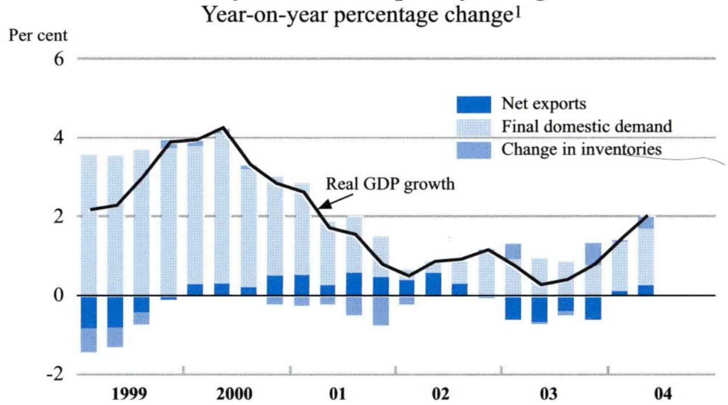

Headline inflation is above the 2 per cent mark
Year-on-year percentage change

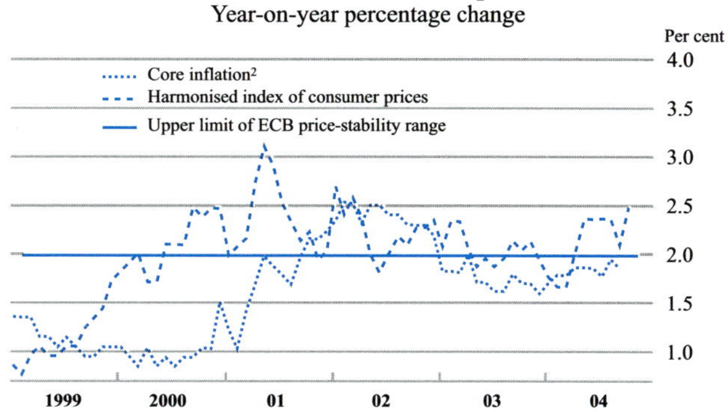

1. Contribution to real GDP growth.
2. Harmonised index of consumer prices excluding energy, food, alcohol and tobacco.
Source: Statistical Office of the European Communities (Eurostat) and OECD Economic Outlook 76 database.

Euro area: Employment, income and inflation

Percentage changes from previous period

	2002	2003	2004	2005	2006
Employment	0.5	0.2	0.7	0.9	1.2
Unemployment rate[a]	8.4	8.8	8.8	8.6	8.3
Compensation per employee[b]	2.4	2.2	1.9	2.2	2.6
Labour productivity[b]	0.5	0.4	1.2	1.1	1.3
Unit labour cost[b]	2.0	1.7	0.7	1.1	1.2
Household disposable income	3.1	2.6	3.0	3.5	3.8
GDP deflator	2.5	2.0	1.9	1.7	1.8
Harmonised index of consumer price	2.3	2.1	2.1	2.0	1.7
Private consumption deflator	2.2	1.9	1.9	2.0	1.7

a) As a percentage of labour force.
b) In the business sector.
Source: OECD Economic Outlook 76 database.

Financial conditions are supportive

Notwithstanding the high oil price, the overall financial situation of the business sector has clearly improved since the onset of the recovery. Wage moderation and the cyclical pick up in labour productivity have helped restore profit margins while balance sheet restructuring has also advanced, albeit not to the same extent as in most English-speaking countries or Japan. The ratio of short to long-term debt in the non-financial corporate sector has fallen while the ratio of total corporate debt to GDP has stabilised. As a result, lending conditions have eased and corporate bond spreads have narrowed. Although investment activity has remained sluggish, current financial conditions are unlikely to act as a brake on capital formation once the uncertainties over demand prospects have ebbed.

The fiscal stance is broadly neutral

The Excessive Deficit Procedure under the European Community Treaty requires governments to take corrective action when the 3 per cent of GDP reference value for the budget deficit has been breached, which is the case for Germany,

Euro area

The fiscal stance is practically neutral

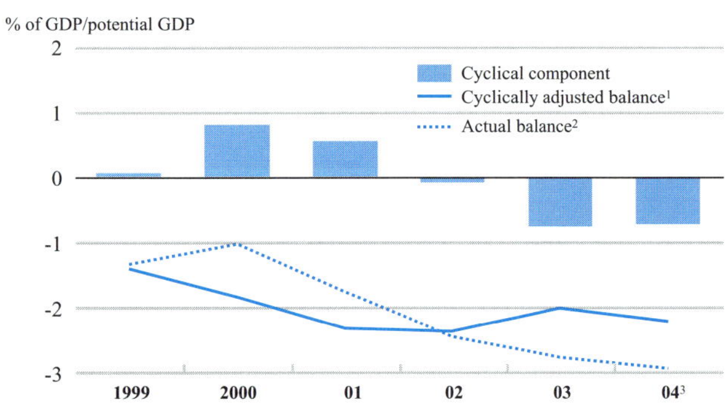

Monetary conditions provide little support

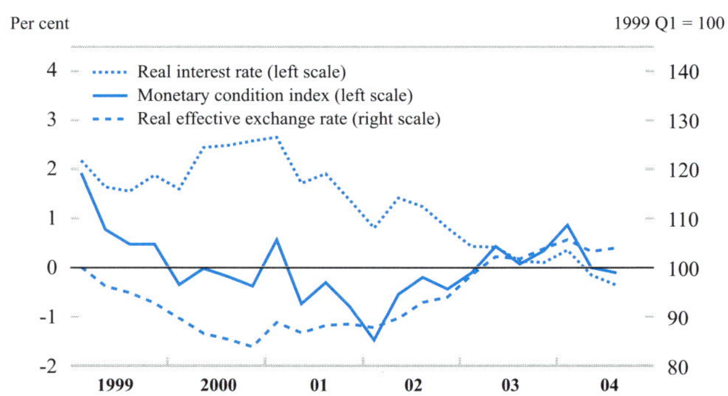

1. Per cent of potential GDP.
2. Actual balance excludes UMTS licence proceeds.
3. OECD estimate.
Source: OECD Economic Outlook 76 database.

Euro area: **Financial indicators**

	2002	2003	2004	2005	2006
Household saving ratio[a]	10.7	10.5	10.5	10.5	10.3
General government financial balance [b]	-2.4	-2.8	-2.9	-2.6	-2.4
Current account balance[b]	0.7	0.4	0.7	0.6	0.9
Short-term interest rate[c]	3.3	2.3	2.1	2.1	2.7
Long-term interest rate[d]	4.9	4.1	4.1	4.1	4.3

a) As a percentage of disposable income.
b) As a percentage of GDP.
c) 3-month interbank rate.
d) 10-year government bonds.
Source: OECD Economic Outlook 76 database.

France, Greece, the Netherlands and Portugal, while Italy is projected to breach the 3 per cent limit in 2005. The European Commission has proposed to the Council of Ministers to ease the terms of the excessive deficit procedure somewhat, thus providing more leeway for governments in breach of the reference value to smooth the required adjustment. In any event, on the basis of currently adopted policies progress in fiscal consolidation is set to be limited. After a minor easing of around ¼ per cent of GDP in 2004, the stance of fiscal policy, as gauged by the area-wide change in the cyclically-adjusted balance, is projected to remain broadly neutral over the projection period.

Monetary policy is assumed to stay easy

Monetary policy has remained easy, with the ECB refinancing rate maintained at a historical low of 2 per cent since June 2003. However, since the exchange rate in real effective terms is some 20 per cent above its level at the start of the downturn in early-2001, monetary conditions have on balance provided little support. Meanwhile, given the large amount of slack that has built up, medium-term inflation risks are small. In fact inflation expectations derived from indexed bonds, although still exceeding the 2 per cent mark, have edged down recently, despite the high oil price. There thus seems to be room to keep the stance of monetary policy accommodative;

Euro area: **Demand and output**

	2001	2002	2003	2004	2005	2006
	Current prices billion €	Percentage changes, volume (1999 prices)				
Private consumption	3 928.0	0.8	1.1	1.2	1.6	2.4
Government consumption	1 372.6	3.1	1.7	1.4	1.1	1.1
Gross fixed investment	1 442.0	-2.3	-0.4	1.9	2.9	3.8
Public	181.1	2.2	0.2	0.0	1.3	2.1
Residential	370.7	-0.9	0.5	1.8	1.9	2.1
Non-residential	890.1	-3.7	-1.0	2.4	3.7	4.9
Final domestic demand	6 742.7	0.6	0.9	1.4	1.8	2.4
Stockbuilding[a]	- 11.6	-0.1	0.3	0.3	0.1	0.0
Total domestic demand	6 731.9	0.5	1.3	1.7	1.9	2.4
Net exports [a]	119.0	0.4	-0.6	0.1	0.1	0.1
Error of estimate[a]	- 0.9		0.0	0.0	0.0	0.0
GDP at market prices	6 850.1	0.9	0.6	1.8	1.9	2.5

a) Contributions to changes in real GDP (percentage of real GDP in previous year), actual amount in the first column.
Source: OECD Economic Outlook 76 database.

Euro area: **External indicators**

	2002	2003	2004	2005	2006
			$ billion		
Foreign balance	177.1	181.2	196.5	199	228
Invisibles, net	- 129.6	- 149.1	- 129.2	- 137	- 132
Current account balance	47.6	32.1	67.4	61	96

Source: OECD Economic Outlook 76 database.

the ECB's refinancing rate is assumed to be maintained at 2 per cent in 2005 and to be raised progressively only in 2006, when underlying inflationary pressures are expected to start rebuilding.

Growth will stay close to potential

Strong growth in world trade, even if easing somewhat from recent highs, should continue to boost exports. Although high energy prices will initially weigh on business and household sentiment, investment should pick up with consumption gradually recovering in its wake. Against this backdrop, real GDP growth is projected to average close to 2 per cent in 2005, about the same as in 2004, before increasing to 2½ per cent in 2006. The unemployment rate is projected to fall slightly to 8¾ per cent in 2005 and 8½ per cent in 2005. With the output gap narrowing only progressively and the impact of the oil price hike waning, inflation is projected to stay close to 2 per cent in 2005, and to fall towards 1½ per cent by the end of the projection period.

Downside risks have increased

Oil price developments could continue to affect the momentum of the recovery. Moreover, global current account imbalances may prompt further realignments between the major currencies and this could result in renewed upward pressure on the euro exchange rate at a time when domestic demand in the euro area has not yet taken off. A sharper than expected increase in long-term interest rates in the United States could spill over to the euro area and crowd out private investment. A correction in housing markets may induce adverse wealth effects on consumption in those euro area countries where house prices have reached very high levels. On the other hand, accelerator mechanisms, underpinned by restored corporate profitability and balance sheets, could spur business investment to levels above those embodied in the projection.

Germany

Based on strong export growth, the German economy is recovering from three years of stagnation. Weak domestic demand is still weighing on activity although there are signs that investment is strengthening. The upswing should broaden in 2005, as consumer confidence gradually improves. In 2006 GDP is projected to grow by 2¼ per cent, above potential. The general government deficit is likely to remain between 3½ and 4 per cent of GDP this year and next, not falling below 3 per cent before 2006.

Significant steps to reform labour and product markets are being phased in. While the short-run impacts on confidence and growth are ambiguous, it is clear that for economic performance to be raised in a durable way these reforms need to be continued and deepened within a coherent framework. Fiscal consolidation needs to be linked to more fundamental spending reform, requiring, inter alia, the untangling of responsibilities across different levels of government, more determined reductions in both subsidies and tax expenditures and continued reform of the social security system.

Strong exports boosted activity in the first half…

GDP grew above potential in the first half of 2004. The upswing was entirely driven by exports, which expanded at double digit rates despite a loss in competitiveness *vis-à-vis* major trading partners outside Europe associated with the appreciation of the euro. Strong external demand for investment goods, in particular in fast growing transition countries, was a major factor behind this development. Also, German exporters gained competitiveness within the euro area owing to relatively lower inflation and a more favourable development of unit labour costs. More recently, however, net exports ceased to contribute to economic growth, reflecting both the adverse effects of higher raw material prices on world trade and accelerating imports. Total domestic demand continued to decline in the first part of the year, but growth turned into positive territory more recently. Private consumption declined as consumer confidence remained subdued and rising unemployment, tighter social security benefits, and accelerating consumer prices reduced disposable income growth. Construction investment slid back into recession, ending the temporary demand push due to special factors that occurred in the second half of 2003. Investment in machinery and equipment also declined in the first half, but strong growth in recent months indicates that the negative investment cycle might have ended.

… but the growth momentum is temporarily easing…

Forward looking indicators suggest that the economy continues to expand, although temporarily on a reduced growth trajectory. Retail sales appear to have stabilised after a protracted period of decline, but consumer confidence has not yet recov-

Germany

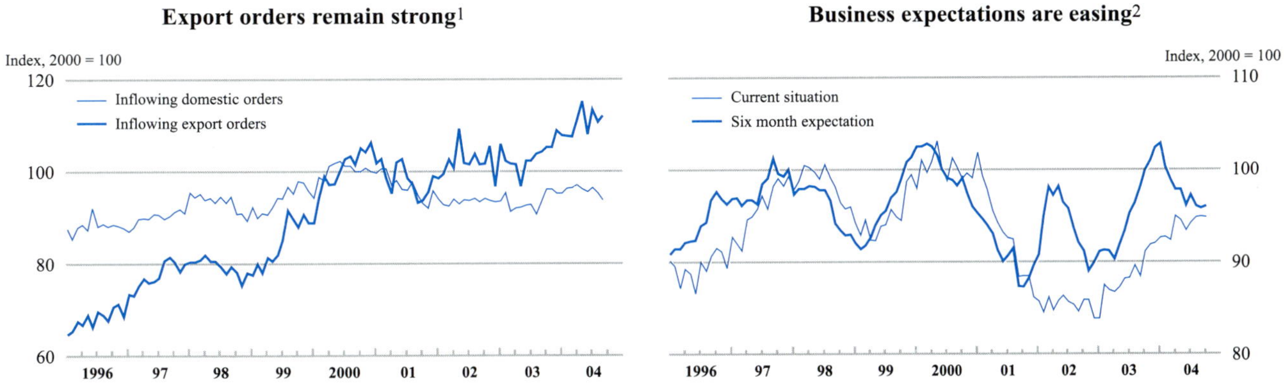

1. Manufacturing, volume.
2. Manufacturing, construction, wholesale and retail trade.
Source: Deutsche Bundesbank; Ifo Institut für Wirtschaftsforschung.

Germany: **Employment, income and inflation**

Percentage changes from previous period

	2002	2003	2004	2005	2006
Employment	-0.6	-1.0	0.2	0.4	1.1
Unemployment rate[a]	8.2	9.1	9.2	9.3	8.9
Compensation of employees	0.8	0.2	0.7	1.4	2.8
Unit labour cost	0.7	0.3	-0.4	0.0	0.4
Household disposable income	0.7	1.2	1.3	1.7	2.0
GDP deflator	1.5	1.1	0.9	0.8	0.9
Harmonised index of consumer price	1.3	1.0	1.7	1.3	0.6
Private consumption deflator	1.1	1.0	1.7	1.2	0.6

a) As a percentage of labour force.
Source: OECD Economic Outlook 76 database.

ered. Domestic orders improved slightly in the first half of the year but have eased more recently. Foreign orders moderated in the autumn following the steep upswing since the middle of last year. In the same vein, business expectations came down from the high levels prevailing at the beginning of the year. But capacity utilisation in manufacturing increased, raising prospects for higher equipment investment.

… and a turnaround on the labour market is not yet achieved

While employment has been rising since the beginning of 2004, accompanied by significant increases in labour force participation, these gains appear to be entirely attributable to strong growth in tax-favoured part-time jobs with few hours worked, and subsidised self-employment schemes for formerly unemployed. At the same time, unemployment has continued to increase unabatedly and shedding of regular employment continues. Diminishing short-shift work and the levelling-off of reductions in vacancies indicate, however, that demand conditions appear to be gradually improving. Wage settlements in major parts of the economy suggest that wage growth will remain moderate, and in some industrial branches social partners agreed to extend working hours without increasing pay. Some recent policy measures, notably stricter means testing and tighter work availability requirements support these developments, which should contribute to making growth more employment-intensive.

Germany

Employment is edging up

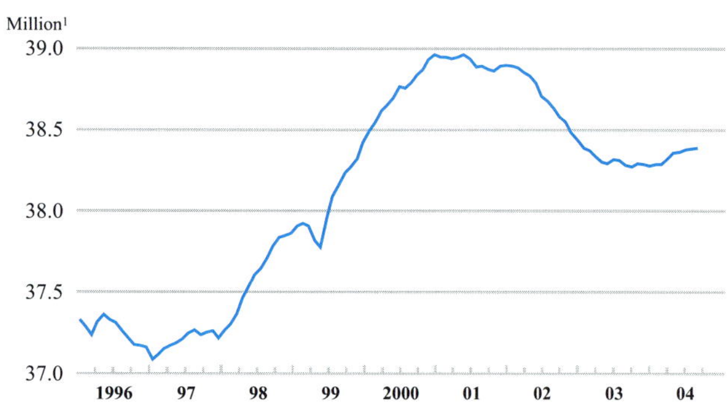

Consumer confidence remains low

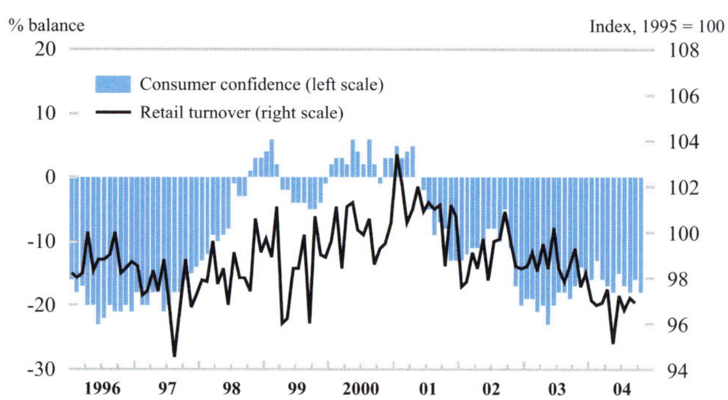

1. Seasonally adjusted employment, domestic concept of the national accounts.
Source: Deutsche Bundesbank ; OECD, *Main Economic Indicators*.

Germany: **Financial indicators**

	2002	2003	2004	2005	2006
Household saving ratio[a]	10.5	10.7	11.1	11.1	10.8
General government financial balance [b]	-3.7 [c]	-3.8	-3.9	-3.5	-2.7
Current account balance[b]	2.1	2.3	3.3	3.9	4.7
Short-term interest rate[d]	3.3	2.3	2.1	2.1	2.7
Long-term interest rate[e]	4.8	4.1	4.1	4.0	4.3

a) As a percentage of disposable income.
b) As a percentage of GDP.
c) Including proceeds of sales of mobile telephone licences (around 2.5 per cent of GDP).
d) 3-month interbank rate.
e) 10-year government bonds.
Source: OECD Economic Outlook 76 database.

Financial conditions are supportive

Headline inflation (harmonised consumer price index) accelerated to 2 per cent year-on-year in summer 2004, driven by both rising oil prices and substantial hikes in administered prices. Significant increases in statutory co-payments for health care services and increases in indirect taxes mainly accounted for the latter. Inflation is set to diminish as these effects are losing significance and unit labour costs decline. Overall, financial conditions appear conducive to higher growth. Returns from buoyant exports and corporate cost cutting are likely to have strengthened corporate balance sheets; real interest rates remain below average historical levels; and banks, having reduced non-performing loans, ceased tightening credit standards, and seem to be making credit more available.

The general government deficit remains close to 4 per cent of GDP…

The general government deficit is projected to remain roughly unchanged at somewhat below 4 per cent of GDP in 2004, exceeding the deficit limit of the Stability and Growth Pact for the third year in a row. While consolidation measures on the spending side of the budget became effective, major income tax reductions are

Germany: **Demand and output**

	2001	2002	2003	2004	2005	2006
	Current prices billion €	Percentage changes, volume (1995 prices)				
Private consumption	1 237.2	-0.7	0.0	-0.7	0.8	1.9
Government consumption	394.2	1.9	0.1	0.1	0.0	0.1
Gross fixed investment	420.6	-6.3	-2.2	-2.0	0.6	3.4
Public	36.8	-2.2	-10.2	-6.0	0.9	-0.7
Residential	131.7	-5.9	-2.7	-2.7	-2.0	-0.2
Non-residential	252.1	-7.1	-0.6	-1.0	1.8	5.6
Final domestic demand	2 052.1	-1.4	-0.4	-0.8	0.6	1.8
Stockbuilding[a]	- 19.3	-0.4	0.9	1.0	0.3	-0.1
Total domestic demand	2 032.8	-1.9	0.5	0.3	0.9	1.8
Exports of goods and services	730.7	4.1	1.8	8.1	5.7	8.1
Imports of goods and services	689.5	-1.6	3.9	6.4	4.9	7.5
Net exports[a]	41.2	1.9	-0.6	0.9	0.6	0.7
GDP at market prices	2 074.0	0.1	-0.1	1.2	1.4	2.3
Memorandum items						
GDP growth without working day adjustments		0.1	-0.1	1.7	1.2	2.1
Investment in machinery and equipment	191.7	-7.2	-0.9	0.0	3.4	7.5
Construction investment	228.9	-5.8	-3.2	-3.7	-2.0	-0.5

Note : Economic activity in 2004, 2005 and 2006 is subject to unusually large changes in the number of working days. The OECD projections are adjusted for this effect so that, other things equal, GDP is lower for 2004 and higher for 2005 and 2006 than in the unadjusted projections
a) Contributions to changes in real GDP (percentage of real GDP in previous year), actual amount in the first column.
Source: OECD Economic Outlook 76 database.

Germany: **External indicators**

	2002	2003	2004	2005	2006
			$ billion		
Goods and services exports	720.5	870.2	1 032.5	1 152	1 255
Goods and services imports	630.7	765.7	897.0	996	1 071
Foreign balance	89.8	104.5	135.5	157	184
Invisibles, net	- 48.3	- 49.7	- 46.5	- 45	- 43
Current account balance	41.5	54.8	89.1	111	141
			Percentage changes		
Goods and services export volumes	4.1	1.8	8.1	5.7	8.1
Goods and services import volumes	- 1.6	3.9	6.4	4.9	7.5
Export performance [a]	1.0	- 2.4	- 0.5	- 2.9	- 0.8
Terms of trade	1.9	1.6	- 0.2	- 0.3	0.8

a) Ratio between export volume and export market of total goods and services.
Source: OECD Economic Outlook 76 database.

reducing government revenues. Higher than expected unemployment-related outlays and unforeseen revenue shortfalls also weigh on the budget. Revenues from a tax amnesty plan fell short of expectations by several billion euro, and increases in tobacco taxes are not likely to yield additional revenues.

... declining slowly in the next couple of years

Consolidation measures scheduled for 2005 and 2006 comprise reductions in both subsidies and tax expenditures and in government employment, and a tightening of social transfers. However, with the final stage of income tax reductions becoming effective in 2005 the deficit is projected to fall only moderately, to 3½ per cent of GDP. Fiscal consolidation will step up in 2006, and the general government deficit will drop to 2¾ per cent of GDP, reflecting a reduction of the structural deficit by 0.4 percentage points and stronger economic growth.

The upswing will broaden in 2005

While export growth will lose some of its momentum over the next couple of quarters, strong foreign demand will remain the main force driving the recovery. With the improvement in domestic demand only narrowly based, GDP growth in 2004 may reach 1¼ per cent. Private consumption will gradually strengthen as employment recovers, although employment gains for the coming months may still be largely confined to part-time jobs with few hours worked and subsidised self-employment schemes. Income tax reductions and the projected decline in inflation will support growth of real disposable incomes and provide some boost to spending in 2005. Rising profits and increasing capacity utilisation will lead to a strengthening of equipment investment, though construction investment will remain a drag on growth. All in all, GDP is likely to grow by 1½ (working-day adjusted) per cent in 2005 and, as the upswing broadens, by 2¼ per cent in 2006, significantly above potential.

Risks to these projections are significant

If world trade were to be weaker or the euro persistently higher valued than what underlies these projections, the adverse impact on German growth could be substantial, as the resilience of the domestic economy to external shocks is still low. On the other hand, confidence of investors and consumers would be reinforced if popular recognition of the need for continued broad-based structural reform were to strengthen.

France

Having slowed in the second half of 2004, the upswing should pick up again in 2005 once the effects of oil price increases begin to wane. Both foreign and private domestic demand remain robust so that employment growth is likely to pick up during 2005 and unemployment should fall. Productivity growth and continued wage moderation allow core inflation to remain low.

Public finances are set to improve slowly, in part reflecting inclusion of a large capital transaction as revenue in the 2005 budget. The 2005 deficit may exceed government plans. Nevertheless, an improvement in government finances should follow from reforms in central government spending control and health care expenditure management. These reforms will require sustained efforts to change underlying incentives if good intentions are not to be undermined. Having shown that lower employers' contributions can improve employment prospects, the government should seek to extend these and other labour market reforms.

Output growth continued in the first half, then faltered

While the first half of 2004 saw real GDP expanding at an annual rate of up to 3 per cent as output responded to strong demand, the third quarter showed an unexpectedly sharp slowdown as GDP barely grew. Earlier in the year, consumer demand, continued export growth, and an upturn in business fixed investment and residential construction had supported GDP, but both private consumption and fixed investment fell in the third quarter.

Productivity increased and core inflation remains contained

Despite the upturn in output growth, total employment continued to fall in early 2004 – though there was a small increase in the third quarter – partly owing to the completed phasing out of some government-supported youth employment schemes, but also owing to quite a sharp increase in labour productivity growth in the private sector. This helped to improve profit margins. The recovery of profits from previously low levels is probably a factor contributing to an acceleration of business investment, which in the past has often occurred only later in the recovery. Although inflation remains relatively low, it has picked up somewhat during the year with year-on-year headline inflation in October at 2.2 per cent, to which increased energy prices contributed 0.6 per cent; core inflation was at 1.3 per cent.

France

Domestic demand is sustaining growth

Contributions to growth[1]

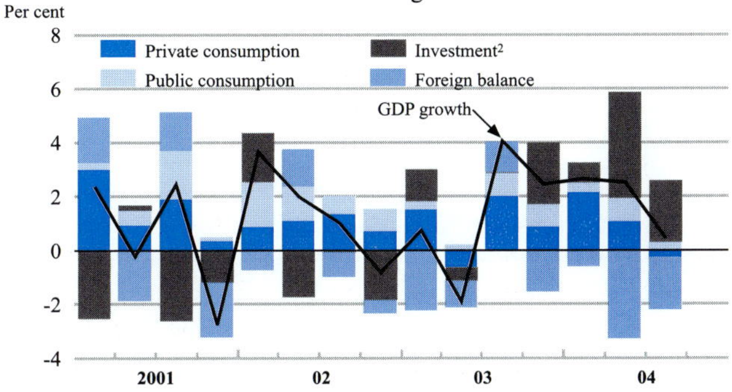

Short-term indicators are contrasting

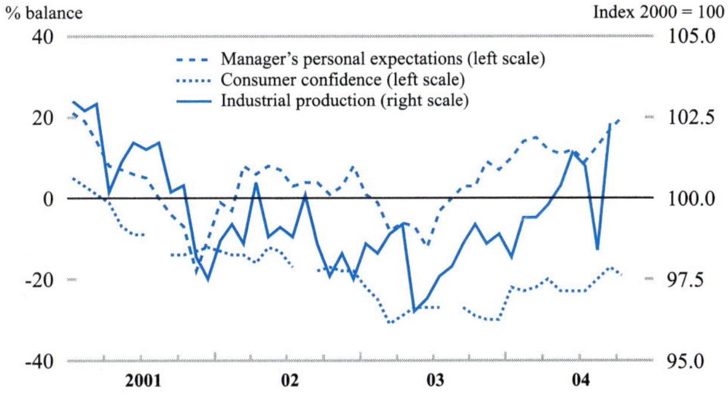

1. At an annual rate.
2. Including changes in stocks.

Source: National Institute for Statistics and Economic Studies (INSEE).

France: Employment, income and inflation

Percentage changes from previous period

	2002	2003	2004	2005	2006
Employment	0.7	-0.1	-0.1	0.4	0.8
Unemployment rate[a]	9.0	9.7	9.8	9.7	9.2
Compensation of employees	3.6	2.3	2.6	3.1	3.6
Unit labour cost	2.5	1.8	0.5	1.1	1.3
Household disposable income	4.3	2.3	2.9	3.5	3.8
GDP deflator	2.4	1.4	1.9	1.8	1.7
Harmonised index of consumer price	1.9	2.2	2.3	1.8	1.8
Private consumption deflator	1.7	1.8	1.5	1.7	1.8

a) As a percentage of labour force.
Source: OECD Economic Outlook 76 database.

Despite the slowdown after mid-year…

According to preliminary data for the third quarter the buoyancy of the first half has apparently evaporated. However, while this may partly be due to further increases in, and renewed uncertainty about, world oil prices, temporary factors have also been at work. Consumer and – especially – business confidence indicators had been pointing to greater optimism, but industrial production fell sharply in August before more than making up for lost ground in September, pointing to the likelihood of renewed growth in the fourth quarter, despite weak consumer expenditure on manufactures in September.

… growth could increase again during 2005

More comfortable company profits, the first half upturn in investment, the likely better-than-budgeted fiscal outturn for 2004, all provide the basis for optimism that the momentum of the recovery can be resumed during 2005. As this occurs, it can be expected that employment will begin to grow again, reinforcing consumer sentiment. This will support consumer demand both through increasing incomes and a further decline in the saving ratio. Although continuing demand growth will no doubt result in strong import growth, the balance of payments should not deteriorate markedly, particularly as France typically benefits strongly from growth in demand from many oil-exporting countries, demand which should come through during 2005 and 2006.

France

Energy and tobacco prices influence inflation[1]

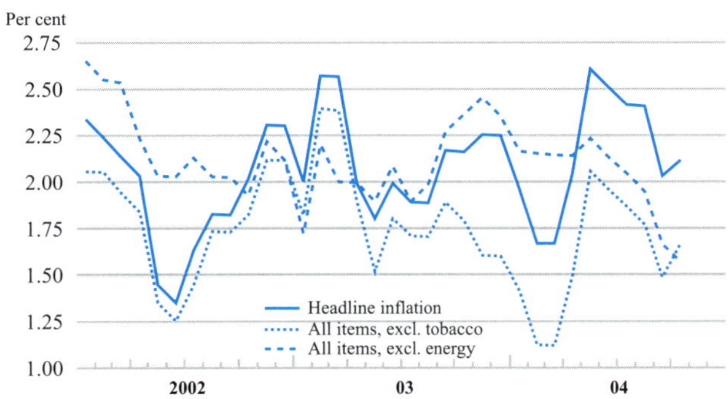

Employment remains weak

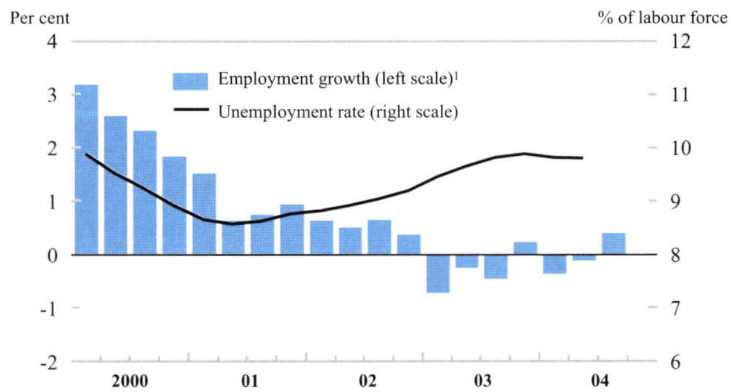

1. Year-on-year percentage changes.
Source: National Institute for Statistics and Economic Studies (INSEE).

France: **Financial indicators**

	2002	2003	2004	2005	2006
Household saving ratio[a]	12.1	11.1	10.2	9.9	9.6
General government financial balance [b]	-3.3	-4.1	-3.7	-3.1	-2.9
Current account balance[b]	1.0	0.4	0.2	0.2	0.6
Short-term interest rate[c]	3.3	2.3	2.1	2.1	2.7
Long-term interest rate[d]	4.9	4.1	4.1	4.1	4.3

a) As a percentage of disposable income.
b) As a percentage of GDP.
c) 3-month interbank rate.
d) 10-year benchmark government bonds.
Source: OECD Economic Outlook 76 database.

The output gap will barely narrow

Growth is not expected consistently to exceed potential before mid-2005, after which there may be some narrowing of the output gap. Renewed employment growth will generate a sustained fall in the unemployment rate, though not as rapidly as in the late 1990s. For most of the projection period unemployment will remain above the level at which it would begin to generate significant pressure on wage inflation, and continued productivity growth should keep unit labour cost growth down, even while real wages grow. The projections would leave the economy at the end of 2006 on the threshold of labour utilisation levels at which renewed wage pressure might be expected. Current estimates suggest that this could occur at an unemployment level of nearly 9 per cent, just below the level projected for late 2006; reforms have reduced structural unemployment from nearly 10 per cent in the late 1990s, but ongoing reforms are needed to allow structural unemployment to fall further.

Underlying public finances improve only slowly…

The general government deficit is likely to be lower in 2004 than planned, owing to stronger revenues generated by higher economic growth, and to an unexpected slowdown in public expenditure on health care in the third quarter. The government budget estimate of a deficit of 2.9 per cent of GDP in 2005 is based on

France: **Demand and output**

	2001	2002	2003	2004	2005	2006
	Current prices billion €	Percentage changes, volume (1995 prices)				
Private consumption	807.2	1.8	1.7	2.3	2.2	2.2
Government consumption	342.8	4.6	2.5	2.3	1.7	1.7
Gross fixed investment	297.2	-1.8	0.1	3.5	3.1	3.3
General government	46.4	1.8	5.8	1.9	1.2	1.1
Household	70.6	0.7	0.7	3.6	4.1	3.5
Other	180.3	-3.7	-1.6	3.9	3.3	3.9
Final domestic demand	1 447.2	1.7	1.6	2.5	2.3	2.3
Stockbuilding[a]	4.5	-0.2	-0.2	0.7	0.3	0.0
Total domestic demand	1 451.7	1.5	1.4	3.2	2.5	2.3
Exports of goods and services	413.2	1.7	-2.6	3.4	6.0	7.5
Imports of goods and services	389.2	3.3	0.3	7.7	7.7	7.5
Net exports[a]	24.1	-0.4	-0.8	-1.2	-0.5	-0.1
GDP at market prices	1 475.8	1.1	0.5	2.1	2.0	2.3

a) Contributions to changes in real GDP (percentage of real GDP in previous year), actual amount in the first column.
Source: OECD Economic Outlook 76 database.

France: **External indicators**

	2002	2003	2004	2005	2006
			$ billion		
Goods and services exports	390.5	455.9	521.1	581	625
Goods and services imports	363.3	435.3	509.9	573	611
Foreign balance	27.3	20.6	11.2	8	15
Invisibles, net	- 13.5	- 13.6	- 7.8	- 4	- 2
Current account balance	13.8	7.1	3.4	4	13
			Percentage changes		
Goods and services export volumes	1.7	- 2.6	3.4	6.0	7.5
Goods and services import volumes	3.3	0.3	7.7	7.7	7.5
Export performance [a]	- 0.6	- 6.3	- 3.9	- 2.1	- 1.3
Terms of trade	2.8	0.3	1.6	0.7	1.1

a) Ratio between export volume and export market of total goods and services.
Source: OECD Economic Outlook 76 database.

slightly higher growth projections than the OECD's, and lower oil prices. On the basis of OECD projections, the deficit may not fall below 3 per cent of GDP until 2006, absent further measures. Budgetary plans for 2005 include, under normal income, the payment from the public electricity company (EDF) to compensate the government for taking over EDF's existing pension liabilities. This amounts to some 0.5 per cent of GDP. While legitimate and accurate under current accounting conventions, this does not reflect the full impact on the budget: while it reduces government debt in the short term, it increases deferred liabilities by exactly the same amount. Without the EDF payment there would be little or no improvement in the structural budget balance in 2005, though a more substantial one in 2006.

... but should be supported by continuing reforms

This prospective improvement in the budget balance depends on government success in reducing employment in the public sector, an area where plans have had to be reined back in the face of implementation difficulties in the past. The same difficulties have arisen with health sector reforms; the success of plans for family doctors to encourage more rational use of resources will depend on the incentives they face.

The recovery remains fragile

Projections of a bounceback from a transitory slowdown in the third quarter of 2004, followed by a sustained recovery, are based on continued consumer and business confidence: households should reduce their saving somewhat, while companies will invest and begin to take on labour. The third quarter outturn and weakening investment intentions underline the fragility of this confidence, however, and represent a downside risk to the projections. Achieving underlying improvements in public sector finances is important for confidence, and continued reforms in labour and product markets will be important in encouraging a sustained upturn in employment growth.

Italy

Exports and investment activity rose markedly in the first half of 2004, ending their protracted slump. Domestic demand will sustain the recovery, though the pass-through of higher oil prices may restrain demand growth temporarily. GDP growth of 1½ to 2 per cent is projected over 2005-06, which would be above the estimated rate of potential. Inflation could start to rise again as the output gap closes.

A planned tax cut in 2005-06 and a pension reform as of 2008 could improve the conditions for growth, but a sustained public debt decline will be a sine qua non for building private agents' confidence, so that more and earlier public spending reforms are needed. Competition reforms in service sectors, including energy, transport, finance and education, could help to narrow the inflation gap with euro area partners, while also spurring innovation and a more competitive export structure.

Recovery thus far has been export-led

In the first half of 2004, exports picked up with the recovery of world demand and market share losses diminished as the euro stabilised against the dollar. Investment growth turned positive following six quarters of decline, and residential construction was buoyant. Imports subsequently surged, encouraged also by weak price competitiveness. Consumption has been more hesitant, with confidence improving only slowly, but it should soon be boosted by better economic prospects including a recovery in employment. Indeed, preliminary estimate for the third quarter suggests a sustained pace of recovery. Industrial production has been exceedingly weak, though leading indicators suggest a recovery toward end-year. GDP growth for 2004 on a working day-adjusted basis is expected to be 1.3 per cent and somewhat above this figure on an unadjusted basis.

Employment growth is robust…

In contrast to previous cycles, employment has grown in the early stages of recovery thanks to labour market reforms. After pausing in the latter half of 2003 as the impact of earlier reforms faded, employment grew strongly again in the first half of 2004, apparently facilitated by new flexible work contracts introduced in late 2003. At the same time, productivity fell over the course of 2001 to mid-2003 and has been rising only slowly since. This in turn has generated unit labour cost growth well above the euro area average. A capacity to pass through costs into prices in

Italy

Productivity growth is weak[1]

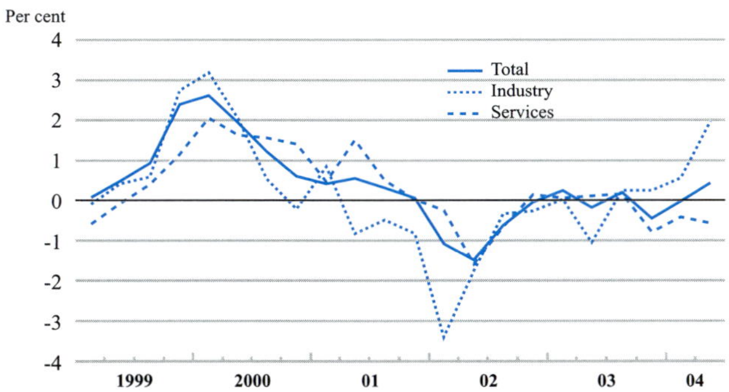

The real exchange rate has appreciated markedly[1]

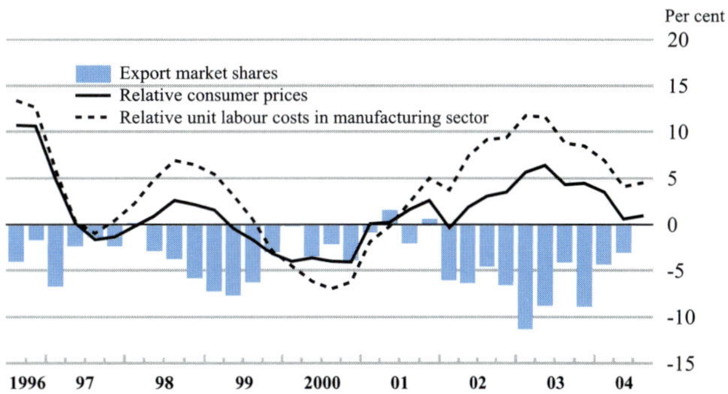

1. Year-on-year percentage changes.
Source: Italian Statistical Office; OECD Economic Outlook 76 database.

Italy: Employment, income and inflation

Percentage changes from previous period

	2002	2003	2004	2005	2006
Employment	1.5	1.0	1.8	1.5	1.1
Unemployment rate[a]	9.1	8.8	8.1	7.5	7.3
Compensation of employees	4.4	4.3	4.4	3.9	3.7
Unit labour cost	4.0	4.0	3.1	2.2	1.6
Household disposable income	3.8	2.4	4.2	3.6	4.0
GDP deflator	3.1	2.9	2.8	2.1	2.0
Harmonised index of consumer price	2.6	2.8	2.1	2.5	2.2
Private consumption deflator	3.1	2.5	2.1	2.4	2.1

a) As a percentage of labour force.
Source: OECD Economic Outlook 76 database.

many service sectors that face weak competitive pressures may explain part of the paradox of firms continuing to hire despite rising unit labour costs.

... and inflation higher than expected

Inflation initially picked up in 2004, reflecting wage increases, in particular in the public sector which has been subject to a not-yet-exhausted bunching of contract implementations and renewals. Against a background of tightening labour markets but weak productivity growth, wage claims are attempting to cover an alleged gap between "perceived" and actual inflation, on top of that between actual and officially forecast inflation, the latter being the basis for national wage agreements. In the summer months, falling food prices led to lower inflation and then in the autumn the government announced administrative measures through end-year to limit consumer price rises. Though only palliative, their intent is to prevent an increase in inflation expectations following the oil price hike. Inflation fell in the third quarter and in October, with inflation expectations also subsiding, and it is likely to remain low through end-year.

Italy

Export and investment volumes are recovering[1]

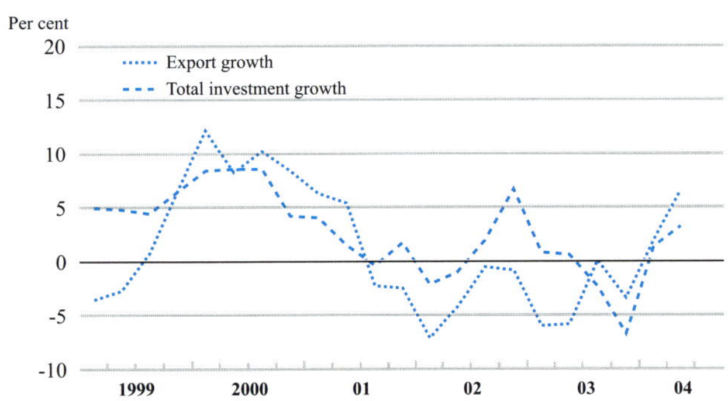

The primary surplus has dwindled[2]

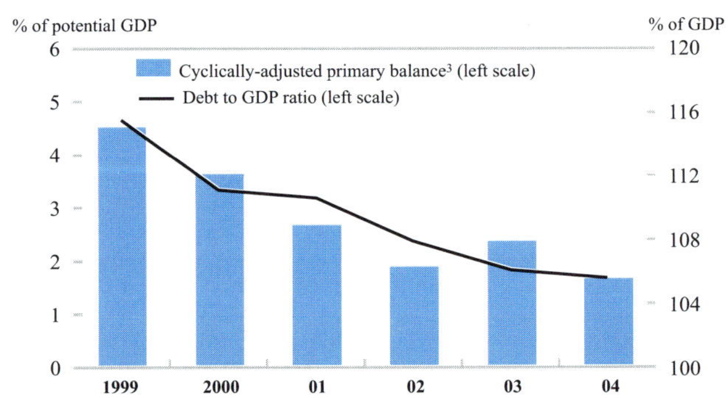

1. Year-on-year percentage changes.
2. Data for 2004 are OECD projections.
3. Corrected for one-off measures.
Source: OECD Economic Outlook 76 database.

Italy: **Financial indicators**

	2002	2003	2004	2005	2006
Household saving ratio[a]	10.6	10.5	11.3	10.9	10.3
General government financial balance [b,c,d]	-2.4	-2.5	-2.9	-3.1	-3.6
Current account balance[b]	-0.8	-1.4	-0.5	-1.6	-1.9
Short-term interest rate[e]	3.3	2.3	2.1	2.1	2.7
Long-term interest rate[f]	5.0	4.3	4.3	4.2	4.4

a) As a percentage of disposable income.
b) As a percentage of GDP.
c) Excludes the impact of swaps and forward rate transactions on interest payments. These operations are however included in the financial balance reported to the European Commission for purposes of the excessive deficit procedure.
d) The deficit of ANAS, the state road agency (around 0.2 per cent of GDP) is included in the projections, pending a decision by the statistical agencies.
e) 3-month interbank rate.
f) 10-year government bonds.
Source: OECD Economic Outlook 76 database.

The policy stance has been supportive

The policy stance has so far been supportive of the recovery. Real interest rates are lower than elsewhere in the euro area, given higher inflation, though the real exchange rate has been appreciating. Credit conditions are easy, and households continue to increase their borrowing to finance housing investment and durable purchases. On the other hand, enterprise credits have been declining, reflecting balance sheet restructuring and still weak industrial production. Fiscal policy has been expansionary as the structural primary surplus has been declining since 2002. Substantial fiscal slippage in the first half of 2004, with the deficit reaching 3½ per cent of GDP, necessitated a mid-year corrective package of current expenditure growth caps, subsidy cuts, and selective tax increases. A greater than planned use of tax amnesties also allowed one-off savings of around 1½ per cent of GDP.

Italy: **Demand and output**

	2001	2002	2003	2004	2005	2006
	Current prices billion €	Percentage changes, volume (1995 prices)				
Private consumption[a]	731.6	0.4	1.2	1.3	1.5	2.6
Government consumption	229.5	1.9	2.2	0.7	0.6	0.3
Gross fixed investment	240.5	1.3	-2.1	3.8	4.9	4.2
Machinery and equipment	140.2	-0.2	-4.9	4.1	4.9	4.5
Construction	100.3	3.3	1.8	3.5	5.0	3.8
Residential	53.9	4.5	2.3	3.7	4.5	3.1
Non-residential	46.4	2.0	1.3	3.3	5.6	4.6
Final domestic demand	1 201.6	0.9	0.7	1.7	2.1	2.5
Stockbuilding [b]	- 0.7	0.5	0.6	-0.4	0.0	0.0
Total domestic demand	1 200.8	1.3	1.3	1.2	2.1	2.5
Exports of goods and services	345.9	-3.4	-3.9	4.5	6.1	5.4
Imports of goods and services	328.4	-0.2	-0.6	4.3	7.5	6.7
Net exports [b]	17.5	-0.9	-0.9	0.1	-0.4	-0.4
GDP at market prices	1 218.3	0.4	0.4	1.3	1.7	2.1

Note: Economic activity in 2004 and 2005 is subject to unusually large changes in the number of working days. The OECD projections are adjusted for this effect, whereas the official government projections are not. Other things equal, the adjusted projections are lower for 2004 and higher for 2005 than the unadjusted projections.
a) Final consumption in the domestic market by households.
b) Contributions to changes in real GDP (percentage of real GDP in previous year), actual amount in the first column.
Source: OECD Economic Outlook 76 database.

Italy: External indicators

	2002	2003	2004	2005	2006
			$ billion		
Goods and services exports	321.6	373.7	437.2	487	521
Goods and services imports	310.1	365.7	427.2	489	529
Foreign balance	11.5	8.0	9.9	- 1	- 8
Invisibles, net	- 21.4	- 29.0	- 19.0	- 27	- 28
Current account balance	- 9.9	- 21.0	- 9.0	- 29	- 36
			Percentage changes		
Goods and services export volumes	- 3.4	- 3.9	4.5	6.1	5.4
Goods and services import volumes	- 0.2	- 0.6	4.3	7.5	6.7
Export performance [a]	- 5.9	- 8.2	- 4.0	- 2.3	- 3.6
Terms of trade	1.7	1.8	0.0	- 1.3	0.1

a) Ratio between export volume and export market of total goods and services.
Source: OECD Economic Outlook 76 database.

Fiscal policy is set to tighten in 2005

The 2005 budget calls for €24 billion (1½ per cent of GDP) in savings in order to counteract the trend deterioration of the deficit and reach the target of 2.7 per cent of GDP, while reducing the use of one-off measures. There are three main deficit-reducing features: *i)* a 2 per cent cap on the growth of non-pension current spending; *ii)* expected receipts from intensified tax scrutiny of small businesses, rental incomes, and value added tax invoices; and *iii)* a programme of real-estate asset securitisations, this being the sole remaining use of one-off measures. The OECD projections suggest a deficit of just over 3 per cent of GDP in 2005, mainly reflecting slower growth than assumed in the budget and the assumption that the State Road Agency (Anas) remains in the general government. The 2006 projection points to a renewed deficit increase unless one-off measures are replaced by permanent ones.

Growth should intensify in 2005 and 2006

Over the next two years, private consumption should take over from investment as the main driver of growth. In 2005, however, households' purchasing power will be curtailed by a renewed rise in inflation, reflecting the removal of administrative measures and full pass-through of the world oil price rise, and also by the budgeted increase in effective taxation. Though a fall in the savings rate could partly cushion these shocks, consumption growth will slow, especially in the first half of the year. Investment demand growth in 2005 is largely unaffected by the oil and tax shocks, but tapers off in 2006 as capacity needs are satisfied and the housing market cools. Export market growth remains robust throughout the projection, but with continuing losses in market share and strong import growth, the contribution of the foreign sector will be negative. All in all, growth is projected to rise to 1¾ per cent in 2005 and then to over 2 per cent in 2006.

But fiscal policy and inflation remain risk factors

Domestic inflation could surprise on the upside. The output gap is closing fast and the labour market is tight in the north-central regions, so that higher oil prices may be passed through into wages and core inflation to a greater extent than expected. Fiscal slippage, stemming from the difficulty of implementing structural measures quickly, larger than expected public sector wage increases, or else from tax cuts not fully financed by structural spending cuts, could impede the recovery of private sector confidence and demand.

United Kingdom

Recent signs that growth is slowing from above-trend rates are welcome as the economy is probably operating close to capacity. Future growth is likely to be less reliant on consumption and more driven by investment, with net exports being much less of a drag. Instability stemming from the housing market remains a risk, although it may be smaller than at previous house price peaks.

The slowdown and continuing low inflation warrant a pause in monetary tightening, although further tightening may be needed during 2005, in particular due to increasing pressures from the labour market. The government deficit is likely to be above 3 per cent of GDP in 2004 and, in the absence of a spontaneous rise in taxes, additional action may be required to achieve a decisive and sustainable reduction.

The recovery is maturing

GDP growth, according to the preliminary estimate, slowed sharply in the third quarter of 2004 to only 0.4 per cent, less than half the average rate over the preceding four quarters. Underlying this slowdown was a fall in industrial production and a decline in the growth rate of retail sales volumes. The cooling of the housing market is likely to be an increasingly important factor in damping growth in private consumption; monthly measures of house prices have flattened since July, following an increase of more than 40 per cent since the beginning of 2002. Nevertheless, the strength of other components of domestic demand, and buoyancy in services sector output and orders caution against extrapolating the weak third quarter growth estimate into subsequent quarters, especially as low preliminary growth estimates are often revised upwards.

Evidence on inflation is mixed

The inflation rate, as measured by the consumer price index, was just over 1 per cent in September and October, the threshold at which the Governor of the Bank of England would be obliged to write to the Chancellor explaining why the 2 per cent target had been undershot. One factor behind this surprisingly low outcome has been falling import prices due to the appreciation of the effective exchange rate, which rose by 6 per cent between the beginning of the year to a peak in early August. However, with more than two-thirds of this appreciation being reversed in the following three months, and oil and metals prices having risen sharply, import prices are push-

United Kingdom

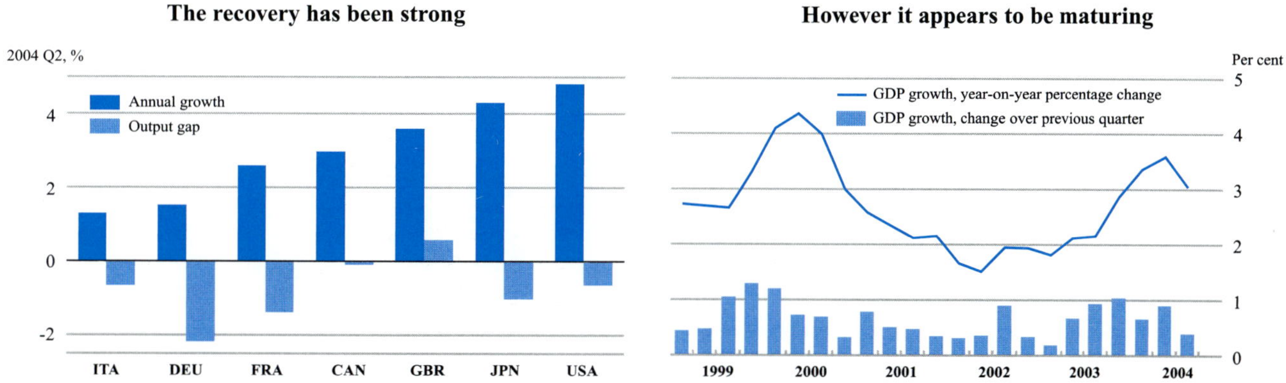

Source: National Statistics and OECD Economic Outlook 76 database.

United Kingdom: Employment, income and inflation

Percentage changes from previous period

	2002	2003	2004	2005	2006
Employment	0.8	0.9	0.9	0.4	0.2
Unemployment rate[a]	5.2	5.0	4.7	4.7	5.0
Compensation of employees	4.4	4.2	6.0	5.5	4.9
Unit labour cost	2.6	1.9	2.7	2.8	2.4
Household disposable income	3.0	4.1	5.5	5.2	4.4
GDP deflator	3.2	3.0	2.1	2.2	2.3
Harmonised index of consumer price[b]	1.3	1.4	1.3	1.7	2.1
Private consumption deflator	1.6	1.8	1.5	2.0	2.2

a) As a percentage of labour force.
b) The HICP is known as the Consumer Price Index in the United Kingdom.
Source: OECD Economic Outlook 76 database.

ing up consumer price inflation in the short term. Pressures are already evident in the producer input and output price indices which are both up strongly since the beginning of 2004. With the unemployment rate falling to just over 4½ per cent, its lowest level since the 1970s and ¾ per cent below the OECD estimate of the structural rate, the rate of increase in private sector average earnings (excluding bonus payments) has also risen steadily over the past year.

On present policies the budget deficit is unlikely to narrow significantly

The general government deficit, on a Maastricht basis, is likely to slightly exceed 3 per cent of GDP in 2004. Increased tax revenues from oil companies due to the higher oil price and lagged effects of the cyclical improvement on corporate tax revenues are likely in 2005, and fiscal drag will also push up income tax revenues. However, as the OECD's assessment differs from the official one, these additional revenues may not be sufficient to compensate for the planned increase in nominal public expenditure of about 12 per cent between 2004 and 2006, so that the deficit is likely to increase slightly.

United Kingdom

Cost pressures have yet to feed into consumer price inflation[1]

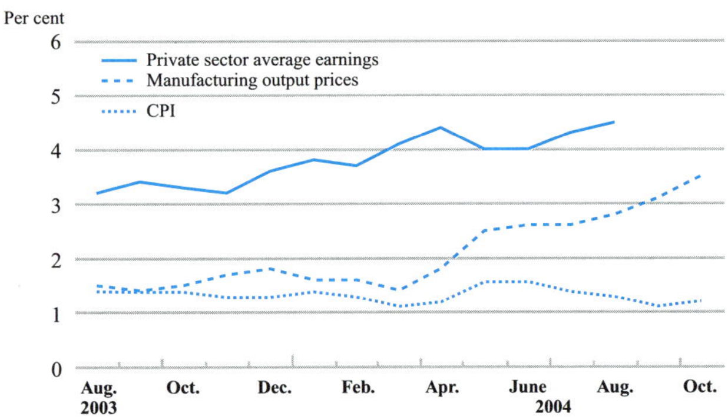

Monetary tightening usually precedes house price falls

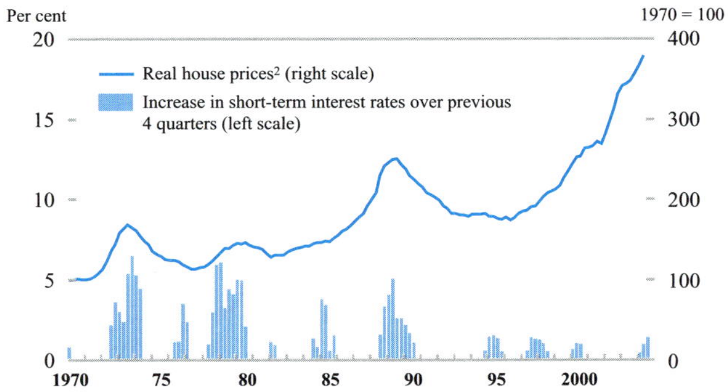

1. Consumer price index. Percentage change year-on-year, average earnings exclude bonuses.
2. Relative to consumers' expenditure deflator (index 1970 = 100).
Source: National Statistics, Office of the Deputy Prime Minister and OECD, Economic Outlook 76 database.

United Kingdom: **Financial indicators**

	2002	2003	2004	2005	2006
Household saving ratio[a]	5.3	5.5	6.4	7.4	7.9
General government financial balance[b]	-1.7	-3.5	-3.2	-3.2	-3.3
Current account balance[b]	-1.7	-1.9	-2.2	-2.4	-2.2
Short-term interest rate[c]	4.0	3.7	4.6	5.5	5.8
Long-term interest rate[d]	4.9	4.5	5.0	5.2	5.2

a) As a percentage of disposable income.
b) As a percentage of GDP.
c) 3-month interbank rate.
d) 10-year government bonds.
Source: OECD Economic Outlook 76 database.

A slowdown in the housing market will raise the saving ratio

The link between the housing market and consumer spending suggests that, with the level of house prices stabilising or even moderately falling, consumption growth may decelerate significantly, in particular as mortgage equity withdrawal becomes less of a supporting factor. This should lead to a rise in the saving ratio by around 1½ percentage points over the coming year to a level closer to its long-run average. With the targeted measure of inflation so low and growth slowing, the Monetary Policy Committee of the Bank of England can afford a wait-and-see approach. Thus, following increases in the repo rate by 1¼ percentage points between November 2003 and August 2004, there should be a pause until next year. Nevertheless, even if the housing market damps growth in consumers' expenditure, other components of domestic demand have considerable momentum: fixed investment was up 7 per cent in the year to the second quarter and surveys of future business investment intentions remain strong; the government's fiscal plans imply continuing rapid growth in public expenditure; and with the relative cyclical position in the major European countries expected to improve over the coming years, net export volumes should act as much less of a drag on activity. Further increases in the repo rate over the course of 2005, totalling around ¾ of a percentage point, should be suf-

United Kingdom: **Demand and output**

	2001	2002	2003	2004	2005	2006
	Current prices billion £	Percentage changes, volume (2001 prices)				
Private consumption	659.9	3.3	2.3	3.0	1.8	1.7
Government consumption	189.7	3.8	3.5	3.8	1.9	2.0
Gross fixed investment	165.5	2.7	2.2	6.5	5.3	3.5
Public[a]	15.9	2.4	22.1	8.5	18.7	4.7
Private residential	39.8	7.6	3.1	6.7	3.1	3.3
Private non-residential	109.8	0.9	-1.1	6.0	3.8	3.3
Final domestic demand	1 015.2	3.3	2.5	3.7	2.4	2.0
Stockbuilding[b]	6.6	-0.4	0.0	0.1	0.0	0.0
Total domestic demand	1 021.7	2.9	2.5	3.8	2.4	2.0
Exports of goods and services	272.4	0.1	0.1	2.6	7.9	8.2
Imports of goods and services	299.8	4.1	1.3	4.7	6.5	6.3
Net exports[b]	- 27.4	-1.2	-0.4	-0.7	0.1	0.2
GDP at market prices	994.3	1.8	2.2	3.2	2.6	2.4

a) Including nationalised industries and public corporations.
b) Contributions to changes in real GDP (percentage of real GDP in previous year), actual amount in the first column.
Source: OECD Economic Outlook 76 database.

United Kingdom: **External indicators**

	2002	2003	2004	2005	2006
			$ billion		
Goods and services exports	411.2	453.6	515.9	575	629
Goods and services imports	458.1	507.1	590.6	659	711
Foreign balance	- 46.9	- 53.5	- 74.7	- 84	- 82
Invisibles, net	19.8	20.1	28.2	29	30
Current account balance	- 27.1	- 33.4	- 46.5	- 54	- 51
			Percentage changes		
Goods and services export volumes	0.1	0.1	2.6	7.9	8.2
Goods and services import volumes	4.1	1.3	4.7	6.5	6.3
Export performance [a]	- 2.5	- 3.5	- 5.3	- 0.4	- 0.6
Terms of trade	2.7	0.8	- 0.4	- 1.4	- 0.4

a) Ratio between export volume and export market of total goods and services.
Source: OECD Economic Outlook 76 database.

ficient to bring the growth rate back to around, or eventually just below, the potential growth rate of 2½ per cent in 2005 and 2006. Demand pressures, particularly stemming from the labour market, will nevertheless lead to a steady rise in the consumer price inflation towards the 2 per cent target in 2006.

The housing market remains a risk

A more pronounced drop in house prices leading to an abrupt fall in consumption remains a risk, although one that may be diminishing as the likelihood of a soft landing for the whole economy increases. The adjustment in real house prices from previous peaks has rarely been gradual, but has normally been triggered by sharp increases in short-term interest rates typically of a magnitude of 4 to 5 percentage points over the previous year. As such a rise in interest rates appears inconceivable in present circumstances, a marked house price fall seems less likely than in the past.

There is uncertainty about potential output

The macroeconomic outlook is inevitably conditioned by views on the underlying supply potential, which is particularly relevant to judgments regarding the scope for manoeuvre for both fiscal and monetary policy. The March budget projections assume an output gap of more than 1 per cent in mid-2004 and although potential growth is estimated to be 2¾ per cent a more cautious estimate of 2½ per cent is used for the fiscal projections. Nevertheless, the expected closing of the gap implies faster growth and additional cyclical buoyancy in revenues which gives greater scope to meet the government's "golden rule", that over the course of the cycle the public sector should only borrow to invest. Conversely, if the output gap has already closed and potential growth is only 2½ per cent (as in the OECD projection), further fiscal retrenchment would almost certainly be required to ensure that the golden rule is met in the cycle that has just begun given that the deficit on current budget in the year to the third quarter is running at nearly 2 per cent of GDP.

Canada

Growth has been higher than expected so far this year, and the economy is now estimated to be operating close to full capacity. The pace of activity should remain buoyant up to the beginning of 2005, before cooling down to near potential growth rates of around 3 per cent. With soaring oil prices and easing capacity constraints, inflation is expected to hover above the mid-point of the target range until next year.

The Bank of Canada needs to continue raising interest rates toward their neutral level to ensure adherence to the inflation target. The government should avoid any easing of the fiscal stance at this juncture, despite the unexpectedly large surplus recorded for the last fiscal year. Great vigilance should be exercised over spending, in particular with regard to additional transfers from federal to lower levels of government.

Activity has picked up strongly…

Real GDP has been growing at a very rapid pace in much of 2004, contrary to the other major countries which all experienced some slowdown. As a result, the Canadian economy is currently operating near to estimated full capacity. Good performance mostly reflected very strong export growth, spurred by a surge in US demand for all major categories of merchandise exports. Imports accelerated as well, but more moderately. As a result, the contribution of foreign demand to GDP growth, which had been braking activity since late 2002 as the dollar appreciated, became positive. In contrast, a broad-based but moderate deceleration in final domestic demand reflected in particular a marked slowdown in consumer spending.

… and economic fundamentals are sound

Recent data and healthy economic fundamentals point to strengthening domestic demand. Solid gains in corporate profits, in part due to rising export prices, especially for energy and metals, should feed through into higher rates of business investment. More vigorous private consumption should flow from job creation and increases in labour incomes. National income has also been boosted by substantial gains in the terms of trade, which have been continuously improving since 2002. But signs of slowing activity are becoming visible in some sectors. Residential investment has decelerated, as housing starts, though still at a high level, have recently been declining. The dynamism of exports seems to have weakened in the third quarter of 2004, no doubt in part because of the further appreciation of the Canadian dollar to levels unseen since 1992.

Canada

Activity has picked up
Year on year

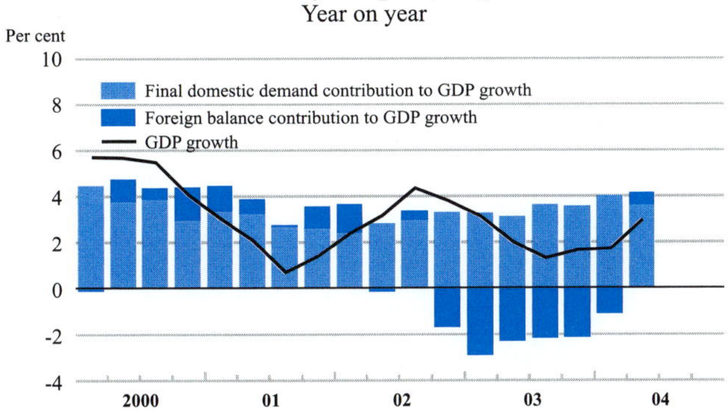

Monetary stimulus is being removed
Per cent

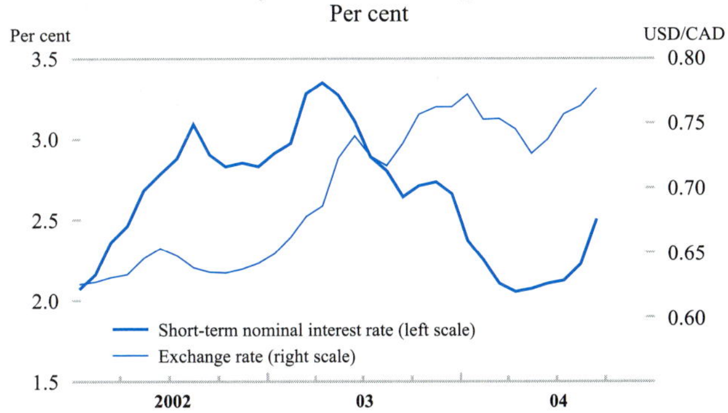

Source: Statistics Canada.

Canada: Employment, income and inflation

Percentage changes from previous period

	2002	2003	2004	2005	2006
Employment	2.2	2.2	1.8	1.4	1.2
Unemployment rate[a]	7.6	7.6	7.2	7.1	7.2
Compensation of employees	4.0	3.5	4.3	4.9	4.7
Unit labour cost	0.5	1.5	1.3	1.6	1.5
Household disposable income	3.8	3.0	5.0	5.0	4.6
GDP deflator	1.0	3.2	3.5	2.8	2.1
Consumer price index	2.2	2.8	1.9	2.0	1.8
Private consumption deflator	2.1	1.6	1.5	1.5	1.4

a) As a percentage of labour force.

Source: OECD Economic Outlook 76 database.

Inflation has risen to the middle part of the target range

Even though the surge in oil prices observed since the summer does not appear to have affected economic activity as yet, it has had a substantial impact on price developments. Headline inflation increased to a year-on-year rate of 2.2 per cent in the second quarter of 2004 but dropped to 2 per cent in the third quarter. The impact on core inflation has been much more subdued, suggesting the absence of second-round effects on prices. Nevertheless, inflation risks are rising: capacity utilisation is now above its long-term average, and the number of firms reporting labour shortages has been increasing.

The removal of monetary stimulus has begun…

Against this background, the Bank of Canada started its tightening cycle this autumn and has increased interest rates by 50 basis points. However, real short-term interest rates remain well below their long-term average and below the outcome that would be predicted by a standard Taylor rule. This suggests that interest rates will have to rise further to remove the existing monetary stimulus and avoid the build-up of inflationary pressures, although the further appreciation of the Canadian dollar in recent weeks will also help.

Canada

Headline inflation is close to the mid point of the target

Year-on-year change

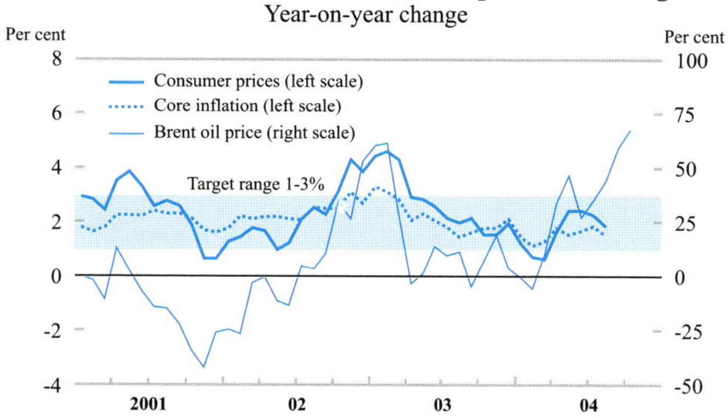

The current account surplus is increasing

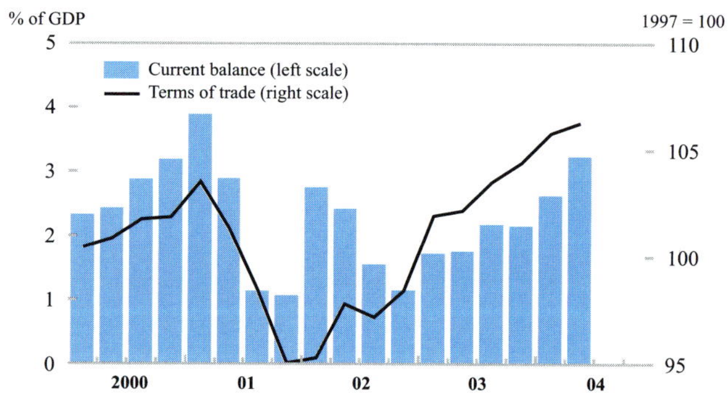

Source: Statistics Canada.

Canada: **Financial indicators**

	2002	2003	2004	2005	2006
Household saving ratio[a]	3.2	1.4	1.5	1.6	1.7
General government financial balance [b]	0.3	0.6	1.1	1.2	1.0
Current account balance[b]	2.0	2.0	3.4	3.9	4.3
Short-term interest rate[c]	2.6	3.0	2.5	3.5	4.2
Long-term interest rate[d]	5.3	4.8	4.7	4.7	5.2

a) As a percentage of disposable income.
b) As a percentage of GDP.
c) 3-month deposit rate.
d) 10-year government bonds.
Source: OECD Economic Outlook 76 database.

… and the fiscal stance is so far prudent

The federal budget surplus for the fiscal year 2003-04 was almost five times larger than expected, with stronger tax receipts and, to a lesser extent, lower outlays than initially planned. However, a number of initiatives announced since the last budget will increase public spending in the next few years. The federal government has announced an additional CAD 500 million aid package to help beef producers hit by Bovine Spongiform Encephalopathy and labour market and education measures were mentioned in the October Speech from the Throne. More importantly, substantial additional federal funding for health care has been provided in the September ten-year Plan for Health. Cyclically-adjusted general government net lending may have risen to about 1 per cent of GDP in 2004 and is projected to stabilise at about this level in 2005 and 2006. Because of longer-term spending pressures from the ageing population, it will be important that the federal government maintains its commitment to pay down the federal debt and resist the temptation of higher public spending at this point in the cycle.

Canada: **Demand and output**

	2001	2002	2003	2004	2005	2006
	Current prices billion CAD	Percentage changes, volume				
Private consumption	622.9	3.4	3.1	3.3	3.2	2.9
Government consumption	211.1	2.8	3.8	2.8	3.1	3.1
Gross fixed investment	217.6	2.4	4.9	6.2	5.3	4.5
Public[a]	26.8	9.2	6.9	3.4	5.4	5.1
Residential	55.4	14.4	7.4	8.8	2.3	0.3
Non-residential	135.5	-4.0	3.2	5.4	7.1	6.8
Final domestic demand	1 051.6	3.1	3.6	3.8	3.6	3.3
Stockbuilding[b]	- 7.0	0.6	0.9	-0.8	0.4	0.0
Total domestic demand	1 044.7	3.7	4.6	3.0	3.9	3.2
Exports of goods and services	483.1	1.1	-2.4	7.7	6.8	5.6
Imports of goods and services	419.5	1.4	3.8	8.4	9.1	6.3
Net exports[b]	63.5	-0.1	-2.4	0.0	-0.7	-0.1
Error of estimate[b]	0.0	0.0	0.0	0.0	0.0	0.0
GDP at market prices	1 108.2	3.4	2.0	3.0	3.3	3.1

Note: National accounts are based on official chain-linked data. This introduces a discrepancy in the identity between real demand components and GDP. For further details see OECD Economic Outlook Sources and Methods, *(http://www.oecd.org/eco/sources-and-methods).*
a) Excluding nationalized industries and public corporations.
b) Contributions to changes in real GDP (percentage of real GDP in previous year), actual amount in the first column.
Source: OECD Economic Outlook 76 database.

Canada: External indicators

	2002	2003	2004	2005	2006
			$ billion		
Goods and services exports	305.4	330.0	390.0	452	487
Goods and services imports	272.8	295.7	335.9	386	414
Foreign balance	32.5	34.2	54.2	66	72
Invisibles, net	- 18.1	- 17.1	- 19.6	- 21	- 20
Current account balance	14.4	17.1	34.5	45	52
			Percentage changes		
Goods and services export volumes	1.1	- 2.4	7.7	6.8	5.6
Goods and services import volumes	1.4	3.8	8.4	9.1	6.3
Export performance [a]	- 2.2	- 6.7	- 2.2	- 1.1	- 2.0
Terms of trade	- 2.5	6.0	4.7	3.1	0.9

a) Ratio between export volume and export market of total goods and services.
Source: OECD Economic Outlook 76 database.

Growth should remain solid in the near term

In the near term, activity is expected to remain robust, as Canada continues to benefit from the strength of the US economy, strong public consumption and non-residential investment, and renewed buoyancy of private consumption. But over the coming two years, higher interest rates will curb real disposable income gains. Moreover, households are expected to rebuild their savings as housing-related wealth effects dissipate. This could damp private consumption increases and reduce residential investment. As a result, although the vigorous expansion of export markets is projected to continue to be a driver of the expansion, the pace of activity is expected to slow over the next two years to rates close to potential growth. Inflation should be in the upper half of the target band until mid-2005, before receding to the mid point of the band. The recent high rates of business investment should also help to ease capacity constraints and enable labour productivity growth in the business sector to recover to an average annual rate of about 2 per cent during the projection period. Boosted by still favourable though slowing terms-of-trade improvements, the current account surplus could steadily rise over the projection horizon, reaching record levels of over 4 per cent of GDP.

Future oil-price developments are the main uncertainty

The main uncertainty in the outlook is the evolution of oil prices: oil export earnings move higher or lower in line with price developments, but these effects would be partially offset by the impact of those prices on US demand and thus Canadian non-oil exports. On the domestic side, inflation may not recede as quickly as expected, leading to greater monetary tightening. This would accentuate the slowdown in private consumption, which in turn depends on how rapidly households might choose to lift their currently low savings rate.

Australia

Economic growth remained robust in the first half of 2004, boosted by domestic spending, and despite the ongoing drag from the foreign balance. Continued strong growth is expected in 2005 and 2006, with improving net exports offsetting the projected weakening in household consumption and residential investment. This should be accompanied by further employment gains and inflation staying within the Reserve Bank's 2 to 3 per cent target band, underpinned by moderate wage increases and solid productivity growth.

The upbeat economic outlook should allow the removal of the remaining monetary stimulus, to safeguard price stability. The projected small fiscal surpluses over coming years are appropriate, leaving room for automatic stabilisers to operate if the global recovery weakens or another drought develops in rural areas.

Economic growth was driven by brisk domestic demand

Private consumption, housing construction and business investment performed strongly in the first half of 2004, reflecting sanguine consumer sentiment and business confidence, supportive financial conditions, a strong labour market and high corporate profitability. The global upturn and improving farm production after the recent drought induced a recovery of exports. But in spite of further sizeable terms-of-trade gains, surging imports kept the current account deficit at close to 6 per cent of GDP in mid-2004. Nearly all current indicators point to continued vigorous economic activity in the second half of 2004.

Unemployment fell close to its structural rate

Employment growth has remained strong so that the unemployment rate fell to around 5½ per cent in recent months, close to estimates of structural unemployment. A higher labour content of economic growth has been reflected in a slowing of labour productivity (per employee basis) and an acceleration in unit labour costs. However, the ongoing moderate growth of the wage cost index bodes well for keeping inflation low, notwithstanding the effective exchange rate depreciation since early 2004.

Monetary policy remains supportive

With the cash rate currently only 100 basis points above its latest cyclical trough of 4¼ per cent, and in view of continued strong borrowing both by households and businesses, monetary policy still appears mildly accommodative. Accordingly, a further gradual tightening of monetary policy is projected for 2005, which should bring the cash rate closer to a "neutral" level of 5½ to 6 per cent.

Fiscal policy aims at small budget surpluses

New policy measures in the 2004-05 Commonwealth budget include personal income tax cuts, additional payments to families, and increased expenditure for aged care and retirement savings incentives. Thanks to buoyant budget revenues, government finances are nevertheless expected to remain in small surplus over the projection period. This should nearly eliminate net government debt by the end of 2006.

Australia

Household debt service has surged

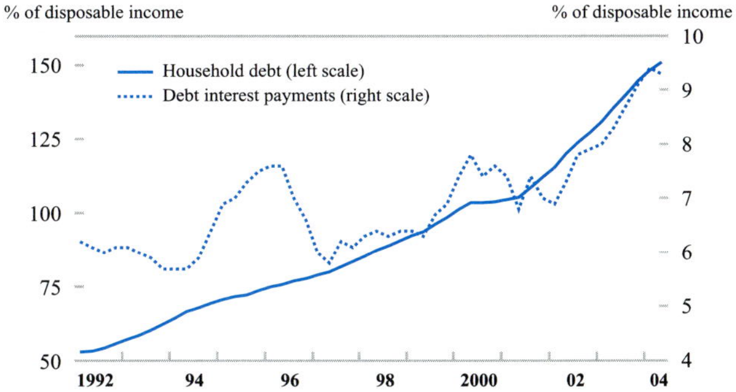

Corporate gearing is low

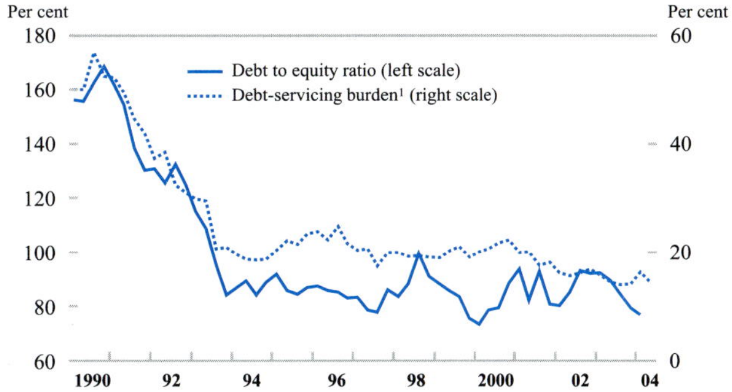

1. Interest payments as a per cent of corporate gross operating surplus.
Source: Reserve Bank of Australia.

Australia: **Demand, output and prices**

	2001	2002	2003	2004	2005	2006
	Current prices billion AUD	Percentage changes, volume				
Private consumption	414.9	4.0	4.1	5.4	3.6	3.3
Government consumption	122.9	3.8	3.8	3.2	3.1	3.2
Gross fixed capital formation	151.1	15.7	8.2	6.1	4.4	4.8
Final domestic demand	688.9	6.5	5.0	5.2	3.7	3.6
Stockbuilding [a]	- 0.1	-0.3	1.1	-0.2	0.1	0.1
Total domestic demand	688.8	6.2	6.1	4.9	3.8	3.7
Exports of goods and services	155.4	0.3	-2.6	6.4	8.3	9.8
Imports of goods and services	152.5	11.9	11.0	13.5	7.6	9.1
Net exports [a]	2.9	-2.3	-2.8	-1.9	-0.3	-0.4
Statistical discrepancy [a]	0.0	-0.2	0.0	0.1	-0.6	-0.1
GDP at market prices	691.7	3.6	3.3	3.6	3.8	3.6
GDP deflator	_	2.8	2.7	3.6	2.5	2.5
Memorandum items						
Consumer price index	_	3.0	2.8	2.3	2.4	2.6
Private consumption deflator	_	2.0	1.7	1.6	2.6	2.7
Unemployment rate	_	6.4	6.0	5.6	5.5	5.5
Household saving ratio [b]	_	-0.4	-2.2	-2.1	-1.8	-1.4
General government financial balance [c]	_	0.3	0.8	0.7	0.4	0.5
Current account balance [c]	_	-4.1	-5.9	-5.5	-4.9	-4.6

Note: National accounts are based on official chain-linked data. This introduces a discrepancy in the identity between real demand components and GDP. For further details see *OECD Economic Outlook* Sources and Methods, *(http:// www.oecd.org/eco/sources-and-methods).*

a) Contributions to changes in real GDP (percentage of real GDP in previous year), actual amount in the first column.

b) As a percentage of disposable income.

c) As a percentage of GDP.

Source: OECD Economic Outlook 76 database.

Economic growth is likely to remain strong…

A continuation of strong growth is expected over the next two years, broadly in line with potential output and accompanied by low inflation. Private consumption is projected to slow, along with the easing in house prices since late 2003, which will reduce the scope for mortgage equity withdrawal. Declining house prices and falling housing loan approvals and building permits so far in 2004 suggest that the dwelling investment boom is already cooling off. On the other hand, high business confidence, healthy profits, the improved environment for equity finance, low corporate debt, and capacity constraints in the resources sector underpin prospects for robust business investment. With the global economy continuing to pick up, the impact of the drought waning, international price competitiveness improving from the exchange rate depreciation during 2004 and the housing cycle turning around, there should also be a rebalancing of growth from domestic demand towards stronger net exports. Together with further terms-of-trade gains, the current balance deficit should thus narrow to about 4½ per cent of GDP in 2006. Further gains in employment are likely to encourage higher labour force participation, keeping unemployment close to its current low level.

… although there are downside risks

The recovery of farm production and exports from the recent drought could be interrupted if the disappointing rainfall in the first half of 2004 were to continue. High levels of household debt and debt-interest payments have made households more vulnerable both to further increases in interest rates and to an abrupt fall in house prices as a possible response to excess supply in the property market. However, the risk of a sudden restructuring of household finances towards higher savings and lower consumption, accompanied by a substantial increase in mortgage arrears and repossessions, is lower than in past episodes, given that sharp increases in interest rates and unemployment are unlikely.

Austria

Output growth is projected to increase gradually, in line with the recovery in the euro area, allowing unemployment to fall in 2006. Notwithstanding progress in reducing the relatively high level of government spending, tax reductions in 2005 and 2006 will be mostly deficit-financed, providing a comparatively large stimulus to growth.

While the planned pension harmonisation will damp ageing-related spending in the future, substantial further reductions in general government outlays are necessary to ensure the long-run sustainability of government finances, while further steps to improve incentives to work among older workers and women would help offset the adverse economic impact of ongoing demographic change.

Exports have led the economic recovery

Economic growth picked up in the first half of 2004, driven by strong external demand. On the back of a favourable unit labour costs trend relative to trading partners in recent years, exports benefited from a surge in sales of intermediate inputs into German exports, as well as from vigorous economic growth in Central and Eastern Europe. Domestic demand was subdued, as investment declined despite tax incentives which will be phased out at the end of the year; and consumption growth remained modest as oil-price rises, pushing year-on-year inflation above 2 per cent, reduced real disposable income growth and as relatively high unemployment weighed on confidence. Employment rose somewhat, but increased labour force participation, in part on account of easier access to the labour market for foreign residents in Austria, delayed the effect of the pickup in activity on unemployment. Vacancies rose in the first months, but levelled off subsequently. Momentum is likely to increase modestly in the near term. Indicators of consumer and business confidence are still subdued although business confidence has improved in recent months. Strong growth in Central and Eastern Europe will continue to provide an additional impetus to trade, though the external stimulus will weaken somewhat in 2005 as slowing German export growth impacts on Austrian intermediate exports.

Fiscal policy is set on an expansionary course…

The government deficit is estimated to have increased slightly this year, reaching 1½ per cent of GDP, as unexpected revenue shortfalls on account of investment tax breaks, more generous R&D tax incentives, weak value-added tax revenues and personal income tax reductions have not been fully offset by higher fuel tax rates, continued cuts in government employment, modest pension adjustments and savings on account of

Austria

Orders have risen

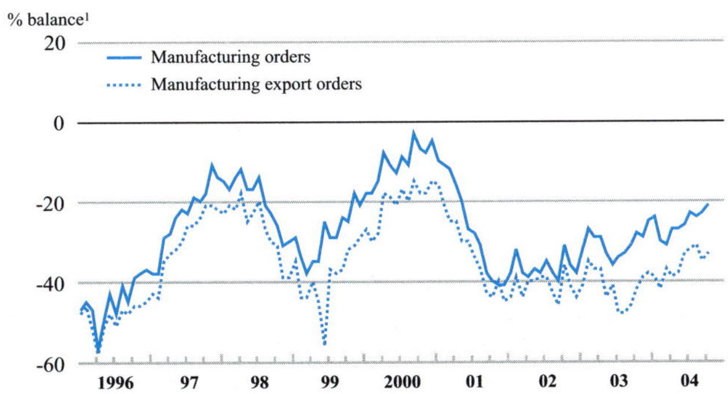

Confidence is still subdued

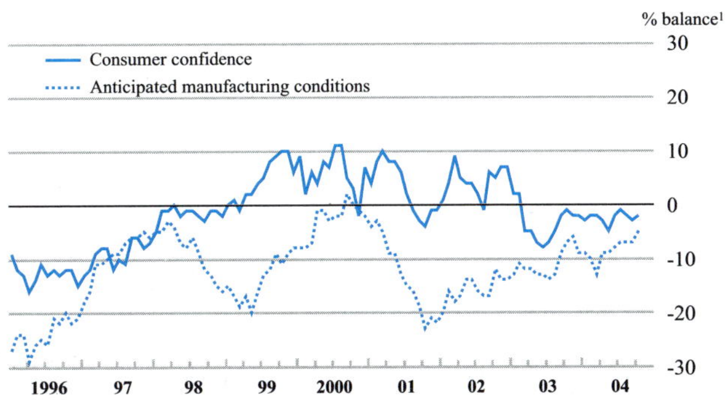

1. Seasonally adjusted balance of positive and negative replies.
Source: OECD, *Main Economic Indicators.*

Austria: **Demand, output and prices**

	2001	2002	2003	2004	2005	2006
	Current prices billion €	Percentage changes, volume (2000 prices)				
Private consumption	123.0	-0.1	0.6	1.4	2.3	2.4
Government consumption	38.8	1.1	0.4	0.2	0.7	1.4
Gross fixed capital formation	47.4	-3.4	6.2	1.6	3.0	4.1
Final domestic demand	209.2	-0.6	1.8	1.2	2.1	2.6
Stockbuilding[a]	1.0	-0.2	0.1	-0.2	0.0	0.0
Total domestic demand	210.2	-0.8	2.0	1.0	2.2	2.6
Exports of goods and services	102.9	3.8	1.4	8.1	8.0	7.9
Imports of goods and services	97.8	-0.2	4.8	7.1	8.1	8.2
Net exports[a]	5.2	1.9	-1.5	0.7	0.2	0.1
GDP at market prices	215.6	1.2	0.8	1.8	2.3	2.6
GDP deflator	_	1.3	1.6	2.1	1.9	1.4
Memorandum items						
Harmonised index of consumer price	_	1.7	1.3	1.9	1.9	1.4
Private consumption deflator	_	1.2	1.5	1.7	1.9	1.4
Unemployment rate[b]	_	5.5	5.7	5.8	5.8	5.5
Household saving ratio[c]	_	8.2	8.5	8.3	8.8	8.8
General government financial balance[d]	_	-0.4	-1.3	-1.5	-2.1	-2.1
Current account balance[d]	_	0.4	-0.4	-0.1	0.0	0.1

a) Contributions to changes in real GDP (percentage of real GDP in previous year), actual amount in the first column.
b) See data annex for details.
c) As a percentage of disposable income.
d) As a percentage of GDP.
Source: OECD Economic Outlook 76 database.

health care reform. The deficit will increase further in 2005, reflecting major personal income and corporate tax relief equivalent to about 1 per cent of GDP. Part of the revenue losses from the tax cuts will arise in 2006, resulting in a further increase in the structural deficit to an estimated 1.7 per cent of GDP. On the other hand, planned pension reform, harmonizing pension schemes across workers in the private and public sectors would, if enacted, lower pension spending in the long term, largely as a result of linking pension increases to inflation. This would provide a welcome step towards fiscal sustainability.

... which will, on balance support domestic demand next year

The tax cuts will raise disposable incomes, boosting consumption, although high oil prices will damp real income growth, and increased private provision for old age will raise private household savings. The phase-out of tax breaks for investment may partly offset the positive impact of the corporate tax reductions on investment, but increased capacity utilisation in manufacturing, the need to replace machinery and low interest rates will support investment throughout the forecasting period.

Recovery is gradual with unemployment falling only in 2006

Recovery should proceed at a moderate pace. Export growth will slow while consumption and investment will provide a larger impetus to activity in 2005 and 2006. Unemployment is expected to fall significantly only in 2006. Inflation will remain relatively high in 2005, but the effect of higher oil prices is expected to fade in the following year.

High deficits might dent confidence

A substantial appreciation of the euro would adversely impact growth, while the accession of neighbouring countries to the European Union could boost growth above projected levels. While pension harmonization could help consumer confidence recover, failure to achieve additional government spending reductions could dent confidence in the sustainability of government finances.

Belgium

Economic growth is expected to ease somewhat in 2005 but strengthen to 2¾ per cent in 2006 as export markets remain buoyant and business investment picks up. The unemployment rate should fall to 7¼ per cent by 2006 with the underlying inflation rate remaining at around 1¾ per cent as the unfavourable effects of the increase in energy prices fade but the economy moves from below to above-potential growth. If the euro were to be stronger than assumed, growth and inflation would be lower.

Further efforts are needed to ensure that the budget remains balanced. Measures should focus on expenditure restraint, as planned, since the high tax burden on labour discourages work effort. Further reforms are also needed to reduce incentives for early retirement and raise the participation rate.

Private consumption and exports have supported the recovery

Economic growth has been robust since mid-2003, reaching 3 per cent (year-on-year) in the second and third quarters of 2004. While private consumption expenditure has been buoyant since late 2002, the economic recovery only took hold when exports also picked up. Business investment remains weak despite improving profitability, favourable demand prospects, low interest rates and stronger corporate balance sheets. Business confidence has stabilised at levels that should support continued economic growth at above the trend rate (estimated to be around 2 per cent). Despite growing employment, unemployment has been stuck at around 7¾ per cent so far this year. Labour force participation has been increasing for females, reflecting a long-term trend, and for workers aged 50 and over, as the minimum age for access to the older unemployed scheme – one of the main routes to early retirement – has been raised to 58.

Wage increases have outpaced those of neighbouring countries

Hourly wage costs in the private sector appear likely to have increased by 5.9 per cent in 2003-04, more than agreed in the wage norm (5.4 per cent) but less than in the previous wage norm period. Abstracting from the reduction in employers' social security contribution rates, the increase was 6.6 per cent. This rate of increase exceeded the average (4.5 per cent) for the three neighbouring countries (Germany, France and the Netherlands), adding to the loss of cost competitiveness against these countries already incurred in previous wage-norm periods. Headline inflation has

Belgium

Exports support the recovery

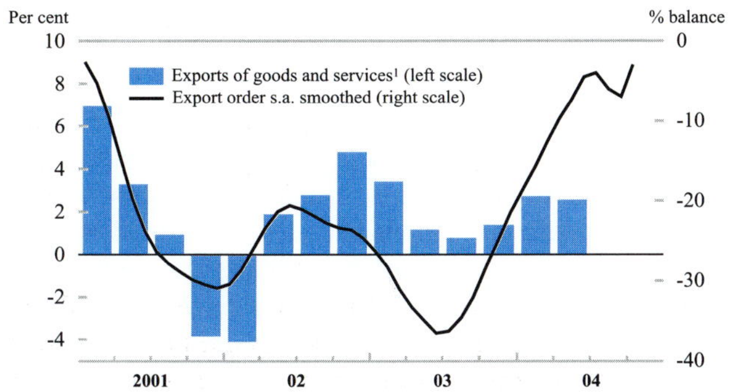

Business confidence is high

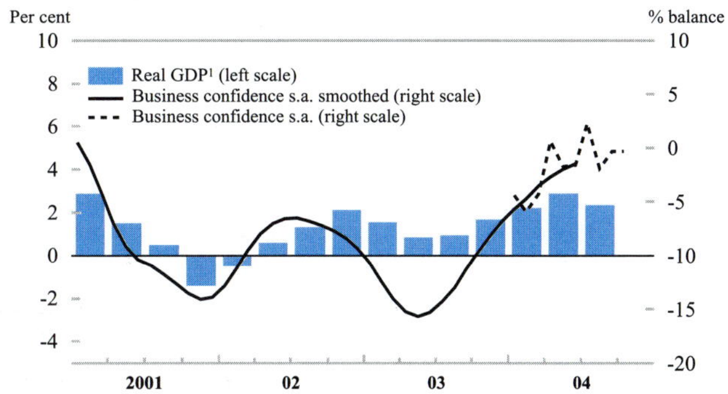

1. Year-on-year percentage change.

Source: National Bank of Belgium and National Accounts Institute.

Belgium: **Demand, output and prices**

	2001	2002	2003	2004	2005	2006
	Current prices billion €	Percentage changes, volume (2000 prices)				
Private consumption	138.4	0.3	2.2	2.2	2.1	2.2
Government consumption	55.1	2.3	2.7	2.5	2.0	2.0
Gross fixed capital formation	53.0	-3.4	-0.6	1.0	2.8	5.1
Final domestic demand	246.6	-0.1	1.7	2.0	2.2	2.7
Stockbuilding [a]	- 1.6	0.7	-0.1	0.4	0.0	0.0
Total domestic demand	244.9	0.6	1.6	2.4	2.2	2.7
Exports of goods and services	218.6	1.3	1.7	3.6	6.3	7.4
Imports of goods and services	209.3	1.0	2.1	3.3	6.2	7.6
Net exports [a]	9.3	0.3	-0.3	0.4	0.3	0.1
GDP at market prices	254.2	0.9	1.3	2.7	2.4	2.7
GDP deflator	_	1.8	2.0	2.3	1.4	1.8
Memorandum items						
Harmonised index of consumer price	_	1.6	1.5	1.9	2.2	1.9
Private consumption deflator	_	1.7	1.8	2.1	2.1	1.9
Unemployment rate	_	7.3	7.9	7.7	7.6	7.3
Household saving ratio [b]	_	14.8	14.2	13.8	13.4	13.9
General government financial balance [c]	_	0.1	0.3	-0.1	-0.4	-0.5
Current account balance [c]	_	5.7	4.2	3.7	3.1	4.0

Note: Corrected for calendar effects.

a) Contributions to changes in real GDP (percentage of real GDP in previous year), actual amount in the first column.

b) As a percentage of disposable income.

c) As a percentage of GDP.

Source: OECD Economic Outlook 76 database.

picked up to 2¼ per cent (year-on-year) owing to rising energy prices. Underlying inflation – excluding energy and unprocessed food prices – has remained around 1¾ per cent.

Further consolidation is needed to keep the budget in balance

The general government budget balance appears likely to have remained near balance in 2004, despite the partial unwinding of non-recurring items that increased the balance in 2003. Such items will decline from 0.6 per cent of GDP in 2004 to 0.3 per cent in 2005 and zero in 2006. Moreover, the government needs to offset the impact of the personal income tax cuts (amounting to 0.6 per cent of GDP over 2005-06, mostly in 2006). Further reductions in social security charges are also programmed, but these are more than compensated by increases in indirect taxes. In addition, there is likely to be a large (temporary) increase in infrastructure investment in 2005-06 to coincide with municipal elections. Based on announced policies, the OECD projects that the budget balance will deteriorate to a deficit of ½ per cent of GDP in 2006. Further measures will be needed to realise the government's announced target of balanced budgets in both 2005 and 2006.

Business investment should begin to support the recovery

Economic growth is projected to ease somewhat as high energy prices and appreciation of the euro put a brake on the pace of recovery, but to strengthen to 2¾ per cent in 2005 as the effects of these factors pass. Initially led by private consumption, exports and surging government investment, the recovery should become more reliant on business investment. Employment growth should continue to strengthen, bringing the unemployment rate down to 7¼ per cent by 2006. Underlying inflation is projected to remain around 1¾ per cent as the unfavourable effects of the increase in energy prices on other input costs fade but the economy moves from below to above potential. The main risks to these projections are that the euro could be stronger than assumed, depressing growth, but also reducing inflation.

Czech Republic

Driven by buoyant exports and strong private investment, output growth has gained momentum and should reach about 4 per cent this year and also in 2005 and 2006. Employment growth is likely to be muted, but nevertheless allow for a slight decline in unemployment. Inflation will remain close to 3 per cent.

The momentum of fiscal reform needs to be boosted. A new budgeting framework has been introduced and needs to be effectively implemented. Also, concrete progress is needed on pension and healthcare reform. Monetary policy looks set to remain neutral in the near term although there are upside risks to inflation. Structural reforms to improve the business environment are needed to enable rapid real convergence.

Strong investment and export growth have boosted output

Real GDP growth is strengthening; it reached 4.1 per cent (year-on-year) in the second quarter, and became more broad-based. Private investment surged, reflecting improving export results and prospects, increasing profitability of firms and low interest rates. Booming exports are driven mainly by capacity increases in the wake of foreign direct investment coming on stream, especially in the sector of information and communication technologies. Entry to the European Union (EU) single market and EU growth recovery helped further. Imports have also soared. Private consumption, on the other hand, has decelerated in response to increasing prices and declining real wage gains. With inflation now at around 3 per cent, the period of undershooting the inflation target band has come to an end, partly due to increases in indirect taxes related to EU accession.

Employment stopped falling

There are some positive signs in employment growth, mainly in private service sectors. In contrast with past experience, jobs were created mostly for dependent workers, while self-employment decreased following changes to the tax treatment of the self-employed. At the same time, restructuring and down-sizing continued in manufacturing, public services and in some private services such as banking, leaving the unemployment rate at its highest level since 2001.

Fiscal consolidation proceeds slowly

A bold programme of fiscal reform was begun in 2003, including the introduction of legally binding three-year spending ceilings as well as intentions to make major reforms to spending on public pensions and health. The 2004 deficit outcome will probably be lower than expected due to higher than expected tax revenues from stronger economic activity, and, once again, likely unrealised capital expenditures. The government aims to bring the general government deficit down to 3 per cent of GDP in 2008, with an intermediate target of 4 per cent in 2006. However, consolida-

Czech Republic

Export capacity is rising

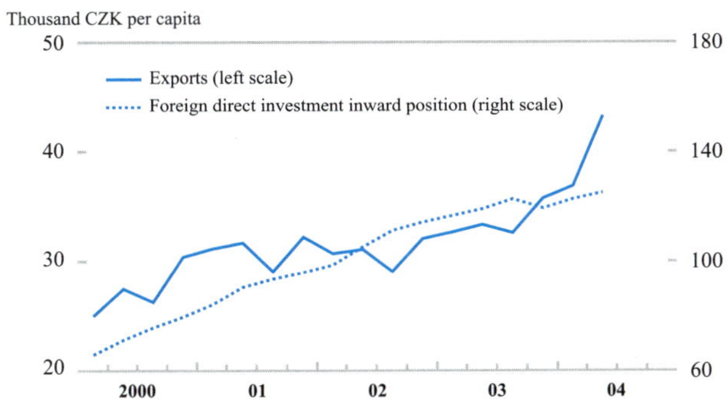

Monetary tightening remains gradual

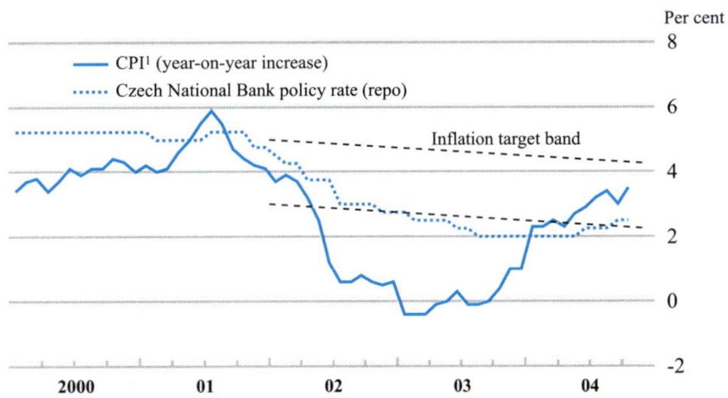

1. Consumer price index.

Source: Czech National Bank; Czech Statistical Office; *OECD, Labour Force Statistics.*

Czech Republic: Demand, output and prices

	2001	2002	2003	2004	2005	2006
	Current prices billion CZK	Percentage changes, volume (1995 prices)				
Private consumption	1 192.3	2.8	4.9	3.5	3.6	3.6
Government consumption	513.0	4.5	2.2	-0.4	-0.2	0.5
Gross fixed capital formation	638.6	3.4	7.4	9.5	7.2	6.0
Final domestic demand	2 343.9	3.3	4.9	4.1	3.7	3.6
Stockbuilding [a]	30.0	0.1	-0.4	0.6	0.0	0.0
Total domestic demand	2 374.0	2.8	4.2	4.5	3.7	3.6
Exports of goods and services	1 539.3	2.7	6.2	16.7	12.0	10.4
Imports of goods and services	1 598.0	4.9	7.8	17.3	11.2	9.6
Net exports [a]	- 58.7	-2.2	-2.2	-2.8	-0.9	-0.7
GDP at market prices	2 315.3	1.5	3.1	3.9	4.2	4.1
GDP deflator	_	2.8	1.7	4.1	2.6	2.5
Memorandum items						
Consumer price index	_	1.8	0.1	2.9	3.1	3.0
Private consumption deflator	_	0.7	-0.7	2.1	2.8	2.6
Unemployment rate	_	7.3	7.8	8.4	8.3	8.2
General government financial balance [b, c]	_	-6.8	-12.6	-4.3	-4.6	-3.9
Current account balance [b]	_	-5.6	-6.2	-6.5	-6.6	-6.5

Note: National accounts are based on official chain-linked data. This introduces a discrepancy in the identity between real demand components and GDP. For further details see *OECD Economic Outlook* Sources and Methods, *(http:// www.oecd.org/eco/sources-and-methods).*

a) Contributions to changes in real GDP (percentage of real GDP in previous year), actual amount in the first column.

b) As a percentage of GDP.

c) Since the change in methodology in 2004, high-risk state guarantees are classified as capital transfers as soon as they are called for the first time. In 2003, the activation of guarantees issued mainly for the banking sector accounted for about 7.7 percentage points of the deficit.

Source: OECD Economic Outlook 76 database.

tion looks set to take place only slowly. Progress in implementing the major spending cuts has been delayed due to the narrow majority of the coalition government. Pension reform has gone back to the drawing board and there are no concrete proposals for reforming the healthcare system.

Monetary policy looks set to remain neutral in the near term

The monetary authorities have responded to higher inflation by gradually tightening the policy stance, increasing the policy rates by 50 basis points overall. Moderate second-round effects of value-added tax (VAT) and excise increases, driven by harmonisation, and increases in regulated prices will affect consumer prices in 2005 and 2006. Overall, little change is projected in interest rates in the near term. However, additional inflation pressures could come from mounting demand pressures resulting from robust output growth, sizeable increases in some public sector wages and oil-price effects.

Real convergence should continue

The momentum of export growth is expected to continue and economic output is projected to grow about 4 per cent over the projection period, while inflation is expected to stabilize at 3 per cent. Export growth is expected to reach double digits in 2004, and will remain high in the two following years. Combined with somewhat slower import growth towards the end of the forecast horizon, this will make for a less negative contribution from net exports. However, the positive effects on the current account will be compensated by increasing repatriation of profits from foreign direct investment. Investment growth will decelerate but remain sustained, while employment creation will be positive but muted. The main risks to the output scenario are balanced. Weaker-than-expected foreign demand would moderate the export activity. Faster restructuring in the context of an improving business environment could boost growth through shifts of resources to more productive uses.

Denmark

The economy has continued to recover in 2004 due to a strong pick-up in private consumption and exports. Prospects look bright for 2005 and 2006, as business investment should add to activity on top of continued solid household spending and fast-growing export demand. The labour market is gradually improving, but inflationary pressures are likely to remain contained until 2006 when labour- and product-market slack is expected to disappear.

The outlook is very much shaped by the 2004 fiscal easing, which provided a large boost to household disposable income. Monetary policy settings are currently supportive of growth, but will become less so by 2006 as the European Central Bank gradually raises interest rates and Denmark follows suit. Further initiatives to increase labour force participation would help to sustain the upturn and bring employment closer to the government's medium-term target.

Exports and household spending continue to drive the recovery

The first half of 2004 saw a substantial pick-up in exports and continued solid growth in private consumption after the boom at the end of 2003. While the increase in demand was largely matched by a huge rise in imports, real GDP grew well above its potential rate. Short-term indicators point to a continued pick-up in growth in the second half of this year, as confidence indicators have risen substantially (even if there has been some recent reversal in manufacturing) and growth in retail and car sales has been brisk. The labour market has turned for the better after the steady worsening last year, and the standardised unemployment rate now stands at 5¾ per cent of the labour force (around 1 percentage point above the structural rate). Wage increases have moderated, reflecting the weaker labour market than in previous years. Consumer price inflation has also remained low, despite significant oil price increases.

Fiscal easing boosts household income

The stimulus from tax cuts implemented at the beginning of 2004 and the spring fiscal package (frontloading tax cuts planned for 2005-07 and suspending Special Pension contributions in 2004 and 2005) is a major driver of growth this year and next. Its main impact is to boost household disposable income. The fiscal easing is expected to push the general government surplus back below 1 per cent of GDP this year, although rising activity and higher employment should help it recover to 1½ per cent of GDP by 2006. After adjusting for the business cycle and certain one-off factors, the structural surplus is projected to remain below the government's

Denmark

Private consumption and exports have picked up

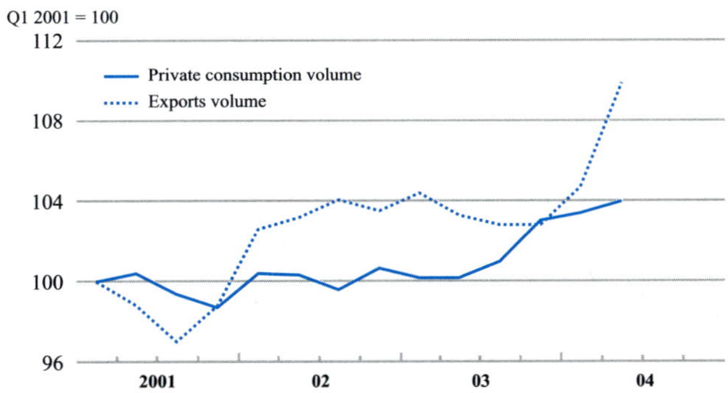

Confidence is strong

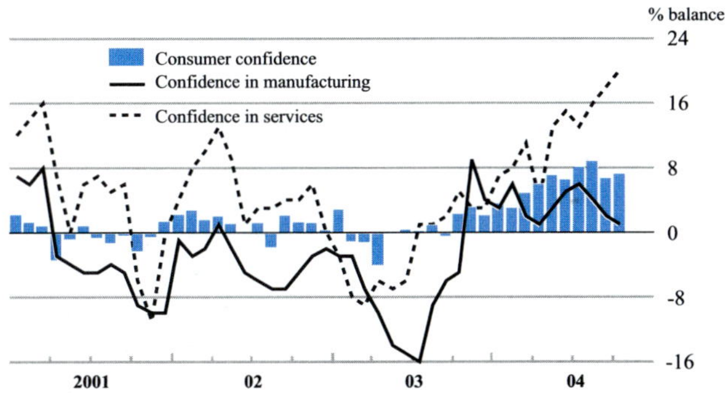

Source: Statistics Denmark, Statbank Database, *www.statbank.dk;* OECD, Quarterly National Accounts database.

Denmark: **Demand, output and prices**

	2001	2002	2003	2004	2005	2006
	Current prices billion DKK	Percentage changes, volume (1995 prices)				
Private consumption	624.5	0.6	0.8	3.6	3.3	2.4
Government consumption	343.3	2.1	1.0	0.7	0.7	0.8
Gross fixed capital formation	271.0	4.5	0.1	3.6	4.7	5.4
Final domestic demand	1 238.7	2.0	0.7	2.8	3.0	2.8
Stockbuilding [a]	1.3	0.0	-0.4	0.2	0.1	0.0
Total domestic demand	1 240.0	1.9	0.3	3.1	3.1	2.8
Exports of goods and services	592.1	4.8	0.0	4.9	6.0	6.4
Imports of goods and services	506.5	7.3	-0.6	6.6	7.0	7.1
Net exports [a]	85.5	-0.8	0.3	-0.5	-0.3	-0.1
GDP at market prices	1 325.5	1.0	0.5	2.4	2.7	2.6
GDP deflator	_	1.6	2.2	1.9	2.0	2.0
Memorandum items						
Consumer price index	_	2.4	2.1	1.2	1.7	2.0
Private consumption deflator	_	2.1	1.8	1.2	1.7	1.9
Unemployment rate	_	4.6	5.6	5.8	5.3	4.9
Household saving ratio [b]	_	0.1	0.3	-0.3	-1.6	-1.3
General government financial balance [c]	_	1.6	1.2	0.9	1.4	1.5
Current account balance [c]	_	2.0	2.7	3.1	3.1	3.4

a) Contributions to changes in real GDP (percentage of real GDP in previous year), actual amount in the first column.
b) As a percentage of disposable income, net of household consumption of fixed capital.
c) As a percentage of GDP.
Source: OECD Economic Outlook 76 database.

target of 1½ to 2½ per cent of GDP over the projection period. A risk to public finances is the restructuring of local governments from 2007, which could involve substantial adjustment costs in 2006 that would be difficult to handle within the spending targets set out in the government's medium-term fiscal framework. Monetary conditions continue to follow euro area developments, with a gradual increase in interest rates projected in 2006 as activity picks up in the euro area. The fiscal stimulus may have pushed Denmark a little ahead in the cycle compared to the euro area, which could make monetary policy there less appropriate for Danish conditions.

Growth depends on household behaviour and export markets

With accommodative fiscal settings, output is projected to increase by just above 2½ per cent per annum from 2004 to 2006. Private consumption seems to have picked up in the second half of 2004 as households reacted to the fiscal package while continued strong exports due to recovering foreign demand have further boosted activity this year. Household spending and exports should remain strong over the next two years, although some moderation of private consumption growth is projected in 2006 as Special Pension contributions are resumed, cutting into disposable incomes. Business investment may provide more support to growth in 2005 and 2006 as firms seek to expand capacity. The unemployment rate is also projected to fall as the business sector starts to increase hiring. Yet wage and price increases should be moderate as output is expected to remain below its potential level until the end of 2005. The main source of uncertainty is the reaction of households to the extra income from previous policy measures. The more of this they decide to spend, the faster capacity constraints may begin to bite, raising inflationary pressure. The strength of the European recovery generates a further uncertainty associated with the outlook, given Denmark's close economic integration with its European Union partners.

Finland

With output close to its potential, Finland is in a more favourable cyclical position than the euro area on average. The pick-up in world trade and a revival in business investment are expected to become increasingly important as drivers of growth, which should average about 3 per cent a year to 2006.

A moderate wage settlement would allow cuts in labour taxation without compromising aggregate fiscal objectives. However, efficiency gains in the public sector and greater private service provision are required to create room for further tax cuts. Additional reforms, particularly a tightening of conditions applying to early retirement schemes, are needed to achieve the government's employment target.

The recovery has gained momentum

The recovery has gained momentum, with GDP growth in the first two quarters of 2004 averaging 3½ per cent at annual rates, and the monthly GDP indicator suggesting growth in the third quarter rising further, in contrast to developments in the euro area as a whole. Business confidence is back at levels not seen since 2000, with business investment recovering, after declining in both 2002 and 2003. Export performance, however, has been disappointing so far; export volumes in the first half of the year were at about the same level as in 2003 despite growth in export markets of nearly 7 per cent. The pick-up in investment provides the first sign that the recovery is becoming less dependent on fiscal stimulus, as until recently public and private consumption – the latter stimulated by tax cuts – have been the only contributors to growth. Government employment has grown briskly, but this has been more than offset by job losses in the private leaving the unemployment rate at 9 per cent. Consumer price inflation has been subdued in 2004, because alcohol taxation was cut by a third in March to counter cross-border trade.

Maintaining a sound budget position will require reforms

Between 2000 and 2004 the general government surplus has declined by more than 5 per cent of GDP, of which a third can be attributed to cyclical factors. From 2005, the government has announced reductions in corporate taxation equal to ¼ per cent of GDP. Further cuts in labour taxation are necessary to improve work incentives. However, the combined balance of central and local government has moved into deficit so that, given the need to respect current fiscal objectives to prepare for ageing, there is no longer room for spending hikes or tax cuts unless they are compensated by savings elsewhere.

Finland

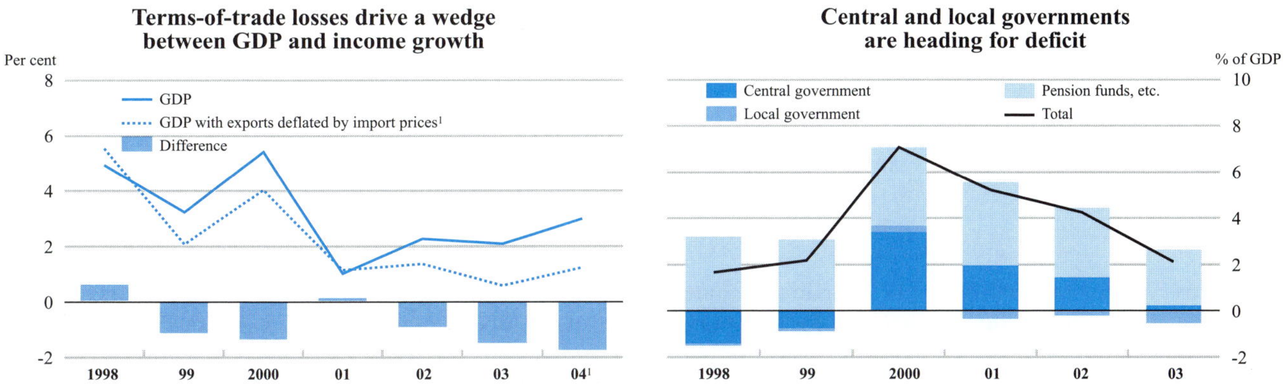

1. This concept is sometimes referred to as "command GDP", *i.e.* the resources that GDP gives command over. It adjusts the real GDP by measuring exports in terms of the volume of imports it can buy: GDP – exports* (1 – export prices/import prices).
2. First half of 2004 at annual rates.

Source: Statistics Finland and OECD Economic Outlook 76 database.

Finland: **Demand, output and prices**

	2001	2002	2003	2004	2005	2006
	Current prices billion €	Percentage changes, volume (2000 prices)				
Private consumption	67.8	1.7	4.5	2.8	2.9	2.4
Government consumption	28.4	3.9	1.6	1.1	1.5	1.5
Gross fixed capital formation	27.8	-3.3	-2.1	4.1	4.1	4.3
Final domestic demand	124.0	1.1	2.4	2.7	2.8	2.6
Stockbuilding [a]	0.1	0.2	-0.2	1.0	-0.9	-0.1
Total domestic demand	124.1	1.3	2.2	3.7	1.8	2.5
Exports of goods and services	54.1	5.2	1.2	2.2	5.8	6.0
Imports of goods and services	42.8	1.7	3.0	0.2	4.0	5.5
Net exports [a]	11.3	1.6	-0.5	0.9	1.2	0.8
GDP at market prices	135.5	2.3	2.1	3.1	2.8	3.1
GDP deflator	_	0.9	0.0	0.8	1.3	1.6
Memorandum items						
Harmonised index of consumer price	_	2.0	1.3	0.2	1.7	1.9
Private consumption deflator	_	3.1	0.6	1.2	2.0	1.9
Unemployment rate	_	9.1	9.1	8.9	8.7	8.2
General government financial balance [b]	_	4.3	2.1	2.3	2.1	2.3
Current account balance [b]	_	7.6	4.1	4.9	4.9	5.0

a) Contributions to changes in real GDP (percentage of real GDP in previous year), actual amount in the first column.
b) As a percentage of GDP.
Source: OECD Economic Outlook 76 database.

Terms-of-trade losses need to be reflected in wage settlements

The government is aiming for a moderate outcome in the central wage negotiations to be concluded in late 2004, in order to provide some scope for tax cuts, but as this is not agreed yet, the forecast is based on a continuation of current real wage trends. A modest agreement would also be appropriate both to allow firm level flexibility and to preserve competitiveness in light of the trend deterioration in the terms of trade, which is mainly due to the weight of information and communication technology (ICT) exports. Indeed, recent output performance is much less impressive if adjusted for the terms of trade loss; "command" GDP, measuring exports in terms of the volume of imports they can buy, has grown by only 1 per cent a year since 2001.

Exports and investment drive activity, but growth of employment is weak

Going forward, output is expected to grow at about 3 per cent a year to 2006. Net exports are projected to add on average 1 percentage points to GDP growth, despite export market share losses. Responding to improved foreign demand, business investment should continue its steady recovery. Stimulated by tax cuts and some recovery in employment, consumption growth is projected to remain strong in 2005, but should weaken in 2006. With potential output now rising only 2 per cent annually, compared with 3 per cent only a few years ago, output is expected to exceed potential by around 1 per cent in 2006. Nevertheless, the unemployment rate will remain above 8 per cent, with employment increasing by about 40 000 from its 2004 low. The government's target for an increase in employment by 100 000 between 2003 and 2007 is therefore unlikely to be met. Consumer price inflation is expected to increase to around 2 per cent in 2006.

Risks are centred on ICT exports and the housing market

Particular uncertainty relates to the growth of electronics exports, which account for about one-quarter of all goods exports. Growth in the mobile phone market could surprise on the upside due to a faster than expected uptake of new products such as third generation mobile phones. On the other hand, it is unclear whether recent losses in market share can be stemmed. Moreover, oil price developments could continue to affect export demand. The housing market could also pose risks, as house prices, in and around Helsinki, have doubled since the mid-1990s.

Greece

Buoyant domestic demand enabled Greece to maintain brisk growth in the first three quarters of 2004. GDP growth is set to ease to 3¼ per cent in 2005, as strong Olympics-related investment comes to an end and fiscal policy tightens, but it should pick up again in 2006. Inflation is expected to increase, reflecting strong demand and higher oil prices, averaging around 3¼ per cent over the next two years.

The recently-revealed sharp deterioration in the fiscal position underlines the need for substantial retrenchment in public expenditure to put public finances on a sustainable path. This should be complemented by improved administrative efficiency and decisive reforms of the pension and health systems. Measures to enhance labour market flexibility and increase product market competition are also required to reduce the inflation differential with the euro area.

Growth has been brisk

The latest indicators suggest a continuation of robust growth in the third quarter of 2004, following a 4 per cent (year-on-year) growth in the first half. Rapid credit expansion in an environment of low real interest rates, buoyant household disposable incomes, and the finalisation of the 2004 Olympic Games-related projects all contributed to the strong growth performance. After a brief dip earlier in the year, consumer price inflation harmonised and core) rose again, reflecting strong demand, higher energy prices, and accelerating unit labour costs. The core inflation differential *vis-à-vis* the euro area average stood at 1.4 percentage points in October. The unemployment rate is expected to remain at around 9 per cent, somewhat below the estimated structural rate of unemployment. The current account deficit has declined, helped by buoyant shipping receipts and tourism income.

Monetary and fiscal conditions have been markedly stimulative

Monetary conditions remain easy with negative real interest rates. Following a marked slowdown since mid-2001, consumer credit accelerated in the course of 2004, after the Bank of Greece lifted remaining consumer credit ceilings in mid-June 2003. Loans to households have been rising at double-digit rates, with total household debt reaching around 30 per cent of GDP by mid-2004, though still well below the euro area average. On the fiscal front, an audit resulted in a significant upward revision of the budget deficits for Greece for the years 2000 to 2003. Official estimates indicate a general government deficit of 5.3 per cent of GDP in 2004, far

Greece

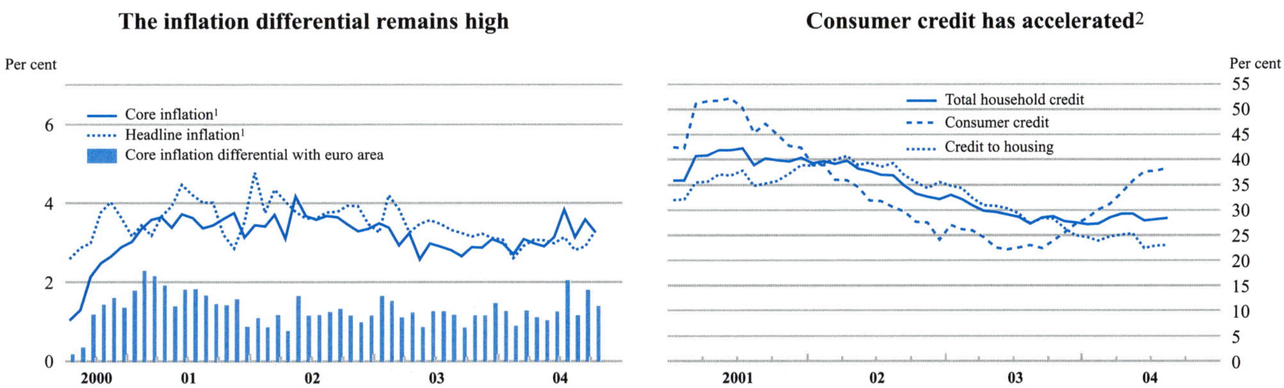

1. Year-on-year percentage changes. Harmonised index of consumer prices. Core inflation excludes energy, food, alcohol and tobacco.
2. Year-on-year percentage changes.
Source: OECD Economic Outlook 76 database; Bank of Greece.

Greece: Demand, output and prices

	2001	2002	2003	2004	2005	2006
	Current prices billion €	Percentage changes, volume (1995 prices)				
Private consumption	89.2	3.1	4.2	3.7	3.4	3.5
Government consumption	22.0	5.3	-2.5	5.2	1.7	0.8
Gross fixed capital formation [a]	31.3	5.7	13.7	5.7	3.1	5.3
Final domestic demand	142.5	4.0	5.5	4.4	3.1	3.6
Stockbuilding [b,c]	- 0.1	0.2	-0.1	-0.4	-0.1	0.0
Total domestic demand	142.5	4.2	5.4	4.0	3.1	3.6
Exports of goods and services	31.2	-7.7	1.0	4.3	7.5	8.7
Imports of goods and services	42.4	-2.9	4.8	5.1	4.1	7.5
Net exports [b]	- 11.1	-0.9	-1.3	-0.7	0.3	-0.5
GDP at market prices	131.3	3.6	4.5	3.8	3.2	3.5
GDP deflator	_	4.0	3.5	3.0	3.4	3.6
Memorandum items	_					
Harmonised index of consumer price	_	3.9	3.4	3.1	3.4	3.2
Private consumption deflator	_	3.6	3.6	3.2	3.5	3.4
Unemployment rate	_	10.2	9.5	9.1	8.9	8.7
General government financial balance [d]	_	-3.8	-4.6	-5.3	-3.5	-3.2
Current account balance [e]	_	-7.6	-6.5	-6.0	-5.8	-5.6

a) Excluding ships operating overseas.
b) Contributions to changes in real GDP (percentage of real GDP in previous year), actual amount in the first column.
c) Including statistical discrepancy.
d) National Account basis, as a percentage of GDP.
e) On settlement basis, as a percentage of GDP.
Source: OECD Economic Outlook 76 database.

above original expectations. This slippage partly reflects overruns in expenditure for the Olympic Games, but current expenditure and revenues also deviated from their targets. The 2005 draft budget aims at a reduction in the general government deficit to 2.8 per cent of GDP, reflecting significantly reined-back expenditure increases. The OECD projects a more gradual fiscal adjustment, with the budget balance moving to a deficit of around 3¼ per cent of GDP in 2006.

Growth should strengthen in 2006, with a risk of inflationary pressures

Growth is expected to slow to 3¼ per cent in 2005, mainly reflecting the end of Olympic Games-related investment spending. It will, however, continue to outpace the euro area average and is expected to pick up again to around 3½ per cent in 2006. Low real interest rates, in combination with still relatively low household debt levels, and a faster implementation of the EU structural funds projects are expected to support domestic demand in the post-Olympics period. Investment spending should be further boosted by the gradual reductions in company tax rates, announced in the 2005 draft budget. Thanks to buoyant export markets, exports are set to pick up strongly over the projection period, despite the erosion of price competitiveness. However, a large current account deficit remains. Given the expected rebound of domestic demand, a major risk attached to the projections is of higher inflationary pressures that would further sap competitiveness. A failure to sufficiently consolidate the budget would pose another risk to the outlook in coming years.

Hungary

Output growth of close to 4 per cent is expected in 2004, easing to around 3½ per cent in 2005 and 2006, with some reduction in the exceptionally rapid pace of export growth and a further slowdown in consumption growth. Inflation is expected to come down rapidly in the near term, as the impact from one-off increases in indirect taxes fades; it is expected to continue to fall, though at a slower pace, in 2005 and 2006, despite higher oil prices.

Although a substantive reduction in the government's budget deficit is expected this year, a big gap between ambitions and outcomes in fiscal policy remains, making co-ordination of macroeconomic policy more difficult and raising risk premia. The new government should switch to a more credible fiscal strategy that sets more realistic targets and backs them up with a stronger commitment to sustainable spending cuts.

Indicators point to a moderation of growth

The driving force of GDP growth over the past year or so has shifted from domestic consumption to external demand with strong growth in exports and, linked to this, strengthening corporate investment. However, a number of indicators suggest an easing in the growth of external demand. Seasonally adjusted monthly export data suggest the pace of export growth has already slowed and this is also seen in monthly production figures. This implies that corporate investment growth is also likely to come down somewhat from its recent high levels. The downward trend in quarterly household consumption growth has continued in 2004, as the end of the series of large wage hikes in the public sector and cutbacks in mortgage residential investment subsidies have begun to damp aggregate household spending power. Price developments have been strongly affected by changes in subsidies and indirect tax increases this year but this effect seems to have already passed its peak.

High interest rates and government deficits continue

The outlook for demand growth also needs to take account of the tempering effects of both high interest rates and budget deficits. The government voted a deficit target of 4.6 per cent of GDP for 2004, which was subsequently revised up to a range of 5.1 to 5.3 per cent. Higher-than-expected debt-servicing costs partly account for the problems with the 2004 deficit. It appears that the government was expecting a more rapid decline in the base rate. The base rate reached 12½ per cent in November 2003 following a 3 percentage point hike in response to exchange rate concerns and

Hungary

The 2004 budget deficit is expected to be well above target

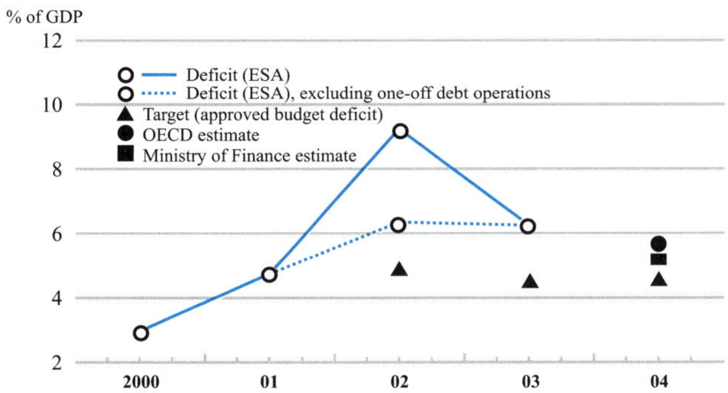

The base rate is being lowered slowly

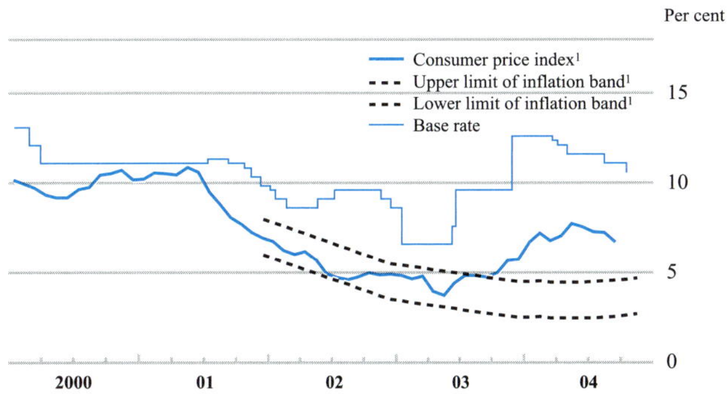

1. Year-on-year percentage change.

Source: Statistical Office of the European Communities (Eurostat), Ministry of Finance, Central Statistical Office, National Bank of Hungary.

Hungary: Demand, output and prices

	2001	2002	2003	2004	2005	2006
	Current prices billion HUF	Percentage changes, volume (2000 prices)				
Private consumption	7 866.5	10.2	7.6	3.5	2.8	2.6
Government consumption	3 231.1	5.0	1.6	1.0	1.0	1.0
Gross fixed capital formation	3 493.0	8.0	3.0	9.0	6.4	6.1
Final domestic demand	14 590.5	8.5	5.2	4.3	3.3	3.2
Stockbuilding[a]	487.9	-2.9	0.3	0.4	0.3	0.0
Total domestic demand	15 078.4	5.4	5.5	4.6	3.5	3.1
Exports of goods and services	10 803.4	3.7	7.2	14.7	12.6	12.2
Imports of goods and services	11 032.0	6.2	10.3	14.7	11.8	11.2
Net exports[a]	- 228.6	-2.0	-2.8	-0.9	-0.2	0.2
GDP at market prices	14 849.8	3.5	2.9	3.9	3.6	3.5
GDP deflator	_	8.9	7.8	5.0	4.4	4.0
Memorandum items						
Consumer price index	_	5.3	4.7	6.9	4.7	4.5
Private consumption deflator	_	3.7	6.0	6.3	4.8	4.5
Unemployment rate	_	5.9	5.9	5.9	5.7	5.6
General government financial balance[b,c]	_	-9.3	-6.2	-5.4	-4.9	-4.5
Current account balance[b]	_	-7.1	-8.9	-9.1	-8.5	-8.2

a) Contributions to changes in real GDP (percentage of real GDP in previous year), actual amount in the first column.
b) As a percentage of GDP.
c) ESA95 accounts provided by the Ministry of Finance for 2001-2003.
Source: OECD Economic Outlook 76 database.

has since been gradually reduced. The government's expectations for faster decline in the base rate is indicative of continuing differences of opinion on the conduct of both monetary and fiscal policy between the central bank and the government. However, unexpected debt-servicing costs do not account for all of the slippage in fiscal outcomes; there is also a continuing failure to reach gross spending and revenue goals. For 2005 the government is discussing a budget with, once again, a deficit target of 4.6 per cent of GDP. If the OECD estimate of a 5.4 per cent deficit for 2004 proves to be accurate, the 2005 target would suggest a consolidation equivalent to 0.8 per cent of GDP. The OECD projection sees this degree of consolidation as unlikely, not least because the government's budget planning is based on an assumption of 4 per cent real GDP growth for 2005 which is at the upper end of the range of projections of other institutions and private-sector analysts.

Growth for 2005 and 2006 will ease but remain robust

For 2005 and 2006, GDP growth is projected to slow to around 3½ per cent. Export growth is projected to ease to just below 12¼ per cent by 2006 and private consumption growth to decelerate by close to 1 percentage point between 2004 and 2006 to about 2½ per cent. Investment growth is also expected to slow down, partly reflecting external demand but also damped residential investment. Despite the reduction in the pace of export growth, the current account deficit is projected to decline somewhat as import growth seems likely to ease more rapidly than export growth.

While export growth may be stronger, there are risks for policy credibility

The main upside risk to the projection lies in external demand as the signs of a slowdown in external demand may turn out to be temporary. The main downside risk is that continuing high interest rates and inadequate fiscal consolidation will induce a further weakening in the credibility of macroeconomic policy and increased exchange rate volatility, both of which could damp foreign investment in Hungary.

Iceland

The economic expansion has continued to gather momentum, broadening from buoyant domestic demand to exports. Even though the economy has not yet entered the most intensive phase of the large-scale aluminium-related investment projects and the labour market is still relatively weak, a sizeable external deficit and inflation pressures have re-emerged.

Further substantial interest-rate increases will be needed to prevent a recurrence of the overheating that took place at the turn of the century. A tight fiscal stance during the investment boom is essential, as it would alleviate the burden on monetary policy to safeguard price stability without the need for excessively high interest rates, upward pressure on the exchange rate and a squeeze on the exposed sector of the economy. Planned tax cuts should therefore be postponed.

Soaring growth has led to tensions and imbalances in the economy

While the upturn, which began two years ago, initially relied exclusively on domestic sources, exports also began to contribute to growth in the first half of 2004, as increased quotas allowed a greater fish catch. Domestic demand continued to expand at a torrid pace, reflecting soaring household spending both on consumption and residential investment (stimulated by surging equity and house prices), as well as the construction of a large power plant (the first stage of the aluminium-related investment projects). Despite strong import growth, the revival of exports (temporarily) stabilised the current account deficit, albeit at a high level. At the same time, however, demand pressures – which so far had mainly taken the form of a rising external imbalance – began to rekindle inflation, pushing the twelve-month rise in the consumer price index toward the Central Bank's upper tolerance limit of 4 per cent by the middle of the year. Although the oil price hike has contributed, core inflation has also easily exceeded the official 2½ per cent target in recent months, due in particular to the housing component of the index.

Policies have moved toward restriction

In response to robust demand and rising inflation expectations, the Central Bank has raised its policy rate by 195 basis points since May (from the historically low level of 5.3 per cent). The Bank's tightening moves have been counteracted by developments in financial and real estate markets, including a considerable reduction in mortgage rates, as offers of cheap loans by commercial and savings banks have been bettered by the public Housing Financing Fund. The planned extension of financing entitlements for homebuyers by the Fund would exacerbate this problem.

Iceland

Economic growth has surged

Real GDP, year-on-year percentage change

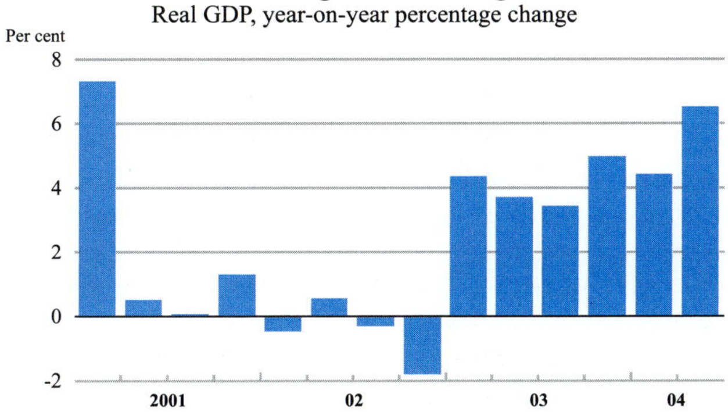

Tensions and imbalances have re-emerged

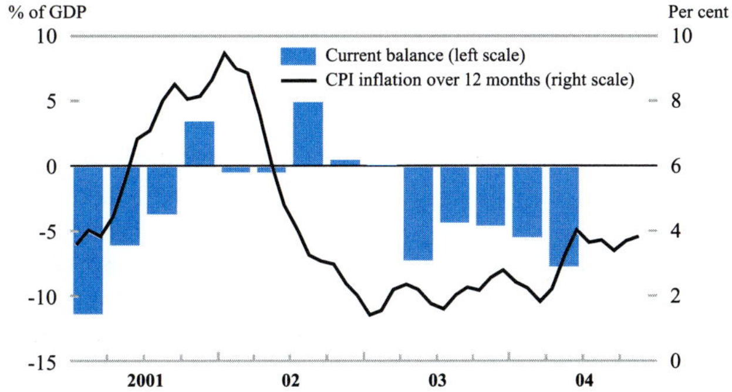

Source: OECD Economic Outlook 76 database.

Iceland: **Demand, output and prices**

	2001	2002	2003	2004	2005	2006
	Current prices billion ISK	Percentage changes, volume (1990 prices)				
Private consumption	408.4	-1.0	6.6	7.3	4.8	4.6
Government consumption	176.7	4.2	3.3	1.9	2.4	2.2
Gross fixed capital formation	165.5	-15.1	17.6	16.9	17.7	10.0
Final domestic demand	750.5	-3.2	8.1	8.2	7.3	5.5
Stockbuilding [a]	- 2.1	0.4	-0.3	0.3	0.0	0.0
Total domestic demand	748.4	-2.8	7.8	8.5	7.4	5.5
Exports of goods and services	303.1	3.6	0.3	6.3	5.1	6.8
Imports of goods and services	307.3	-2.5	9.7	12.5	11.0	8.1
Net exports [a]	- 4.2	2.3	-3.6	-2.6	-2.8	-1.1
GDP at market prices	744.2	-0.5	4.1	5.9	5.2	4.8
GDP deflator	_	5.3	-0.5	1.9	3.6	3.2
Memorandum items						
Consumer price index	_	5.2	2.1	3.1	3.9	3.9
Private consumption deflator	_	3.7	0.7	2.5	3.3	3.4
Unemployment rate	_	3.3	3.4	3.1	2.9	2.6
General government financial balance [b]	_	-0.4	-1.6	0.1	1.2	1.0
Current account balance [b]	_	1.1	-4.1	-8.5	-11.0	-11.6

a) Contributions to changes in real GDP (percentage of real GDP in previous year), actual amount in the first column.
b) As a percentage of GDP.
Source: OECD Economic Outlook 76 database.

Following a considerable loosening in the fiscal stance in the first year of the recovery, budgetary policy has also moved toward restriction. The likely return to financial balance by the general government in 2004 is partly attributable to buoyant tax receipts but also to discretionary measures, notably a sharp cutback in public investment. Government consumption growth has slowed, too, albeit less than intended. But transfers, in particular, have risen much more than envisaged. Current budget plans call for fiscal surpluses over the next two years. However, those will be modest compared to the overheating episode of the late 1990s, with tax cuts over 2005-07 – though back-loaded – bringing fiscal tightening (in terms of the change in the cyclically-adjusted budget balance) to a halt in 2006, just when the construction projects reach their peak.

Preserving economic stability will be a challenge

After approaching 6 per cent in 2004, economic growth is projected to average 5 per cent in the two following years, with a marked deceleration towards the end of this period. This reflects a gradual cooling in household demand as the assumed substantial rise in interest rates begins to bite, as well as a more pronounced slowdown in investment activity when the mega-projects begin to gear down. With a significant positive output gap emerging, inflation is projected to temporarily exceed 4 per cent, while the current account deficit could approach 12 per cent of GDP, more than seen even at the end of the last economic boom. A major risk to the outlook is that budget restraint will be insufficient to prevent severe overheating and the development of a wage/price spiral, since wage negotiations can be re-opened if inflation exceeds assumptions underlying multi-year agreements. This would necessitate even higher interest rates than projected and might entail a hard landing of the economy.

Ireland

Output is estimated to rise by 5 per cent in 2004 and is set to expand roughly at that pace in 2005 and 2006, driven by buoyant net exports and consumption. With excess demand persisting, inflationary pressures are expected to rebuild gradually. The economy is vulnerable to a rise in the euro exchange rate or in interest rates.

Curbing inflation pressures in the medium term should rely on unleashing market forces in services, including in network industries and the liberal professions, and easing regulations in retail trade. Wage moderation should also be encouraged.

The economy has bounced back

After a mild slowdown in 2003, output rose by an estimated 5 per cent in 2004, as net exports and private investment picked up. A buoyant residential construction sector has been an important driver of growth in private investment. Domestic demand has also been fuelled by government and private consumption and, in the second half of the year, by government capital spending. Consumer confidence has been steadily improving from its trough in mid-2003 while retail sales trended upward. The rebound in demand has enabled the absorption of labour force growth that is about three times faster than in the euro area while the unemployment rate remained steady and low at 4.4 per cent. Despite edging up in the last months of 2004 as a result of the oil price hike, harmonised consumer price inflation decelerated in 2004 for the second year in a row.

The fundamentals remain strong

The Irish economy thus continues to experience an impressive performance in terms of employment and labour productivity growth. The main forces that prompted the 2001-03 slowdown – a downturn in the information and communication technology markets and the appreciation of the euro – have largely worked their way through and the economy is rebounding. Trend growth should stabilise at around 5 per cent per annum, as the "Celtic tiger" era of double digit growth rates spurred by foreign direct investment belongs to the past.

Policy conditions are easy

Monetary conditions remain easy, with real short-term interest rates remaining negative. This has contributed to sustaining the sharp upward trend in house prices

Ireland

Real wages are accelerating | **The housing market is still booming**

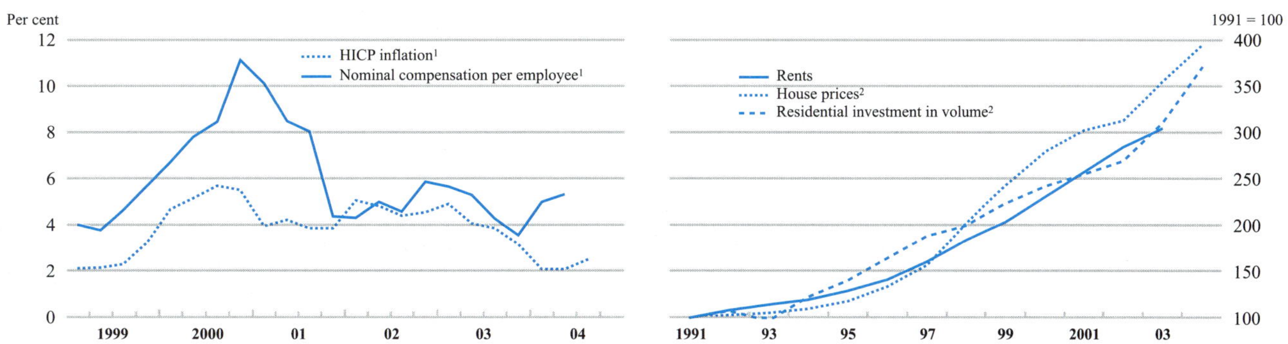

1. Harmonised index of consumer prices. Year-on-year percentage changes.
2. Estimates for 2004.
Source: OECD, *National Accounts* and OECD, *Main Economic Indicators*; European Mortgage Federation, HypoStat 2003.

Ireland: **Demand, output and prices**

	2001	2002	2003	2004	2005	2006
	Current prices billion €	Percentage changes, volume (1995 prices)				
Private consumption	53.5	2.6	2.6	2.7	3.8	3.9
Government consumption	16.2	8.8	2.6	3.2	4.8	4.9
Gross fixed capital formation	27.0	3.1	3.6	7.1	5.6	3.6
Final domestic demand	96.8	3.8	2.8	3.9	4.4	4.0
Stockbuilding [a]	0.4	-0.2	0.5	0.0	0.0	0.0
Total domestic demand	97.2	3.5	3.4	3.9	4.4	4.0
Exports of goods and services	113.6	5.7	-0.9	6.6	8.8	7.2
Imports of goods and services	96.3	3.4	-2.3	6.0	8.6	6.9
Net exports [a]	17.3	3.1	1.1	1.8	1.9	1.8
GDP at market prices	115.4	6.1	3.6	4.9	5.5	4.9
GDP deflator	_	4.5	1.6	3.5	2.9	2.8
Memorandum items						
Harmonised index of consumer price	_	4.7	4.0	2.4	2.8	2.9
Private consumption deflator	_	6.0	4.0	2.7	2.9	3.8
Unemployment rate	_	4.4	4.6	4.4	4.1	4.0
General government financial balance [b]	_	-0.2	0.2	0.2	-0.1	-0.4
Current account balance [b]	_	-1.3	-1.4	-0.6	-0.1	0.1

a) Contributions to changes in real GDP (percentage of real GDP in previous year), actual amount in the first column.
b) As a percentage of GDP.
Source: OECD Economic Outlook 76 database.

and construction. Leading indicators for housing starts kept rising during 2004, suggesting that construction activity will initially remain strong in 2005, even if parts of the housing market are showing signs of saturation. Fiscal policy is also supportive as outlays are set to expand faster than revenues in 2005 and beyond.

Robust growth heightens inflationary pressures

GDP growth is projected to peak at 5½ per cent in 2005. Against an estimated potential growth of 5 per cent, this implies an increasingly positive output gap. Wage gains, which overshot the wage agreement in the business sector in 2004, are expected to remain buoyant in 2005 as skilled labour shortages start to bite. Combined with the carry-over from the oil price hike of end-2004, these developments should translate into a consumer price inflation rate of 3 per cent in 2005 and 2006. The faster pace of unit labour cost increases will erode Ireland's competitiveness *vis-à-vis* its main trading partners, thus holding back net export growth in 2006, which will contribute to GDP growth easing somewhat to just below 5 per cent.

House prices pose a downside risk

The projection is based on the assumption of a soft landing in the housing market. This presupposes that the recent surge in dwelling construction permits will not translate into oversupply. However, if house prices were to fall in real terms, the associated adverse wealth effects would dent confidence and private consumption. The negative impact on GDP growth would be exacerbated by a further fall of the dollar *vis-à-vis* the euro, as this would raise *ex post* real interest rates in addition to weakening foreign demand. On the other hand, the fiscal stance could be more expansionary than projected, hence further supporting domestic demand, as political pressure is building up to cut income taxes and to increase spending, particularly on health care.

Korea

Exports, driven in large part by China, are sustaining the expansion during a period of weak private consumption in the wake of the household credit bubble. Although export growth is now moderating, a pick-up in domestic demand, led initially by investment, is expected to maintain economic growth in the 4 to 5 per cent range in 2005 and 2006. A slowdown in world trade growth before domestic demand revives would pose a threat to a continued expansion.

Given the structural causes of weak domestic demand, further progress in the reform agenda, notably by increasing flexibility in the labour market and addressing the problems of the credit card companies, should be the top priority. Monetary policy should maintain its expansionary stance until domestic demand recovers, while automatic fiscal stabilisers should be allowed to function.

Despite an export-led upturn, consumption is still falling…

Buoyant export growth has driven the recovery from the 2003 recession. China, including Hong Kong, has been the key market, with exports rising 60 per cent year-on-year (in dollar terms) during the first half of 2004. Strong external demand has spilled over to investment and is reversing the decline in employment recorded in 2003. However, improved labour market conditions did not prevent a fall in private consumption, which was also damped by a deterioration in consumer sentiment to its lowest level since 2000. The confidence of households, as well as of firms, has weakened in part as a result of rising oil prices, which boosted headline inflation to a 4½ per cent year-on-year rate in mid-2004. The increase in core inflation, which is still near 3 per cent, has been relatively small.

… due to the household debt overhang

Private consumption has fallen under the weight of the earlier sharp run-up in household debt, which is leading to an upward trend in the saving rate. Encouraged by deregulation and tax incentives to promote the use of credit cards and a shift in banks' lending behaviour, debt increased from 87 per cent of household disposable income in 1999 to 131 per cent in 2002. The saving rate dropped from 16 per cent to only 1.5 per cent over the same period. With the rise in debt, nearly 4 million persons – almost a fifth of the labour force – are delinquent in their credit repayments. Private consumption has also been negatively effected by a slowdown in wage growth in 2004 and falling real estate prices.

Korea

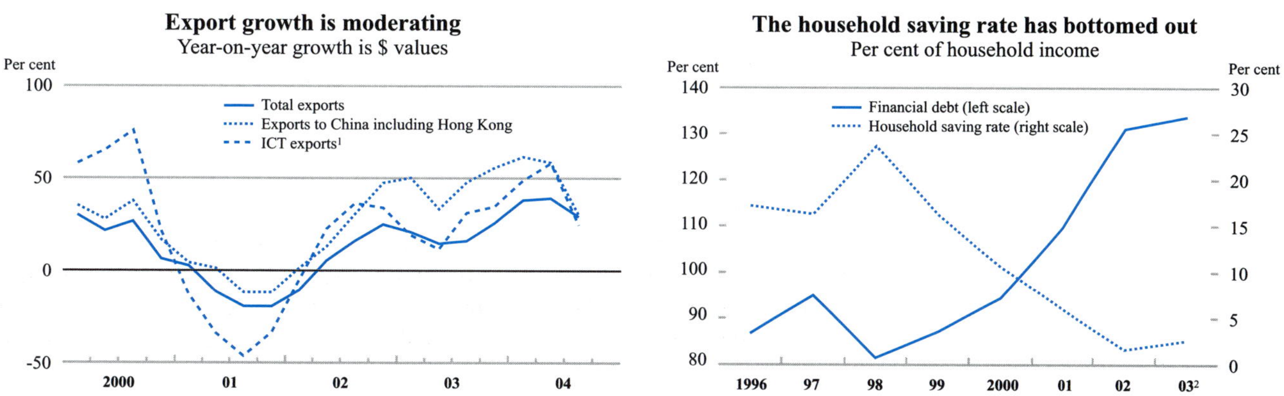

1. Information and communication technology products, including semi-conductors.
2. OECD projection.
Source: Bank of Korea and Korea National Statistical Office.

Korea: Demand, output and prices

	2001	2002	2003	2004	2005	2006
	Current prices trillion KRW	Percentage changes, volume (2000 prices)				
Private consumption	343.4	7.9	-1.4	-0.5	2.0	3.2
Government consumption	80.3	6.0	3.7	3.7	3.5	3.4
Gross fixed capital formation	183.8	6.6	3.6	3.5	4.3	3.8
Final domestic demand	607.5	7.3	0.8	1.3	2.9	3.4
Stockbuilding [a]	- 1.3	-0.2	-0.6	0.0	0.0	0.0
Total domestic demand	606.2	7.0	0.1	1.3	2.9	3.4
Exports of goods and services	235.2	13.3	15.7	21.1	13.3	15.3
Imports of goods and services	220.9	15.2	9.7	14.0	12.8	14.5
Net exports [a]	14.3	-0.2	2.8	4.0	1.5	1.9
Statistical discrepancy [a]	1.7	0.4	0.2	-0.3	0.4	0.0
GDP at market prices	622.1	7.0	3.1	5.0	4.5	5.0
GDP deflator	_	2.8	2.3	1.1	0.2	1.0
Memorandum items						
Consumer price index	_	2.8	3.5	3.7	3.5	3.0
Private consumption deflator	_	2.8	3.4	3.6	3.4	3.0
Unemployment rate	_	3.1	3.4	3.5	3.5	3.4
Household saving ratio [b]	_	1.5	2.5	3.4	3.7	5.1
Consolidated central government balance [c]	_	3.3	1.1	0.4	0.7	1.3
Current account balance [c]	_	1.0	2.0	3.7	2.7	2.7

a) Contributions to changes in real GDP (percentage of real GDP in previous year), actual amount in the first column.

b) As a percentage of disposable income.

c) As a percentage of GDP.

Source: OECD Economic Outlook 76 database.

Monetary and fiscal policies are supporting the expansion…

Both monetary and fiscal policies have been eased to support domestic demand. The Bank of Korea cut its short-term policy rate in August 2004 to a record low of 3½ per cent, below the rate of inflation. The easing of monetary conditions, though, was partly offset by the 4 per cent appreciation in the effective exchange rate during the course of 2004. Fiscal policy is aimed at supporting domestic demand with a 7½ per cent rise in spending in 2005 and a 1 percentage point reduction in income tax rates. Nevertheless, the government expects a strong rise in total tax revenue to increase the consolidated central government surplus from 0.4 per cent of GDP in 2004 to 0.7 per cent in 2005. Progress in reducing the bad debt of the credit card companies is helping to stabilise credit conditions for households.

… which is projected to continue, though at a slower pace

While economic growth may reach Korea's potential rate of about 5 per cent in 2004, maintaining this pace will depend on the resiliency of export growth and the timing of a rebound in private consumption. Export growth already began to moderate in the third quarter of 2004, reflecting a slowdown in China, which accounts for nearly a third of Korean exports. While private consumption may stop declining in the latter part of 2004, the rebound is likely to be very gradual as the household sector increases its saving rate at the same time. Hence, growth may slow to around 4½ per cent in 2005, with core inflation falling to the midpoint of the 2½ to 3½ per cent medium-term target zone. With the falling contribution from external demand, the current account surplus is likely to narrow from 3¾ per cent of GDP in 2004 to around 2¾ per cent in 2005. The main risk to a continued expansion would be a slowdown in world trade, in the context of a further rise in oil prices. However, a rebound in consumer confidence could result in a stronger-than-expected rise in private consumption.

Luxembourg

Export-led growth has resulted in a brisk economic upswing with GDP growth rates expected to exceed 4 per cent in 2004 and the following two years. The trend rise in unemployment is likely to come to an end as of early 2005.

The government should take advantage of the economic upturn both to revise its spending programmes in line with more moderate medium-term growth prospects and to tackle structural unemployment.

The economy is recovering strongly

As a small open economy, which is strongly integrated internationally, Luxembourg benefits immediately from the surge in world trade, which was particularly strong in the second quarter of this year. As a consequence, economic growth, which already turned out to be stronger than expected in 2003, is expected to accelerate further in 2004. The recovery of the financial sector is clearly gaining strength, with revenues on commissions, exports of financial services, profits and employment picking up again. The confidence indicator for the industry has gone up sharply since the middle of this year in response to a more favourable economic outlook. Consumer confidence is following the same upward trend, although more cautiously, as there are signs that employment prospects may start improving soon following an extended period of labour market adjustments. The unemployment rate has reached an average of 4.2 per cent in 2004, reflecting modest job creation in a combination with strong competition from trans-border workers filling in 2/3 of the new jobs created, and increasing female labour force participation. As a consequence of modest wage growth in 2003, there has been a further slowdown in the underlying inflation rate. However, this is not reflected in the development of the consumer price index, which has been adversely affected by the surge in oil prices.

The pressures for fiscal tightening have eased

Contrary to all earlier predictions, Luxembourg managed to maintain a budget surplus, reaching 0.8 per cent of GDP in 2003. Tax revenues have been boosted by value-added tax payments by electronic service providers with headquarters in Luxembourg. In addition, the European Savings Directive obliges the government to levy taxes on interest revenues earned by European non-nationals in Luxembourg. These new sources of tax revenues slow down the projected structural deterioration of the fiscal balance. The latter is attributable to structurally high expenditure growth – which outpaces revenue growth at normal economic growth rates of around 4 per

Luxembourg

Exports are picking up strongly
Year-on-year percentage change

Confidence has improved

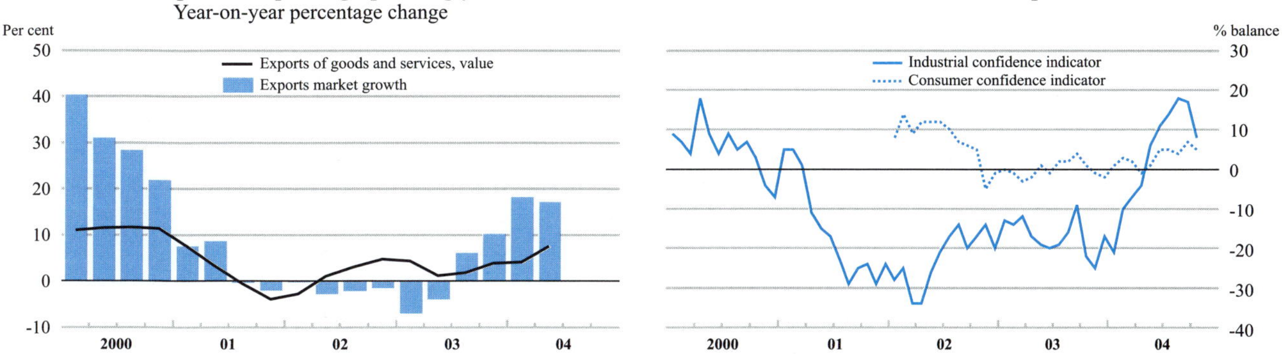

Source: Central bank of Luxembourg and Central Service for Statistics and Economic Studies (STATEC).

Luxembourg: Demand, output and prices

	2001	2002	2003	2004	2005	2006
	Current prices billion €	Percentage changes, volume (1995 prices)				
Private consumption	9.2	3.2	1.6	2.0	2.8	3.0
Government consumption	3.7	3.2	5.0	3.8	2.8	2.3
Gross fixed capital formation	5.0	-1.1	-6.3	7.0	8.0	5.8
Final domestic demand	18.0	2.0	0.2	3.7	4.2	3.6
Stockbuilding [a]	0.2	-1.8	2.0	0.0	0.0	0.0
Total domestic demand	18.2	-0.2	2.6	3.6	4.1	3.5
Exports of goods and services	33.7	-0.6	1.8	6.7	7.4	7.7
Imports of goods and services	29.9	-2.6	1.6	6.9	7.7	7.7
Net exports [a]	3.8	2.5	0.6	1.1	1.3	1.6
GDP at market prices	22.0	2.5	2.9	4.2	4.5	4.3
GDP deflator	_	1.1	2.1	2.2	2.1	1.9
Memorandum items						
Harmonised index of consumer price	_	2.1	2.5	3.5	2.3	2.0
Private consumption deflator	_	2.1	1.9	2.2	2.0	1.9
Unemployment rate	_	3.0	3.8	4.2	4.2	4.2
General government financial balance [b]	_	2.8	0.8	-0.4	-0.8	-1.2

a) Contributions to changes in real GDP (percentage of real GDP in previous year), actual amount in the first column.
b) As a percentage of GDP.
Source: OECD Economic Outlook 76 database.

cent – in combination with recent reforms lowering the tax burden on personal and corporate income and a contraction of the corporate income tax base following several years of low profits.

Export-led growth will gain further momentum

In view of a rapid expansion of world trade and export markets, GDP growth is projected to accelerate further to about 4½ per cent in 2005 and 2006. Domestic demand, in particular private consumption and investment, will reinforce economic growth. The benefits of a sustained economic recovery will finally spill over to the labour market, resulting in an acceleration of employment creation and a stabilisation of the unemployment rate at 4.2 per cent as of early 2005. In addition, inflationary pressures are likely to persist for some time because the current oil shock is transmitted to wages and prices by the automatic wage indexation mechanism. There is a risk that a stronger than expected appreciation of the euro exchange rate would temper export growth and inflation. But conversely, stronger-than-projected recovery of world financial markets would boost financial service exports and overall growth, while also strengthening consumer confidence via the prospect of an increase in high-wage jobs.

Mexico

A strong recovery is finally under way, fuelled by the upturn in the US manufacturing sector and high oil prices. Growth prospects are expected to remain bright as domestic demand offsets the projected slowdown of foreign demand. Headline inflation has risen, mostly reflecting erratic factors, but core inflation has also turned up.

Faced with rising inflation expectations, the successive moves to tighten the monetary policy stance during 2004 have been appropriate. On the fiscal front, the 2004 budget target will be easily met, thanks to higher-than-projected oil revenues. The supportive revenue environment should continue to be used to consolidate public finances. A revenue-enhancing tax reform is required to reduce the vulnerability of public finances to oil price changes.

Both private domestic demand and net exports have been strong

Real GDP growth picked up strongly in the first half of 2004, led by the upturn in external demand and a strong recovery in private investment. Household consumption was bolstered by the recovery in employment in the formal sector. The current account deficit narrowed again, helped by terms-of-trade gains on account of oil prices, while net foreign direct investment inflows continued on a large scale. The peso has depreciated against the dollar in the course of 2004 (by 4 per cent over the first 10 months). Year-on-year inflation, as measured by the consumer price index, has been steadily rising to 5.4 per cent in October 2004, mainly because of rising food, energy and other commodity prices.

Monetary policy remains cautious…

Core inflation has also turned up since June 2004, although it has remained below 4 per cent. And inflation expectations have been creeping up, to above 5 per cent for December 2004 in the case of consumer price inflation, compared with the central bank target of 3 per cent (plus or minus 1 per cent). The central bank has responded swiftly, tightening the policy stance on 7 instances between February and October. As a result, short-term interest rates rose above 8 per cent in early November. They are assumed to remain high over the projection period, in line with US rates. This should help put consumer price inflation back on a declining path, but the inflation target now is unlikely to be reached before 2005.

Mexico

Inflation has risen above the 2004 target[1] | **Strong US industrial production has boosted exports**

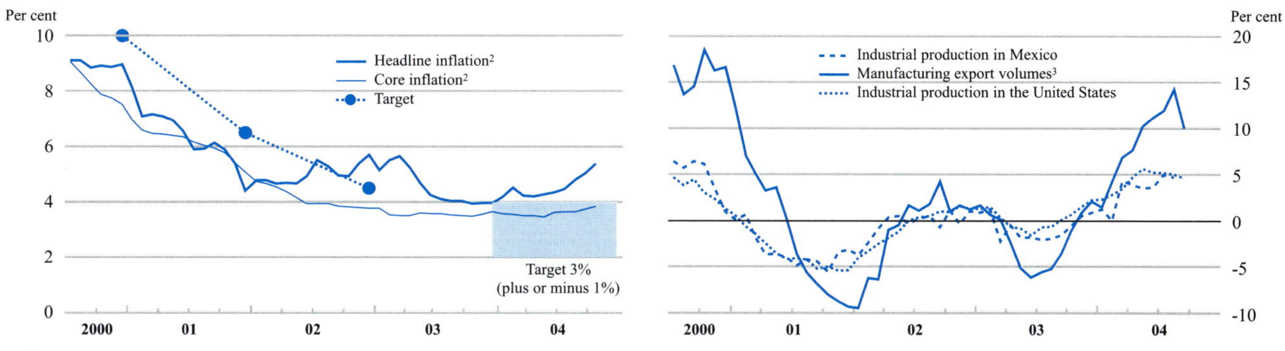

1. The target is based on the consumer price index headline inflation.
2. Year-on-year percentage change. Core inflation excludes food and other items with erratic developments.
3. At constant prices of 1993. Year-on-year percentage change. 3-month moving average.

Source: Bank of Mexico; OECD, *Main Economic Indicators*.

Mexico: Demand, output and prices

	2001	2002	2003	2004	2005	2006
	Current prices billion MXN	Percentage changes, volume (1993 prices)				
Private consumption	4 044.9	1.3	3.0	4.5	4.2	4.2
Government consumption	683.4	0.1	2.5	0.0	1.1	2.0
Gross fixed capital formation	1 162.0	-1.0	-0.4	6.4	5.8	6.0
Final domestic demand	5 890.2	0.7	2.3	4.5	4.2	4.4
Stockbuilding [a]	55.1	0.0	-1.7	-0.7	0.1	0.2
Total domestic demand	5 945.3	0.7	0.5	3.7	4.3	4.5
Exports of goods and services	1 598.5	1.5	1.1	12.4	8.4	8.4
Imports of goods and services	1 730.4	1.4	-1.0	10.5	9.1	8.9
Net exports [a]	- 131.9	0.0	0.7	0.4	-0.4	-0.4
GDP at market prices	5 813.4	0.7	1.3	4.2	3.9	4.2
GDP deflator	_	6.9	6.5	6.0	4.2	3.4
Memorandum items						
Consumer price index	_	5.0	4.5	4.6	4.5	3.4
Private consumption deflator	_	5.4	5.0	3.9	3.7	3.3
Unemployment rate [b]	_	2.4	2.5	2.4	2.3	2.3
Current account balance [c]	_	-2.2	-1.4	-1.4	-1.5	-1.9

a) Contributions to changes in real GDP (percentage of real GDP in previous year), actual amount in the first column.
b) Based on National Employment Survey. Data not comparable with previous issues of the *OECD Economic Outlook*.
c) As a percentage of GDP.
Source: OECD Economic Outlook 76 database.

... and fiscal policy aims for budget balance in 2005

The public sector borrowing requirement (PSBR) is expected to be just above 3 per cent of GDP in 2004.[1] In the first half of the year, cost-reduction measures were implemented in the public administration. Over the year as a whole, extra oil-related revenue will finance additional infrastructure investment and social spending, as well as a rise in the primary surplus. Transfers will also be made to the oil stabilisation fund. The 2005 draft budget envisages balanced public sector accounts (narrow definition) and a decline in the PSBR. An oil price fall of about $6 per barrel in 2005 is built into the draft budget. Based on the OECD assumption for a more gradual decline in oil prices, budget targets should be easy to achieve.

Growth is expected to remain around 4 per cent

Export growth is expected to slow in line with foreign demand, but strong investment, including public-private investment schemes (PIDIREGAS), should provide some stimulus to activity. Employment in the formal sector should strengthen, helping sustain the expansion of household consumption. Overall, GDP growth should remain at around 4 per cent, with some acceleration in the election year 2006, but hardly enough to raise average per capita incomes significantly. The current account deficit is expected to widen somewhat as domestic demand picks up, reaching just above 2 per cent of GDP by 2006, comfortably financed by foreign direct investment. The standstill on the reform agenda is the main factor holding back growth in the near term, and there are risks attached to the projections, mostly related to the vulnerability of public finances to world oil price changes.

1. Including spending related to the voluntary retirement programme but excluding the favourable impact of accounting adjustments related to the banking sector debt, and excluding non-recurrent revenue.

Netherlands

The economy is gradually recovering from a long and severe recession. Real GDP is likely to grow by 1¼ per cent in 2004 and 2005, accelerating to 2¼ per cent in 2006, which would still leave a large negative output gap. Modest wage growth, needed to restore international competitiveness, and only gradually accelerating employment account for the delayed return of private consumption to trend growth. The unemployment rate will increase temporarily as a consequence of supply-side reforms, helping core inflation to edge down further.

There is a risk that the additional labour supply resulting from the current social benefit reforms may not be fully absorbed at current wage rates. Hence, the government should complement these reforms with measures increasing wage flexibility, aimed at enhancing employment prospects for low-skilled workers.

Exports have been leading the recovery…

Real GDP grew by 1.4 per cent during the first half of 2004 (seasonally-adjusted annual rate), a pace falling short of that in the euro area. Net exports contributed heavily to growth as exports as well as re-exports accelerated markedly and outpaced imports for domestic use. Domestic demand lost half of the ground gained in late 2003, reflecting lower business investment, de-stocking and a turnaround in public expenditure in the wake of several consolidation packages. GDP growth at 0.8 per cent remained below potential in the third quarter as industrial production was volatile and retail sales edged down, though other service activities held up well.

… while domestic demand remained fragile

Private consumption expenditure is picking up slowly, having underperformed in 2001-02, under the effect of sharply decelerating house price increases and falling stock prices, and decreased in 2003 due to falling real disposable income. Precautionary saving continued to rise in 2004, spurred by the weak labour market and wage deceleration. However, both employment and registered unemployment stabilised during the summer. Real disposable income is not expected to repeat its 2003 fall because the decline in consumer price inflation, which averaged 1.1 per cent (year-on-year) in the August-October period, has helped to stabilise purchasing power.

Fiscal policy reacted rapidly to respect the 3 per cent threshold

The general government budget deficit reached 3.2 per cent of GDP in 2003 and needs to come down to 3 per cent or less by no later than in 2005 according to the Excessive Deficit Procedure. It is likely that this goal will already be achieved in 2004. In the spring the government took further consolidation measures amounting to 0.4 per cent of GDP for 2004 and 2005. Half of the improvement in 2004 represents either revenues brought forward from 2005 or postponed investment expenditure, so that the improve-

Netherlands

Private consumption is slowly picking up

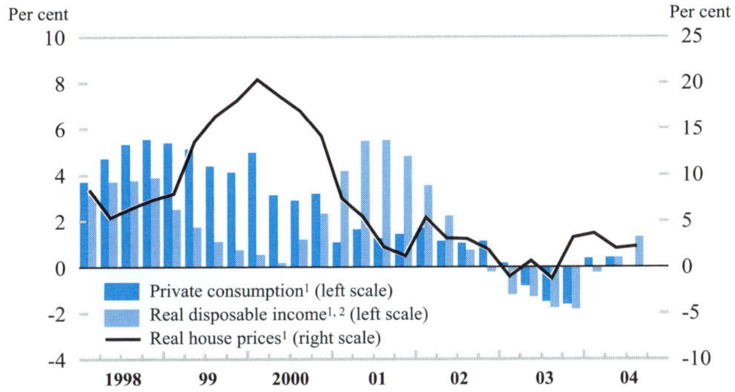

Expectations are improving in all sectors
Survey indicators

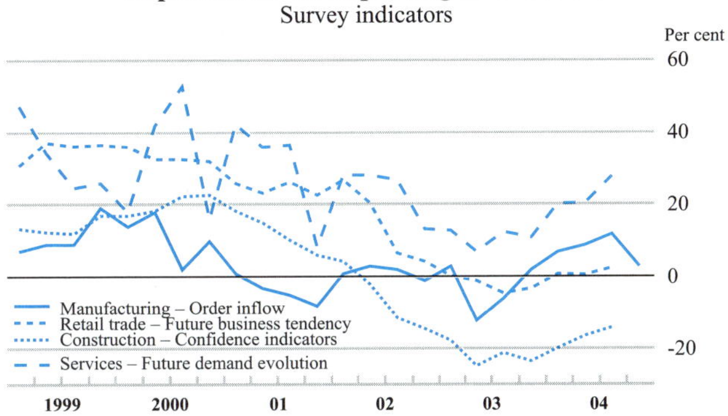

1. Year-on-year percentage change.
2. 2004: estimations.
Source: OECD, *Main Economic Indicators* and OECD, *National Accounts*.

Netherlands: **Demand, output and prices**

	2001	2002	2003	2004	2005	2006
	Current prices billion €	Percentage changes, volume				
Private consumption	212.8	1.3	-0.9	0.1	0.2	1.7
Government consumption	100.9	3.6	1.8	0.3	0.3	0.5
Gross fixed capital formation	92.9	-3.6	-3.1	0.2	0.5	3.1
Final domestic demand	406.6	0.7	-0.7	0.2	0.3	1.7
Stockbuilding [a]	0.0	-0.2	0.2	0.1	0.1	0.2
Total domestic demand	406.6	0.5	-0.5	0.3	0.4	1.9
Exports of goods and services	280.0	0.8	0.0	6.4	7.1	7.5
Imports of goods and services	257.3	0.8	0.6	5.3	6.4	7.6
Net exports [a]	22.7	0.1	-0.4	1.1	0.9	0.5
GDP at market prices	429.3	0.6	-0.9	1.2	1.2	2.4
GDP deflator	_	3.1	3.0	0.8	0.6	1.0
Memorandum items						
Harmonised index of consumer price	_	3.9	2.2	1.3	2.1	1.6
Private consumption deflator	_	2.7	2.3	1.1	2.1	1.6
Unemployment rate	_	2.9	4.1	4.9	5.2	5.0
Household saving ratio [b]	_	10.0	10.1	10.7	10.7	9.9
General government financial balance [c]	_	-1.9	-3.2	-2.9	-2.7	-1.9
Current account balance [c]	_	2.5	2.9	4.2	4.2	4.4

Note: National accounts are based on official chain-linked data. This introduces a discrepancy in the identity between real demand components and GDP. For further details see *OECD Economic Outlook* Sources and Methods, (*http:// www.oecd.org/eco/sources-and-methods*).

a) Contributions to changes in real GDP (percentage of real GDP in previous year), actual amount in the first column.

b) As a percentage of disposable income, including savings in life insurance and pension schemes.

c) As a percentage of GDP.

Source: OECD Economic Outlook 76 database.

ment of the cyclically-adjusted balance in 2005 is expected to be smaller. The measures decided for 2005 are structural, however, with one half relating to lower social expenditure (tighter access rules to unemployment and disability benefit, lower sickness reintegration subsidies and introduction of no-claim rules reducing consumption by health funds). The other half originates in higher marginal income taxes for middle-income earners and higher energy taxes, which more than offset tax reductions for corporations and self-employed amounting to 0.4 per cent of GDP. The further improvement of the structural balance in 2006 reflects consolidation commitments made in 2003.

The recovery continues to depend on exports but should broaden in 2006

As the upswing strengthens in the euro area and is sustained in other trading partner regions, GDP growth is expected to firm from spring 2005, when the damping effects from high oil and commodity prices should start fading. With world trade growth remaining high and low wage increases helping to restore cost competitiveness further, exports will continue to be the driving force. Better sales prospects will improve companies' financial situation along with an increase in capacity utilisation, so that business investment should gradually gain strength and employment start growing moderately in 2005 and at a faster pace in 2006. The turnaround in employment is supported by the reforms increasing labour supply, which will also raise the unemployment rate temporarily. With real house price increases having stabilised at moderately positive rates and households further improving their balance sheets, the growth of private consumption is expected to exceed that of real disposable income, especially in 2006.

External risks are to the downside but domestic risks are balanced

With the expansion relying strongly on exports, euro appreciation and slower-than-expected international trade represent downside risks to the outlook. Private consumption remains vulnerable to a decline in house prices but could also grow faster than projected should households decide to spend a greater share of their savings.

New Zealand

The economy grew very rapidly in the first half of the year, adding to an already positive output gap and inflation pressures. However, the pace of activity is now starting to slow, as higher interest rates damp domestic demand and the effects of exchange rate appreciation continue to spread through the economy. Labour shortages persist and real wage growth may accelerate, although capacity constraints will be eased through high rates of investment.

The economy is on track for a soft landing, and successive moves taken to tighten monetary policy during 2004 should prove to be sufficient. Additional fiscal stimulus at this point in the cycle would be unhelpful and would anyway need to be offset by higher interest rates in order to bring the economy back onto a sustainable growth path.

The economy is starting to cool…

Domestic demand steamed ahead in the first half of 2004 but is now showing signs of slowing. Household consumption has come back to a more moderate rate of expansion, as higher interest rates start to bite. The housing market has softened, property prices may have peaked and houses are taking longer to sell. Lower net immigration has eased pressures on residential construction. Meanwhile, exporters have benefited from the recovery in foreign markets, but this has been partly offset by the effects of the exchange-rate appreciation. These continue to diffuse through the economy, although terms-of-trade gains have tempered the impact on national income. Cheaper import prices for capital goods have been a boon for producers facing both buoyant demand and labour shortages, and business investment rates have been exceptionally high. These external sector developments have pushed the current account balance further into deficit.

… but inflationary pressures remain strong

Inflationary pressures have mounted with major contributions from housing, some transportation costs and food prices. Inflation expectations have also risen. However, price declines in tradeables, attributable to the higher exchange rate, have played a major role in moderating overall inflation, though this is likely to prove short-lived in view of the recent steep climb in oil prices. But while activity is cooling, the labour market remains very tight, with the unemployment rate well below its estimated structural level and wage growth is now showing signs of acceleration.

Monetary conditions have tightened considerably…

The Reserve Bank has raised official interest rates by 1½ percentage points since the beginning of the year, and the currency appreciation has also contributed to tighter monetary conditions. These moves should be enough to bring the economy

New Zealand

The exchange rate remains high and the terms of trade have improved

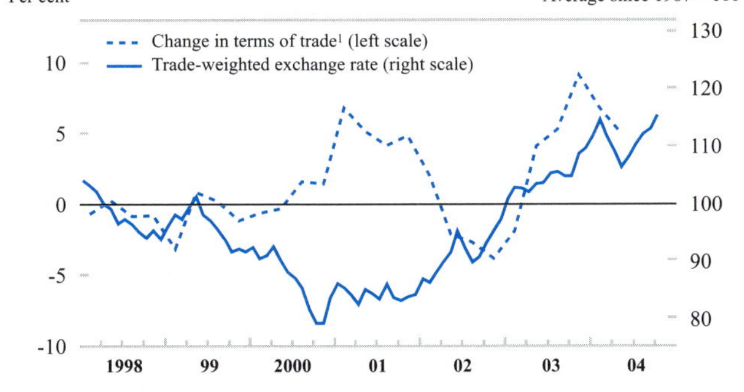

Inflationary pressures have risen
Year-on-year percentage change

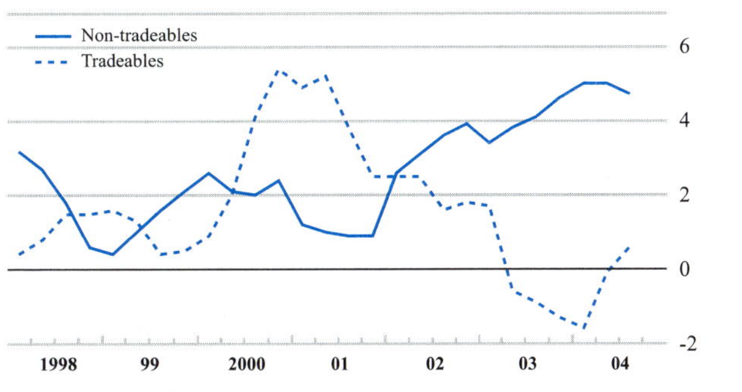

1. Year-on-year change.
Source: Reserve Bank of New Zealand and OECD, Economic Outlook 76 database.

New Zealand: **Demand, output and prices**

	2001	2002	2003	2004	2005	2006
	Current prices billion NZD	Percentage changes, volume				
Private consumption	71.2	4.4	4.8	5.5	1.1	1.7
Government consumption	21.4	2.3	2.5	7.4	3.2	5.0
Gross fixed capital formation	23.8	8.3	13.1	13.5	4.7	2.9
Final domestic demand	116.4	4.8	6.1	7.6	2.3	2.6
Stockbuilding [a]	1.6	0.2	-0.3	0.1	0.2	0.0
Total domestic demand	118.1	5.1	5.7	7.3	2.5	2.6
Exports of goods and services	43.5	6.3	1.7	6.3	4.3	7.6
Imports of goods and services	39.8	8.4	9.2	14.6	5.2	7.2
Net exports [a]	3.7	-0.5	-2.3	-2.8	-0.5	-0.2
GDP (expenditure) at market prices	121.8	4.5	3.2	4.8	2.1	2.6
GDP deflator	_	0.5	2.1	2.9	2.2	2.0
Memorandum items						
GDP (production)	_	4.6	3.4	4.9	2.1	2.6
Consumer price index	_	2.7	1.8	2.3	3.0	2.8
Private consumption deflator	_	1.9	0.7	1.4	2.4	2.0
Unemployment rate	_	5.2	4.6	4.1	4.2	4.2
General government financial balance [b]	_	2.5	3.1	2.9	2.1	1.9
Current account balance [b]	_	-3.1	-4.2	-5.1	-5.3	-5.0

Note: National accounts are based on official chain-linked data. This introduces a discrepancy in the identity between real demand components and GDP. For further details see *OECD Economic Outlook* Sources and Methods, (*http:// www.oecd.org/eco/sources-and-methods*).

a) Contributions to changes in real GDP (percentage of real GDP in previous year), actual amount in the first column.

b) As a percentage of GDP.

Source: OECD Economic Outlook 76 database.

back onto a more sustainable path, and a "wait and see" stance is projected going forward. The government recorded an unexpectedly large financial surplus for the last fiscal year, largely for cyclical reasons. Despite various calls for additional spending initiatives or tax cuts, the government has reiterated its commitment to maintaining a fiscally prudent approach.

... and should bring about a soft landing

The economy is projected to expand by less than potential in 2005 and 2006, thereby eliminating excess demand. Following near-term weakness, exports are expected to rebound, albeit less vigorously than export market growth. Private consumption growth may be less buoyant over the next few quarters as households adjust to higher interest rates and the end of capital gains in housing, before gradually picking up pace again. Residential investment could continue to shrink, allowing a switch of construction capacity to non-residential activity. Business investment may continue expanding vigorously, boosting potential output. Real wage growth could remain slightly ahead of productivity improvements, and labour shortages are unlikely to ease significantly. Inflation pressures may not start to dissipate until some way through next year.

Risks tend to be on the downside

There are several risks to this outlook. Weaker-than-projected export market growth or a more pronounced household reaction to the turnaround of the housing market would worsen prospects. More persistent inflation could require tighter monetary policy to avoid inflation expectations gaining ground. Changes to labour legislation could be another source of downside risk if concerns about their impact on overall costs and labour market flexibility were to undermine business confidence.

Norway

A domestic-demand-led recovery is gaining momentum, based on strengthened oil investments, low interest rates and an expansionary fiscal policy. The negative output gap is expected to reverse in 2005. The external sector should start contributing positively to growth. Core inflation is projected to rise as a result of excess demand but is expected to reach the middle of the range targeted by the Central Bank only by end-2006.

Monetary policy should be geared towards reaching the inflation target by maintaining low interest rates throughout the projection period. Fiscal policy should return rapidly to the fiscal rule to help avoid overheating and Krone appreciation, and to contribute to a more equitable use of oil resources over time.

Activity is supported by domestic demand

Activity continued to expand briskly in the first half of 2004, led by a further surge in domestic demand. The growth contribution of net exports was negative, as import penetration continued to increase and the competitiveness of Norwegian manufacturing industry to suffer. Coincident and leading indicators suggest that growth will remain strong through to the end of 2004. Employment and, especially, unemployment are responding only sluggishly to strong activity, pointing to still unabsorbed labour hoarding. Recent wage round outturns have been characterised by moderate settlements compared with the recent past.

Inflation is nonetheless subdued

Benign labour market developments, falling import prices of some consumer goods, increased price competition in retail trade and a deceleration of electricity prices and housing rents all contributed to low headline inflation until October. Core inflation is also low and well beneath the target band of 1½ to 3½ per cent. After a series of cuts from December 2002 to March 2004, the policy interest rate remains at a historically low level of 1.75 per cent, below the rate prevailing in the euro area. The interest rate differential with the euro area is expected to be narrowed only slowly as core inflation could remain lower than 2.5 per cent (the middle level of the inflation target range) through 2005 and into 2006.

Fiscal policy is supportive

The non-oil structural deficit deteriorated markedly in 2004 representing a further step away from the fiscal rule (structural non-oil deficit equal to the expected real return on the petroleum fund over time). The 2005 budget bill has introduced new tax measures

Norway

Competitiveness is still weak

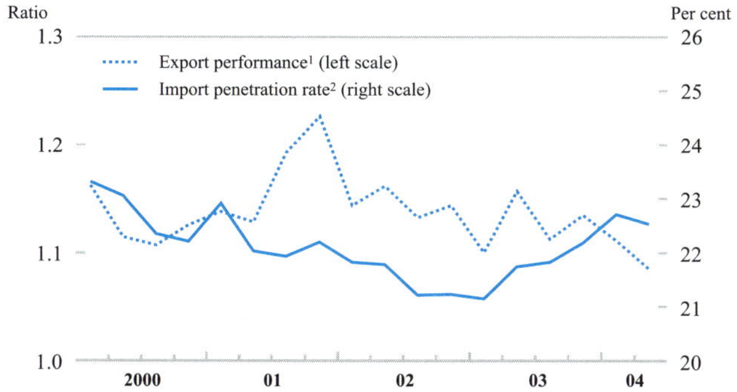

Household debt is rising

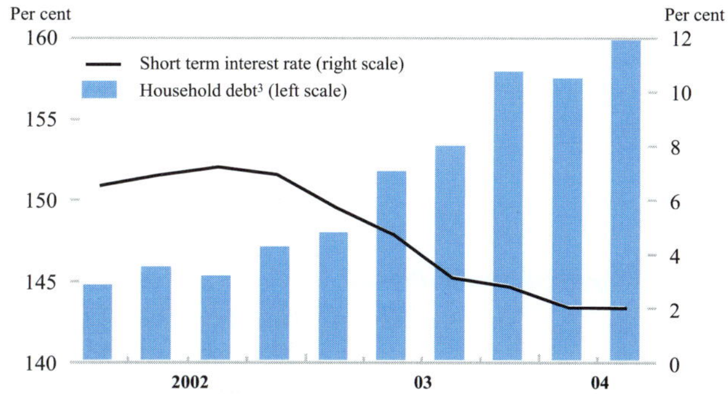

1. Defined as the ratio between export volumes and export markets weighted by Norway's trade shares.
2. Imports of goods and services as a percentage of demand (calculated as the sum of gross domestic product and imports).
3. As a percentage of disposable income.
Source: OECD Economic Outlook 76 database and Norges Bank.

Norway: **Demand, output and prices**

	2001	2002	2003	2004	2005	2006
	Current prices billion NOK	Percentage changes, volume (2001 prices)				
Private consumption	651.3	3.6	3.8	4.0	3.8	3.1
Government consumption	314.8	3.1	1.4	2.2	1.8	1.8
Gross fixed capital formation	278.9	-3.4	-3.7	5.4	5.4	2.5
Final domestic demand	1 245.1	1.9	1.6	3.8	3.6	2.7
Stockbuilding[a]	20.7	0.4	-0.8	0.9	0.2	0.0
Total domestic demand	1 265.7	2.4	0.6	4.8	3.7	2.6
Exports of goods and services	697.3	0.1	1.2	2.4	2.6	3.8
Imports of goods and services	436.8	2.3	2.2	6.8	3.7	3.3
Net exports[a]	260.5	-0.6	-0.1	-0.9	0.1	0.7
GDP at market prices	1 526.2	1.4	0.4	3.2	3.2	2.9
GDP deflator	_	-1.6	2.3	5.6	6.3	2.4
Memorandum items						
Mainland GDP at market prices[b]	_	1.7	0.6	3.7	3.2	2.9
Consumer price index	_	1.3	2.5	0.5	1.9	2.1
Private consumption deflator	_	0.8	2.3	0.8	2.2	2.2
Unemployment rate	_	3.9	4.5	4.4	4.2	4.1
Household saving ratio[c]	_	9.2	7.6	7.5	7.7	7.8
General government financial balance[d]	_	9.1	8.3	8.2	10.5	11.4
Current account balance[d]	_	12.9	12.9	14.2	16.3	16.4

a) Contributions to changes in real GDP (percentage of real GDP in previous year), actual amount in the first column.
b) GDP excluding oil and shipping.
c) As a percentage of disposable income.
d) As a percentage of GDP.
Source: OECD Economic Outlook 76 database.

mainly shifting the burden from income to consumption. Annual inflows to the petroleum fund in 2004-2005 are estimated to be almost one quarter higher than in 2003, which could make the fiscal rule easier to attain. The budget measures are slightly expansionary, however, so that the fiscal policy still deviates significantly from the fiscal rule.

The short-term outlook is favourable

Thanks to accommodating policies and high oil prices, domestic demand is expected to grow strongly in 2005 and the negative output gap will reverse. Higher oil prices should stimulate investment in the oil sector as well. As oil investment feeds through into higher production and exports, while the associated capital goods imports decelerate, net exports should begin to contribute positively to growth since the start of the year. An assumed more neutral policy stance in 2006 implies that growth will develop more in line with potential. Labour demand should gather strength during 2005 and this will progressively translate into lower unemployment. A moderate carry-over from previous contracts suggests modest wage developments in the short term, while in the medium term real earnings are expected to grow broadly in line with productivity. Prices are likely to accelerate in 2005 because of demand pressure as well as the increase of value added tax rates introduced by the 2005 budget. Still, core inflation is likely to reach 2.5 per cent only by end-2006.

There are risks on both sides

Risks are evenly balanced. Demand, including that coming from the public sector, could overheat resulting in unexpected price acceleration and an early monetary policy tightening. As Norwegian household debt has increased significantly in the past quarters because of low interest rates, an early reversal of the monetary stance could have a negative impact on private consumption and housing investment. On the upside, if high oil prices persist, oil investment could well be much stronger than projected, although the opposite risk could stem from a bigger than assumed fall in oil prices.

Poland

GDP increased markedly in the first half of 2004, driven by strong increases in inventories and exports. Activity should continue to be robust in 2005, although less so than in the beginning of 2004. Export growth should decrease slightly, in part due to recent zloty appreciation. An investment recovery is under way but is likely to gain force only in 2006. Employment is expected to expand moderately in 2005 and more robustly in 2006 as investment picks up.

The effect on the budget deficit of a relaxation of government spending in 2004 has been partly offset by robust growth; with the moderation of GDP growth projected by the OECD, public expenditure targets will need to be monitored closely and even reinforced if medium-term fiscal sustainability is to be preserved. Although the upturn in headline inflation may be only temporary, increases in central bank interest rates have been appropriate in the light of wage growth and the budgetary position. Further increases may be necessary if inflationary pressures continue.

Inventories sustained growth in early 2004

Economic activity accelerated markedly in the first half of 2004, with real GDP increasing by 6.5 per cent (year-over-year), though growth showed some signs of moderation in the third quarter. A large part of this acceleration is accounted for by a strong increase in inventories. Other components of domestic demand did not accelerate: household consumption continued to expand at moderate rates. Investment recovered slowly from its decline in 2003 while exports expanded strongly in the first quarter, they slowed in the second and imports continued to grow rapidly so that the external growth contribution diminished. The real effective depreciation that was at work until May reversed as the zloty started to appreciate. Industrial production has grown less robustly since May and, although household and business confidence have stabilised at high levels, short term indicators point to some deceleration in activity in the latter part of the year.

Employment began to improve and inflation rose temporarily

The labour market has shown signs of improvement since early 2004, but the corner has not yet been turned. After falling by 1.2 per cent in 2003, total employment rose in the first two quarters of 2004. The standardised unemployment rate has slowly decreased, to 18.7 per cent in August. Wage growth in the enterprise sector increased markedly, to over 4 per cent in the first half of the year before moderating to 3.7 per cent in September. Inflation rose in the second quarter mainly due to food prices, value added tax chapes and oil prices. It subsequently fell back slightly to 4.5 per cent. In July-August the National Bank of Poland increased policy rates twice, by 1¼ percentage points altogether. Core inflation reached 2.4 per cent in September (year-on-year), well within the central bank's official target of 2.5±1 per cent.

Poland

Stockbuilding has boosted activity

Contributions to growth[1]

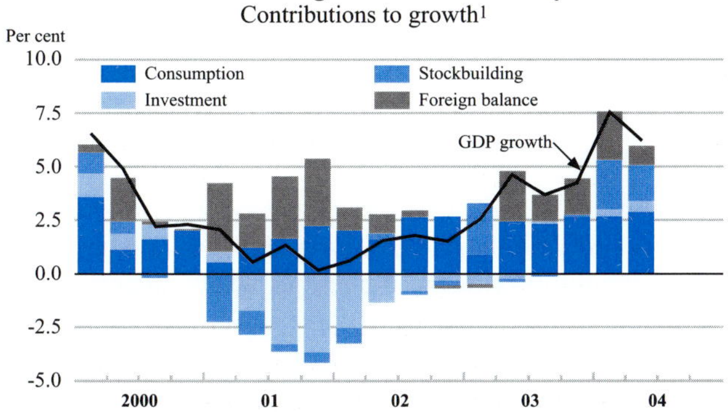

The labour market is improving

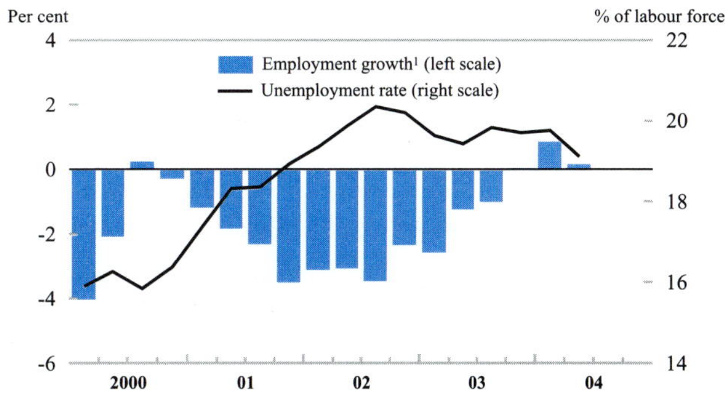

1. Percentage change from same period of previous year.
Source: Central Statistical Office.

Poland: **Demand, output and prices**

	2001	2002	2003	2004	2005	2006
	Current prices billion PLZ	Percentage changes, volume				
Private consumption	493.7	3.4	3.1	4.0	4.0	3.7
Government consumption	137.1	0.4	0.4	2.0	1.5	1.6
Gross fixed capital formation	157.2	-5.8	-0.9	3.9	7.2	8.8
Final domestic demand	788.1	1.0	1.9	3.6	4.2	4.3
Stockbuilding [a]	0.5	-0.2	0.6	1.3	0.1	0.2
Total domestic demand	788.6	0.9	2.4	4.7	4.2	4.5
Exports of goods and services	210.6	4.8	14.7	13.4	12.2	12.6
Imports of goods and services	238.6	2.6	9.3	10.4	11.2	11.9
Net exports [a]	- 28.0	0.5	1.3	0.6	0.0	0.0
GDP at market prices	760.6	1.4	3.8	5.4	4.3	4.5
GDP deflator	_	1.3	0.5	3.9	2.5	3.2
Memorandum items						
Consumer price index	_	1.9	0.7	3.3	3.0	3.4
Private consumption deflator	_	1.6	0.6	3.5	3.2	3.4
Unemployment rate	_	19.9	19.6	19.1	18.4	17.6
General government financial balance [b]	_	-4.9	-3.8	-5.4	-4.7	-4.3
Current account balance [b]	_	-2.6	-2.0	-1.5	-2.1	-2.2

Note: National accounts are based on official chain-linked data. This introduces a discrepancy in the identity between real demand components and GDP. For further details see *OECD Economic Outlook* Sources and Methods, *(http:// www.oecd.org/eco/sources-and-methods).*

a) Contributions to changes in real GDP (percentage of real GDP in previous year), actual amount in the first column.

b) As a percentage of GDP.

Source: OECD Economic Outlook 76 database.

Fiscal policy eased substantially in 2004

The general government deficit should remain over 5 per cent of GDP in 2004, following the substantial relaxation of spending, even though revenues benefited from the acceleration of GDP. The effect on the government budget from entry in the European Union (EU) may not be strong, as agriculture payments pass directly to the farm sector, and flows of structural funds will be a function of corresponding additional investment projects. The deficit should nevertheless diminish in 2005 provided spending controls are effective. If this is not the case, government debt may rise to levels that would trigger more drastic measures under constitutional provisions designed to limit the stock of debt.

The recovery should continue

After slowing from the high growth of early 2004, GDP should expand by 4.3 per cent in 2005. Private consumption should grow robustly, sustained by employment growth, real wage increases and EU transfers, while investment is to continue to recover modestly. Export growth should weaken somewhat. Still-robust domestic demand should be reflected in strong imports. The current account deficit should widen but so should foreign direct investment inflows. Robust labour productivity growth should keep a lid on unit labour cost despite real wage increases. As a result, inflation should remain moderate. As the recovery continues, investment will accelerate and, along with stronger world growth and slowly declining oil prices, will lead to strengthening GDP growth in 2006.

Public finance and structural reforms remain vital

The main downside risk remains the ability of the government to adhere to its planned public expenditure limits and the possible effect on confidence; significant slippage would not only undermine public finance objectives while raising doubts about fiscal sustainability, but also further encourage wage inflation and threaten hard-won price stability. The continued upturn in employment and investment could be threatened if structural reforms to improve the investment climate are not pursued. On the upside, investment dynamics could be stronger than projected – especially in view of growing access to EU structural funds.

Portugal

The Portuguese economy emerged from recession in 2004, driven by exports and private domestic demand. Real GDP growth is expected to pick up further and reach 2¾ per cent in 2006. By any measure, the economy would still not be operating at its potential at the end of the projection period. As a result the inflation differential vis-à-vis *the euro area should remain small.*

Fiscal consolidation remains a challenge for policymakers. Reliance on large one-off measures to keep the deficit below 3 per cent of GDP has become the norm since 2002. These should be replaced by strict controls on spending and the implementation of already-approved reforms should be accelerated. A radical reform of the pension system is also needed to ensure the long-term sustainability of public finances.

Growth has picked up

The Portuguese economy came out of recession in 2004. Activity picked up sharply in the first half, reflecting both temporary factors, such as the impact of the European Soccer Championship (Euro 2004), and more durable ones, such as stronger export markets and the end of retrenchment in the private sector. Most recent short-term indicators point to a slowdown in the second half of the year. Overall, GDP growth is estimated to reach 1½ per cent in 2004. Employment has stopped falling but has not yet picked up and the unemployment rate reached 6½ per cent at mid-year. After a temporary widening in June and July, related to the Euro 2004 and some public service price readjustments, the year-on-year inflation differential with the euro area disappeared in September. Reflecting strong domestic demand and slightly unfavourable terms of trade, the trade deficit has started to widen, and the current account deficit is expected to increase to more than 6 per cent of GDP in 2004.

Fiscal consolidation still relies on one-off measures

In 2004 the fiscal deficit is expected to be below 3 per cent of GDP, thanks to one-off measures (real estate sales and the integration of the assets of a pension fund) equivalent to 2 percentage points of GDP. Tax receipts were higher than budgeted, reflecting stronger activity; and recent structural reforms in health spending and public administration have started to generate savings. However, other current expenditure, especially on public pensions, grew faster than budgeted. The underlying consolidation effort – calculated by adjusting the change in the structural deficit for

Portugal

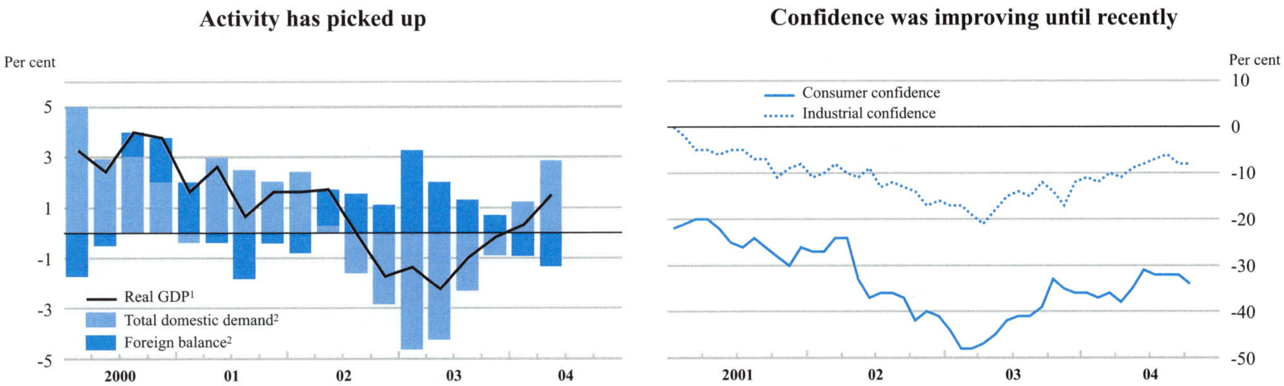

1. Year-on-year percentage changes.
2. Contributions to annual per cent change in real GDP. Percentage points.
Source: OECD Economic Outlook 76 database; European Commission.

Portugal: **Demand, output and prices**

	2001	2002	2003	2004	2005	2006
	Current prices billion €	Percentage changes, volume (1995 prices)				
Private consumption	75.3	1.0	-0.5	2.0	1.9	2.6
Government consumption	25.6	2.2	-0.4	0.5	0.5	0.9
Gross fixed capital formation	33.3	-4.9	-9.8	2.6	4.9	6.4
Final domestic demand	134.1	-0.3	-2.7	1.8	2.3	3.2
Stockbuilding[a]	0.9	-0.1	0.0	0.0	-0.1	0.0
Total domestic demand	135.0	-0.4	-2.8	1.9	2.2	3.2
Exports of goods and services	37.5	2.0	4.0	7.3	6.1	6.2
Imports of goods and services	50.0	-0.3	-0.9	7.1	5.5	6.4
Net exports[a]	- 12.5	0.8	1.8	-0.5	-0.2	-0.6
GDP at market prices	122.5	0.4	-1.2	1.5	2.2	2.8
GDP deflator	_	4.5	2.3	1.8	1.9	2.0
Memorandum items						
Harmonised index of consumer price	_	3.7	3.3	2.5	2.0	1.8
Private consumption deflator	_	3.5	3.4	2.4	2.0	1.8
Unemployment rate	_	5.0	6.3	6.5	6.6	6.1
Household saving ratio[b]	_	12.7	13.0	12.8	12.8	12.4
General government financial balance[c]	_	-2.7	-2.8	-2.9	-3.0	-3.8
Current account balance[c]	_	-6.7	-5.1	-6.3	-6.3	-6.3

a) Contributions to changes in real GDP (percentage of real GDP in previous year), actual amount in the first column.
b) As a percentage of disposable income.
c) As a percentage of GDP.
Source: OECD Economic Outlook 76 database.

the impact of one-off measures – is estimated at 0.2 percentage points of GDP. The budget proposal for 2005 targets a deficit of 2.8 per cent of GDP. It includes personal income tax cuts, a relaxation of the freezes on public sector wages and employment, an 11 per cent increase in public investment, and 1.4 per cent of GDP from one-off revenue measures (which still have to be cleared by Eurostat). According to OECD estimates the deficit would reach 3 per cent of GDP in 2005 and would widen to above 3.5 per cent of GDP in 2006. Stronger control of public spending and the postponement of some tax cuts would be preferable to reliance on one-off measures to contain the deficit, and negative short-term effects on growth would be less of a problem now that economic recovery is under way.

Growth will strengthen in 2005 and 2006

Activity is expected to strengthen in 2005 and 2006, driven by private consumption and investment. The contribution of external demand to growth is expected to be negative, despite strong export growth driven by demand from Europe and oil-producing countries. Although narrowing, the negative output gap will still be large at end-2006. Unemployment is expected to start to decrease in 2005, but would remain high, while the inflation differential *vis-à-vis* the euro area should remain low. The main risk to the forecast comes from the public finances ahead of the 2006 elections. The combination of a pre-election period and higher revenues as growth accelerates might result in a larger slippage in expenditure than projected. As with other OECD oil-importing countries, a key uncertainty surrounding the forecast is the evolution of oil prices and its impact on world growth.

Slovak Republic

Activity is broadening and growth close to 5 per cent over the projection horizon is exceeding previous expectations. Headline inflation will drop significantly from currently high levels once the effects of administered price adjustments, tax reform and European Union accession-related food price increases start to fade in 2005. Unemployment will also begin to fall to a rate of 16 per cent by the end of 2006.

For fiscal policy to remain credibly committed to the adoption of the euro in 2009, the substantial government spending cuts already budgeted should be implemented as planned. The monetary authorities should specify and communicate their strategy for euro-area entry as soon as one-off effects on inflation dissipate.

Domestic demand is becoming the driving force for growth

GDP accelerated to almost 5½ per cent in the first half of 2004, and monthly indicators suggest that strong growth continued after the summer. Private consumption, benefiting from real income growth, and investment developed strongly and replaced net exports as the driving force of growth. While exports, especially of machinery and vehicles, continued to gain momentum, import growth was even stronger because of significant investment involved in the construction of new manufacturing plants. The widening trade deficit and outflows of dividends to foreign investors shifted the current account balance to the negative side, but the deficit remained fully financed by foreign direct investment (FDI) inflows. Unemployment peaked in the first half of 2004, as a result of ongoing restructuring in industry and public services and lagged seasonal hiring in agriculture and tourist industries. Headline inflation was at around 8 per cent over the first three quarters of 2004, of which 4 percentage points resulted from administered price adjustments and the implementation of a uniform value-added tax rate. Food price inflation as a consequence of European Union (EU) accession exceeded expectations and further added to price dynamics. Real wage increases remained well below productivity growth in the first half of 2004, but recent collective agreements in several industries imply a marked acceleration in wage growth. Even so, headline inflation is likely to decelerate markedly as the impact of temporary factors wanes.

Slovakia remains a top reformer

With the adoption of the health reform and fiscal decentralization packages in autumn 2004, the Slovak government has continued to implement its ambitious reform programme. The measures launched earlier in 2004 are aimed at providing a favourable business environment and stimulating FDI through low direct taxes and labour costs. A new manufacturing plant of a third multinational car producer is scheduled to start production in 2006.

Slovak Republic

Domestic demand is driving GDP growth again

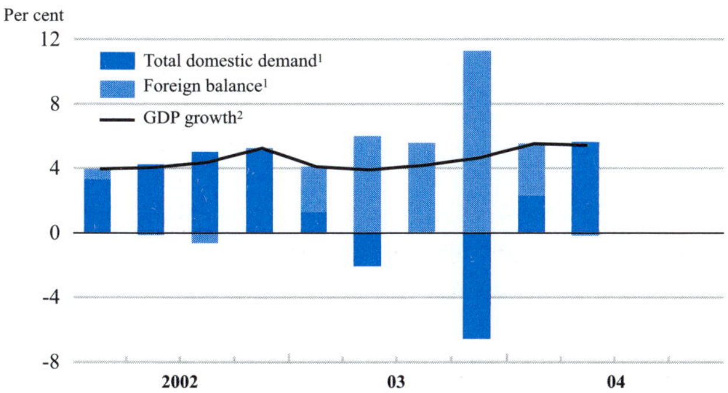

Real wage growth is picking up markedly in several sectors²

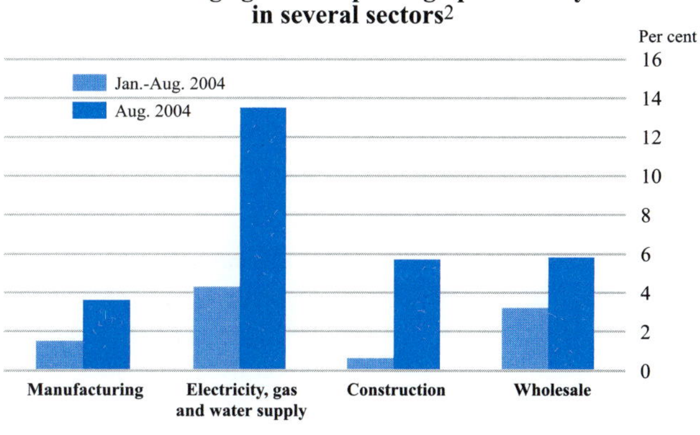

1. Contribution to annual GDP growth in percentage points.
2. Percentage change from same period of previous year.
Source: Statistical Office of the Slovak Republic and OECD, *National Accounts*.

Slovak Republic: **Demand, output and prices**

	2001	2002	2003	2004	2005	2006
	Current prices billion SKK	Percentage changes, volume (1995 prices)				
Private consumption	585.9	5.3	-0.4	3.2	3.7	3.9
Government consumption	203.4	4.7	2.9	1.4	1.6	0.8
Gross fixed capital formation	291.0	-0.9	-1.2	3.7	8.6	5.6
Final domestic demand	1 080.3	3.5	0.0	3.0	4.6	3.7
Stockbuilding [a]	12.0	0.8	-2.3	1.3	0.5	-0.1
Total domestic demand	1 092.3	4.2	-2.2	4.3	5.0	3.6
Exports of goods and services	741.0	5.5	22.6	14.5	12.3	13.0
Imports of goods and services	823.5	5.2	13.8	14.0	12.7	11.9
Net exports [a]	- 82.4	0.0	6.4	0.8	-0.1	1.6
GDP at market prices	1 009.8	4.4	4.2	4.9	4.8	5.0
GDP deflator	_	4.0	4.7	5.3	2.6	2.9
Memorandum items						
Consumer price index	_	3.1	8.6	7.7	3.6	3.1
Private consumption deflator	_	2.5	7.7	7.0	2.7	2.8
Unemployment rate	_	18.6	17.5	18.2	17.5	16.5
General government financial balance [b, c]	_	-5.7	-3.7	-3.9	-3.8	-3.9
Current account balance [b]	_	-7.9	-0.9	-2.6	-3.0	-1.9

a) Contributions to changes in real GDP (percentage of real GDP in previous year), actual amount in the first column.
b) As a percentage of GDP.
c) Includes the cost of transfering contributions to the second pillar of the pension system.
Source: OECD Economic Outlook 76 database.

Fiscal and monetary policy are committed to euro adoption in 2009

With stronger-than-expected tax revenues and continuing spending discipline, the fiscal deficit target of 3.9 per cent for 2004 is within reach. Fiscal policy remains committed to the convergence programme that envisages a gradual reduction of the budget deficit to 3 per cent by 2007 (taking into account the costs related to the pension reform). This would pave the way for the adoption of the euro in 2009, but meeting the Maastrict criteria remains conditional on the implementation of substantial spending cuts. The first-time agreement on a multi-annual budget, as well as the support of independent members of parliament for major reforms, gives credibility to government consolidation plans. The central bank continues to pursue a cautious route. It has gradually lowered its basic refinancing rate by a cumulative 150 basis points in 2004 in response to the temporary character of inflation and appreciation pressures on the koruna. The central bank expects marked disinflation over the coming years; however a more specific communication strategy for the run-up to the euro adoption is necessary.

Growth remains strong and broadly based…

Output growth is projected to remain close to 5 per cent over the forecast horizon, driven primarily by investment and production for export. Improving labour-market conditions will sustain household consumption. The current account deficit is expected to widen temporarily as a result of projected increases in machinery and equipment imports following FDI-investment in the car industry. Marked disinflation will start in 2005 with the fading of the effects of administered price adjustments and EU accession. Modest employment increases are foreseen over the medium term.

… but there are some downside risks

The risk that inflationary one-off measures will have second-round effects remains in the near term, as witnessed by recent collective wage agreements. This may put pressure on competitiveness and interest rates, damping growth. The main downside risks for fiscal policy relate to the costs of the ongoing pension reforms and the impact of the tax reform on fiscal revenues, possibly requiring additional fiscal restraint. Growth and foreign trade forecasts in 2006 are sensitive to the advancement of the new car manufacturing plant; if the administrative approval of construction plans delays the start of production, GDP growth and net export figures in 2006 would have to be revised downwards.

Spain

Domestic demand sustained activity during the first half of 2004, but net foreign demand weakened. Inflation has risen due to the oil price shock leaving the positive differential with the euro area at around 1 percentage point. Although some weakness can be expected in the short term because of the oil price hike, activity should accelerate again to close to 3 per cent over the projection period.

Monetary conditions remain relaxed, while the budget for 2005 implies a broadly neutral fiscal stance. Reforms to raise competition in some sectors and to improve the wage bargaining system should be adopted with the aim of raising productivity growth and reducing the inflation differential with other countries.

The recovery paused in the course of 2004, despite buoyant domestic demand

Although the recovery seems to have paused in 2004, domestic demand remains strong. In the first half of the year, consumption and construction investment remained buoyant while equipment investment started to recover. Part of the strength in domestic demand was absorbed by rapidly growing imports, continuing a trend already observed in 2003. Exports also recovered, pulled by a more dynamic international environment, but this did not suffice to dent the large negative contribution of external demand to growth of more than 1 per cent. More recently, the tourist season has been weak and private consumption has become less buoyant, but investment indicators have been recovering rapidly and point to a strong surge in demand. House prices continue to rise very rapidly and household debt has increased to close to 70 per cent of GDP. Job creation is expanding at around 2.5 per cent, while the labour force is also growing rapidly but at a lower rate. The unemployment rate has thus declined.

Oil prices are pushing inflation up

Headline inflation started to accelerate in the second quarter due to the increase in energy prices and reached 3½ per cent in October. Core inflation has already been affected by second round effects from the oil price shock and stands at close to 3 per cent. On the other hand, there is no evidence yet that higher inflation has affected wage growth.

The policy stance will remain relaxed

Due to an inflation rate which is higher than in the rest of the euro area, short-term real interest rates remain negative and monetary conditions relaxed. The official projection points to a deficit of about 1 per cent of GDP for the general government

Spain

Net exports are a drag on activity

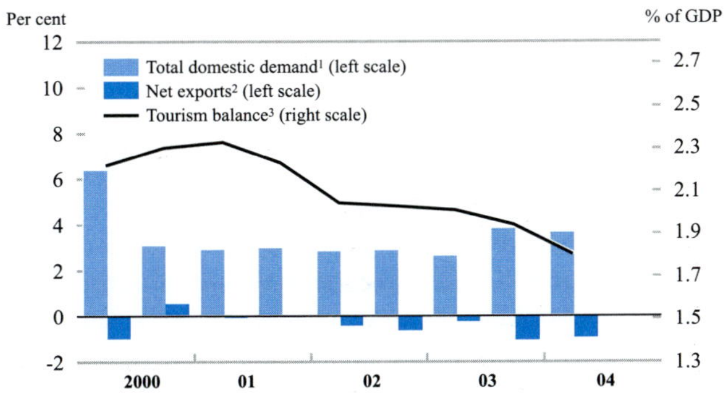

Household debt is rising rapidly

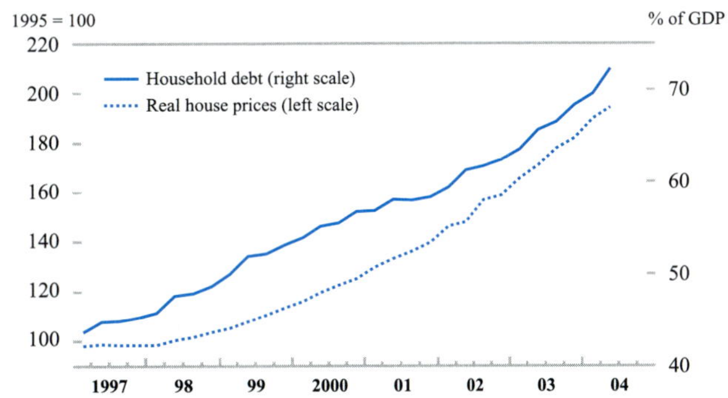

1. Year-on-year percentage changes.
2. Contribution to GDP growth.
3. Seasonally adjusted by the OECD Secretariat.

Source: Bank of Spain and OECD, *Quarterly National Accounts*.

Spain: **Demand, output and prices**

	2001	2002	2003	2004	2005	2006
	Current prices billion €	Percentage changes, volume (1995 prices)				
Private consumption	381.9	2.9	2.9	3.2	2.7	3.3
Government consumption	115.1	4.1	3.9	4.0	3.3	3.0
Gross fixed capital formation	165.4	1.7	3.2	3.3	4.1	4.1
Final domestic demand	662.4	2.8	3.1	3.4	3.1	3.4
Stockbuilding [a]	1.9	0.0	0.1	0.0	0.0	0.0
Total domestic demand	664.3	2.8	3.2	3.4	3.1	3.5
Exports of goods and services	195.6	1.2	2.6	5.3	7.6	7.4
Imports of goods and services	206.0	3.1	4.8	7.4	8.2	8.1
Net exports [a]	- 10.4	-0.6	-0.8	-0.9	-0.5	-0.6
GDP at market prices	653.9	2.2	2.5	2.6	2.7	3.0
GDP deflator	_	4.5	4.0	3.1	3.6	3.6
Memorandum items						
Harmonised index of consumer price	_	3.6	3.1	3.0	3.2	2.7
Private consumption deflator	_	3.4	3.1	2.9	3.2	2.7
Unemployment rate [b]	_	11.4	11.3	10.9	10.7	10.4
Household saving ratio [c]	_	10.6	10.6	10.7	11.0	11.0
General government financial balance [d]	_	-0.1	0.4	-1.1	-0.1	-0.1
Current account balance [d]	_	-2.4	-2.8	-4.2	-4.7	-4.8

a) Contributions to changes in real GDP (percentage of real GDP in previous year), actual amount in the first column.

b) Spanish data on labour force, employment and unemployment are revised since 1976 using the methodology applied by the Labour Force Survey as from 2002. Revisions are made by the OECD based on information from the official Statistical Office in Spain. They imply a downward revision of the unemployment rate by 2.5 points in 2001.

c) As a percentage of disposable income.

d) As a percentage of GDP.

Source: OECD Economic Outlook 76 database.

accounts in 2004, but it includes one-off measures, such as the recognition of past debts. Excluding these adjustments, the accounts would be balanced. The budget for 2005, which is based on a growth projection of 3 per cent, also aims at a balanced budget, despite large increases in some outlays such as spending on social transfers, education and research. In the OECD's projection, a balanced budget is expected, which implies a broadly neutral fiscal stance, even though inflation pressures have mounted.

After a lull, activity should rebound again

Private consumption is expected to decelerate moderately in the first half of 2005 as higher oil prices bite into households' real incomes, while construction investment should also slow down somewhat. Equipment investment, on the other hand, should help maintain the momentum of domestic demand, which could grow at more than 3 per cent in 2005. Imports will continue to rise swiftly, but stronger exports due to the international recovery should reduce the negative contribution of the external sector to growth. Overall, following a lull in the coming quarters, GDP growth should firm again to close to 3 per cent, which is slightly above potential growth. The labour market is likely to remain strong, with high employment creation and a moderate fall in unemployment. However, productivity growth will probably remain weak and may recover only slowly reflecting the build-up of equipment investment. Inflation could accelerate over the coming months as catch-up clauses of wages are activated and second round effects of the oil price shock set in. Apart from the risks associated with the oil price hike and the international environment, there is the negative risk that housing prices continue to surge for some time, but then fall, forcing consumer retrenchment.

Sweden

The economic expansion is gathering pace, with output growing faster than its potential rate, driven by strong exports and a rebound in investment. Export growth is projected to remain robust, and household consumption will be boosted by tax cuts and rising house prices. Those factors should drive the long-awaited improvement in employment, which will also support domestic demand.

Inflation is likely to pick up, as spare capacity will be absorbed by the end of this year. The central bank will therefore need to begin raising interest rates soon. In September, the government added a substantial fiscal stimulus to an already-buoyant economy. This will make the job of monetary policy more difficult and risks jeopardising the government's medium-term fiscal target.

Activity has rebounded strongly

The economy has been gaining momentum for more than a year, with activity expanding at well above its potential rate. Export growth has been especially vigorous, reflecting higher international demand and a recovery in the telecommunications and motor vehicle sectors. An upturn in investment is also clearly under way. Low interest rates, high rates of capacity utilisation and the telecommunications expansion have supported machinery and equipment investment in particular. In addition, the strength of the housing market has driven up residential construction and house prices. However, the upswing has taken an unusually long time to feed through to the labour market. One reason is that productivity growth has remained remarkably strong, but it also reflects an increase in the average number of hours worked per employee, with firms expanding production by calling on their existing workers rather than through new recruitment.

Investment and consumption will drive growth

The recovery is expected to continue, but with investment and consumption playing bigger roles. Businesses will seek to reduce capacity constraints by investing in new capital equipment, bringing the investment rate back towards its historical average. In addition, households will enjoy healthy gains in their disposable incomes as their job prospects improve and as a result of the tax and spending measures announced in the 2005 budget. They will also feel wealthier because of the recent increases in house prices. Wage growth, on the other hand, will be moderate through to the end of 2005, reflecting the restrained agreements negotiated in the first few months of this year. Most deals were settled on the basis of more generous wage increases for 2006. The combination of these forces should deliver sturdy consumption growth in 2005 and even stronger rises the year after. Exports should also remain buoyant due to continuing robust demand from abroad. This economic

Sweden

Exports are growing strongly

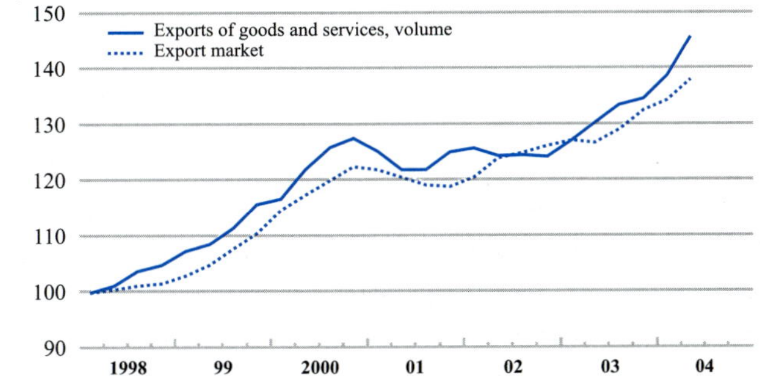

Employment remains weak but hours are picking up

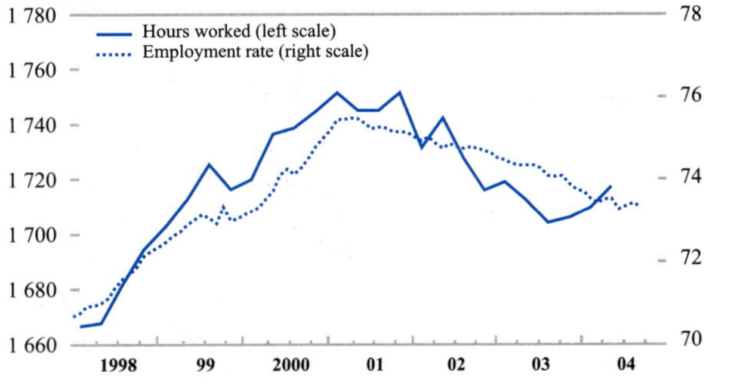

Source: Statistics Sweden.

Sweden: Demand, output and prices

	2001	2002	2003	2004	2005	2006
	Current prices billion SEK	Percentage changes, volume				
Private consumption	1 108.4	1.4	1.9	2.3	2.8	2.8
Government consumption	613.3	3.2	0.6	1.2	1.1	1.1
Gross fixed capital formation	395.6	-3.0	-2.0	2.7	7.2	5.5
Final domestic demand	2 117.4	1.1	0.8	2.1	3.1	2.8
Stockbuilding [a]	6.6	-0.2	0.4	-0.8	0.4	0.0
Total domestic demand	2 123.9	0.9	1.3	1.2	3.5	2.8
Exports of goods and services	1 039.5	1.0	5.3	10.7	8.0	7.8
Imports of goods and services	897.1	-1.9	5.0	6.9	9.3	7.5
Net exports [a]	142.5	1.2	0.6	2.4	0.3	1.0
GDP at market prices	2 266.4	2.0	1.7	3.3	3.3	3.2
GDP deflator	_	1.5	2.2	1.1	1.5	2.2
Memorandum items						
Consumer price index	_	2.2	1.9	0.4	1.8	2.5
Private consumption deflator	_	1.8	2.5	1.0	1.8	2.3
Unemployment rate [b]	_	4.0	4.9	5.6	4.9	4.3
Household saving ratio [c]	_	9.7	8.5	8.3	7.8	7.1
General government financial balance [d,e]	_	-0.3	0.1	0.5	0.7	1.2
Current account balance [d]	_	5.3	6.4	7.4	6.4	6.5

Note: National accounts are based on official chain-linked data. This introduces a discrepancy in the identity between real demand components and GDP. For further details see *OECD Economic Outlook* Sources and Methods, *(http://www.oecd.org/eco/sources-and-methods)*.

a) Contributions to changes in real GDP (percentage of real GDP in previous year), actual amount in the first column.

b) Based on monthly Labour Force Surveys.

c) As a percentage of disposable income.

d) As a percentage of GDP.

e) Maastricht definition.

Source: OECD Economic Outlook 76 database.

strength should significantly improve the job market, with the unemployment rate projected to fall back below 4½ per cent by the end of 2006.

A significant fiscal expansion has been planned

The government announced a large fiscal expansion in its 2005 budget. The key measures include reductions in income and wealth taxes, and increases in child allowances and transfers to local government. The policy decisions amount to 1 per cent of GDP in 2005 and another ½ per cent the following year. Although many of the budget measures are welcome, the timing is awkward when considering the state of the business cycle: they will boost household incomes and economic activity at a time when growth would have been brisk anyway. Moreover, the general government surplus is projected to fall well short of the government's target of 2 per cent of GDP in cyclically-adjusted terms.

Interest rates need to rise soon

Inflation has remained low throughout the expansion, reflecting weak import prices and strong productivity growth. However, the economy had only a small amount of spare capacity by the middle of 2004, and this is expected to be used up by the end of the year. With demand projected to exceed supply for the rest of the projection period, inflation pressures are likely to re-emerge. They will be given a further boost in 2006 as wage growth accelerates. The central bank will therefore need to begin lifting interest rates by the end of this year.

Future productivity growth is uncertain

A key uncertainty is the extent to which the recent high rate of productivity growth will persist. If it remains impressive, then the immediate outlook for employment will be less buoyant and there will be less urgency for the central bank to lift interest rates. The inflationary impact of oil prices is likely to be modest, since wages for most of the private sector are already agreed until 2006, thereby limiting any second-round effects on inflation.

Switzerland

Underpinned by relaxed monetary and fiscal policies, the economy picked up in 2004, with GDP growth set to be close to 2 per cent. The expansion should continue through 2005 and 2006 at much the same pace, slightly above potential, thanks to the more dynamic external environment. These developments, which should contribute to an improvement in the labour market as of 2005, are likely to be accompanied by continuing moderate inflation.

Continuing gradual monetary tightening is projected, with financial conditions becoming more neutral as spare production capacity is reduced. The consolidation of Federal finances as of 2005 remains necessary, even if budget outturns in 2004 prove better than expected. The improved cyclical situation must not lead to a weakening of the efforts made to stimulate domestic competition and increase potential growth.

The recovery looks firm, despite a fragile labour market

The recovery, which began in the second semester of 2003, continued into the first half of 2004 at a stable annual rate of some 2 per cent. Expansionary fiscal and monetary policies have sustained firm domestic demand, reflecting increases in both private consumption and investment. According to recent indicators, this cyclical upswing seems to be benefiting both the industrial and services sectors and should continue into the second half, though without accelerating to any great extent. Household confidence remains relatively subdued and has not picked up since the beginning of 2004. Registered unemployment, which reached 3.8 per cent in October 2004, has hardly fallen at all since last autumn. This reflects continuing modest job creation, despite the recovery, stemming from a cyclical rebound in productivity after it had fallen in recent years. Because of the rise in oil prices, inflation reached 1.3 per cent (year-on-year) in October 2004, but the underlying rate is still only ½ per cent.

The degree of monetary expansion has been reduced

While maintaining an expansionary stance, the National Bank, having kept interest rates at an exceptionally low ¼ per cent since March 2003, raised the 3-month LIBOR rate by ¼ point on two occasions, in June and September 2004, bringing it to ¾ per cent. This slight monetary tightening was warranted by the firming of the recovery and the need to regain some room for manoeuvre in case of

Switzerland

Despite a slight tightening, monetary policy remains easy | **Growth has recovered**

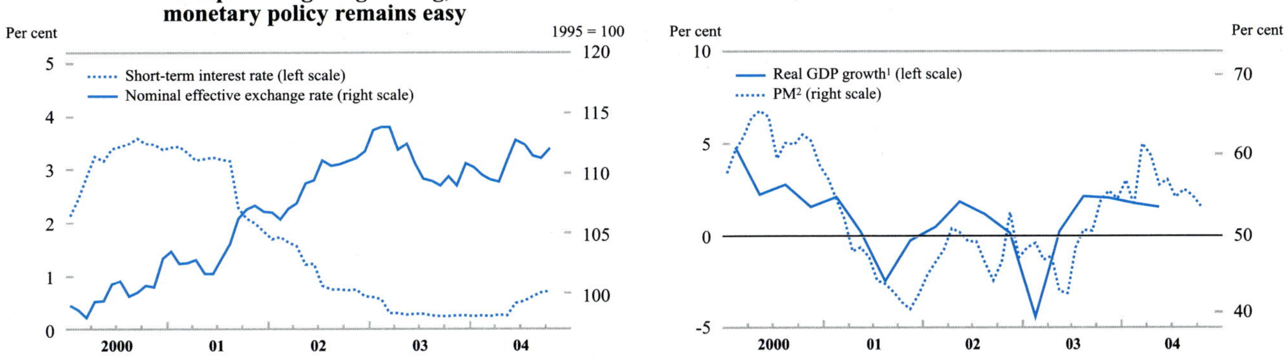

1. Percentage changes over the previous quarter, at annual rates.
2. The Purchasing Managers' Index (PMI) is an index on the response of 200 managers at Swiss industrial companies about their performance in the current month compared with the prior month. An index below 50 indicates that industrial production is falling.

Source: National Swiss Bank; OECD, *Quarterly National Accounts*.

Switzerland: Demand, output and prices

	2001	2002	2003	2004	2005	2006
	Current prices billion CHF	Percentage changes, volume (2000 prices)				
Private consumption	255.2	0.3	0.5	1.8	1.6	1.9
Government consumption	49.0	3.2	1.4	1.0	0.2	0.4
Gross fixed capital formation	93.8	0.3	-0.3	5.0	4.2	3.8
Final domestic demand	398.0	0.7	0.4	2.4	2.0	2.2
Stockbuilding[a]	6.1	-1.4	-0.2	-0.4	0.1	-0.1
Total domestic demand	404.1	-0.8	0.2	2.0	2.2	2.0
Exports of goods and services	190.8	-0.2	0.0	4.1	5.1	5.6
Imports of goods and services	172.3	-2.8	1.4	4.7	6.1	6.0
Net exports[a]	18.4	1.1	-0.5	0.0	-0.2	0.1
GDP at market prices	422.5	0.3	-0.4	1.9	1.9	2.0
GDP deflator	_	1.7	0.9	1.1	1.1	1.0
Memorandum items						
Consumer price index	_	0.6	0.6	0.8	1.2	0.9
Private consumption deflator	_	1.6	0.6	0.8	1.2	0.9
Unemployment rate	_	3.1	4.0	4.0	3.6	2.8
General government financial balance[b]	_	0.2	-0.8	-1.0	-0.6	-0.2
Current account balance[b]	_	8.4	13.2	12.8	12.4	12.6

a) Contributions to changes in real GDP (percentage of real GDP in previous year), actual amount in the first column.
b) As a percentage of GDP.
Source: OECD Economic Outlook 76 database.

renewed pressure on the franc. The projections point to a further rise in short rates as the output gap narrows, which is likely to curb the buoyancy of domestic demand.

Fiscal tightening is expected as of 2005

The general government deficit, which may have reached between ¾ and 1 per cent of GDP in 2003, is expected to widen slightly in 2004, though not as much as projected by the authorities. The sharper than expected acceleration in growth should partly offset the expansionary impact on the budget of the fall in unemployment insurance contributions. As of 2005, however, fiscal policy is set to become more restrictive since the federal government has planned to phase out the structural deficit by 2007, mainly through expenditure cuts.

Growth should remain stable

The growth of the economy could stabilise at around 2 per cent in 2005 and 2006. The buoyancy of domestic demand will probably be hampered by the gradual tightening of monetary and fiscal policy and, in the shorter term, by the rise in oil prices, all of which is likely to counterbalance the positive effect of the recovery. The increase in investment could slacken, while the gradual upturn in employment and downturn in unemployment will contribute to a more robust private consumption in 2006. With the output gap closing, inflation could settle at around 1 per cent in 2005 and 2006. A steeper than expected increase in oil prices would raise inflation, while depressing growth. Even so, inflationary pressures could be limited by the moderating effect on wages owing to the entry into force of the second phase of the free movement of persons with the European Union countries.

Turkey

Driven by buoyant private business investment and household consumption, GDP growth reached nearly 12 per cent at an annual rate in the first half of 2004 and should approach 10 per cent for the year. It is likely to slow to a more sustainable rate of around 6 per cent in 2005 and 2006, with exports and domestic demand remaining robust.

The authorities should adhere to their strict monetary and fiscal policies and fully implement their ambitious structural reform agenda, continuing to improve domestic and international confidence. Fiscal gains from strong growth should be devoted to public debt reduction in order to improve fiscal sustainability and rein in the growing current account deficit.

The economy is growing very rapidly…

GDP growth was exceptionally strong in the first half of 2004 and should approach 10 per cent for the whole year. Business investment, household consumption and soaring exports have been driving growth, while contracting government spending has not undermined the recovery. Headline inflation has continued to fall thus far through 2004, in line with targets, and should undershoot the end-of-the-year objective of 12 per cent. Private demand remains robust, in spite of high unemployment and moderate wage growth, as declining real interest rates and improving consumer confidence have underpinned strong growth of consumer credit. Enterprises restored profit margins and borrowed massively, including from foreign sources, to raise machinery and equipment investments by more than 90 per cent in the first half of 2004 and this investment drive continues. Sentiment was fuelled further by positive signals on the possible opening of accession negotiations with the European Union.

… but the external deficit has risen and the labour market remains weak

Amid this firm recovery, which has generated a 25 per cent cumulative increase in GDP since 2001, the current account deficit has widened significantly. It reached more than 7 per cent of GDP in the first half (on a non-seasonally-adjusted basis), because of a deepening trade deficit driven by industrial machinery and car imports, before improving in the summer months thanks to rapidly growing tourism revenues and a deceleration of car imports (tax incentives for car renewals, introduced in 2003, were phased out). The deficit is unlikely to fall below 5 per cent of GDP for the year. Its financing continues to be based on debt creation, generating concerns about its sustainability, while foreign direct investment remains weak (consisting mainly of real estate purchases by foreign households). Another weak spot is very slow job creation. Employment grew by only 0.4 per cent in the first half despite double-digit growth. The unemployment rate fell to about 9 per cent in the first half, from above 10 per cent in 2003, but this was mainly due to falling – although already low – labour force participation by discouraged workers and

Turkey

The risk premium has continued to fall and investment has picked up sharply

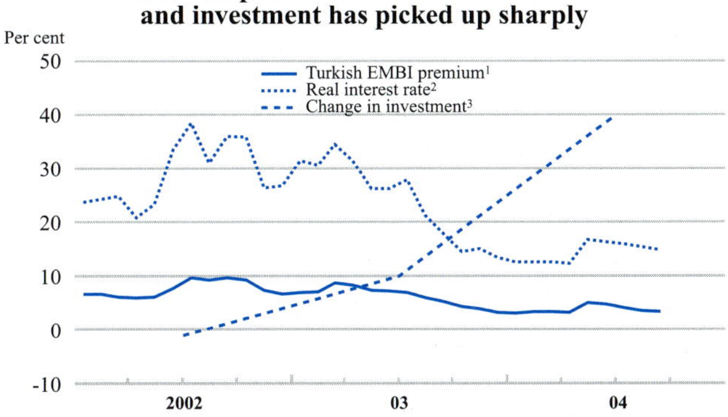

The current account deficit has deteriorated

Cumulative last 12 months

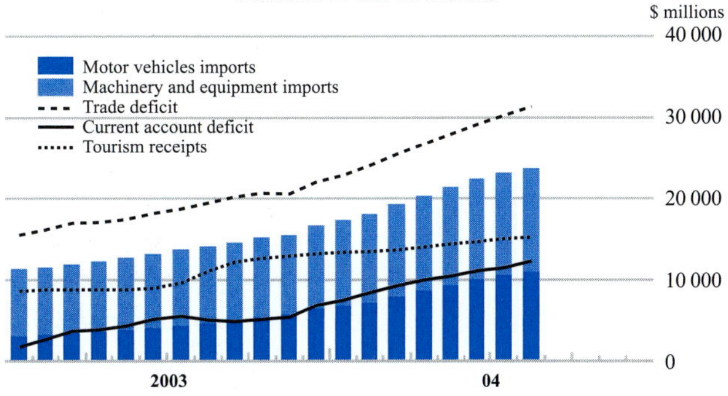

1. Interest rate differential between US dollar Turkish government bonds and US treasury rate.
2. Treasury auction rate discounted by inflation expectations.
3. Real annual per cent change, OECD projection for 2004.

Sources: Central Bank of Turkey, J.P. Morgan and OECD.

Turkey: Demand, output and prices

	2001	2002	2003	2004	2005	2006
	Current prices trillion TRL	Percentage changes, volume (1987 prices)				
Private consumption	128 513	2.1	6.6	9.2	4.5	5.2
Government consumption	25 405	5.4	-2.4	2.2	2.8	-0.2
Gross fixed capital formation	32 409	-1.1	10.0	39.9	10.2	8.0
Final domestic demand	186 327	1.7	6.5	15.3	5.9	5.6
Stockbuilding [a]	-2 475	7.1	3.0	1.2	-0.1	0.1
Total domestic demand	183 852	9.3	9.3	15.2	5.4	5.3
Exports of goods and services	60 151	11.1	16.0	14.5	13.9	12.6
Imports of goods and services	55 862	15.8	27.1	27.0	12.1	11.2
Net exports [a]	4 289	-0.9	-3.1	-5.0	0.4	0.4
Statistical discrepancy [a]	-9 729	0.1	0.0	-0.2	0.4	0.0
GDP at market prices	178 412	7.9	5.8	9.8	6.4	5.8
GDP deflator	_	44.1	22.5	6.5	7.6	6.2
Memorandum items						
Consumer price index	_	45.0	25.3	10.7	8.6	6.3
Private consumption deflator	_	40.6	21.8	8.2	6.6	5.8
Unemployment rate	_	10.1	10.3	9.5	10.0	10.5
Current account balance [b]	_	-0.8	-2.9	-5.2	-4.5	-3.8

a) Contributions to changes in real GDP (percentage of real GDP in previous year), actual amount in the first column.
b) As a percentage of GDP.
Source: OECD Economic Outlook 76 database.

women. Unemployment would be likely to pick up should the participation rate increase. The corollary of weak job creation has been extremely strong labour productivity growth, which rose by nearly 7 per cent in 2003 for the overall economy and may rise by 9 per cent in 2004; such gains are helping to preserve the competitiveness of exporters despite real currency appreciation as measured by relative consumer prices.

Maintaining a rigorous policy stance will be key

Rigorous monetary and fiscal policies are expected to remain on track and continue to back the recovery. Monetary policy remains focused on the targeted disinflation path, which should attain single-digit territory in 2005 with an end-year objective of 8 per cent. If disinflation remains entrenched – with no disruption from adverse exchange rate movements – the central bank may further reduce policy rates, after a 200 points decrease in September. Fiscal policy remains anchored on a primary surplus objective of 6.5 per cent of GDP for 2005, for a third year in a row. This objective will be attained in 2004 but, given an *ex post* growth rate nearly double the 2004 budget plans, this could be seen as a loosening fiscal stance (on a cyclically adjusted basis). However, this is not due to an intended policy stimulus but to oil tax cuts effected in 2004 in order to offset the effect of the oil price hike on consumer prices. In future, the authorities should devote the additional revenue gains from stronger growth to government debt reduction, in order to improve debt sustainability and keep a firm fiscal stance. This would help to tame the current boom and mitigate any additional pressures on the current account and on domestic prices.

Turkey may face a "positive" supply shock

GDP is expected to keep growing at rates of around 6 per cent in 2005 and 2006. Yet, if the European Council follows the Commission advice issued in October and decides in its meeting in December to open accession negotiations with Turkey, an additional positive supply shock may ensue, lifting capital inflows, investment, consumption and GDP growth. This could put upward pressure on the currency and domestic prices. Fiscal policy would then have to play a pivotal role, even if additional tightening is politically difficult. Conversely, should domestic and international confidence falter, higher risk premia, weaker currency and declining sentiment would push the economy onto a less favourable path.

III. DEVELOPMENTS IN SELECTED NON-MEMBER ECONOMIES

The growth of foreign trade in the Asian area slackened markedly in the first half of 2004 under the influence of a tightening of economic polices in China but recovered somewhat in the second half of the year. The rebound has been sufficiently strong to ensure that output growth in China is unlikely to slow this year. In 2005, the increase in oil prices will weigh particularly heavily on this group of economies. At the same time, inflation may pick up somewhat, especially outside of China – a development that adds to the pressure for a change in the exchange rate policies of a number of economies.

South America is set to grow by more than 4 per cent in 2004. Growth in Brazil remains particularly robust and the economy has become less vulnerable to external shocks. Area-wide growth has become more balanced across sectors. Private investment and consumption are picking up, taking over from net exports as the main drivers of growth. Inflation is expected to remain tame. Imports surged in the first half of the year in the major economies, albeit from a low level, and are likely to continue to grow more rapidly than exports. The external current account surplus is therefore expected to shrink in 2005-06.

Russia's oil-driven growth is set to continue at relatively high rates, boosted by very strong domestic demand and expansionary fiscal policy. However, growth will slow over the projection period, owing partly to slower growth of export volumes while imports continue to rise rapidly. A loss of confidence in the future course of structural policy reform, could also weaken investment growth. Nonetheless, prices of oil and other commodities will benefit Russia and other hydrocarbon producers among the Newly Independent States. Russian growth will also benefit other states in the region, which depend largely on trade with, and, in some cases, remittances from, Russia. Growth in South-eastern Europe, which largely depends on developments in the European Union, is set to continue, but at rates well below those found among the Newly Independent States.

Strong domestic demand in Dynamic Asia outweighs weaker external trends

The pick-up in economic activity that began late last year continued in the first half of 2004 as the Dynamic Asian economies grew rapidly, led by a combination of domestic and external demand. Demand has been buoyant enough to maintain overall growth momentum despite the rise in oil prices and a slowing of exports to China. Much of the buoyancy in these economies has come from the increasing strength of private consumption and business investment, the latter more so than at any time since the Asian financial crisis, thus more than offsetting the moderation in export growth to China – despite the fact that greater integration makes some of these economies (particularly Chinese Taipei and Hong Kong, China) very dependent on developments in China. The current oil price projections point to a negative shock to the area of as much as 1 to 2 percentage points of GDP for the most intensive oil-importing countries in Asia: Thailand, Malaysia, the Philippines, and Singapore, with Indonesia being insulated through its oil and gas exports. Nevertheless, growth in the region during 2005, at around 5½ per cent, should still be strong enough to generate sustained demand for imports from OECD economies and even to keep alive concerns about rising inflation affecting competitiveness.

South America's recovery is now well entrenched

Economic growth accelerated in most of South America in 2004. In Brazil, GDP rose at a rapid pace in the first half of 2004, exceeding market expectations. Chile's economic performance remains strong, buoyed by commodity exports, particularly copper, and the recovery in private consumption. Investment is also on the rise. By contrast, Argentina's recovery appears to be losing steam as private consumption is decelerating and uncertainty surrounding debt restructuring and the regulatory framework for setting utility prices continues to weigh heavily on private investment.

Growth remains strong in South-eastern Europe and the Newly Independent States

The first half of 2004 saw a further acceleration of growth across South-eastern Europe (SEE) and the Newly Independent States (NIS) while growth in Russia remains strong. SEE growth rose to roughly 5 per cent in the first half of this year and NIS growth reached about 8 per cent. As in 2003, growth in the region is being driven by both exports and strong domestic demand. Export growth in the NIS has been driven largely by hydrocarbons and metals, reflecting strong demand from China, while SEE has benefited from recovery in the European Union. Accelerating output and rising commodity prices have also contributed to a pick-up in inflation in much of the region, while strong domestic demand has stimulated an acceleration of import growth, which should, however, moderate somewhat over the projection period. Several countries, though not Russia, are running high current account deficits which suggest that they will not be able to sustain import growth at the rates seen in recent quarters.

China

Real GDP growth is losing momentum in China...

After a period of very rapid expansion that lasted until the beginning of 2004, the economy stalled in the middle of the year but rebounded sharply in the second half. The deceleration in output was particularly pronounced in the industries producing inputs to investment projects and sectors such as automobiles where sales had become particularly reliant on credit. A marked tightening in the stance of macroeconomic policy drove this slowdown. Administrative actions resulted in the growth in lending to the non-bank sector almost coming to halt by mid-year. Interest rates were also raised in October but such a move is unlikely to have much impact on demand, as the effective rate of interest implied by credit rationing is much higher than the level of official interest rates. The government also moderated the growth of its infrastructure spending. At the same time, the central government has been rigorously enforcing land zoning and other regulations that apply to new investment, with the objective of reducing the growth of capital formation in a number of industries where it has judged that outlays were excessive. Following the initial disruption from these measures, companies appear to have found ways to moderate the impact of the administrative actions and output growth has recovered sharply. As a result, in 2004 economic growth appears likely to be unchanged at 9¼ per cent.

... but inflation has risen

Although economic activity weakened for a time, the inflation rate has continued to accelerate, though some signs of stabilisation could be observed by the autumn. The increase in inflation was widespread both for consumption, where prices for food were particularly strong, and for investment goods. Strong prices for a wide range of imported commodities drove this increase. In particular, higher oil prices boosted the GDP deflator, given the significant extent of domestic oil production, which will increase in value by around 1 per cent of GDP. Although the increase in the value of domestic oil production represents an internal transfer of income within the economy, it is still likely to depress demand. Most of the oil is owned by state-controlled companies and the government is unlikely to spend its

Table III.1. **Projections for China**

	2003	2004	2005	2006
Real GDP growth	9.3	9.2	8.0	8.5
Inflation	1.2	4.2	4.0	4.0
Fiscal balance (per cent of GDP)	-2.5	-2.0	-1.7	-1.7
Current account balance ($ billion)	45.9	18.8	33.8	45.6
Current account balance (per cent of GDP)	3.1	1.1	1.8	2.2

Note: The figures given for GDP and inflation are percentage changes from the previous year. Inflation refers to the consumer price index.

Source: Data for 2003 are from national sources. Data for 2004-06 are OECD estimates and projections.

share of increased revenues while, in the short-term, the companies are more likely to repay debt than increase domestic investment. In addition, the value of oil imports will increase by almost 2 per cent of GDP between 2003 and 2005, adding to the downward pressure on demand coming from the restrictive stance of economic policy. Higher commodity and oil prices are also largely responsible for the reduction in the current account surplus to 1 per cent of GDP in 2004.

A tight policy stance and higher oil prices may slow output growth…

The extent of the slowdown in growth engendered by tight policies and higher oil prices will be limited by a number of factors. Investment in the state-dominated power generation sector is likely to continue its rapid increase, as there has been a noticeable shortage of capacity in this area. Demand for real estate is being boosted by negative real interest rates that are leading to a marked reluctance of consumers to commit saving to traditional assets such as bank deposits. The supply of new houses has been adversely affected by tightened government regulations, thereby boosting prices, but incomes are still rising faster than prices in most parts of the country, thus underpinning demand. In the rest of the private sector, investment is mainly financed through retained earnings which have been particularly buoyant in 2004, insulating to some extent this sector from the tightening of monetary policy. Consumption should also be aided by the strongest increase in rural incomes in the past seven years. Finally, export demand seems likely to be buoyant as foreign direct investment boosts outsourcing from OECD economies, competitiveness remains strong in the face of stable exchange rate and flat unit labour costs and as the Multi-Fibre Agreement, which has limited textile exports, draws to an end in 2005. Overall, growth is likely to be somewhat below potential in 2005 before recovering in 2006. The projected slowdown in the growth of world commodity prices should result in a slowing in inflation.

… with a risk that a downturn in inflation will not materialise

There are a number of risks that point to the possibility of a less benign outcome to the current economic cycle. The abrupt slowing in bank lending has disrupted the provision of working capital and could lead to a greater than expected rundown in inventories and hence output which might set off a downward revision of industrial investment plans. Initially such a downward movement might be accompanied by higher than expected inflation especially if the accumulation of foreign exchange reserves continues to boost liquidity in the economy and if real interest rates on bank deposits remain negative, so fuelling the real estate boom. Such adverse risks could be moderated by a change in the policy mix, with less reliance on administrative control of bank lending, higher deposit rates, and greater flexibility in the exchange rate. The recent decision to allow banks complete freedom in determining interest rates on lending is a first step in that direction and will allow them to move towards setting interest rates in line with risk.

Brazil

The recovery is firmly established in Brazil

The Brazilian economy is bouncing back more strongly than anticipated. GDP grew by nearly 6 per cent in the second quarter of 2004 relative to the same period in 2003, with domestic demand taking over as the main driver of growth. The upturn in private consumption is underpinned by the steady expansion of credit to the private sector, falling unemployment, and increasing real wages. An improving climate for business is providing further impetus for private investment. The trade and external current account balances have also strengthened beyond market expectations. Robust domestic demand has boosted imports, in particular of fuels and intermediate goods, but exports continue to exhibit considerable dynamism. The external adjustment is on-going, reducing vulnerability, strengthening fundamentals, and making the economy more resilient to adverse shocks. On the supply side, agriculture and manufacturing continue to perform strongly while activity is gathering pace in the services sector on the back of the recovery in private consumption.

Monetary easing has come to an end

The cycle of monetary easing that started in mid-2003 has now ended. Underscoring continued prudence in macroeconomic management, the policy interest rate was raised by 125 basis points in September-November to 17.25 per cent. This was in response to concern about shrinking economic slack and an uptick in inflation in the second quarter associated with rising commodity, food, and utility prices. Inflation expectations for 2005 have also deteriorated, motivating the monetary tightening. To accommodate part of the inflationary inertia estimated to be inherited from 2004, the central bank has announced that it would accept a somewhat higher level of inflation in 2005 – 5.1 per cent against an official target of 4.5 per cent (+/–2.5 percentage points). The exchange rate has appreciated recently, after weakening in the second quarter, and financial market conditions remain favourable: sovereign risk premia have come down and credit ratings have been upgraded.

The primary surplus target has been raised

Fiscal performance has been stronger than expected. This, together with favourable market conditions, has contributed to a continued reduction in the ratio of public debt to GDP in the course of the year. The consolidated primary surplus target has been raised by 0.25 percentage points to 4.5 per cent of GDP in 2004, in order to save part of the cyclical revenue windfall while accommodating some additional spending on much-needed infrastructure investment. Progress has been made in debt management to continue to reduce the government's exposure to foreign-exchange risk. The share in public debt of securities indexed to the exchange rate (including foreign exchange swaps) is now coming down towards 10 per cent, its lowest level since the floating of

Table III.2. **Projections for Brazil**

	2003	2004	2005	2006
Real GDP growth	-0.2	4.5	3.6	3.5
Inflation	9.3	7.3	6.0	5.0
Fiscal balance (per cent of GDP)	-5.2	-3.0	-2.8	-2.3
Primary fiscal balance (per cent of GDP)	4.4	4.5	4.3	4.3
Current account balance ($ billion)	4.0	8.5	2.5	-1.0
Current account balance (per cent of GDP)	0.8	1.5	0.4	-0.2

Note: Real GDP growth and inflation are defined in percentage change from the previous period. Inflation refers to the end-year consumer price index (IPCA).

Source: Data for 2003 are from national sources. Data for 2004-06 are OECD estimates and projections.

the *Real* in 1999. The regional governments (states and municipalities) and the public enterprises continue to contribute to this strong fiscal performance.

The pace of reforms has slowed

Congressional approval is pending for several important elements of the government's structural reform agenda. This includes legislation on public-private partnerships, the upgrading of bankruptcy legislation, and a new legal framework for the regulatory agencies. The legislative calendar has been affected by the municipal elections in October, taking a toll on the pace of reform. Further structural reform remains essential to make the economy more resilient in response to adverse shocks and to support growth on a sustainable basis over the longer term.

The outlook is by and large positive

Following the strong performance in 2004, economic growth is likely to moderate in 2005-06, with domestic demand expected to continue to be the main engine of growth. A further decline in unemployment and rising real wages will sustain the recovery in private consumption, and the positive outlook is set to continue to encourage private investment. Overall, GDP growth may continue at about 3.5 per cent over the projection period. The external adjustment is also expected to continue, facilitated by the recovery in the world economy, but the trade surplus is set to taper off, owing predominantly to rising imports fuelled by the recovery in domestic demand. As a result, the external current account surplus is expected to shrink during 2005-06. The outlook is contingent on the maintenance of sound policies in pursuit of the inflation and fiscal targets.

But there are risks

This outlook is not without risks. On the external front, market sentiment may deteriorate in light of the adverse impact of persistently high oil prices on the world economy, affecting the buoyancy of overseas demand. Domestically, high oil prices and the emergence of supply bottlenecks in many manufacturing sectors may affect the inflation outlook adversely, calling for corrective action.

The Russian Federation

Growth in the Russian Federation remains strong but has begun to slow

Strong growth has continued in 2004, although the pace of expansion has begun to slow. On the demand side, growth has been driven chiefly by very strong household demand on the back of a further accelerating consumption boom. With import growth remaining strong and export volume growth slowing markedly, the contribution of net exports to GDP growth has become significantly negative, even though strongly improving terms of trade have sustained a large current-account surplus. Slower export growth is primarily related to negative developments in the oil sector, in particular the effects on output of a decline in production growth among large private oil producers, such as Yukos and Sibneft.

Disinflation is becoming palpably more difficult

The central bank continues to pursue partly contradictory goals in trying to bring inflation down while preventing an overly rapid appreciation of the real exchange rate. This task has been made somewhat easier in 2004 by the operation of the newly established stabilisation fund, which has sterilised a large share of the foreign exchange inflows resulting from the ballooning current account surplus. In addition, a sharp pick-up in net private capital outflows – which reflects, among other things, a deterioration in the investment climate – has also helped. Yet despite slower money supply growth, inflation re-accelerated somewhat during mid-2004 to slightly over 11 per cent and it will most likely be above the authorities' 8 to 10 per cent target range for the year.

Table III.3. **Projections for the Russian Federation**

	2003	2004	2005	2006
Real GDP growth	7.3	6.4	5.5	5.5
Inflation	12.0	11.0	10.5	9.5
Fiscal balance (per cent of GDP)[a]	1.2	3.5	2.0	1.5
Primary fiscal balance (per cent of GDP)[b]	3.4	6.0	5.0	4.5
Current account balance ($ billion)	39.5	55.5	73.0	54.0
Current account balance (per cent of GDP)	8.3	10.2	11.1	6.8

Note: Real GDP growth and inflation are defined in percentage change from the previous period. Inflation refers to the end-year consumer price index.

a) General government.

b) Federal Budget only.

Source: Data for 2003 are from national sources. Data for 2004-06 are OECD estimates and projections.

The fiscal stance is being loosened

The budget remains in surplus despite fiscal easing, thanks chiefly to the impact on revenues of very high oil prices. Significantly, while the 2004 budget would probably have remained in rough balance even at average oil prices, the draft budget for 2005 would not, despite rather ambitious assumptions about expenditure cuts. The authorities anticipate spending a substantial portion of windfall revenues generated by high oil prices to cover the deficit that the Pension Fund is expected to run with respect to current pension payments, following the planned cut in the unified social tax. Such pro-cyclical fiscal loosening breaks with the practice of recent years of ensuring that budgets would balance at long-term average oil prices.

Progress on structural reform has slowed markedly

Structural reforms appear largely to have stalled in 2004, not least as a result of delays arising from the overhaul of the federal executive. The central bank has continued work on implementing reforms in the banking sector, but turbulence in the sector during the early summer has highlighted how difficult this will be. The banking "mini-crisis" also underscored apparent differences in the federal authorities' approach to banking reform. Electricity reform has slowed markedly, with many decisions being delayed, and there is little sign of any readiness to advance gas-sector reform. The long-awaited liberalisation of the market in Gazprom shares is now in prospect and would indeed be a welcome development. However, the implications of Gazprom's acquisition of the state-owned oil company Rosneft – which is seen by the authorities as a necessary pre-cursor to share-market liberalisation – are mixed at best, as are its ambitious plans for expansion into the power sector as well. More generally, these moves must be seen in the context of an on-going drive by the state to tighten its grip on key industrial sectors – especially resource sectors. Greater state control over resource-exporting industries is likely to lead to less efficiency, more rent-seeking and slower growth in the very sectors that have been driving growth in recent years.

Growth will continue, but will slow gradually over the projection period

Real GDP growth is projected to moderate gradually over the projection period. The consumption boom will continue, supported by the planned fiscal loosening in 2005. However, with export growth slowing and consumption driving import growth, the negative contribution of net exports is set to grow. While the current account surplus is expected to remain fairly large over the projection period, thanks to projected high prices for oil and other export commodities, pressure for further fiscal easing, lack of progress on structural reforms and a worsening investment climate point to downside risks, which would be exacerbated should the terms of trade become less favourable.

IV. OIL PRICE DEVELOPMENTS: DRIVERS, ECONOMIC CONSEQUENCES AND POLICY RESPONSES

Introduction

The price of oil has risen significantly

At the end of October the oil price had more than doubled in dollar terms since the late 1990s, while increasing substantially, though somewhat less, in terms of the other major currencies (Figure IV.1). The chapter begins by investigating the fundamentals driving longer-term oil market developments and the implications for the long-run equilibrium price. It then identifies short-term influences which may have

Figure IV.1. **Oil prices: a historical perspective**

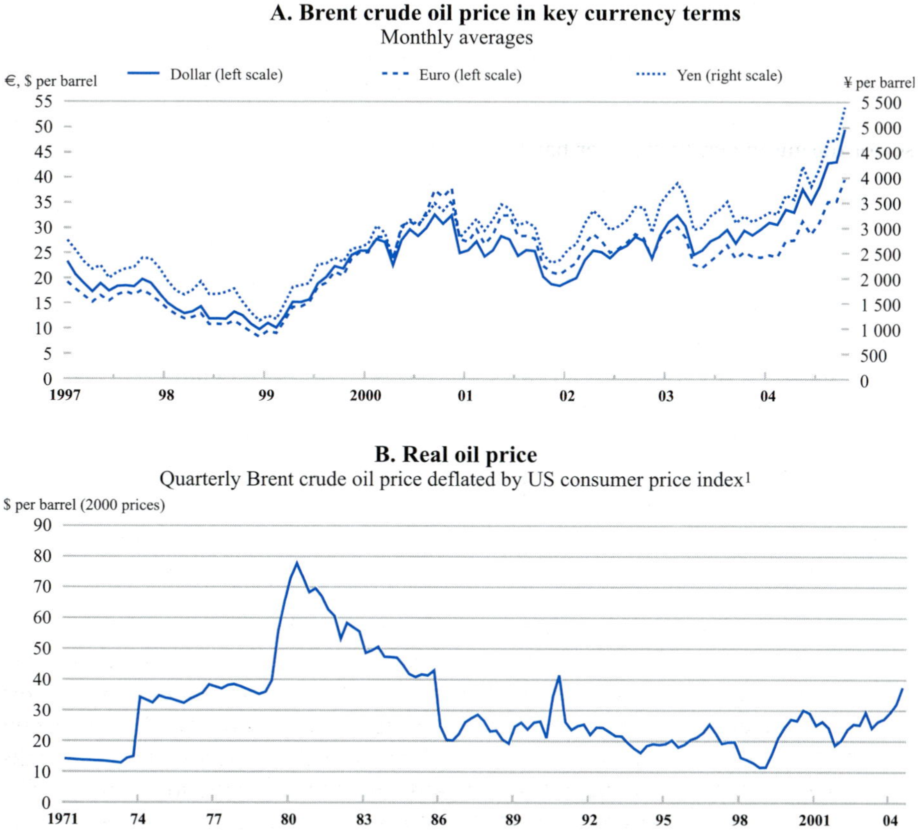

1. Before May 1987, oil prices are OECD estimates for crude oil of the same quality as Brent.
Source: OECD Economic Outlook 76 database.

caused risk premia to rise, volatility to increase, and the oil price to diverge from its equilibrium. It concludes with an assessment of the impact of higher oil prices on OECD growth and inflation and the implications for economic policy.

The main points to emerge from the analysis are as follows:

Global dependence on oil will continue...

– Notwithstanding more efficient use of oil in production, oil is likely to retain its importance as a fuel in the longer term, increasingly for transport. In addition to expected strong demand in North America, strong oil demand growth from rapidly growing and energy-intensive non-OECD countries would entail an upward structural shift in the demand for oil per increment of global GDP.

...with growing reliance on OPEC...

– While global oil reserves are probably relatively ample, their distribution is likely to be increasingly concentrated on the Middle Eastern members of OPEC, which already account for around two-thirds of global proved reserves. Outside the Middle East, newly-discovered resources have tended to become smaller and more expensive to develop, being increasingly offshore.

... and a likely trend rise in the oil price...

– The OECD baseline scenario used here generates a trend rise in the real oil price from $27 per barrel in 2003 to $35 a barrel by 2030, both prices expressed in year 2000 dollars, if initial OPEC/non-OPEC market shares are maintained over the projection horizon.

... the more so if growth is strong and oil-intensive

– Higher GDP growth assumptions, or higher income elasticities of demand, especially in China and the rest of the non-OECD, could imply that prices rise significantly more than in the baseline scenario, or that OPEC is prepared to increase its market share significantly (from 38 per cent in 2003 to around 55 per cent by 2030).

Non-OPEC supply and demand responses limit OPEC's market power...

– Over the longer term, behavioural responses to higher prices could constrain cartel-like behaviour, particularly given the endogenous but non-reversible nature of technological progress in non-conventional supply and in oil consumption.

... but volatility and uncertainty depresses investment...

– In the short run, the low price elasticities of global demand and non-OPEC supply make oil prices highly sensitive to supply and demand shifts. Price volatility, compounded by geopolitical tensions, raises uncertainty about underlying price trends that may depress oil exploration. OPEC's excess capacity is currently the lowest in three decades, providing little cushion to raise supply in the event of unexpected oil market disruptions.

... and bottlenecks have put upward pressure on prices

– Transportation bottlenecks have emerged recently as the changing geographical composition of demand has put pressure on the tanker fleet. In addition, regional mismatches between the grade of oil supplied and demanded have seen premia on low sulphur oil rise.

The current price shock could be prolonged

– It is not clear how rapidly short-term factors boosting the oil price will endure, hampering the return to long-term equilibrium prices. However, some stickiness seems to be indicated by the far futures prices, which have risen to historical highs.

The link between the oil price and core inflation has weakened...

– The pass-though from oil price increases to core inflation has been very limited in recent years, consistent with the increasing focus of monetary authorities on core inflation as the measure to be monitored or targeted and hence with expectations that monetary policy will respond to offset any pass-through from headline inflation to wages and non-energy prices. Going forward, the established credibility of monetary policies should ensure that oil price rises do not become embedded into inflation expectations to an extent requiring a significant rise in nominal interest rates.

– Traditional model analysis suggests that the likely impact on OECD output following an oil price hike of the magnitude experienced recently is relatively moderate in the short run. However, such models may not pick up supply-side effects and may not allow for asymmetries, where price increases have a more significant effect on output than do price decreases.

... and oil price shocks tend to have only a moderate impact on output

– A high tax component of the final price reduces oil intensity and hence the terms-of-trade and inflation impacts of such shocks. Using fiscal policy to stabilise end-user prices may hinder adjustment that could reduce an economy's oil dependence.

Economic policy should respond cautiously to oil price shocks

Longer-term prospects for the oil market

The oil intensity of production has fallen...

World oil demand (measured as *ex post* supply net of stock movements) has decelerated significantly over the past thirty years, largely reflecting a decline in the oil intensity of production – total oil consumption per unit of output – in OECD countries (Figure IV.2). This is an outcome of more efficient use of oil, as ongoing fuel-saving technical change has contributed to continuing reductions of energy intensities, an increasing utilisation of alternative energy sources, such as natural gas in power generation, and a shift in the composition of output towards less oil intensive sectors. By contrast, in non-OECD countries oil intensities have generally increased slightly up to the mid 1990s – partly reflecting a change in production structure towards manufacturing and increasing vehicle ownership – before falling marginally.

... but the global economy will remain reliant on oil...

Looking forward, and on the assumption that global growth will average around 3 per cent per annum over the period from 2000 to 2030, the International Energy Agency (IEA) has projected that global oil demand will increase by around 1 per

Figure IV.2. **Oil intensity of production has fallen in the OECD area**

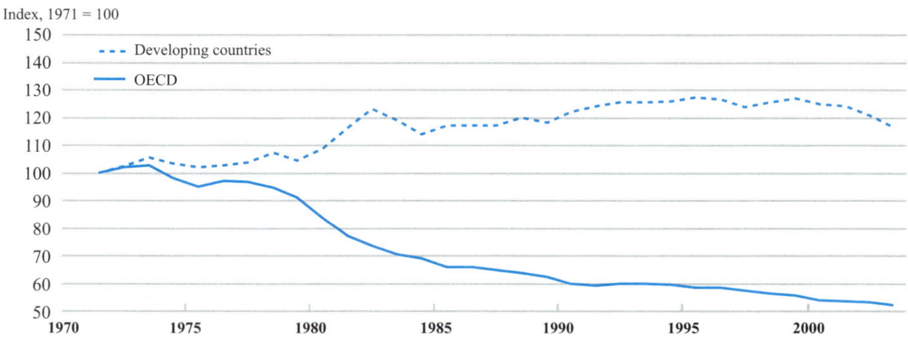

Note: Oil intensity is defined as total primary oil use per unit of output (GDP).
Source: OECD Economic Outlook 76 database and International Energy Agency.

cent annually over the same period, leading to a two-thirds rise in the global demand for oil, to 120 million barrels per day (mbd).[1] This is seen as consistent with an \$8 per barrel rise in the real oil price.[2] The largest absolute increase in oil demand is expected to continue to come from North America, with demand from China and elsewhere in Asia also increasing strongly (Figure IV.3). More rapid economic growth in the more energy-intensive non-OECD countries would entail an upward structural shift in the demand for oil per increment of global GDP compared with recent decades, given the large regional differences in oil intensities. Transport is expected to remain the principal consumer of oil, accounting for two-thirds of the increment in oil demand between 2002 and 2030, raising its share in oil consumption by 7 percentage points to 54 per cent. As a result of these geographical and sectoral demand patterns, the share of oil in both global and OECD primary energy supply would remain broadly stable, at almost two-fifths.

... of which there are ample reserves...

At current production rates, existing reserves would be exhausted in around 40 years. However, the reserves-to-production ratio has changed little over the past two decades notwithstanding increasing production as reserves have also increased, and there remains considerable scope for substantial additions to reserves.[3] The concept of proved reserves is linked to commercial viability and therefore reserves have increased in response both to oil price shifts and to technological changes, which have both allowed the extraction of new sources and increased the share of oil within a deposit that can be extracted. However, newly-discovered resources have tended to be smaller and more expensive to develop, being increasingly offshore, and the costs of exploration, development and production are higher than in the reserve-rich Middle East.

... but largely in the Middle East...

Against this background, and while oil reserves will probably remain relatively ample, their distribution is likely to be increasingly concentrated on the Middle Eastern members of OPEC, which already account for around two-thirds of global proved reserves (Figure IV.4). However, with reserves concentrated in a limited number of

Figure IV.3. **Oil demand is projected to increase in most North America and China**

Absolute increase in regional oil demand, 2000-30

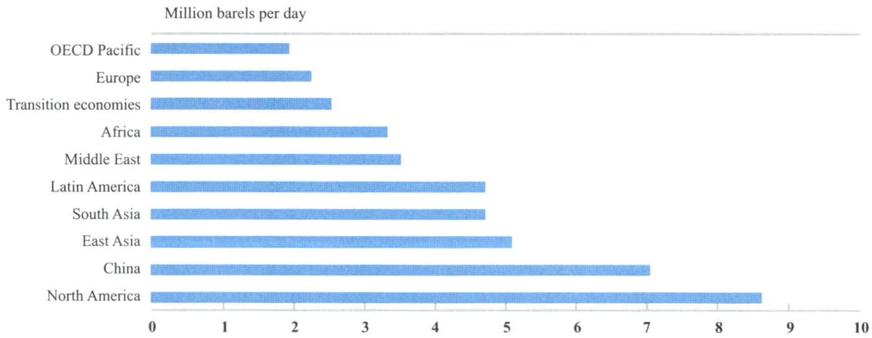

Source: International Energy Agency.

1. International Energy Agency (2002).
2. From its then-assumed average 2002-10 level of \$21 per barrel in 2000 prices, given certain assumptions about the geographical origin of supply.
3. US Geological Survey (2000).

Figure IV.4. **Proved oil reserves appear adequate for the next few decades relative to current production**

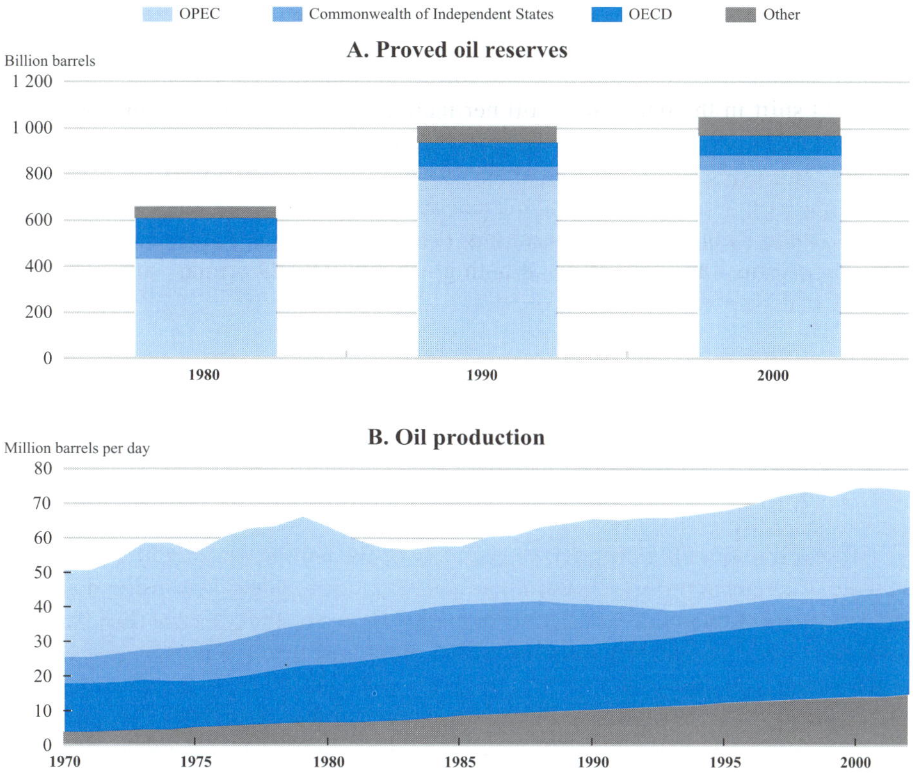

Source: BP and International Energy Agency.

OPEC countries, where investment is not allocated according to market forces, investment in the energy sector may not be sufficient.[4]

... affording OPEC potential market power

Global investment, supply and price extrapolations are contingent upon the extent to which OPEC (or a subset of OPEC countries) will exercise its market power. Exploration, development, and extraction costs in the Middle East are reported to be less than \$5 per barrel, while short-run marginal costs are generally estimated to be below \$2 per barrel.[5] Other suppliers face much higher, and probably more steeply increasing marginal costs than OPEC and the reserve-rich producers in the Middle East have incentives to exploit this cost advantage by trading off market share for a higher price. The less elastic global oil demand and non-OPEC supply are in the long run, the greater are OPEC's incentives to restrict output and thus raise prices in the face of rising world demand.

4. International Energy Agency (2003) contains a "restricted investment outlook" that considers the impact of lower investment in the Middle East, resulting in a lower supply and higher price (rising to \$35 from \$29 per barrel in the baseline). Kohl (2002) documents some of the deterioration in public finances in many OPEC countries. In the future, demographic pressures may also place additional strain on the public finances of OPEC members.
5. Maurice (2001).

... though this is limited, especially in the longer run

The longer-run supply and demand characteristics of the oil market are thus crucial determinants of future price trends. First, estimates of the long-run non-OPEC price elasticity of supply vary from a low of 0.1 to a relatively high 0.6. Second, the elasticity of non-OPEC supply may be non-linear insofar as at a certain point the oil price would be pushed up sufficiently to encourage investment to promote the production of (ample) non-conventional oil in other countries or alternative backstop technology, such as the liquefaction of other plentiful fossil fuels. For example, the cost of extraction of oil from tar sands in Canada has fallen considerably over past decades, and expectations of a sustained high oil price may trigger investment in expanding such activity. Third, higher prices induce investment in (non-reversible) energy-saving technology or substitution between fuels, tending to make the price elasticity of demand for oil asymmetric.

Oil price scenarios to 2030

In the baseline scenario the oil price rises to $35 in 2030...

To explore possible oil price scenarios over the coming quarter of a century, a number of longer-term oil-price simulations have been undertaken, using a simplified spreadsheet model of the global oil market (see Appendix IV.1).[6] The baseline scenario is one in which initial market shares are maintained (38 per cent for OPEC) over the projection horizon and the non-OPEC price elasticity of supply is assumed to be in the middle of the range of estimated elasticities.[7] With market shares constant while demand is steadily growing, non-OPEC producers are assumed to pass into oil prices the expected rise in long-run marginal costs, as new additions to reserves and enhanced recovery techniques are increasingly required to raise their production levels. On the basis of these assumptions, and using the potential growth rates embodied in the OECD's Medium-term Reference Scenario for the period up to 2010, the baseline generates a rise in the real oil price to $35 by the end of the projection period (2030), from $27.4 per barrel in 2003.

... which might be seen as an equilibrium price...

The baseline could be interpreted as an estimate of the equilibrium long-term price (contingent upon the elasticities adopted) only under certain assumptions. First, and most importantly, the starting point for the oil price (in 2003) would itself have to be considered as a long-run equilibrium. The 2003 price of $27 per barrel was achieved against the background of an already volatile oil market, so the spot price may already have included a short-term risk premium, but it was one where supply and demand were relatively well matched. Second, an oil market evolution based on a stable OPEC market share would need to be seen as the most likely supply side outcome.

... though this depends on OPEC behaviour

The equilibrium price could well differ quite substantially according to the OPEC supply and pricing strategy adopted (Table IV.1). Keeping the elasticity of non-OPEC supply unchanged and allowing OPEC supply to meet the additional

6. The model is designed specifically to examine the impact of aggregate demand and supply developments on the oil price and should not be confused with the IEA's more comprehensive and disaggregated World Energy Model. For further discussion see Brook *et al.* (2004).
7. The assumption of constant market shares is adopted as being consistent with the maintenance of the existing diversification of supply. The long-term projections of oil demand also assume that there will be no major changes in the structure of energy supply.

Table IV.1. **OPEC's market share under different assumptions**

Oil price[a]	OPEC supply (Mbd)	OPEC market share (%)	Per cent change in OPEC supply
	Baseline value in 2030		
$35	53.3	38.4	..
	Deviations from baseline in 2030		
$25	23.8	11.6	45
$30	11.9	6.1	22
$40	-11.9	-6.8	-22

a) Constant 2000 dollars.
Source: OECD calculations.

demand, OPEC's share of the oil market would have to rise by around 6 percentage points compared with the baseline to limit the oil price to $30 in 2030. It would have to rise by a further 5 to 6 percentage points to achieve and maintain a price of $25. This would take the OPEC share to around 50 per cent, which would not be unusual historically.

Price extrapolations are sensitive to assumptions…

The results summarised in Table IV.2 explore the sensitivity of the oil price extrapolations to different assumptions about GDP growth, income and price elasticities of oil demand, and non-OPEC supply elasticities. In Part A of the table (the first four columns), the scenarios are based on the assumption that OPEC targets a constant market share (38 per cent) regardless of the price implications.

… about growth rates, income elasticities of demand…

The first two scenarios suggest that oil price projections may be particularly sensitive to assumptions about the demand for oil. Moderate variations in global growth (½ per cent per annum stronger except in China, where the variation is 1 per cent) could push the oil price up by an additional $4.50 by 2030 (scenario group 1), while an increase of 0.2 in the income elasticity of oil demand could lead to an oil price some $13 higher (scenario group 2). In both cases, the magnitude of the shock imposed is plausible; any GDP growth projections over a 25-year horizon will have significant error bounds associated with them, and the range of estimates for long-run elasticities of demand with respect to income is sufficiently wide to suggest that a 0.2 percentage point change relative to the baseline assumption is possible. Although the scenarios presented in Table IV.2 are for positive shocks to growth and the income elasticity, negative shocks are equally plausible (with the impact approximated by reversing the signs in Table IV.2). As discussed in the annex, the model already assumes that the income elasticity of demand has declined since the 1970s, consistent with falling oil intensity and on-going technological change. But this process could continue over the next 25 years, resulting in even lower income elasticities.

… and the price elasticities of demand and non-OPEC supply

The next two scenarios suggest that oil price projections are sensitive to assumptions about the price elasticity of demand (scenario group 3) and the non-OPEC supply elasticity (scenario group 4). In the baseline scenario, the price path is relatively flat and the effect of changed elasticity assumptions on the oil price relatively small. In both cases the magnitude of shock assumed (0.2) seems reasonably significant relative to the range of estimates in the economic literature, and this magnitude of shock affects the oil price by around $1 by 2030. However, the

Table IV.2. Oil price extrapolations under selected demand and supply scenarios

Deviations from baseline [a]

	A. Oil price in constant 2000 dollars (fixed OPEC market share target - 38%)				B. OPEC target price band +/- 10% from baseline 2030	
	2004	2010	2020	2030	OPEC Supply (Mbd)	OPEC Market share (percentage points)
1. Higher growth						
OECD (+1/2%)	0.2	0.6	1.0	1.4	0.6	0.0
China (+1%)	0.1	0.3	0.7	1.3	0.5	0.0
Rest of the world (+1/2%)[b]	0.2	0.5	1.1	1.9	0.8	0.0
World	0.4	1.5	3.0	4.6	4.5	1.5
2. Higher income elasticities						
OECD (+0.2)	0.7	1.9	3.1	4.1	2.6	0.6
OECD and China (+0.2)	0.9	2.6	4.5	6.5	9.6	3.9
World (+0.2 for ROW)	1.4	4.6	8.7	13.2	29.0	11.7
3. Lower price elasticities of demand						
OECD (+0.2)	0.0	0.0	0.2	0.4	0.2	0.0
China (+0.2)	0.0	0.0	0.0	0.1	0.0	0.0
Rest of the world (+0.2)[b]	0.0	0.0	0.1	0.4	0.2	0.0
World	0.0	0.0	0.5	1.2	0.5	0.0
4. Different non-OPEC price elasticities of supply						
Higher (+0.2)	0.0	-0.1	-0.3	-0.6	0.3	0.0
Lower (-0.2)	0.0	-0.1	0.4	0.9	-0.5	0.0
5. Higher growth and income elasticities in non-OECD countries[c]						
China	0.3	1.1	2.6	4.8	5.0	1.8
World excluding OECD	1.1	4.0	8.7	14.9	34.4	13.6
6. Higher growth and income elasticities and lower price elasticities of demand[c]						
China	0.3	1.1	2.8	5.3	6.3	2.5
Rest of the world[b]	0.8	3.1	7.3	13.2	24.9	10.3
World excluding OECD	1.2	4.5	10.9	20.1	38.9	15.1

a) Assumptions in the left column are also shown as deviations from baseline. Since price elasticities are negative a positive change implies a lower elasticity (in absolute terms).

b) Rest of the World is defined as the total world less China and the OECD.

c) Scenarios 5 and 6 are simulated as combinations of scenarios 1, 2 and 3 where relevant, for the country or region concerned.

Source: OECD calculations.

non-OPEC supply elasticity becomes much more important in scenarios where the price increases significantly and remains at the new level.

There is particular uncertainty about non-OECD demand

In terms of the global composition of oil demand, there is significant uncertainty about the likely path of oil demand from non-OECD countries. The risk of exceptionally strong demand from the non-OECD region is addressed in the final two scenarios, which combine the high growth scenario with higher income elasticities of demand in China and the rest of the world (scenario group 5), and with the additional effect of lower long-run price elasticities (scenario group 6). These results suggest that stronger demand and a higher income elasticity in China alone would be sufficient to push prices up by an additional $5 per barrel by 2030, with the rest of the world pushing prices up by a further $10. In the most extreme case, the final scenario in the table suggests that the oil price could rise by around $20 relative to the baseline price of $35 per barrel.[8]

OPEC has an interest in preventing large price movements…

The consequences of an alternative OPEC reaction function have been investigated in the last two columns of Table IV.2 (Part B). Instead of aiming at a fixed market share, OPEC is assumed to behave in a way that mimics OPEC's declared policy of attempting to maintain oil prices within a band. In particular, OPEC is assumed to adjust supply in order to prevent the price from moving by more than 10 per cent from the baseline price. In this context, some events, such as a ½ per cent *per annum* increase in OECD growth or a change to the price elasticity of demand, could be accommodated without an increase in OPEC share. But more significant shocks such as slower reductions in oil intensities, or combination scenarios, could require OPEC to adjust supply substantially. In order to restrict price rises to no more than 10 per cent, the scenarios that incorporate robust, oil intensive and price inelastic growth in non OECD countries (scenario groups 5 and 6) would require OPEC to increase output significantly. The most extreme scenario suggests that OPEC would need to increase supply by 39 million barrels per day (relative to 51 million bpd in the baseline). In turn this would imply that global dependence on OPEC would increase from around 38 per cent to 53 per cent.

… and is likely to prevent the price rising too far…

The OPEC reaction function – and in particular the question of whether OPEC responds to demand shifts by allowing the price to rise or by a matching supply shift – is obviously crucial to any long-term oil price projection. In this context, it may be interesting to note that, comparing the revenue outcomes of the two strategies, the illustrative scenarios tentatively suggest that stabilising the price while expanding output (as in scenario 6 of Part B of the simulations), might result in significantly higher revenues than would accrue if OPEC's share were fixed.[9] This implies that the longer term price elasticities of non OPEC supply and of global oil demand could act as "softeners" on cartel like behaviour. This would apply all the more if the demand elasticity is asymmetric, as it appears to have been in the past, being higher when prices move up than when they decline. Such a response is not built into the spreadsheet model. However, any conclusion about the relative benefits of stabilising market share or price would seem to be heavily contingent on the choice of supply and demand elasticities, which remains unavoidably somewhat arbitrary.[10]

… but short-term price volatility and uncertainty can depress investment

In the short term both the global demand and non-OPEC supply elasticities are very low, leading to considerable price volatility, and this may depress investment in exploration and development needed to ensure that supply is elastic in the longer term. Higher oil prices do indeed appear to induce greater investment activity by non-OPEC producers in identifying and developing new reserves. However, price volatility may increase long-term price uncertainty, prompting oil companies to require a greater rate of return on their investment. In this respect, current uncertainties about oil prices may limit the hike in investment activity by non-OPEC oil pro-

8. In interpreting this result it should be kept in mind that the model does not embody the availability of considerable backstop supplies at a particular price level.
9. In scenario A6 OPEC achieves a 56 per cent increase in the oil price while supply rises by 15 per cent; in scenario B6 the oil price rises by 10 per cent while supply increases by 82 per cent. The incremental revenue calculations which result from these shifts would need to be evaluated with respect to costs and option values to determine which strategy was optimal.
10. Gately (2004), in an investigation of possible OPEC strategies, finds that a competitive market strategy, which would see OPEC's market share rising constantly over time, would be inferior for its members to one that restricts output. An optimal OPEC strategy in one of Gately's central scenarios would result in an OPEC market share of 37 per cent.

ducers that would otherwise follow from current high prices. And one consequence of the reduced investment over the 1990s could be limited flexibility in the supply response to higher prices over the near-term horizon. The next section considers the role of supply and demand shocks and associated volatility in driving the oil price away from its trend level and how long such price spikes might last.

Short-term influences on oil price movements

The oil price has increased far more than implied by fundamentals…

So far in 2004, oil prices have increased significantly more than would be implied by longer-term fundamentals, reaching levels similar (in real terms) to those attained in the mid-to-late 1970s following the first oil shock, while being still much below the real oil price of the early 1980s. Spikes in oil prices are not unusual and are, to some extent, symptomatic of a gradual upward trend in daily oil price volatility since the early 1980s. In this regard, crude oil prices have become more volatile than the prices of other commodities since 1987, most of which have been less volatile than over the 1974 to 1986 period (Table IV.3).

… and is driven by stronger than anticipated demand…

An important contributor to the recent spike in oil prices has been unexpectedly strong demand for oil. The difficulties of forecasting global economic activity are well known, and misjudgements can, at times, have an important impact on oil prices.[11] In the most recent episode, oil demand was particularly underestimated in China, where strong demand has been related to the vigorous investment cycle over the recent past (Table IV.4). This has been exacerbated by an inadequate electricity distribution network, which has prompted significant investment in diesel generators.

… a limited ability to respond on the supply side…

OPEC's excess capacity, currently estimated to be just over 1 million barrels per day, is at its lowest level since the early 1990's, providing little cushion in the event of unexpected oil market disruptions (Figure IV.5, panel A). This state of affairs has been

Table IV.3. **Crude oil prices have become more volatile than the price of other commodities**

Standard deviation of monthly percentage changes

	1974-1986	1987-2004	Difference
Agricultural raw materials	3.1	2.5	-0.6
Food and beverages	5.5	3.1	-2.3
Food	6.0	3.5	-2.5
Tropical beverages	6.1	6.5	0.4
Vegetable oil	6.8	4.8	-2.0
Minerals and metals	3.3	3.7	0.4
Gold bullion	6.0	3.7	-2.3
Crude oil	**4.4**	**9.2**	**4.8**

Source: Datastream.

11. For example, in 1997, the sharp and unexpected slowdown in the Asian economies coincided with an increase in the OPEC production target, and the oil price tumbled from almost $25 to just below $10 per barrel between early 1997 and early 1999 (Adelman, 2002).

Table IV.4. **The United States and China have been major of incremental oil demand since 1995**

	Oil demand (level)			Share of incremental demand
	Million barrels per day			*Per cent*
	1995	2000	2004	1995-2004
United States	18.0	20.0	20.5	19.9
China	3.3	4.6	6.3	24.3
India	1.7	2.3	2.5	6.5
Dynamic Asia[a]	3.7	4.3	5.0	9.8
OECD (excl. US)	26.9	27.8	28.8	15.7
Rest of the world	16.2	17.3	19.1	23.7
Total	69.8	76.2	82.2	100

a) Includes Chinese Taipei; Hong-Kong, China; Indonesia; Malaysia; the Philippines; Singapore and Thailand.
Source: International Energy Agency.

largely attributed to insufficient investment in new extraction capacity over recent years and may result from mistaken expectations together with the long gestation lags applying to capital investment. Furthermore, restraints on foreign direct investment and on the role of the enterprise sector in financing energy projects may be playing a role. Some of the price volatility noted above could be associated with a lack of transparency that deprives the market of reliable up to date information on global supply. As a result, OPEC "news" can move oil prices sharply, exacerbating oil price volatility and contributing to greater uncertainty about longer term price trends.

... low oil industry inventories...

The number of days of forward cover provided by OECD industry stocks has been on a longer-term downward trend, and though inventories have picked up in 2004, it is not yet clear whether the increase will be sufficient to halt that trend (Figure IV.5, panel B). Globally, by historical standards, the industry margin to meet unexpected demand increases remains relatively low. In this context, low stocks could mean that the market is more exposed than normal to potential disruptions and regional supply imbalances, and hence to persisting volatility, which may be pushing the oil price (see Appendix IV.2). Volatility increases the demand for stocks (by increasing the value of the convenience yield which attaches to the physical ownership of oil), and thus pushes up the spot price relative to the forward price. This state of strong "backwardation" has been an unusually persistent characteristic of the oil market during the current episode, implying that the futures price has been a poor predictor of the actual future price. There may be an element of unstable dynamics here, by which the combination of supply uncertainty, high inventory demand and low stocks causes persistent price volatility.

... transportation bottlenecks...

Transportation bottlenecks for both crude and refined oil products also seem to have put upward pressure on oil tanker rates (Figure IV.5, panel C), with likely consequences for crude oil prices. Tight capacity is partly a result of unexpectedly high demand, and partly due to changes in the global composition of demand and supply, with more tankers required to meet longer supply lines. New orders of tankers are currently high, although there is a significant time delay (three to four years) to bring new capacity into service.

... and regional supply imbalances

Even when the global supply of oil is sufficient to meet global demand, there are often regional mismatches between the grade of oil supplied and that demanded. For example, recent final product price volatility and widening premia on types of

Figure IV.5. **Short-term influences on the oil price**

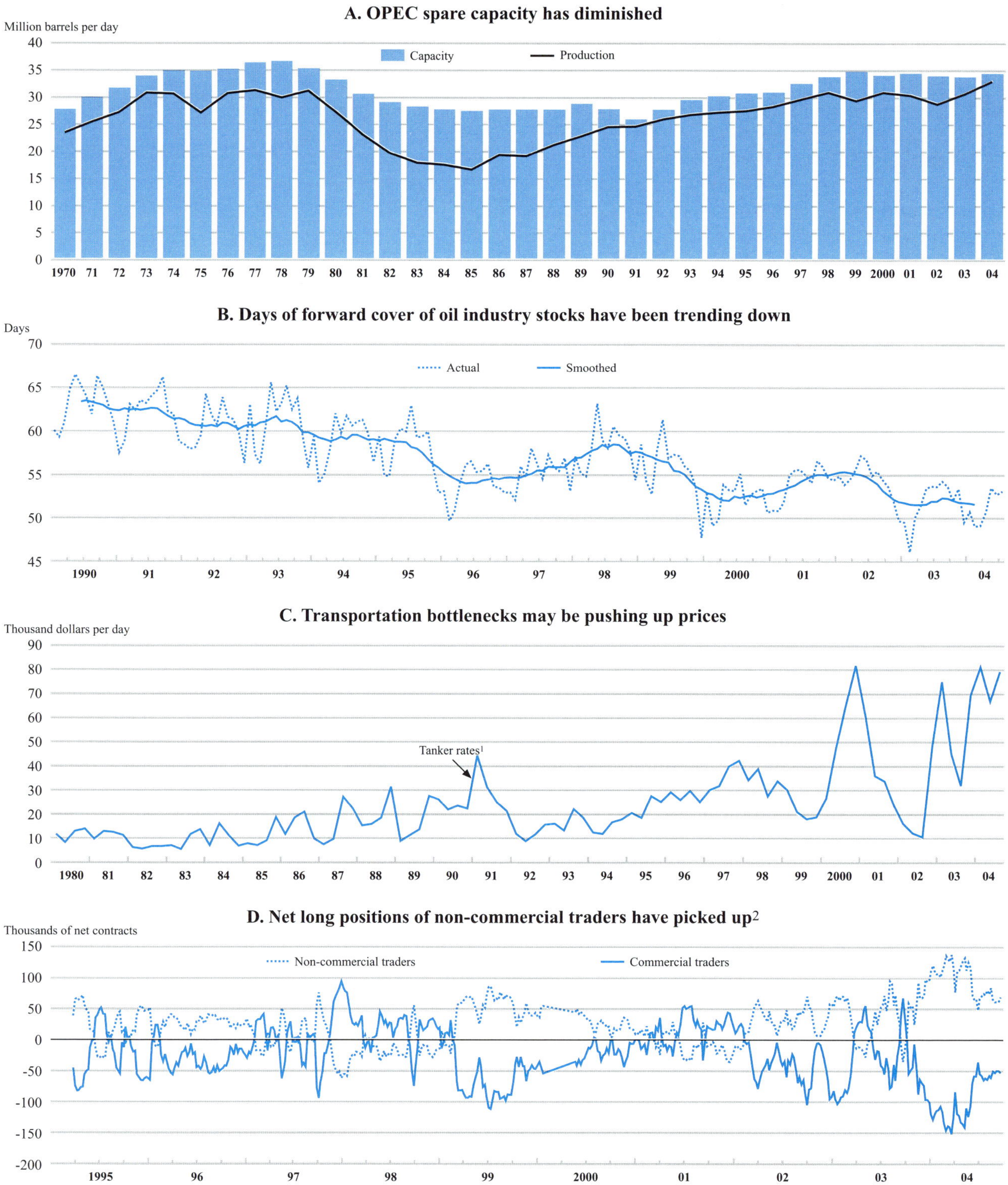

1. Quarterly average very large crude carrier (VLCC) rates for key routes.
2. Data include futures and options contracts. Each contract is for one thousand barrels. Data from February 1st to mid-may 2000 are unavailable.

Source: International Energy Agency, P.F. Bassøe AS, US Securities and Exchange Commission.

crude oil reflect tightening regulations on fuel quality and short-run constraints on refinery capacity, especially in the United States. In particular, the available heavy, high-sulphur oil in early 2004 was of relatively little use for gasoline production, raising the premium on light, low-sulphur oil.

In addition, geopolitical tensions have raised uncertainty…

Geopolitical tensions and uncertainty stemming from acts of sabotage on oil facilities in the Middle East and fears of disruption in other oil producing counties have added an additional "risk premium" to the oil price, related to the possibility of a significant disruption to supply capabilities, of a magnitude experienced in the major oil shocks of the past.[12] Given this risk, Box IV.1 examines the possible impact of a severe supply disruption based on previous supply shocks.

… and speculation may have played a role

One gauge of speculative pressure is the volume of oil futures and options contracts traded on the New York Mercantile Exchange, where registration of all traders with large positions allows the data to be broadly separated into commercial and

Box IV.1. The impact of an oil supply crisis

To investigate the possible consequences of a serious supply disruption, the model was used to simulate the impact of a severe disruption of global oil supply by 7 per cent.[1] In the first simulation (the "bad case" scenario), post-crisis output is assumed to recover linearly to baseline levels over the following decade. In this case, using the baseline parameter assumptions described in the Annex, the results suggest that the oil price would need to rise by around $20 per barrel in the first year in order to equilibrate demand and supply. Prices would then fall back to their baseline level relatively quickly.

In the second simulation (the "worse case" scenario) the recovery is assumed to be slower, with production remaining at its initial post-disturbance level for ten years before recovering linearly to the pre-crisis production level over the following decade. In this case the short-term spike in prices would be the same as in the bad case scenario. However, since production remains permanently below baseline, the price would remain around 20 – 25 per cent above the baseline price throughout the projection horizon. Finally, it is worth noting that these simulations capture only the increase in the price that would be required to equilibrate demand and supply given the reduction in supply, and as such they probably underestimate the total short-term price shock. This is because the uncertainty and risks that would accompany such a supply shock may also provoke a significant increase in the risk premium.

An oil supply crisis could push prices up significantly

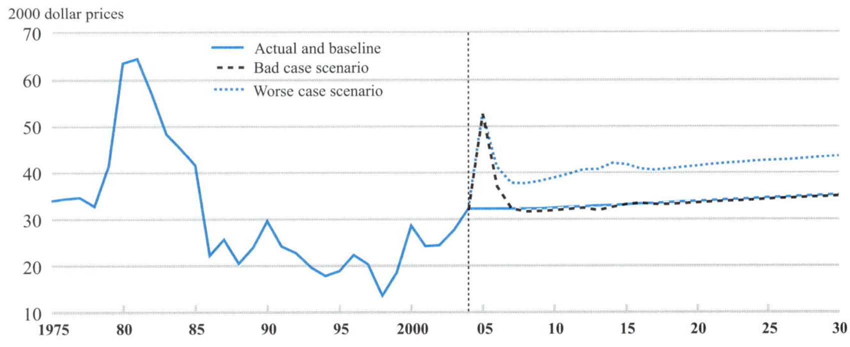

1. This magnitude of the disruption approximates the size of past exogenous supply shocks (see Hamilton, 2003).

12. Estimates of the "risk premium" are typically derived from a subjective analysis of what the oil price would be in the absence of geopolitical tensions.

Box IV.2. The impact of speculation

Concerns have surfaced repeatedly about the possibly destabilising role of speculative hedge funds, or commodity pools, which may shift large sums of "hot money" between different markets at the first sign of a possible higher rate of return elsewhere.[1] In this sense, the term "speculators" usually refers to investors who trade oil futures with a view to profiting from the rise or fall of prices; they have no exposure to the physical oil commodity.[2] In contrast, hedgers generally have sizable spot or forward market commitments and trade futures contracts in order to minimise their exposure to price fluctuations.

Although the positions held by non-commercial traders make up only a relatively small proportion of total futures and options contracts traded, their net positions can be very significant and any sudden changes in these net positions could have an important influence on prices from time to time. Thus, speculation may exacerbate price *volatility*, particularly when news about the fundamentals is itself changing rapidly. At the same time, if speculators are successful, then the amplitude of the price cycle may be reduced. This would be the case if speculators correctly anticipate a turning point in prices and clip the peaks and troughs by selling or buying just prior to the turning point.

It is very difficult to judge whether speculators have any impact on the average *level* of prices. There are two reasons for this. First, it is not easy to distinguish between a situation in which hedgers move market prices (and speculators merely take the other side of the market) and the opposite one, where speculators are behind price movements. Second, changes in market fundamentals should affect both oil prices and the desired futures positions of hedgers and speculators. Thus, any correlation between prices and changes in speculators positions does not necessarily imply that that speculation has caused the price movements. Most robust empirical studies have found little evidence that speculation plays a role in price determination in the oil futures market.[3] Even if speculators can temporarily raise prices by buying futures contracts, they cannot unload these positions at the higher price without a change in market fundamentals. In fact, the very action of unwinding their large positions would cause prices to fall.

1. Dale and Zyren, 1996.
2. Ederington and Lee, 2000.
3. Weiner, 2002.

non-commercial categories. On this basis, there was a significant increase in the net long positions of non-commercial traders in late 2003, supporting the view that there was a pick-up in speculative activity (Figure IV.5, panel D). More recently, the extent of speculative demand seems to have fallen back somewhat, consistent with prices having risen and speculators taking profits. However, the net impact of speculation on the oil price is likely to be small (Box IV.2).

The deviation from the "equilibrium" price could be prolonged

The degree of persistence will most likely depend on whether fears about future oil shortages prove to be valid. If, for example, a lasting solution were to be found for current geopolitical concerns, it is likely that the current spot price would fall back significantly. The speed of the price fall would depend on the gap between actual and desired inventories. If, on the other hand, the current state of uncertainty turns out to be prolonged, a relatively high spot price (and high volatility) may well persist. Indeed, the probability that there is a degree of expected persistence in the current price spike is supported by the fact that the far futures price of oil, which reflects the price for contracts six to seven years out has also increased quite sharply. Moreover, rising oil company share prices reflect a revaluation of their oil assets over the past few years which is consistent with an increase in longer-term oil price projections of around $5 per barrel.

The economic effects of oil price movements

Oil price shocks have become less inflationary…

The quantitative relationship between oil prices, economic activity and inflation is complex (Box IV.3) but seems to have weakened over time for a number of reasons. First, the weight of oil and oil products in price indices has fallen. Second,

Box IV.3. Channels of oil price effects on the economy

Terms of trade effects. The first, and principal, impact of oil price shifts on activity arises from changes in purchasing power between oil-importing and oil-exporting nations. The extent to which oil-importing countries will suffer a reduction in purchasing power will depend on the oil-intensity of production and the degree to which the demand for oil is price inelastic. The income of oil-producers would increase correspondingly. The global demand impact would depend on how much of the extra revenue accruing to oil exporters is respent; typically, such revenues are not fully respent in the short term. Terms-of-trade changes have been quite large in the past but have generally been quite moderate in the current episode, with some OECD economies experiencing an improvement.

since oil is an input into many goods both consumers and producers would bear losses. To the extent that producers are affected, profit margins and returns on capital will fall, with effects on the allocation of capital. While capital is the most flexible and footloose of the factors of production in the longer run, and would move from energy-intensive areas to areas with higher rates of return, in the short term capital in energy-intensive sectors is relatively inflexible, which makes it bear an income loss.

Supply-side implications: impact on output and employment; The impact on output and employment is determined by the relative supply responses of labour and capital. To the extent that labour market institutions inhibit the adjustment

Terms of trade losses due to oil price increases in OECD countries

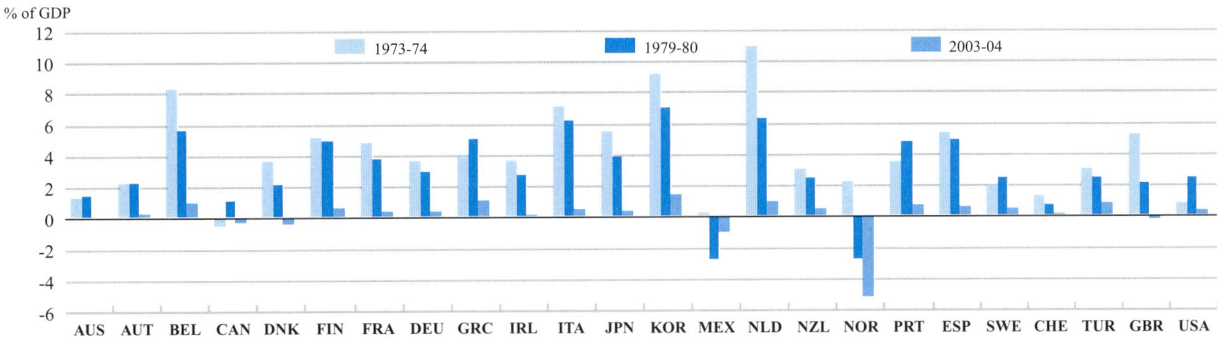

Source: OECD Economic Outlook 76 database and International Energy Agency.

Effect on domestic prices and inflation. Inflation effects mirror terms-of-trade changes in their impact on producer prices. As far as headline consumer price inflation is concerned, taxes on oil products help to insulate the price level from oil price changes, fundamentally by helping to reduce oil intensity in the longer run, but also statistically in the short term, since the proportional impact of an oil price rise is inversely related to the tax content of the retail price. Whether the increase in the price level translates into a shift in core inflation depends on the "second round" effects – *i.e.* whether workers and/or enterprises are able to compensate for the income loss through higher wages and prices – which, in turn, depends on the monetary policy regime in place.

Domestic demand effects: who bears the income loss? Domestically, the income loss arising from the price increase would be borne by consumers to the extent that the demand for oil and oil price products is inelastic in the short run. This would be the case for final consumption products such as gasoline. However, where oil is an input into price-elastic final goods, the negative revenue effects would initially be borne by producers in a competitive market, since they would be unable to pass on the higher costs. More generally,

of real wages to shocks – *i.e.* higher oil prices imply higher input prices which reduce profitability – the deterioration in the terms of trade following an oil shock can affect equilibrium employment, since it creates a wedge between value-added and consumer prices. In general, the short-term economic impact of an oil shock on output and employment would be smaller, the higher the proportion of the price rise that can be passed on to consumers and/or the more flexible are wages if the price rise cannot be passed on.

Longer-term outcomes. The negative impact of an oil price rise on domestic demand and income will diminish over time as consumers and producers modify their behaviour (the longer-run price elasticity of demand is higher than the short-run elasticity). However, research seems to indicate that there is an asymmetric effect, insofar as oil demand does not revert to its initial level as oil prices fall. In that case, the income losses experienced by energy importers may eventually be partly reversed. Where fluctuations in oil prices create uncertainty, there may be a reduction in trend investment activity, but it is less clear that the effects on profitability or capacity utilisation are asymmetric.

many economies have raised specific taxes on gasoline, which reduces the impact of a per-barrel rise in the oil price. Third, the wage formation process has become less responsive to fluctuations in oil prices. Fourth, heightened competition has helped to reduce the secondary impact on core inflation from changes in oil prices. In this context, the impact of oil prices on headline inflation expectations also appears to have become smaller over time, indicating that these tend to be formed from extrapolations of core rather than headline inflation.

... and will tend to have a smaller effect when indirect taxes are higher

Taking account of the weight of oil and oil products and the impact of the tax structure, and assessing the impact of a 10 per cent oil price hike, Table IV.5 suggests that the mechanical impact would be greatest for the United States and least for Japan, with the euro area impact being intermediate. The weight of transport fuel and lubricants in the consumer price inflation is 4.2 per cent in the euro area, but two-thirds of the price is made up of taxation, so the effect of a 10 per cent energy price hike is to raise the price level by 0.14 per cent (Table IV.5). In the United States, with its lower tax component, the mechanical impact would be a somewhat larger 0.23 per cent and in Japan somewhat smaller. The actual effect on inflation in different regions will, however, depend on exchange rate movements, the grade of crude oil being imported, pricing behaviour, the price response of other energy sources to oil price rises, and the impact of lower activity on prices.[13]

The oil price/output relationship has weakened

Simulation results from large-scale macroeconomic models suggest that the impact of higher oil prices on inflation and output is quite small in the short term. Table IV.6 summarises the results from a sustained $15 increase in the price of oil (from $32 to $47 per barrel) over the short-term, using the OECD's INTERLINK model.[14] The effects on inflation are close to those expected from the rules of thumb above. However, apart from the size and duration of the shock, the eventual impact

Table IV.5. **The mechanical impact of a 10 per cent oil price change on consumer price inflation**

	Weight of transport fuel and lubricants in CPI, per cent	Share of excise taxes in final transport fuel price, per cent	Change in CPI inflation as a result of a 10 per cent change in oil price, percentage points
United States	3.1	25	0.23
Japan	1.8	53	0.08
Euro area	4.2	67	0.14

Source: OECD calculations.

13. Price developments during 2004 are broadly consistent with the rules of thumb, bearing in mind the lags between oil price and consumer price movements. However, the impact on consumer prices in Japan is more muted. This is mainly due to the different price dynamics of the main oil imported by Japan, Dubai crude, which trades at a discount to low sulphur oils such as Brent. The spread between Brent and Dubai widened to $14 per barrel during 2004 from an average of $2 per barrel over the previous 5 years.

14. The rise in the oil price has been chosen to represent the scale of the oil price shock embodied in the projections in this *Outlook*. For these simulations, the country weights of energy in export prices have been updated to their 2002 levels. Due to the model structure this mechanically updates the energy content of import prices and consequently the response of domestic inflation.

Table IV.6. **Impacts of a sustained $15 increase in the price of oil**

Deviation from baseline levels, per cent, unless otherwise stated

	2004	2005
A. Assuming constant real interest rates		
United States		
GDP level	-0.45	-0.55
Inflation (percentage points)	0.70	0.40
Total domestic demand	-0.65	-0.75
Current account (% of GDP)	-0.15	-0.15
Japan		
GDP level	-0.60	-0.60
Inflation (percentage points)	0.40	0.10
Total domestic demand	-0.55	-0.50
Current account (% of GDP)	-0.35	-0.45
Euro area		
GDP level	-0.50	-0.35
Inflation (percentage points)	0.60	0.20
Total domestic demand	-0.50	-0.60
Current account (% of GDP)	-0.45	-0.30
OECD		
GDP level	-0.45	-0.45
Inflation (percentage points)	0.65	0.25
Total domestic demand	-0.50	-0.60
Current account (% of GDP)	-0.10	-0.10
B. Assuming constant nominal interest rates		
United States		
GDP level	-0.15	-0.30
Inflation (percentage points)	0.70	0.45
Total domestic demand	-0.20	-0.40
Current account (% of GDP)	-0.30	-0.25
Japan		
GDP level	-0.35	-0.35
Inflation (percentage points)	0.40	0.15
Total domestic demand	-0.40	-0.40
Current account (% of GDP)	-0.30	-0.40
Euro area		
GDP level	-0.20	-0.20
Inflation (percentage points)	0.65	0.30
Total domestic demand	-0.25	-0.40
Current account (% of GDP)	-0.40	-0.30
OECD		
GDP level	-0.20	-0.25
Inflation (percentage points)	0.65	0.35
Total domestic demand	-0.20	-0.35
Current account (% of GDP)	-0.15	-0.15

Source: OECD calculations (INTERLINK model simulation).

on inflation and output depends crucially on the extent to which the country/area is an oil producer, the assumed nature of the wage price formation process, the reaction function of the monetary authorities and the degree to which higher oil revenues are respent by oil exporting countries:[15]

– If real interest rates, measured in terms of headline inflation, were to be held constant, as in panel A, the price shock leads to a negative impact on OECD

15. The simulations reported here assume that two-thirds of oil revenues are respent within two years, leaving the remainder to be recycled through capital markets. Fiscal policy is assumed to be neutral, maintaining public expenditure constant in real terms.

GDP of –0.4 per cent in the first year, with a slightly larger impact in Japan and the euro area than in the United States. The impact on output is felt longer in the United States, partly as a result of benefiting less than others from the respending of oil-exporting countries. The impact on headline inflation is significant in the first year at 0.6 percentage point for the OECD area, but this fades in the following year.

– The negative short-term impact on output of an oil price shock would be reduced if nominal interest rates remain unchanged (panel B), since real interest rates (nominal rates less headline inflation) would fall, with a slight cost in terms of higher inflation in the subsequent year.

Price increases may have a larger impact than falls

These impacts would tend to be amplified if supply-side channels were to be taken into account and would not necessarily apply where the oil price were to fall. Reduced-form econometric evidence points to more powerful links between oil prices and economic activity and to non-linear reactions which are conditional on the recent history of oil price shocks. Price increases appear to have a larger impact on activity than oil price declines. The relatively high estimated impact from reduced-form macroeconomic models may be due to the inclusion of supply-side channels that can have slower-acting effects on potential output.

Monetary policy can be cautious in responding to oil prices…

It is likely that the increasing independence of central banks and the growing adoption of price stability objectives, often based on inflation targeting, have helped to improve the response of monetary policy, and price-setting behaviour more generally, to oil price shocks. In particular, inflation targeting, or its approximation in practice, has helped to anchor inflation expectations among economic agents, preventing temporary inflationary shocks from becoming embedded into a more generalised and enduring increase in the inflation rate. Indeed, inflation expectations have been affected to only a small extent by the current oil price shock. As a result, it is now generally accepted that transitory spikes in headline inflation caused by movements in oil prices can be ignored, or "looked through". This is likely to remain the case, making it unnecessary for nominal interest rates to respond to headline inflation, although monetary policy needs to remain vigilant towards any second round inflationary effects that show up in core inflation.

… fiscal policy generally should be guided by long-term goals…

As for the role of fiscal policy vis-à-vis an oil shock, while it might be possible to smooth final prices by adjusting energy taxes, there are a number of reasons why such a policy may be problematic. First, it is very difficult *ex ante* to determine whether a change in the oil price is a temporary shock or a more permanent response to changes in market fundamentals. If it turns out to be a prolonged shock, then lower taxes would simply impede the beneficial medium-term adjustment of demand and supply to price changes, thus raising long-term oil dependence. More specifically, lowering taxes might impede the effect that higher prices have on incentives to switch to alternative energy sources and increase the efficiency of the capital stock. Second, if many countries adopt such a practice, then the "global" effect would be to reduce the price elasticity of the demand faced by OPEC – inviting them to cut supply or raise prices further. Third, even if the smoothing of adjustment costs (and therefore slowing adjustment) is a legitimate policy aim, the effectiveness of tax policy as a means of smoothing oil price movements may be compromised by political economy considerations, thus jeopardising the achievement of budget goals.

... and structural policies should promote the development of markets

Against the background that the uncertainties associated with the oil market have probably acted to depress investment activity, greater market transparency would seem essential for creating a better match between supply and demand. This would allow market participants to make better informed decisions and help to damp the effects of "news". Better information would probably be instrumental in reducing the convenience yield while allowing the more effective use of hedging activity to reduce exposure to price volatility. In addition, given the apparent role of tightening regulation in creating demand and supply mismatches, governments need to examine whether they can remove regulatory or other obstacles to the development of new oil resources, refining capacity, energy substitutes and energy saving technology.

Appendix IV.1: The oil spreadsheet model

The impact on oil prices of different assumptions about economic growth or supply and demand elasticities is assessed using a "calibrated" spreadsheet model of global oil demand and supply.[16] World oil demand is comprised of three main regions: the OECD area (which is split into the three largest economies – the United States, the euro area and Japan – and other OECD countries); China, which is among the most dynamic and oil intensive developing economies; and the rest of the world (ROW). On the supply side, two groups of producer countries are distinguished: OPEC and non OPEC. Non OPEC producers are assumed to be "price takers" *i.e.* to produce until marginal costs equal the world price of oil. In contrast, the OPEC cartel may adjust production to influence prices.

The only exogenous variable is real GDP in each of the main oil consumer countries or regions.

- Real GDP growth in OECD countries up to 2009 is derived from the OECD's Medium Term Baseline projections (3.3 per cent in the United States, 1.9 per cent in the euro area and 1.3 per cent in Japan).[17] From 2010 to 2030, GDP is assumed to be driven by trend labour productivity growth, as defined at the end of the Medium Term Baseline, and potential employment growth based on United Nations projections of population growth. Labour force participation rates are based on those contained in earlier OECD research into long term labour supply trends.[18] This results in potential GDP growth rates slowing after 2010 to around 3 per cent in the United States, 1.4 per cent in the Euro area and 1 per cent in Japan.
- China's GDP growth, projected at 8.5 per cent in 2004, is assumed to decline progressively to 5 per cent in 2020-2030.[19] In ROW, real GDP is assumed to grow at 5.4 per cent from 2004 to 2009 and at 5 per cent thereafter.[20]

The remaining assumptions underpinning the baseline scenario are:

- The long run price and income elasticities of demand for oil were based on existing estimates,[21] though adjusted downwards somewhat to reflect the fact that these elasticities have probably fallen slightly over recent decades. The long-run income elasticities of demand are 0.4 for the OECD, 0.7 for China and 0.6 for ROW. The long-run price elasticities of demand are –0.6 for the OECD and –0.2 for both China and ROW.
- The price elasticities of non-OPEC supply are assumed to be 0.04 in the short run and 0.35 in the long run. The OPEC share of supply remains constant at its 2003 level of 38.4 per cent. This implies that both OPEC and non-OPEC supply are growing at the same rate as oil demand.
- In calibrating the model, it is has been assumed that the structural adjustment of demand and supply to prices takes place over ten years. In addition, in line with existing estimates,[22] short run price elasticities are assumed to be very low (-0.02 for the United States and Japan, -0.04 for the Euro area and –0.01 for China and ROW).
- Oil demand is estimated to rise from 79.4 million barrels a day in 2003 to 134 million in 2030.

16. For a fuller exposition, see Brook *et al.* (2004).
17. See OECD (2004).
18. Burniaux, Duval and Jaumotte (2003).
19. Using purchasing power parity estimates, GDP *per capita* in China is estimated in 2003 at around 13 per cent of that of the United States. According to the projections embodied in the baseline scenario and to United Nations population projections, this figure would rise to 27 per cent in 2030.
20. Based on data in International Monetary Fund (2004).
21. Gately and Huntington (2002).
22. See for example Gately (2004).

Appendix IV.2: Price volatility, inventories and the oil price

Volatility affects the level of oil prices and inventories in two main ways. First, when the market is volatile, refiners and consumers will usually have a higher desired level of inventories, which, *ceteris paribus*, raises prices in the short run. Second, volatility *per se* raises the value of the call option held by oil producers of being able to extract oil from the ground. This increases the opportunity cost of current production and can result in decreased oil supply, unless the spot price increases sufficiently relatively to the futures price to make continuing production and running down inventories worthwhile. Higher demand for inventories and reduced supply will thus push prices up. Although the impact of the first channel will be temporary, as inventories adjust to their new higher level, the higher price that results from the second channel will persist as long as the higher level of volatility persists.

Compared with other markets for traded assets (such as bonds), the oil market is distinguished by the existence of a "convenience yield", which refers to the services that accrue to the owner of the physical stock of oil, but not to the owner of a contract for future delivery of the oil. Intuitively the convenience yield can be thought of as the premium that purchasers of the physical commodity are prepared to pay to avoid counterparty risk. The size of this convenience yield determines whether the futures price is greater or smaller than the spot price.[23] When the convenience yield is sufficiently high that the spot price exceeds the futures price, the market is described as being in strong backwardation. While some degree of backwardation of normal, a very strong degree of backwardation may be encountered when price volatility is high.[24] The futures market is said to be in contango when the spot price is lower than the futures price. For an extractive resource commodity like crude oil, the futures market would be expected to normally exhibit weak or strong backwardation most of the time, in order to provide producers with an incentive to extract now, rather than to wait.

However, the recent period has been one of strong backwardation, which has persisted for longer than earlier episodes in 1990 and 1996. Under normal circumstances, such strong backwardation would provide important incentives for refineries and consumers to run down their inventory levels, since it would suggest that the future spot price of oil should be lower than the current spot price. However, when the risk premium is large and volatility persistent futures prices often provide poor forecasts of subsequent spot prices, as in present circumstances. Market participants may not interpret strong backwardation in the six-month futures price as a sign that the spot price of oil will necessarily fall. In conjunction with geopolitical uncertainties and capacity constraints, low stocks and the price volatility noted above could imply only a partial and slow return to long-term equilibrium prices. This may be accompanied by unstable dynamics, which exacerbate fluctuations, as when a high spot price leads to strong backwardation and a run-down in inventories, such as has been seen recently. If lower inventories were interpreted as a signal of excess demand, this could cause spot prices to rise, exacerbating the strong backwardation and further discouraging inventory accumulation. Hence, spot and short-term futures prices can rise very dramatically when supply disruptions occur and inventories are low.[25]

23. The spread between the spot and futures price gives an approximation of the convenience yield, though for an accurate representation this should be adjusted to take into account the risk free rate and the costs of oil storage.
24. Pindick (2001).
25. See Farrel *et al.* (2001).

BIBLIOGRAPHY

ADELMAN, M. (2002), "World oil production and prices", *The Quarterly Review of Economics and Finance*, No. 42.

BROOK, A., R. PRICE, D. SUTHERLAND, N. WESTERLUND and C. ANDRÉ (2004), "Oil price developments: drivers, economic consequences and policy responses", *OECD Economics Department Working Papers*, No. 412.

BURNIAUX, J-M., R. DUVAL and F. JAUMOTTE (2003), "Coping with ageing: a dynamic approach to quantify the impact of alternative policy options on future labour supply in OECD countries", *OECD Economics Department Working Papers,* No. 371.

DALE, C. and J. ZYREN (1996), "Noncommercial trading in the energy futures market", *Energy Information Administration/Petroleum Marketing Monthly*, May.

EDERINGTON, L. and J.H. LEE (2000), "Who trades futures and how: evidence from heating oil futures markets", *Journal of Business*, No. 75(2).

FARRELL, G., B. KAHN and F. VISSER (2001), "Price determination in international oil markets: developments and prospects", *South African Reserve Bank Quarterly Bulletin*, March.

GATELY, D. (2004), "OPEC's incentives for faster output growth", *Energy Journal*, 25.

GATELY, D. and H. HUNTINGTON (2002), "The asymmetric effects of changes in price and income on energy and oil demand" *The Energy Journal*, 23.

HAMILTON, J. (2003), "What is an oil price shock?", *Journal of Econometrics*, 113.

INTERNATIONAL ENERGY AGENCY (2002), *World Energy Outlook*, Paris.

INTERNATIONAL ENERGY AGENCY (2003), *World Energy Investment Outlook*, Paris.

INTERNATIONAL MONETARY FUND (2004), *World Economic Outlook,* April, Washington.

KOHL, W. (2002), "OPEC behavior, 1998-2001", *Quarterly Review of Economics and Finance*, 42.

MAURICE, J. (2001), *Prix du Pétrole*, Conseil d'analyse économique, Paris.

OECD (2004), *OECD Economic Outlook*, No. 75, Paris.

PINDYCK, R. (2001), "The dynamics of commodity spot and futures markets: a primer", *The Energy Journal,* Vol. 22(3).

US GEOLOGICAL SURVEY (2000), *World Petroleum Assessment, 2000*, Digital Data Series 60.

WEINER, R. (2002), "Sheep in wolves' clothing? Speculators and price volatility in petroleum futures", *The Quarterly Review of Economics and Finance*, No. 42.

V. SAVING BEHAVIOUR AND THE EFFECTIVENESS OF FISCAL POLICY

Introduction

Private saving behaviour has important consequences for the effectiveness of fiscal policy…

Fiscal policy has been used as an antidote to weak activity during the most recent downturn and fiscal consolidation has been delayed in some countries because of its perceived costs in terms of lower activity. However, the impact of fiscal policy on aggregate demand depends on the responses of private saving to changes in fiscal stance. In certain circumstances budget deficit shifts can be offset by simultaneous compensating changes in private saving. This chapter examines the possible extent of such offsets, focusing on the case where co-movements in private and public saving may be related to uncertainties about how long a budget deficit can be sustained and the consequent need to provide against future tax "surprises".[1] Even though conscious "tax discounting" may be rare, experience in many OECD economies suggests that fiscal adjustments made for stabilisation purposes can often be associated with inverse movements in private saving. Depending on their extent, such responses raise important issues for policy-makers.

… and this may be through various channels…

Identifying the direct offsetting effects of budget deficits on saving is not easy because fiscal actions can be offset by private saving responses through a variety of channels besides tax discounting. The most direct, incorporated into most conventional aggregate demand models, may arise because a fiscal stimulus boosts disposable income and the propensity to consume out of an extra dollar of income is generally significantly less than one in the long term. More indirectly, private saving may rise because higher budget deficits drive up interest rate, which may cause financial "crowding out". In some countries, this effect would be accompanied by the negative effects on asset prices ("wealth effects") accompanying the accumulation of government debt. Because of these other channels of influence, as well as the links running from private to public saving, simple correlations between public and private saving cannot be used as evidence of direct expectations-generated private/public saving offsets.

… depending on country-specific factors and fiscal composition

The approach used here is to estimate the direct effects of budget deficits on saving from pooled cross-country and time-series data, controlling for income, interest-rate and wealth factors. This allows the identification of OECD-wide behaviour patterns. However, the analysis also investigates whether there are country-specific differences in the behaviour of private agents to changes in the budget and whether the composition of the fiscal action – revenue, current spending or public investment – affects the private saving offset.

1. For a full discussion of the methodology and results see de Mello *et al.* (2004).

Figure V.1. Private and public saving: deviations from averages

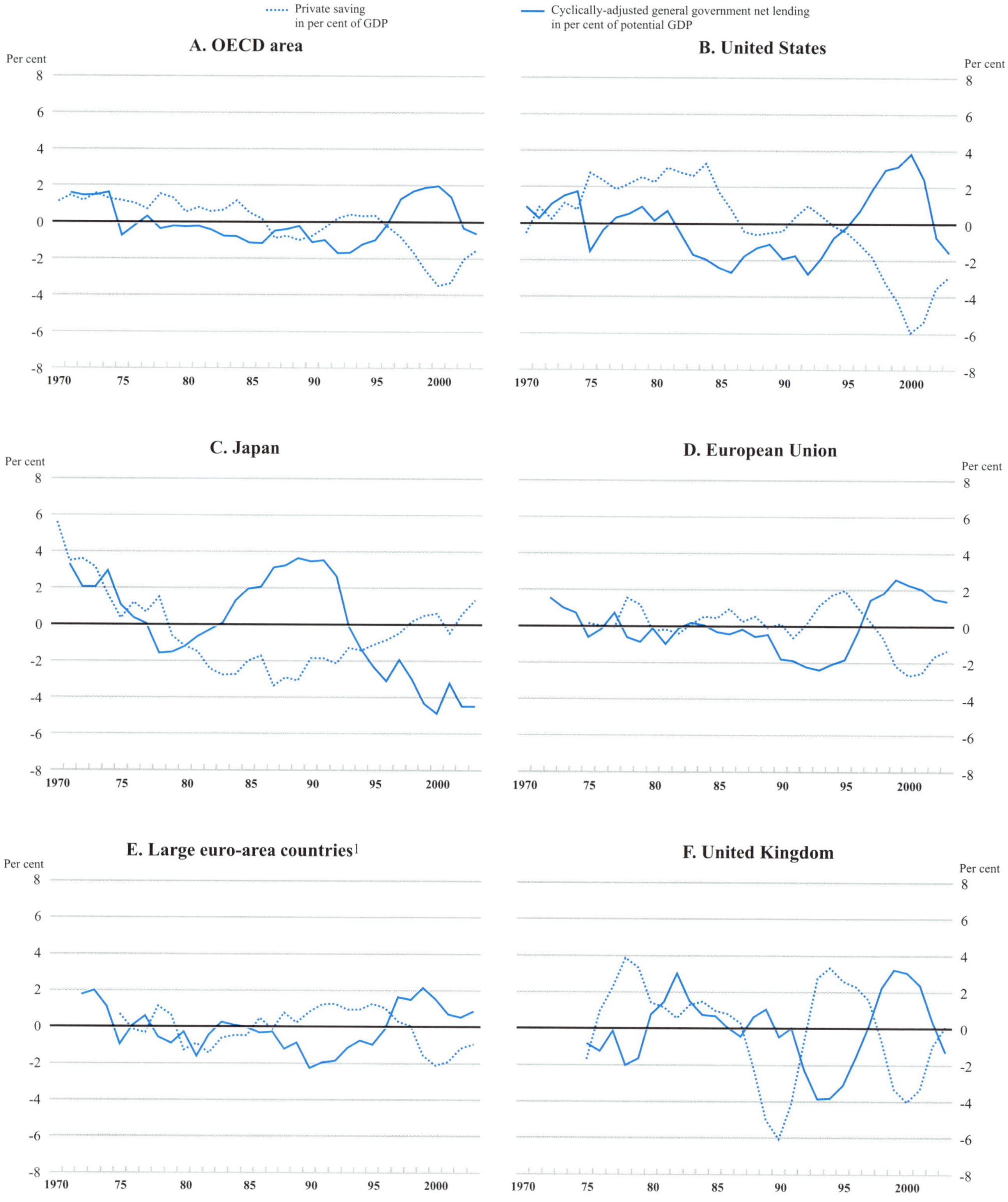

1. France, Germany and Italy.

Source: OECD Economic Outlook 76 database.

The main findings are as follows:

- The evidence of partial, yet substantial, direct offsetting movements in private saving is strong. The aggregate initial offset is about half in the short term after allowing for income, interest rate and wealth effects (which have an important impact on saving), rising to around 70 per cent in the long term.

There appears to be a direct private saving offset…

- Private saving appears to respond in relatively equal proportion to changes in current revenue and expenditure in the longer run, although the short-run saving offset is greater for changes in revenue.

… which applies to revenue and current spending…

- Public investment does not elicit an offsetting saving response, consistent with such investment – where properly defined in the public accounts – yielding either a financial rate of return or a social return, accruing to future tax-payers.

… but public investment does not elicit a saving response

- The private saving response to deficits appears, exceptionally, to be positive in the United States over the longer term. Otherwise, there is no evidence of differential country behaviour.

The United States may be an exception

Co-movements in private and public saving

Co-movements in private and public saving tend to be strong…

OECD countries have experienced considerable swings in private and public saving over time (Figure V.1). However, establishing the direction of causality is complicated by a number of conceptual issues, in particular those related to measurement problems and the need to account for automatic stabilisers (see Box V.1). Because of these complications, raw correlations between public and private saving should not necessarily be taken to indicate the extent to which there is an behavioural relationship through which private saving offsets shifts in public saving. With this proviso, across regions, changes in fiscal stance have often coincided with opposite co-movements in private saving, thus smoothing fluctuations in national saving. This is confirmed by a correlation between changes in private saving and the cyclically-adjusted budget balance which is around –0.5 for OECD countries on average (Figure V.2). A closer look at the 1990s reveals that the countries included in the sample (excluding Japan) experienced a significant improvement in the cyclically-adjusted government balance, with movements in private saving going in the opposite direction (France, Norway and Sweden being exceptions). However, the magnitude of the co-movements differed considerably (Figure V.3).

… but are not necessarily causally-related

The above developments have also coincided with a number of secular influences which could have served to disguise any causal relationship between private and public saving or throw up a spuriously inverse one. Capital market liberalisation would have been an exogenous factor pushing down private saving, while lower inflation has reduced government dissaving. If budget deficits are adjusted for the effect of inflation on debt and debt service payments (*i.e.* if the inflation tax, measuring the erosion caused by inflation of the real value of government debt, is included as a government receipt), the improvement in budget balances in recent decades is, in some cases, significantly reduced (Figure V.4).

Box V.1. Conceptual issues

The definition and measurement of saving matters

The measurement of private and public saving is fraught with conceptual problems. The treatment of capital gains, inflation, the aggregation of household and corporate saving, and the classification of capital and current spending all affect the relationship between public and private saving:

- Realised capital gains are not included in personal income in the National Accounts. But taxes paid on them are recorded as negative personal income and included in government revenue, thus potentially inducing a spurious negative correlation between public and private saving.
- Inflation raises nominal interest payments and receipts, which are recorded in the National Accounts, while eroding the real value of debt and transferring wealth from creditors to debtors, which is not. The budget deficit will thus be overstated and private saving overstated by ignoring the wealth effects of this "inflation tax".
- The boundary between personal and corporate saving is somewhat arbitrary.[1] Aggregating the household and corporate sectors is therefore not without problems. Corporate saving is typically much higher than household saving, and saving motives tend to differ between households and corporations.[2] This may, in particular, be the case for public and foreign-controlled enterprises, which play a non-negligible role in some countries.
- The distinction between current and capital outlays in the National Accounts is not always relevant from an economic point of view.[3] Some public sector projects may have a negative present value and still be treated as investment, while public consumption and capital expenditure are often complementary (*e.g.* building hospitals and paying for health professionals), making the distinction less relevant from the viewpoint of tax-payers. Reclassifying households' purchases of durable goods and spending on human capital and Research & Development (R&D) as investment would raise saving rates and affect saving patterns, as purchases of durable goods (and to some extent R&D) in particular fluctuate significantly over the business cycle.

The cyclically-adjusted budget balance is the most relevant indicator

In addition there is the problem of which budget-balance concept is most appropriate for tracking private sector responses. To the extent that the actual budget balance incorporates the effects of automatic stabilisers, causality will run from shifts in private saving to government saving, creating endogeneity biases. Moreover, forward-looking, rational individuals should not react to changes in fiscal stance stemming from automatic stabilisers, as these should reflect tax smoothing and not changes in the total tax take (and hence debt accumulation) over the cycle. The structural, or cyclically-adjusted, budget balance may thus be more relevant than the actual one for determining private sector expectations.[4] It is the concept used here. However, the estimates of the private saving offset presented below do not change significantly in magnitude when the budget balance itself is used. Nor does the offset coefficient vary significantly in magnitude when the fiscal stance is measured by the primary budget balance (adjusted for the cycle).

1. See Gale and Sabelhaus (1999), for further discussion.
2. In the United States, for example, corporate saving has accounted for around 80 per cent of private saving since 1995.
3. Spending on human capital (*e.g.* education and health care) or on research and development (R&D), for example, is recorded as consumption, although rates of return may be comparable to those of investment in physical capital.
4. Furthermore, large one-off items (*e.g.* revenues from sale of licences for third-generation mobile phones, UMTS) -- which are taken into account by the OECD when calculating fiscal aggregates on a cyclically-adjusted basis – may imply significant disguised shifts in fiscal aggregates from year to year, exaggerating changes in future tax obligations.

Figure V.2. Private and public saving: raw correlations[1]

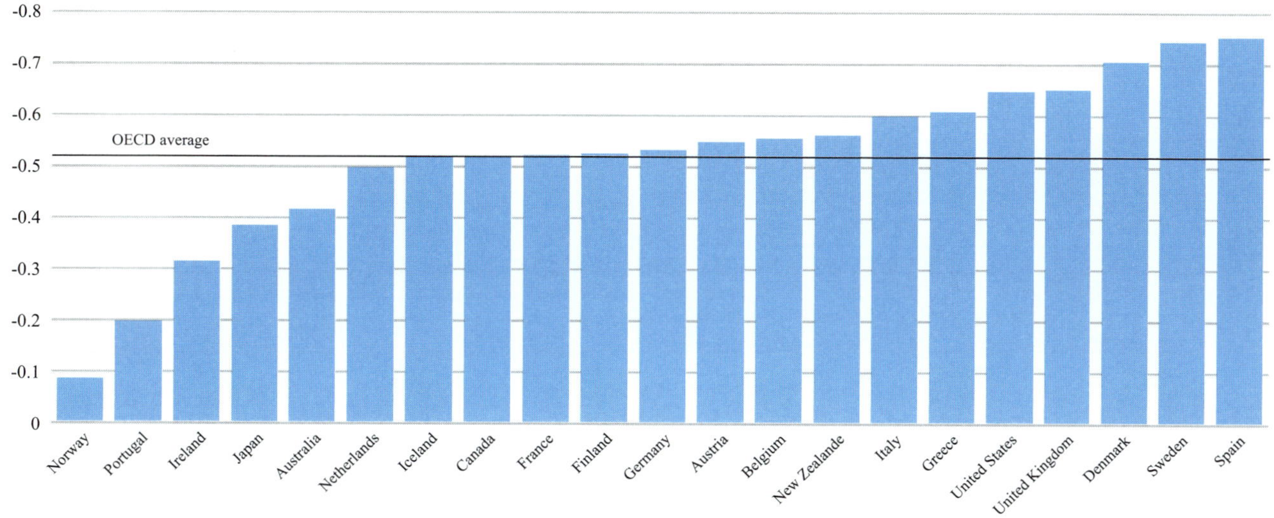

1. Correlation between changes in private saving and in the cyclically-adjusted budget balance between 1970-2003 (data range varies according to data availability).
Source: OECD Economic Outlook 76 database.

Figure V.3. Change in private and public saving

Per cent of GDP

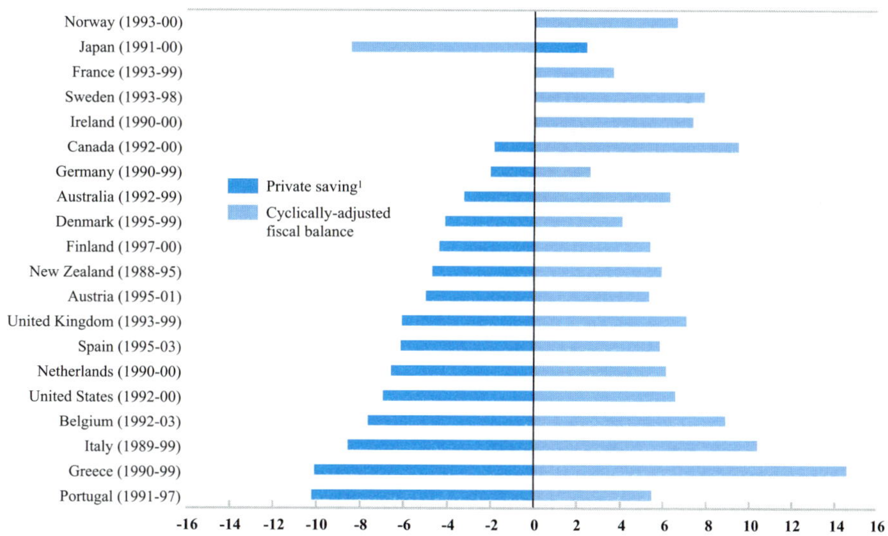

Note: For each country, the period of analysis (in parentheses) was selected on the basis of the most recent episode of fiscal expansion (consolidation), defined as the years over which changes in the cyclically-adjusted budget balance trended down (up).

1. In the case of Norway, France and Sweden changes in private saving were positive over the selected period (4.6, 0.9 and 0.7 respectively) and therefore do not show on this chart.

Source: OECD Economic Outlook 76 database.

Figure V.4. **Public saving: inflation adjustment**

Per cent of potential GDP

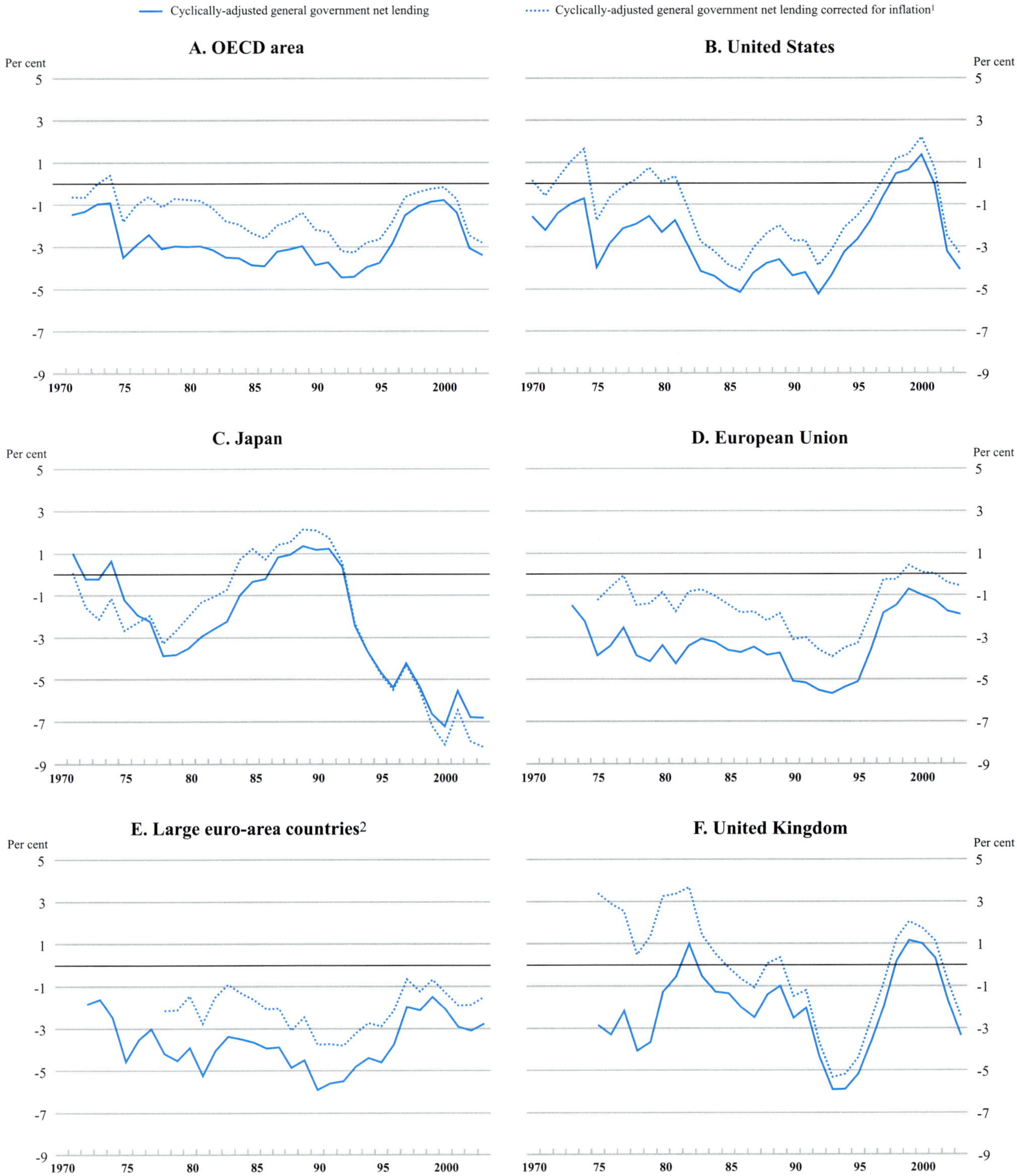

1. The adjusted fiscal balance-to-GDP ratio is equal to the raw ratio plus the percentage change of a 3-year moving average of inflation (based on GDP deflator) times net public debt in the previous year.
2. France, Germany and Italy.

Source: OECD Economic Outlook 76 database.

Episodes of sharp swings in fiscal stance

Fiscal corrections can be expansionary and vice versa…

A number of case studies can be used to illustrate how compensating shifts in private saving can make fiscal contractions expansionary or fiscal expansions contractionary. In particular, when fiscal policy becomes unsustainable, leading to accelerating inflation and rising interest rates, a fiscal correction, based on either higher taxes or lower government spending, can have a positive, stabilising effect.[2] This type of movement appears not to occur in a linear fashion but to be associated with "trigger points", linked to large and unsustainable fiscal imbalances.[3]

… as evidenced by a number of extreme episodes…

Two cases of expansionary fiscal consolidation relate to Denmark and Ireland in the 1980s. The Danish fiscal stabilisation of 1983-86 was achieved by retrenching real government consumption, cutting back public investment and raising taxes. The reduction in the deficit was accompanied by a boom in private consumption and investment. In Ireland, the post-1987 stabilisation programme – accomplished by slashing government consumption and investment – was the trigger for higher growth. Conversely, the massive increase in the budget deficit in Sweden in the early 1990s was offset by rising private saving, in part due to the negative wealth effects associated with the concomitant fall in housing prices. A common characteristic of these episodes is the presence of strong exogenous wealth effects, but it is likely that direct fiscally-induced effects, related to perceptions about fiscal sustainability, were also present.

… but also when policies are not perceived as unsustainable

There is also evidence of strongly offsetting movements in private and public saving in less extreme cases, when fiscal policies are not deemed unsustainable, although again separating pure fiscal responses from other wealth factors is very difficult. The United States experience during the 1990s provides an example of a fiscal consolidation – based on public spending restraint and revenue windfalls on realised capital gains – associated with a significant decline in private saving. However, while fiscal consolidation provided some of the room for productive investment associated with the asset-price boom, other ("new economy") factors were probably more important. Similarly, the fiscal expansion in Japan over the same period, which was predominantly expenditure-based, saw the private saving ratio rise substantially. But again, the substantial negative wealth effects which occurred were more closely related to exogenous factors, in the form of the decline in equity and land prices, than to fiscal easing.

Wealth effects play an important role

Two inferences may be drawn from these episodes. On the one hand, exogenous wealth effects may obscure the presence of budget effects on saving behaviour. On the other hand, budget deficit shifts may themselves elicit wealth responses, and associated private saving developments, which are difficult to distinguish from pure tax discounting. Such wealth responses seem to depend on the nature and composition of changes in fiscal stance and the policy actions with which they are packaged.

---

2. The European Commission (2003) provides a comprehensive study of the effects of past fiscal adjustments in the European Union, as well as a survey of existing studies. Among the episodes of fiscal consolidation identified, this study concludes that around half of them have been expansionary.
3. The traditional channel for these non-Keynesian effects is private consumption (Giavazzi and Pagano, 1996, Giavazzi *et al.*, 2000). But non-linear effects may also take place through private investment, as discussed by Alesina *et al.* (2002).

In particular, from case-study evidence, consolidation based on spending cuts may generate greater private saving offsets than when based on tax increases because the resulting wealth and crowding-in effects are stronger.[4] Correspondingly, expansions (whether tax or spending induced) may have negative wealth and confidence effects, depending on the initial fiscal and economic conditions.

Private saving offsets: the empirical evidence

The private saving offset can be measured more formally

The conditions for strict debt neutrality (which is also known as Ricardian equivalence), where movements in private saving fully offset changes in public saving, are difficult to meet (see Box V.2). However, a test of the existence, and extent, of private saving offsets in response to movements in public saving can be carried out using panel data analysis. Being based on pooled cross-country and time-series data, the objective of the empirical analysis is, at this stage, to highlight OECD-wide trends. The dataset covers 16 OECD countries spanning the period 1970-2002.

An error-correction procedure is used

There are several options for estimating the relationship between private and public saving. The specification preferred here is a reduced-form error-correction one, in which private saving is regressed on public saving and short- and long-term dynamics are modeled explicitly.[5] The saving equation can be estimated as follows:

$$S_{it}^{priv} = \alpha_0 + \alpha_1 S_{it}^{pub} + \alpha_2 X_{it} + e_{it} \quad (1)$$

$$\Delta S_{it}^{priv} = \beta_0 + \beta_1 \Delta S_{i,t-1}^{priv} + \beta_2 e_{i,t-1} + \beta_3 \Delta S_{it}^{pub} + \beta_4 \Delta X_{it} + v_{it},$$

$$\text{with } \beta_2 < 0 \quad (2)$$

Where S_{it}^{priv} and S_{it}^{pub} denote, respectively, the private and the public saving ratios in country i at time t, X_{it} is a vector of control variables, e and v are disturbance terms, and Δ is the first-difference operator.

Equations (1) and (2) can be estimated jointly by solving Equation (1) for $e_{i,t-1}$ and substituting for it into Equation (2), which allows for the inclusion in the estimating equation of the right-hand-side variables in first-differences and in lagged levels, such that:

$$\Delta S_{it}^{priv} = (\beta_0 - \beta_2\alpha_0) + \beta_1 \Delta S_{i,t-1}^{priv} + \beta_2 S_{i,t-1}^{priv} + \beta_3 \Delta S_{it}^{pub} - \beta_2\alpha_1 S_{i,t-1}^{pub} + \beta_4 \Delta X_{itit}$$

$$- \beta_2\alpha_2 X_{i,t-1} + v_{it} \quad (3)$$

4. Zaghini (1999) suggests that shifting the composition of retrenchment toward expenditure cuts increases the probability of success. Alesina and Perotti (1995), McDermott and Wescott (1996), Alesina and Ardagna (1998), Alesina *et al.* (1998) report similar findings. Giavazzi *et al.* (2000) suggest that offsetting saving responses are stronger during large fiscal contractions, but particularly when based on tax measures. Wealth effects are strengthened if interest rates come down as a result of the fiscal consolidation, to the extent that corrective measures, if credible, contribute to reducing risk premia (Blanchard, 1990, and Zaghini, 1999).

5. A more conventional approach is to estimate the reduced-form saving equation in a partial equilibrium set-up, in which the lagged dependent variable is included in the set of regressors primarily to deal with inertia in saving behaviour. However, the error-correction specification is preferred because the partial-equilibrium set-up only allows for very simple dynamics, making the estimation of long-term private saving offsets often unrealistically high.

Box V.2. Private saving responses to budget deficits

The existence of Ricardian equivalence has been much debated…

According to the life cycle/permanent income hypothesis, households make spending decisions based on lifetime wealth, which incorporates expectations about future income, rather than on current disposable income. Linked expressly to fiscal policy and the issuance of government debt to finance public consumption, together with an infinite planning horizon based on the bequest motive, this leads to the concept of debt neutrality (Ricardian equivalence). Forward-looking private agents will, under certain conditions, fully internalise the fact that, to satisfy the government's intertemporal budget constraint, public borrowing implies higher future debt service and, hence, deferred taxation (tax discounting). In this case, the impact of fiscal policy is summarised by the path of expenditures, while the timing of taxes – as implied by budget deficits – has no effect on the economy.[1]

The existence of Ricardian equivalence has been much debated theoretically and the hypothesis is much tested in empirical work.[2] There are strong theoretical objections to the existence of completely offsetting movements in private saving in response to changes in the timing of taxes, focused on the relatively strict conditions underlying the model. These include the requirement of a perfect credit market, non-distortionary taxes, and certainty about future taxes, income, and other variables. Also, current consumption decisions need to be based on infinite planning horizons, with positive transfers to future generations based on altruism. These assumptions would not be expected to hold in general. Nonetheless, significant, yet partial, offsetting effects may exist and the practical relevance of Ricardian equivalence becomes an empirical issue.

… and institutional factors may be important

Empirical validation of debt neutrality is constrained by the difficulties of testing the validity of the different postulates on which the theoretical model rests and of disentangling all the channels through which offsetting movements in private and public saving may take place. As noted in Box V.1, there are particular difficulties of endogeneity bias and spurious correlation which need to be taken into account in the definition of saving. Moreover, individuals should in principle react to *news* about current and future fiscal developments, but constructing an accurate forward-looking budget indicator is difficult.[3] In practice, implementation of political plans is often surrounded by significant uncertainty and may fail to be credible. Where fiscal consolidation programmes have enjoyed strong political commitment (as in many European Union countries in the run-up to European Monetary Union), the conditions for private saving to respond in anticipation are more likely to obtain. Systems relying on multi-year budgeting, may similarly anchor private expectations. Differences in the extent of private saving offset (identified below) may thus be ascribed to institutional factors surrounding the budget.

1. The postulate that the timing of taxes has no real effects on the economy is in particular linked to a seminal paper by Barro (1974). See also Barro (1989).
2. For recent surveys see, for example, Seater (1985, 1993), Elmendorf and Mankiw (1999), Hemming *et al.* (2002), and Ricciuti (2003).
3. One possibility could be to rely on information from consumer confidence indicators, and in particular the sub-index on households' expectations of future developments in government finances.

The private saving offset is estimated at about one-half in the short term…

The main empirical findings presented in Table V.1 control for other main determinants of private saving (see Appendix for fuller discussion).[6] The private saving offset is estimated at about one-half in the short term, while the corresponding long-term offset is estimated at about 70 per cent.[7] The magnitudes of these estimated offsets suggest that, in response to a fiscal tightening of approximately 5 per cent of GDP – comparable to that of the OECD area as a whole in the previous upturn, between 1993-2000 – private saving would be expected to fall by about 3½ per cent of GDP

6. The control variables affect the private saving dynamics as follows: *i)* fluctuations in the terms of trade are positively associated with private saving in the short term (an improvement increasing saving); *ii)* broad money affects private saving negatively in the short term (increased liquidity reducing saving); and *iii)* the old-age dependency ratio and the equity market index affect private saving negatively in the long term. The proxies for wealth effects appear to have a statistically significant effect on private saving, with an increase in housing and equity prices acting to reduce private saving in both the short and long terms.
7. The long-term private saving offset can be calculated by dividing the estimated coefficient on $S^{pub}_{i,t-1}$ by minus the estimated coefficient on $S^{priv}_{i,t-1}$.

Table V.1. **Response of private saving to fiscal stance**

Dep. Var.: Private saving (in per cent of GDP, National Accounts definition): [a]

	Estimated coefficients
Private saving	
Lagged first difference	0.11 **
	(0.047)
Lagged level	-0.27 ***
	(0.034)
Public saving (net lending[b])	
First difference	-0.51 ***
	(0.048)
Lagged level	-0.19 ***
	(0.034)
Controls	
Broad money (first difference)	-0.10 ***
	(0.271)
Change in terms of trade (first difference)	0.04 ***
	(0.012)
Old-age dependency ratio (lagged level)	-0.28 ***
	(0.057)
Per capita GDP growth (first difference)	0.32
	(0.027)
Housing price index (first difference)	-0.02 ***
	(0.008)
Housing price index (lagged level)	-0.02 ***
	(0.004)
Equity market index (lagged level)	-0.01 ***
	(0.001)
Memorandum items:	
Implied long-term offset	-0.70
No. of observations	275
No. of cross-sectional units	16
Second-order autocorrelation (*p* -value)	0.40

a) All models are estimated using the Arellano-Bond difference-GMM estimator and include a common intercept (not reported). Standard errors are reported in parentheses. Statistical significance at the 1, 5, and 10 per cent levels is denoted by respectively (***), (**), and (*). The null hypothesis of the Sargan tests for overidentifying restrictions is not rejected at classical levels of significance.

b) Net lending is cyclically adjusted.

Source: OECD Economic Outlook 74 database.

over the period. The effect on national saving of a fiscal easing of this magnitude, all else unchanged, is therefore of a rise of about 1½ per cent of GDP.

... abstracting from wealth effects

As noted, these estimates of the direct effects of budget deficits on saving abstract from the wealth effects of budget deficits on saving which may themselves be significant. Normally, declining deficits would be expected to have positive wealth effects. In the late 1990s, falling budget deficits were associated with a decline in private saving rates, related to increasing household net worth (Figure V.5). However, examples of higher budget deficits coinciding with growing private sector net worth can also be found, as in the United States during the 1980s.[8]

8. In this particular case, the tax reforms with which the deficit was associated may have been instrumental in generating positive wealth effects. See International Monetary Fund (2003), for further discussion and empirical evidence for the United States.

Figure V.5. **Public debt and net financing wealth in selected OECD countries**

Source: OECD Economic Outlook 76 database.

Table V.2. Response of private saving to fiscal stance: selected countries

Dep. Var.: Private saving (in per cent of GDP, National Accounts definition): [a]

	Private saving	Net lending		Net lending times country dummy
	Lagged level	Lagged first difference	Lagged level	Lagged level
Canada	-0.27 ***	-0.51 ***	-0.21 ***	0.10
France	-0.27 ***	-0.51 ***	-0.19 ***	0.07
Germany	-0.27 ***	-0.51 ***	-0.19 ***	0.00
Italy	-0.27 ***	-0.51 ***	-0.19 ***	0.04
Japan	-0.27 ***	-0.51 ***	-0.19 ***	-0.03
United Kingdom	-0.27 ***	-0.51 ***	-0.18 ***	-0.17
United States	-0.29 ***	-0.51 ***	-0.22 ***	0.44 ***

a) All models are estimated using the Arellano-Bond difference-GMM estimator and include a common intercept and the full set of controls (not reported). (***) denotes statistical significance at the 1 per cent level. The null hypothesis of the Sargan tests for overidentifying restrictions is never rejected at classical levels of significance. There is no evidence of second-order serial correlation in all models.

Source: OECD Economic Outlook 74 database.

The United States seems to be an exception

To test whether the degree of offset varies from country to country the cyclically-adjusted budget balance (measuring public saving) was interacted with a dummy variable taking value "1" for selected countries and "0" for all other countries in the panel. Based on this methodology, the private saving response appears to be positive in the United States over the longer term (Table V.2).[9] This finding should be interpreted with caution,[10] but could reflect either a greater confidence that deficits will not ultimately be reflected in higher taxes or an association between higher deficits and positive wealth effects not identified in the controls. Applying the same procedure to other major OECD countries indicates rather consistent behaviour, although differences in the level of public debt might be expected to affect the offset.

Composition effects

The role of composition effects: revenues vs. expenditures

The analysis can be extended to decompose public saving into its revenue and expenditure components. Based on the findings reported in Table V.3, the OECD experience suggests that, in general, private saving rises only slightly less in response to current expenditure hikes (for a given level of revenue) than to shifts in taxation (for a given level of spending). Specifically, private saving is estimated to rise by about 0.8 per cent of GDP in the long term in response to a tax cut of 1 per

9. Based on the parameters reported in Table V.2, the long-term private saving offset is estimated at about three-quarters in the United States (–(–0.22 + 0.44)/–0.29).
10. It may still be the case that a strong complementarity between public and private consumption is overriding a truly Ricardian behaviour in reaction to tax changes. But this would be an original and surprising configuration.

Table V.3. **Response of private saving to fiscal stance: composition effects**

Dep. Var.: Private saving (in per cent of GDP, National Accounts definition): [a]

	Estimated coefficients
Private saving	
Lagged first difference	0.11 **
	(0.048)
Lagged level	-0.26 ***
	(0.034)
Current revenue	
Lagged first difference	-0.81 ***
	(0.077)
Lagged level	-0.21 ***
	(0.058)
Current spending	
Lagged first difference	0.37 ***
	(0.077)
Lagged level	0.18 ***
	(0.041)
Public investment	
Lagged first difference	-0.10
	(0.261)
Lagged level	0.10
	(0.166)
Public investment * high debt	
Memorandum item:	
Implied long-term offset	
Current revenue	-0.81
Current spending	0.69
No. of observations	256
No. of cross-sectional units	16
Second-order autocorrelation (*p* -value)	0.41

a, All models are estimated using the Arellano-Bond difference-GMM estimator and include a common intercept and the full set of controls (not reported). Standard errors are reported in parentheses. Statistical significance at the 1, 5, and 10 per cent levels is denoted by respectively (***), (**), and (*). Current revenue and expenditure are cyclically adjusted. The null hypothesis of the Sargan tests for overidentifying restrictions is not rejected at classical levels of significance.

Source: OECD Economic Outlook 74 database.

cent of GDP, keeping expenditure unchanged, and by about 0.7 per cent in response to an increase in current spending of the same magnitude, keeping the tax take constant. The short-run response of private saving to taxation is, however, significantly stronger than that to current spending. The results do not point to observable offsetting saving effects with respect to public investment, in line with the arguments advanced above, unless the debt-to-GDP ratio is relatively high.

Appendix: Estimating the private saving offset

Equation (3) in the main text allows for the direct estimation of the private saving offset.[11] The set of control variables, discussed in greater detail in Box V.3, is standard in empirical literature,[12] and includes the old-age dependency ratio, the real interest rate, consumer price inflation, changes in the terms of trade, the ratio of broad money (M2) to GDP, and the growth rate of *per capita* GDP.

Several estimators have been used to estimate reduced-form equations such as Equation (3), including the pooled mean group (PMG) estimator, which allows for cross-country heterogeneity in the coefficients, and a variety of GMM estimators, which deal with persistence in saving dynamics and joint endogeneity among the regressors. Although appealing, the possibility of slope heterogeneity may be exaggerated in the case of public saving, the main parameter of interest in this analysis.[13]

Table V.1 (main text) reports the results of the estimation of Equation (3) for a panel of at most 16 OECD countries spanning the period 1970-2002. The data set includes Australia, Austria, Belgium, Canada, Denmark, Finland, France, Germany, Greece, Iceland, Ireland, Itlay, Japan, Netherlands, New Zealand, Norway, Portugal, Spain, Sweden, United Kingdom and United States. Country selection was contingent on data availability. The main source of data is the OECD Economic Outlook 74 database. The regressions are estimated using the Arellano-Bond (1991) difference-GMM estimator to take account of inertia in saving behaviour and the joint endogeneity of the explanatory variables.[14] The preferred specification includes proxies for wealth effects (equity market and housing price indices), in addition to the conventional controls.[15] The baseline estimates of a private saving offset of about 50 per cent in the short term and 70 per cent in the long term are discussed in the main text.[16] When the conventional controls are included, the Sargan test of overidentifying restrictions does not reject the orthogonality of the instruments and the error terms, thus underscoring the appropriateness of the model specifications. The tests of first- and second-order serial correlation of the first-differenced error terms also confirm the adequacy of the lags of the explanatory variables used as instruments in the models reported.

11. The advantage of using a reduced-form saving equation in the empirical analysis is that it allows for the estimation of the private saving offset with a large set of control variables. Structural models, on the other hand, have the advantage oftesting more directly the different premises on which different theoretical models rest, based on first-order conditions, but do not allow for the inclusion of a large number of controls. The advantages and shortcomings of different estimation strategies are discussed in greater detail in, for example, Haque *et al.* (1999), Elmendorf and Mankiw (1999), and Ricciuti (2003).
12. Empirical studies have also focused on the association between public saving and private consumption, such as Giavazzi and Pagano (1996), on the one hand, and national saving, as in Giavazzi *et al.* (2000), on the other. Previous empirical studies focusing on private, rather than national, saving as a left hand-side variable in a reduced-form saving equation include Loayza *et al.* (2000), and de Serres and Pelgrin (2003). Exclusive focus on household, rather than private or national, saving, such as Callen and Thimann (1997), is relatively uncommon in empirical literature.
13. Evidence reported using the pooled mean group estimator does not suggest that the response of private saving to public saving differs significantly across countries (Haque *et al.*, 1999; de Serres and Pelgrin, 2003).
14. First-step estimates are reported throughout. A variety of unit root and cointegration tests were carried out for the individual time series and the panel as a whole, suggesting that the variables of interest are non-stationary. Cointegration tests were also carried out, suggesting that there is a stable long-term relationship between private and public saving. This error-correction specification is also used by Cotis *et al.* (2004).
15. An alternative to the use of proxies for wealth effects is to use direct measures of net household financial wealth, but data are only available for a small sub-sample of countries, as depicted in Figure V.5 (Canada, France, Japan, Italy, United Kingdom, and United States).
16. The estimated private saving offset is greater in magnitude in the short-term than that reported by Loayza *et al.* (2000) for OECD countries (about 0.1), using a comparable GMM estimator, but lower than those reported by Haque *et al.* (1999) and De Serres and Pelgrin (2003) using error-correction mean group estimators (about 0.9 and 0.7, respectively); by Masson *et al.* (1998), using a static fixed-effects estimator (about 0.8), and by Edwards (1996), for both industrial and developing countries using an instrumental variables estimator (about 0.6).

Box V.3. Private saving equations: conventional control variables

The set of control variables includes conventional determinants of private saving, such as the *old-age dependency ratio*, the *real interest rate*, *inflation*, proxies for *financial deepening* (*e.g.* credit-to-GDP ratio, M2-to GDP ratio, interest rate spread, etc.), *changes in the terms of trade* and the *per capita GDP growth rate*. These controls have been used extensively in the empirical literature based on reduced-form equations, including Haque *et al.* (1999); Masson *et al.* (1998); Loayza *et al.* (2000), and de Serres and Pelgrin (2003).

The old-age dependency ratio is expected in principle to be negatively correlated with private saving through life-cycle effects, although when aggregate, rather than household-level, saving ratios are used, the correlation may be affected by interactions between generations, such as bequests to younger cohorts, which may reduce aggregate saving even though older cohorts may not dissave. The effects of inflation and the real interest rate are ambiguous, since they depend on the extent of credit constraints and on the relative magnitude of income and substitution effects.[1] Higher, and/or accelerating, inflation erodes the real value of debt and raises private saving, but also discourages holdings of assets that are not inflation-indexed, which may make it difficult to identify a direct link between the level of government debt and private saving. The effect of financial liberalisation, as measured by M2, on private saving may be positive to the extent that it measures greater access to credit and liquidity, although the removal of bank portfolio allocation constraints, which often accompanies financial liberalisation, may result in higher real interest rates, which encourages saving.[2]

Other control variables can also be considered, based on recent empirical literature. In principle, household wealth is expected to affect consumption/saving decisions based on permanent income considerations. Data are not readily available for most countries, but both the housing price and equity market index are used here. The extent and coverage of government-run social security, to the extent that it crowds out privately-run alternatives, which are more likely to encourage private thrift, might also be considered, but data limitations are often difficult to overcome. Income distribution can also be considered as an additional explanatory variable, on the grounds that it allows for greater consumer heterogeneity. To the extent that the distributions of income and wealth differ significantly, poorer individuals are less able to smooth consumption over their lifetime, whereas wealthier individuals smooth consumption not only throughout their own life but also across generations via bequests.[3] In the same vein, precautionary motives are important determinants of saving but quantifiable proxies are often difficult to come by.[4] Productivity could also be considered, to the extent that it affects long-term income growth and hence current consumption/investment decisions, with a drop in productivity being expected to lead to higher saving.

Terms of trade shocks are expected to be positively correlated with private saving to the extent that they are perceived as temporary, through the Harberger-Metzler effect. Permanent shocks should not affect private saving. Moreover, the external current account balance might be taken as an additional determinant, and this has become customary in large cross-sectional studies which include developing countries subject to external borrowing constraints, to assess the extent to which foreign saving crowds out domestic private saving.

1. Using a panel of 19 OECD countries, Perotti (1999) shows that, in more credit-constrained economies, based on the ratio of mortgage loan to property value, the transmission mechanism of government spending shocks to private consumption is weaker than in economies with less severe credit constraints. Masson *et al.* (1998) also report correlations between private saving and real interest rates that are not robust.
2. Pozzi *et al.* (2003) do not find a strong correlation between financial liberalisation and private consumption in a panel of OECD countries.
3. It can also be argued that the distribution of income and wealth is affected by fiscal policy to the extent that higher debt is associated to higher interest payments, which accrue to higher-income individuals, who are net savers, widening the gap between low-income spenders and high-income savers. For further discussion, see Mankiw (2000).
4. See Carroll (1997), for further discussion on buffer-stock saving behaviour.

BIBLIOGRAPHY

ALESINA, A. and S. ARDAGNA (1998), "Tales of fiscal contractions", *Economic Policy*, No. 27.

ALESINA, A. and R. PEROTTI (1995), "Fiscal expansions and adjustments in OECD countries", *Economic Policy*, No. 21.

ALESINA, A., R. PEROTTI and J. TAVARES (1998), "The political economy of fiscal adjustments", *Brookings Papers on Economic Activity*, Vol. 1998, No. 1.

ALESINA, A., S. ARDAGNA, R. PEROTTI and F. SCHIANTARELLI (2002), "Fiscal policy, profits, and investment", *American Economic Review*, Vol. 92.

ARELLANO, M. and S.R. BOND (1991). "Some Tests of Specification for Panel Data: Monte Carlo Evidence and an Application to Employment Equations", *Review of Economic Studies*, Vol. 58.

BARRO, R. (1974), "Are government bonds net wealth?", *Journal of Political Economy*, Vol. 82.

BARRO, R. (1989), "The Ricardian approach to budget deficits", *Journal of Economic Perspectives*, Vol. 3.

BLANCHARD, O. (1990), "Comment on Giavazzi and Pagano (1990)", in O. Blanchard and S. Fisher (eds.), *NBER Macroeconomics Annual.*

CALLEN, T. and C. THIMANN (1997), "Empirical determinants of household saving: evidence from OECD countries", *IMF Working Paper*, No. 97/181.

CARROLL, C.D. (1997), "Buffer-stock saving and the life cycle/permanent income hypothesis", *Quarterly Journal of Economics*, Vol. 112.

COTIS, J.P., J. COPPEL and L. DE MELLO (2004), "Is the U.S. prone to over-consumption?", presented at the Federal Reserve Bank of Boston Economic Conference on the Macroeconomics of Fiscal Policy, Chatham, Massachusetts, June 14-16.

DE MELLO, L., P.M. KONGSRUD, and R.W.R. PRICE, (2004) "Saving behaviour and the effectiveness of fiscal policy", *Economics Department Working Paper* No. 397.

DE SERRES, A. and F. PELGRIN (2003), "The decline in private saving rates in the 1990s in OECD countries: how much can be explained by non-wealth determinants?", *OECD Economic Studies*, No. 36.

EDWARDS, S. (1996), "Why are Latin America's saving rates so low: an international comparative analysis", *Journal of Development Economics*, Vol. 51.

ELMENDOF, D.W. and N.G. MANKIW (1999), "Government debt", in J.B. Taylor and M. Woodford (eds.) *Handbook of Macroeconomics*, Amsterdam: North-Holland.

EUROPEAN COMMISSION (2003), "Public finances in the EMU 2003", No. 3.

GALE, W.G. and J. SABELHAUS (1999), "Perspectives on the household saving rate", *Brookings Papers on Economic Activity*, Vol. 1999.

GIAVAZZI, F. and M. PAGANO (1996), "Non-Keynesian effects of fiscal policy changes: international evidence and Swedish experience", *Swedish Economic Policy Review*, Vol. 3.

GIAVAZZI, F., T. JAPPELLI and M. PAGANO (2000), "Searching for non-linear effects of fiscal policy: evidence from industrial and developing countries", *European Economic Review*, Vol. 44.

HAQUE, N., M.H. PESARAN and S. SHARMA (1999), "Neglected heterogeneity and dynamics in cross-country savings regressions", *IMF Working Paper*, No. 09/128.

HEMMING, R., M. KELL and S. MAHFOUZ (2002), "The effectiveness of fiscal policy in stimulating economic activity – a review of the literature", *IMF Working Paper*, No. 02/208.

INTERNATIONAL MONETARY FUND (IMF) (2003), "United States of America: Selected Issues", *IMF Country Report*, No. 03/245.

LOAYZA, N., K. SCHMIDT-HEBBEL and L. SERVEN (2000), "What drives private saving across the world?", *Review of Economics and Statistics*, Vol. 82.

MASSON, P.R., T. BAYOUMI and H. SAMIEI, 1998, "International evidence on the determinants of private saving", *The World Bank Economic Review*, Vol. 12.

MANKIW, N.G. (2000), "The savers-spenders theory of fiscal policy", AEA Papers and Proceedings, Vol. 90.

McDERMOTT, C.J. and R.F. WESCOTT (1996), "An empirical analysis of fiscal adjustments", *IMF Staff Papers*, Vol. 43.

PEROTTI, R. (1999), "Fiscal policy in good times and bad", *Quarterly Journal of Economics*, Vol. 114.

POZZI, L., F. HEYLEN and M. DOSSCHE (2003), "Government debt and the excess sensitivity of private consumption to current income: an empirical analysis for OECD countries", *Working Papers of Faculty of Economics and Business Administration*, No. 02.155, Ghent University.

RICCIUTI, R. (2003), "Assessing Ricardian equivalence", *Journal of Economic Surveys*, Vol. 17.

SEATER, J.J. (1985), "Does government debt matter?", *Journal of Monetary Economics*, Vol. 16.

SEATER, J.J. (1993), "Ricardian equivalence", *Journal of Economic Literature*, Vol. 31.

ZAGHINI, A. (1999), "The economic policy of fiscal consolidations: the European experience", Banca d'Italia, Temi di Discussione, No. 355.

Special chapters in recent issues of *OECD Economic Outlook*

No. 75, June 2004

Housing markets, wealth and the business cycle
The challenges of narrowing the US current account deficit
Asset price cycles, "one-off" factors and structural budget balances
Enhancing income convergence in central Europe after EU accession

No. 74, December 2003

Fiscal stance over the cycle: the role of debt, institutions, and budget constraints
Fiscal relations across levels of government
Enhancing the cost effectiveness of public spending

No. 73, June 2003

After the telecommunication bubble
Structural policies and growth
Trends in foreign direct investment in OECD countries
Foreign direct investment restrictions in OECD countries
Policy influences on foreign direct investment

No. 72, December 2002

Fiscal sustainability: the contribution of fiscal rules
Increasing employment: the role of later retirement
Product market competition and economic performance
Inflation persistence in the euro area

No. 71, June 2002

Economic consequences of terrorism
Ongoing changes in the business cycle
Intra-industry and intra-firm trade and the internationalisation of production
Productivity and innovation: the impact of product and labour market policies

No. 70, December 2001

Saving and investment: determinants and policy implications
Investment in human capital through post-compulsory education and training
The cross-market effects of product and labour market policies
Agricultural policy reform: the need for further progress

No. 69, June 2001

Fiscal implications of ageing: projections of age-related spending
Challenges for tax policy in OECD countries
Encouraging environmentally sustainable growth: experience in OECD countries
Productivity and firm dynamics: evidence from microdata

No. 68, December 2000

Links between policy and growth: cross-country evidence
Revised OECD measures of structural unemployment
House prices and economic activity
Trends in immigration and economic consequences

Statistical Annex

This annex contains data on some main economic series which are intended to provide a background to the recent economic developments in the OECD area described in the main body of this report. Data for 2004 to 2006 are OECD estimates and projections. The data on some of the tables have been adjusted to internationally agreed concepts and definitions in order to make them more comparable as between countries, as well as consistent with historical data shown in other OECD publications. Regional totals and sub totals are based on those countries in the table for which data are shown. Aggregate measures contained in the Annex, except the series for the euro area (see below), are computed on the basis of 2000 GDP weights expressed in 2000 purchasing power parities (see following page for weights). Aggregate measures for external trade and payments statistics, on the other hand, are based on current year exchange for values and base year exchange rates for volumes.

The OECD projection methods and underlying statistical concepts and sources are described in detail in documentation that can be downloaded from the OECD Internet site:

- *OECD Economic Outlook* Sources and Methods (*www.oecd.org/eco/sources-and-methods*).
- *OECD Economic Outlook* Database Inventory (*www.oecd.org/pdf/M00024000/M00024521.pdf*).
- The construction of macroeconomic series of the euro area (*www.oecd.org/pdf/M00017000/M00017861.pdf*).

NOTE ON NEW FORECASTING FREQUENCIES
AND THE STATISTICAL TREATMENT OF GERMANY, THE CZECH REPUBLIC,
HUNGARY, POLAND, THE SLOVAK REPUBLIC
AND THE EURO AREA AGGREGATE

- The OECD projections are carried out on a working-day adjusted basis. In some countries, official forecasts of annual figures do not include any such adjustment. For Germany and Italy in particular, this makes for a marked difference over the projection period. Even when official forecasts do adjust for working days, the size of the adjustment may in some cases differ from that used by the OECD.
- OECD is now making quarterly projections on a seasonal and working day-adjusted basis for selected key variables. This implies that differences between adjusted and unadjusted annual data may occur, though these in general are quite small.
- Data up to end 1990 are for western Germany only; unless otherwise indicated, they are for the whole of Germany from 1991 onwards. In tables showing percentage changes from the previous year, data refer to the whole of Germany from 1992 onwards. When data are available for western Germany only, a special mention is made in a footnote to the table.
- For the Czech Republic, Hungary, Poland and the Slovak Republic data are available from 1993 onwards. In tables showing percentage changes from the previous year, the Czech Republic, Hungary, Poland and the Slovak Republic are included from 1994 onwards.
- Greece entered the euro area on 1 January 2001. In order to ensure comparability of the euro area data over time, Greeace has been included in the calculation of the eura area throughout.

Country classification

	OECD
Seven major OECD countries	Canada, France, Germany, Italy, Japan, United Kingdom and United States.
Euro area	Austria, Belgium, Finland, France, Germany, Greece, Ireland, Italy, Luxembourg, Netherlands, Portugal and Spain.
	Non-OECD
Africa and the Middle East	Africa and the following countries (Middle East): Bahrain, Cyprus, Iran, Iraq, Jordan, Kuwait, Lebanon, Oman, Qatar, Saudi Arabia, Syrian Arab Republic, United Arab Emirates and Yemen.
Dynamic Asian Economies (DAEs)	Chinese Taipei; Hong Kong, China; Indonesia; Malaysia; the Philippines; Singapore and Thailand.
Other Asia	Non-OECD Asia and Oceania, excluding China, the DAEs and the Middle East.
Latin America	Central and South America.
Central and Eastern Europe	Albania, Bulgaria, Romania, the Newly Independent States of the former Soviet Union, and the Baltic States.

Weighting scheme for aggregate measures

Per cent

Australia	1.82	Mexico	3.29
Austria	0.84	Netherlands	1.59
Belgium	0.98	New Zealand	0.29
Canada	3.29	Norway	0.60
Czech Republic	0.55	Poland	1.45
Denmark	0.56	Portugal	0.65
Finland	0.49	Slovak Republic	0.21
France	5.68	Spain	3.01
Germany	7.56	Sweden	0.87
Greece	0.65	Switzerland	0.80
Hungary	0.45	Turkey	1.68
Iceland	0.03	United Kingdom	5.49
Ireland	0.39	United States	36.35
Italy	5.28	Total OECD	100.00
Japan	12.18	*Memorandum items:*	
Korea	2.88	Euro area	27.21
Luxembourg	0.08		

Note: Based on 2000 GDP and purchasing power parities (PPPs).

Irrevocable euro conversion rates

National currency unit per euro

Austria	13.7603	Ireland	0.787564
Belgium	40.3399	Italy	1 936.27
Finland	5.94573	Luxembourg	40.3399
France	6.55957	Netherlands	2.20371
Germany	1.95583	Portugal	200.482
Greece	340.750	Spain	166.386

Source: European Central Bank.

National accounts reporting systems and base-years

Many countries are changing from the SNA68/ESA79 methodology for the national accounts data.
In the present edition of the OECD Economic Outlook, *the status of national accounts in the OECD countries is as follows :*

	Expenditure accounts	Household accounts	Government accounts	Use of chain weighted price indices	Benchmark/ base year
Australia	SNA93 (1959)	SNA93 (1959)	SNA93 (1959)	YES	2002/2003
Austria	ESA95 (1988)	ESA95 (1995)	ESA95 (1976)	YES	2000
Belgium	ESA95 (1970)	ESA95 (1995)	ESA95 (1970)	NO	2000
Canada	SNA93 (1955)	SNA93 (1955)	SNA93 (1981)	YES	1997
Czech Republic	SNA93 (1994)	SNA93 (1994)	SNA93 (1992)	YES	2000
Denmark	ESA95 (1988)	ESA95 (1988)	ESA95 (1971)	NO	1995
Finland	ESA95 (1995)	ESA95 (1995)	ESA95 (1995)	NO	2000
France	ESA95 (1978)	ESA95 (1978)	ESA95 (1978)	NO	1995
Germany[b]	ESA95 (1960)	ESA95 (1970)	ESA95 (1980)	NO	1995
Greece	ESA95 (1960)	Not available	ESA95 (1960)	YES	1995
Hungary	SNA93 (1995)	SNA93 (1995)	SNA93 (1991)	NO	2000
Iceland	SNA93 (1970)	Not available	SNA93 (1990)	NO	1990
Ireland	ESA95 (1990)	ESA95 (1990)	ESA95 (1990)	NO	1995
Italy	ESA95 (1982)	ESA95 (1980)	ESA95 (1980)	NO	1995
Japan	SNA93 (1980q1)[c]	SNA93 (1990)[c]	SNA93 (1990)[c]	NO	1995
Korea	SNA93 (1995)	SNA93 (1975)	SNA93 (1975)	NO	2000[a]
Luxembourg	ESA95 (1970)	Not available	ESA95(1990)	NO	1995
Mexico	SNA93 (1980)	Not available	Not available	NO	1993
Netherlands	ESA95 (1977)	ESA95 (1980)	ESA95 (1969)	YES	1995
New Zealand	SNA93 (1987)	SNA93 (1987)	SNA93 (1976)	YES	1995/96
Norway	SNA93 (1978)	SNA93 (1978)	SNA93 (1978)	NO	2001[a]
Poland	SNA93 (1991)	SNA93 (1991)	SNA93 (1995)	YES	2000
Portugal	ESA95 (1995)	ESA95(1995)	ESA95 (1977)	NO	1995
Slovak Republic	SNA93 (1993)	SNA93 (1994)	SNA93 (1993)	NO	1995
Spain	ESA95 (1995)	ESA95 (1995)	ESA95 (1995)	NO	1995
Sweden	ESA95 (1980)	ESA95 (1993)	ESA95 (1993)	YES	2000[a]
Switzerland	SNA93 (1960)	SNA93 (1990)	SNA93 (1990)	YES	2000[a]
Turkey	SNA68	SNA68	SNA68	NO	1987
United Kingdom	ESA95 (1987)	ESA95 (1987)	ESA95 (1987)	YES	2001
United-States	NIPA (SNA93)[d]	NIPA (SNA93)[d]	NIPA (SNA93)[d]	YES	2000[a]

a) SNA: System of National Accounts. ESA: European Standardised Accounts. NIPA: National Income and Product Accounts. GFS: Government Financial Statistics. The numbers in brackets indicate the starting year for the time series.

b) Data prior to 1991 refer to the new SNA93/ESA95 accounts for western Germany data..

c) Spliced to SNA68.

d) 1960q1.

Annex Tables

Interest Rates and Exchange Rates

External Trade and Payments

Other Background Data

Annex Table 1. **Real GDP**

Percentage change from previous year

	Average 1980-90	1991	1992	1993	1994	1995	1996	1997	1998	1999	2000	2001	2002	2003	2004	2005	2006	Fourth quarter 2004	2005	2006
Australia	3.2	-0.7	2.3	3.9	4.7	3.9	4.0	3.7	5.4	4.3	3.3	2.7	3.6	3.3	3.6	3.8	3.6	3.3	3.4	3.8
Austria	2.3	3.6	2.4	0.3	2.7	1.9	2.6	1.8	3.6	3.3	3.4	0.7	1.2	0.8	1.8	2.3	2.6	..	..	..
Belgium	2.0	1.8	1.3	-0.7	3.3	2.3	0.8	3.8	2.1	3.2	3.7	0.9	0.9	1.3	2.7	2.4	2.7	2.7	2.5	2.8
Canada	2.8	-2.1	0.9	2.3	4.8	2.8	1.6	4.2	4.1	5.5	5.2	1.8	3.4	2.0	3.0	3.3	3.1	3.6	3.1	3.1
Czech Republic	..	..	..	..	4.2	5.9	4.3	-0.7	-1.1	1.2	3.9	2.6	1.5	3.1	3.9	4.2	4.1	..	..	..
Denmark	1.6	1.1	0.6	0.0	5.5	2.8	2.5	3.0	2.5	2.6	2.8	1.6	1.0	0.5	2.4	2.7	2.6	2.7	2.9	2.5
Finland	3.1	-6.4	-4.2	-1.2	4.1	3.5	3.7	6.5	4.9	3.2	5.4	1.0	2.3	2.1	3.1	2.8	3.1	3.5	3.0	2.9
France	2.4	1.0	1.3	-0.9	1.9	1.8	1.0	1.9	3.6	3.2	4.2	2.1	1.1	0.5	2.1	2.0	2.3	2.1	2.1	2.3
Germany	2.3	5.1	1.8	-1.1	2.4	1.8	0.8	1.5	1.7	1.9	3.1	1.0	0.1	-0.1	1.2	1.4	2.3	1.2	1.9	2.5
Greece	0.7	3.1	0.7	-1.6	2.0	2.1	2.4	3.6	3.4	3.4	4.5	4.3	3.6	4.5	3.8	3.2	3.5	3.1	4.1	4.0
Hungary	..	..	..	..	2.9	1.5	1.3	4.6	4.9	4.2	5.2	3.8	3.5	2.9	3.9	3.6	3.5	..	..	..
Iceland	2.7	-0.2	-3.3	0.8	4.0	0.1	5.2	4.7	5.5	4.1	5.7	2.2	-0.5	4.1	5.9	5.2	4.8	5.8	5.9	4.5
Ireland	3.6	1.9	3.3	2.7	5.8	9.8	8.1	10.8	8.7	11.1	9.9	6.0	6.1	3.6	4.9	5.5	4.9	..	..	..
Italy	2.3	1.4	0.7	-0.9	2.3	3.0	1.0	2.0	1.7	1.7	3.2	1.7	0.4	0.4	1.3	1.7	2.1	1.7	1.8	2.2
Japan	3.9	3.4	1.0	0.2	1.1	1.9	3.4	1.9	-1.1	0.1	2.8	0.4	-0.3	2.5	4.0	2.1	2.3	2.6	2.4	2.1
Korea	8.6	9.2	5.5	5.4	8.3	9.0	7.0	4.7	-6.9	9.5	8.5	3.8	7.0	3.1	5.0	4.5	5.0	3.9	4.5	5.2
Luxembourg	5.0	8.6	1.8	4.2	3.8	1.4	3.3	8.3	6.9	7.8	9.0	1.5	2.5	2.9	4.2	4.5	4.3	..	..	..
Mexico	1.8	4.2	3.6	2.0	4.5	-6.2	5.1	6.8	4.9	3.7	6.6	-0.1	0.7	1.3	4.2	3.9	4.2	4.4	4.0	4.2
Netherlands	2.2	2.4	1.5	0.7	2.9	3.0	3.0	3.8	4.3	4.0	3.5	1.4	0.6	-0.9	1.2	1.2	2.4	1.1	1.8	2.4
New Zealand	2.5	-1.9	0.8	4.7	6.2	3.9	3.5	2.9	0.2	4.9	3.6	2.7	4.5	3.2	4.8	2.1	2.6	4.2	1.7	3.4
Norway	2.4	3.6	3.3	2.7	5.3	4.4	5.3	5.2	2.6	2.1	2.8	2.7	1.4	0.4	3.2	3.2	2.9	2.6	4.2	2.4
Poland	..	..	..	..	5.3	7.0	6.0	6.8	4.8	4.1	4.0	1.0	1.4	3.8	5.4	4.3	4.5	..	..	..
Portugal	3.3	4.4	1.1	-2.0	1.0	4.3	3.5	4.0	4.6	3.8	3.4	1.6	0.4	-1.2	1.5	2.2	2.8	2.4	2.7	2.9
Slovak Republic	..	..	..	..	6.2	5.8	6.1	4.6	4.2	1.5	2.0	3.8	4.4	4.2	4.9	4.8	5.0	..	..	..
Spain	2.9	2.5	0.9	-1.0	2.4	2.8	2.4	4.0	4.3	4.2	4.4	2.8	2.2	2.5	2.6	2.7	3.0	2.6	2.9	3.0
Sweden	2.2	-1.1	-1.3	-2.0	4.0	4.2	1.3	2.6	3.7	4.3	4.4	1.2	2.0	1.7	3.3	3.3	3.2	3.4	3.4	3.2
Switzerland	2.1	-0.8	0.0	-0.2	1.1	0.4	0.5	1.9	2.8	1.3	3.6	1.0	0.3	-0.4	1.9	1.9	2.0	..	..	..
Turkey	5.2	0.9	6.0	8.0	-5.5	7.2	7.0	7.5	3.1	-4.7	7.4	-7.5	7.9	5.8	9.8	6.4	5.8	..	..	..
United Kingdom	2.6	-1.4	0.2	2.3	4.4	2.9	2.8	3.3	3.1	2.9	3.9	2.3	1.8	2.2	3.2	2.6	2.4	2.7	2.7	2.1
United States	3.3	-0.2	3.3	2.7	4.0	2.5	3.7	4.5	4.2	4.4	3.7	0.8	1.9	3.0	4.4	3.3	3.6	3.8	3.3	3.6
Euro area	2.4	2.5	1.2	-0.9	2.4	2.3	1.4	2.4	2.8	2.8	3.7	1.7	0.9	0.6	1.8	1.9	2.5	1.9	2.3	2.5
Total OECD	3.2	1.3	2.1	1.4	3.3	2.5	3.1	3.6	2.7	3.3	3.9	1.1	1.6	2.2	3.6	2.9	3.1	3.1	3.1	3.1

Note: The adoption of new national account systems, SNA93 or ESA95, has been proceeding at an uneven pace among OECD member countries, both with respect to variables and the time period covered. As a consequence, there are breaks in many national series. Moreover, some countries are using chain-weighted price indices to calculate real GDP and expenditures components. See Table "National Account Reporting Systems and Base-years" at the beginning of the Statistical Annex and *OECD Economic Outlook* Sources and Methods *(http://www.oecd.org/eco/sources-and-methods)*.

These numbers are working-day adjusted and hence may differ from the basis used for official projections. The differences are particularly marked for certain countries -- see the notes to the "Demand and Output" table in the country notes for Germany and Italy.

Source: OECD Economic Outlook 76 database.

Annex Table 2. **Nominal GDP**

Percentage change from previous year

	Average 1980-90	1991	1992	1993	1994	1995	1996	1997	1998	1999	2000	2001	2002	2003	2004	2005	2006	Fourth quarter 2004	2005	2006
Australia	11.1	1.6	3.7	5.1	5.6	5.5	6.4	5.4	5.7	4.9	7.7	6.1	6.5	6.1	7.3	6.4	6.2	6.7	6.0	6.3
Austria	5.9	7.5	6.1	3.1	5.4	3.9	3.6	1.8	3.9	4.0	5.2	2.5	2.5	2.3	3.9	4.2	4.1	..	..	..
Belgium	6.4	4.7	4.8	3.3	5.5	3.6	2.0	5.3	3.8	4.6	5.0	2.6	2.7	3.3	5.0	3.8	4.6	5.1	3.8	4.4
Canada	8.0	0.8	2.2	3.8	6.0	5.1	3.3	5.5	3.7	7.4	9.6	2.9	4.5	5.3	6.5	6.2	5.3	8.5	5.0	5.3
Czech Republic	..	..	..	..	14.0	16.8	13.2	7.5	9.9	4.0	5.3	7.7	4.3	4.9	8.2	6.9	6.7	..	..	..
Denmark	7.9	3.9	3.5	1.4	7.3	4.6	5.1	5.2	3.5	4.5	5.9	3.6	2.7	2.8	4.4	4.8	4.6	4.6	4.7	4.8
Finland	10.4	-4.2	-2.3	1.1	5.9	8.4	3.3	8.7	8.6	3.2	8.4	4.1	3.1	2.1	3.8	4.2	4.7	4.3	4.4	4.6
France	8.7	4.0	3.3	1.5	3.7	3.6	2.5	3.2	4.4	3.7	5.0	3.8	3.6	2.0	4.0	3.8	4.0	4.0	3.9	4.2
Germany	5.2	8.8	7.0	2.5	5.0	3.9	1.8	2.2	2.8	2.4	2.8	2.3	1.6	1.0	2.1	2.2	3.3	2.0	2.8	3.5
Greece	20.4	23.5	15.6	12.6	13.4	12.1	9.9	10.7	8.8	6.5	8.0	7.9	7.7	8.2	6.8	6.6	7.2	5.8	6.8	8.2
Hungary	..	..	..	..	23.0	27.4	22.8	23.9	18.1	12.9	15.6	12.7	12.7	11.0	9.2	8.1	7.7	..	..	..
Iceland	36.5	8.2	-0.1	3.1	6.2	3.0	7.3	8.0	10.7	7.1	8.7	12.3	4.7	3.7	7.9	8.9	8.1	8.5	10.6	7.6
Ireland	10.9	3.8	6.2	8.0	7.5	13.0	10.2	15.7	15.7	15.3	15.2	12.0	10.9	5.3	8.6	8.5	7.9	..	..	..
Italy	13.1	9.1	5.3	3.0	5.9	8.1	6.4	4.5	4.5	3.3	5.4	4.4	3.4	3.3	4.1	3.8	4.1	4.6	3.9	4.4
Japan	6.2	6.4	2.6	0.8	1.2	1.4	2.6	2.1	-1.2	-1.4	0.8	-1.1	-1.4	-0.1	1.6	0.9	2.0	1.0	1.3	2.3
Korea	16.8	21.1	13.5	12.9	16.6	16.7	12.5	9.5	-1.4	9.4	9.3	7.5	10.0	5.4	6.1	4.7	6.0	1.6	9.2	4.0
Luxembourg	9.3	10.6	5.6	10.4	7.5	3.8	5.4	11.2	9.8	10.2	13.6	3.5	3.6	5.0	6.5	6.7	6.3	..	..	..
Mexico	65.7	28.5	18.6	11.6	13.3	29.3	37.5	25.7	21.0	19.5	19.5	5.8	7.7	7.9	10.5	8.3	7.8	11.6	6.8	8.0
Netherlands	4.2	5.3	3.9	2.5	5.2	5.1	4.2	5.9	6.1	5.6	7.5	6.7	3.7	2.0	2.0	1.8	3.4	1.4	2.6	3.6
New Zealand	12.6	-1.4	2.3	7.8	7.3	6.4	6.0	3.4	1.4	5.1	6.4	7.4	5.0	5.4	7.9	4.4	4.7	7.3	3.9	5.3
Norway	8.7	5.9	2.7	5.1	5.2	7.3	9.5	8.2	1.9	8.9	19.1	3.9	-0.3	2.7	9.0	9.7	5.4	12.5	6.5	4.8
Poland	..	..	..	..	44.5	36.9	25.7	21.6	16.9	10.7	10.9	5.1	2.7	4.3	9.5	6.9	7.9	..	..	..
Portugal	21.2	14.9	12.7	5.2	8.3	7.9	6.7	7.9	8.5	7.0	7.0	6.1	4.9	1.1	3.3	4.1	4.8	3.2	4.8	4.8
Slovak Republic	..	..	..	..	20.5	16.3	10.7	11.6	9.6	8.0	10.7	8.1	8.6	9.1	10.5	7.5	8.1	..	..	..
Spain	12.6	9.7	7.7	3.5	6.4	7.8	6.0	6.4	6.8	7.1	8.0	7.1	6.8	6.6	5.8	6.4	6.7	5.1	7.5	5.9
Sweden	10.0	7.8	-0.2	1.0	6.6	7.6	2.5	4.0	4.4	5.3	5.7	3.3	3.6	3.9	4.4	4.8	5.5	4.1	5.8	5.5
Switzerland	6.0	4.8	2.2	2.1	2.6	1.2	0.5	1.8	2.5	2.0	4.4	1.7	2.0	0.5	3.0	3.0	3.1	..	..	..
Turkey	54.0	60.3	73.5	81.3	95.2	100.7	90.3	95.2	81.1	48.2	60.9	43.2	55.6	29.6	17.0	14.5	12.4	..	..	..
United Kingdom	9.2	5.1	4.2	5.1	6.0	5.6	6.2	6.2	6.0	5.2	5.2	4.6	5.0	5.3	5.4	4.8	4.7	4.6	5.1	4.4
United States	7.6	3.3	5.7	5.0	6.2	4.6	5.7	6.2	5.3	6.0	5.9	3.2	3.5	4.9	6.5	5.2	5.4	6.0	5.2	5.4
Euro area	8.7	7.4	5.7	2.7	5.2	5.2	3.6	4.0	4.6	3.9	5.1	4.1	3.4	2.6	3.7	3.7	4.3	3.6	4.1	4.3
European Union	8.8	7.0	5.2	3.0	5.4	5.3	4.0	4.4	4.8	4.2	5.2	4.1	3.7	3.1	4.0	3.9	4.4	3.8	4.3	4.4
Total OECD	10.7	7.0	6.4	5.5	7.6	7.5	7.3	7.2	5.8	5.7	6.7	4.0	4.2	4.2	5.4	4.6	4.9	5.1	4.8	4.9
Memorandum item																				
OECD *less* high inflation countries[a]	8.3	5.5	4.9	3.9	5.6	4.9	4.8	5.1	4.0	4.4	5.3	3.2	3.2	3.6	5.0	4.2	4.6	4.5	4.5	4.6

Note: The adoption of new national account systems, SNA93 or ESA95, has been proceeding at an uneven pace among OECD member countries, both with respect to variables and the time period covered. As a consequence there are breaks in many national series. See Table "National Account Reporting Systems and Base-years" at the beginning of the Statistical Annex and *OECD Economic Outlook* Sources and Methods *(http://www.oecd.org/eco/sources-and-methods).* Working-day adjusted -- see note to Table on Real GDP.

a) High inflation countries are defined as countries which have had 10 per cent or more inflation in terms of the GDP deflator on average during the last 10 years based on historical data. Consequently, Hungary, Mexico, Poland and Turkey are excluded from the aggregate.

Source: OECD Economic Outlook 76 database.

Annex Table 3. **Real private consumption expenditure**

Percentage change from previous year

	Average 1980-90	1991	1992	1993	1994	1995	1996	1997	1998	1999	2000	2001	2002	2003	2004	2005	2006	Fourth quarter 2004	Fourth quarter 2005	Fourth quarter 2006
Australia	3.1	0.6	2.5	1.6	3.7	4.7	3.2	4.0	4.5	4.9	3.1	2.9	4.0	4.1	5.4	3.6	3.3	4.3	3.4	3.3
Austria	2.6	3.6	3.6	-0.3	3.3	0.4	3.4	0.0	1.6	2.0	3.9	1.0	-0.1	0.6	1.4	2.3	2.4	..	..	..
Belgium	2.0	3.0	1.7	-0.3	2.4	1.0	1.0	2.2	3.1	2.3	3.4	0.7	0.3	2.2	2.2	2.1	2.2	2.5	2.0	2.2
Canada	2.7	-1.6	1.5	1.8	3.0	2.1	2.6	4.6	2.8	3.8	4.0	2.7	3.4	3.1	3.3	3.2	2.9	3.6	3.2	2.7
Czech Republic	..	..	..	..	4.5	5.9	7.9	1.3	-1.5	2.1	2.9	2.6	2.8	4.9	3.5	3.6	3.6	..	..	..
Denmark	1.0	1.6	1.9	0.5	6.5	1.2	2.5	2.9	2.3	0.7	-0.7	-0.2	0.6	0.8	3.6	3.3	2.4	3.1	2.8	2.3
Finland	3.4	-3.8	-4.1	-3.8	2.7	4.1	3.1	3.9	4.2	3.3	3.2	1.7	1.7	4.5	2.8	2.9	2.4	2.4	2.7	2.3
France	2.1	0.7	0.8	-0.2	0.9	1.3	1.3	0.2	3.6	3.5	2.9	2.8	1.8	1.7	2.3	2.2	2.2	2.5	2.1	2.3
Germany	2.1	4.6	2.3	0.2	1.1	2.3	0.9	0.7	1.7	3.6	2.2	1.8	-0.7	0.0	-0.7	0.8	1.9	0.0	1.3	2.2
Greece	2.2	2.9	2.3	-0.8	1.9	2.5	2.4	2.7	3.5	2.5	2.2	2.8	3.1	4.2	3.7	3.4	3.5	..	..	..
Hungary	..	..	..	..	0.2	-7.1	-4.3	1.9	4.8	5.4	3.8	5.7	10.2	7.6	3.5	2.8	2.6	..	..	..
Iceland	2.7	2.9	-3.1	-4.5	3.2	2.3	5.1	5.0	9.9	7.3	4.0	-3.8	-1.0	6.6	7.3	4.8	4.6	7.4	5.1	3.9
Ireland	1.9	1.8	2.9	2.9	4.4	3.5	6.4	7.2	7.0	9.6	8.5	5.2	2.6	2.6	2.7	3.8	3.9	..	..	..
Italy	2.7	2.9	1.9	-3.6	1.5	1.7	1.3	3.2	3.2	2.6	2.8	0.8	0.4	1.2	1.3	1.5	2.6	1.5	2.0	2.7
Japan	3.7	2.9	2.6	1.4	2.7	1.8	2.5	0.9	-0.1	0.2	1.0	1.7	1.0	0.8	3.4	2.2	1.7	3.3	1.9	1.6
Korea	7.9	8.0	5.5	5.6	8.2	9.6	6.7	3.3	-13.4	11.5	8.4	4.9	7.9	-1.4	-0.5	2.0	3.2	0.4	2.3	4.0
Luxembourg	2.9	7.0	-2.3	2.1	4.0	1.9	4.3	3.9	6.6	2.6	4.6	5.1	3.2	1.6	2.0	2.8	3.0	..	..	..
Mexico	1.8	4.7	4.7	1.5	4.6	-9.5	2.2	6.5	5.4	4.3	8.2	2.5	1.3	3.0	4.5	4.2	4.2	5.2	4.3	4.1
Netherlands	1.2	2.7	0.5	0.3	1.4	2.9	4.0	3.0	4.8	4.7	3.5	1.4	1.3	-0.9	0.1	0.2	1.7	0.2	0.8	2.1
New Zealand	2.1	-1.3	0.1	2.8	5.8	4.0	5.1	2.3	2.5	3.7	2.1	2.2	4.4	4.8	5.5	1.1	1.7	3.6	1.1	2.0
Norway	1.7	2.3	2.2	2.4	3.3	3.7	6.5	3.2	2.7	3.3	3.9	1.8	3.6	3.8	4.0	3.8	3.1	3.6	4.2	2.5
Poland	..	..	..	..	3.9	3.7	8.5	6.9	4.8	5.2	2.8	2.0	3.4	3.1	4.0	4.0	3.7	..	..	..
Portugal	2.8	4.2	4.7	1.1	1.0	0.6	3.0	3.3	5.0	5.1	2.9	1.2	1.0	-0.5	2.0	1.9	2.6	1.7	2.3	2.7
Slovak Republic	..	..	..	..	1.0	5.4	7.9	5.5	6.5	3.2	-0.8	4.7	5.3	-0.4	3.2	3.7	3.9	..	..	..
Spain	2.4	2.9	2.2	-1.9	1.1	1.7	2.2	3.2	4.4	4.7	4.1	2.8	2.9	2.9	3.2	2.7	3.3	3.0	2.8	3.4
Sweden	1.7	1.1	-1.3	-3.5	1.9	1.0	1.6	2.7	3.0	3.8	5.0	0.4	1.4	1.9	2.3	2.8	2.8	2.5	2.9	2.6
Switzerland	1.5	1.7	0.4	-0.6	1.0	0.7	1.0	1.5	2.4	2.3	2.3	2.0	0.3	0.5	1.8	1.6	1.9	..	..	..
Turkey	3.1	2.7	3.2	8.6	-5.4	4.8	8.5	8.4	0.6	-2.6	6.2	-9.2	2.1	6.6	9.2	4.5	5.2	..	..	..
United Kingdom	3.5	-1.5	0.5	2.9	3.1	1.6	3.6	3.6	3.9	4.4	4.6	2.9	3.3	2.3	3.0	1.8	1.7	2.6	1.8	1.6
United States	3.5	0.2	3.3	3.3	3.7	2.7	3.4	3.8	5.0	5.1	4.7	2.5	3.1	3.3	3.6	3.1	3.1	3.3	2.9	3.2
Euro area	2.2	2.8	1.7	-0.9	1.3	1.9	1.6	1.6	3.0	3.5	2.9	1.9	0.8	1.1	1.2	1.6	2.4	1.5	1.9	2.5
Total OECD	3.2	1.5	2.5	1.8	2.9	2.1	3.0	3.0	3.0	3.9	3.8	2.1	2.3	2.2	2.9	2.5	2.7	2.8	2.7	2.7

Note: The adoption of new national account systems, SNA93 or ESA95, has been proceeding at an uneven pace among OECD member countries, both with respect to variables and the time period covered. As a consequence there are breaks in many national series. Moreover, some countries are using chain-weighted price indices to calculate real GDP and expenditures components. See Table "National Account Reporting Systems and Base-years" at the beginning of the Statistical Annex and *OECD Economic Outlook* Sources and Methods *(http://www.oecd.org/eco/sources-and-methods)*. Working-day adjusted -- see note to Table on Real GDP.

Source: OECD Economic Outlook 76 database.

Annex Table 4. **Real public consumption expenditure**

Percentage change from previous year

	Average 1980-90	1991	1992	1993	1994	1995	1996	1997	1998	1999	2000	2001	2002	2003	2004	2005	2006	Fourth quarter 2004	2005	2006
Australia	3.7	3.0	0.4	0.3	3.1	4.0	2.9	2.6	3.5	2.2	4.8	0.6	3.8	3.8	3.2	3.1	3.2	3.1	3.1	3.2
Austria	1.6	2.6	2.8	3.2	2.6	3.0	1.5	3.0	2.3	3.0	0.2	-1.4	1.1	0.4	0.2	0.7	1.4	..	..	..
Belgium	1.0	3.6	1.6	-0.3	1.6	1.7	2.1	0.4	1.1	3.5	2.3	2.7	2.3	2.7	2.5	2.0	2.0	2.5	1.9	1.9
Canada	2.4	2.9	1.0	0.0	-1.2	-0.6	-1.2	-1.0	3.2	2.1	3.1	3.7	2.8	3.8	2.8	3.1	3.1	2.7	3.2	2.9
Czech Republic	..	..	..	..	1.4	-4.3	3.6	1.4	-1.0	5.4	0.2	3.8	4.5	2.2	-0.4	-0.2	0.5	..	..	..
Denmark	0.8	0.6	0.8	4.1	3.0	2.1	3.4	0.8	3.1	2.0	0.9	2.7	2.1	1.0	0.7	0.7	0.8	1.6	-0.2	1.2
Finland	3.2	2.0	-2.5	-4.3	0.8	2.0	2.7	2.8	2.0	1.4	0.2	2.2	3.9	1.6	1.1	1.5	1.5	1.1	1.5	1.5
France	2.7	2.6	3.6	4.3	0.5	0.0	2.2	2.1	-0.1	1.5	3.0	2.9	4.6	2.5	2.3	1.7	1.7	1.4	2.1	1.6
Germany	1.4	1.9	5.0	0.1	2.4	1.5	1.8	0.3	1.9	0.8	1.1	1.0	1.9	0.1	0.1	0.0	0.1	-0.1	0.2	0.2
Greece	1.4	-1.5	-3.0	2.6	-1.1	5.6	0.9	3.0	1.7	2.1	14.8	-3.1	5.3	-2.5	5.2	1.7	0.8	..	..	..
Hungary	..	..	..	..	-7.4	-5.7	-1.9	3.1	2.8	1.7	1.4	6.2	5.0	1.6	1.0	1.0	1.0	..	..	..
Iceland	5.1	3.1	-0.7	2.3	4.0	1.8	1.2	2.5	3.4	4.9	4.4	3.1	4.2	3.3	1.9	2.4	2.2	1.4	1.9	2.5
Ireland	0.1	2.7	3.0	0.1	4.1	3.9	3.4	5.1	5.3	4.4	9.9	11.4	8.8	2.6	3.2	4.8	4.9	..	..	..
Italy	2.9	1.7	0.6	-0.2	-0.9	-2.2	1.0	0.2	0.2	1.3	1.7	3.9	1.9	2.2	0.7	0.6	0.3	-0.4	0.9	0.4
Japan	3.5	4.1	2.5	3.0	3.2	4.3	2.9	1.0	2.0	4.6	4.9	3.0	2.4	1.0	1.9	2.1	2.0	2.2	2.0	2.0
Korea	5.3	7.2	5.9	4.6	1.9	0.8	8.0	2.6	2.3	2.9	1.6	4.9	6.0	3.7	3.7	3.5	3.4	3.6	3.9	3.0
Luxembourg	4.4	4.0	3.2	5.2	1.0	4.7	5.6	3.0	1.3	7.3	4.8	6.5	3.2	5.0	3.8	2.8	2.3	..	..	..
Mexico	2.7	5.4	1.9	2.4	2.9	-1.3	-0.7	2.9	2.3	4.7	2.4	-2.0	0.1	2.5	0.0	1.1	2.0	4.9	-5.3	4.0
Netherlands	2.8	2.9	2.9	1.6	1.5	1.5	-0.4	3.2	3.6	2.5	2.0	4.8	3.6	1.8	0.3	0.3	0.5	-0.5	0.1	0.5
New Zealand	1.7	-0.6	1.1	1.3	0.8	4.8	2.3	6.6	0.0	6.4	-3.0	4.4	2.3	2.5	7.4	3.2	5.0	8.6	0.0	8.1
Norway	2.7	5.4	5.6	2.7	1.5	1.5	3.1	2.5	3.3	3.2	1.3	5.8	3.1	1.4	2.2	1.8	1.8	1.6	2.5	1.4
Poland	..	..	..	..	1.2	4.8	2.3	3.3	2.0	1.9	1.3	0.6	0.4	0.4	2.0	1.5	1.6	..	..	..
Portugal	5.0	9.6	-0.9	-0.2	4.3	1.0	3.4	2.2	4.1	5.6	4.1	3.3	2.2	-0.4	0.5	0.5	0.9	0.6	0.7	0.7
Slovak Republic	..	..	..	..	-10.7	3.6	17.2	-5.4	12.5	-7.1	1.6	4.6	4.7	2.9	1.4	1.6	0.8	..	..	..
Spain	5.0	6.0	3.5	2.7	0.5	2.4	1.3	2.9	3.7	4.2	5.6	3.5	4.1	3.9	4.0	3.3	3.0	3.3	3.5	2.7
Sweden	1.7	3.4	1.7	0.1	-0.8	-0.4	0.6	-0.9	3.4	1.7	-1.2	0.9	3.2	0.6	1.2	1.1	1.1	1.4	0.9	1.3
Switzerland	3.2	4.3	1.7	-0.7	2.0	1.0	0.9	-0.1	-0.9	0.3	2.6	4.2	3.2	1.4	1.0	0.2	0.4	..	..	..
Turkey	8.8	3.7	3.6	8.6	-5.5	6.8	8.6	4.1	7.8	6.5	7.1	-8.5	5.4	-2.4	2.2	2.8	-0.2	..	..	..
United Kingdom	0.9	3.0	0.7	-0.7	1.0	1.4	1.3	-0.4	1.2	3.5	2.3	2.6	3.8	3.5	3.8	1.9	2.0	1.6	2.7	1.0
United States	2.8	1.3	0.4	-0.3	0.3	0.2	0.4	1.8	1.6	3.1	1.7	3.1	4.0	2.9	1.8	1.6	1.2	1.8	1.4	1.2
Euro area	2.4	2.6	2.9	1.3	1.2	0.8	1.7	1.4	1.4	1.8	2.5	2.5	3.1	1.7	1.4	1.1	1.1	0.9	1.3	1.1
Total OECD	2.8	2.6	1.8	1.0	0.9	1.1	1.5	1.5	1.8	2.9	2.5	2.6	3.4	2.2	1.9	1.7	1.5	2.0	1.2	1.6

Note: The adoption of new national account systems, SNA93 or ESA95, has been proceeding at an uneven pace among OECD member countries, both with respect to variables and the time period covered. As a consequence, there are breaks in many national series. Moreover, some countries are using chain-weighted price indices to calculate real GDP and expenditures components. See Table "National Account Reporting Systems and Base-years" at the beginning of the Statistical Annex and *OECD Economic Outlook* Sources and Methods *(http://www.oecd.org/eco/sources-and-methods)*. Working-day adjusted -- see note to Table on Real GDP.

Source: OECD Economic Outlook 76 database.

Annex Table 5. **Real total gross fixed capital formation**

Percentage change from previous year

	Average 1980-90	1991	1992	1993	1994	1995	1996	1997	1998	1999	2000	2001	2002	2003	2004	2005	2006	Fourth quarter 2004	Fourth quarter 2005	Fourth quarter 2006
Australia	3.5	-8.3	1.3	5.4	11.2	1.9	3.9	9.3	8.3	6.4	0.6	-1.9	15.7	8.2	6.1	4.4	4.8	3.2	4.6	4.8
Austria	1.9	8.1	0.2	-1.2	5.2	-1.0	2.6	1.4	3.5	2.3	6.5	-2.1	-3.4	6.2	1.6	3.0	4.1	..	..	..
Belgium	2.3	-3.9	0.6	-1.7	0.0	3.6	-0.3	8.3	3.5	4.5	3.4	0.6	-3.4	-0.6	1.0	2.8	5.1	1.6	6.3	4.6
Canada	3.5	-5.4	-2.7	-2.0	7.5	-2.1	4.4	15.2	2.4	7.3	4.7	4.1	2.4	4.9	6.2	5.3	4.5	5.4	5.2	4.2
Czech Republic	..	..	..	..	10.2	19.8	8.2	-3.4	-1.1	-3.5	4.9	5.4	3.4	7.4	9.5	7.2	6.0	..	..	..
Denmark	1.9	-3.3	-2.0	-4.0	7.6	11.6	4.0	10.9	10.1	1.5	6.9	4.9	4.5	0.1	3.6	4.7	5.4	0.9	4.7	5.7
Finland	3.5	-18.6	-16.5	-14.8	-3.6	11.3	5.8	13.8	9.0	2.3	4.1	4.0	-3.3	-2.1	4.1	4.1	4.3	4.1	4.6	4.0
France	2.6	-1.5	-1.8	-6.6	1.6	2.2	-0.1	-0.2	7.2	8.3	8.4	2.1	-1.8	0.1	3.5	3.1	3.3	3.9	3.0	3.4
Germany	1.6	5.2	3.4	-4.6	4.2	-0.5	-0.6	0.7	2.3	3.8	3.4	-4.0	-6.3	-2.2	-2.0	0.6	3.4	-2.9	1.7	4.0
Greece	-0.9	4.2	-3.5	-4.0	-3.1	4.1	8.4	6.8	10.6	11.0	8.0	6.5	5.7	13.7	5.7	3.1	5.3	..	..	..
Hungary	..	..	..	..	12.5	-4.3	6.7	9.2	13.3	5.9	6.7	5.0	8.0	3.0	9.0	6.4	6.1	..	..	..
Iceland	0.8	1.8	-11.1	-10.7	0.6	-1.1	25.7	10.0	32.8	-3.0	14.8	-7.6	-15.1	17.6	16.9	17.7	10.0	13.9	12.3	9.6
Ireland	0.9	-7.0	0.0	-5.1	11.8	15.8	17.4	18.0	16.3	15.5	7.1	-1.8	3.1	3.6	7.1	5.6	3.6	..	..	..
Italy	1.9	1.1	-1.7	-10.9	0.3	6.2	3.4	2.1	3.8	5.1	7.3	1.6	1.3	-2.1	3.8	4.9	4.2	6.2	5.1	3.5
Japan	5.0	2.3	-2.4	-2.8	-1.5	0.8	6.4	0.9	-3.9	-0.9	2.7	-1.1	-6.1	3.2	2.8	1.2	2.2	-0.6	2.4	2.0
Korea	11.9	13.4	-0.7	6.1	10.9	12.0	8.4	-2.3	-22.9	8.3	12.2	-0.2	6.6	3.6	3.5	4.3	3.8	2.8	4.7	3.5
Luxembourg	3.9	15.8	-15.1	20.6	0.0	-1.5	3.8	12.7	11.8	14.6	-3.5	10.0	-1.1	-6.3	7.0	8.0	5.8	..	..	..
Mexico	-1.2	11.0	10.8	-2.5	8.4	-29.0	16.4	21.0	10.3	7.7	11.4	-5.6	-1.0	-0.4	6.4	5.8	6.0	8.2	5.5	6.4
Netherlands	2.2	0.3	0.7	-3.2	2.1	4.1	6.3	6.6	4.2	7.8	1.4	0.2	-3.6	-3.1	0.2	0.5	3.1	-2.2	3.2	2.8
New Zealand	4.0	-18.3	0.2	14.5	15.3	12.2	7.8	0.6	-5.4	6.8	8.2	0.6	8.3	13.1	13.5	4.7	2.9	12.4	3.1	2.9
Norway	-0.6	-3.0	-1.1	6.5	5.3	3.9	10.3	15.5	13.1	-5.6	-3.6	-0.7	-3.4	-3.7	5.4	5.4	2.5	14.0	6.0	0.4
Poland	..	..	..	..	9.2	16.6	19.7	21.7	14.2	6.8	2.7	-8.8	-5.8	-0.9	3.9	7.2	8.8	..	..	..
Portugal	3.0	3.3	4.5	-5.5	2.7	6.6	5.7	13.9	11.5	6.4	3.8	0.8	-4.9	-9.8	2.6	4.9	6.4	5.1	6.0	6.5
Slovak Republic	..	..	..	..	-2.5	0.6	29.1	15.0	11.0	-19.6	-7.2	13.9	-0.9	-1.2	3.7	8.6	5.6	..	..	..
Spain	5.3	1.7	-4.1	-8.9	1.9	7.7	2.1	5.0	10.0	8.8	5.7	3.0	1.7	3.2	3.3	4.1	4.1	2.9	4.2	4.1
Sweden	3.8	-8.5	-11.3	-14.6	6.6	9.9	4.5	-0.3	7.8	8.2	5.6	-1.0	-3.0	-2.0	2.7	7.2	5.5	5.3	7.5	4.4
Switzerland	3.6	-2.2	-8.0	-2.9	6.5	4.4	-1.7	2.0	6.5	1.2	4.3	-3.1	0.3	-0.3	5.0	4.2	3.8	..	..	..
Turkey	10.2	0.4	6.4	26.4	-16.0	9.1	14.1	14.8	-3.9	-15.7	16.9	-31.5	-1.1	10.0	39.9	10.2	8.0	..	..	..
United Kingdom	4.3	-8.2	-0.9	0.3	4.7	3.1	5.7	6.8	12.7	1.6	3.6	2.6	2.7	2.2	6.5	5.3	3.5	6.2	5.1	2.8
United States	3.4	-5.1	4.9	6.0	7.3	5.7	8.1	8.1	9.1	8.2	6.1	-1.7	-3.1	4.5	8.9	5.8	5.9	7.7	4.9	6.3
Euro area	2.3	1.1	-0.3	-6.3	2.4	2.5	1.3	2.6	5.1	6.0	5.4	0.0	-2.3	-0.4	1.9	2.9	3.8	1.7	3.6	3.8
Total OECD	3.6	-1.5	1.3	0.7	4.7	3.1	6.2	6.2	5.2	5.3	5.6	-1.3	-1.9	2.7	6.0	4.5	4.7	4.8	4.7	4.6

Note: The adoption of new national account systems, SNA93 or ESA95, has been proceeding at an uneven pace among OECD member countries, both with respect to variables and the time period covered. As a consequence, there are breaks in many national series. Moreover, some countries are using chain-weighted price indices to calculate real GDP and expenditures components. See Table "National Account Reporting Systems and Base-years" at the beginning of the Statistical Annex and *OECD Economic Outlook* Sources and Methods *(http://www.oecd.org/eco/sources-and-methods)*. Working-day adjusted -- see note to Table on Real GDP.
Source: OECD Economic Outlook 76 database.

Annex Table 6. **Real gross private non-residential fixed capital formation**

Percentage change from previous year

	Average 1980-90	1991	1992	1993	1994	1995	1996	1997	1998	1999	2000	2001	2002	2003	2004	2005	2006	Fourth quarter 2004	2005	2006
Australia	5.4	-11.2	-2.3	2.4	11.4	7.3	10.1	7.8	7.1	6.0	-1.4	0.4	15.2	8.2	5.5	6.4	7.4	2.4	7.2	7.3
Austria	3.5	8.8	-3.5	-4.9	4.7	-5.0	4.5	10.0	7.2	5.2	12.8	1.3	-4.3	10.0	2.5	3.6	4.8	..	..	..
Belgium	5.5	-3.3	-1.4	-4.6	-2.5	4.3	3.8	8.5	5.2	2.3	4.4	3.6	-3.8	-1.9	0.5	2.4	5.0	2.1	4.4	5.3
Canada	3.6	-3.3	-7.8	-1.4	9.4	4.8	4.4	22.6	5.3	7.2	4.7	0.7	-4.0	3.2	5.4	7.1	6.8	5.4	7.6	6.3
Denmark	5.4	-1.4	-4.2	-8.3	7.6	13.9	2.7	13.7	13.5	1.9	6.6	6.9	4.2	-1.1	2.8	5.6	6.2	-1.7	5.1	6.8
Finland	4.6	-23.5	-18.6	-18.0	-4.6	26.7	5.8	8.0	13.5	0.7	6.8	9.4	-7.2	-7.6	3.3	3.7	4.4	3.6	4.7	4.0
France	4.2	-1.0	-2.6	-8.0	0.7	3.4	-0.2	1.0	10.2	9.2	9.7	3.1	-3.7	-1.6	3.9	3.3	3.9	4.4	3.2	4.0
Germany	1.7	6.0	-1.0	-9.2	1.0	1.2	-0.4	2.5	3.7	4.6	7.9	-3.3	-7.1	-0.6	-1.0	1.8	5.6	-1.2	3.2	6.5
Greece	-0.5	5.2	0.7	1.1	0.9	2.9	14.7	5.4	12.0	16.7	9.6	8.5	6.8	16.2	7.9	8.0	8.3	..	..	..
Iceland	0.2	4.2	-17.8	-25.4	1.8	11.9	52.0	19.2	45.6	-5.1	14.9	-15.1	-22.6	25.9	28.4	25.4	13.0	21.8	17.5	11.8
Ireland	2.3	-11.6	-3.1	-5.4	7.8	18.2	18.4	20.1	21.7	15.8	5.3	-7.3	1.3	2.6	4.8	7.4	5.2	..	..	..
Italy	2.4	0.1	-2.3	-14.3	5.1	10.7	3.5	3.7	4.0	6.1	8.8	1.0	0.0	-5.0	4.4	5.9	4.9	7.3	6.3	3.9
Japan	7.8	4.3	-7.1	-10.3	-5.7	2.7	4.7	11.3	-2.0	-4.0	9.6	1.1	-7.2	9.6	9.0	3.4	4.0	3.4	4.2	3.7
Korea	11.6	13.5	0.1	5.1	15.1	14.1	8.0	-3.6	-29.2	13.8	18.9	-4.5	5.4	3.1	3.3	5.0	4.2	2.9	4.9	3.9
Mexico	0.6	22.6	22.8	-5.6	-0.4	-38.9	45.8	34.0	18.3	8.8	10.0	-4.3	-3.7	-3.5	7.0	6.2	6.3	12.3	6.2	6.3
Netherlands	3.9	2.0	-3.2	-5.1	-0.4	5.5	7.0	9.7	5.2	9.9	1.0	-2.7	-6.4	-3.4	0.0	0.2	3.4	-2.9	2.1	3.7
New Zealand	4.9	-18.9	8.2	23.1	17.0	15.0	7.3	-6.7	-3.3	8.0	19.0	-0.4	6.0	13.4	17.2	7.5	4.6	15.3	5.7	4.1
Norway	-0.4	-3.3	-0.7	12.5	2.7	2.1	13.5	15.8	15.3	-8.6	-4.1	-4.1	-4.5	-6.5	4.8	5.4	2.5	16.4	8.6	-1.1
Spain	4.8	3.7	-1.0	-13.5	3.5	12.4	3.6	6.4	9.1	9.6	7.8	3.4	-1.3	3.3	3.1	4.4	4.8	3.3	4.4	4.9
Sweden	5.4	-16.1	-15.9	-9.5	22.2	23.2	8.0	4.8	9.5	8.5	8.2	-2.9	-7.0	-2.5	0.5	9.0	6.4	3.1	9.1	4.9
Switzerland	..	-2.0	-11.1	-4.4	4.9	8.5	1.3	3.1	9.4	1.3	4.9	-2.1	-2.2	-1.7	6.0	5.2	4.8	..	..	..
United Kingdom	7.6	-4.6	-3.0	-7.0	4.5	9.7	10.8	11.9	21.9	2.2	4.8	1.8	0.9	-1.1	6.0	3.8	3.3	5.4	3.3	3.2
United States	3.2	-5.4	3.2	8.7	9.2	10.5	9.3	12.1	11.1	9.2	8.7	-4.2	-8.9	3.3	10.2	9.9	9.8	9.9	9.2	9.6
Euro area	3.0	1.4	-2.1	-9.6	1.7	4.7	1.9	4.5	6.7	6.9	7.8	0.4	-3.7	-1.0	2.4	3.7	4.9	2.3	4.4	4.9
Total OECD	4.3	-0.8	-0.2	-1.2	4.9	6.1	7.7	10.2	7.5	6.2	8.3	-1.5	-5.2	2.3	6.9	6.4	6.7	6.1	6.5	6.5

Note: The adoption of new national account systems, SNA93 or ESA95, has been proceeding at an uneven pace among OECD member countries, both with respect to variables and the time period covered. As a consequence, there are breaks in many national series. Moreover, some countries are using chain-weighted price indices to calculate real GDP and expenditures components. Some countries, United States, Canada and France use hedonic price indices to deflate current-price values of investment in certain information and communication technology products such as computers. See Table "National Account Reporting Systems and Base-years" at the beginning of the Statistical Annex. National account data do not always have a sectoral breakdown of investment expenditures, and for some countries data are estimated by the OECD. See also *OECD Economic Outlook* Sources and Methods, *(http://www.oecd.org/eco/sources-and-methods)*. Working-day adjusted -- see note to Table on Real GDP.

Source: OECD Economic Outlook 76 database.

Annex Table 7. **Real gross private residential fixed capital formation**

Percentage change from previous year

	Average 1980-90	1991	1992	1993	1994	1995	1996	1997	1998	1999	2000	2001	2002	2003	2004	2005	2006	Fourth quarter 2004	2005	2006
Australia	0.0	-5.7	11.4	12.8	12.1	-7.6	-10.6	15.3	14.9	5.2	3.3	-10.0	24.4	7.5	7.6	-0.9	-1.8	3.9	-2.3	-1.1
Austria	0.2	8.9	9.6	3.7	7.6	10.0	2.6	-1.6	-2.4	-2.7	-4.5	-6.8	-4.7	-4.4	-0.2	1.4	2.5	..	..	..
Belgium	0.3	-9.0	4.9	1.8	5.5	4.3	-8.2	10.4	0.2	5.7	1.0	-3.4	-3.3	2.6	1.5	1.8	1.2	2.8	1.3	1.2
Canada	3.2	-14.4	6.9	-3.8	3.9	-14.9	9.7	8.2	-3.6	3.6	5.2	10.5	14.4	7.4	8.8	2.3	0.3	6.5	1.0	0.1
Denmark	-2.9	-10.1	0.1	6.3	8.9	8.5	5.8	7.1	4.2	-1.0	7.7	-5.3	10.5	5.2	7.5	2.2	3.2	6.0	4.1	2.3
Finland	1.7	-17.2	-18.3	-7.9	-6.7	-4.2	3.6	25.9	8.9	7.8	2.9	-9.4	0.9	8.5	9.1	6.1	5.3	7.2	5.5	5.0
France	-0.5	-6.9	-3.7	-5.2	4.4	2.1	0.5	0.9	3.8	7.1	3.4	0.8	0.7	0.7	3.6	4.1	3.5	5.0	3.6	3.3
Germany	2.8	7.4	10.8	4.7	12.0	0.4	-0.2	0.4	0.3	1.6	-2.6	-6.2	-5.9	-2.7	-2.7	-2.0	-0.2	-4.9	-0.9	0.1
Greece	-2.4	-0.3	-15.6	-10.5	-11.3	2.6	-1.2	6.6	8.8	3.8	-4.3	4.8	8.8	7.3	-4.4	-0.7	2.3	..	..	..
Iceland	-0.1	-3.7	-3.4	-5.2	4.1	-8.7	7.1	-9.3	1.3	0.3	15.2	17.8	5.2	13.3	10.4	7.0	3.6	14.6	1.7	3.7
Ireland	1.8	0.7	8.0	-11.9	24.0	14.5	18.3	15.8	7.2	12.3	6.5	0.8	6.0	15.2	14.9	2.0	-0.3	..	..	..
Italy	0.1	3.3	1.2	-1.5	-2.2	0.0	-1.6	-2.8	-0.7	1.9	5.5	1.3	4.5	2.3	3.7	4.5	3.1	6.2	4.0	2.6
Japan	3.3	-5.4	-5.9	1.1	7.2	-4.7	11.9	-12.0	-14.3	0.1	0.6	-5.4	-4.2	-0.8	2.0	1.0	-0.2	1.8	0.7	-0.8
Korea	13.9	10.8	-7.3	11.2	-1.7	8.3	2.8	-4.9	-13.4	-6.1	-9.3	12.9	11.4	4.1	2.7	0.0	2.6	-0.7	3.7	2.0
Mexico	2.8	7.6	2.9	5.2	4.0	-7.9	2.5	4.5	3.4	3.0	6.4	-10.6	-4.8	-12.5	12.4	4.4	5.2	10.3	5.0	5.2
Netherlands	0.1	-4.7	6.9	1.2	7.6	1.3	3.9	5.3	1.4	4.2	-0.3	2.0	-4.3	-4.3	1.5	1.1	3.2	0.4	6.0	2.0
New Zealand	4.7	-15.5	3.8	17.1	13.1	3.3	5.9	6.7	-13.5	7.8	1.3	-9.7	19.5	20.7	11.5	-0.3	-0.4	10.9	-1.8	0.0
Norway	-2.9	-15.2	-9.2	-0.8	24.5	10.6	2.9	12.1	7.8	3.0	5.6	8.2	-2.3	-5.2	12.4	8.9	4.0	16.9	6.1	2.8
Spain	2.1	-3.7	-4.0	-4.1	0.4	7.1	9.3	3.0	10.2	9.9	7.7	0.8	5.3	4.4	4.3	3.7	3.2	0.7	4.8	2.4
Sweden	2.6	-2.4	-11.6	-33.5	-34.1	-23.9	8.9	-11.5	-0.6	10.8	10.0	4.2	5.7	3.6	15.5	6.4	5.9	15.8	5.6	5.7
Switzerland	..	-6.6	-2.5	2.5	12.3	-2.0	-8.7	-0.1	2.8	-5.5	-2.7	-4.0	17.4	4.4	4.1	2.2	2.0	..	..	..
United Kingdom	0.8	-16.7	-1.7	9.2	1.8	-3.9	8.4	4.5	-4.7	0.5	-0.5	0.3	7.6	3.1	6.7	3.1	3.3	5.8	3.9	3.0
United States	2.2	-9.6	13.8	8.2	9.6	-3.2	8.0	1.9	7.6	6.0	0.8	0.4	4.8	8.8	9.8	0.6	0.4	6.6	-1.8	1.7
Euro area	0.9	0.0	2.9	0.1	6.3	1.7	0.6	1.3	1.9	3.8	1.1	-2.2	-0.9	0.5	1.8	1.9	2.1	1.2	2.4	1.9
Total OECD	2.6	-5.6	5.4	4.2	7.0	-2.4	5.6	0.4	1.3	3.7	1.0	-1.0	2.9	3.8	6.2	1.4	1.3	4.4	0.7	1.6

Note: The adoption of new national account systems, SNA93 or ESA95, has been proceeding at an uneven pace among OECD member countries, both with respect to variables and the time period covered. As a consequence, there are breaks in many national series. Moreover, some countries are using chain-weighted price indices to calculate real GDP and expenditures components. See Table "National Account Reporting Systems and Base-years" at the beginning of the Statistical Annex and *OECD Economic Outlook* Sources and Methods *(http://www.oecd.org/eco/sources-and-methods)*. Working-day adjusted -- see note to Table on Real GDP.

Source: OECD Economic Outlook 76 database.

Annex Table 8. **Real total domestic demand**

Percentage change from previous year

	Average 1980-90	1991	1992	1993	1994	1995	1996	1997	1998	1999	2000	2001	2002	2003	2004	2005	2006	Fourth quarter 2004	Fourth quarter 2005	Fourth quarter 2006
Australia	3.3	-2.0	2.4	2.9	4.9	4.3	3.1	3.2	6.9	5.2	2.1	1.3	6.2	6.1	4.9	3.8	3.7	4.0	3.7	3.7
Austria	2.2	3.5	2.2	-0.5	3.6	1.8	2.4	0.9	2.3	2.7	3.2	-0.3	-0.8	2.0	1.0	2.2	2.6	..	..	..
Belgium	1.7	1.8	1.8	-0.9	2.1	2.2	0.8	2.8	3.2	2.5	3.6	0.2	0.6	1.6	2.4	2.2	2.7	0.5	3.8	2.2
Canada	2.9	-1.9	0.3	1.4	3.4	1.8	1.3	6.2	2.5	4.3	4.8	1.2	3.7	4.6	3.0	3.9	3.2	3.1	3.7	3.0
Czech Republic	..	..	..	..	6.7	8.3	7.0	-0.9	-1.8	0.9	3.8	3.6	2.8	4.2	4.5	3.7	3.6	..	..	..
Denmark	1.2	-0.1	0.9	-0.3	7.0	4.2	2.2	4.9	4.0	0.1	2.4	1.0	1.9	0.3	3.1	3.1	2.8	2.8	2.7	2.9
Finland	3.2	-8.4	-6.1	-5.8	3.7	4.3	2.0	6.2	5.4	1.4	3.7	1.6	1.3	2.2	3.7	1.8	2.5	3.8	2.0	2.5
France	2.4	0.5	0.6	-1.7	1.9	1.8	0.7	0.7	4.2	3.7	4.5	2.0	1.5	1.4	3.2	2.5	2.3	3.4	2.3	2.4
Germany	1.9	4.4	2.4	-1.1	2.3	1.7	0.3	0.6	2.2	2.7	2.1	-0.6	-1.9	0.5	0.3	0.9	1.8	0.3	1.0	2.1
Greece	1.3	3.5	-0.5	-1.0	1.1	3.5	3.3	3.5	4.5	3.8	5.5	2.4	4.2	5.4	4.0	3.1	3.6	..	..	..
Hungary	..	..	..	..	1.9	-3.5	0.6	4.0	8.2	4.1	5.3	1.9	5.4	5.5	4.6	3.5	3.1	..	..	..
Iceland	2.6	3.5	-4.5	-3.6	2.3	2.3	6.8	5.4	13.4	4.2	6.9	-4.2	-2.8	7.8	8.5	7.4	5.5	8.6	6.6	5.1
Ireland	1.7	0.1	-0.5	1.1	5.6	7.4	8.0	9.9	9.3	8.5	9.0	3.7	3.5	3.4	3.9	4.4	4.0	..	..	..
Italy	2.4	2.1	0.8	-5.1	1.7	2.0	0.8	2.7	3.1	3.2	2.4	1.4	1.3	1.3	1.2	2.1	2.5	1.6	2.5	2.5
Japan	4.1	3.0	0.6	0.2	1.3	2.5	3.9	0.9	-1.5	0.2	2.4	1.2	-1.0	1.8	3.2	1.9	1.9	2.3	2.1	1.8
Korea	8.6	9.3	3.5	6.4	7.4	9.4	8.2	0.1	-17.4	13.9	8.2	3.3	7.0	0.1	1.3	2.9	3.4	2.2	3.4	3.7
Luxembourg	3.9	8.5	-4.3	5.6	2.4	1.1	5.0	6.5	7.2	6.3	4.8	4.5	-0.2	2.6	3.6	4.1	3.5	..	..	..
Mexico	1.2	5.7	6.0	1.1	5.6	-14.0	5.6	9.6	6.1	4.3	8.3	0.6	0.7	0.5	3.7	4.3	4.5	4.4	4.2	4.5
Netherlands	1.7	2.0	1.3	-1.7	2.3	3.6	2.8	3.9	4.8	4.3	2.6	1.8	0.5	-0.5	0.3	0.4	1.9	-0.2	1.2	2.0
New Zealand	2.6	-6.2	2.0	4.8	7.1	5.4	4.7	2.6	-0.1	6.0	1.9	2.4	5.1	5.7	7.3	2.5	2.6	6.4	1.4	3.3
Norway	1.6	1.5	2.1	3.2	4.3	4.8	3.9	6.6	5.7	0.3	2.4	0.8	2.4	0.6	4.8	3.7	2.6	6.0	4.0	1.8
Poland	..	..	..	..	4.1	7.2	8.5	9.8	6.2	4.8	2.8	-1.5	0.9	2.4	4.7	4.2	4.5	..	..	..
Portugal	3.2	6.1	3.4	-2.1	1.5	4.1	3.0	5.1	6.7	5.9	2.9	1.6	-0.4	-2.8	1.9	2.2	3.2	2.3	2.9	3.2
Slovak Republic	..	..	..	..	-4.5	9.9	18.2	3.7	7.2	-6.3	0.1	7.4	4.2	-2.2	4.3	5.0	3.6	..	..	..
Spain	3.4	3.0	1.0	-3.3	1.5	3.1	1.9	3.5	5.7	5.6	4.6	2.9	2.8	3.2	3.4	3.1	3.5	2.8	3.4	3.4
Sweden	2.2	-1.4	-1.3	-4.6	2.9	2.4	1.0	1.4	4.4	2.8	4.1	-0.1	0.9	1.3	1.2	3.5	2.8	1.5	3.4	2.6
Switzerland	2.7	-1.0	-2.3	-0.8	2.8	1.6	0.2	0.5	4.0	0.3	2.1	2.3	-0.8	0.2	2.0	2.2	2.0	..	..	..
Turkey	4.9	-0.6	5.6	14.2	-12.5	11.4	7.6	9.0	0.6	-3.7	9.8	-18.5	9.3	9.3	15.2	5.4	5.3	..	..	..
United Kingdom	3.0	-2.1	0.8	2.0	3.5	1.7	3.1	3.5	4.8	3.9	3.8	2.9	2.9	2.5	3.8	2.4	2.0	2.8	2.5	1.7
United States	3.4	-0.8	3.3	3.2	4.4	2.4	3.8	4.8	5.3	5.3	4.4	0.9	2.5	3.3	4.7	3.4	3.5	4.3	3.2	3.6
Euro area	2.3	2.3	1.2	-2.1	2.1	2.1	1.1	1.8	3.5	3.4	3.2	1.1	0.5	1.3	1.7	1.9	2.4	1.6	2.1	2.5
Total OECD	..	0.9	2.1	1.4	3.2	2.2	3.2	3.5	3.1	3.9	4.0	0.8	1.8	2.5	3.6	2.8	3.0	3.1	3.0	2.9

Note: The adoption of new national account systems, SNA93 or ESA95, has been proceeding at an uneven pace among OECD member countries, both with respect to variables and the time period covered. As a consequence, there are breaks in many national series. Moreover, some countries are using chain-weighted price indices to calculate real GDP and expenditures components. See Table "National Account Reporting Systems and Base-years" at the beginning of the Statistical Annex and *OECD Economic Outlook* Sources and Methods *(http://www.oecd.org/eco/sources-and-methods)*. Working-day adjusted -- see note to Table on Real GDP.

Source: OECD Economic Outlook 76 database.

Annex Table 9. **Foreign balance contributions to changes in real GDP**

As a per cent of real GDP in the previous period, seasonally adjusted at annual rates

	Average 1980-90	1991	1992	1993	1994	1995	1996	1997	1998	1999	2000	2001	2002	2003	2004	2005	2006	Fourth quarter 2004	2005	2006
Australia	-0.1	2.2	-0.2	0.7	-0.6	-0.4	0.5	0.3	-1.2	-0.9	0.6	1.3	-2.3	-2.8	-1.9	-0.3	-0.4	0.1	-0.7	-0.2
Austria	0.2	-0.6	0.0	0.8	-1.6	0.0	-0.1	1.2	1.2	0.3	0.3	0.9	1.9	-1.5	0.7	0.2	0.1	..	..	..
Belgium	0.4	0.0	-0.5	0.2	1.2	0.2	0.0	1.1	-1.0	0.8	0.2	0.6	0.3	-0.3	0.4	0.3	0.1	2.7	-0.4	0.7
Canada	-0.2	-0.2	0.7	1.0	1.6	1.1	0.4	-1.7	1.7	1.5	0.7	0.7	-0.1	-2.4	0.0	-0.7	-0.1	-0.6	-0.1	0.1
Czech Republic	..	..	..	..	-2.2	-2.6	-3.2	0.2	0.6	0.1	-0.7	-1.8	-2.2	-2.2	-2.8	-0.9	-0.7	..	..	..
Denmark	0.6	1.2	-0.2	0.3	-1.0	-1.2	0.4	-1.7	-1.4	2.6	0.5	0.6	-0.8	0.3	-0.5	-0.3	-0.1	-1.1	0.0	-0.3
Finland	-0.3	1.7	2.0	3.4	0.8	0.9	0.1	1.3	1.0	1.1	2.4	-0.5	1.6	-0.5	0.9	1.2	0.8	1.3	1.0	0.7
France	-0.1	0.5	0.7	0.7	0.0	0.1	0.4	1.2	-0.5	-0.4	-0.2	0.1	-0.4	-0.8	-1.2	-0.5	-0.1	-0.3	-0.1	0.0
Germany	0.6	-5.2	-0.6	0.0	0.1	0.1	0.5	0.9	-0.5	-0.8	1.0	1.6	1.9	-0.6	0.9	0.6	0.7	4.1	0.8	0.5
Greece	-0.6	-0.7	1.3	-0.6	0.9	-1.6	-1.1	-0.1	-1.6	-0.8	-1.7	1.7	-0.9	-1.3	-0.7	0.3	-0.5	..	..	..
Hungary	..	..	..	..	0.9	5.2	0.8	0.5	-3.4	0.0	-0.3	1.9	-2.0	-2.8	-0.9	-0.2	0.2	..	..	..
Iceland	0.1	-3.8	1.4	4.8	2.0	-2.0	-1.8	-0.8	-7.8	-0.4	-1.6	6.7	2.3	-3.6	-2.6	-2.8	-1.1	-4.1	-1.0	-0.5
Ireland	1.5	1.8	3.4	1.8	1.0	3.9	1.2	2.5	-0.1	4.3	2.2	3.0	3.1	1.1	1.8	1.9	1.8	..	..	..
Italy	-0.4	-0.8	-0.1	4.4	0.6	1.0	0.2	-0.6	-1.2	-1.4	0.8	0.3	-0.9	-0.9	0.1	-0.4	-0.4	-0.3	-0.5	-0.1
Japan	0.1	0.4	0.4	0.1	-0.2	-0.5	-0.4	1.0	0.3	-0.1	0.5	-0.7	0.7	0.7	0.9	0.3	0.4	0.4	0.4	0.5
Korea	-0.1	-2.6	0.6	0.5	-2.5	-1.4	-1.8	4.2	11.3	-2.9	0.3	0.5	-0.2	2.8	4.0	1.5	1.9	3.7	1.7	1.7
Luxembourg	0.7	0.8	5.9	0.2	2.0	1.0	-0.9	3.1	1.0	2.6	5.3	-2.0	2.5	0.6	1.1	1.3	1.6	..	..	..
Mexico	0.2	-1.6	-2.6	0.8	-1.4	8.5	-0.3	-2.5	-1.1	-0.5	-1.8	-0.7	0.0	0.7	0.4	-0.4	-0.4	-0.4	-0.3	-0.5
Netherlands	0.5	0.5	0.2	2.2	0.7	-0.3	0.4	0.2	-0.2	-0.1	1.1	-0.3	0.1	-0.4	1.1	0.9	0.5	1.3	0.3	0.5
New Zealand	0.1	3.9	-0.9	0.0	-0.5	-1.3	-1.1	0.5	0.2	-1.0	1.8	0.3	-0.5	-2.3	-2.8	-0.5	-0.2	1.0	-0.1	0.0
Norway	1.0	2.3	1.5	0.1	1.9	0.6	2.0	0.0	-2.2	1.8	1.0	2.0	-0.6	-0.1	-0.9	0.1	0.7	-0.7	0.5	1.1
Poland	..	..	..	..	0.4	0.1	-3.4	-1.9	-1.8	-1.1	0.7	2.8	0.5	1.3	0.6	0.0	0.0	..	..	..
Portugal	0.0	-1.8	-2.4	0.2	-0.6	-0.1	0.3	-1.5	-2.6	-2.6	0.1	-0.2	0.8	1.8	-0.5	-0.2	-0.6	0.5	-0.7	-0.6
Slovak Republic	..	..	..	..	10.9	-3.5	-11.6	0.6	-3.5	8.4	1.9	-3.7	..	6.4	0.8	-0.1	1.6	..	..	..
Spain	-0.4	-0.6	-0.1	2.4	0.9	-0.3	0.5	0.6	-1.3	-1.4	-0.3	-0.2	-0.6	-0.8	-0.9	-0.5	-0.6	-0.7	-0.4	-0.6
Sweden	0.0	0.9	0.2	2.9	0.8	1.5	0.3	1.0	-0.6	1.6	0.5	1.3	1.2	0.6	2.4	0.3	1.0	-0.7	0.7	1.3
Switzerland	0.0	0.2	2.2	0.5	-1.5	-1.2	0.2	1.3	-1.1	1.0	1.5	-1.2	1.1	-0.5	0.0	-0.2	0.1	..	..	..
Turkey	-0.4	1.8	-0.3	-6.2	8.6	-4.7	-0.6	-1.9	2.6	-0.9	-3.0	12.4	-0.9	-3.1	-5.0	0.4	0.4	..	..	..
United Kingdom	-0.3	0.9	-0.5	0.2	0.7	0.8	-0.2	-0.3	-1.6	-1.0	-0.1	-0.7	-1.2	-0.4	-0.7	0.1	0.2	-0.2	0.1	0.3
United States	0.0	0.6	0.0	-0.5	-0.4	0.1	-0.1	-0.3	-1.1	-1.0	-0.9	-0.2	-0.7	-0.5	-0.6	-0.3	-0.1	-0.3	-0.1	-0.1
Euro area	0.1	-1.5	0.0	1.2	0.3	0.2	0.4	0.6	-0.6	-0.6	0.5	0.6	0.4	-0.6	0.1	0.1	0.1	1.1	0.2	0.2
Total OECD	0.0	-0.1	0.0	0.2	0.0	0.3	-0.1	0.1	-0.3	-0.6	-0.1	0.3	-0.2	-0.4	-0.1	0.0	0.1	0.5	0.1	0.2

Note: The adoption of new national account systems, SNA93 or ESA95, has been proceeding at an uneven pace among OECD member countries, both with respect to variables and the time period covered. As a consequence there are breaks in many national series. Moreover, some countries are using chain-weighted price indices to calculate real GDP and expenditures components. See Table "National Account Reporting Systems and Base-years" at the beginning of the Statistical Annex and *OECD Economic Outlook* Sources and Methods *(http://www.oecd.org/eco/sources-and-methods)*. Working-day adjusted -- see note to Table on Real GDP.

Source: OECD Economic Outlook 76 database.

Annex Table 10. **Output gaps**

Deviations of actual GDP from potential GDP as a per cent of potential GDP

	1987	1988	1989	1990	1991	1992	1993	1994	1995	1996	1997	1998	1999	2000	2001	2002	2003	2004	2005	2006
Australia	-1.2	-0.7	-0.2	-2.4	-5.6	-5.5	-4.0	-2.0	-1.4	-1.0	-0.9	0.8	1.3	1.0	0.4	0.8	0.5	0.6	0.6	0.4
Austria	-2.5	-1.3	-0.2	1.5	2.1	1.4	-0.9	-0.6	-0.8	-0.2	0.0	1.2	2.0	2.7	1.0	-0.3	-1.8	-2.1	-1.8	-1.3
Belgium	-3.1	-0.6	0.5	1.4	0.4	-0.5	-3.0	-2.1	-1.6	-2.6	-0.8	-0.6	0.4	2.0	0.8	-0.5	-1.2	-0.7	-0.4	0.2
Canada	0.8	3.0	2.9	0.9	-3.1	-4.1	-3.9	-1.6	-1.5	-2.8	-2.4	-2.1	-0.3	1.3	-0.2	0.4	-0.2	-0.1	0.2	0.1
Denmark	2.3	1.4	-0.2	-0.8	-1.3	-2.4	-4.3	-1.4	-1.1	-0.6	0.2	0.4	0.7	1.4	1.0	0.0	-1.5	-1.0	-0.2	0.4
Finland	2.2	4.1	6.3	3.4	-4.4	-9.6	-12.2	-10.0	-8.5	-6.6	-2.8	-1.0	-0.6	1.7	-0.3	-0.8	-1.1	-0.2	0.3	1.2
France	-2.4	-0.5	1.5	2.1	1.1	0.7	-1.8	-1.5	-1.4	-2.4	-2.7	-1.4	-0.5	1.2	0.9	-0.2	-1.7	-1.6	-1.6	-1.4
Germany	-1.2	0.6	2.0	4.3	2.1	1.3	-2.0	-1.6	-1.1	-1.6	-1.5	-0.9	-0.2	1.6	1.1	-0.6	-2.2	-2.4	-2.5	-1.6
Greece	-3.4	-0.3	1.9	0.1	0.9	-0.4	-3.7	-3.7	-3.5	-3.6	-2.7	-1.7	-1.3	0.1	0.7	0.8	1.1	1.1	0.5	-0.1
Iceland	6.5	2.9	0.7	0.2	-1.9	-6.6	-6.9	-4.2	-5.5	-2.6	-1.1	-0.2	-0.4	0.8	-0.4	-3.2	-1.8	0.6	1.2	1.3
Ireland	-3.6	-2.0	0.0	3.6	0.2	-2.4	-5.1	-5.7	-3.7	-3.3	-0.8	-0.2	2.6	4.4	3.2	2.3	0.4	0.0	0.3	0.2
Italy	-1.8	0.0	0.6	0.2	-0.5	-1.4	-3.6	-2.7	-1.3	-1.6	-1.0	-0.6	-0.3	1.3	1.4	0.4	-0.6	-0.6	-0.4	0.1
Japan	-2.1	0.6	2.1	4.1	4.0	2.1	0.3	-0.3	-0.3	1.4	1.9	-0.8	-2.2	-1.0	-2.3	-4.1	-3.3	-1.0	-0.1	0.9
Netherlands	-1.8	-1.2	1.1	2.7	2.4	1.2	-0.9	-0.6	-0.2	0.4	1.4	2.7	3.5	4.2	2.7	0.4	-2.5	-3.2	-3.7	-3.2
New Zealand	0.9	-0.7	-0.8	-2.5	-5.5	-5.8	-2.8	0.3	1.4	2.1	1.0	-1.5	0.2	1.1	0.8	1.7	1.2	2.4	1.0	0.3
Norway [a]	1.3	-1.7	-4.9	-5.3	-4.8	-4.4	-3.7	-2.5	-1.7	-0.4	1.4	2.6	2.5	1.9	1.4	0.7	-1.2	-0.1	0.4	0.3
Portugal	-4.8	-0.6	2.5	3.3	4.5	2.5	-2.2	-3.5	-1.6	-0.5	0.7	2.3	2.9	3.0	1.5	-0.7	-3.7	-3.8	-3.3	-2.4
Spain	-0.6	1.6	2.8	3.3	2.6	0.6	-3.0	-3.0	-3.2	-3.9	-2.8	-1.4	-0.1	1.0	0.8	0.0	-0.5	-0.8	-0.9	-0.7
Sweden	1.5	1.6	1.3	-0.2	-2.9	-5.1	-7.7	-5.5	-3.4	-3.7	-2.7	-1.0	0.8	2.2	0.3	-0.3	-1.1	-0.1	0.6	1.2
Switzerland	-0.2	0.6	2.5	3.9	0.5	-1.3	-2.5	-2.4	-2.9	-3.3	-2.2	-0.3	-0.7	1.3	0.9	-0.1	-1.7	-1.1	-0.5	0.0
United Kingdom	1.3	3.7	3.6	1.8	-2.0	-3.7	-3.6	-1.6	-1.2	-1.1	-0.5	-0.3	-0.3	0.9	0.7	-0.1	-0.3	0.4	0.5	0.3
United States	-0.2	0.8	1.4	0.5	-2.4	-1.8	-2.0	-1.0	-1.7	-1.5	-0.7	-0.1	0.8	1.1	-1.3	-2.1	-1.9	-0.6	-0.3	-0.1
Euro area	-1.5	0.3	1.8	2.7	1.4	0.4	-2.5	-2.1	-1.5	-2.0	-1.5	-0.7	0.1	1.7	1.2	-0.1	-1.5	-1.6	-1.6	-1.1
Total OECD	-0.7	0.9	1.7	1.7	-0.5	-0.9	-2.1	-1.4	-1.4	-1.3	-0.7	-0.4	0.1	1.0	-0.4	-1.4	-1.7	-0.8	-0.6	-0.2

Note: Potential output for all countries except Portugal is calculated using the "production function method" described in Giorno et al, "Potential Output, Output Gaps, and Structural Budget Balances", *OECD Economic Studies,* No. 24, 1995/I. Using this methodology, two broad changes have been made to the calculation of potential output since the last *OECD Economic Outlook.* First, the "smoothing parameters" applied in the calculations have been standardised across the OECD countries. Second, as was previously the case for the major seven economies only, the calculations now incorporate trend working hours for other Member economies also, excepting Austria and Portugal where the data span is insufficient. Potential output for Portugal is calculated using a Hodrick-Prescott filter of actual output. See also *OECD Economic Outlook* Sources and Methods *(http://www.oecd.org/eco/sources-and-methods).* Working-day adjusted -- see note to Table on Real GDP.

a) Mainland Norway.

Source: OECD Economic Outlook 76 database.

Annex Table 11. **Compensation per employee in the business sector**

Percentage change from previous period

	Average 1978-1987	1988	1989	1990	1991	1992	1993	1994	1995	1996	1997	1998	1999	2000	2001	2002	2003	2004	2005	2006
Australia	8.7	6.5	8.1	7.6	2.8	4.3	2.6	2.3	2.7	5.6	4.0	3.6	2.8	2.8	4.1	3.9	3.4	4.0	4.1	3.9
Austria	6.2	4.2	4.5	5.2	6.0	5.5	4.3	3.7	3.9	1.0	2.9	1.8	1.5	2.7	3.5	2.2	2.3	2.1	2.4	2.7
Belgium	6.7	2.6	5.2	6.9	7.1	5.1	4.2	3.8	1.8	1.5	2.7	1.0	3.7	1.9	3.6	3.6	2.5	2.9	2.5	2.7
Canada	7.1	7.6	5.6	4.3	4.9	3.2	2.3	0.5	2.3	2.9	5.9	2.9	3.1	4.8	2.0	1.5	1.7	2.6	3.6	3.3
Czech Republic	..	..	..	..	..	..	..	..	..	18.1	4.3	9.5	4.5	6.4	6.9	2.3	7.6	9.4	7.0	6.8
Denmark	8.5	4.3	4.6	4.1	4.2	4.2	2.1	2.9	3.9	3.2	3.4	3.8	3.1	3.5	4.3	1.8	3.7	3.5	3.4	3.8
Finland	10.1	9.6	10.7	9.0	4.8	1.7	1.1	4.6	4.0	2.3	2.3	5.0	2.3	4.2	5.2	1.3	3.1	3.1	4.3	3.9
France	10.0	4.3	4.0	3.8	3.9	3.7	1.9	0.7	1.4	1.7	1.6	0.6	2.1	1.8	3.1	2.2	2.3	2.7	3.0	3.1
Germany	4.4	2.8	2.8	4.7	5.7	10.4	3.5	3.1	3.5	1.0	0.7	0.9	1.0	2.2	1.7	1.4	1.7	1.0	1.2	1.8
Greece	19.1	20.5	22.6	16.3	16.3	12.7	8.7	11.8	11.8	11.2	11.3	4.7	6.9	5.4	5.3	7.0	3.6	6.1	5.9	6.2
Hungary	..	..	..	..	..	..	..	..	23.6	21.5	18.7	12.7	2.2	17.5	14.7	10.7	8.1	9.3	6.8	6.0
Iceland	44.7	26.1	13.4	16.1	15.6	0.6	-3.7	3.7	4.9	8.1	5.7	9.7	9.1	8.5	6.6	7.2	3.9	5.1	7.9	6.2
Ireland	12.6	5.2	6.8	1.9	3.3	7.8	4.9	1.7	2.8	1.9	6.0	3.3	5.8	5.2	5.5	3.4	1.9	5.2	5.8	5.7
Italy	14.2	7.3	8.8	8.3	9.0	6.2	5.2	3.1	4.8	4.8	3.2	-0.8	2.5	2.9	3.0	2.4	3.3	2.5	3.1	3.2
Japan	4.4	3.0	3.8	3.7	4.6	0.8	0.6	1.4	1.0	0.2	1.5	-0.8	-1.2	0.3	-1.1	-2.3	-0.9	-0.3	0.2	0.6
Korea	16.3	17.5	10.0	16.3	16.2	11.2	12.1	11.3	15.4	11.0	3.1	2.4	1.6	3.4	6.6	4.8	3.9	2.6	3.9	5.7
Luxembourg	5.2	3.8	8.5	3.1	5.6	6.5	5.5	4.1	0.9	1.1	1.9	2.1	4.6	5.3	4.0	3.1	1.3	2.6	2.7	2.9
Mexico	..	..	..	..	..	20.6	11.4	9.9	4.8	21.2	18.7	19.5	13.5	11.5	9.3	5.2	5.0	4.7	4.6	4.4
Netherlands	3.4	1.1	0.5	2.9	4.1	4.1	2.7	1.9	0.3	1.6	2.0	3.9	3.2	4.5	4.8	5.6	3.2	1.8	1.4	1.6
New Zealand	..	11.8	7.1	1.9	0.9	2.3	3.2	2.4	0.9	2.4	1.6	1.9	1.2	3.2	0.9	2.4	2.7	3.2	3.7	3.9
Norway	8.7	8.6	4.5	4.0	6.4	4.4	2.7	3.1	3.2	2.6	2.5	7.6	6.2	4.7	7.2	4.1	4.1	3.7	4.1	4.7
Poland	..	..	..	..	..	..	..	..	..	29.6	20.7	14.8	14.7	9.8	12.6	0.7	-1.8	2.8	4.8	5.0
Portugal	19.0	9.9	12.8	17.4	18.6	16.0	7.1	5.9	6.7	9.0	3.8	4.3	4.0	6.9	5.2	3.8	3.1	2.7	2.7	2.8
Spain	14.7	7.2	7.3	10.0	10.3	10.4	8.3	4.0	3.5	5.5	3.5	2.5	2.5	3.6	4.4	4.6	4.8	4.5	4.2	3.9
Sweden	9.2	8.1	12.3	9.7	6.2	3.2	8.5	7.2	2.4	6.4	4.6	3.6	0.9	7.6	4.5	2.2	2.1	2.8	3.8	4.2
Switzerland	4.7	3.6	4.6	5.4	6.6	4.3	3.0	3.1	2.3	0.3	3.1	0.2	2.1	2.7	3.3	0.8	0.8	1.1	1.5	1.8
Turkey	..	83.2	86.2	81.9	86.1	57.7	73.0	49.8	62.5	93.8	102.4	68.2	74.1	48.9	40.6	33.4	27.2	20.3	18.2	13.5
United Kingdom	10.3	6.6	9.1	10.0	8.1	4.0	2.3	2.6	2.4	2.4	4.0	6.1	5.1	5.5	5.5	3.3	4.1	5.6	4.7	4.8
United States	6.5	4.7	3.2	4.6	4.0	6.2	2.0	1.8	2.3	3.0	4.0	5.4	4.5	6.8	2.6	3.0	3.7	4.1	4.0	4.1
Euro area	7.5	4.6	4.9	6.1	6.6	8.2	5.3	3.2	3.8	1.7	1.6	1.0	1.4	2.3	2.6	2.4	2.2	1.9	2.2	2.6
Total OECD	7.2	6.6	6.1	7.1	7.0	7.2	4.7	3.6	4.2	5.2	5.5	4.9	4.4	5.4	3.6	2.8	3.0	3.2	3.4	3.5
Memorandum item																				
OECD *less* high inflation countries [a]	7.2	5.2	4.6	5.7	5.5	5.9	3.2	2.5	3.0	2.6	3.0	3.1	2.7	4.2	2.5	2.2	2.6	2.9	3.0	3.3

Note: The business sector is in the OECD terminology defined as total economy less the public sector. Hence business sector employees are defined as total employees less public sector employees. See also *OECD Economic Outlook* Sources and Methods *(http://www.oecd.org/eco/sources-and-methods).*

a) High inflation countries are defined as countries which have had 10 per cent or more inflation in terms of the GDP deflator on average during the last 10 years based on historical data. Consequently, Hungary, Mexico, Poland and Turkey are excluded from the aggregate.

Source: OECD Economic Outlook 76 database.

Annex Table 12. **Labour productivity in the business sector**

Percentage change from previous period

	Average 1978-1987	1988	1989	1990	1991	1992	1993	1994	1995	1996	1997	1998	1999	2000	2001	2002	2003	2004	2005	2006
Australia	1.7	0.8	-0.3	-0.2	1.6	3.5	4.1	1.6	-0.4	3.0	3.2	4.0	2.8	0.6	1.7	1.6	0.9	2.1	2.0	1.8
Austria	2.2	3.3	2.6	3.5	2.5	2.5	1.1	3.3	2.3	3.7	2.1	2.8	2.2	3.0	0.2	1.5	1.0	1.5	1.8	1.8
Belgium	2.4	3.1	1.8	2.0	1.2	1.4	-0.2	3.8	1.8	0.4	3.2	0.4	2.1	1.9	-0.9	1.6	1.4	2.4	1.8	1.7
Canada	0.8	2.0	0.5	-0.5	-0.2	2.1	1.8	3.1	0.8	0.7	1.8	1.5	3.0	2.9	0.7	1.5	0.1	1.4	2.2	2.3
Czech Republic	..	..	..	..	..	..	..	..	..	4.3	-0.8	-0.2	3.7	5.3	2.8	0.4	3.4	4.9	4.7	4.4
Denmark	1.1	-0.4	2.0	0.5	2.1	1.3	3.2	7.7	0.5	1.8	1.7	2.8	2.1	3.1	1.7	0.9	2.1	2.9	2.6	2.4
Finland	3.4	4.5	4.9	0.0	-0.6	4.1	6.2	7.0	1.8	2.9	3.6	3.1	0.5	3.5	-0.6	1.8	2.6	3.8	2.7	2.7
France	2.5	3.8	3.0	2.0	1.1	2.5	0.7	2.1	1.1	0.6	1.5	2.2	1.2	1.5	0.2	0.4	0.8	2.8	1.8	1.6
Germany	1.1	2.6	2.3	2.8	2.4	4.6	0.1	2.8	1.6	1.1	1.6	0.8	0.8	1.0	0.3	0.7	0.9	1.0	1.1	1.3
Greece	0.0	2.8	3.9	-1.5	6.4	-0.9	-2.7	0.1	1.4	3.1	4.8	-0.9	3.8	5.2	5.2	4.0	3.4	2.5	2.4	2.5
Hungary	..	..	..	..	..	..	..	..	-2.4	1.4	4.7	9.2	0.5	3.5	3.8	4.4	1.6	3.0	2.8	2.8
Iceland	1.8	3.4	2.3	1.7	-0.2	-3.6	1.1	3.8	-3.5	6.0	5.3	1.3	0.4	4.1	0.6	1.2	4.6	6.8	3.4	2.1
Ireland	3.2	6.4	6.8	4.5	2.5	3.2	1.3	2.7	5.2	4.4	7.6	0.2	5.1	5.4	3.2	4.8	2.1	3.5	4.1	3.7
Italy	2.3	3.4	3.0	1.0	0.7	1.6	2.5	3.9	3.3	0.7	1.7	0.7	1.1	1.5	0.1	-1.0	-0.2	0.3	0.6	1.4
Japan	2.6	5.3	3.5	3.6	1.6	-0.1	0.0	1.1	1.7	2.9	0.9	-0.8	0.6	3.2	0.8	0.9	2.9	4.0	2.0	2.1
Korea	5.5	8.0	2.0	6.3	6.7	3.8	4.5	5.4	6.4	5.0	3.0	-1.1	8.3	4.4	1.9	4.2	3.3	3.3	3.1	3.3
Luxembourg	..	..	..	..	4.8	-0.9	2.6	1.3	-1.4	0.5	5.5	2.7	3.0	3.4	-4.3	-0.8	1.0	2.1	2.1	2.0
Mexico	..	..	..	..	..	-0.1	-1.9	0.9	-8.1	1.3	0.3	2.2	2.7	4.7	-0.3	-2.0	0.1	2.6	1.3	1.7
Netherlands	0.6	1.3	2.5	1.2	0.6	0.2	0.4	2.6	0.8	0.8	0.7	1.9	1.5	1.4	-0.7	0.2	-0.6	2.6	0.7	1.1
New Zealand	1.1	3.3	4.5	-0.9	-0.5	0.3	3.4	1.5	-0.8	0.5	1.5	0.5	3.0	2.0	-0.1	1.9	1.3	2.5	1.3	1.9
Norway	1.5	-0.4	2.0	3.0	4.9	3.5	4.0	2.3	1.1	1.7	2.0	2.3	3.3	2.2	2.3	1.7	1.8	4.3	2.6	2.3
Poland	..	..	..	..	..	..	..	..	..	5.6	6.4	4.1	9.6	6.4	3.7	5.2	5.6	5.4	3.9	4.1
Portugal	1.7	5.3	4.8	1.9	1.5	0.5	-0.2	1.2	5.7	3.6	2.0	2.5	2.8	1.3	-0.4	-0.2	-1.2	1.6	1.5	1.5
Spain	2.7	1.8	1.4	0.0	1.6	2.8	2.1	3.2	1.0	1.5	1.1	0.1	0.6	0.8	0.4	0.7	1.0	0.7	0.8	1.0
Sweden	2.2	1.5	1.4	0.1	0.5	4.2	5.9	6.1	2.8	2.5	4.7	2.4	2.4	1.2	-1.0	2.4	2.5	4.5	1.8	1.9
Switzerland	0.3	0.6	1.6	0.6	-3.0	0.2	0.8	1.8	0.5	0.5	2.1	1.7	0.1	2.5	-0.7	-0.2	-0.3	1.8	1.1	0.9
United Kingdom	2.6	0.2	-0.5	0.3	1.7	2.6	3.0	3.4	1.2	1.4	1.1	2.0	1.7	2.8	1.7	1.1	1.7	2.7	2.4	2.5
United States	1.1	1.0	1.2	0.7	0.7	3.9	0.9	1.3	0.3	2.0	2.3	2.1	2.8	2.3	1.0	3.7	3.4	3.7	2.0	2.2
Euro area	2.0	3.0	2.8	1.8	1.6	2.6	1.1	3.0	1.8	1.0	1.7	0.9	0.8	1.4	0.2	0.5	0.4	1.2	1.1	1.3
Total OECD	1.8	2.3	1.8	1.6	1.2	2.7	1.4	1.9	0.9	1.9	2.0	1.4	2.0	2.5	0.7	2.1	2.2	3.0	1.9	2.1
Memorandum item																				
OECD *less* high inflation countries[a]	1.8	2.4	1.9	1.5	1.3	2.8	1.2	2.2	1.2	1.8	1.9	1.3	2.0	2.2	0.8	2.0	2.1	2.2	2.2	2.2

Note: The business sector is in the OECD terminology defined as total economy less the public sector. Hence business sector employees are defined as total employees less public sector employees. See also *OECD Economic Outlook* Sources and Methods *(http://www.oecd.org/eco/sources-and-methods)*.

a) High inflation countries are defined as countries which have had 10 per cent or more inflation in terms of the GDP deflator on average during the last 10 years based on historical data. Consequently, Hungary, Mexico, Poland and Turkey are excluded from the aggregate.

Source: OECD Economic Outlook 76 database.

Annex Table 13. **Unemployment rates: commonly used definitions**

Per cent of labour force

	2001 Unemployment thousands	1991	1992	1993	1994	1995	1996	1997	1998	1999	2000	2001	2002	2003	2004	2005	2006	Fourth quarter 2004	Fourth quarter 2005	Fourth quarter 2006
Australia	667	9.1	10.4	10.7	9.4	8.3	8.2	8.3	7.8	6.9	6.3	6.8	6.4	6.0	5.6	5.5	5.5	5.5	5.4	5.5
Austria	205	4.5	4.7	5.4	5.3	5.3	5.6	5.7	5.7	5.3	4.7	4.8	5.5	5.7	5.8	5.8	5.5	..	..	..
Belgium	300	6.4	7.1	8.6	9.8	9.7	9.5	9.2	9.3	8.6	6.9	6.7	7.3	7.9	7.7	7.6	7.3	7.7	7.6	7.2
Canada	1 172	10.3	11.2	11.4	10.3	9.4	9.6	9.1	8.3	7.6	6.8	7.2	7.6	7.6	7.2	7.1	7.2	7.1	7.1	7.2
Czech Republic	418	..	..	4.3	4.3	4.1	3.9	4.8	6.5	8.8	8.9	8.2	7.3	7.8	8.4	8.3	8.2	..	..	..
Denmark	124	7.9	8.6	9.6	7.7	6.8	6.3	5.3	4.9	4.8	4.4	4.3	4.6	5.6	5.8	5.3	4.9	5.6	5.2	4.7
Finland	238	6.6	11.7	16.4	16.6	15.4	14.6	12.7	11.4	10.3	9.8	9.1	9.1	9.1	8.9	8.7	8.2	8.8	8.5	7.9
France	2 322	9.4	10.3	11.6	12.0	11.4	12.0	12.1	11.5	10.7	9.4	8.7	9.0	9.7	9.8	9.7	9.2	9.8	9.5	9.0
Germany	3 109	5.3	6.2	7.5	8.0	7.7	8.4	9.2	8.7	8.0	7.3	7.4	8.2	9.1	9.2	9.3	8.9	9.3	9.2	8.7
Greece	462	7.7	8.7	9.7	9.6	9.1 |	9.8	9.8	11.1	11.9	11.2	10.5	10.2	9.5	9.1	8.9	8.7	..	..	..
Hungary	234	..	..	12.1	11.0	10.4	10.1	8.9	7.9	7.1	6.5	5.8	5.9	5.9	5.9	5.7	5.6	..	..	..
Iceland	4	2.6	4.3	5.3	5.3	4.7	3.7	3.9	2.7	2.0	2.3	2.3	3.3	3.4	3.1	2.9	2.6	2.6	1.8	1.5
Ireland	70	14.1	14.7	15.4	14.4	11.9	11.4	10.1	7.6	5.6	4.3	3.9	4.4	4.6	4.4	4.1	4.0	..	..	..
Italy	2 267	8.6	8.8	10.2	11.2	11.7	11.7	11.8	11.9	11.5	10.7	9.6	9.1	8.8	8.1	7.5	7.3	7.9	7.4	7.2
Japan	3 396	2.1	2.2	2.5	2.9	3.2	3.4	3.4	4.1	4.7	4.7	5.0	5.4	5.3	4.8	4.5	4.2	4.8	4.4	4.0
Korea	845	2.4	2.5	2.9	2.5	2.1	2.0	2.6	7.0	6.3	4.1	3.8	3.1	3.4	3.5	3.5	3.4	3.6	3.5	3.3
Luxembourg	5	1.4	1.6	2.1	2.7	3.0	3.3	3.6	3.1	2.9	2.6	2.6	3.0	3.8	4.2	4.2	4.2	4.2	4.2	4.2
Mexico[a]	837	3.0	3.1	3.2	3.5	5.8	4.3	3.4	2.9	2.1	2.2	2.1	2.4	2.5	2.4	2.3	2.3	2.3	2.3	2.3
Netherlands	215	5.2	5.2	6.3	7.2	6.8	6.3	5.4	4.2	3.5	3.0	2.5	2.9	4.1	4.9	5.2	5.0	4.9	5.3	4.9
New Zealand	104	10.3	10.3	9.5	8.1	6.2	6.1	6.6	7.4	6.8	6.0	5.3	5.2	4.6	4.1	4.2	4.2	4.0	4.2	4.2
Norway	84	5.5	5.9	6.0	5.4	4.9	4.8	4.0	3.2	3.2	3.4	3.6	3.9	4.5	4.4	4.2	4.1	4.4	4.2	4.1
Poland	3 170	..	..	14.0	14.4	13.3	12.3	11.2	10.6	13.9	16.1	18.2	19.9	19.6	19.1	18.4	17.6	..	..	..
Portugal	214	4.3 |	4.1	5.5	6.8	7.2	7.3	6.7	5.0	4.4	4.0	4.0	5.0	6.3	6.5	6.6	6.1	6.7	6.5	5.7
Slovak Republic	508	..	..	..	13.7	13.1	11.3	11.9	12.6	16.4	18.8	19.3	18.6	17.5	18.2	17.5	16.5	..	..	..
Spain[b]	1 869	11.8	13.0	16.6	18.4	18.1	17.5	16.6	15.0	12.8	11.0	10.5	11.4	11.3	10.9	10.7	10.4	10.9	10.6	10.4
Sweden	176	3.0	5.3	8.2	8.0	7.7	8.0	8.0	6.5	5.6	4.7	4.0	4.0	4.9	5.6	4.9	4.3	5.5	4.5	4.2
Switzerland	107	1.9	2.9	3.8	3.7	3.3	3.8	4.0	3.4	2.9	2.5	2.5	3.1	4.0	4.0	3.6	2.8	..	..	..
Turkey[c]	1 967	8.0	8.3	8.7	8.4	7.5	6.5	6.7	6.7	7.5	6.3	8.2	10.1	10.3	9.5	10.0	10.5	..	..	..
United Kingdom	1 488	8.0	9.9	10.4	9.5	8.6	8.1	7.0	6.2	6.0	5.5	5.1	5.2	5.0	4.7	4.7	5.0	4.7	4.8	5.2
United States	6 834	6.8	7.5	6.9 |	6.1	5.6	5.4	4.9	4.5	4.2	4.0	4.8	5.8	6.0	5.5	5.3	5.1	5.4	5.3	5.0
Euro area	11 275	7.5	8.3	9.9	10.6	10.4	10.7	10.7	10.2	9.4	8.4	8.0	8.4	8.8	8.8	8.6	8.3	8.8	8.6	8.2
Total OECD	33 409	6.1	6.8	7.5	7.4	7.1	7.0	6.7	6.6	6.4	5.9	6.2	6.7	6.9	6.6	6.5	6.3	6.5	6.4	6.2

Note: Labour market data are subject to differences in definitions across countries and to many series breaks, though the latter are often of a minor nature. For information about definitions, sources, data coverage, break in series and rebasings, see *OECD Economic Outlook* Sources and Methods *(http://www.oecd.org/eco/sources-and-methods).*

a) Based on National Employment Survey. Data not comparable with previous issues of the OECD Economic Outlook; see *OECD Economic Outlook* Sources and Methods.

b) Spanish data on unemployment are revised since 1976 using the methodology to be applied by the LFS as from 2002. Revisions are OECD calculations based on information from INE in Spain.

c) The figures incorporate important revisions to Turkish data; see *OECD Economic Outlook* Sources and Methods.

Source: OECD Economic Outlook 76 database.

Annex Table 14. **Standardised unemployment rates**[a]

Per cent of civilian labour force

	1985	1986	1987	1988	1989	1990	1991	1992	1993	1994	1995	1996	1997	1998	1999	2000	2001	2002	2003
Australia	8.3	7.9	7.9	7.0	6.0	6.7	9.3	10.5	10.6	9.5	8.2	8.2	8.3	7.7	6.9	6.3	6.8	6.4	6.1
Austria	..	..	..	..	..	..	..	..	4.0	3.8	3.9	4.4	4.4	4.5	4.0	3.7	3.6	4.2	4.3
Belgium	10.1	10.0	9.8	8.8	7.4	6.6	6.4	7.1	8.6	9.8	9.7	9.5	9.2	9.3	8.6	6.9	6.7	7.3	7.9
Canada	10.7	9.6	8.8	7.8	7.5	8.1	10.3	11.2	11.4	10.4	9.4	9.6	9.1	8.3	7.6	6.8	7.2	7.7	7.6
Czech Republic	..	..	..	..	..	..	..	..	4.4	4.3	4.1	3.9	4.8	6.3	8.6	8.6	8.0	7.3	7.8
Denmark	6.6	5.0	5.0	5.7	6.8	7.2	7.9	8.6	9.6	7.7	6.8	6.3	5.3	4.9	4.8	4.4	4.3	4.6	5.6
Finland	6.0	6.7	4.9	4.2	3.1	3.2	6.7	11.6	16.4	16.8	15.2	14.6	12.7	11.4	10.2	9.7	9.1	9.1	9.0
France	9.7	9.8	9.9	9.4	8.9	8.5	9.0	9.9	11.1	11.7	11.1	11.6	11.5	11.1	10.5	9.1	8.4	8.9	9.4
Germany[b]	7.2	6.5	6.3	6.2	5.6	4.8	4.2	6.4	7.7	8.2	8.0	8.7	9.7	9.1	8.4	7.8	7.8	8.7	9.6
Greece	7.0	6.6	6.6	6.9	6.7	6.3	6.9	7.8	8.6	8.9	9.1	9.7	9.6	11.0	11.8	11.0	10.4	10.0	9.3
Hungary	..	..	..	..	..	..	..	9.9	12.1	11.0	10.4	9.6	9.0	8.4	6.9	6.3	5.6	5.6	5.7
Ireland	16.8	16.8	16.6	16.2	14.7	13.4	14.7	15.4	15.6	14.3	12.3	11.7	9.9	7.5	5.6	4.3	3.9	4.3	4.6
Italy	8.1	8.9	9.6	9.7	9.7	8.9	8.5	8.7	10.1	11.0	11.5	11.5	11.6	11.7	11.3	10.4	9.4	9.0	8.6
Japan	2.6	2.8	2.8	2.5	2.3	2.1	2.1	2.2	2.5	2.9	3.1	3.4	3.4	4.1	4.7	4.7	5.0	5.4	5.3
Korea	..	..	..	..	..	..	..	..	..	..	..	..	..	..	..	4.4	4.0	3.3	3.6
Luxembourg	2.9	2.6	2.5	2.0	1.8	1.6	1.6	2.1	2.6	3.2	2.9	2.9	2.7	2.7	2.4	2.3	2.1	2.8	3.7
Netherlands	7.9	7.8	7.7	7.2	6.6	5.9	5.5	5.3	6.2	6.8	6.6	6.0	4.9	3.8	3.2	2.9	2.5	2.7	3.8
New Zealand	4.2	4.1	4.1	5.6	7.1	7.8	10.3	10.4	9.5	8.1	6.3	6.1	6.6	7.4	6.8	6.0	5.3	5.2	4.6
Norway	2.6	2.0	2.1	3.2	5.4	5.8	6.0	6.6	6.6	6.0	5.5	4.8	4.0	3.2	3.2	3.4	3.6	3.9	4.5
Poland	..	..	..	..	..	..	..	..	14.0	14.4	13.3	12.3	10.9	10.2	13.4	16.4	18.5	19.8	19.2
Portugal	9.2	8.8	7.2	5.8	5.2	4.8	4.2	4.3	5.6	6.9	7.3	7.3	6.8	5.2	4.5	4.1	4.0	5.0	6.2
Slovak Republic	..	..	..	..	..	..	..	..	..	13.7	13.1	11.3	11.9	12.6	16.8	18.7	19.4	18.7	17.5
Spain	17.7	17.4	16.7	15.8	13.9	13.1	13.2	14.9	18.6	19.8	18.8	18.1	17.0	15.2	12.8	11.3	10.6	11.3	11.3
Sweden	2.9	2.7	2.2	1.8	1.5	1.7	3.1	5.6	9.0	9.4	8.8	9.6	9.9	8.2	6.7	5.6	4.9	4.9	5.6
Switzerland	..	..	..	..	..	..	1.9	3.0	3.9	3.9	3.5	3.9	4.2	3.6	3.0	2.7	2.6	3.2	4.1
United Kingdom	11.2	11.2	10.3	8.5	7.1	6.9	8.6	9.8	10.0	9.2	8.5	8.0	6.9	6.2	5.9	5.4	5.0	5.1	5.0
United States	7.2	7.0	6.2	5.5	5.3	5.6	6.8	7.5	6.9	6.1	5.6	5.4	4.9	4.5	4.2	4.0	4.7	5.8	6.0
Euro area	..	..	..	..	..	..	7.9	8.6	10.1	10.8	10.6	10.8	10.8	10.2	9.4	8.4	8.0	8.4	8.9
Total OECD	..	..	..	..	..	..	..	..	..	7.7	7.3	7.2	7.0	6.9	6.7	6.3	6.5	7.0	7.1

Note: In so far as possible, the data have been adjusted to ensure comparability over time and to conform to the guidelines of the International Labour Office. All series are benchmarked to labour-force-survey-based estimates. In countries with annual surveys, monthly estimates are obtained by interpolation/extrapolation and by incorporating trends in administrative data, where available. The annual figures are then calculated by averaging the monthly estimates (for both unemployed and the labour force). For countries with monthly or quarterly surveys, the annual estimates are obtained by averaging the monthly or quarterly estimates, respectively. For several countries, the adjustment procedure used is similar to that of the Bureau of Labor Statistics, U.S. Department of Labor. For EU countries, the procedures are similar to those used in deriving the Comparable Unemployment Rates (CURs) of the Statistical Office of the European Communities. Minor differences may appear mainly because of various methods of calculating and applying adjustment factors, and because EU estimates are based on the civilian labour force.

a) See technical notes in OECD *Quarterly Labour Force Statistics.*

b) Prior to 1993 data refers to Western Germany.

Source: OECD, *Quarterly Labour Force Statistics.*

Annex Table 15. **Labour force, employment and unemployment**

Millions

	1988	1989	1990	1991	1992	1993	1994	1995	1996	1997	1998	1999	2000	2001	2002	2003	2004	2005	2006
Labour force																			
Major seven countries	303.7	307.8	312.0	322.7	325.0	326.2	328.6	330.3	333.2	337.3	339.9	342.7	347.1	349.1	350.9	353.2	354.8	357.6	360.3
Total of smaller countries[a]	129.3	132.2	134.5	137.9	139.9	167.2	172.6	176.3	178.6	181.8	184.1	186.1	187.8	189.9	192.6	193.8	195.5	198.3	201.2
Euro area	120.1	121.0	122.5	131.9	131.8	131.7	132.5	133.0	134.0	135.3	137.0	138.6	140.3	141.8	143.1	144.2	145.1	146.2	147.5
Total OECD[a]	433.0	440.0	446.5	460.7	464.9	493.3	501.2	506.6	511.8	519.1	524.0	528.8	535.0	539.1	543.5	547.0	550.3	555.8	561.5
Employment																			
Major seven countries	285.6	290.9	295.1	302.5	302.5	302.8	305.8	308.4	310.9	315.3	318.5	321.9	327.5	328.6	328.1	329.6	332.3	335.5	338.9
Total of smaller countries[a]	95.0	97.4	99.4	122.6	131.0	153.8	158.5	162.0	165.3	169.0	171.0	173.0	175.6	177.1	178.8	179.5	181.5	184.2	187.3
Euro area	109.5	111.3	113.4	122.0	120.9	118.7	118.4	119.1	119.7	120.8	123.1	125.6	128.6	130.5	131.2	131.4	132.3	133.6	135.2
Total OECD[a]	380.6	388.3	394.5	425.2	433.4	456.6	464.3	470.4	476.2	484.3	489.5	495.0	503.1	505.6	506.8	509.1	513.7	519.7	526.2
Unemployment																			
Major seven countries	18.1	16.9	16.9	20.2	22.6	23.4	22.9	22.0	22.3	22.0	21.4	20.8	19.6	20.6	22.8	23.7	22.5	22.1	21.4
Total of smaller countries[a]	7.5	7.1	6.9	8.1	8.9	13.5	14.1	14.2	13.3	12.8	13.1	13.1	12.2	12.8	13.9	14.3	14.1	14.0	13.9
Euro area	10.6	9.7	9.0	9.9	10.9	13.0	14.1	13.9	14.3	14.5	13.9	13.0	11.8	11.3	12.0	12.8	12.7	12.6	12.2
Total OECD[a]	25.6	24.0	23.8	28.3	31.5	36.9	37.0	36.2	35.7	34.8	34.5	33.9	31.8	33.4	36.7	37.9	36.6	36.1	35.3

a) The aggregate measures include Mexico as of 1987. There is a potential bias in the aggregates thereafter because of the limited coverage of the Mexican National Survey of Urban Employment.
Source: OECD Economic Outlook 76 database.

Annex Table 16. **GDP deflators**

Percentage change from previous year

	Average 1980-90	1991	1992	1993	1994	1995	1996	1997	1998	1999	2000	2001	2002	2003	2004	2005	2006	Fourth quarter 2004	2005	2006
Australia	7.6	2.3	1.4	1.2	0.9	1.6	2.3	1.6	0.3	0.7	4.3	3.4	2.8	2.7	3.6	2.5	2.5	3.3	2.5	2.4
Austria	3.5	3.8	3.6	2.7	2.7	1.9	1.0	0.0	0.3	0.6	1.8	1.7	1.3	1.6	2.1	1.9	1.4	..	..	..
Belgium	4.3	2.9	3.4	4.0	2.1	1.2	1.2	1.4	1.7	1.4	1.3	1.8	1.8	2.0	2.3	1.4	1.8	2.4	1.3	1.5
Canada	5.1	3.0	1.3	1.4	1.1	2.3	1.6	1.2	-0.4	1.7	4.1	1.1	1.0	3.2	3.5	2.8	2.1	4.7	1.9	2.1
Czech Republic	..	..	..	..	9.4	10.2	8.6	8.3	11.2	2.8	1.4	4.9	2.8	1.7	4.1	2.6	2.5	..	..	..
Denmark	6.2	2.8	2.9	1.4	1.7	1.8	2.5	2.2	1.0	1.8	3.0	2.1	1.6	2.2	1.9	2.0	2.0	1.9	1.8	2.2
Finland	7.1	2.3	1.9	2.3	1.8	4.7	-0.4	2.1	3.5	0.0	2.9	3.1	0.9	0.0	0.8	1.3	1.6	0.8	1.4	1.7
France	6.2	3.0	2.0	2.4	1.8	1.7	1.4	1.3	0.8	0.4	0.7	1.7	2.4	1.4	1.9	1.8	1.7	1.9	1.8	1.8
Germany	2.9	3.5	5.0	3.7	2.5	2.0	1.0	0.7	1.1	0.5	-0.3	1.3	1.5	1.1	0.9	0.8	0.9	0.8	0.9	1.0
Greece	19.6	19.8	14.8	14.4	11.2	9.8	7.4	6.8	5.2	3.0	3.4	3.5	4.0	3.5	3.0	3.4	3.6	2.6	2.6	4.0
Hungary	..	..	..	..	19.5	25.6	21.2	18.5	12.6	8.4	9.9	8.6	8.9	7.8	5.0	4.4	4.0	..	..	..
Iceland	32.9	8.5	3.3	2.3	2.1	2.9	2.0	3.2	5.0	2.8	2.8	9.9	5.3	-0.5	1.9	3.6	3.2	2.6	4.5	3.0
Ireland	7.0	1.8	2.8	5.2	1.7	2.9	1.9	4.4	6.4	3.7	4.8	5.7	4.5	1.6	3.5	2.9	2.8	..	..	..
Italy	10.6	7.6	4.5	3.9	3.5	5.0	5.3	2.4	2.7	1.6	2.2	2.7	3.1	2.9	2.8	2.1	2.0	2.9	2.0	2.2
Japan	2.2	2.9	1.6	0.5	0.1	-0.5	-0.8	0.3	-0.1	-1.5	-2.0	-1.5	-1.2	-2.5	-2.3	-1.3	-0.3	-1.6	-1.1	0.2
Korea	7.5	10.9	7.6	7.1	7.7	7.1	5.1	4.6	5.8	-0.1	0.7	3.5	2.8	2.3	1.1	0.2	1.0	-2.2	4.5	-1.2
Luxembourg	4.1	1.8	3.7	6.0	3.5	2.3	2.0	2.7	2.7	2.2	4.2	1.9	1.1	2.1	2.2	2.1	1.9	..	..	..
Mexico	62.8	23.3	14.4	9.5	8.5	37.9	30.7	17.7	15.4	15.2	12.1	5.9	6.9	6.5	6.0	4.2	3.4	6.9	2.7	3.6
Netherlands	2.0	2.9	2.3	1.9	2.3	2.0	1.2	2.0	1.7	1.6	3.9	5.2	3.1	3.0	0.8	0.6	1.0	0.3	0.8	1.1
New Zealand	9.8	0.5	1.4	3.0	1.1	2.4	2.4	0.5	1.2	0.3	2.6	4.6	0.5	2.1	2.9	2.2	2.0	2.9	2.2	1.9
Norway	6.2	2.2	-0.6	2.3	-0.1	2.9	4.1	2.9	-0.7	6.6	15.9	1.1	-1.6	2.3	5.6	6.3	2.4	9.6	2.3	2.4
Poland	..	..	..	..	37.2	28.0	18.6	13.9	11.6	6.4	6.7	4.0	1.3	0.5	3.9	2.5	3.2	..	..	..
Portugal	17.3	10.1	11.4	7.4	7.3	3.4	3.0	3.8	3.8	3.1	3.5	4.4	4.5	2.3	1.8	1.9	2.0	0.8	2.1	1.9
Slovak Republic	..	..	..	..	13.4	9.9	4.3	6.7	5.2	6.5	8.5	4.2	4.0	4.7	5.3	2.6	2.9	..	..	..
Spain	9.4	6.9	6.7	4.5	3.9	4.9	3.5	2.3	2.4	2.8	3.4	4.2	4.5	4.0	3.1	3.6	3.6	2.4	4.5	2.9
Sweden	7.6	9.0	1.1	3.0	2.4	3.2	1.2	1.4	0.7	0.9	1.2	2.0	1.5	2.2	1.1	1.5	2.2	0.7	2.3	2.2
Switzerland	3.7	5.7	2.2	2.4	1.5	0.8	-0.1	-0.1	-0.3	0.7	0.8	0.6	1.7	0.9	1.1	1.1	1.0	..	..	..
Turkey	46.4	58.8	63.7	67.8	106.5	87.2	77.8	81.5	75.7	55.6	49.9	54.8	44.1	22.5	6.5	7.6	6.2	..	..	..
United Kingdom	6.4	6.6	4.0	2.7	1.5	2.6	3.2	2.9	2.8	2.3	1.3	2.2	3.2	3.0	2.1	2.2	2.3	1.9	2.3	2.3
United States	4.2	3.5	2.3	2.3	2.1	2.0	1.9	1.7	1.1	1.4	2.2	2.4	1.7	1.8	2.0	1.8	1.7	2.2	1.8	1.7
Euro area	6.2	4.8	4.4	3.6	2.8	2.8	2.1	1.5	1.7	1.1	1.4	2.4	2.5	2.0	1.9	1.7	1.8	1.7	1.8	1.8
Total OECD	7.8	5.8	4.4	3.9	4.7	5.3	4.4	3.8	3.3	2.5	2.8	3.0	2.6	2.0	1.8	1.7	1.7	1.9	1.7	1.7
Memorandum item																				
OECD *less* high inflation countries[a]	4.9	4.2	3.0	2.6	2.2	2.2	1.8	1.6	1.3	1.0	1.5	1.9	1.7	1.5	1.5	1.4	1.5	1.5	1.6	1.5

Note: The adoption of new national account systems, SNA93 or ESA95, has been proceeding at an uneven pace among OECD member countries, both with respect to variables and the time period covered. As a consequence there are breaks in many national series. See Table "National Account Reporting Systems and Base-years" at the beginning of the Statistical Annex and *OECD Economic Outlook* Sources and Methods *(http://www.oecd.org/eco/sources-and-methods).*

a) High inflation countries are defined as countries which have had 10 per cent or more inflation in terms of the GDP deflator on average during the last 10 years based on historical data. Consequently, Hungary, Mexico, Poland and Turkey are excluded from the aggregate.

Source: OECD Economic Outlook 76 database.

Annex Table 17. **Private consumption deflators**

Percentage change from previous year

	Average 1980-90	1991	1992	1993	1994	1995	1996	1997	1998	1999	2000	2001	2002	2003	2004	2005	2006	Fourth quarter 2004	2005	2006
Australia	7.8	4.4	2.2	2.2	1.2	2.3	1.9	1.6	1.3	1.0	3.4	3.6	2.0	1.7	1.6	2.6	2.7	2.2	2.6	2.7
Austria	3.5	3.5	3.8	3.4	2.7	2.0	1.9	1.5	0.3	0.7	2.5	1.9	1.2	1.5	1.7	1.9	1.4	..	..	..
Belgium	4.2	2.8	1.9	2.5	2.3	2.1	2.1	1.8	0.9	1.2	2.3	2.5	1.7	1.8	2.1	2.1	1.9	2.7	1.8	1.9
Canada	5.7	5.0	1.7	2.3	1.1	1.3	1.6	1.6	1.2	1.7	2.2	1.8	2.1	1.6	1.5	1.5	1.4	2.0	1.4	1.4
Czech Republic	..	..	..	..	9.6	9.2	8.4	8.6	8.7	2.6	3.0	3.5	0.7	-0.7	2.1	2.8	2.6	..	..	..
Denmark	5.9	2.8	1.9	2.0	3.0	1.9	2.1	2.2	1.3	2.4	2.6	2.5	2.1	1.8	1.2	1.7	1.9	1.4	1.8	2.0
Finland	6.3	5.8	3.8	4.5	0.8	0.7	1.7	1.9	2.1	1.4	3.2	3.6	3.1	0.6	1.2	2.0	1.9	2.2	1.6	2.0
France	6.4	3.5	2.5	2.5	2.2	2.0	1.9	1.4	0.6	0.2	1.2	1.4	1.7	1.8	1.5	1.7	1.8	1.6	1.7	1.9
Germany	2.5	3.8	4.4	3.9	2.6	1.9	1.7	2.0	1.1	0.3	1.5	1.6	1.1	1.0	1.7	1.2	0.6	1.8	0.8	0.7
Greece	19.0	19.7	15.7	14.1	11.0	9.0	8.2	5.6	4.5	2.3	3.1	3.5	3.6	3.6	3.2	3.5	3.4	..	..	..
Hungary	..	..	..	..	19.7	27.0	23.8	18.0	13.7	10.4	10.9	8.2	3.7	6.0	6.3	4.8	4.5	..	..	..
Iceland	33.7	6.5	3.6	3.6	1.5	2.0	2.5	1.9	1.0	2.5	4.4	8.9	3.7	0.7	2.5	3.3	3.4	3.1	3.4	3.1
Ireland	7.2	2.7	2.9	2.2	2.7	2.7	2.7	2.6	3.8	3.1	4.1	4.3	6.0	4.0	2.7	2.9	3.8	..	..	..
Italy	10.0	7.0	5.5	5.5	4.9	6.0	4.4	2.2	2.1	2.1	2.9	2.7	3.1	2.5	2.1	2.4	2.1	1.9	2.7	1.9
Japan	2.2	2.7	1.6	1.0	0.5	-0.3	-0.1	1.0	-0.1	-0.7	-1.3	-1.6	-1.3	-1.4	-1.5	-0.6	0.3	-1.3	-0.1	0.5
Korea	6.2	12.1	8.9	8.0	9.7	7.0	6.2	6.0	6.7	3.3	4.8	4.8	2.8	3.4	3.6	3.4	3.0	4.0	2.4	3.4
Luxembourg	4.8	3.4	4.2	4.0	2.6	2.0	1.4	1.4	1.1	1.5	2.6	3.2	2.1	1.9	2.2	2.0	1.9	..	..	..
Mexico	64.2	24.3	15.4	10.1	7.6	34.0	30.7	16.5	20.5	14.0	10.4	7.2	5.4	5.0	3.9	3.7	3.3	3.2	3.6	3.3
Netherlands	2.4	3.3	3.2	2.1	2.9	1.4	1.9	2.0	1.7	1.8	3.3	4.6	2.7	2.3	1.1	2.1	1.6	1.0	2.3	1.3
New Zealand	10.5	2.2	1.1	1.2	1.2	2.6	2.2	1.9	1.9	0.6	2.3	2.2	1.9	0.7	1.4	2.4	2.0	2.3	2.3	1.8
Norway	7.4	3.8	2.5	2.4	1.2	2.4	1.4	2.3	2.5	2.0	3.0	2.3	0.8	2.3	0.8	2.2	2.2	1.2	2.2	2.5
Poland	..	..	..	..	37.9	27.2	19.4	14.5	11.2	6.5	9.0	4.7	1.6	0.6	3.5	3.2	3.4	..	..	..
Portugal	17.2	11.8	9.2	6.9	5.6	4.3	3.7	2.9	2.8	2.1	3.3	3.8	3.5	3.4	2.4	2.0	1.8	2.7	1.9	1.8
Slovak Republic	..	..	..	..	13.4	9.2	5.0	6.0	5.8	8.6	10.8	5.9	2.5	7.7	7.0	2.7	2.8	..	..	..
Spain	9.2	6.4	6.6	5.3	4.9	4.8	3.5	2.6	2.2	2.4	3.1	3.3	3.4	3.1	2.9	3.2	2.7	3.3	2.7	2.7
Sweden	8.0	10.4	2.1	6.3	2.7	2.8	1.3	1.9	0.8	1.2	1.1	2.4	1.8	2.5	1.0	1.8	2.3	0.8	2.1	2.4
Switzerland	3.4	5.8	3.8	3.1	0.5	1.6	0.6	0.7	-0.4	0.3	0.6	0.4	1.6	0.6	0.8	1.2	0.9	..	..	..
Turkey	47.0	60.7	65.6	65.9	108.9	92.4	67.8	82.1	83.0	59.0	50.0	58.8	40.6	21.8	8.2	6.6	5.8	..	..	..
United Kingdom	6.2	7.8	4.9	3.5	2.1	3.4	3.4	2.5	2.6	1.7	1.1	2.4	1.6	1.8	1.5	2.0	2.2	1.5	2.1	2.2
United States	4.5	3.6	2.9	2.3	2.1	2.1	2.2	1.7	0.9	1.7	2.5	2.1	1.4	1.9	2.1	1.8	1.6	2.4	1.6	1.6
Euro area	6.2	5.1	4.6	4.1	3.3	3.0	2.5	2.0	1.4	1.1	2.1	2.3	2.2	1.9	1.9	2.0	1.7	2.0	1.8	1.7
Total OECD	7.9	6.2	4.9	4.3	5.0	5.4	4.6	4.0	3.5	2.7	3.1	3.0	2.2	2.0	1.8	1.8	1.7	2.1	1.5	1.9
Memorandum item																				
OECD *less* high inflation countries[a]	5.0	4.6	3.4	3.0	2.5	2.3	2.2	1.9	1.3	1.2	1.9	1.8	1.4	1.5	1.5	1.6	1.6	1.7	1.5	1.6

Note: The adoption of new national account systems, SNA93 or ESA95, has been proceeding at an uneven pace among OECD member countries, both with respect to variables and the time period covered. As a consequence there are breaks in many national series. See Table "National Account Reporting Systems and Base-years" at the beginning of the Statistical Annex and *OECD Economic Outlook* Sources and Methods (*http://www.oecd.org/eco/sources-and-methods*).

a) High inflation countries are defined as countries which have had 10 per cent or more inflation in terms of the GDP deflator on average during the last 10 years based on historical data. Consequently, Hungary, Mexico, Poland and Turkey are excluded from the aggregate.

Source: OECD Economic Outlook 76 database.

Annex Table 18. **Consumer price indices**

Percentage change from previous year

	Average 1980-90	1991	1992	1993	1994	1995	1996	1997	1998	1999	2000	2001	2002	2003	2004	2005	2006	Fourth quarter 2004	2005	2006
Australia	8.1	3.2	1.0	1.8	1.9	4.6	2.6	0.3	0.9	1.5	4.5	4.4	3.0	2.8	2.3	2.4	2.6	2.4	2.5	2.7
Austria	3.5	3.1	3.4	3.2	2.7	1.6	1.8	1.2	0.8	0.5	2.0	2.3	1.7	1.3	1.9	1.9	1.4	..	..	..
Belgium	4.5	4.2	2.2	2.5	2.4	1.3	1.8	1.5	0.9	1.1	2.7	2.4	1.6	1.5	1.9	2.2	1.9	2.6	1.8	1.9
Canada	5.9	5.6	1.5	1.9	0.2	2.2	1.6	1.6	1.0	1.7	2.7	2.5	2.2	2.8	1.9	2.0	1.8	2.4	1.8	1.8
Czech Republic	..	..	..	..	10.0	9.1	8.8	8.5	10.7	2.1	3.9	4.7	1.8	0.1	2.9	3.1	3.0	..	..	..
Denmark	5.9	2.4	2.1	1.3	2.0	2.1	2.1	2.2	1.8	2.5	2.9	2.4	2.4	2.1	1.2	1.7	2.0	1.7	1.8	2.1
Finland	6.6	4.6	3.2	3.3	1.6	0.4	1.1	1.2	1.4	1.3	3.0	2.7	2.0	1.3	0.2	1.7	1.9	1.4	1.6	2.0
France	6.3	3.4	2.5	2.2	1.7	1.8	2.1	1.3	0.7	0.6	1.8	1.8	1.9	2.2	2.3	1.8	1.8	2.0	1.7	1.9
Germany	2.6	4.1	5.1	4.4	2.7	1.7	1.2	1.5	0.6	0.6	1.4	1.9	1.3	1.0	1.7	1.3	0.6	1.8	0.8	0.6
Greece	19.0	19.5	15.9	14.4	10.9	8.9	7.9	5.4	4.5	2.1	2.9	3.7	3.9	3.4	3.1	3.4	3.2	..	..	..
Hungary	..	..	..	..	18.9	28.3	23.5	18.3	14.2	10.0	9.8	9.2	5.3	4.7	6.9	4.7	4.5	..	..	..
Iceland [a]	33.8	6.8	3.9	4.0	1.6	1.7	2.3	1.8	1.7	3.2	5.1	6.4	5.2	2.1	3.1	3.9	3.9	3.5	3.9	3.6
Ireland	7.7	3.2	3.1	1.4	2.3	2.5	2.2	1.2	2.1	2.5	5.3	4.0	4.7	4.0	2.4	2.8	2.9	..	..	..
Italy	9.6	6.2	5.0	4.5	4.2	5.4	4.0	1.9	2.0	1.7	2.6	2.3	2.6	2.8	2.1	2.5	2.2	2.1	2.8	2.1
Japan	2.0	3.2	1.7	1.3	0.7	-0.1	0.1	1.7	0.7	-0.3	-0.7	-0.7	-0.9	-0.3	-0.1	0.1	0.6	0.0	0.3	0.7
Korea	..	9.3	6.2	4.8	6.3	4.5	4.9	4.4	7.5	0.8	2.3	4.1	2.8	3.5	3.7	3.5	3.0	4.0	3.0	3.0
Luxembourg	4.4	3.1	3.2	3.6	2.2	1.9	1.2	1.4	1.0	1.0	3.8	2.4	2.1	2.5	3.5	2.3	2.0	..	..	..
Mexico	65.1	22.7	15.5	9.8	7.0	35.0	34.4	20.6	15.9	16.6	9.5	6.4	5.0	4.5	4.6	4.5	3.4	4.9	3.9	3.4
Netherlands	2.4	3.2	2.8	1.6	2.1	1.4	1.4	1.9	1.8	2.0	2.3	5.1	3.9	2.2	1.3	2.1	1.6	1.2	2.3	1.3
New Zealand	10.7	2.6	1.0	1.3	1.7	3.8	2.3	1.2	1.3	-0.1	2.6	2.6	2.7	1.8	2.3	3.0	2.8	2.6	3.0	2.6
Norway	7.6	3.4	2.3	2.3	1.4	2.4	1.2	2.6	2.3	2.3	3.1	3.0	1.3	2.5	0.5	1.9	2.1	1.2	2.1	2.3
Poland	..	..	..	..	33.2	28.1	19.8	14.9	11.6	7.2	9.9	5.4	1.9	0.7	3.3	3.0	3.4	..	..	..
Portugal	17.1	11.4	8.9	5.9	5.0	4.0	2.9	1.9	2.2	2.2	2.8	4.4	3.7	3.3	2.5	2.0	1.8	2.0	2.0	1.8
Slovak Republic	..	..	..	..	13.4	9.8	5.8	6.1	6.7	10.6	12.0	7.3	3.1	8.6	7.7	3.6	3.1	..	..	..
Spain	9.3	5.9	5.9	4.9	4.6	4.6	3.6	1.9	1.8	2.2	3.5	2.8	3.6	3.1	3.0	3.2	2.7	3.4	2.9	2.7
Sweden	7.6	9.4	2.4	4.7	2.2	2.5	0.5	0.7	-0.3	0.5	0.9	2.4	2.2	1.9	0.4	1.8	2.5	0.6	2.4	2.6
Switzerland	3.4	5.9	4.0	3.3	0.9	1.8	0.8	0.5	0.0	0.8	1.6	1.0	0.6	0.6	0.8	1.2	0.9	..	..	..
Turkey [b]	45.1	66.0	70.1	66.1	105.2	89.1	80.4	85.7	84.6	64.9	54.9	54.4	45.0	25.3	10.7	8.6	6.3	..	..	..
United Kingdom [c]	6.1	7.5	4.2	2.5	2.0	2.7	2.5	1.8	1.6	1.3	0.8	1.2	1.3	1.4	1.3	1.7	2.1	1.3	1.8	2.2
United States [d]	4.7	4.2	3.0	3.0	2.6	2.8	2.9	2.3	1.5	2.2	3.4	2.8	1.6	2.3	2.6	2.4	2.1	3.2	2.1	2.1
Euro area	6.3	5.0	4.6	4.0	3.2	2.9	2.4	1.7	1.2	1.2	2.1	2.4	2.3	2.1	2.1	2.0	1.7	2.1	1.8	1.6

Note: Consumer price index. For the euro area countries, the euro area aggregate and the United Kingdom: harmonised index of consumer prices (HICP).
a) Excluding rent, but including imputed rent.
b) Until 1981: Istanbul index (154 items); from 1982, Turkish index.
c) Known as the CPI in the United Kingdom.
d) The methodology for calculating the Consumer Price Index has changed considerably over the past years, lowering measured inflation substantially.
Source: OECD Economic Outlook 76 database.

Annex Table 19. **Oil and other primary commodity markets**

	1989	1990	1991	1992	1993	1994	1995	1996	1997	1998	1999	2000	2001	2002	2003	2004	2005	2006
Oil market conditions[a]																		
(in million barrels per day)																		
Demand																		
OECD[b]	41.2	41.4	41.8	42.9	43.2	44.4	44.8	45.9	46.7	46.9	47.8	47.9	47.9	48.0	48.7	49.4	49.6	..
of which: North America	21.0	20.7	20.5	20.8	21.1	21.7	21.6	22.2	22.7	23.1	23.8	24.1	24.0	24.1	24.6	25.0	25.3	..
Europe[c]	13.5	13.6	14.0	14.2	14.2	14.3	14.6	14.9	15.0	15.3	15.2	15.1	15.3	15.2	15.4	15.7	15.7	..
Pacific	6.7	7.1	7.4	7.9	7.9	8.4	8.6	8.8	9.0	8.5	8.8	8.7	8.7	8.6	8.8	8.7	8.6	..
Non-OECD[d]	24.7	24.8	25.2	24.7	24.8	24.3	25.2	26.0	27.0	27.5	28.2	28.7	29.4	29.9	31.0	33.0	34.2	..
Total	65.9	66.3	67.0	67.6	67.9	68.7	70.0	71.9	73.7	74.4	76.0	76.6	77.3	77.9	79.7	82.4	83.8	..
Supply																		
OECD[b]	18.9	19.0	19.5	19.8	20.0	20.8	21.1	21.7	22.1	21.9	21.4	21.9	21.8	21.8	21.6	21.4	21.3	..
OPEC total	23.8	25.1	25.3	26.5	26.9	27.6	27.9	28.7	30.2	31.0	29.6	30.9	30.4	28.8	30.7	..	..	..
Former USSR	12.2	11.5	10.4	8.9	7.9	7.2	7.1	7.1	7.2	7.3	7.5	7.9	8.6	9.4	10.3	11.2	11.8	..
Other non-OECD[d]	11.2	11.4	11.6	12.1	12.6	13.4	14.5	15.0	15.4	15.7	16.0	16.2	16.4	16.9	17.1	..	..	..
Total	66.1	66.9	66.8	67.2	67.5	69.1	70.6	72.5	74.9	75.9	74.5	76.9	77.2	76.9	79.6	..	..	..
Trade																		
OECD net imports[b]	22.5	22.7	22.3	23.1	23.4	23.8	23.4	24.2	25.0	25.3	25.6	26.2	26.4	25.9	27.4	28.3	28.3	..
Former USSR net exports	3.5	3.1	2.2	2.0	2.0	2.7	2.8	3.1	3.4	3.6	3.9	4.3	4.9	5.9	6.7	7.5	8.0	..
Other non-OECD net exports[d]	19.0	19.6	20.1	21.1	21.4	21.0	20.6	21.1	21.5	21.8	21.7	21.9	21.5	20.0	20.7	20.8	20.3	..
Prices[e]																		
Brent crude oil import price (cif, $ per bl)	18.2	23.7	20.0	19.3	17.0	15.8	17.0	20.7	19.1	12.7	17.9	28.4	24.5	25.0	28.8	39.0	46.2	44.6
Prices of other primary commodities[e]																		
($ indices)																		
Food and tropical beverages	137	123	116	111	113	155	158	153	167	142	112	100	91	102	109	109	109	109
of which: Food	130	116	112	118	119	129	136	160	143	118	100	100	97	108	118	137	121	125
Tropical beverages	142	129	118	107	109	172	172	148	183	158	121	100	87	98	103	106	106	107
Agricultural raw materials	114	125	108	110	105	120	139	120	113	97	94	100	86	85	104	114	110	111
Minerals, ores and metals	130	119	106	102	89	102	121	108	110	93	89	100	92	90	102	138	145	151
Total	125	123	109	108	102	123	138	124	126	107	97	100	89	91	105	126	141	148

a) Based on data published in in varoius issues of International Energy Agency, Oil Market Report and Annual Statistical Supplement, August 2004.
b) Excluding Czech Republic, Hungary, Korea, Mexico and Poland.
c) European Union countries and Iceland, Norway, Switzerland and Turkey.
d) Including Czech Republic, Hungary, Korea, Mexico and Poland.
e) Indices through 2003 are based on data compiled by International Energy Agency for oil and by Hamburg Institute for Economic Research for the prices of other primary commodities; OECD estimates and projections for 2004 to 2006.
Source: OECD Economic Outlook 76 database.

Annex Table 20. **Employment rates, participation rates and labour force**

	Employment rates						Labour force participation rates						Labour force					
	Average 1983-85	Average 1993-95	2003	2004	2005	2006	Average 1983-85	Average 1993-95	2003	2004	2005	2006	Average 1983-92	Average 1993-02	2003	2004	2005	2006
	Per cent						*Per cent*						*Percentage change*					
Australia	63.8	67.2	71.3	71.7	71.9	72.3	70.1	74.2	75.8	75.9	76.1	76.5	2.2	1.6	1.8	1.2	1.6	1.9
Austria	73.7	73.8	74.0	74.3	74.8	75.4	76.4	77.9	78.5	78.9	79.3	79.8	0.8	0.4	0.1	0.6	0.7	0.7
Belgium	55.2	57.8	61.6	61.7	61.9	62.3	61.8	63.8	66.9	66.9	67.0	67.2	0.3	0.7	0.7	0.2	0.6	0.7
Canada	65.7	68.1	73.3	73.7	73.7	73.7	74.0	76.0	79.4	79.4	79.4	79.4	1.5	1.6	2.2	1.3	1.3	1.3
Czech Republic	..	69.4	65.1	64.8	64.8	64.9	..	72.5	70.7	70.7	70.7	70.7	..	0.0	-0.1	0.2	0.1	0.1
Denmark	73.4	73.2	75.7	75.8	76.2	76.5	79.4	79.6	80.3	80.5	80.5	80.4	0.9	0.1	0.1	0.3	0.1	0.1
Finland	72.3	60.7	67.6	67.3	67.7	68.1	76.3	72.4	74.4	73.9	74.1	74.1	-0.1	0.6	-0.4	-0.5	0.6	0.4
France	60.4	59.2	63.3	63.0	62.9	63.2	66.8	67.0	70.1	69.8	69.7	69.6	0.5	0.8	0.7	0.0	0.2	0.2
Germany	63.9	67.3	69.1	69.3	69.7	70.6	68.4	72.9	76.0	76.4	76.8	77.5	3.8	0.5	0.0	0.3	0.5	0.7
Greece	56.4	55.0	57.9	58.9	59.5	60.2	61.3	60.8	64.0	64.8	65.4	65.9	0.5	0.7	0.6	0.9	0.8	0.9
Hungary	..	52.5	..	..	..	..	..	59.1	..	..	..	..	..	-0.1	1.3	0.9	0.7	0.6
Iceland	83.9	81.3	82.8	81.7	81.7	82.2	85.5	85.6	85.6	84.3	84.1	84.5	1.3	1.3	0.2	-0.3	1.9	2.3
Ireland	53.8	54.9	67.5	67.9	68.3	68.7	63.8	63.8	70.8	71.0	71.3	71.5	0.4	3.0	2.1	1.4	1.3	1.3
Italy	54.9	51.6	56.3	57.4	58.3	58.9	59.9	57.9	61.7	62.4	63.0	63.6	0.4	0.6	0.6	1.0	0.9	0.9
Japan	70.6	74.1	73.4	73.9	74.4	75.2	72.5	76.3	77.5	77.6	78.0	78.5	1.2	0.1	-0.3	-0.2	0.0	-0.1
Korea	56.0	63.0	64.7	65.3	65.6	66.0	58.3	64.6	66.9	67.7	68.0	68.3	2.9	1.6	0.2	1.9	1.3	1.4
Luxembourg	59.3	60.0	63.6	63.8	64.1	64.4	60.3	61.6	66.1	66.6	66.9	67.2	1.0	1.8	1.9	1.7	1.5	1.3
Mexico	..	57.3	56.9	57.0	57.3	57.5	..	59.8	58.4	58.4	58.6	58.9	..	2.4	1.3	1.5	2.4	2.5
Netherlands	60.1	66.6	75.5	74.8	75.0	75.7	66.6	71.4	78.7	78.6	79.1	79.7	1.2	1.6	0.8	0.2	1.0	1.1
New Zealand	74.9	68.5	73.7	..	..	..	78.5	74.4	77.3	..	..	..	0.5	1.8	1.7	2.1	1.0	1.0
Norway	74.5	72.8	76.1	75.8	76.0	76.0	76.9	77.0	79.7	79.3	79.3	79.3	0.6	1.2	-0.1	0.2	0.9	0.8
Poland	..	58.3	51.2	51.2	51.3	51.5	..	67.7	63.7	63.3	62.9	62.5	..	0.1	-1.6	-0.3	-0.3	-0.3
Portugal	63.5	68.1	71.9	71.5	71.6	72.3	69.4	72.8	76.8	76.5	76.7	77.0	1.0	1.1	0.9	0.3	0.9	0.9
Slovak Republic	..	59.9	57.3	57.1	57.8	58.6	..	69.2	69.4	69.8	70.1	70.2	..	0.8	0.4	0.8	0.4	0.4
Spain	47.2	47.7	60.7	61.6	62.5	63.4	55.9	58.0	68.5	69.2	70.0	70.7	1.2	2.5	2.6	2.0	2.1	2.0
Sweden	78.7	70.8	72.8	72.2	72.7	73.2	81.2	76.9	76.5	76.5	76.5	76.5	0.2	0.3	0.7	0.5	0.7	0.8
Switzerland	77.6	83.6	83.9	83.7	84.1	84.8	78.3	86.7	87.4	87.2	87.2	87.2	2.2	0.5	0.9	0.2	0.4	0.5
Turkey	60.0	53.1	47.1	46.5	46.0	45.6	64.7	57.8	52.5	51.4	51.2	51.0	2.1	1.7	-0.7	-0.3	2.0	2.1
United Kingdom	65.0	68.3	72.6	72.8	72.7	72.5	73.2	75.5	76.4	76.4	76.3	76.3	0.7	0.5	0.8	0.6	0.4	0.5
United States	66.4	72.1	70.9	..	..	..	72.3	76.8	75.4	..	..	..	1.6	1.3	1.1	0.6	1.4	1.2
Euro area	58.6	59.4	64.3	64.6	65.1	65.8	64.4	66.2	70.6	70.9	71.3	71.7	1.5	0.9	0.7	0.6	0.8	0.9
Total OECD	63.1	65.0	66.0	64.4	64.6	65.0	68.2	70.1	70.9	69.3	69.5	69.7	2.3	1.1	0.6	0.6	1.0	1.0

Note: Employment rates are calculated as the ratio of total employment to the population of working age. The working age population concept used here and in the labour force participation rate is defined as all persons of the age 15 to 64 years (16 to 65 years for Spain). This definition does not correspond to the commonly-used working age population concepts for the United States (16 years and above), Hungary and New Zealand (15 years and above). Hence for these countries no projections are available. For information about sources and definitions, see *OECD Economic Outlook* Sources and Methods *(http://www.oecd.org/eco/sources-and-methods).*

Source: OECD Economic Outlook 76 database.

Annex Table 21. **Potential GDP, employment and capital stock**

Percentage change from previous period

	Potential GDP						Employment						Capital stock					
	Average 1983-92	Average 1993-02	2003	2004	2005	2006	Average 1983-92	Average 1993-02	2003	2004	2005	2006	Average 1983-92	Average 1993-02	2003	2004	2005	2006
Australia	3.4	3.4	3.6	3.4	3.9	3.8	2.2	2.1	2.3	1.6	1.8	1.9	3.5	3.0	4.0	4.2	4.5	4.9
Austria	2.4	2.3	2.3	2.1	2.1	2.1	0.6	0.4	-0.1	0.5	0.7	1.0	4.1	4.0	4.3	4.2	4.2	4.2
Belgium	2.2	2.0	2.1	2.1	2.1	2.2	0.7	0.9	0.1	0.4	0.7	1.1	3.1	2.7	2.3	2.2	2.2	2.4
Canada	2.3	3.2	2.6	2.8	3.0	3.2	1.6	2.0	2.2	1.8	1.4	1.2	2.7	2.7	1.2	1.6	2.4	3.0
Czech Republic	..	..	..	..	..	..	..	-0.3	-0.7	-0.4	0.2	0.3	..	..	..	..	..	..
Denmark	1.7	2.2	2.0	1.9	2.0	2.0	0.9	0.7	-1.0	0.2	0.5	0.5	3.4	3.5	3.7	3.6	3.6	3.7
Finland	2.4	2.4	2.4	2.1	2.3	2.1	-0.9	1.5	-0.3	-0.4	0.9	0.9	2.9	0.8	0.7	0.8	0.9	1.1
France	2.0	2.1	2.1	1.9	2.0	2.0	0.3	1.2	-0.1	-0.1	0.4	0.8	4.3	3.2	2.7	2.8	2.8	2.9
Germany	3.7	1.4	1.5	1.5	1.5	1.5	3.9	0.4	-1.0	0.2	0.4	1.1	4.4	1.8	0.8	1.2	0.9	1.3
Greece	1.2	2.7	4.2	3.8	3.8	4.0	0.4	0.6	1.3	1.4	0.9	1.1	2.0	4.1	6.8	6.1	6.3	6.6
Hungary	..	3.6	3.8	3.9	4.0	4.2	..	0.6	1.3	0.9	0.9	0.8	..	..	..	..	..	..
Iceland	2.7	3.0	2.6	3.4	4.5	4.7	1.0	1.5	0.1	0.0	2.0	2.6	2.6	3.4	3.7	5.8	7.6	8.2
Ireland	3.8	7.6	5.5	5.4	5.1	5.1	0.4	4.4	1.9	1.7	1.6	1.5	2.4	4.5	4.6	4.5	4.6	4.5
Italy	2.2	1.4	1.4	1.3	1.4	1.6	0.2	0.7	1.0	1.8	1.5	1.1	3.3	2.5	2.3	2.5	2.6	2.7
Japan	3.6	1.6	1.6	1.5	1.3	1.2	1.3	-0.2	-0.2	0.3	0.2	0.3	6.5	3.5	1.7	1.2	0.9	1.6
Korea	..	..	..	..	..	..	3.1	1.6	-0.1	1.8	1.3	1.6	..	..	..	..	..	..
Luxembourg	..	..	..	..	..	..	1.0	1.7	1.0	1.2	1.5	1.3	..	..	..	..	..	..
Mexico	..	..	..	..	..	..	..	2.5	1.1	1.7	2.5	2.5	..	..	..	..	..	..
Netherlands	2.1	2.8	2.1	1.9	1.8	1.7	1.9	2.0	-0.4	-0.6	0.6	1.4	2.3	2.7	1.9	1.8	1.7	1.8
New Zealand	1.6	2.9	3.8	3.7	3.5	3.3	0.0	2.3	2.3	2.7	0.9	0.9	2.9	2.7	4.2	5.3	5.3	5.1
Norway	2.2	2.8	2.5	2.5	2.8	2.9	0.3	1.5	-0.8	0.3	1.1	0.9	1.7	2.7	1.5	1.7	1.8	1.9
Poland	..	..	..	..	..	..	..	-0.8	-1.2	0.5	0.6	0.7	..	..	..	..	..	..
Portugal	2.8	2.8	1.9	1.6	1.7	1.8	1.4	1.1	-0.5	0.1	0.7	1.5	..	..	..	..	..	..
Slovak Republic	..	..	..	..	..	..	..	-0.1	1.8	0.0	1.2	1.7	..	..	..	..	..	..
Spain	2.8	2.9	3.0	2.9	2.8	2.8	1.3	3.2	2.7	2.4	2.3	2.4	4.0	3.8	3.2	3.0	3.0	3.1
Sweden	2.0	2.2	2.6	2.3	2.6	2.6	0.0	0.8	-0.2	-0.3	1.5	1.4	3.1	3.0	2.2	2.1	2.4	2.7
Switzerland	2.0	1.2	1.3	1.2	1.3	1.5	2.0	0.5	-0.1	0.2	0.9	1.2	2.8	2.6	2.3	2.5	2.7	2.8
Turkey	..	..	..	..	..	..	2.0	1.6	-0.9	0.6	1.4	1.6	..	..	..	..	..	..
United Kingdom	2.2	2.6	2.4	2.5	2.5	2.5	0.9	1.1	0.9	0.9	0.4	0.2	2.8	3.9	3.6	3.8	3.8	3.7
United States	3.0	3.3	2.8	3.0	3.1	3.3	1.8	1.4	0.9	1.1	1.6	1.5	2.8	3.2	1.9	2.5	3.0	3.5
Euro area	2.7	2.0	2.0	1.9	1.9	2.0	1.5	1.1	0.2	0.7	0.9	1.2	..	..	..	..	..	..
Total OECD	2.9	2.6	2.4	2.4	2.5	2.5	1.6	1.1	0.4	0.9	1.2	1.2	3.6	3.1	2.1	2.4	2.6	2.9

Note: Potential output is estimated using a Cobb-Douglas production function approach. For information about definitions, sources and data coverage, see *OECD Economic Outlook* Sources and Methods *(http://www.oecd.org/eco/sources-and-methods).*

Source: OECD Economic Outlook 76 database.

Annex Table 22. **Structural unemployment, wage shares and unit labor costs**

	Structural unemployment rate						Wage shares in the business sector						Unit labour costs in the business sector					
	Average 1983-85	Average 1993-95	2003	2004	2005	2006	Average 1983-85	Average 1993-95	2003	2004	2005	2006	Average 1983-92	Average 1993-02	2003	2004	2005	2006
	Per cent						*Per cent of business GDP*						*Percentage change*					
Australia	5.6	6.8	5.6	5.5	5.4	5.4	44.0	43.9	45.0	44.4	44.4	44.3	4.8	1.5	2.5	1.9	2.0	2.0
Austria	3.0	4.8	4.9	4.9	4.9	4.9	55.1	52.7	52.4	51.9	51.4	51.4	2.7	0.2	1.3	0.5	0.6	0.8
Belgium	7.4	7.3	7.2	7.2	7.2	7.2	49.4	50.8	49.7	49.3	49.2	49.1	3.2	1.0	1.1	0.5	0.7	1.0
Canada	7.8	8.1	7.3	7.3	7.3	7.3	44.2	46.4	47.2	46.3	45.8	45.4	3.9	1.1	1.6	1.2	1.3	1.0
Czech Republic	..	..	..	..	..	..	..	43.0	41.6	41.9	42.3	42.9	..	3.7	4.1	4.3	2.2	2.3
Denmark	5.6	6.6	4.8	4.8	4.8	4.8	41.1	40.0	39.0	38.6	38.4	38.4	4.2	0.8	1.6	0.6	0.8	1.4
Finland	3.9	8.7	8.6	8.6	8.5	8.4	47.8	40.6	41.3	40.9	41.1	41.2	4.7	0.9	0.5	-0.6	1.6	1.1
France	7.6	10.3	9.1	9.0	8.9	8.8	50.6	43.4	41.9	41.6	41.6	41.8	2.2	0.5	1.5	0.1	1.1	1.5
Germany	4.1	6.3	7.7	7.7	7.6	7.6	52.3	52.1	52.2	51.9	51.9	51.9	2.2	0.5	0.7	-0.1	0.1	0.5
Greece	6.3	8.8	10.5	10.5	10.5	10.3	54.8	45.4	42.0	42.3	42.4	42.6	15.4	5.2	0.2	3.5	3.4	3.6
Hungary	..	..	..	..	..	..	..	47.1	41.2	42.7	42.7	42.5	..	9.6	6.4	6.2	3.9	3.1
Iceland	1.5 |	3.9	2.8	2.8	2.8	2.8	46.7	49.2	52.1	50.7	51.6	52.4	22.0 |	4.8	-0.6	-1.6	4.4	3.9
Ireland	12.5	12.4	5.7	5.5	5.4	5.2	56.4	49.3	36.4	35.8	35.4	35.2	1.4	-0.3	-0.2	1.6	1.6	1.9
Italy	6.7	9.3	9.3	9.1	8.9	8.7	54.4	49.4	47.2	47.0	47.3	47.4	6.1	1.5	3.5	2.3	2.5	1.8
Japan	2.4	3.0	3.9	3.9	3.9	3.9	65.9	59.5	54.9	54.0	53.9	53.4	0.2	-1.4	-3.6	-4.2	-1.8	-1.5
Korea	..	..	..	..	..	..	76.8	72.1	62.0	61.1	61.4	62.4	5.2	2.3	0.5	-0.7	0.7	2.3
Luxembourg	..	..	..	..	..	..	..	47.2	46.5	46.2	45.9	45.7	7.4	1.9	0.3	0.3	0.9	1.0
Mexico	..	..	..	..	..	..	..	..	..	..	..	..	..	12.3	4.9	2.1	3.2	2.7
Netherlands	6.9	5.8	3.3	3.2	3.2	3.2	45.6	47.6	49.1	48.5	48.8	48.8	1.0	2.0	3.8	-0.8	0.7	0.5
New Zealand	3.6	7.5	5.7	5.7	5.6	5.6	..	43.7	40.5	39.7	39.6	39.7	2.2	0.8	1.4	0.7	2.4	2.0
Norway	2.5	4.5	4.1	4.1	4.1	4.1	39.7	36.4	34.1	32.5	31.2	31.3	4.8	2.4	2.3	-0.6	1.5	2.3
Poland	..	..	..	..	..	..	..	45.6	43.0	40.9	40.7	40.2	..	5.8	-7.0	-2.5	0.8	0.9
Portugal	5.9	4.4	4.1	4.2	4.1	4.1	57.7	51.3	51.3	51.1	50.9	51.0	13.4	3.4	4.3	1.1	1.2	1.4
Slovak Republic	..	..	..	..	..	..	..	36.7	35.8	36.4	36.3	36.3	..	5.3	2.5	6.0	2.4	2.3
Spain	10.6	13.1	11.0	10.7	10.6	10.5	51.2	48.8	47.9	48.1	48.0	47.7	7.0	2.7	3.8	3.8	3.4	2.8
Sweden	2.4	4.4	4.7	4.7	4.7	4.7	39.8	39.0	43.6	42.6	43.2	43.5	5.8	1.7	-0.5	-1.6	2.0	2.3
Switzerland	0.3	2.4	2.2	2.2	2.2	2.2	50.5	53.6	56.3	55.5	55.3	55.4	4.2	1.1	1.1	-0.7	0.5	0.9
Turkey	..	..	..	..	..	..	..	..	..	..	..	..	74.5	61.1	18.5	10.0	12.7	9.0
United Kingdom	7.5	7.4	5.4	5.3	5.3	5.3	50.9	53.0	55.0	55.6	55.8	55.8	5.4	2.2	2.4	2.8	2.3	2.3
United States	6.3	5.5	4.8	4.8	4.8	4.8	49.9	48.9	49.5	49.1	49.3	49.5	2.8	1.7	0.3	0.4	2.0	1.9
Euro area	6.5	8.4	8.2	8.2	8.1	8.0	52.7	50.2	48.3	48.0	47.9	47.9	3.8	1.0	1.7	0.7	1.1	1.2
Total OECD	5.8	6.2	5.9	5.8	5.8	5.8	53.2	51.2	50.0	49.5	49.6	49.6	4.4	2.6	0.8	0.3	1.5	1.4

Note: The structural unemployment rate corresponds to "NAIRU". For more information about sources and definitions, see *OECD Economic Outlook* Sources and Methods (*http://www.oecd.org/eco/sources-and-methods*).
Source: OECD Economic Outlook 76 database.

Annex Table 23. **Household saving rates**

Per cent of disposable household income

	1987	1988	1989	1990	1991	1992	1993	1994	1995	1996	1997	1998	1999	2000	2001	2002	2003	2004	2005	2006
Net savings																				
Australia	8.2	7.0	8.7	9.3	6.2	5.7	5.0	5.8	4.9	5.8	3.9	1.9	1.5	2.9	2.5	-0.4	-2.2	-2.1	-1.8	-1.4
Austria	13.9	11.9	12.8	14.0	14.9	12.0	10.9	11.8	11.7	9.9	7.4	8.4	8.3	8.4	7.5	8.2	8.5	8.3	8.8	8.8
Canada	11.9	12.3	13.0	13.0	13.3	13.0	11.9	9.5	9.2	7.0	4.9	4.9	4.0	4.7	4.6	3.2	1.4	1.5	1.6	1.7
Denmark	..	-1.2	-0.2	3.2	3.0	2.0	0.5	-3.6	-0.1	-1.7	-4.4	-3.2	-8.0	-5.7	-1.2	0.1	0.3	-0.3	-1.6	-1.3
Finland	3.1	-1.0	-1.4	1.8	7.1	10.0	7.8	1.9	4.8	0.4	2.2	0.4	1.5	-1.4	-1.2	-0.2	0.4	1.6	1.1	0.8
France	6.4	6.9	7.2	7.8	8.7	9.7	10.4	9.8	11.2	10.0	11.3	10.8	10.4	10.9	11.5	12.1	11.1	10.2	9.9	9.6
Germany	12.9	13.2	12.7	13.9	13.0	13.0	12.3	11.6	11.2	10.8	10.4	10.3	9.8	9.7	10.2	10.5	10.7	11.1	11.1	10.8
Hungary	..	..	..	..	..	..	9.9	12.7	15.6	19.4	20.1	21.3	17.4	16.0	17.7	17.7	17.3	17.3	17.7	17.7
Ireland	11.0	8.1	6.2	7.9	9.0	8.5	11.4	7.6	11.3	9.7	10.6	13.3	12.2	9.9	10.4	10.3	8.3	8.2	8.2	8.2
Italy	24.6	24.0	23.7	24.0	22.9	21.4	20.8	19.2	17.9	18.9	15.4	12.2	9.8	9.2	10.3	10.6	10.5	11.3	10.9	10.3
Japan	13.9	13.0	13.1	13.9	15.0	14.2	13.7	12.6	11.9	9.8	10.0	11.0	10.7	9.5	6.6	6.4	6.3	5.1	5.0	5.0
Korea	22.7	24.9	23.5	22.0	24.4	23.3	20.6	20.3	18.0	17.1	16.3	23.7	16.2	10.5	6.0	1.5	2.5	3.4	3.7	5.1
Netherlands	13.5	13.4	15.3	17.5	13.8	16.1	13.5	14.3	14.4	13.0	13.4	12.9	9.6	6.8	9.5	10.0	10.1	10.7	10.7	9.9
New Zealand	4.0	3.3	2.9	0.7	2.1	0.8	-0.2	-3.1	-3.8	-2.5	-4.1	-4.2	-5.1	-4.1	-4.4	-5.2	-6.5	-8.1	-7.1	-6.3
Norway	-4.6	-1.2	1.1	2.2	2.9	5.0	6.1	5.2	4.6	2.2	2.8	5.8	5.5	5.2	4.1	9.2	7.6	7.5	7.7	7.8
United States	7.0	7.3	7.1	7.0	7.3	7.7	5.8	4.8	4.6	4.0	3.6	4.3	2.4	2.3	1.8	2.0	1.4	0.8	0.5	1.2
Gross savings																				
Belgium	15.2	15.4	15.0	17.3	17.4	18.4	19.5	19.5	18.6	16.9	15.6	14.4	14.4	13.1	14.4	14.8	14.2	13.8	13.4	13.9
Portugal	..	..	..	..	..	..	..	..	13.6	11.8	10.3	9.9	8.6	10.9	11.9	12.7	13.0	12.8	12.8	12.4
Spain	10.6	11.0	10.2	12.3	13.4	11.9	14.4	11.9	16.2	14.2	13.4	12.2	11.1	10.7	10.3	10.6	10.6	10.7	11.0	11.0
Sweden	-1.0	-3.0	-2.9	1.6	5.0	9.5	11.6	10.2	9.0	6.6	4.1	3.1	2.0	2.9	8.3	9.7	8.5	8.3	7.8	7.1
Switzerland	..	..	..	9.6	10.0	10.7	11.2	11.1	11.6	11.3	10.5	10.7	10.0	11.8	11.9	8.2	8.2	8.0	8.0	8.0
United Kingdom	6.4	4.9	6.7	8.0	10.2	11.6	10.8	9.3	10.0	9.4	9.4	6.1	4.9	5.0	6.5	5.3	5.5	6.4	7.4	7.9

Note: The adoption of new national account systems, SNA93 or ESA95, has been proceeding at an uneven pace among OECD member countries, both with respect to variables and the time period covered. As a consequence, there are breaks in many national series. See Table "National Account Reporting Systems and Base-years" at the beginning of the Statistical Annex and *OECD Economic Outlook* Sources and Methods *(http://www.oecd.org/eco/sources-and-methods)*. Countries differ in the way household disposable income is reported (in particular whether private pension benefits less pension contributions are included in disposable income or not), but the calculation of household saving is adjusted for this difference. Most countries are reporting household saving on a net basis (i.e. excluding consumption of fixed capital by households and unincorporated businesses). In most countries the households saving include saving by non-profit institutions (in some cases referred to as personal saving). Other countries (Czech Republic, Finland, France, Japan and New Zealand) report saving of households only.

Source: OECD Economic Outlook 76 database.

Annex Table 24. **Gross national saving**

Per cent of nominal GDP

	1985	1986	1987	1988	1989	1990	1991	1992	1993	1994	1995	1996	1997	1998	1999	2000	2001	2002	2003
Australia	18.8	19.4	21.3	22.6	21.7	18.1	16.2	17.2	18.6	17.5	17.8	18.9	19.0	18.6	19.1	19.0	19.7	19.0	..
Austria	23.1	23.2	23.3	23.9	24.4	25.0	24.8	23.9	22.4	22.3	21.6	21.4	21.3	21.8	21.2	22.0	21.7	22.9	22.4
Belgium	17.9	19.0	19.8	22.5	23.6	23.9	23.1	23.5	24.6	25.9	25.8	24.6	25.7	25.7	26.1	25.7	24.5	24.7	23.7
Canada	20.2	18.8	20.0	20.8	20.1	17.6	14.9	13.6	14.2	16.5	18.6	19.1	19.9	19.4	21.0	24.1	22.8	22.3	..
Czech Republic	..	..	..	..	..	..	..	27.9	28.1	27.3	29.9	27.4	26.1	27.8	25.4	24.4	..	..	..
Denmark	17.4	18.3	18.6	19.2	19.5	20.7	20.0	20.3	19.2	19.1	20.4	20.4	21.2	20.8	21.5	22.5	23.6	22.9	22.7
Finland	24.4	23.8	23.7	26.2	26.1	24.8	17.1	14.4	15.5	18.8	22.2	21.1	24.5	25.8	25.8	27.8	27.5	26.4	24.2
France	18.1	19.4	19.6	20.8	21.6	21.5	20.9	20.5	19.0	19.2	19.5	19.2	20.4	21.4	22.3	22.4	22.0	20.9	..
Germany	23.1	24.6	23.8	24.9	26.1	26.1	23.3	23.1	21.9	21.9	21.8	21.3	21.4	21.5	20.8	20.6	20.2	21.1	20.4
Greece	22.6	22.4	18.9	21.3	19.0	19.1	20.7	20.0	18.5	19.4	18.0	17.4	17.9	17.8	16.8	17.6	17.8	18.8	19.5
Iceland	15.9	19.0	16.6	16.3	16.2	17.4	16.8	16.6	18.2	18.4	17.7	17.9	18.5	17.9	15.6	14.3	17.9	18.4	15.8
Ireland	13.5	13.4	14.5	14.7	15.0	18.0	17.7	15.6	17.7	18.0	20.8	22.3	24.2	25.9	24.7	25.2	22.8	20.5	..
Italy	22.6	22.4	21.9	21.8	21.0	20.7	19.6	18.3	19.2	19.7	21.6	21.9	21.6	21.2	20.7	20.0	20.0	19.7	18.4
Japan	32.0	32.1	32.3	33.5	33.6	33.8	34.5	33.7	32.3	30.4	29.5	29.8	30.1	29.1	27.9	27.8	26.4	25.7	..
Korea	30.6	34.6	38.4	40.7	37.6	37.6	37.4	36.5	36.2	35.6	35.4	33.7	33.3	33.7	32.6	32.2	30.1	29.1	..
Mexico	25.8	19.1	24.5	21.3	20.3	20.3	18.7	16.6	15.1	14.8	19.3	22.4	24.0	20.5	20.5	20.7	18.0	..	..
Netherlands	23.9	24.2	23.9	25.6	27.2	26.1	25.4	24.5	24.6	26.2	27.4	26.7	27.9	25.2	26.6	27.1	25.2	22.6	..
New Zealand	18.6	18.9	18.0	18.6	17.8	16.2	13.0	13.9	16.6	17.3	17.2	16.2	15.8	15.4	14.0	15.4	18.2	..	..
Norway	31.1	25.4	25.6	25.0	26.0	25.7	24.7	23.7	23.8	24.8	26.4	28.4	30.1	27.3	29.1	36.5	35.0	32.3	30.8
Portugal	8.7	10.6	11.9	11.6	12.4	11.1	8.6	8.0	5.0	4.1	4.7	3.8	3.7	4.3	3.1	0.6	0.4	0.7	..
Spain	21.9	22.9	22.6	23.5	22.9	22.9	22.3	20.5	20.5	20.0	22.3	22.0	22.5	22.4	22.5	22.5	22.6	22.8	..
Sweden	20.6	21.4	21.7	22.4	23.1	21.6	18.5	15.7	14.0	17.7	20.7	20.2	20.5	21.3	21.7	22.6	22.1	21.8	21.6
Switzerland	31.8	31.4	31.1	33.2	34.0	33.7	31.6	29.1	30.0	29.6	29.9	29.4	31.3	32.3	33.1	34.9	31.5	..	..
Turkey	20.7	23.9	24.3	28.9	26.4	21.5	17.7	18.5	18.7	18.9	20.1	22.6	21.6	20.6	13.7	15.2	12.6	18.7	..
United Kingdom	18.1	17.2	17.3	17.2	17.1	16.2	15.3	14.0	13.9	15.5	15.7	15.8	16.9	17.7	15.5	15.4	15.3	14.9	14.7
United States	17.2	15.4	15.9	17.2	16.7	15.9	16.1	15.1	15.0	15.8	16.4	16.7	17.6	18.3	17.9	18.0	16.1	14.6	..

Note: Based on SNA93 or ESA95 except Turkey that reports on SNA68 basis.
Source: OECD Annual National Accounts database.

Annex Table 25. **General government total outlays**

Per cent of nominal GDP

	1987	1988	1989	1990	1991	1992	1993	1994	1995	1996	1997	1998	1999	2000	2001	2002	2003	2004	2005	2006
Australia	38.9	36.3	35.5	36.2	37.9	39.7	39.8	39.3	39.1	37.9	36.8	36.7	35.8	35.7	37.2	36.3	36.0	35.7	35.8	35.4
Austria	54.4	53.2	51.9	51.6	52.3	53.2	56.4	56.0	56.0	55.4	53.1	53.4	53.2	51.4	50.9	50.6	50.8	49.9	49.4	48.2
Belgium	57.0	55.1	53.4	53.4	54.4	54.7	55.7	53.4	52.9	53.1	51.4	50.7	50.0	49.3	49.3	50.2	51.0	49.2	49.5	49.1
Canada	46.1	45.4	45.8	48.8	52.3	53.3	52.2	49.7	48.5	46.6	44.3	44.4	42.5	41.1	41.8	40.9	40.5	39.4	38.9	38.9
Czech Republic [a]	..	..	..	..	..	..	..	..	54.4	42.8	42.4	43.8	42.9	42.1	45.0	46.9	54.5	46.1	45.8	45.2
Denmark	55.0	57.2	57.3	57.0	57.8	59.0	61.7	61.6	60.3	59.8	58.0	57.6	56.3	54.9	55.3	55.8	56.1	55.6	54.6	54.1
Finland	48.5	47.0	45.1	48.7	57.6	62.9	64.1	62.8	59.5	59.8	56.4	52.8	52.1	49.1	49.1	50.1	51.0	50.5	50.6	50.4
France	51.9	51.4	50.4	50.7	51.5	53.0	55.3	55.0	55.1	55.4	54.9	53.7	53.5	52.5	52.5	53.4	54.5	54.5	54.4	53.9
Germany [b]	45.8	45.3	44.0	44.5	47.1	48.1	49.3	49.0	49.4	50.3	49.3	48.8	48.7	45.7	48.3	48.7	48.8	47.8	47.2	46.1
Greece	45.1	44.0	45.4	50.2	46.7	49.4	52.0	49.9	51.0	49.2	47.8	47.8	47.6	52.1	50.2	49.1	48.3	49.8	48.4	48.1
Hungary	..	..	..	..	56.7	60.3	59.8	63.4	56.9	53.9	51.8	52.5	50.2	47.8	49.0	52.6	49.7	51.3	50.7	50.0
Iceland	37.4	42.5	45.0	42.4	43.7	44.6	44.5	44.3	43.7	43.2	41.6	42.4	43.5	43.1	44.1	45.8	48.0	45.9	44.5	43.6
Ireland	52.0	48.5	42.1	43.2	44.8	45.3	45.1	44.3	41.5	39.6	37.1	34.9	34.5	32.0	33.5	33.8	34.3	33.9	34.0	34.3
Italy	50.8	51.5	52.8	54.4	55.5	56.7	57.7	54.5	53.4	53.2	51.1	49.9	48.9	46.9	48.7	48.0	48.9	48.7	48.3	48.7
Japan [c]	31.5	30.9	30.2	31.7	31.5	32.5	34.2	34.8	35.8	36.3	35.1	36.1	37.7	38.2	37.7	38.1	37.6	36.7	37.2	37.5
Korea	17.7	17.9	19.0	19.5	20.6	21.8	21.4	20.9	20.8	21.8	22.4	24.7	23.9	23.8	25.0	24.8	27.3	27.9	28.2	28.3
Luxembourg	..	..	..	43.2	44.4	46.0	45.7	44.5	45.5	45.6	43.3	42.0	41.2	38.7	38.8	43.1	44.9	45.3	45.6	45.6
Netherlands [d]	58.4	56.6	54.5	54.8	54.8	55.8	56.0	53.6	51.4	49.6	48.2	47.2	46.9	45.3	46.7	47.8	49.0	48.9	48.6	47.8
New Zealand	53.6	52.7	51.9	53.3	51.5	49.5	46.0	43.0	41.9	41.0	41.7	42.7	41.0	39.8	38.6	38.5	38.3	38.2	38.7	39.1
Norway	50.5	52.6	52.2	54.0	54.9	56.2	55.1	54.1	51.5	49.0	47.2	49.6	48.1	42.7	44.3	47.4	48.7	46.7	45.1	45.3
Poland	..	..	..	..	..	..	..	..	51.3	51.2	50.2	48.5	48.1	44.9	47.6	48.9	48.2	47.7	46.6	45.1
Portugal	40.0	38.5	38.8	42.1	45.1	46.2	47.8	46.0	45.0	45.8	44.8	44.1	45.3	45.2	46.3	45.9	47.7	48.0	47.3	47.3
Slovak Republic	..	..	..	..	..	..	..	57.8	54.1	61.5	65.0	60.8	56.9	59.9	51.5	51.0	39.4	39.2	39.0	38.1
Spain	41.0	40.9	42.2	43.4	44.9	45.9	49.4	47.3	45.0	43.7	41.8	41.4	40.2	40.0	39.6	39.9	39.6	41.0	40.2	40.1
Sweden	62.3	62.5	62.4	63.5	65.5	70.2	72.9	70.9	67.6	65.2	62.9	60.7	60.3	57.3	57.0	58.2	58.2	57.5	57.2	56.7
Switzerland	..	..	..	30.0	31.8	33.9	34.8	34.8	34.6	35.3	35.6	36.1	34.6	34.0	34.8	35.4	36.0	36.0	35.7	35.2
United Kingdom	43.6	41.1	40.5	42.2	44.0	46.1	46.1	45.3	45.0	43.0	41.4	40.2	39.7	37.5	41.0	41.8	43.7	44.4	45.0	45.2
United States [e]	37.0	36.1	36.0	37.0	37.8	38.5	38.0	37.0	36.9	36.5	35.3	34.6	34.2	34.0	35.1	36.0	36.1	35.6	35.6	35.7
Euro area	48.9	48.4	47.9	48.7	50.1	51.3	52.9	51.8	51.4	51.5	50.2	49.3	48.9	47.1	48.1	48.5	48.9	48.6	48.2	47.7
Total OECD	40.4	39.6	39.3	40.3	41.5	42.6	43.1	42.3	42.3	41.9	40.7	40.3	40.0	39.2	40.2	40.8	41.1	40.6	40.5	40.4

Note: Total outlays are defined as current outlays plus capital outlays. Data refer to the general government sector, which is a consolidation of accounts for the central, state and local governments plus social security. One-off revenues from the sale of mobile telephone licenses are recorded as negative capital outlays for countries listed in the note to Table 27. See *OECD Economic Outlook* Sources and Methods *(http://www.oecd.org/eco/sources-and-methods)*.

a) In 1995 data reflect the large privatisation campaign which transferred some public enterprises to private ownership through vouchers distributed to the population. In 2003 the activation of State guarantees, mainly for the banking sector, accounts for about 7.7 per cent of total outlays.

b) The 1995 outlays are net of the debt taken on this year from the Inherited Debt Funds.

c) The 1998 outlays would be 5.3 percentage points of GDP higher if it included central government's assumption of the debt of the Japan Railway Settlement Corporation and the National Forest Special Account. The 2000 outlays include capital transfers to the Deposit Insurance Company.

d) The 1995 outlays would be 4.9 percentage points of GDP higher if capital transfers to a housing agency offering rentals to low income people were taken into account.

e) These data include outlays net of operating surpluses of public enterprises.

Source: OECD Economic Outlook 76 database.

Annex Table 26. **General government total tax and non-tax receipts**

Per cent of nominal GDP

	1987	1988	1989	1990	1991	1992	1993	1994	1995	1996	1997	1998	1999	2000	2001	2002	2003	2004	2005	2006
Australia	36.4	35.5	34.9	34.5	33.6	33.3	33.9	34.5	35.2	35.7	36.4	37.4	37.8	36.5	36.4	36.6	36.8	36.4	36.2	35.8
Austria	50.3	50.3	49.3	49.7	50.0	51.6	52.5	51.3	50.3	51.4	51.1	51.0	50.8	49.8	51.0	50.2	49.5	48.4	47.3	46.1
Belgium	49.0	47.7	45.7	46.6	46.9	46.6	48.3	48.3	48.5	49.3	49.4	50.0	49.6	49.5	49.9	50.3	51.3	49.1	49.1	48.6
Canada	40.6	41.0	41.2	43.0	43.9	44.2	43.5	43.0	43.2	43.8	44.5	44.5	44.1	44.1	42.9	41.2	41.2	40.6	40.1	39.9
Czech Republic	..	..	..	..	..	..	..	..	41.0	39.7	40.0	38.8	39.2	38.5	39.1	40.2	41.9	41.7	41.2	41.3
Denmark	57.5	58.7	57.6	56.0	55.4	56.8	58.9	59.1	58.0	58.8	58.3	58.7	59.5	57.4	58.2	57.4	57.3	56.5	56.0	55.6
Finland	50.1	52.3	52.0	54.2	56.6	57.3	56.9	57.1	55.7	56.9	55.1	54.5	54.3	56.1	54.3	54.4	53.2	52.8	52.7	52.6
France	49.9	49.0	48.6	48.6	49.1	48.8	49.3	49.4	49.6	51.3	51.8	51.1	51.7	51.1	50.9	50.2	50.4	50.7	51.2	51.0
Germany	44.0	43.3	44.1	42.5	44.1	45.5	46.2	46.6	46.1	46.9	46.6	46.6	47.3	47.1	45.5	45.1	45.0	43.9	43.7	43.3
Greece	35.5	32.4	31.8	34.5	35.6	37.2	38.6	40.7	40.9	41.7	43.7	45.3	45.8	47.9	46.5	45.3	43.6	44.5	44.9	44.9
Hungary	..	..	..	..	53.7	53.2	53.2	52.3	49.3	48.1	44.6	44.5	44.6	44.8	44.3	43.2	43.6	45.9	45.8	45.5
Iceland	36.5	40.5	40.5	39.0	40.7	41.8	40.0	39.6	40.7	41.6	41.6	42.9	45.9	45.6	44.3	45.3	46.3	46.0	45.7	44.6
Ireland	43.9	44.2	40.4	40.4	42.0	42.3	42.3	42.3	39.4	39.5	38.6	37.2	36.9	36.4	34.5	33.6	34.5	34.1	33.9	33.9
Italy	39.1	40.2	41.1	42.6	43.8	46.1	47.4	45.2	45.8	46.1	48.4	46.8	47.1	46.2	46.0	45.6	46.4	45.7	45.2	45.1
Japan [a]	31.9	32.0	32.0	33.8	33.3	33.2	31.9	31.0	31.1	31.2	31.3	30.6	30.5	30.7	31.6	30.2	29.9	30.2	30.7	31.2
Korea	20.1	21.1	22.1	22.7	22.2	23.1	23.6	23.7	24.6	25.2	25.7	26.5	26.7	29.3	29.6	30.3	31.4	31.3	31.6	31.7
Luxembourg	..	..	..	48.0	45.6	46.2	47.3	47.3	47.6	47.5	46.5	45.1	44.9	44.7	45.2	45.9	45.6	44.9	44.8	44.4
Netherlands	53.2	52.4	49.5	49.4	52.2	51.6	53.2	50.1	47.3	47.8	47.1	46.4	47.6	47.5	46.6	45.9	45.8	46.0	45.9	45.9
New Zealand	51.0	48.8	48.3	48.9	47.7	46.3	44.7	45.4	44.9	43.9	43.5	43.0	41.7	41.3	40.6	41.0	41.4	41.2	40.8	40.9
Norway	55.1	55.3	54.0	56.2	55.0	54.4	53.7	54.4	54.9	55.6	55.0	53.1	54.3	58.2	57.9	56.5	57.1	54.9	55.6	56.7
Poland	..	..	..	..	..	..	..	..	47.4	46.5	45.7	44.5	44.9	42.5	43.8	43.9	44.3	42.3	41.9	40.8
Portugal	32.8	34.8	35.7	35.5	37.5	41.5	39.7	38.3	39.6	41.0	41.2	41.0	42.4	42.3	41.9	43.2	44.9	45.1	44.3	43.5
Slovak Republic	..	..	..	..	..	..	..	51.7	53.3	54.1	58.8	57.1	49.8	47.6	45.5	45.3	35.6	35.3	35.2	34.2
Spain	38.0	37.8	39.6	39.5	40.3	42.3	42.4	40.8	38.4	38.8	38.6	38.3	39.0	39.1	39.2	39.8	40.0	40.0	40.0	40.0
Sweden	66.2	65.5	67.3	67.2	63.6	62.6	61.5	61.6	60.7	62.4	61.9	62.6	62.6	62.4	59.9	58.0	58.3	58.0	57.9	57.8
Switzerland	..	..	..	30.6	30.6	31.5	32.1	32.8	33.3	33.9	33.2	34.7	34.7	36.3	35.7	35.6	35.2	35.0	35.0	35.0
United Kingdom	41.8	41.6	41.3	40.7	40.9	39.6	38.1	38.6	39.1	38.8	39.2	40.2	40.7	41.3	41.7	40.1	40.2	41.2	41.8	41.9
United States [b]	32.7	32.5	32.8	32.7	32.9	32.7	33.0	33.4	33.8	34.3	34.5	35.0	35.1	35.7	34.7	32.2	31.5	31.2	31.4	31.5
Euro area	44.3	44.0	44.1	44.1	45.1	46.2	47.2	46.7	46.3	47.2	47.5	47.0	47.6	47.1	46.4	46.0	46.2	45.7	45.6	45.3
Total OECD	37.2	37.0	37.2	37.4	37.7	38.0	38.1	38.1	38.3	38.8	39.1	39.1	39.3	39.5	39.0	37.6	37.4	37.1	37.3	37.3

Note: Data refer to the general government sector, which is a consolidation of accounts for central, state and local governments plus social security. Non-tax receipts consist of property income (including dividends and other transfers from public enterprises), fees, charges, sales, fines, capital tranfers received by the general government, etc. See *OECD Economic Outlook* Sources and Methods *(http://www.oecd.org/eco/sources-and-methods)*.

a) Includes deferred tax payments on postal savings accounts in 2000, 2001 and 2002.

b) Excludes the operating surpluses of public enterprises.

Source: OECD Economic Outlook 76 database.

Annex Table 27. **General government financial balances**

Surplus (+) or deficit (-) as a per cent of nominal GDP

	1987	1988	1989	1990	1991	1992	1993	1994	1995	1996	1997	1998	1999	2000	2001	2002	2003	2004	2005	2006
Australia	-2.6	-0.9	-0.6	-1.7	-4.3	-6.4	-5.8	-4.8	-3.9	-2.2	-0.4	0.7	2.0	0.8	-0.8	0.3	0.8	0.7	0.4	0.5
Austria	-4.0	-2.8	-2.6	-2.0	-2.3	-1.6	-3.9	-4.7	-5.7	-4.0	-2.0	-2.5	-2.3	-1.6	0.1	-0.4	-1.3	-1.5	-2.1	-2.1
Belgium	-7.9	-7.3	-7.7	-6.8	-7.5	-8.1	-7.4	-5.1	-4.4	-3.8	-2.0	-0.7	-0.4	0.2	0.6	0.1	0.3	-0.1	-0.4	-0.5
Canada	-5.4	-4.3	-4.6	-5.8	-8.4	-9.1	-8.7	-6.7	-5.3	-2.8	0.2	0.1	1.6	2.9	1.1	0.3	0.6	1.1	1.2	1.0
Czech Republic	..	..	..	..	..	..	..	..	-13.4	-3.1	-2.4	-5.0	-3.6	-3.7	-5.9	-6.8	-12.6	-4.3	-4.6	-3.9
Denmark	2.5	1.5	0.3	-1.0	-2.4	-2.2	-2.9	-2.4	-2.3	-1.0	0.4	1.1	3.2	2.5	2.8	1.6	1.2	0.9	1.4	1.5
Finland	1.6	5.3	6.9	5.5	-1.0	-5.5	-7.2	-5.7	-3.9	-2.9	-1.3	1.6	2.2	7.1	5.2	4.3	2.1	2.3	2.1	2.3
France	-2.0	-2.5	-1.8	-2.1	-2.4	-4.2	-6.0	-5.5	-5.5	-4.1	-3.0	-2.7	-1.8	-1.4	-1.5	-3.3	-4.1	-3.7	-3.1	-2.9
Germany	-1.8	-2.0	0.1	-2.0	-2.9	-2.6	-3.1	-2.4	-3.3	-3.4	-2.7	-2.2	-1.5	1.3	-2.8	-3.7	-3.8	-3.9	-3.5	-2.7
Greece[a]	-9.6	-11.6	-13.6	-15.7	-11.0	-12.2	-13.4	-9.3	-10.2	-7.4	-4.0	-2.5	-1.8	-4.2	-3.7	-3.8	-4.6	-5.3	-3.5	-3.2
Hungary	..	..	..	..	-3.0	-7.1	-6.6	-11.0	-7.6	-5.9	-7.2	-8.0	-5.6	-3.0	-4.7	-9.3	-6.2	-5.4	-4.9	-4.5
Iceland	-0.9	-2.0	-4.6	-3.3	-3.0	-2.9	-4.5	-4.8	-3.0	-1.6	0.0	0.5	2.4	2.5	0.2	-0.4	-1.6	0.1	1.2	1.0
Ireland	-8.1	-4.2	-1.7	-2.8	-2.9	-3.0	-2.7	-2.0	-2.1	-0.1	1.5	2.3	2.5	4.4	1.0	-0.2	0.2	0.2	-0.1	-0.4
Italy	-11.8	-11.3	-11.7	-11.8	-11.7	-10.7	-10.3	-9.3	-7.6	-7.1	-2.7	-3.1	-1.8	-0.7	-2.7	-2.4	-2.5	-2.9	-3.1	-3.6
Japan	0.3	1.1	1.8	2.1	1.8	0.8	-2.4	-3.8	-4.7	-5.1	-3.8	-5.5	-7.2	-7.5	-6.1	-7.9	-7.7	-6.5	-6.4	-6.3
Korea	2.4	3.2	3.1	3.2	1.6	1.3	2.2	2.8	3.8	3.4	3.3	1.7	2.9	5.4	4.6	5.5	4.1	3.4	3.4	3.4
Luxembourg	..	..	..	4.8	1.2	0.2	1.5	2.7	2.1	1.9	3.2	3.2	3.7	6.0	6.4	2.8	0.8	-0.4	-0.8	-1.2
Netherlands	-5.3	-4.2	-5.0	-5.3	-2.7	-4.2	-2.8	-3.5	-4.2	-1.8	-1.1	-0.8	0.7	2.2	-0.1	-1.9	-3.2	-2.9	-2.7	-1.9
New Zealand	-2.6	-4.0	-3.6	-4.3	-3.9	-3.3	-1.3	2.5	3.0	2.9	1.9	0.3	0.6	1.5	2.0	2.5	3.1	2.9	2.1	1.9
Norway	4.6	2.6	1.8	2.2	0.1	-1.9	-1.4	0.3	3.4	6.5	7.7	3.6	6.2	15.6	13.6	9.1	8.3	8.2	10.5	11.4
Poland	..	..	..	..	..	..	..	..	-3.9	-4.7	-4.5	-4.0	-3.2	-2.4	-3.8	-4.9	-3.8	-5.4	-4.7	-4.3
Portugal	-7.2	-3.8	-3.1	-6.6	-7.6	-4.8	-8.1	-7.7	-5.5	-4.8	-3.6	-3.2	-2.9	-2.9	-4.4	-2.7	-2.8	-2.9	-3.0	-3.8
Slovak Republic	..	..	..	..	..	..	..	-6.1	-0.9	-7.4	-6.2	-3.8	-7.1	-12.3	-6.0	-5.7	-3.7	-3.9	-3.8	-3.9
Spain	-3.1	-3.1	-2.6	-3.9	-4.6	-3.7	-7.0	-6.5	-6.6	-5.0	-3.2	-3.0	-1.2	-0.9	-0.4	-0.1	0.4	-1.1	-0.1	-0.1
Sweden	3.8	2.9	4.8	3.8	-1.9	-7.6	-11.4	-9.3	-6.9	-2.8	-1.0	1.9	2.3	5.1	2.9	-0.3	0.1	0.5	0.7	1.2
Switzerland	..	..	..	0.6	-1.1	-2.4	-2.7	-1.9	-1.2	-1.4	-2.4	-1.5	0.0	2.3	0.9	0.2	-0.8	-1.0	-0.6	-0.2
United Kingdom	-1.8	0.5	0.8	-1.6	-3.1	-6.5	-7.9	-6.8	-5.8	-4.2	-2.2	0.1	1.0	3.8	0.7	-1.7	-3.5	-3.2	-3.2	-3.3
United States	-4.3	-3.6	-3.2	-4.2	-4.9	-5.8	-4.9	-3.6	-3.1	-2.2	-0.8	0.4	0.9	1.6	-0.4	-3.8	-4.6	-4.4	-4.1	-4.2
Euro area	-4.5	-4.4	-3.7	-4.6	-5.0	-5.1	-5.8	-5.1	-5.1	-4.3	-2.6	-2.3	-1.3	0.1	-1.7	-2.4	-2.8	-2.9	-2.6	-2.4
Total OECD	-3.2	-2.6	-2.1	-2.9	-3.7	-4.6	-5.0	-4.2	-4.0	-3.1	-1.7	-1.2	-0.8	0.3	-1.2	-3.2	-3.7	-3.5	-3.2	-3.2
Memorandum items																				
General government financial balances excluding social security																				
United States	-4.8	-4.4	-4.2	-5.3	-5.8	-6.6	-5.6	-4.4	-3.9	-3.1	-1.9	-0.8	-0.6	0.1	-2.0	-5.4	-6.0	-5.7	-5.6	-5.8
Japan[b]	-2.5	-2.0	-1.4	-1.4	-0.9	-1.7	-4.6	-5.7	-6.6	-6.8	-5.6	-6.9	-8.3	-8.0	-6.2	-7.7	-7.4	-6.2	-6.1	-6.1

Note: Financial balances include one-off revenues from the sale of the mobile telephone licenses. These revenues are substantial in a number of countries including Australia (2000-2001), Austria (2000), Belgium (2001), Denmark (2001), France (2001-2002), Germany (2000), Greece (2001), Ireland (2002), Italy (2000), Netherlands (2000), New Zealand (2001), Portugal (2000), Spain (2000) and the United Kingdom (2000). As data are on a national account basis, the government financial balance may differ from the numbers reported to the European Commission under the Excessive Deficit Procedure for some EU countries. For more details see footnotes to Annex Tables 25 and 26 and *OECD Economic Outlook* Sources and Methods *(http://www.oecd.org/eco/sources-and-methods)*.

a) Recent revisions to Greek budgetary data suggest deficits of 6.6, 4.3 and 3.4 per cent of GDP in 1997-1999 respectively. At the cut-off date for information, no data were available for the underlying changes to the spending and revenue components.

b) Prior to 1991, when SNA93 was adopted, these data included private pension funds.

Source: OECD Economic Outlook 76 database.

Annex Table 28. **Cyclically-adjusted general government balances**

Surplus (+) or deficit (-) as a per cent of potential GDP

	1987	1988	1989	1990	1991	1992	1993	1994	1995	1996	1997	1998	1999	2000	2001	2002	2003	2004	2005	2006
Australia	-2.2	-0.7	-0.5	-1.1	-2.6	-4.7	-4.6	-4.2	-3.4	-1.9	-0.2	0.5	1.6	0.3	-1.1	0.1	0.6	0.5	0.2	0.4
Austria	-3.3	-2.5	-2.5	-2.4	-2.9	-2.0	-3.6	-4.5	-5.5	-4.0	-2.0	-2.8	-2.9	-2.8	-0.2	-0.3	-0.7	-0.9	-1.6	-1.7
Belgium	-5.8	-7.0	-8.0	-7.8	-7.7	-7.8	-5.3	-3.7	-3.3	-2.1	-1.4	-0.3	-0.7	-1.1	-0.1	0.4	1.1	0.3	-0.2	-0.6
Canada	-5.8	-5.6	-5.9	-6.2	-6.8	-7.0	-6.8	-5.9	-4.6	-1.6	1.2	0.9	1.7	2.4	1.2	0.1	0.7	1.2	1.1	1.0
Denmark	0.8	0.4	0.4	-0.4	-1.4	-0.3	0.6	-1.3	-1.4	-0.5	0.2	0.8	2.7	1.5	1.8	1.6	2.4	1.6	1.6	1.3
Finland	0.3	2.8	3.3	3.4	2.1	1.8	2.2	2.1	2.3	1.9	0.7	2.3	2.6	6.1	5.4	4.7	2.8	2.4	1.9	1.5
France	-1.0	-2.3	-2.4	-2.9	-2.9	-4.5	-5.2	-4.9	-4.9	-3.0	-1.9	-2.1	-1.5	-1.9	-2.0	-3.2	-3.4	-3.1	-2.5	-2.4
Germany	-1.2	-2.3	-0.9	-4.0	-3.5	-3.2	-2.1	-1.6	-2.8	-2.6	-1.9	-1.7	-1.4	-2.0	-3.4	-3.4	-2.7	-2.6	-2.3	-1.9
Greece	-8.1	-11.5	-14.4	-15.8	-11.4	-12.1	-11.6	-7.6	-8.5	-5.8	-2.9	-1.7	-1.2	-4.2	-4.5	-4.2	-5.2	-5.9	-3.7	-3.2
Iceland	-3.1	-3.2	-4.8	-3.4	-2.2	-0.1	-1.7	-3.1	-0.8	-0.6	0.4	0.6	2.6	2.2	0.3	0.9	-0.8	-0.1	0.7	0.5
Ireland	-6.4	-3.4	-1.7	-4.2	-2.9	-2.0	-0.6	0.4	-0.6	1.1	1.7	2.4	1.7	3.1	-0.1	-1.1	0.0	0.2	-0.2	-0.5
Italy	-10.9	-11.3	-12.0	-11.9	-11.4	-9.9	-8.3	-7.9	-7.0	-6.3	-2.2	-2.8	-1.6	-2.5	-3.3	-2.6	-2.2	-2.7	-3.0	-3.7
Japan [a]	0.8	0.9	1.3	1.2	1.2	0.3	-2.4	-3.7	-4.6	-5.4	-4.2	-5.3	-6.7	-7.2	-5.5	-6.8	-6.8	-6.3	-6.4	-6.6
Netherlands	-3.7	-3.2	-5.9	-7.5	-4.7	-5.2	-2.1	-3.0	-4.0	-2.1	-2.1	-2.7	-1.8	-1.4	-1.9	-2.2	-1.4	-0.6	0.0	0.3
New Zealand	-3.2	-3.6	-3.2	-2.8	-0.6	0.1	0.3	2.3	2.3	1.9	1.4	1.1	0.5	1.0	1.6	1.7	2.5	1.8	1.7	1.7
Norway [b]	0.7	1.2	0.9	-0.7	-3.3	-5.3	-5.6	-4.4	-1.3	-1.4	-1.2	-2.3	-1.0	1.1	0.2	-2.7	-3.0	-3.8	-2.7	-1.3
Portugal	-5.7	-3.6	-3.9	-7.8	-9.3	-5.7	-7.2	-6.4	-4.9	-4.6	-3.8	-4.0	-3.9	-4.4	-5.0	-2.4	-1.4	-1.4	-1.7	-2.9
Spain	-2.8	-3.8	-3.8	-5.2	-5.7	-3.9	-5.6	-5.2	-5.2	-3.3	-2.0	-2.5	-1.1	-1.7	-0.7	-0.1	0.6	-0.7	0.2	0.2
Sweden	2.8	1.8	3.9	3.9	0.2	-3.6	-5.2	-5.0	-4.4	-0.1	0.9	2.6	1.8	3.6	2.7	-0.1	0.9	0.6	0.3	0.3
United Kingdom	-2.5	-1.4	-1.0	-2.5	-2.1	-4.4	-5.9	-5.9	-5.2	-3.6	-2.0	0.2	1.2	1.0	0.3	-1.7	-3.4	-3.4	-3.4	-3.5
United States	-4.2	-3.8	-3.6	-4.4	-4.2	-5.2	-4.4	-3.3	-2.6	-1.8	-0.6	0.5	0.6	1.3	-0.1	-3.2	-4.1	-4.2	-4.0	-4.2
Euro area	-3.8	-4.6	-4.6	-5.9	-5.7	-5.2	-4.4	-4.0	-4.3	-3.3	-1.9	-2.0	-1.4	-1.8	-2.3	-2.4	-2.0	-2.1	-1.8	-1.8
Total OECD	-3.2	-3.1	-3.0	-3.8	-3.8	-4.4	-4.3	-3.8	-3.6	-2.8	-1.5	-1.1	-0.9	-0.8	-1.4	-3.1	-3.4	-3.4	-3.3	-3.3

Note: Cyclically-adjusted balances exclude one-off revenues from the sale of mobile telephone licenses for those countries listed in the note to Table 27. For details on the methodology used for estimating the cyclical component of government balances see *OECD Economic Outlook* Sources and Methods *(http://www.oecd.org/eco/sources-and-methods)*.

a) Includes deferred tax payments on postal savings accounts in 2000, 2001 and 2002. The 2000 outlays include capital transfers to the Deposit Insurance Company.

b) As a percentage of mainland potential GDP. The financial balances shown exclude net revenues from petroleum activities.

Source: OECD Economic Outlook 76 database.

Annex Table 29. **General government primary balances**

Surplus (+) or deficit (-) as a per cent of nominal GDP

	1987	1988	1989	1990	1991	1992	1993	1994	1995	1996	1997	1998	1999	2000	2001	2002	2003	2004	2005	2006
Australia	1.5	3.0	3.3	1.7	-1.1	-2.7	-2.7	-0.6	0.2	1.2	2.4	3.0	4.2	2.9	1.1	2.0	2.3	2.2	1.8	1.9
Austria	-1.3	0.0	0.2	0.8	0.7	1.4	-0.8	-1.7	-2.5	-0.6	1.2	0.6	0.6	1.3	2.9	2.2	1.1	1.0	0.1	0.2
Belgium	2.2	2.6	3.2	4.4	3.3	2.6	3.2	4.1	4.5	4.7	5.7	6.7	6.3	6.7	6.8	5.8	5.5	4.6	4.0	3.6
Canada	-1.2	-0.1	0.0	-0.7	-3.1	-3.8	-3.4	-1.5	0.4	2.5	5.0	4.9	5.9	6.0	4.0	2.8	2.4	2.4	2.3	2.0
Denmark	7.5	5.8	4.3	2.8	1.6	1.0	0.6	0.9	0.9	1.9	3.3	3.6	5.7	4.6	4.6	3.1	2.3	1.9	2.2	2.2
Finland	0.7	4.4	5.7	3.7	-2.9	-7.5	-7.6	-4.6	-3.0	-1.5	0.7	3.4	3.8	8.1	5.9	4.5	2.3	2.2	2.0	2.1
France	0.2	-0.3	0.4	0.3	0.1	-1.4	-3.0	-2.4	-2.2	-0.7	0.1	0.4	1.1	1.4	1.2	-0.5	-1.6	-1.2	-0.6	-0.4
Germany	0.7	0.4	2.4	0.3	-0.6	0.1	-0.3	0.4	-0.1	-0.2	0.5	1.0	1.6	4.3	0.0	-0.9	-1.1	-1.2	-0.8	0.0
Greece	-3.1	-4.4	-6.3	-5.9	-1.7	-1.0	-1.1	4.2	2.0	4.0	4.2	5.8	5.6	3.3	3.0	2.2	0.9	-0.1	1.8	2.5
Iceland	-0.9	-1.3	-3.8	-2.0	-1.7	-1.8	-3.2	-3.4	-1.3	0.0	1.3	2.1	3.8	3.6	1.3	-0.7	-1.2	0.7	1.6	1.5
Ireland	-1.2	2.2	4.5	3.4	2.8	2.2	2.1	2.6	1.9	3.1	4.1	4.7	3.9	5.3	1.1	0.0	0.4	0.3	0.1	-0.2
Italy	-4.2	-3.3	-2.7	-1.8	-0.4	1.5	2.3	1.7	3.3	3.8	6.1	4.7	4.4	5.3	3.3	2.9	2.3	1.8	1.5	1.3
Japan	2.4	2.9	3.3	3.3	2.9	1.9	-1.2	-2.5	-3.4	-3.7	-2.5	-4.1	-5.8	-6.0	-4.7	-6.4	-6.2	-5.0	-4.7	-4.3
Korea	2.3	3.1	2.8	2.7	1.1	0.7	1.8	2.4	3.3	2.7	2.4	0.7	2.0	4.4	3.8	4.6	2.8	2.3	2.5	2.5
Luxembourg	..	..	..	2.6	-0.9	-1.7	0.0	1.5	0.9	1.0	2.4	2.2	3.0	5.1	5.1	1.7	-0.3	-1.4	-1.8	-2.1
Netherlands	-0.5	0.5	-0.8	-1.1	1.8	0.3	1.7	1.0	0.6	2.9	3.3	3.4	4.5	5.3	2.6	0.5	-0.9	-0.6	-0.4	0.4
New Zealand	1.4	-0.6	0.0	-0.1	-0.7	-0.5	1.2	3.9	4.4	3.7	2.5	0.7	0.7	1.6	1.9	2.2	2.8	2.6	1.8	1.5
Norway	1.7	-0.8	-1.6	-1.3	-3.6	-5.3	-4.2	-1.9	1.1	4.3	5.7	1.4	3.9	13.0	10.4	5.5	4.8	4.7	6.1	5.9
Poland	..	..	..	..	..	..	..	..	1.5	-0.5	-0.7	-0.3	-0.4	0.0	-1.2	-1.6	-0.8	-2.3	-1.4	-1.0
Portugal	0.3	2.9	3.1	2.0	1.2	3.8	-0.3	-1.1	0.8	0.6	0.7	0.3	0.4	0.4	-1.2	0.3	0.1	0.0	0.0	-0.9
Slovak Republic	..	..	..	..	..	..	..	-4.9	-0.1	-6.5	-5.0	-2.4	-5.7	-10.0	-3.4	-2.8	-2.4	-2.0	-2.0	-2.2
Spain	-0.6	-0.4	0.2	-0.8	-1.2	0.0	-2.3	-1.9	-1.8	0.0	1.2	0.9	2.2	2.2	2.4	2.4	2.6	1.2	2.0	1.9
Sweden	4.3	2.7	4.1	2.7	-3.0	-8.6	-11.8	-8.5	-5.5	-1.2	1.0	3.3	3.7	5.9	3.6	0.6	0.0	0.2	0.5	1.0
Switzerland	..	..	..	1.0	-0.7	-1.8	-2.1	-1.3	-0.5	-0.6	-1.6	-0.7	0.9	2.9	1.6	0.9	-0.1	-0.3	0.1	0.5
United Kingdom	1.6	3.5	3.6	1.1	-0.7	-4.1	-5.5	-4.1	-2.9	-1.3	0.9	3.1	3.4	6.0	2.5	-0.2	-1.9	-1.6	-1.7	-1.8
United States	-1.2	-0.5	0.1	-0.8	-1.3	-2.2	-1.5	-0.2	0.4	1.2	2.4	3.5	3.6	4.1	1.9	-1.7	-2.8	-2.6	-2.2	-2.0
Euro area	-0.6	-0.4	0.4	-0.1	-0.2	0.1	-0.5	-0.1	0.0	0.8	2.0	2.0	2.5	3.7	1.8	0.8	0.3	0.0	0.3	0.6
Total OECD	-0.1	0.5	1.0	0.3	-0.4	-1.1	-1.5	-0.8	-0.4	0.4	1.6	1.9	2.0	2.8	1.1	-1.0	-1.7	-1.5	-1.2	-1.0

Note: The primary balance is the difference between the financial balance and net interest payments. For more details see footnotes to Annex Tables 27 and 31 and *OECD Economic Outlook* Sources and Methods (*http://www.oecd.org/eco/sources-and-methods*) .

Source: OECD Economic Outlook 76 database.

Annex Table 30. **Cyclically-adjusted general government primary balances**

Surplus (+) or deficit (-) as a per cent of potential GDP

	1987	1988	1989	1990	1991	1992	1993	1994	1995	1996	1997	1998	1999	2000	2001	2002	2003	2004	2005	2006
Australia	1.8	3.1	3.3	2.3	0.3	-1.2	-1.6	-0.1	0.6	1.5	2.6	2.8	3.9	2.4	0.8	1.8	2.2	2.0	1.7	1.8
Austria	-0.7	0.4	0.3	0.5	0.1	1.1	-0.5	-1.5	-2.3	-0.6	1.2	0.3	0.1	0.2	2.7	2.2	1.6	1.5	0.6	0.5
Belgium	4.0	2.9	2.9	3.7	3.1	2.9	4.9	5.3	5.4	6.2	6.2	7.0	6.1	5.6	6.2	6.0	6.2	5.0	4.2	3.5
Canada	-1.5	-1.3	-1.1	-1.0	-1.6	-1.9	-1.6	-0.8	1.0	3.6	5.8	5.6	6.0	5.5	4.0	2.6	2.5	2.5	2.2	2.0
Denmark	5.9	4.8	4.4	3.3	2.5	2.8	3.9	2.0	1.7	2.4	3.1	3.3	5.1	3.5	3.7	3.1	3.4	2.6	2.4	1.9
Finland	-0.6	1.9	2.0	1.6	0.3	0.1	1.9	3.1	3.1	3.3	2.5	4.0	4.2	7.1	6.1	5.0	3.0	2.3	1.8	1.4
France	1.1	-0.1	-0.1	-0.5	-0.3	-1.7	-2.3	-1.8	-1.7	0.2	1.2	0.9	1.3	0.9	0.8	-0.5	-0.9	-0.6	0.0	0.1
Germany	1.3	0.2	1.5	-1.7	-1.2	-0.5	0.7	1.2	0.4	0.6	1.3	1.5	1.7	1.0	-0.5	-0.6	0.0	0.0	0.4	0.8
Greece	-1.9	-4.3	-7.0	-6.0	-2.0	-0.9	0.2	5.4	3.2	5.2	5.1	6.4	6.1	3.2	2.3	1.8	0.4	-0.5	1.6	2.6
Iceland	-3.2	-2.4	-4.1	-2.1	-1.0	0.9	-0.4	-1.7	0.8	1.0	1.7	2.1	4.0	3.3	1.4	0.6	-0.4	0.5	1.1	0.9
Ireland	0.2	3.0	4.5	2.1	2.7	3.1	3.9	4.6	3.2	4.2	4.3	4.8	3.1	4.0	0.1	-0.9	0.3	0.3	0.0	-0.3
Italy	-3.5	-3.2	-3.0	-1.9	-0.2	2.0	3.8	2.8	3.8	4.4	6.4	4.9	4.5	3.6	2.7	2.7	2.5	2.0	1.7	1.2
Japan[a]	2.8	2.8	2.9	2.5	2.3	1.5	-1.2	-2.5	-3.3	-4.1	-2.9	-3.9	-5.2	-5.8	-4.1	-5.4	-5.4	-4.8	-4.7	-4.5
Netherlands	0.9	1.5	-1.6	-3.2	-0.1	-0.7	2.4	1.5	0.7	2.6	2.4	1.6	2.2	1.9	0.8	0.2	0.9	1.6	2.2	2.6
New Zealand	0.9	-0.3	0.5	1.3	2.4	2.8	2.7	3.7	3.8	2.7	1.9	1.5	0.6	1.1	1.5	1.4	2.2	1.4	1.3	1.3
Norway[b]	-2.6	-2.5	-2.8	-4.6	-7.5	-9.2	-8.7	-6.9	-4.0	-4.1	-3.7	-4.8	-3.9	-2.4	-3.9	-7.2	-7.4	-8.1	-8.3	-8.3
Portugal	1.5	3.0	2.4	1.1	-0.1	3.1	0.4	0.0	1.3	0.8	0.4	-0.5	-0.6	-1.1	-1.8	0.6	1.5	1.4	1.1	0.0
Spain	-0.4	-0.9	-0.8	-2.1	-2.3	-0.2	-1.1	-0.7	-0.5	1.4	2.2	1.5	2.2	1.5	2.1	2.4	2.8	1.5	2.3	2.1
Sweden	3.2	1.6	3.2	2.8	-0.9	-4.5	-5.6	-4.2	-3.0	1.5	2.9	4.0	3.2	4.4	3.4	0.8	0.7	0.3	0.1	0.2
United Kingdom	1.0	1.8	1.9	0.3	0.3	-2.1	-3.5	-3.3	-2.3	-0.7	1.1	3.2	3.5	3.2	2.1	-0.1	-1.8	-1.9	-1.9	-1.9
United States	-1.2	-0.7	-0.3	-1.0	-0.7	-1.8	-1.0	0.1	0.9	1.6	2.6	3.6	3.4	3.9	2.2	-1.2	-2.3	-2.5	-2.1	-2.0
Euro area	0.0	-0.6	-0.4	-1.3	-0.8	-0.1	0.7	0.9	0.7	1.8	2.7	2.4	2.5	1.9	1.2	0.9	1.0	0.8	1.1	1.1
Total OECD	0.0	0.1	0.4	-0.4	-0.3	-0.8	-0.8	-0.3	0.0	0.8	1.9	2.1	2.0	1.9	1.0	-0.9	-1.4	-1.4	-1.2	-1.1

Note: The cyclically-adjusted primary balance is the difference between the cyclically adjusted balance and net interest payments. It excludes one-off revenues from the sale of mobile telephone licenses. See *OECD Economic Outlook* Sources and Methods *(http://www.oecd.org/eco/sources-and-methods)* for details on the methodology used for estimating the cyclical component of government balances.

a) Includes deferred tax payments on postal savings accounts in 2000, 2001 and 2002. The 2000 outlays include capital transfers to the Deposit Insurance Company.

b) As a percentage of mainland potential GDP. The financial balances shown exclude net revenues from petroleum activities.

Source: OECD Economic Outlook 76 database.

Annex Table 31. **General government net debt interest payments**

Per cent of nominal GDP

	1987	1988	1989	1990	1991	1992	1993	1994	1995	1996	1997	1998	1999	2000	2001	2002	2003	2004	2005	2006
Australia	4.1	3.8	3.9	3.5	3.1	3.7	3.2	4.2	4.1	3.4	2.8	2.2	2.2	2.1	1.9	1.7	1.5	1.5	1.4	1.4
Austria	2.7	2.9	2.8	2.8	2.9	3.0	3.2	3.1	3.2	3.4	3.1	3.0	2.9	2.9	2.8	2.6	2.3	2.4	2.2	2.2
Belgium	10.1	9.9	10.9	11.3	10.8	10.8	10.6	9.2	8.9	8.5	7.7	7.3	6.7	6.5	6.2	5.7	5.2	4.7	4.4	4.1
Canada	4.2	4.2	4.6	5.2	5.3	5.3	5.3	5.2	5.7	5.3	4.8	4.8	4.3	3.1	2.9	2.5	1.8	1.3	1.1	1.0
Denmark	5.0	4.3	4.0	3.8	4.0	3.2	3.5	3.3	3.1	2.9	2.9	2.5	2.4	2.1	1.8	1.6	1.1	1.0	0.8	0.7
Finland	-0.9	-0.9	-1.2	-1.7	-1.9	-1.9	-0.3	1.1	0.9	1.5	1.9	1.7	1.6	1.1	0.7	0.2	0.2	-0.1	0.0	-0.1
France	2.2	2.1	2.2	2.4	2.6	2.7	3.0	3.1	3.3	3.3	3.2	3.1	2.9	2.8	2.8	2.7	2.6	2.5	2.5	2.5
Germany [a]	2.5	2.5	2.3	2.2	2.3	2.7	2.8	2.8	3.2	3.2	3.2	3.3	3.1	2.9	2.8	2.7	2.8	2.7	2.8	2.8
Greece	6.5	7.2	7.3	9.8	9.4	11.2	12.2	13.5	12.1	11.5	8.2	8.2	7.4	7.5	6.7	6.0	5.5	5.3	5.2	5.7
Iceland	-0.1	0.7	0.8	1.3	1.2	1.0	1.4	1.4	1.7	1.6	1.3	1.6	1.4	1.1	1.1	-0.3	0.5	0.6	0.4	0.4
Ireland	6.9	6.5	6.2	6.2	5.7	5.2	4.8	4.5	4.0	3.2	2.6	2.4	1.4	0.9	0.2	0.2	0.2	0.2	0.2	0.2
Italy	7.6	8.0	9.0	9.9	11.3	12.2	12.6	11.0	10.9	10.9	8.8	7.8	6.2	6.0	5.9	5.3	4.8	4.7	4.7	4.9
Japan [b]	2.0	1.8	1.5	1.3	1.1	1.1	1.2	1.2	1.3	1.3	1.3	1.4	1.5	1.5	1.4	1.5	1.5	1.5	1.7	2.1
Korea	-0.1	-0.1	-0.3	-0.5	-0.5	-0.5	-0.5	-0.4	-0.5	-0.7	-0.8	-1.1	-0.9	-1.1	-0.8	-0.9	-1.3	-1.1	-0.9	-0.8
Luxembourg	..	..	..	-2.2	-2.0	-1.9	-1.6	-1.3	-1.1	-0.9	-0.8	-0.9	-0.7	-0.9	-1.3	-1.1	-1.0	-1.0	-1.0	-0.9
Netherlands	4.7	4.7	4.2	4.3	4.5	4.5	4.6	4.4	4.7	4.7	4.4	4.2	3.8	3.1	2.7	2.5	2.4	2.3	2.3	2.4
New Zealand	4.0	3.3	3.7	4.2	3.2	2.8	2.5	1.4	1.4	0.8	0.6	0.4	0.1	0.1	-0.1	-0.3	-0.4	-0.4	-0.4	-0.4
Norway	-2.9	-3.5	-3.4	-3.5	-3.7	-3.4	-2.8	-2.2	-2.3	-2.2	-2.1	-2.1	-2.3	-2.6	-3.1	-3.6	-3.6	-3.4	-4.4	-5.6
Poland	..	..	..	..	..	..	..	..	5.3	4.2	3.9	3.7	2.8	2.4	2.6	3.3	3.1	3.1	3.3	3.3
Portugal	7.5	6.6	6.1	8.6	8.8	8.5	7.7	6.6	6.3	5.4	4.2	3.5	3.2	3.3	3.2	3.1	3.0	2.9	2.9	2.9
Slovak Republic	..	..	..	..	..	..	..	1.3	0.8	0.9	1.2	1.3	1.5	2.3	2.6	2.9	1.4	1.8	1.9	1.7
Spain	2.5	2.8	2.9	3.1	3.3	3.7	4.7	4.6	4.9	5.0	4.4	4.0	3.3	3.1	2.8	2.5	2.2	2.2	2.1	2.0
Sweden	0.4	-0.3	-0.7	-1.1	-1.1	-1.0	-0.4	0.8	1.4	1.6	2.0	1.4	1.4	0.8	0.8	0.9	-0.1	-0.3	-0.2	-0.2
Switzerland	..	..	..	0.4	0.4	0.6	0.6	0.7	0.8	0.7	0.8	0.8	0.9	0.5	0.7	0.7	0.7	0.7	0.7	0.7
United Kingdom	3.5	3.1	2.8	2.7	2.4	2.4	2.5	2.7	2.9	2.9	3.1	3.0	2.4	2.2	1.8	1.5	1.6	1.5	1.5	1.5
United States	3.1	3.1	3.3	3.4	3.6	3.5	3.4	3.4	3.6	3.4	3.2	3.1	2.7	2.5	2.3	2.1	1.8	1.8	2.0	2.2
Euro area	3.9	4.0	4.2	4.5	4.8	5.2	5.3	5.0	5.0	5.1	4.6	4.3	3.8	3.6	3.5	3.2	3.0	3.0	3.0	3.0
Total OECD	3.1	3.1	3.1	3.2	3.3	3.4	3.4	3.4	3.5	3.5	3.2	3.1	2.7	2.5	2.3	2.2	2.0	1.9	2.0	2.1

Note: In the case of Ireland and New Zealand where net interest payments are not available, net property income paid is used as a proxy. For Denmark, net interest payments include dividends received. See *OECD Economic Outlook* Sources and Methods *(http://www.oecd.org/eco/sources-and-methods)*.

a) Includes interest payments on the debt of the Inherited Debt Funds from 1995 onwards.

b) Includes interest payments on the debt of the Japan Railway Settlement Corporation and the National Forest Special Account from 1998 onwards.

Source: OECD Economic Outlook 76 database.

Annex Table 32. **General government gross financial liabilities**

Per cent of nominal GDP

	1987	1988	1989	1990	1991	1992	1993	1994	1995	1996	1997	1998	1999	2000	2001	2002	2003	2004	2005	2006
Australia	..	27.5	25.0	23.1	23.9	28.7	32.2	42.6	44.6	41.4	39.6	34.1	28.4	25.2	22.1	20.7	19.6	20.6	18.2	18.0
Austria	58.1	59.2	58.2	57.6	57.6	57.3	62.1	65.0	69.7	69.9	69.9	67.4	69.8	69.4	70.2	71.9	69.7	69.5	69.9	70.2
Belgium	128.7	129.1	125.7	129.7	131.4	140.5	144.3	141.2	138.8	136.1	129.9	124.7	120.3	115.0	113.5	110.4	104.9	100.4	100.1	96.6
Canada	71.5	71.1	72.3	74.5	82.1	89.9	96.9	98.2	100.8	100.3	96.2	93.9	89.5	81.8	81.0	77.7	73.3	70.6	67.2	64.8
Czech Republic	..	..	..	..	..	..	..	..	..	..	12.2	12.9	13.4	18.2	25.3	28.8	37.8	39.1	41.1	42.5
Denmark	72.2	70.7	69.0	69.8	70.8	74.9	88.9	82.4	78.4	74.5	70.4	67.1	61.1	54.4	53.7	54.1	49.5	48.4	46.8	45.2
Finland	20.3	19.1	16.9	16.7	25.1	45.1	58.3	60.9	65.7	66.6	64.8	61.4	55.9	53.2	51.3	50.8	51.5	51.8	52.5	53.0
France	40.1	40.0	39.9	39.5	40.3	44.7	51.6	55.3	63.9	67.5	69.4	71.1	67.3	66.2	64.9	68.7	71.2	74.0	76.2	77.4
Germany [a]	41.8	42.3	40.9	41.5	38.8	41.8	47.4	47.9	57.1	60.3	61.8	63.2	61.6	60.9	60.5	62.9	65.1	67.0	68.6	69.1
Greece [b]	53.0	62.7	65.7	79.6	82.2	87.8	110.1	107.9	108.7	111.3	108.2	105.8	105.2	114.0	114.7	112.5	109.9	112.1	111.4	107.2
Hungary	..	..	..	..	..	..	..	..	..	..	67.3	64.9	66.4	60.2	60.1	61.1	60.3	57.1	58.8	60.2
Iceland	28.1	31.5	37.3	36.9	39.1	47.2	54.2	56.9	60.3	57.6	54.3	49.3	44.5	41.9	47.4	43.6	41.6	37.1	33.9	31.9
Ireland	111.7	108.1	98.7	94.0	95.4	92.4	95.0	89.5	81.9	73.4	64.6	53.7	48.7	38.3	35.9	32.7	32.1	29.3	26.9	25.3
Italy	98.1	100.3	103.3	112.5	116.5	126.0	127.9	134.4	133.5	135.7	133.0	133.4	128.4	124.5	122.0	121.5	120.9	120.0	119.5	119.3
Japan [c]	76.4	74.1	70.8	68.6	64.8	68.7	74.9	79.7	87.1	93.9	100.3	112.2	125.7	134.1	142.3	149.3	157.5	163.5	170.0	175.4
Korea	12.6	9.6	8.8	7.7	6.7	6.3	5.6	5.2	5.5	5.9	7.5	13.1	15.6	16.3	17.4	16.6	18.7	19.3	20.0	21.3
Luxembourg	..	..	..	5.4	4.6	5.5	6.8	6.3	6.7	7.2	6.8	6.3	6.0	5.5	5.5	5.7	5.3	5.2	5.2	5.4
Netherlands	85.4	87.5	88.2	87.8	88.9	92.8	97.7	87.7	90.8	89.8	84.5	82.9	74.2	66.7	62.1	62.1	63.2	66.1	68.1	68.7
New Zealand	..	..	..	..	..	..	70.8	62.7	56.9	50.8	50.1	49.7	47.1	44.7	42.2	40.2	37.4	34.6	33.2	32.3
Norway	33.7	32.8	32.8	29.3	27.5	32.2	40.5	36.9	34.4	30.7	27.5	26.2	26.8	30.0	29.2	35.7	35.2	34.9	31.1	26.8
Poland	..	..	..	..	..	..	..	..	..	..	45.6	41.8	43.2	40.0	41.0	46.7	51.6	53.2	57.0	58.5
Portugal	..	..	..	..	..	..	..	..	72.5	71.8	68.0	64.2	62.8	61.4	65.1	68.1	70.3	70.6	71.8	73.9
Slovak Republic	..	..	..	..	..	..	..	..	..	30.6	33.1	34.0	47.2	49.9	48.7	43.4	42.8	40.1	38.9	37.7
Spain	..	..	..	48.8	50.7	53.0	66.8	65.4	70.3	77.1	76.0	76.1	70.3	67.3	63.5	61.3	59.4	58.4	56.3	54.2
Sweden	62.5	56.1	51.0	46.8	55.5	74.0	79.0	83.5	82.2	84.7	82.8	81.2	71.6	64.2	63.2	62.1	61.9	61.2	60.3	59.0
United Kingdom	48.9	42.8	36.9	33.0	33.6	39.8	49.6	47.8	52.7	52.6	53.2	53.8	48.8	45.9	41.2	41.5	42.0	43.4	44.9	46.5
United States	64.1	64.8	65.1	66.6	71.3	73.7	75.4	74.6	74.2	73.4	70.9	67.7	64.1	58.2	57.9	60.2	62.5	63.5	64.9	66.8
Euro area	59.5	60.1	60.3	62.7	63.3	66.8	72.2	73.3	78.7	82.7	82.6	82.7	79.2	77.0	75.5	76.6	77.4	78.3	79.0	78.9
Total OECD	61.9	60.8	60.1	60.8	62.7	66.3	70.4	71.2	73.9	75.5	74.3	74.6	73.4	70.9	71.1	73.2	75.4	76.8	78.4	79.8

Note: Gross debt data are not always comparable across countries due to different definitions or treatment of debt components. Notably, they include the funded portion of government employee pension liabilities for some OECD countries, including Australia and the United States. The debt position of these countries is thus overstated relative to countries that have large unfunded liabilities for such pensions which according to ESA95/SNA93 are not counted in the debt figures, but rather as a memorandum item to the debt. General government financial liabilities presented here are defined according to ESA95/SNA93 for all countries with the exception of the Czech Republic, Greece, Ireland, Luxembourg and the Slovak Republic where debt measures follow the definition of debt applied under the Maastricht Treaty. Maastricht debt for European Union countries is shown in Annex Table 60. For more details see *OECD Economic Outlook* Sources and Methods *(http://www.oecd.org/eco/sources-and-methods).*

a) Includes the debt of the Inherited Debt Fund from 1995 onwards.

b) Recent revisions to Greek budgetary data suggest gross debt data of 114.0, 112.4 and 112.3 per cent of GDP in 1997-1999 respectively.

c) Includes the debt of the Japan Railway Settlement Corporation and the National Forest Special Account from 1998 onwards.

Source: OECD Economic Outlook 76 database.

Annex Table 33. **General government net financial liabilities**

Per cent of nominal GDP

	1987	1988	1989	1990	1991	1992	1993	1994	1995	1996	1997	1998	1999	2000	2001	2002	2003	2004	2005	2006
Australia	..	16.3	11.9	10.9	11.7	16.5	22.6	27.5	28.2	22.3	22.5	17.0	15.9	9.9	5.8	4.1	2.4	1.9	1.4	0.9
Austria	34.6	36.4	35.9	35.4	35.3	36.4	41.1	43.2	47.8	47.3	48.0	44.2	44.5	43.1	43.6	45.2	43.4	43.2	43.6	43.9
Belgium	120.2	120.6	117.2	116.9	118.2	125.2	127.9	126.2	125.6	123.3	118.3	112.8	107.7	102.5	100.1	97.9	95.3	90.8	90.5	87.0
Canada	39.3	38.2	41.1	43.3	50.0	58.5	64.4	67.4	69.3	67.5	63.5	60.8	53.5	44.8	40.5	37.9	34.3	31.1	28.1	25.7
Denmark	18.7	19.8	18.6	18.4	21.0	23.1	25.3	25.6	25.9	24.5	21.3	21.1	12.6	8.7	6.5	7.9	4.7	3.6	2.0	0.4
Finland [a]	-28.0	-29.2	-33.4	-35.6	-34.1	-24.9	-16.1	-16.3	-3.8	-6.5	-7.4	-15.0	-51.5	-31.5	-32.5	-32.3	-33.8	-34.8	-35.5	-36.1
France	13.3	15.1	15.7	17.5	18.8	20.4	27.1	28.3	38.9	42.6	43.3	41.7	33.6	34.9	36.7	42.3	44.1	46.1	47.6	48.7
Germany [b]	21.1	22.0	20.5	21.0	20.2	24.5	28.1	29.3	39.6	42.5	43.4	46.1	45.3	42.4	44.1	48.6	51.9	54.7	57.1	58.0
Hungary	..	..	..	..	..	..	..	..	..	..	24.0	30.6	32.7	30.9	33.5	39.8	39.7	41.8	43.5	44.9
Iceland	8.2	9.9	17.9	19.4	20.1	27.1	35.3	38.4	40.4	40.2	38.2	31.7	24.1	24.0	26.9	23.4	23.5	22.7	20.6	18.6
Italy	88.8	91.0	93.9	84.1	89.0	97.8	106.0	111.3	109.2	110.9	107.0	108.2	103.7	98.9	96.9	97.7	97.1	96.2	95.8	95.5
Japan [c]	55.6	46.9	38.3	24.6	12.6	14.3	17.7	20.3	24.5	29.7	35.2	45.8	53.6	59.1	65.2	71.4	79.1	84.4	90.1	94.7
Korea	-9.3	-12.8	-15.4	-16.3	-15.1	-14.6	-15.3	-16.0	-17.4	-19.0	-21.5	-23.1	-23.9	-27.0	-30.0	-31.8	-29.0	-30.7	-32.7	-34.3
Netherlands	25.6	29.2	32.5	33.4	34.6	40.6	45.3	44.2	54.1	52.9	50.7	48.0	36.6	35.1	33.3	35.3	36.8	39.0	41.1	41.6
New Zealand	..	..	..	..	..	..	47.9	40.8	34.7	30.7	28.4	25.8	23.8	20.7	20.3	18.0	13.9	9.9	7.4	5.2
Norway	-42.6	-42.7	-41.9	-41.7	-37.9	-35.6	-32.4	-31.0	-32.6	-36.5	-42.9	-46.9	-52.7	-60.6	-71.9	-72.5	-78.9	-80.5	-83.9	-91.1
Portugal	..	..	..	..	..	..	..	..	26.4	28.6	28.7	28.3	27.2	27.1	29.5	33.2	35.4	35.7	36.9	39.0
Spain	..	..	..	30.7	32.7	33.2	41.5	43.5	48.9	53.1	52.3	51.7	46.2	43.3	41.8	39.9	38.0	37.0	34.9	32.8
Sweden	6.3	0.2	-5.9	-7.8	-5.0	4.5	10.3	20.4	25.3	25.7	23.1	20.0	9.4	1.4	-2.9	4.8	4.5	3.8	2.9	1.6
United Kingdom	25.8	20.5	15.6	14.9	15.5	22.5	32.3	33.0	38.9	40.5	42.6	43.7	39.8	36.9	33.5	34.3	34.9	36.3	37.8	39.4
United States	46.5	47.6	47.7	48.9	52.5	55.9	58.4	57.9	57.2	56.3	53.1	49.3	44.3	39.0	38.0	40.7	42.8	44.3	45.7	47.6
Euro area	35.4	36.9	37.3	36.1	37.5	40.6	45.4	46.6	53.1	56.4	55.8	55.8	50.8	49.0	49.1	51.5	52.5	53.4	54.0	54.0
Total OECD	39.9	38.6	37.2	35.4	36.1	39.6	43.4	44.3	46.9	48.0	47.0	46.7	43.5	40.8	40.6	43.1	45.2	46.6	48.0	49.2

Note: Net debt measures are not always comparable across countries due to different definitions or treatment of debt (and asset) components. First, the treatment of government liabilities in respect of their employee pension plans may be different (see note to Annex Table 32). Second, a range of items included as general government assets differs across countries. For example, equity holdings are excluded from government assets in some countries whereas foreign exchange, gold and SDR holdings are considered as assets in the United States and the United Kingdom. For details see *OECD Economic Outlook* Sources and Methods *(http://www.oecd.org/eco/sources-and-methods).*

a) From 1995 onwards housing corporation shares are no longer classified as financial assets.

b) Includes the debt of the Inherited Debt Fund from 1995 onwards.

c) Includes the debt of the Japan Railway Settlement Corporation and the National Forest Special Account from 1998 onwards.

Source: OECD Economic Outlook 76 database.

Annex Table 34. **Short-term interest rates**

Per cent, per annum

	1990	1991	1992	1993	1994	1995	1996	1997	1998	1999	2000	2001	2002	2003	2004	2005	2006	Fourth quarter 2004	2005	2006
Australia	14.5	10.2	6.5	5.2	5.7	7.7	7.2	5.4	5.0	5.0	6.2	4.9	4.7	4.9	5.5	5.9	6.1	5.5	6.1	6.1
Austria	9.0	9.5	9.5	7.0	5.1	4.6	3.4	3.5	3.6											
Belgium	9.6	9.4	9.4	8.2	5.7	4.8	3.2	3.4	3.6											
Canada	13.0	9.0	6.7	5.0	5.5	7.1	4.5	3.6	5.1	4.9	5.7	4.0	2.6	3.0	2.5	3.5	4.2	3.0	3.7	4.4
Czech Republic	..	..	..	13.1	9.1	10.9	12.0	15.9	14.3	6.9	5.4	5.2	3.5	2.3	2.4	3.0	3.2	2.9	3.0	3.3
Denmark	10.9	9.7	11.0	10.4	6.1	6.1	3.9	3.7	4.1	3.3	4.9	4.6	3.5	2.4	2.1	2.2	2.7	2.2	2.2	3.1
Finland	14.0	13.1	13.3	7.8	5.4	5.8	3.6	3.2	3.6											
France	10.3	9.6	10.3	8.6	5.8	6.6	3.9	3.5	3.6											
Germany	8.5	9.2	9.5	7.3	5.4	4.5	3.3	3.3	3.5											
Greece	23.0	23.3	21.7	21.3	19.3	15.5	12.8	10.4	11.6	8.9	4.4									
Hungary	..	..	..	17.2	26.9	32.0	24.0	20.1	18.0	14.7	11.0	10.8	8.9	8.2	11.5	10.0	8.7	10.9	9.6	8.1
Iceland	14.8	14.6	10.5	8.8	4.9	7.0	7.0	7.1	7.4	8.6	11.2	11.0	8.0	5.0	6.2	8.7	8.8	7.8	9.0	8.0
Ireland	11.3	10.4	14.3	9.1	5.9	6.2	5.4	6.1	5.4											
Italy	12.2	12.2	14.0	10.2	8.5	10.5	8.8	6.9	5.0											
Japan	7.7	7.4	4.5	3.0	2.2	1.2	0.6	0.6	0.7	0.2	0.2	0.1	0.1	0.0	0.0	0.0	0.4	0.0	0.0	0.5
Korea	..	18.3	16.4	13.0	13.3	14.1	12.7	13.4	15.2	6.8	7.1	5.3	4.8	4.3	3.8	3.7	3.9	3.6	3.9	3.9
Luxembourg	9.6	9.4	9.4	8.2	5.7	4.8	3.2	3.4	3.6											
Mexico	35.0	19.8	15.9	15.5	14.6	48.2	32.9	21.3	26.2	22.4	16.2	12.2	7.5	6.5	6.8	7.8	8.1	7.5	7.9	8.3
Netherlands	8.7	9.3	9.4	6.9	5.2	4.4	3.0	3.3	3.5											
New Zealand	13.9	10.0	6.7	6.3	6.7	9.0	9.3	7.7	7.3	4.8	6.5	5.7	5.7	5.4	6.1	6.7	6.7	6.6	6.7	6.7
Norway	11.5	10.6	11.8	7.3	5.9	5.5	4.9	3.7	5.8	6.5	6.7	7.2	6.9	4.1	2.0	2.0	2.6	2.0	2.0	3.0
Poland	..	..	..	34.9	31.8	27.7	21.3	23.1	19.9	14.7	18.9	15.7	8.8	5.7	6.4	7.5	7.5	7.3	7.3	7.1
Portugal	16.9	17.7	16.1	12.5	11.1	9.8	7.4	5.7	4.3											
Slovak Republic	..	..	..	..	..	..	11.5	20.2	18.1	14.8	8.2	7.5	7.5	5.9	4.6	4.4	4.1	4.5	4.3	4.0
Spain	15.2	13.2	13.3	11.7	8.0	9.4	7.5	5.4	4.2											
Sweden	13.7	11.6	12.9	8.4	7.4	8.7	5.8	4.1	4.2	3.1	4.0	4.0	4.1	3.0	2.1	3.2	4.6	2.0	4.0	4.7
Switzerland	8.9	8.2	7.9	4.9	4.2	2.9	2.0	1.6	1.5	1.4	3.2	2.9	1.1	0.3	0.5	1.6	2.4	0.7	1.9	2.4
Turkey	..	..	..	..	..	..	..	..	..	..	38.9	92.4	59.5	38.5	22.5	14.7	12.5	15.7	14.4	12.6
United Kingdom	14.8	11.5	9.6	5.9	5.5	6.7	6.0	6.8	7.3	5.4	6.1	5.0	4.0	3.7	4.6	5.5	5.8	5.0	5.8	5.8
United States	8.2	5.9	3.8	3.2	4.7	6.0	5.4	5.7	5.5	5.4	6.5	3.7	1.8	1.2	1.5	2.8	3.8	2.1	3.2	4.2
Euro area	10.7	10.6	11.2	8.6	6.3	6.5	4.8	4.3	3.9	3.0	4.4	4.3	3.3	2.3	2.1	2.1	2.7	2.1	2.1	3.0

Note: Three-month money market rates where available, or rates on proximately similar financial instruments. See *OECD Economic Outlook* Sources and Methods *(http://www.oecd.org/eco/sources-and-methods).*
Individual euro area countries are not shown after 1998 (2000 for Greece) since their short term interest rates are equal to the euro area rate.

Source: OECD Economic Outlook 76 database.

Annex Table 35. **Long-term interest rates**

Per cent, per annum

	1990	1991	1992	1993	1994	1995	1996	1997	1998	1999	2000	2001	2002	2003	2004	2005	2006	Fourth quarter		
																		2004	2005	2006
Australia	13.2	10.7	9.2	7.3	9.0	9.2	8.2	6.9	5.5	6.1	6.3	5.6	5.8	5.4	5.7	5.9	6.4	5.6	6.1	6.5
Austria	8.7	8.5	8.1	6.7	7.0	7.1	6.3	5.7	4.7	4.7	5.6	5.1	5.0	4.2	4.2	4.1	4.3	4.0	4.2	4.5
Belgium	10.1	9.3	8.7	7.2	7.7	7.4	6.3	5.6	4.7	4.7	5.6	5.1	4.9	4.1	4.1	4.1	4.4	4.0	4.2	4.5
Canada	10.7	9.5	8.1	7.2	8.4	8.2	7.2	6.1	5.3	5.5	5.9	5.5	5.3	4.8	4.7	4.7	5.2	4.7	4.8	5.3
Denmark	10.6	9.3	9.0	7.3	7.8	8.3	7.2	6.3	5.0	4.9	5.7	5.1	5.1	4.3	4.3	4.3	4.5	4.2	4.4	4.7
Finland	13.2	11.7	12.0	8.8	9.0	8.8	7.1	6.0	4.8	4.7	5.5	5.0	5.0	4.1	4.1	4.1	4.4	3.9	4.1	4.5
France	9.9	9.0	8.6	6.8	7.2	7.5	6.3	5.6	4.6	4.6	5.4	4.9	4.9	4.1	4.1	4.1	4.3	3.9	4.2	4.5
Germany	8.7	8.5	7.9	6.5	6.9	6.9	6.2	5.7	4.6	4.5	5.3	4.8	4.8	4.1	4.1	4.0	4.3	3.9	4.1	4.4
Greece	..	..	..	..	..	..	..	9.8	8.5	6.3	6.1	5.3	5.0	4.3	4.2	4.1	4.4	4.0	4.2	4.5
Iceland	..	..	13.1	13.4	7.0	9.7	9.2	8.7	7.7	8.5	11.2	10.4	8.0	6.7	7.5	9.0	9.0	8.1	9.2	8.8
Ireland	10.3	9.4	9.3	7.6	8.0	8.2	7.2	6.3	4.7	4.8	5.5	5.0	5.0	4.1	4.1	4.1	4.4	4.0	4.2	4.6
Italy	13.5	13.3	13.3	11.2	10.5	12.2	9.4	6.9	4.9	4.7	5.6	5.2	5.0	4.3	4.3	4.2	4.4	4.0	4.3	4.6
Japan	7.0	6.3	5.3	4.3	4.4	3.4	3.1	2.4	1.5	1.7	1.7	1.3	1.3	1.1	1.5	1.8	2.5	1.5	2.0	2.8
Korea	15.1	16.5	15.1	12.1	12.3	12.4	10.9	11.7	12.8	8.7	8.5	6.7	6.5	5.0	4.8	4.8	5.3	4.6	5.0	5.3
Luxembourg	..	..	..	..	7.2	7.2	6.3	5.6	4.7	4.7	5.5	4.9	4.7	3.3	3.1	3.3	3.6	3.2	3.3	3.7
Mexico	34.9	19.7	16.1	15.6	13.8	39.9	34.4	22.4	24.8	24.1	16.9	13.8	8.5	7.4	7.6	8.5	8.9	8.3	8.6	9.1
Netherlands	8.9	8.7	8.1	6.4	6.9	6.9	6.2	5.6	4.6	4.6	5.4	5.0	4.9	4.1	4.1	4.0	4.3	3.9	4.1	4.5
New Zealand	12.4	10.1	8.4	6.9	7.6	7.8	7.9	7.2	6.3	6.4	6.9	6.4	6.5	5.9	6.1	6.0	6.0	6.1	6.0	6.0
Norway	10.7	10.0	9.6	6.9	7.4	7.4	6.8	5.9	5.4	5.5	6.2	6.2	6.4	5.0	4.5	4.9	5.6	4.5	5.3	6.2
Portugal	..	..	..	..	10.5	11.5	8.6	6.4	4.9	4.8	5.6	5.2	5.0	4.2	4.2	4.2	4.5	4.1	4.3	4.6
Slovak Republic	..	..	..	..	..	..	9.7	9.4	21.7	16.2	9.8	8.1	6.9	5.0	5.1	5.2	5.3	5.1	5.3	5.4
Spain	14.6	12.8	11.7	10.2	10.0	11.3	8.7	6.4	4.8	4.7	5.5	5.1	5.0	4.1	4.1	4.1	4.3	3.9	4.1	4.5
Sweden	13.2	10.7	10.0	8.5	9.5	10.2	8.0	6.6	5.0	5.0	5.4	5.1	5.3	4.6	4.5	5.2	5.6	4.3	5.6	5.6
Switzerland	6.4	6.2	6.4	4.6	5.0	4.5	4.0	3.4	3.0	3.0	3.9	3.4	3.2	2.7	2.8	3.3	3.6	3.0	3.3	3.7
Turkey	..	..	..	..	..	..	..	..	..	..	37.7	99.6	63.5	44.1	24.2	16.5	12.6	20.7	14.3	12.8
United Kingdom	11.8	10.1	9.1	7.5	8.2	8.2	7.8	7.1	5.5	5.1	5.3	4.9	4.9	4.5	5.0	5.2	5.2	5.1	5.2	5.2
United States	8.6	7.9	7.0	5.9	7.1	6.6	6.4	6.4	5.3	5.6	6.0	5.0	4.6	4.0	4.3	4.7	5.3	4.2	4.9	5.5
Euro area	..	10.3	9.8	7.9	8.0	8.4	7.1	5.9	4.7	4.6	5.4	5.0	4.9	4.1	4.1	4.1	4.3	3.9	4.1	4.5

Note: 10-year benchmark government bond yields where available or yield on proximately similar financial instruments (for Korea a 5-year bond is used). See also *OECD Economic Outlook* Sources and Methods *(http://www.oecd.org/eco/sources-and-methods).*

Source: OECD Economic Outlook 76 database.

Annex Table 36. **Nominal exchange rates (*vis-à-vis* the US dollar)**

Average of daily rates

	Monetary unit	1994	1995	1996	1997	1998	1999	1999	2000	2001	2002	2003	Estimates and assumptions[a]		
													2004	2005	2006
Australia	*Dollar*	1.369	1.350	1.277	1.348	1.592	1.550	1.550	1.727	1.935	1.841	1.542	1.363	1.325	1.325
Austria	*Schilling*	11.42	10.08	10.58	12.20	12.38	12.91								
Belgium	*Franc*	33.46	29.50	30.98	35.76	36.30	37.86								
Canada	*Dollar*	1.366	1.372	1.364	1.385	1.483	1.486	1.486	1.485	1.548	1.570	1.400	1.300	1.198	1.198
Czech Republic	*Koruny*	28.79	26.54	27.15	31.70	32.28	34.59	34.59	38.64	38.02	32.73	28.13	25.85	24.45	24.450
Denmark	*Krone*	6.360	5.604	5.798	6.604	6.699	6.980	6.980	8.088	8.321	7.884	6.577	6.006	5.731	5.731
Finland	*Markka*	5.223	4.367	4.592	5.187	5.345	5.580								
France	*Franc*	5.552	4.991	5.116	5.837	5.899	6.157								
Germany	*Deutschemark*	1.623	1.433	1.505	1.734	1.759	1.836								
Greece	*Drachma*	242.2	231.6	240.7	272.9	295.3	305.7								
Hungary	*Forint*	105.1	125.7	152.6	186.6	214.2	237.0	237.0	282.1	286.4	257.3	224.2	203.4	190.9	190.9
Iceland	*Krona*	69.99	64.77	66.69	70.97	71.17	72.43	72.43	78.84	97.67	91.59	76.69	70.67	67.68	67.68
Ireland	*Pound*	0.670	0.624	0.625	0.660	0.703	0.739								
Italy	*Lira*	1613	1629	1543	1703	1736	1817								
Japan	*Yen*	102.2	94.1	108.8	121.0	130.9	113.9	113.9	107.8	121.5	125.3	115.9	108.4	105.7	105.7
Korea	*Won*	804.3	771.4	804.4	950.5	1 400.5	1 186.7	1 186.7	1 130.6	1 290.4	1 251.0	1 191.0	1 152.3	1 111.6	1 111.6
Luxembourg	*Franc*	33.46	29.50	30.98	35.76	36.30	37.86								
Mexico	*Peso*	3.389	6.421	7.601	7.924	9.153	9.553	9.553	9.453	9.344	9.660	10.790	11.306	11.428	11.428
Netherlands	*Guilder*	1.820	1.605	1.686	1.951	1.983	2.068								
New Zealand	*Dollar*	1.687	1.524	1.454	1.513	1.869	1.892	1.892	2.205	2.382	2.163	1.724	1.515	1.448	1.448
Norway	*Krone*	7.057	6.337	6.457	7.072	7.545	7.797	7.797	8.797	8.993	7.986	7.078	6.767	6.368	6.368
Poland	*Zloty*	2.273	2.425	2.695	3.277	3.492	3.964	3.964	4.346	4.097	4.082	3.888	3.675	3.330	3.330
Portugal	*Escudo*	166.0	149.9	154.2	175.2	180.1	188.2								
Slovak Republic	*Koruna*	32.0	29.74	30.65	33.62	35.23	41.36	41.36	46.23	48.35	45.30	36.76	32.44	31.02	31.020
Spain	*Peseta*	134.0	124.7	126.7	146.4	149.4	156.2								
Sweden	*Krona*	7.716	7.134	6.707	7.635	7.947	8.262	8.262	9.161	10.338	9.721	8.078	7.380	7.008	7.008
Switzerland	*Franc*	1.367	1.182	1.236	1.450	1.450	1.503	1.503	1.688	1.687	1.557	1.345	1.246	1.178	1.178
Turkey	*Lira*	29 778	45 738	81 281	151 595	260 473	418 984	418 984	624 325	1 228 269	1 512 342	1 502 542	1 437 340	1 526 498	1 579 354
United Kingdom	*Pound*	0.653	0.634	0.641	0.611	0.604	0.618	0.618	0.661	0.694	0.667	0.612	0.548	0.539	0.539
United States	*Dollar*	1.000	1.000	1.000	1.000	1.000	1.000	1.000	1.000	1.000	1.000	1.000	1.000	1.000	1.000
Euro area	*Euro*	..	..	..	..	..	..	0.939	1.086	1.118	1.062	0.886	0.808	0.772	0.772
	SDR	0.699	0.659	0.689	0.726	0.737	0.731	0.731	0.758	0.785	0.773	0.714	0.677	0.665	0.665

Note: No rate are shown for individual euro area countries after 1999.

a) On the technical assumption that exchange rates remain at their levels of 5 November 2004, except for Turkey, where exchange rates vary according to official exchange rate policy.

Source: OECD Economic Outlook 76 database.

Annex Table 37. **Effective exchange rates**

Indices 1995 = 100, average of daily rates

	1991	1992	1993	1994	1995	1996	1997	1998	1999	2000	2001	2002	2003	Estimates and assumptions[a]		
														2004	2005	2006
Australia	111.9	104.8	99.5	107.2	103.9	113.9	115.4	107.5	107.7	100.0	93.8	97.2	108.6	116.9	117.8	117.9
Austria	90.2	92.4	95.5	97.7	102.4	101.4	99.5	101.6	102.3	100.0	100.5	101.0	104.1	105.1	106.0	106.1
Belgium	93.0	95.9	98.0	102.3	108.1	106.3	102.1	104.6	104.1	100.0	101.2	102.9	108.0	109.6	111.1	111.2
Canada	118.9	112.9	107.8	102.8	102.0	103.9	104.3	99.4	99.0	100.0	97.0	95.5	105.8	112.6	121.4	121.4
Czech Republic	..	..	94.7	98.1	98.8	100.4	97.4	99.0	98.7	100.0	104.9	116.7	116.0	115.8	117.4	117.4
Denmark	90.8	93.6	98.0	100.3	105.5	104.6	102.1	104.8	104.2	100.0	101.8	103.0	107.5	108.9	109.9	109.9
Finland	100.5	88.2	79.4	90.0	103.6	101.0	98.8	101.7	104.7	100.0	102.1	103.9	109.1	110.8	111.9	111.9
France	89.8	93.6	97.5	100.4	104.5	104.9	102.1	104.6	103.8	100.0	100.9	102.5	107.1	108.7	110.1	110.2
Germany	84.9	89.0	93.9	98.5	106.0	104.5	100.9	104.6	104.5	100.0	101.2	103.0	109.0	111.0	112.5	112.7
Greece	136.6	128.6	119.9	114.5	113.1	111.3	109.3	106.2	107.0	100.0	100.8	102.5	106.9	108.3	109.5	109.6
Hungary	..	..	214.0	192.4	152.7	130.1	120.5	109.2	105.4	100.0	101.8	108.8	107.5	109.3	112.0	112.0
Iceland	103.2	102.9	96.9	92.7	93.1	92.6	94.6	97.2	98.9	100.0	84.7	86.7	91.3	92.0	92.9	92.9
Ireland	108.9	113.6	107.9	109.7	111.7	114.6	114.4	111.1	107.8	100.0	101.3	103.7	113.6	115.6	118.4	118.4
Italy	116.4	115.4	99.4	99.3	91.4	100.6	102.0	104.1	103.8	100.0	101.2	103.1	108.0	109.6	110.9	111.1
Japan	55.4	60.1	74.4	86.4	92.5	80.7	77.1	80.1	91.9	100.0	92.3	88.4	91.2	94.8	95.9	96.0
Korea	128.7	119.9	118.1	119.4	119.8	121.8	112.7	81.6	93.4	100.0	92.4	95.5	94.7	93.9	95.7	95.7
Luxembourg	96.4	98.5	99.1	101.9	105.3	104.1	101.8	102.9	102.7	100.0	100.4	101.6	105.0	106.3	107.1	107.2
Mexico	259.1	259.4	272.5	263.9	138.7	117.8	115.6	102.7	97.9	100.0	102.8	99.6	87.0	81.8	80.3	80.3
Netherlands	88.9	92.4	96.9	101.5	108.5	107.0	101.8	105.4	105.3	100.0	101.4	103.7	110.3	112.6	114.2	114.2
New Zealand	104.6	97.3	102.0	109.4	116.8	124.2	127.2	114.3	110.3	100.0	99.0	106.9	121.0	128.5	131.4	131.5
Norway	99.2	101.0	99.9	100.7	104.4	104.5	105.5	102.4	102.2	100.0	103.3	112.1	109.5	105.6	107.9	108.0
Poland	..	..	170.4	139.1	122.6	114.3	106.2	103.9	97.0	100.0	110.3	105.5	94.9	92.6	98.0	98.0
Portugal	100.5	106.2	102.5	101.6	104.8	104.5	103.0	103.0	102.4	100.0	100.9	101.9	104.7	105.4	106.3	106.3
Slovak Republic	..	..	95.7	94.6	97.8	98.7	103.2	104.2	98.3	100.0	97.6	97.9	103.4	107.5	107.5	107.6
Spain	125.5	124.2	111.0	105.7	106.0	107.1	102.8	104.0	103.1	100.0	101.1	102.6	106.4	107.6	108.6	108.7
Sweden	109.8	112.5	92.6	93.7	94.1	103.6	100.3	100.0	99.8	100.0	92.0	94.3	99.7	101.2	103.0	103.0
Switzerland	83.5	83.0	86.9	95.7	104.1	102.8	96.9	101.1	101.8	100.0	104.1	109.4	111.1	111.5	114.0	114.0
Turkey	9 935.6	5 929.3	4 152.4	1 684.0	970.6	569.2	338.4	204.5	136.9	100.0	56.4	41.7	36.5	35.4	32.2	31.1
United Kingdom	84.8	82.8	76.5	79.0	76.4	78.1	91.0	97.0	97.4	100.0	99.0	100.1	96.5	101.1	99.7	99.7
United States	67.0	68.3	72.6	76.9	78.4	82.8	88.7	97.9	97.6	100.0	105.4	105.7	99.2	94.7	91.4	91.4
Euro area	90.6	96.5	95.5	102.1	111.0	113.2	106.1	111.8	109.9	100.0	102.5	106.1	118.7	122.9	126.1	126.4

Note: For details on the method of calculation, see the section on exchange rates and competitiveness indicators in *OECD Economic Outlook* Sources and Methods *(http://www.oecd.org/eco/sources-and-methods).*

a) On the technical assumption that exchange rates remain at their levels of 5 November 2004, except for Turkey, where exchange rates vary according to official exchange rate policy.

Source: OECD Economic Outlook 76 database.

Annex Table 38. **Export volumes of goods and services**

National accounts basis, percentage changes from previous year

	1987	1988	1989	1990	1991	1992	1993	1994	1995	1996	1997	1998	1999	2000	2001	2002	2003	2004	2005	2006
Australia	12.2	3.5	2.9	8.5	13.1	5.4	8.0	9.0	5.0	10.6	11.5	-0.2	4.7	10.9	1.8	0.3	-2.6	6.4	8.3	9.8
Austria	2.3	9.8	10.1	8.2	3.0	1.5	-2.6	5.5	6.3	4.8	11.4	8.6	5.7	10.5	6.8	3.8	1.4	8.1	8.0	7.9
Belgium	4.6	10.3	8.8	4.6	2.8	2.4	0.9	9.0	4.8	2.2	6.2	5.7	5.3	8.2	1.8	1.3	1.7	3.6	6.3	7.4
Canada	2.9	8.9	1.0	4.7	1.8	7.2	10.8	12.7	8.5	5.6	8.3	9.1	10.7	8.9	-2.8	1.1	-2.4	7.7	6.8	5.6
Czech Republic	..	..	..	..	..	..	..	3.9	16.7	8.2	8.5	10.6	5.7	16.8	11.8	2.7	6.2	16.7	12.0	10.4
Denmark	4.3	11.2	4.2	6.2	6.1	-0.9	-1.5	7.0	3.1	4.3	4.1	4.3	12.2	13.4	4.4	4.8	-0.0	4.9	6.0	6.4
Finland	3.0	2.9	3.0	1.6	-7.4	10.0	16.2	13.5	8.6	5.5	13.8	9.2	6.1	19.4	-0.8	5.2	1.2	2.2	5.8	6.0
France[a]	2.7	8.6	10.6	4.9	5.4	5.2	-0.1	7.9	7.7	3.2	12.0	8.4	4.2	13.4	1.9	1.7	-2.6	3.4	6.0	7.5
Germany	0.7	5.5	10.3	13.2	-7.3	-2.0	-5.4	7.7	6.0	5.3	11.4	6.4	5.1	14.2	6.1	4.1	1.8	8.1	5.7	8.1
Greece	6.0	-2.1	2.0	-3.5	4.1	10.0	-2.6	7.4	3.0	3.5	20.0	5.3	18.1	14.1	-1.0	-7.7	1.0	4.3	7.5	8.7
Hungary	..	..	..	..	..	..	..	13.7	13.4	8.4	26.4	16.7	13.1	21.8	7.8	3.7	7.2	14.7	12.6	12.2
Iceland	3.3	-3.6	2.9	-0.0	-5.9	-2.0	6.5	9.5	-2.3	9.9	5.3	2.1	4.0	5.0	7.7	3.6	0.3	6.3	5.1	6.8
Ireland	13.7	9.0	10.3	8.7	5.7	13.9	9.7	15.1	20.0	12.2	17.4	22.0	15.2	20.4	8.5	5.7	-0.9	6.6	8.8	7.2
Italy	4.5	5.1	7.8	7.5	-1.4	7.3	9.0	9.8	12.6	0.6	6.4	3.4	0.1	9.7	1.6	-3.4	-3.9	4.5	6.1	5.4
Japan	-0.8	5.3	9.3	6.7	4.1	3.9	-0.1	3.6	4.1	6.4	11.4	-2.4	1.5	12.4	-6.1	8.0	10.1	14.4	7.4	8.0
Korea	22.7	12.2	-4.3	4.1	11.2	11.3	11.3	16.1	24.6	12.2	21.6	12.7	14.6	19.1	-2.7	13.3	15.7	21.1	13.3	15.3
Luxembourg	3.3	11.1	12.6	5.6	9.2	2.7	4.8	7.7	4.6	5.8	14.7	14.1	14.8	17.3	1.8	-0.6	1.8	6.7	7.4	7.7
Mexico	9.5	5.8	5.7	5.3	5.1	5.0	8.1	17.8	30.2	18.2	10.7	12.1	12.4	16.4	-3.8	1.5	1.1	12.4	8.4	8.4
Netherlands	3.5	8.1	7.5	5.6	5.6	1.8	4.8	9.7	8.8	4.6	8.8	7.4	5.1	11.3	1.6	0.8	-0.0	6.4	7.1	7.5
New Zealand	5.6	6.1	-1.4	4.9	10.8	3.7	4.6	10.0	3.8	3.7	3.9	1.8	8.1	6.0	2.5	6.3	1.7	6.3	4.3	7.6
Norway	1.1	6.4	11.0	8.6	6.1	4.7	3.2	8.4	4.9	10.2	7.7	0.6	2.8	4.0	5.0	0.1	1.2	2.4	2.6	3.8
Poland	..	..	..	..	..	..	..	13.1	22.9	12.0	12.2	14.3	-2.6	23.2	3.1	4.8	14.7	13.4	12.2	12.6
Portugal	11.2	8.2	12.2	9.5	1.2	3.2	-3.3	8.4	8.8	7.1	7.1	9.1	2.9	7.8	1.0	2.0	4.0	7.3	6.1	6.2
Slovak Republic	..	..	..	..	..	..	..	14.8	4.5	-1.1	17.6	12.8	5.0	13.7	6.3	5.5	22.6	14.5	12.3	13.0
Spain	5.3	3.8	1.4	4.7	8.3	7.5	7.8	16.7	9.4	10.4	15.3	8.2	7.7	10.1	3.6	1.2	2.6	5.3	7.6	7.4
Sweden	4.3	2.8	3.2	1.8	-1.9	2.2	8.3	13.8	11.3	4.1	13.3	8.5	8.2	11.1	0.4	1.0	5.3	10.7	8.0	7.8
Switzerland	1.4	6.2	6.1	2.8	-1.3	3.1	1.3	1.9	0.5	3.6	11.1	3.9	6.5	12.2	0.2	-0.2	0.0	4.1	5.1	5.6
Turkey	26.4	18.4	-0.3	2.6	3.7	11.0	7.7	15.2	8.0	22.0	19.1	12.0	-7.0	19.2	7.4	11.1	16.0	14.5	13.9	12.6
United Kingdom	6.1	0.7	4.5	5.5	-0.1	4.3	4.4	9.2	9.3	8.6	8.4	2.8	4.3	9.4	2.9	0.1	0.1	2.6	7.9	8.2
United States[a]	10.8	16.0	11.5	9.0	6.6	6.9	3.2	8.7	10.1	8.4	11.9	2.4	4.3	8.7	-5.4	-2.3	1.9	8.9	9.2	10.0
Total OECD	4.7	7.8	7.8	7.3	2.3	4.3	4.6	8.9	8.9	6.7	11.0	5.2	5.4	11.6	-0.0	1.9	2.4	8.3	7.8	8.5

Note: Regional aggregates are calculated *inclusive* of intra-regional trade as the sum of volumes expressed in 2000 $.

a) Volume data use hedonic price deflators for certain components.

Source: OECD Economic Outlook 76 database.

Annex Table 39. **Import volumes of goods and services**

National accounts basis, percentage changes from previous year

	1987	1988	1989	1990	1991	1992	1993	1994	1995	1996	1997	1998	1999	2000	2001	2002	2003	2004	2005	2006
Australia	2.7	17.1	20.6	-4.0	-2.4	7.1	4.2	14.3	7.9	8.3	10.5	6.0	9.3	7.5	-4.2	11.9	11.0	13.5	7.6	9.1
Austria	4.8	9.3	9.6	7.6	4.6	1.6	-4.8	10.2	6.0	5.0	7.8	5.6	5.0	10.1	5.0	-0.2	4.8	7.1	8.1	8.2
Belgium	6.8	10.7	10.0	4.8	2.8	3.1	0.5	7.4	4.8	2.3	5.0	7.3	4.5	8.3	1.0	1.0	2.1	3.3	6.2	7.6
Canada	5.3	13.5	5.9	2.0	2.5	4.7	7.4	8.0	5.7	5.1	14.2	5.1	7.8	8.1	-5.0	1.4	3.8	8.4	9.1	6.3
Czech Republic	..	..	..	..	..	..	..	8.7	21.2	13.4	7.0	8.4	5.0	16.2	12.9	4.9	7.8	17.3	11.2	9.6
Denmark	-3.1	8.3	4.1	1.2	3.0	-0.4	-2.7	12.3	7.5	3.5	10.0	8.9	5.5	13.5	3.4	7.3	-0.6	6.6	7.0	7.1
Finland	9.2	9.4	9.6	0.0	-13.2	0.4	2.1	12.3	6.6	6.2	11.7	7.7	3.7	16.3	0.6	1.7	3.0	0.2	4.0	5.5
France[a]	7.6	8.6	8.4	5.5	2.4	1.7	-3.8	8.6	7.6	1.7	7.2	11.5	6.1	15.2	1.6	3.3	0.3	7.7	7.7	7.5
Germany	4.7	5.7	8.5	10.7	12.3	0.5	-5.4	7.4	5.8	3.3	8.4	8.6	8.1	11.1	1.4	-1.6	3.9	6.4	4.9	7.5
Greece	2.1	7.3	10.5	8.4	5.8	1.1	0.6	1.5	8.9	7.0	14.2	9.2	15.0	15.1	-5.2	-2.9	4.8	5.1	4.1	7.5
Hungary	..	..	..	..	..	..	..	8.8	-0.7	6.2	24.6	22.8	12.3	21.1	5.1	6.2	10.3	14.7	11.8	11.2
Iceland	23.3	-4.6	-10.3	1.0	5.3	-6.0	-7.8	4.1	3.9	16.5	7.7	23.4	4.2	8.0	-9.0	-2.5	9.7	12.5	11.0	8.1
Ireland	6.2	4.9	13.5	5.1	2.4	8.2	7.5	15.5	16.4	12.5	16.8	26.1	12.1	21.3	6.7	3.4	-2.3	6.0	8.6	6.9
Italy	12.2	5.9	8.9	11.5	2.3	7.4	-10.9	8.1	9.7	-0.3	10.1	8.9	5.6	7.1	0.5	-0.2	-0.6	4.3	7.5	6.7
Japan	13.6	18.5	16.9	7.8	-1.1	-0.7	-1.4	7.9	12.5	13.1	1.0	-6.6	3.3	9.2	0.1	1.9	5.0	9.9	7.1	6.9
Korea	19.9	13.7	17.1	13.9	19.2	5.3	6.2	21.6	22.4	14.3	3.5	-21.8	27.8	20.1	-4.2	15.2	9.7	14.0	12.8	14.5
Luxembourg	7.3	10.5	9.1	5.0	9.1	-3.1	5.2	6.7	4.2	7.6	13.9	15.3	14.6	15.4	3.7	-2.6	1.6	6.9	7.7	7.7
Mexico	5.1	36.7	18.0	19.7	15.2	19.6	1.9	21.3	-15.0	22.9	22.7	16.6	14.1	21.5	-1.6	1.4	-1.0	10.5	9.1	8.9
Netherlands	3.7	6.4	7.7	3.8	4.9	1.5	0.3	9.4	10.5	4.4	9.5	8.5	5.8	10.5	2.2	0.8	0.6	5.3	6.4	7.6
New Zealand	8.6	-0.9	13.5	3.6	-5.2	8.3	5.3	13.1	9.0	7.7	2.2	1.3	11.7	0.3	1.7	8.4	9.2	14.6	5.2	7.2
Norway	-6.5	-2.4	2.2	2.5	0.5	1.6	4.9	5.8	5.7	8.8	12.4	8.5	-1.8	2.7	0.9	2.3	2.2	6.8	3.7	3.3
Poland	..	..	..	..	..	..	..	11.3	24.2	28.0	21.4	18.5	1.0	15.6	-5.3	2.6	9.3	10.4	11.2	11.9
Portugal	23.1	18.0	5.9	14.5	7.2	10.7	-3.3	8.8	7.4	4.9	10.0	14.2	8.5	5.5	1.1	-0.3	-0.9	7.1	5.5	6.4
Slovak Republic	..	..	..	..	..	..	..	-4.7	11.6	19.7	14.2	16.5	-6.7	10.5	11.0	5.2	13.8	14.0	12.7	11.9
Spain	24.8	16.1	17.7	9.6	10.3	6.8	-5.2	11.4	11.1	8.0	13.3	13.2	12.6	10.5	3.9	3.1	4.8	7.4	8.2	8.1
Sweden	7.6	4.5	7.7	0.7	-4.9	1.5	-2.2	12.0	7.2	3.7	12.0	11.3	4.9	11.5	-2.6	-1.9	5.0	6.9	9.3	7.5
Switzerland	6.1	5.0	5.8	3.2	-1.9	-3.8	-0.1	7.7	4.3	3.2	8.3	7.5	4.3	9.6	3.2	-2.8	1.4	4.7	6.1	6.0
Turkey	23.0	-4.5	6.9	33.0	-5.2	10.9	35.8	-21.9	29.6	20.5	22.4	2.3	-3.7	25.4	-24.8	15.8	27.1	27.0	12.1	11.2
United Kingdom	7.9	12.8	7.4	0.5	-4.5	6.8	3.3	5.8	5.6	9.7	9.8	9.3	7.9	9.1	4.9	4.1	1.3	4.7	6.5	6.3
United States[a]	5.9	3.9	4.4	3.6	-0.6	6.9	8.7	11.9	8.0	8.7	13.6	11.6	11.5	13.1	-2.7	3.4	4.4	10.1	7.7	7.3
Total OECD	7.5	8.8	8.8	6.0	2.6	4.0	3.0	9.4	8.1	7.4	10.1	7.4	8.4	11.9	-0.3	2.6	3.6	8.4	7.6	7.7

Note: Regional aggregates are calculated *inclusive* of intra-regional trade as the sum of volumes expressed in 2000 $.

a) Volume data use hedonic price deflators for certain components.

Source: OECD Economic Outlook 76 database.

Annex Table 40. **Export prices of goods and services**

National accounts basis, percentage changes from previous year, national currency terms

	1987	1988	1989	1990	1991	1992	1993	1994	1995	1996	1997	1998	1999	2000	2001	2002	2003	2004	2005	2006
Australia	3.8	8.0	6.0	1.1	-5.1	2.0	1.0	-4.0	6.0	-2.6	-0.1	2.4	-5.1	13.1	6.9	-2.1	-5.2	3.0	1.9	0.8
Austria	-1.7	2.2	2.5	1.0	0.7	0.1	0.5	1.3	2.0	1.1	1.2	0.4	0.7	1.4	0.8	0.6	0.1	1.2	1.2	0.8
Belgium	-3.3	3.8	6.9	-1.6	-0.8	-0.9	-1.5	1.3	1.6	1.7	4.8	-1.3	0.0	9.6	1.4	-1.1	-1.2	1.9	1.2	0.8
Canada	2.0	0.3	2.1	-0.7	-3.6	2.9	4.4	5.9	6.4	0.6	0.2	-0.3	1.1	6.2	1.3	-1.9	-1.3	1.8	0.2	2.0
Czech Republic	..	..	..	..	..	..	..	6.8	6.4	2.1	5.5	3.8	0.8	2.9	-0.7	-6.1	0.8	4.2	1.3	1.1
Denmark	-1.3	-0.8	6.8	0.7	1.7	2.5	-0.3	0.6	1.4	1.7	3.0	-2.6	-1.0	8.0	0.6	-2.7	0.4	1.3	0.2	0.4
Finland	1.7	4.8	5.7	0.4	-0.3	5.9	6.8	1.3	4.9	-0.3	-0.7	-0.9	-5.1	3.3	-2.4	-4.9	-3.1	1.4	-0.2	-1.3
France[a]	-0.5	2.6	3.7	-1.3	-0.6	-1.7	-2.2	-0.1	0.7	1.6	2.0	-1.4	-1.4	2.3	-0.1	-1.7	0.2	0.9	0.5	0.2
Germany	-1.0	1.7	2.5	-0.2	1.3	1.0	0.7	1.0	2.0	0.1	1.2	0.2	-0.8	3.0	0.9	0.1	-0.8	0.2	0.9	0.8
Greece	8.9	11.9	13.9	15.9	14.0	10.1	9.1	8.6	8.7	5.6	3.6	4.1	1.9	8.0	1.3	2.4	2.2	0.7	0.9	0.8
Hungary	..	..	..	..	..	..	..	18.5	33.7	23.1	11.5	13.7	3.8	9.1	2.9	-4.4	-0.1	-0.1	0.3	1.1
Iceland	12.0	18.3	26.3	17.6	6.9	-1.3	4.8	5.9	4.8	-0.2	2.4	4.9	-0.1	4.0	21.5	-1.7	-7.1	3.7	2.9	2.0
Ireland	0.5	5.6	7.3	-8.1	-0.3	-2.0	6.8	0.2	1.9	-0.3	1.2	2.8	2.3	5.8	4.1	-0.3	-5.0	-0.1	1.8	1.6
Italy	1.0	3.4	6.6	3.0	3.9	0.9	10.4	3.3	8.8	1.0	0.3	1.0	0.0	6.3	3.2	1.8	1.0	2.2	0.4	1.4
Japan	-4.2	-1.8	3.3	1.7	-2.3	-2.5	-6.6	-3.1	-1.8	2.9	1.6	0.6	-8.4	-3.9	1.4	-1.7	-4.2	-1.9	0.5	0.4
Korea	2.9	1.0	-0.3	5.1	2.4	3.1	1.1	1.4	1.7	-3.1	4.7	24.7	-19.3	-4.2	2.4	-9.4	-1.4	2.9	-2.6	-2.1
Luxembourg	-2.1	2.0	4.3	0.1	1.2	1.8	5.7	3.1	1.5	1.5	4.0	2.7	2.6	8.0	2.4	-2.2	-1.3	2.0	2.0	2.0
Mexico	150.6	64.5	18.9	25.2	7.6	5.2	3.3	5.9	79.6	22.8	7.1	9.4	6.6	3.5	-2.5	3.4	13.2	8.7	6.2	2.5
Netherlands	-5.0	0.2	4.0	-0.8	0.1	-2.0	-2.1	0.5	0.9	0.5	2.7	-1.4	-0.7	8.2	1.5	-1.0	0.0	0.9	0.8	-0.1
New Zealand	4.9	2.8	9.4	-0.2	-2.9	5.5	2.2	-2.7	-0.4	-2.6	-2.4	5.1	-0.2	15.5	7.6	-8.1	-7.5	-0.9	-0.8	0.8
Norway	1.8	0.6	10.7	3.0	-1.2	-7.0	2.0	-2.7	1.9	6.9	2.0	-7.9	10.7	35.7	-3.2	-10.2	1.9	11.2	8.6	0.9
Poland	..	..	..	..	..	..	..	31.7	19.6	7.6	13.9	13.2	5.9	1.7	1.3	4.8	5.8	11.4	1.0	3.0
Portugal	10.8	11.7	11.8	6.3	3.4	0.5	4.9	6.4	5.6	-1.7	2.6	0.8	0.2	5.4	1.9	0.3	-1.8	0.1	1.3	0.8
Slovak Republic	..	..	..	..	..	..	..	10.7	8.4	4.0	-0.3	2.1	5.7	12.3	5.4	0.7	-3.3	-1.0	0.4	0.3
Spain	3.5	4.7	6.0	0.8	1.5	2.9	5.0	4.6	5.9	1.5	3.3	0.6	0.4	7.3	2.7	1.1	0.7	0.3	2.0	1.6
Sweden	2.6	5.1	6.5	1.8	1.6	-2.8	9.1	3.9	7.2	-4.9	0.3	-1.2	-2.4	2.9	2.3	-1.7	-1.9	-0.1	0.4	0.2
Switzerland	0.3	2.0	5.9	0.5	3.3	1.6	1.7	-0.0	-0.1	-0.8	0.7	-0.4	-0.7	2.1	0.2	-0.2	0.6	2.0	-0.6	0.1
Turkey	30.8	74.9	53.2	38.2	61.0	62.5	59.9	164.8	73.0	69.0	87.0	60.1	52.1	39.9	86.9	21.4	4.7	5.6	5.6	3.0
United Kingdom	2.9	0.3	8.2	4.4	1.6	1.6	8.8	1.0	3.2	1.3	-4.0	-3.8	-0.6	2.2	-0.8	0.4	1.3	-0.8	1.6	1.1
United States[a]	2.5	5.2	1.7	0.7	1.3	-0.4	0.0	1.1	2.3	-1.3	-1.7	-2.3	-0.6	1.7	-0.4	-0.4	2.1	3.6	2.7	1.4
Total OECD	3.7	4.6	4.8	1.9	1.1	0.7	0.5	2.4	5.2	1.6	1.5	0.9	-1.2	3.7	1.3	-0.8	0.2	1.7	1.4	0.9

Note: Regional aggregates are calculated *inclusive* of intra-regional trade. They are calculated as the geometric averages of prices weighted by 2000 trade volumes expressed in $.

a) Certain components are estimated on a hedonic basis.

Source: OECD Economic Outlook 76 database.

Annex Table 41. **Import prices of goods and services**

National accounts basis, percentage changes from previous year, national currency terms

	1987	1988	1989	1990	1991	1992	1993	1994	1995	1996	1997	1998	1999	2000	2001	2002	2003	2004	2005	2006
Australia	3.0	-4.0	-1.4	4.1	1.3	4.2	5.7	-4.3	3.4	-6.6	-1.7	6.8	-4.5	7.3	5.8	-4.6	-8.9	-5.3	-0.4	-0.1
Austria	-2.0	2.3	3.1	0.5	1.1	0.5	0.8	1.2	0.9	2.4	1.8	0.3	0.6	2.8	0.4	-1.2	-0.9	1.3	1.0	0.3
Belgium	-4.1	2.4	5.8	-1.3	-1.0	-2.4	-2.6	1.7	1.4	2.5	5.6	-2.2	0.7	12.0	1.3	-2.1	-1.0	2.5	2.0	0.9
Canada	-1.2	-2.1	0.2	1.4	-1.6	4.4	6.4	6.6	3.4	-1.1	0.8	3.7	-0.2	2.1	3.0	0.6	-7.0	-2.8	-2.8	1.1
Czech Republic	..	..	..	..	..	..	..	5.5	5.8	0.7	5.2	-1.8	1.6	6.2	-2.6	-8.4	-0.5	1.8	2.0	1.5
Denmark	-1.6	-1.4	6.8	-0.6	2.8	-0.8	-0.5	0.7	1.2	-0.0	2.2	-2.5	-2.4	6.8	0.4	-3.1	-1.7	0.7	-0.6	-0.1
Finland	-0.2	2.4	4.4	0.6	2.9	8.2	7.4	0.1	0.5	0.4	0.7	-2.1	-2.1	6.9	-2.7	-2.8	0.4	5.2	2.5	0.1
France[a]	-1.4	1.7	6.0	-1.6	-0.1	-3.1	-3.2	0.4	0.6	2.4	1.6	-2.8	-1.6	5.2	-1.1	-4.4	-0.2	-0.7	-0.2	-0.9
Germany	-4.8	1.8	5.3	-0.9	2.2	-1.2	-1.0	0.6	0.8	0.5	3.1	-2.0	-1.0	7.4	0.8	-1.7	-2.4	0.4	1.2	0.0
Greece	6.9	9.2	14.7	13.7	12.3	12.3	7.4	5.6	7.5	5.0	2.8	3.8	1.7	9.3	1.8	0.9	1.4	1.9	2.1	0.4
Hungary	..	..	..	..	..	..	..	15.6	32.8	24.3	12.0	12.6	6.4	10.8	2.4	-5.3	0.2	1.0	0.6	1.1
Iceland	7.4	19.2	31.5	19.3	3.3	-0.8	9.1	5.6	3.5	3.1	0.3	-0.7	0.7	6.8	21.2	-2.2	-3.0	4.6	1.8	2.0
Ireland	1.3	6.4	6.2	-3.7	2.4	-1.2	4.5	2.4	3.8	-0.5	0.7	2.5	2.5	7.5	3.6	-1.0	-4.5	-0.3	1.2	1.9
Italy	-1.7	4.8	6.9	-1.8	0.5	1.1	14.8	4.8	11.1	-2.9	1.4	-1.3	0.2	14.2	2.6	0.1	-0.8	2.2	1.7	1.4
Japan	-8.9	-3.9	5.6	7.3	-5.1	-5.1	-8.3	-4.5	-1.1	8.6	5.9	-3.0	-8.2	1.5	2.9	-1.9	-1.9	1.2	2.9	1.3
Korea	0.2	-1.6	-5.4	7.3	1.9	3.5	0.3	1.0	4.3	3.0	11.4	27.2	-16.8	5.9	5.8	-8.9	1.2	6.2	0.9	-0.6
Luxembourg	-1.2	0.8	3.8	1.6	2.5	2.7	3.2	2.1	1.3	0.9	3.6	1.2	2.3	7.7	3.4	-2.1	-1.8	1.6	1.8	2.0
Mexico	131.5	68.4	14.9	16.2	9.1	4.3	3.7	5.3	95.2	21.2	3.6	12.2	3.3	0.1	-2.8	2.3	14.4	8.5	5.5	2.7
Netherlands	-3.0	-0.2	4.6	-1.3	0.3	-1.1	-2.1	0.1	0.2	1.2	2.2	-1.5	0.5	8.3	0.5	-1.0	-0.7	2.3	2.3	0.1
New Zealand	-4.9	-3.2	8.1	1.5	2.3	6.2	-1.4	-3.9	-1.8	-3.7	-0.5	5.6	0.7	14.7	2.3	-6.5	-11.1	-4.3	0.2	0.8
Norway	6.9	4.4	7.0	1.2	-0.4	-1.8	1.5	0.9	0.8	1.0	0.3	1.4	-1.1	6.6	0.3	-6.7	1.8	6.1	1.7	1.0
Poland	..	..	..	..	..	..	..	27.0	18.0	10.4	15.7	10.8	7.1	7.7	1.3	5.2	6.9	12.1	2.4	3.5
Portugal	9.5	11.7	10.6	4.1	1.0	-4.2	4.4	4.3	3.9	1.6	2.7	-1.2	-0.3	8.2	0.0	-2.1	-1.2	1.3	1.9	0.7
Slovak Republic	..	..	..	..	..	..	..	12.3	7.3	7.2	0.3	-0.2	8.1	11.6	8.4	-0.2	-3.4	0.6	0.5	-0.2
Spain	-2.8	0.1	1.9	-2.8	-1.5	1.2	6.1	5.8	4.4	0.7	3.5	-0.3	0.7	9.7	0.5	-1.3	-0.2	3.3	3.2	0.9
Sweden	3.8	4.1	5.7	3.3	0.3	-2.4	13.9	4.2	5.7	-4.8	1.2	-0.5	1.1	4.7	4.2	-0.0	-2.2	1.4	2.9	1.1
Switzerland	-3.6	4.3	8.6	-1.1	0.9	2.3	-1.8	-4.5	-2.4	-0.1	3.5	-1.8	-0.2	5.7	0.6	-4.0	-1.5	0.5	-0.4	-0.1
Turkey	33.1	79.0	66.7	28.4	60.2	63.1	48.9	163.3	85.0	80.4	74.1	62.5	48.2	50.6	89.2	31.7	1.9	3.8	4.9	2.2
United Kingdom	2.4	-0.9	6.5	3.3	0.3	-0.0	8.6	3.0	5.9	0.1	-7.1	-5.8	-1.2	3.1	-0.3	-2.3	0.5	-0.4	3.1	1.5
United States[a]	6.1	4.8	2.2	2.8	-0.4	0.1	-0.9	0.9	2.7	-1.8	-3.6	-5.4	0.6	4.2	-2.5	-1.2	3.4	5.1	4.1	1.9
Total OECD	3.2	4.2	4.9	2.4	0.7	0.4	0.1	2.7	5.8	1.9	1.4	-0.5	-0.7	6.0	1.0	-1.5	0.2	2.3	2.2	1.0

Note: Regional aggregates are calculated *inclusive* of intra-regional trade. They are calculated as the geometric averages of prices weighted by 2000 trade volumes expressed in $.

a) Certain components are estimated on a hedonic basis.

Source: OECD Economic Outlook 76 database.

Annex Table 42. Competitive positions: relative consumer prices

Indices, 1995 = 100

	1987	1988	1989	1990	1991	1992	1993	1994	1995	1996	1997	1998	1999	2000	2001	2002	2003	2004
Australia	108.7	119.7	127.4	125.3	122.8	110.9	102.4	107.5	105.7	115.6	114.5	104.7	105.0	100.0	96.2	101.5	114.7	123.7
Austria	106.0	105.3	103.2	105.4	103.7	105.2	106.5	106.6	109.6	107.2	103.5	103.8	102.7	100.0	100.2	100.4	102.9	103.7
Belgium	109.3	106.3	104.1	108.3	107.2	107.9	107.8	109.5	113.2	110.4	105.0	105.8	104.2	100.0	100.8	101.9	106.3	107.8
Canada	121.7	129.0	134.5	134.1	138.1	127.6	118.9	109.2	106.9	107.0	106.3	100.3	99.4	100.0	96.9	96.0	106.9	112.9
Czech Republic	..	..	..	..	..	..	77.2	81.1	83.8	89.3	90.8	99.5	98.1	100.0	106.6	118.3	115.2	115.3
Denmark	104.4	103.8	101.0	104.9	101.0	101.6	102.5	102.2	105.8	104.2	101.5	103.7	103.8	100.0	101.4	103.0	107.6	108.3
Finland	134.2	138.3	144.9	148.7	142.0	122.6	102.5	106.4	114.2	107.5	103.4	104.7	104.6	100.0	101.4	102.2	105.8	105.4
France	112.2	109.8	106.7	110.3	106.9	108.4	109.5	109.4	111.6	110.9	106.4	107.1	104.9	100.0	99.7	101.0	105.5	106.9
Germany	110.0	107.1	103.3	106.4	105.0	109.6	113.3	114.0	118.3	113.5	108.0	109.1	106.5	100.0	99.9	100.4	104.9	106.0
Greece	89.1	91.0	91.0	95.5	96.8	99.4	100.1	100.9	104.1	107.0	107.7	106.3	107.0	100.0	100.9	103.6	109.2	111.2
Hungary	..	..	..	..	..	..	95.8	93.5	88.8	89.7	95.2	95.8	98.7	100.0	108.1	119.1	120.8	128.3
Iceland	106.1	112.4	105.3	102.4	104.6	104.6	98.4	92.2	90.8	90.1	91.6	93.7	96.5	100.0	88.1	93.5	98.6	100.9
Ireland	122.5	117.9	114.4	119.5	115.6	119.2	110.6	110.3	111.2	113.0	111.6	108.3	104.8	100.0	104.0	109.6	121.6	123.5
Italy	118.8	117.5	119.3	123.9	124.6	122.5	103.4	100.5	93.3	103.3	103.7	105.1	104.1	100.0	101.1	103.2	108.5	110.0
Japan	86.7	91.9	82.4	74.7	80.5	82.9	96.1	103.8	105.6	88.3	83.3	84.2	94.4	100.0	89.5	83.7	84.6	85.4
Korea	105.0	108.6	121.0	118.2	117.7	110.7	107.5	108.7	110.0	113.9	107.4	81.9	93.0	100.0	94.6	99.5	100.6	101.5
Luxembourg	104.5	103.0	101.3	104.4	103.4	104.4	104.3	105.6	108.2	105.6	102.5	102.7	102.0	100.0	100.5	101.8	105.3	106.5
Mexico	56.9	71.9	75.2	77.7	86.1	93.3	99.7	95.3	64.6	72.1	83.4	84.2	92.1	100.0	106.5	106.6	95.3	91.4
Netherlands	114.9	111.9	105.9	108.2	106.0	107.8	108.3	108.3	112.4	109.3	103.5	106.3	105.7	100.0	102.9	106.4	113.2	114.5
New Zealand	123.6	130.9	122.6	121.0	114.8	104.0	106.5	112.2	120.2	127.4	129.8	116.0	110.3	100.0	99.1	108.1	122.2	129.9
Norway	111.6	114.6	113.7	111.9	108.1	108.0	104.0	101.2	103.6	102.4	103.6	100.9	101.4	100.0	103.8	111.8	109.8	104.6
Poland	..	..	..	..	..	..	73.3	74.0	79.1	84.8	87.8	93.2	90.7	100.0	112.9	107.8	95.6	94.2
Portugal	82.4	82.8	85.2	89.7	95.5	104.0	100.9	99.3	102.8	102.6	101.3	102.1	102.2	100.0	102.5	104.8	108.6	109.3
Slovak Republic	..	..	..	..	..	..	83.7	82.8	84.7	84.5	89.2	91.1	90.7	100.0	101.2	102.3	115.3	126.0
Spain	101.8	106.9	113.1	119.9	121.4	121.0	107.8	102.9	104.4	106.1	101.4	102.3	102.2	100.0	102.1	104.5	109.2	111.4
Sweden	114.5	117.4	119.5	124.0	129.9	130.0	106.8	105.3	104.4	112.4	106.7	103.6	101.7	100.0	91.6	93.9	99.0	99.0
Switzerland	106.7	104.6	97.4	104.2	103.9	102.1	104.0	108.7	115.2	111.1	102.6	104.3	103.0	100.0	102.1	105.7	105.7	104.5
Turkey	73.4	70.4	76.1	85.1	86.7	83.3	89.4	65.7	71.2	71.9	76.8	84.6	89.4	100.0	81.7	88.7	95.9	100.5
United Kingdom	80.9	87.1	86.6	89.7	91.6	88.2	78.6	79.0	76.1	77.3	90.6	97.4	97.2	100.0	98.0	98.6	95.8	101.1
United States	95.4	89.2	89.2	87.4	85.8	84.0	85.2	85.3	84.1	86.7	91.1	98.4	97.0	100.0	105.7	105.8	99.4	95.3
Euro area	112.3	107.5	103.1	112.7	109.0	113.2	106.4	106.0	109.8	108.7	99.1	101.2	111.3	100.0	101.9	105.5	117.7	121.4

Note: Competitiveness-weighted relative consumer prices in dollar terms. Competitiveness weights take into account the structure of competition in both export and import markets of the manufacturing sector of 42 countries. An increase in the index indicates a real effective appreciation and a corresponding deterioration of the competitive position. For details on the method of calculation see Durand, M., C. Madaschi and F. Terribile (1998), "Trends in OECD Countries' International Competitiveness: The Influence of Emerging Market Economies", *OECD Economics Department Working Papers,* No. 195. See also *OECD Economic Outlook* Sources and Methods *(http://www.oecd.org/eco/sources-and-methods).*

Source: OECD Economic Outlook 76 database.

Annex Table 43. **Competitive positions: relative unit labour costs**

Indices, 1995 = 100

	1987	1988	1989	1990	1991	1992	1993	1994	1995	1996	1997	1998	1999	2000	2001	2002	2003	2004
Australia	188.1	184.7	187.2	171.1	152.2	132.4	116.3	118.0	114.8	118.9	119.9	106.6	104.9	100.0	92.8	99.4	114.0	126.0
Austria	166.7	158.4	149.9	149.6	145.5	148.0	150.1	138.6	137.8	140.6	126.7	113.0	109.2	100.0	95.8	96.2	98.8	97.7
Belgium	110.1	107.1	104.9	111.5	111.3	111.3	110.5	111.0	114.6	109.4	101.8	104.2	106.0	100.0	101.9	103.3	108.2	110.8
Canada	112.0	120.7	124.8	128.2	131.8	120.6	107.8	100.4	102.7	108.7	109.1	103.2	102.1	100.0	100.5	101.3	113.3	120.0
Czech Republic	..	..	..	..	..	..	81.0	89.5	84.6	90.3	89.1	98.0	99.6	100.0	102.4	108.8	106.4	102.2
Denmark	94.5	95.6	89.8	97.9	94.0	96.3	101.3	96.9	100.9	104.7	99.3	104.3	104.7	100.0	101.4	103.6	109.8	112.2
Finland	150.9	155.9	163.3	171.6	164.8	129.1	98.5	104.2	120.3	113.2	107.0	109.6	110.5	100.0	103.8	103.5	107.5	108.9
France	131.3	126.4	121.8	129.3	123.6	121.3	123.1	122.0	121.4	120.9	114.4	109.5	106.1	100.0	97.7	99.6	102.8	101.7
Germany	89.5	89.1	86.2	88.8	89.6	96.3	98.2	99.5	107.7	104.9	99.8	101.8	103.4	100.0	101.2	101.1	104.9	106.8
Greece	86.2	95.2	101.1	107.7	99.2	95.6	89.5	93.5	101.6	104.3	107.4	102.5	104.5	100.0	99.7	102.6	107.6	114.0
Hungary	..	..	..	..	..	..	154.4	154.2	126.8	117.2	117.5	108.3	108.8	100.0	109.4	125.1	131.0	136.4
Iceland	79.6	87.0	77.0	74.3	80.9	81.3	74.2	72.9	73.4	72.7	76.6	82.9	91.9	100.0	86.0	91.7	96.6	98.3
Ireland	247.0	226.0	212.7	224.6	212.4	205.3	188.8	179.3	160.8	155.9	132.5	128.3	117.4	100.0	98.8	93.2	100.7	103.1
Italy	116.7	113.8	114.2	113.5	116.4	114.7	105.0	100.0	87.7	98.1	99.4	104.5	106.2	100.0	100.9	108.5	117.4	122.8
Japan	68.3	70.6	64.0	59.7	65.4	72.2	86.5	95.8	97.3	82.4	78.0	84.5	96.6	100.0	93.2	85.7	83.8	82.9
Korea	89.1	109.5	129.5	125.9	128.4	118.3	114.4	117.8	131.2	141.0	126.6	88.0	93.9	100.0	93.0	97.9	97.8	96.6
Luxembourg	139.7	126.8	119.9	120.8	118.2	118.1	116.9	115.2	113.5	108.7	104.7	104.6	100.3	100.0	104.2	103.6	105.9	107.8
Mexico	86.2	89.5	99.2	100.9	112.8	125.6	135.3	132.0	82.2	83.6	91.8	89.0	92.3	100.0	106.5	110.1	98.3	96.3
Netherlands	113.6	111.3	103.8	105.5	103.9	106.9	106.3	102.7	106.7	103.1	99.8	103.7	104.3	100.0	102.6	109.0	119.8	120.6
New Zealand	93.0	103.5	96.1	96.2	95.3	85.3	88.6	96.9	103.9	115.4	121.1	111.6	111.9	100.0	97.0	106.8	122.0	132.5
Norway	78.3	82.8	81.3	80.3	79.1	78.0	76.3	80.3	85.0	84.5	91.2	94.9	97.7	100.0	102.0	116.0	116.3	111.6
Poland	..	..	..	..	..	..	84.8	90.5	99.0	100.9	101.3	106.6	100.2	100.0	103.5	93.5	76.8	68.4
Portugal	85.3	88.7	96.5	91.6	93.5	102.6	93.5	97.0	102.2	93.3	94.6	96.3	99.0	100.0	102.4	105.1	109.1	110.5
Slovak Republic	..	..	..	..	..	..	78.6	77.7	82.8	90.9	98.6	102.5	99.8	100.0	96.4	98.3	105.0	112.3
Spain	78.8	83.9	90.4	101.7	102.7	105.4	96.0	93.1	93.9	98.0	96.8	99.4	99.5	100.0	102.2	105.4	110.0	114.8
Sweden	140.7	146.3	153.4	158.2	160.9	157.8	112.7	106.6	106.5	118.9	111.9	107.5	101.9	100.0	96.5	93.1	96.0	99.0
Switzerland	87.5	89.0	84.0	90.3	90.7	88.2	87.8	96.4	105.5	101.2	96.3	99.0	100.4	100.0	104.9	111.9	114.7	115.2
Turkey	52.2	47.7	72.0	102.2	112.4	101.5	101.2	65.9	59.1	59.2	66.5	74.1	87.1	100.0	71.3	70.0	73.0	77.2
United Kingdom	74.7	79.8	77.1	79.8	82.1	76.1	67.3	68.7	68.4	71.1	86.2	95.4	96.9	100.0	97.1	101.6	97.3	102.0
United States	103.5	95.9	96.8	94.1	92.4	89.0	88.1	87.3	82.7	83.6	87.7	95.3	95.5	100.0	102.1	99.4	94.2	88.7
Euro area	106.2	101.7	96.5	105.6	103.3	107.9	103.7	101.2	104.9	105.4	95.6	97.2	110.8	100.0	101.4	107.1	120.4	126.2

Note: Competitiveness-weighted relative unit labour costs in the manufactoring sector in dollar terms. Competitiveness weights take into account the structure of competition in both export and import markets of the manufacturing sector of 42 countries. An increase in the index indicates a real effective appreciation and a corresponding deterioration of the competitive position. For details on the method of calculation see Durand, M., C. Madaschi and F. Terribile (1998), "Trends in OECD Countries' International Competitiveness: The Influence of Emerging Market Economies", *OECD Economics Department Working Papers,* No. 195. See also *OECD Economic Outlook* Sources and Methods *(http://www.oecd.org/eco/sources-and-methods).*

Source: OECD Economic Outlook 76 database.

Annex Table 44. **Export performance for total goods and services**

Percentage changes from previous year

	1987	1988	1989	1990	1991	1992	1993	1994	1995	1996	1997	1998	1999	2000	2001	2002	2003	2004	2005	2006
Australia	3.1	-6.5	-6.8	1.7	8.3	0.1	2.7	-1.1	-5.9	0.8	4.1	2.7	-3.0	-1.7	2.4	-5.1	-8.6	-4.2	-1.2	-0.6
Austria	-2.7	3.2	2.5	2.6	0.7	3.5	-1.8	-1.9	-1.1	-0.4	1.7	1.2	-0.5	-1.5	4.4	2.0	-3.4	-0.6	-0.1	-0.9
Belgium	-1.4	2.6	0.9	-0.8	-1.0	0.3	1.5	1.0	-2.9	-3.0	-3.0	-2.3	-1.6	-3.3	0.1	-0.8	-1.4	-3.7	-1.4	-0.9
Canada	-2.9	3.7	-4.0	0.8	1.4	0.9	2.9	1.1	0.1	-2.9	-3.8	-0.6	0.2	-3.6	-0.8	-2.2	-6.7	-2.2	-1.1	-2.0
Czech Republic	..	..	..	..	..	..	..	-2.7	8.0	1.3	-1.4	2.3	1.1	4.2	8.9	0.8	0.2	7.1	3.2	1.0
Denmark	-1.2	4.5	-3.0	1.8	4.5	-2.3	-1.8	-1.7	-4.4	-1.8	-5.6	-3.6	5.7	2.0	3.7	3.2	-3.8	-2.5	-1.6	-1.4
Finland	-1.7	-4.0	-3.9	-0.7	-7.0	15.0	14.1	5.0	0.2	-0.9	3.7	3.7	1.0	6.2	-2.7	1.7	-4.4	-6.7	-3.1	-3.2
France	-3.4	0.9	2.5	-0.4	1.4	2.4	-0.3	0.4	-0.1	-2.6	2.0	1.3	-2.7	2.4	0.3	-0.6	-6.3	-3.9	-2.1	-1.3
Germany	-5.2	-2.1	2.5	8.6	-7.9	-3.4	-6.8	-0.6	-2.4	-1.2	1.3	-0.6	-1.0	1.8	4.4	1.0	-2.4	-0.5	-2.9	-0.8
Greece	0.9	-8.0	-4.4	-6.5	3.5	12.5	-4.5	0.0	-4.2	-2.7	9.1	-1.4	10.9	2.1	-2.3	-10.5	-3.7	-4.3	-1.1	-0.3
Hungary	..	..	..	..	..	..	..	5.5	5.4	3.1	16.1	9.2	6.9	8.8	5.1	2.1	2.4	5.9	4.3	3.2
Iceland	-3.1	-11.7	-5.1	-4.7	-7.5	-4.1	6.3	1.1	-9.5	2.5	-3.3	-4.1	-2.6	-5.0	6.3	1.3	-2.8	-1.1	-2.0	-0.6
Ireland	6.4	0.6	2.2	3.6	3.3	9.9	8.7	6.3	11.2	5.3	7.3	14.3	7.2	8.2	7.4	3.0	-4.0	-0.9	1.0	-0.8
Italy	-1.0	-2.3	0.1	2.9	-4.4	7.8	7.7	2.0	4.3	-5.4	-3.1	-3.0	-6.0	-2.3	-0.1	-5.9	-8.2	-4.0	-2.3	-3.6
Japan	-8.6	-4.1	1.5	-0.1	-2.9	-3.6	-7.5	-7.5	-6.3	-2.1	0.8	-2.3	-6.9	-2.0	-4.3	2.7	3.5	2.8	-2.2	-2.3
Korea	14.4	1.4	-11.9	-1.5	5.7	5.2	4.2	5.4	12.5	2.2	11.2	12.6	6.8	4.6	-2.1	7.8	7.8	8.6	3.0	4.1
Luxembourg	-2.8	3.2	4.4	0.3	5.7	0.5	5.4	-0.6	-2.7	0.9	5.2	5.1	7.7	5.3	0.3	-2.1	-0.8	-0.3	0.2	-0.1
Mexico	3.3	1.1	1.1	1.4	4.6	-1.9	-0.2	5.5	20.2	9.1	-2.4	1.1	1.9	3.3	-1.5	-1.2	-3.1	2.1	0.5	0.9
Netherlands	-2.7	0.1	-0.6	-0.4	1.4	-0.2	5.8	1.7	1.4	-0.5	-0.1	-0.1	-1.4	0.0	0.2	-0.8	-3.3	-0.7	-0.3	-0.7
New Zealand	-1.2	-5.2	-11.7	1.0	8.0	-1.7	-0.1	-1.0	-5.7	-5.0	-4.5	0.3	-0.1	-5.2	4.0	0.3	-4.6	-4.1	-4.2	-1.8
Norway	-4.9	-2.0	3.2	4.8	5.0	1.8	2.1	-0.3	-2.6	3.8	-2.1	-7.1	-3.9	-6.7	3.9	-2.2	-1.6	-4.4	-4.7	-3.6
Poland	..	..	..	..	..	..	..	5.4	14.1	6.5	3.3	8.3	-6.8	9.4	-0.8	2.1	8.5	3.5	3.0	2.9
Portugal	3.3	-0.2	3.1	3.4	-3.7	-0.4	-1.8	0.1	1.1	1.5	-2.7	-0.1	-4.5	-2.8	-1.1	0.1	0.9	0.3	-1.4	-1.8
Slovak Republic	..	..	..	..	..	..	..	6.3	-4.6	-7.2	7.8	5.1	0.0	0.3	1.5	2.8	15.6	3.5	2.8	3.3
Spain	-1.6	-3.8	-5.4	-1.5	4.2	3.8	8.8	8.4	1.6	5.1	5.0	-0.4	1.6	-0.7	2.2	-0.1	0.1	-2.1	-0.1	-0.8
Sweden	0.3	-3.9	-3.6	-2.3	-3.9	0.7	6.7	5.0	3.1	-2.6	2.8	1.6	2.4	-0.3	-0.8	-2.1	1.3	2.4	0.2	-0.5
Switzerland	-4.8	-1.4	-1.9	-3.4	-5.7	0.4	1.3	-5.9	-7.2	-2.2	1.5	-1.9	-0.4	0.3	-0.5	-2.4	-3.9	-3.9	-2.9	-3.0
Turkey	22.1	11.2	-6.7	0.5	2.2	17.6	7.1	8.2	1.0	15.4	9.8	7.2	-12.1	6.7	3.9	7.1	10.1	5.2	3.7	1.9
United Kingdom	0.5	-5.8	-3.0	0.3	-3.8	1.8	3.0	0.4	0.7	2.3	-1.4	-4.3	-2.7	-2.4	2.0	-2.5	-3.5	-5.3	-0.4	-0.6
United States	3.6	3.1	2.6	2.7	0.6	0.7	-1.3	-1.5	2.6	-0.2	0.6	-0.7	-1.9	-3.2	-4.7	-4.4	-2.0	-0.8	-0.1	0.7
Total OECD	-1.6	-0.7	0.1	1.9	-1.3	0.7	-0.1	-0.3	0.5	-0.5	0.6	-0.3	-1.6	-0.6	-0.3	-1.0	-2.0	-0.7	-0.8	-0.5
Memorandum items																				
China	..	..	..	..	9.4	11.8	10.6	13.3	-3.7	8.4	13.9	8.7	5.7	12.5	7.3	21.1	20.3	8.6	8.7	8.9
Dynamic Asia[a]	..	..	..	..	6.2	6.4	4.5	1.9	0.8	-4.5	-2.0	-2.3	-1.8	-1.7	-4.7	1.4	1.6	-0.3	1.0	0.0
Other Asia	..	..	..	..	7.1	4.8	4.8	0.7	2.5	0.5	2.8	5.5	1.9	8.4	4.3	5.7	-0.6	0.8	4.2	4.8
Latin America	..	..	..	..	-4.4	1.6	5.3	-5.3	-3.5	-1.0	-1.5	1.2	-2.8	-4.7	4.9	1.3	3.1	1.4	-2.1	-2.6
Africa & Middle-East	..	..	..	..	-4.9	4.1	3.4	-3.6	-7.5	-3.1	-2.1	1.1	-0.5	-4.5	1.2	-1.9	2.1	-5.8	-3.7	-2.4
Central & East Europe[b]	..	..	..	..	-10.9	-8.3	15.5	-7.8	-6.5	-4.6	-4.2	0.1	3.7	-4.9	2.1	4.8	2.3	-0.2	-0.9	-1.2

Note: Regional aggregates are calculated *inclusive* of intra-regional trade. Export performance is the ratio between export volumes and export markets for total goods and services. The calculation of export markets is based on a weighted average of import volumes in each exporting country's markets, with weights based on trade flows in 2000.

a) Dynamic Asia includes Chinese Taipei; Hong Kong, China; Indonesia; Malaysia; Philippines; Singapore and Thailand.

b) Data prior to 1996 are OECD estimates.

Source: OECD Economic Outlook 76 database.

Annex Table 45. **Shares in world exports and imports**

Percentage, values for goods and services, national accounts basis

	1991	1992	1993	1994	1995	1996	1997	1998	1999	2000	2001	2002	2003	2004	2005	2006
A. Exports																
Canada	3.5	3.4	3.6	3.6	3.5	3.6	3.7	3.8	4.1	4.2	4.1	3.8	3.6	3.6	3.6	3.5
France	6.1	6.2	5.6	5.5	5.6	5.4	5.2	5.6	5.3	4.8	4.9	4.9	4.9	4.7	4.6	4.5
Germany	10.8	10.7	9.4	9.3	9.6	9.1	8.6	9.2	8.9	8.1	8.6	9.0	9.4	9.4	9.2	9.0
Italy	5.0	5.1	4.7	4.6	4.7	4.8	4.5	4.6	4.3	3.9	4.1	4.0	4.1	4.0	3.9	3.7
Japan	8.0	8.0	8.4	8.2	7.7	6.9	6.7	6.2	6.4	6.5	5.7	5.6	5.5	5.5	5.4	5.2
United Kingdom	5.5	5.5	5.2	5.2	5.1	5.3	5.5	5.6	5.5	5.2	5.2	5.2	4.9	4.7	4.6	4.5
United States	13.8	13.7	13.9	13.6	12.9	13.1	13.9	14.1	14.1	14.0	13.6	12.6	11.3	10.8	10.5	10.6
Other OECD countries	24.0	24.0	24.0	24.4	25.4	25.4	24.9	26.0	26.0	25.3	26.0	26.3	26.9	27.1	27.0	26.7
Total OECD	76.6	76.5	74.9	74.5	74.5	73.5	73.0	75.1	74.5	71.9	72.2	71.4	70.7	69.8	68.7	67.8
Non-OECD Asia	11.6	12.5	13.7	14.6	14.9	15.3	15.8	14.7	15.1	16.3	16.0	16.8	17.1	17.3	17.8	18.8
Latin America	2.6	2.6	2.8	2.9	2.8	2.8	3.0	2.9	2.8	2.9	2.9	2.7	2.7	2.7	2.8	2.8
Other non-OECD countries[a]	9.2	8.4	8.6	8.0	7.9	8.4	8.2	7.2	7.6	9.0	8.9	9.0	9.6	10.2	10.7	10.7
Non-OECD	23.4	23.5	25.1	25.5	25.5	26.5	27.0	24.9	25.5	28.1	27.8	28.6	29.3	30.2	31.3	32.2
B. Imports																
Canada	3.5	3.4	3.6	3.6	3.3	3.2	3.5	3.6	3.7	3.7	3.6	3.4	3.2	3.1	3.1	3.0
France	6.1	6.1	5.2	5.2	5.3	5.1	4.7	5.1	4.9	4.6	4.6	4.6	4.8	4.7	4.6	4.4
Germany	10.8	10.8	9.5	9.4	9.5	8.9	8.3	8.8	8.7	8.0	8.1	7.9	8.4	8.2	8.0	7.7
Italy	5.0	5.1	4.1	4.0	4.1	4.0	3.9	4.1	4.0	3.7	3.9	3.9	4.0	3.9	3.9	3.8
Japan	6.7	6.3	6.4	6.5	6.6	6.6	6.2	5.2	5.5	5.7	5.3	5.0	4.8	4.8	4.7	4.6
United Kingdom	5.8	5.7	5.5	5.5	5.3	5.4	5.6	5.9	5.9	5.5	5.7	5.8	5.5	5.4	5.3	5.1
United States	14.3	14.4	15.4	15.6	14.6	14.8	15.7	16.7	17.9	18.8	18.4	18.0	16.9	16.4	16.0	15.8
Other OECD countries	23.9	24.0	23.6	24.0	24.5	24.8	24.3	25.2	25.2	24.6	24.7	25.2	26.0	26.2	26.2	25.8
Total OECD	76.1	75.8	73.4	73.8	73.1	72.9	72.3	74.6	75.8	74.6	74.3	73.8	73.5	72.6	71.7	70.2
Non-OECD Asia	11.3	12.4	14.2	14.9	15.5	15.7	15.8	13.7	13.9	15.3	14.9	15.5	15.8	16.6	17.0	17.9
Latin America	2.3	2.5	3.0	3.0	3.2	3.1	3.5	3.6	3.0	3.0	3.0	2.5	2.3	2.4	2.5	2.5
Other non-OECD countries[a]	10.3	9.3	9.5	8.2	8.2	8.3	8.4	8.0	7.3	7.2	7.9	8.2	8.4	8.4	8.8	9.3
Non-OECD	23.9	24.2	26.6	26.2	26.9	27.1	27.7	25.4	24.2	25.4	25.7	26.2	26.5	27.4	28.3	29.8

Note: Regional aggregates are calculated *inclusive* of intra-regional trade.

a) Central and Eastern Europe data prior to 1995 are OECD estimates.

Source: OECD Economic Outlook 76 database.

Annex Table 46. **Geographical structure of world trade growth**

Average of export and import volumes

	1991	1992	1993	1994	1995	1996	1997	1998	1999	2000	2001	2002	2003	2004	2005	2006
A. Trade growth by main regions (percentage changes from previous year)																
NAFTA[a]	3.2	7.2	6.5	11.1	8.3	8.9	12.8	7.9	8.9	11.5	-3.7	1.1	2.5	9.6	8.3	8.0
OECD Europe	1.7	3.0	-0.2	8.3	8.0	5.3	10.1	8.2	5.8	11.7	2.6	1.6	1.8	6.4	7.0	7.6
OECD Asia & Pacific[b]	3.9	3.2	1.6	8.6	10.6	10.3	7.6	-3.9	7.0	12.6	-3.0	7.6	8.7	13.6	9.0	9.9
Total OECD	2.4	4.2	1.9	9.2	8.5	7.1	10.5	6.3	6.9	11.8	-0.1	2.2	3.0	8.4	7.7	8.1
China	15.3	22.7	24.3	20.2	12.9	22.8	17.3	1.9	17.2	25.5	6.0	23.1	26.5	20.1	16.7	18.5
Non-OECD Asia excluding China	12.8	12.4	12.0	13.6	13.4	6.6	8.2	-6.3	5.7	15.9	-4.6	6.8	7.2	11.4	11.1	11.6
Latin America	9.1	13.5	16.0	8.7	11.0	5.2	15.6	8.0	-5.2	5.9	3.4	-5.7	5.5	14.3	9.4	8.4
Other non-OECD countries[c]	-4.9	-4.5	7.2	-0.1	1.3	4.7	5.5	-0.0	5.2	9.1	5.8	6.5	8.6	8.0	10.8	12.1
Non-OECD[c]	4.1	5.7	11.3	8.3	8.9	7.2	9.0	-1.8	5.3	13.7	0.7	7.5	10.4	12.2	11.9	12.8
World	2.9	4.6	4.5	8.9	8.6	7.1	10.1	4.0	6.5	12.3	0.1	3.6	5.1	9.5	9.0	9.5
B. Contribution to World Trade growth by main regions (percentage points)																
NAFTA[a]	0.6	1.4	1.3	2.3	1.7	1.8	2.7	1.7	2.0	2.6	-0.9	0.2	0.5	2.0	1.7	1.7
OECD Europe	0.7	1.3	-0.1	3.4	3.2	2.1	4.0	3.2	2.4	4.8	1.0	0.7	0.7	2.5	2.7	2.9
OECD Asia & Pacific[b]	0.4	0.4	0.2	0.9	1.1	1.1	0.8	-0.4	0.7	1.3	-0.3	0.7	0.9	1.4	1.0	1.1
Total OECD	1.8	3.0	1.4	6.5	6.1	5.0	7.5	4.5	5.1	8.7	-0.1	1.6	2.2	5.9	5.4	5.6
China	0.2	0.3	0.4	0.4	0.3	0.5	0.5	0.1	0.5	0.8	0.2	0.8	1.1	1.0	0.9	1.1
Non-OECD Asia excluding China	1.3	1.4	1.4	1.7	1.8	0.9	1.1	-0.8	0.7	1.9	-0.6	0.8	0.9	1.4	1.4	1.5
Latin America	0.2	0.4	0.5	0.3	0.4	0.2	0.5	0.3	-0.2	0.2	0.1	-0.2	0.2	0.4	0.3	0.2
Other non-OECD countries[c]	-0.6	-0.5	0.8	-0.0	0.1	0.4	0.5	-0.0	0.4	0.8	0.5	0.6	0.8	0.7	1.0	1.1
Non-OECD[c]	1.1	1.5	3.1	2.4	2.5	2.0	2.6	-0.5	1.4	3.6	0.2	2.0	2.9	3.6	3.6	3.9
World	2.9	4.6	4.5	8.9	8.6	7.1	10.1	4.0	6.5	12.3	0.1	3.6	5.1	9.5	9.0	9.5

Note: Regional aggregates are calculated *inclusive* of intra-regional trade as the sum of volumes expressed in 2000 $.

a) Canada, Mexico and United States.

b) Australia, Japan, Korea and New Zealand.

c) Central and Eastern Europe data prior to 1996 are OECD estimates.

Source: OECD Economic Outlook 76 database.

Annex Table 47. **Trade balances for goods and services**

$ billion, national accounts basis

	1987	1988	1989	1990	1991	1992	1993	1994	1995	1996	1997	1998	1999	2000	2001	2002	2003	2004	2005	2006
Australia	-2.1	-3.0	-7.7	-3.2	1.1	-0.9	-1.5	-4.5	-5.2	-0.7	1.5	-6.5	-10.7	-4.6	1.5	-5.6	-15.4	-16.5	-14.4	-13.6
Austria	0.4	0.7	0.7	1.5	0.3	-0.0	1.3	-1.6	-0.7	-1.9	0.4	3.1	3.6	2.7	4.6	10.5	10.1	13.2	15.3	16.9
Belgium	2.3	3.8	3.9	4.0	4.3	5.8	7.3	10.1	12.5	10.7	11.2	10.5	10.8	6.8	8.3	11.1	12.1	13.0	12.6	12.9
Canada	5.0	3.8	0.2	0.8	-3.4	-2.2	0.0	6.7	18.9	24.7	12.6	12.3	24.2	41.6	41.1	32.5	34.2	54.2	66.0	72.5
Czech Republic	..	..	..	..	..	..	-0.3	-1.0	-2.4	-3.7	-3.1	-0.7	-0.7	-1.7	-1.5	-1.6	-2.0	-1.3	-1.5	-1.3
Denmark	1.9	3.2	3.3	6.8	7.9	9.7	9.4	8.1	7.4	9.0	6.0	3.5	8.3	9.4	10.3	9.8	13.9	15.3	16.8	17.8
Finland	0.1	-0.8	-2.3	-2.2	-1.1	1.0	4.1	5.7	10.2	9.7	9.9	11.4	10.8	11.2	10.1	11.2	10.6	11.0	11.6	11.6
France	-8.9	-8.1	-9.1	-11.8	-5.4	8.1	19.4	18.4	22.7	25.7	41.3	38.8	32.3	17.3	21.6	27.3	20.6	11.2	7.6	14.8
Germany	54.9	59.5	59.2	90.8	-3.9	-4.7	3.4	6.6	15.9	24.8	28.7	32.1	17.0	7.7	37.0	89.8	104.5	135.5	156.5	184.2
Greece	-2.5	-3.7	-5.3	-8.3	-8.6	-8.2	-7.6	-6.3	-8.6	-9.9	-8.9	-10.2	-10.7	-11.9	-10.0	-11.4	-15.5	-18.9	-20.1	-21.0
Hungary	..	..	..	..	..	..	-3.1	-2.4	-0.1	0.2	0.4	-0.7	-1.3	-1.8	-0.8	-1.6	-3.5	-5.2	-6.0	-5.9
Iceland	-0.1	-0.1	0.1	0.1	-0.1	-0.0	0.2	0.3	0.3	0.0	0.0	-0.4	-0.4	-0.6	-0.1	0.2	-0.3	-0.7	-1.1	-1.2
Ireland	1.4	2.3	2.1	2.2	2.4	4.1	5.3	5.4	7.6	8.5	10.0	10.0	13.0	12.4	15.5	20.1	23.5	28.3	33.9	36.9
Italy	3.6	0.6	-1.6	0.6	-0.2	-1.3	32.1	35.7	44.6	60.8	47.4	40.6	24.4	10.7	15.8	11.5	8.0	9.9	-1.4	-7.9
Japan	72.8	64.4	45.5	28.5	56.2	82.2	97.0	96.5	74.8	23.4	47.4	72.4	69.4	68.0	26.2	51.3	69.1	86.7	83.9	91.8
Korea	10.5	14.2	5.6	-2.1	-8.0	-3.8	1.2	-3.4	-5.7	-19.2	-4.3	44.0	29.8	16.2	11.1	7.4	15.4	27.6	22.1	21.8
Luxembourg	-0.0	0.1	0.4	0.4	0.3	1.0	1.3	1.8	2.2	2.1	2.4	2.8	3.3	4.1	3.4	4.0	5.1	6.1	7.0	7.7
Mexico	10.8	2.5	-0.1	-2.9	-9.1	-18.3	-15.8	-20.3	7.6	6.9	-0.4	-9.0	-7.8	-11.3	-14.1	-12.1	-10.5	-8.0	-9.1	-11.9
Netherlands	4.2	6.9	6.3	11.0	11.9	11.6	18.0	21.2	24.7	23.7	22.3	21.4	17.4	19.3	20.4	21.5	25.7	29.6	30.1	30.8
New Zealand	0.2	1.5	0.2	0.1	1.3	0.8	1.2	1.1	0.7	0.3	0.2	0.2	-0.5	0.5	1.6	1.0	0.5	-0.5	-1.1	-1.1
Norway	-2.0	-0.5	3.6	7.7	9.5	8.8	7.7	7.7	9.2	14.3	13.1	2.8	11.8	28.8	29.0	26.5	30.1	36.4	47.5	50.2
Poland	..	..	..	..	..	..	0.8	2.1	3.0	-2.2	-6.1	-8.3	-9.9	-10.9	-6.8	-6.4	-5.2	-4.9	-6.7	-7.5
Portugal	-2.0	-4.0	-3.1	-4.7	-5.8	-7.3	-6.0	-6.2	-6.7	-7.4	-8.2	-9.9	-11.9	-12.0	-11.2	-9.8	-9.7	-12.1	-13.6	-14.6
Slovak Republic	..	..	..	..	..	..	-0.6	0.9	0.5	-2.2	-2.0	-2.4	-0.9	-0.5	-1.7	-1.7	-0.5	-1.0	-1.4	-1.0
Spain	-0.2	-4.3	-13.6	-17.6	-17.9	-17.2	-4.0	-0.8	-1.1	3.1	5.7	0.3	-7.5	-12.5	-9.3	-8.6	-13.9	-30.4	-40.8	-44.5
Sweden	3.3	3.3	1.3	1.2	4.2	4.5	7.3	9.7	16.8	17.8	17.9	15.6	15.5	13.9	13.8	15.6	20.2	27.0	25.2	26.4
Switzerland	3.7	3.3	1.8	3.2	5.5	10.9	14.3	14.9	16.2	15.5	14.6	13.2	14.9	14.1	10.9	19.0	22.8	27.3	28.4	29.8
Turkey	-1.8	0.8	-1.6	-6.4	-4.1	-4.7	-10.2	0.5	-7.3	-11.4	-11.0	-7.4	-6.3	-14.9	3.1	-2.7	-7.9	-18.3	-18.2	-17.9
United Kingdom	-8.3	-30.4	-34.6	-25.2	-10.9	-13.3	-9.8	-7.3	-5.6	-5.3	1.7	-14.1	-25.8	-29.5	-39.5	-46.9	-53.5	-74.7	-83.8	-81.8
United States	-145.2	-110.4	-88.2	-78.0	-27.5	-33.3	-65.0	-93.6	-91.4	-96.3	-101.6	-160.0	-260.5	-379.5	-367.0	-424.9	-498.1	-607.8	-681.2	-715.8
Euro area	53.2	52.9	37.4	66.0	-23.7	-7.1	74.5	89.9	123.4	149.8	162.1	150.9	102.5	55.9	106.2	177.1	181.2	196.5	198.8	227.8
Total OECD	1.8	5.6	-33.1	-3.2	-1.2	33.3	107.3	106.0	161.1	121.1	149.0	105.5	-48.4	-207.0	-176.8	-162.9	-209.6	-267.9	-335.6	-321.1

Source: OECD Economic Outlook 76 database.

Annex Table 48. **Investment income, net**

$ billion

	1987	1988	1989	1990	1991	1992	1993	1994	1995	1996	1997	1998	1999	2000	2001	2002	2003	2004	2005	2006
Australia	-5.8	-8.6	-10.4	-13.2	-12.2	-10.1	-8.1	-12.4	-14.0	-15.2	-13.8	-11.4	-11.6	-10.8	-9.9	-11.0	-14.6	-17.3	-17.1	-18.3
Austria	-0.8	-0.9	-0.9	-0.9	-1.4	-1.4	-1.5	-1.7	-2.4	-0.9	-1.5	-2.0	-2.9	-2.5	-3.1	-1.6	-1.8	-2.5	-2.6	-2.9
Belgium[a]	1.8	2.1	4.0	4.8	5.7	6.4	6.9	7.4	7.3	6.8	6.3	6.9	6.6	5.9	5.6	7.6	7.9	9.2	11.2	13.7
Canada	-17.1	-17.5	-20.5	-19.4	-17.4	-17.5	-20.8	-18.9	-22.7	-21.5	-20.9	-20.0	-22.6	-22.3	-25.4	-18.3	-16.8	-19.3	-20.5	-19.9
Czech Republic	..	..	..	..	..	..	-0.1	-0.0	-0.1	-0.7	-0.8	-1.1	-1.4	-1.4	-2.2	-3.6	-4.2	-6.0	-7.0	-7.7
Denmark	-4.1	-3.7	-3.8	-5.1	-5.1	-4.9	-3.8	-3.8	-3.8	-3.7	-3.4	-2.8	-2.5	-4.1	-3.0	-3.5	-3.9	-3.5	-3.5	-3.4
Finland	-1.6	-1.7	-2.7	-3.7	-4.7	-5.5	-4.9	-4.4	-4.4	-3.7	-2.5	-3.1	-2.4	-1.8	-0.9	-0.5	-2.4	-1.4	-0.5	0.3
France	-1.7	-1.0	-0.3	-1.6	-3.3	-6.0	-6.6	-6.0	-8.4	-1.9	7.2	9.2	18.9	15.6	14.5	4.3	7.0	9.8	11.9	13.9
Germany	5.2	9.4	14.3	20.6	20.3	21.8	16.6	2.9	0.1	1.2	-1.5	-7.6	-10.3	-2.4	-9.5	-15.8	-14.0	-9.2	-4.3	0.0
Greece	-1.7	-1.8	-1.9	-2.0	-2.0	-2.4	-1.7	-1.4	-1.8	-2.1	-1.7	-1.6	-0.7	-0.9	-1.9	-2.0	-2.9	-3.5	-4.0	-4.3
Hungary	..	..	..	..	..	..	-0.1	0.1	0.0	0.0	-2.7	-3.0	-2.9	-2.6	-2.9	-3.6	-4.4	-5.6	-6.2	-6.5
Iceland	-0.2	-0.2	-0.2	-0.2	-0.2	-0.2	-0.1	-0.2	-0.2	-0.2	-0.2	-0.2	-0.2	-0.2	-0.3	-0.1	-0.1	-0.2	-0.4	-0.5
Ireland	-3.1	-3.9	-4.3	-5.0	-4.6	-5.6	-5.3	-5.4	-7.3	-8.2	-9.7	-10.6	-13.7	-13.5	-16.4	-22.2	-26.2	-30.5	-35.0	-37.4
Italy	-4.9	-5.5	-7.2	-14.6	-17.5	-21.9	-17.4	-16.9	-15.9	-15.2	-10.3	-11.2	-11.1	-11.9	-10.4	-14.5	-19.4	-13.7	-19.0	-19.4
Japan	16.6	20.9	23.0	22.7	26.0	35.6	40.7	40.6	44.2	53.3	58.1	54.9	58.1	60.6	69.3	65.5	71.1	82.3	91.6	99.8
Korea	-1.6	-1.3	-0.6	-0.1	-0.2	-0.4	-0.4	-0.5	-1.3	-1.8	-2.5	-5.6	-5.2	-2.4	-1.2	0.4	0.6	-0.3	0.1	1.5
Luxembourg	..	..	..	..	..	..	..	..	1.6	1.3	0.5	0.2	-0.5	-1.3	-1.6	-2.3	-3.0	-3.4	-3.9	-4.3
Mexico	-6.8	-7.3	-8.3	-8.7	-8.6	-9.6	-11.4	-13.0	-13.3	-14.0	-12.8	-13.3	-12.9	-14.8	-14.0	-12.4	-12.7	-15.0	-16.5	-17.5
Netherlands	1.4	1.2	2.9	-0.6	0.4	-1.0	0.9	3.6	7.3	3.5	7.0	-2.7	3.5	-2.2	-2.8	-1.0	-2.2	4.0	7.2	9.9
New Zealand	-2.0	-2.1	-1.9	-1.6	-2.5	-2.5	-2.9	-3.4	-4.0	-4.7	-4.9	-2.6	-3.1	-3.2	-3.0	-3.0	-3.9	-4.5	-4.6	-4.5
Norway	-1.4	-2.5	-2.8	-3.4	-3.9	-2.8	-2.7	-2.2	-1.8	-1.9	-1.6	-1.2	-1.9	-1.6	-1.1	0.7	1.5	-0.1	3.1	3.2
Poland[b]	..	..	..	..	..	..	-3.4	-2.6	-2.0	-1.1	-1.1	-1.2	-1.0	-1.5	-1.4	-1.9	-3.1	-3.9	-4.8	-5.3
Portugal	-0.8	-0.8	-0.6	-0.1	0.2	0.6	0.2	-0.6	-0.0	-1.0	-1.5	-1.6	-1.8	-3.0	-3.0	-2.1	-2.4	-2.1	-2.1	-2.3
Slovak Republic	..	..	..	..	..	..	-0.0	-0.1	-0.0	-0.0	-0.1	-0.2	-0.3	-0.3	-0.3	-0.5	-0.1	-0.6	-0.5	-0.5
Spain	-2.6	-3.3	-2.8	-3.5	-4.3	-5.8	-3.6	-7.8	-4.1	-6.1	-6.8	-7.5	-9.5	-8.3	-9.8	-10.6	-11.9	-13.1	-14.7	-15.9
Sweden	-1.6	-1.8	-2.3	-4.5	-6.4	-10.0	-8.8	-5.9	-5.5	-6.3	-4.9	-3.2	-2.0	-1.4	-1.4	-1.1	0.3	0.6	1.1	1.8
Switzerland	6.8	8.9	8.1	8.8	8.8	8.3	9.1	7.9	11.9	12.6	16.2	17.6	20.2	21.9	14.0	10.9	26.4	25.7	27.6	28.7
Turkey	-2.1	-2.5	-2.3	-2.5	-2.7	-2.6	-2.7	-3.3	-3.2	-2.9	-3.0	-3.0	-3.5	-4.0	-5.0	-4.6	-5.4	-3.7	-3.9	-4.1
United Kingdom	1.4	1.3	-1.2	-5.1	-5.9	0.2	-0.3	5.1	3.3	1.8	6.4	21.4	-1.8	8.0	16.8	32.7	36.2	47.2	48.8	51.1
United States	14.3	18.7	19.8	28.5	24.1	24.2	25.3	17.1	20.9	22.3	12.6	3.8	13.2	20.6	23.6	7.2	33.3	18.4	-3.4	-26.2
Euro area	-8.7	-6.0	0.5	-6.6	-11.2	-20.7	-16.3	-30.1	-28.0	-26.4	-14.5	-31.5	-23.7	-26.4	-39.3	-60.7	-71.5	-56.4	-55.9	-48.7
Total OECD	-12.4	-3.8	-3.0	-10.4	-17.3	-12.8	-6.9	-25.5	-19.6	-10.3	6.0	-2.4	-5.2	14.0	13.3	-6.7	28.5	37.9	28.1	22.9

Note: The classification of non-factor services and investment income is affected by the change in reporting system to the International Monetary Fund, *Fifth Balance of Payments Manual.*

a) Including Luxembourg until 1994.

b) Data in 1993 are OECD estimates.

Source: OECD Economic Outlook 76 database.

Annex Table 49. **Total transfers, net**

$ billion

	1987	1988	1989	1990	1991	1992	1993	1994	1995	1996	1997	1998	1999	2000	2001	2002	2003	2004	2005	2006
Australia	0.0	0.0	0.2	0.4	0.1	-0.1	-0.1	-0.2	-0.1	0.1	-0.0	-0.3	-0.0	-0.0	0.0	-0.1	-0.1	-0.1	-0.0	-0.0
Austria	-0.1	-0.0	-0.1	-0.0	-0.1	-1.0	-1.0	-1.1	-1.7	-1.8	-1.7	-1.9	-2.0	-1.3	-1.2	-1.8	-2.3	-2.7	-3.2	-3.8
Belgium[a]	-1.4	-1.7	-1.8	-2.0	-2.1	-2.5	-2.6	-3.3	-4.2	-4.1	-3.7	-4.3	-4.6	-3.9	-4.1	-4.3	-6.6	-6.7	-6.5	-5.2
Canada	-0.9	-0.9	-1.0	-0.8	-1.1	-0.9	-0.6	-0.3	-0.1	0.5	0.5	0.6	0.5	0.8	1.0	0.6	0.2	0.4	0.3	0.3
Czech Republic	..	..	..	..	..	..	0.1	0.1	0.6	0.4	0.4	0.5	0.6	0.4	0.5	0.9	0.5	0.5	0.6	0.7
Denmark	-0.2	-1.0	-1.2	-1.2	-1.6	-1.7	-1.7	-2.0	-2.4	-2.6	-1.8	-2.3	-2.7	-3.0	-2.6	-3.0	-3.9	-4.3	-5.0	-5.0
Finland	-0.5	-0.5	-0.8	-1.0	-1.0	-0.8	-0.5	-0.5	-0.5	-0.9	-0.7	-1.1	-1.0	-0.7	-0.7	-0.7	-1.1	-1.4	-1.2	-1.2
France	-5.4	-6.7	-7.7	-9.8	-9.3	-11.1	-8.2	-11.5	-5.9	-7.4	-1.8	-1.8	-2.8	-0.9	-1.2	-1.8	-2.9	-3.9	-1.6	-1.6
Germany	-16.5	-18.7	-18.5	-21.9	-35.4	-32.8	-33.3	-36.8	-38.7	-33.9	-30.5	-30.3	-26.7	-26.2	-24.6	-26.3	-32.4	-37.2	-38.5	-38.2
Greece[b]	3.0	3.6	4.0	4.7	6.2	6.5	6.5	6.9	8.0	8.0	8.3	7.9	4.1	3.4	3.4	3.6	4.3	5.1	5.6	5.7
Hungary	..	..	..	..	..	..	0.8	0.9	0.2	-0.0	0.2	0.2	0.4	0.4	0.4	0.5	0.7	-0.0	-0.1	-0.1
Iceland	0.0	-0.0	-0.0	-0.0	-0.0	-0.0	-0.0	-0.0	-0.0	-0.0	-0.0	-0.0	-0.0	-0.0	-0.0	0.0	-0.0	-0.0	0.0	0.0
Ireland	1.3	1.4	1.5	2.4	2.6	2.1	1.9	1.7	1.8	2.2	2.0	1.5	1.3	0.9	0.3	0.7	0.5	0.8	0.7	0.5
Italy	-1.3	-2.3	-3.9	-4.0	-7.6	-7.8	-7.3	-7.2	-4.2	-6.6	-4.2	-7.4	-5.4	-4.3	-5.8	-5.5	-8.1	-7.6	-9.1	-9.1
Japan	-3.1	-3.3	-3.1	-4.8	-12.0	-3.8	-5.1	-6.1	-7.7	-9.0	-8.9	-8.8	-12.1	-9.8	-7.9	-4.9	-7.4	-8.2	-8.5	-8.5
Korea	1.8	2.3	1.1	1.1	0.8	1.1	1.2	1.3	0.2	-0.0	0.7	3.4	1.9	0.7	-0.4	-1.6	-2.8	-1.6	-2.5	-3.0
Luxembourg	..	..	..	..	..	..	..	..	-0.6	-0.6	-0.5	-0.4	-0.6	-0.5	-0.5	-0.2	-0.5	-0.9	-0.8	-0.6
Mexico	1.9	2.3	2.6	3.8	3.0	3.4	3.6	3.8	4.0	4.4	5.3	6.0	6.3	7.1	9.2	10.3	13.8	14.4	14.9	15.2
Netherlands	-2.0	-1.9	-1.9	-2.9	-4.1	-4.3	-4.5	-5.2	-6.4	-6.8	-6.1	-7.2	-6.4	-6.3	-6.7	-6.2	-7.7	-9.4	-10.7	-11.6
New Zealand	0.2	0.2	0.2	0.2	0.2	0.2	0.2	0.3	0.3	0.6	0.3	0.3	0.2	0.2	0.2	0.1	0.1	0.0	0.1	0.1
Norway	-1.0	-1.0	-1.0	-1.2	-1.2	-1.5	-1.3	-1.7	-2.1	-1.5	-1.4	-1.5	-1.4	-1.4	-1.6	-2.4	-3.1	-2.6	-2.7	-2.7
Poland[c]	..	..	..	..	..	..	0.9	1.3	1.0	1.7	2.0	2.9	2.2	2.4	2.9	3.3	4.2	5.0	5.5	6.0
Portugal[b]	3.8	4.3	4.6	5.5	6.0	7.8	6.7	5.4	7.2	4.4	3.8	4.1	3.9	3.4	3.4	2.8	3.4	4.1	4.6	5.1
Slovak Republic	..	..	..	..	..	..	0.1	0.1	0.1	0.2	0.2	0.4	0.2	0.1	0.2	0.2	0.2	0.4	0.5	0.5
Spain	2.6	4.5	4.6	2.7	2.7	2.1	1.3	1.3	4.7	2.4	2.8	3.3	3.0	1.4	1.6	2.3	0.4	1.4	2.7	2.7
Sweden	-1.3	-1.4	-1.8	-1.9	-2.0	-1.4	-1.3	-1.2	-2.6	-2.0	-2.4	-2.6	-2.7	-2.5	-2.4	-2.8	-2.0	-2.7	-2.1	-2.1
Switzerland	-1.5	-1.7	-1.7	-2.3	-2.6	-3.0	-2.7	-3.4	-4.2	-4.0	-3.4	-3.7	-4.1	-2.9	-5.2	-5.7	-5.2	-5.5	-5.9	-5.9
Turkey	2.4	2.2	3.5	4.5	5.1	4.1	3.8	3.1	4.5	4.4	4.9	5.7	5.2	5.2	3.8	3.5	2.1	3.4	4.4	5.7
United Kingdom	-5.9	-6.3	-7.3	-8.8	-2.2	-9.9	-7.9	-8.2	-11.9	-7.4	-9.7	-13.9	-11.9	-14.7	-9.5	-12.9	-16.1	-19.0	-19.4	-20.7
United States	-23.3	-25.3	-26.2	-26.7	10.7	-33.1	-37.1	-36.8	-34.1	-38.6	-40.4	-48.4	-46.8	-55.7	-46.6	-59.4	-67.4	-77.1	-79.7	-85.6
Euro area	-16.3	-17.9	-20.0	-26.2	-42.3	-41.9	-41.1	-50.3	-40.6	-45.1	-32.4	-37.5	-37.2	-34.8	-36.1	-37.5	-53.0	-58.4	-57.9	-57.2
Total OECD	-47.1	-51.8	-55.5	-63.7	-45.0	-88.5	-88.2	-99.5	-95.0	-98.0	-86.1	-99.0	-101.5	-107.6	-94.0	-110.9	-139.1	-155.5	-157.5	-162.2

a) Including Luxembourg until 1994.
b) Breaks between 1998 and 1999 for Greece and between 1995 and 1996 for Portugal, reflecting change in methodology to the International Monetary Fund, *Fifth Balance of Payments Manual* (capital transfers from European Union are excluded from the current account).
c) Data in 1993 are OECD estimates.
Source: OECD Economic Outlook 76 database.

Annex Table 50. **Current account balances**

$ billion

	1987	1988	1989	1990	1991	1992	1993	1994	1995	1996	1997	1998	1999	2000	2001	2002	2003	2004	2005	2006
Australia	-8.0	-11.6	-17.9	-15.9	-11.0	-11.1	-9.7	-17.1	-19.3	-15.8	-12.4	-18.1	-22.3	-15.4	-8.3	-16.7	-30.1	-34.1	-32.7	-33.1
Austria	-0.2	-0.3	0.3	1.2	-0.0	-0.7	-1.4	-3.4	-6.2	-5.3	-6.5	-5.2	-6.4	-4.8	-3.7	0.7	-1.1	-0.4	0.1	0.3
Belgium[a]	4.1	5.2	5.1	6.2	7.2	9.9	13.0	14.2	15.3	13.8	13.8	13.3	12.9	9.0	8.9	14.1	12.8	13.1	11.9	16.0
Canada	-13.5	-14.9	-21.8	-19.8	-22.4	-21.1	-21.7	-13.0	-4.4	3.4	-8.2	-7.7	1.7	19.7	16.2	14.4	17.1	34.5	45.1	52.1
Czech Republic	..	..	..	..	..	..	0.5	-0.8	-1.4	-4.1	-3.6	-1.3	-1.5	-2.7	-3.3	-4.2	-5.7	-6.9	-7.9	-8.3
Denmark	-3.0	-1.6	-1.7	0.6	1.2	3.2	3.9	2.3	1.2	2.7	0.7	-1.6	3.1	2.3	4.9	3.4	5.7	7.5	8.3	9.4
Finland	-1.7	-2.8	-5.7	-6.9	-6.9	-5.2	-1.2	1.1	5.4	5.0	6.6	7.4	7.2	8.9	8.7	10.1	6.6	9.1	9.8	10.6
France	-4.5	-4.6	-4.6	-9.8	-5.7	4.8	9.6	7.4	11.0	20.8	37.6	39.3	41.4	18.8	21.9	13.8	7.1	3.4	3.7	12.9
Germany	43.8	50.7	55.4	44.6	-22.0	-19.0	-13.9	-29.3	-27.0	-13.7	-9.4	-12.3	-24.0	-25.3	1.6	41.5	54.8	89.1	111.2	141.0
Greece[b]	-1.9	-1.6	-3.4	-4.8	-2.8	-3.8	-2.1	-1.5	-4.7	-6.6	-5.3	-3.8	-7.7	-9.9	-11.3	-10.1	-11.2	-12.1	-13.0	-13.5
Hungary	..	..	..	..	..	..	-2.0	-1.9	0.1	0.2	-2.0	-3.4	-3.8	-4.0	-3.2	-4.7	-7.3	-9.0	-9.8	-10.1
Iceland	-0.2	-0.2	-0.1	-0.1	-0.3	-0.2	0.0	0.1	0.1	-0.1	-0.1	-0.6	-0.6	-0.8	-0.3	0.1	-0.4	-1.1	-1.5	-1.8
Ireland	-0.1	-0.0	-0.6	-0.4	0.3	0.6	1.8	1.5	1.7	2.0	1.9	0.7	0.3	-0.3	-0.7	-1.5	-2.2	-1.1	-0.2	0.2
Italy	-2.5	-7.6	-11.8	-16.5	-23.5	-28.8	7.5	12.6	24.8	39.7	33.3	22.8	8.0	-6.1	-1.0	-9.9	-21.0	-9.0	-28.8	-35.7
Japan	84.3	78.8	66.2	46.6	69.3	108.6	131.1	130.4	113.4	64.8	97.8	119.5	114.3	118.8	89.6	111.7	135.3	164.5	167.6	183.6
Korea	10.1	14.5	5.4	-2.0	-8.3	-3.9	1.0	-3.9	-8.5	-23.0	-8.2	40.4	24.5	12.2	8.0	5.4	12.3	24.2	19.7	20.3
Luxembourg	..	..	..	..	..	..	..	..	2.5	2.3	1.9	1.8	1.8	2.7	1.8	2.5	2.3	2.8	3.7	4.1
Mexico	4.3	-2.3	-5.7	-7.6	-14.5	-24.4	-23.4	-29.6	-1.4	-2.6	-7.5	-16.1	-13.9	-17.8	-18.3	-14.0	-9.0	-8.9	-10.9	-14.5
Netherlands	4.2	7.0	9.4	8.1	7.4	6.9	13.2	17.3	25.8	21.5	25.1	13.0	15.7	7.3	7.5	10.5	15.1	24.2	25.5	28.0
New Zealand	-1.7	-0.4	-1.6	-1.4	-1.1	-1.6	-1.7	-2.0	-3.1	-3.9	-4.4	-2.1	-3.5	-2.5	-1.3	-1.9	-3.3	-4.9	-5.6	-5.5
Norway	-4.4	-4.0	-0.2	3.1	4.2	4.2	3.4	3.8	5.3	11.0	10.1	0.0	8.3	24.8	26.3	24.8	28.5	36.0	48.0	50.8
Poland[c]	..	..	..	..	..	..	-4.6	0.9	0.8	-3.3	-5.8	-6.9	-12.5	-10.0	-5.4	-5.0	-4.1	-3.7	-6.0	-6.9
Portugal[b]	0.4	-1.0	0.2	-0.2	-0.7	-0.3	0.3	-2.3	-0.2	-4.2	-6.1	-7.8	-9.7	-11.6	-10.4	-8.1	-7.5	-10.4	-11.4	-12.0
Slovak Republic	..	..	..	..	..	..	-0.6	0.7	0.5	-2.0	-1.8	-2.0	-1.0	-0.7	-1.7	-1.9	-0.3	-1.0	-1.4	-0.9
Spain	-0.2	-3.7	-10.9	-18.1	-19.9	-21.6	-5.7	-6.4	0.8	0.4	2.5	-3.0	-13.8	-19.4	-16.4	-15.9	-23.6	-41.3	-50.9	-55.7
Sweden	-0.0	-0.6	-3.1	-6.3	-4.7	-7.4	-2.7	2.5	8.5	9.7	10.3	9.7	10.7	9.9	9.7	12.8	19.4	25.6	24.2	26.1
Switzerland	7.6	9.1	7.1	8.8	10.7	15.3	19.2	17.3	21.3	22.0	25.5	25.9	30.3	31.7	20.0	23.6	42.6	46.0	48.4	50.9
Turkey	-0.8	1.6	0.9	-2.6	0.3	-1.0	-6.4	2.6	-2.3	-2.4	-2.6	2.0	-1.3	-9.8	3.4	-1.5	-6.9	-15.3	-14.3	-12.9
United Kingdom	-12.7	-35.4	-43.1	-39.1	-19.0	-22.9	-17.9	-10.3	-14.3	-10.9	-1.6	-6.6	-39.6	-36.2	-32.2	-27.1	-33.4	-46.5	-54.3	-51.4
United States	-160.7	-121.2	-99.5	-79.0	3.7	-48.0	-82.0	-118.0	-109.5	-120.2	-136.0	-209.6	-296.8	-413.5	-385.7	-473.9	-530.7	-669.0	-761.3	-825.5
Euro area	41.5	41.4	33.2	3.5	-66.5	-57.2	21.3	11.2	49.3	75.7	95.4	66.0	25.5	-30.7	6.9	47.6	32.1	67.4	61.5	96.1
Total OECD	-57.2	-46.7	-81.8	-111.4	-58.5	-67.5	7.8	-24.7	36.3	1.0	45.5	-12.5	-178.3	-324.9	-274.7	-307.1	-338.0	-395.1	-483.0	-481.7

Note: The balance-of-payments data in this table are based on the concepts and definition of the International Monetary Fund, *Fifth Balance of Payments Manual*.

a) Including Luxembourg until 1994.

b) Breaks between 1998 and 1999 for Greece and between 1995 and 1996 for Portugal, reflecting change in methodology to the International Monetary Fund, *Fifth Balance of Payments Manual* (capital transfers from European Union are excluded from the current account).

c) Data in 1993 are OECD estimates.

Source: OECD Economic Outlook 76 database.

Annex Table 51. **Current account balances as a percentage of GDP**

	1987	1988	1989	1990	1991	1992	1993	1994	1995	1996	1997	1998	1999	2000	2001	2002	2003	2004	2005	2006
Australia	-3.9	-4.4	-6.1	-5.2	-3.5	-3.7	-3.3	-5.1	-5.4	-3.9	-3.1	-5.0	-5.7	-4.0	-2.3	-4.1	-5.9	-5.5	-4.9	-4.6
Austria	-0.2	-0.2	0.2	0.7	0.0	-0.3	-0.7	-1.6	-2.6	-2.2	-3.1	-2.4	-3.0	-2.5	-1.9	0.4	-0.4	-0.1	0.0	0.1
Belgium[a]	2.8	3.3	3.2	3.1	3.6	4.4	6.0	6.0	5.6	5.1	5.6	5.3	5.1	3.9	3.9	5.7	4.2	3.7	3.1	4.0
Canada	-3.2	-3.0	-3.9	-3.4	-3.7	-3.6	-3.9	-2.3	-0.8	0.5	-1.3	-1.2	0.3	2.7	2.3	2.0	2.0	3.4	3.9	4.3
Czech Republic	..	..	..	..	..	..	1.2	-1.8	-2.5	-6.7	-6.3	-2.1	-2.5	-4.9	-5.4	-5.6	-6.2	-6.5	-6.6	-6.5
Denmark	-2.8	-1.4	-1.6	0.4	0.9	2.1	2.8	1.5	0.7	1.5	0.4	-0.9	1.8	1.5	3.0	2.0	2.7	3.1	3.1	3.4
Finland	-1.9	-2.6	-4.9	-5.0	-5.5	-4.8	-1.4	1.1	4.2	3.9	5.4	5.7	5.6	7.4	7.2	7.6	4.1	4.9	4.9	5.0
France	-0.5	-0.5	-0.5	-0.8	-0.4	0.4	0.8	0.5	0.7	1.3	2.7	2.7	2.9	1.4	1.7	1.0	0.4	0.2	0.2	0.6
Germany	3.9	4.1	4.6	2.9	-1.2	-1.0	-0.7	-1.4	-1.1	-0.6	-0.4	-0.6	-1.1	-1.4	0.1	2.1	2.3	3.3	3.9	4.7
Greece[b]	-3.3	-2.5	-5.1	-5.7	-3.0	-3.7	-2.3	-1.5	-4.0	-5.3	-4.4	-3.1	-6.2	-8.7	-9.7	-7.6	-6.5	-6.0	-5.8	-5.6
Hungary	..	..	..	..	..	..	-5.0	-4.6	0.4	0.5	-4.4	-7.2	-7.8	-8.7	-6.3	-7.1	-8.9	-9.1	-8.5	-8.2
Iceland	-3.3	-3.7	-1.9	-2.1	-4.1	-2.4	0.7	2.0	0.8	-1.8	-1.7	-6.9	-7.0	-10.1	-4.0	1.1	-4.1	-8.5	-11.0	-11.6
Ireland	-0.2	-0.0	-1.5	-0.8	0.7	1.0	3.7	2.7	2.6	2.8	2.4	0.8	0.3	-0.4	-0.7	-1.3	-1.4	-0.6	-0.1	0.1
Italy	-0.3	-0.9	-1.4	-1.5	-2.0	-2.3	0.8	1.2	2.3	3.2	2.8	1.9	0.7	-0.6	-0.1	-0.8	-1.4	-0.5	-1.6	-1.9
Japan	3.5	2.7	2.2	1.5	2.0	2.9	3.0	2.7	2.1	1.4	2.3	3.0	2.6	2.5	2.2	2.8	3.1	3.5	3.5	3.7
Korea	7.1	7.6	2.3	-0.8	-2.7	-1.2	0.3	-0.9	-1.6	-4.2	-1.3	11.8	5.5	2.4	1.7	1.0	2.0	3.7	2.7	2.7
Luxembourg	..	..	..	..	..	..	..	..	13.9	12.7	11.0	9.4	8.9	13.7	9.0	11.8	8.2	8.8	10.6	11.1
Mexico	2.8	-1.3	-2.6	-2.9	-4.6	-6.7	-5.8	-7.0	-0.5	-0.8	-1.9	-3.8	-2.9	-3.1	-2.9	-2.2	-1.4	-1.4	-1.5	-1.9
Netherlands	1.8	2.9	3.9	2.7	2.4	2.1	4.1	5.0	6.2	5.2	6.6	3.3	3.9	2.0	1.9	2.5	2.9	4.2	4.2	4.4
New Zealand	-4.8	-0.9	-3.7	-3.1	-2.7	-4.1	-3.8	-3.9	-5.1	-5.9	-6.5	-4.0	-6.2	-4.8	-2.4	-3.1	-4.2	-5.1	-5.3	-5.0
Norway	-4.8	-4.1	-0.1	2.5	3.6	3.3	2.9	3.0	3.6	6.9	6.4	0.0	5.3	14.9	15.5	12.9	12.9	14.2	16.3	16.4
Poland[c]	..	..	..	..	..	..	-4.9	0.9	0.6	-2.2	-3.8	-4.1	-7.6	-6.0	-2.9	-2.6	-2.0	-1.5	-2.1	-2.2
Portugal[b]	1.0	-2.0	0.3	-0.3	-0.8	-0.2	0.4	-2.4	-0.1	-3.8	-5.7	-6.9	-8.5	-10.9	-9.5	-6.7	-5.1	-6.3	-6.3	-6.3
Slovak Republic	..	..	..	..	..	..	-4.3	4.7	2.7	-9.4	-8.6	-9.0	-4.8	-3.4	-8.2	-7.9	-0.9	-2.6	-3.0	-1.9
Spain	-0.0	-1.0	-2.8	-3.5	-3.6	-3.6	-1.1	-1.3	0.1	0.1	0.5	-0.5	-2.3	-3.4	-2.8	-2.4	-2.8	-4.2	-4.7	-4.8
Sweden	-0.0	-0.3	-1.5	-2.6	-1.9	-2.8	-1.3	1.1	3.4	3.6	4.2	3.9	4.3	4.1	4.4	5.3	6.4	7.4	6.4	6.5
Switzerland	4.3	4.7	3.8	3.7	4.5	6.1	7.9	6.4	6.7	7.3	9.7	9.7	11.5	12.9	8.0	8.4	13.2	12.8	12.4	12.6
Turkey	-0.9	2.1	0.9	-1.7	0.2	-0.6	-3.5	2.7	-1.6	-1.3	-1.3	1.2	-1.0	-4.9	2.5	-0.8	-2.9	-5.2	-4.5	-3.8
United Kingdom	-1.8	-4.2	-5.1	-4.0	-1.8	-2.1	-1.9	-1.0	-1.3	-0.9	-0.1	-0.5	-2.7	-2.5	-2.3	-1.7	-1.9	-2.2	-2.4	-2.2
United States	-3.4	-2.4	-1.8	-1.4	0.1	-0.8	-1.2	-1.7	-1.5	-1.5	-1.6	-2.4	-3.2	-4.2	-3.8	-4.5	-4.8	-5.7	-6.2	-6.4
Euro area	1.1	1.0	0.8	0.1	-1.1	-0.9	0.4	0.2	0.7	1.1	1.5	1.0	0.4	-0.5	0.1	0.7	0.4	0.7	0.6	0.9
Total OECD	-0.4	-0.3	-0.5	-0.6	-0.3	-0.3	0.0	-0.1	0.2	0.0	0.2	-0.1	-0.7	-1.3	-1.1	-1.2	-1.1	-1.2	-1.4	-1.3

a) Including Luxembourg until 1994.
b) Breaks between 1998 and 1999 for Greece and between 1995 and 1996 for Portugal, reflecting change in methodology to the International Monetary Fund, *Fifth Balance of Payments Manual* (capital transfers from European Union are excluded from the current account).
c) Data in 1993 are OECD estimates.
Source: OECD Economic Outlook 76 database.

Annex Table 52. **Structure of current account balances of major world regions**

$ billion

	1990	1991	1992	1993	1994	1995	1996	1997	1998	1999	2000	2001	2002	2003	2004	2005	2006
Goods and services trade balance[a]																	
OECD	-3	-1	33	107	106	161	121	149	105	-48	-207	-177	-163	-210	-268	-336	-321
Non-OECD *of which:*	16	-27	-34	-57	-18	-57	-17	-11	-10	105	219	152	200	274	332	393	345
Non-OECD Asia *of which:*	7	10	3	-14	-5	-24	-10	23	83	91	81	84	115	125	86	104	125
China	11	12	5	-11	8	12	18	43	44	31	29	28	37	36	14	34	47
Dynamic Asia[b]	10	9	9	9	3	-12	0	4	62	80	72	71	91	106	93	87	87
Other Asia	-13	-10	-12	-12	-16	-24	-28	-24	-23	-19	-20	-15	-13	-18	-21	-18	-9
Latin America	27	14	3	-6	-7	-19	-17	-32	-46	-16	-3	-9	21	38	43	39	35
Africa & Middle-East	2	-50	-37	-34	-11	-14	8	5	-43	6	92	48	38	77	155	188	134
Central & East Europe[c]	-20	-1	-4	-3	6	1	2	-7	-4	24	48	29	26	34	49	62	52
World[d]	12	-28	-1	50	88	105	104	138	95	57	12	-25	37	64	64	57	24
Investment income, net																	
OECD	-10	-17	-13	-7	-26	-20	-10	6	-2	-5	14	13	-7	28	38	28	23
Non-OECD *of which:*	-38	-33	-39	-46	-44	-59	-69	-72	-81	-82	-90	-85	-89	-94	-103	-117	-119
Non-OECD Asia *of which:*	-8	-9	-10	-12	-9	-20	-24	-20	-27	-26	-29	-25	-25	-14	-13	-15	-14
China	1	1	0	-1	-1	-12	-12	-11	-17	-14	-15	-19	-15	-8	-11	-16	-17
Dynamic Asia[b]	-3	-4	-4	-4	-3	-2	-6	-2	-4	-5	-6	0	-2	4	9	12	16
Other Asia	-5	-6	-6	-6	-6	-6	-6	-7	-7	-7	-7	-6	-8	-10	-11	-12	-12
Latin America	-26	-23	-21	-23	-24	-28	-29	-35	-37	-39	-38	-41	-38	-44	-49	-60	-65
Africa & Middle-East	0	2	-2	-5	-8	-6	-8	-6	-3	-7	-12	-10	-14	-17	-18	-17	-14
Central & East Europe[c]	-5	-3	-6	-5	-2	-5	-7	-11	-14	-10	-11	-8	-11	-20	-24	-24	-27
World[d]	-49	-50	-51	-53	-69	-79	-79	-66	-83	-87	-76	-72	-95	-65	-65	-89	-96
Total transfers, net																	
OECD	-64	-45	-89	-88	-99	-95	-98	-86	-99	-102	-108	-94	-111	-139	-155	-158	-162
Non-OECD *of which:*	12	-1	33	29	27	28	35	42	35	41	44	49	61	69	79	85	90
Non-OECD Asia *of which:*	9	11	14	13	16	14	19	26	19	23	26	27	37	44	49	49	50
China	0	1	1	1	0	1	2	5	4	5	6	8	13	18	15	15	16
Dynamic Asia[b]	0	1	2	1	1	-2	-2	-2	-4	-4	-4	-5	-5	-5	1	1	1
Other Asia	8	9	10	11	15	15	19	23	19	22	24	24	29	32	33	33	33
Latin America	5	7	8	7	9	11	10	10	11	13	13	15	17	19	23	27	30
Africa & Middle-East	-5	-26	6	3	-1	-1	1	2	1	-0	-1	0	-1	-3	-4	-4	-4
Central & East Europe[c]	3	7	5	5	3	4	4	4	4	5	6	6	7	9	11	13	14
World[d]	-51	-46	-56	-59	-73	-67	-63	-44	-64	-61	-63	-45	-50	-70	-76	-73	-73
Current account balance																	
OECD	-111	-58	-68	8	-25	36	1	46	-13	-178	-325	-275	-307	-338	-395	-483	-482
Non-OECD *of which:*	-10	-61	-40	-73	-36	-87	-51	-41	-56	64	173	116	172	250	308	361	316
Non-OECD Asia *of which:*	8	12	7	-13	1	-30	-16	29	74	88	78	86	127	155	122	137	161
China	12	13	6	-12	7	2	7	37	31	21	21	17	35	46	18	34	46
Dynamic Asia[b]	7	6	8	6	1	-16	-8	0	54	71	61	66	83	105	103	100	104
Other Asia	-11	-7	-7	-7	-7	-15	-15	-8	-11	-4	-3	3	8	4	1	4	12
Latin America	6	-3	-10	-22	-22	-36	-36	-57	-72	-41	-28	-35	0	14	17	6	-0
Africa & Middle-East	-3	-73	-32	-36	-21	-21	1	1	-44	-1	79	38	23	57	132	167	116
Central & East Europe[c]	-21	3	-4	-3	6	-0	-0	-13	-14	18	43	27	23	24	36	50	39
World[d]	-122	-119	-107	-66	-60	-51	-50	5	-69	-114	-152	-159	-135	-88	-87	-122	-166

Note: Historical data for the OECD area are aggregates of reported balance-of-payments data of each individual country. Because of various statistical problems as well as a large number of non-reporters among non-OECD countries, trade and current account balances estimated on the basis of these countries' own balance-of-payments records may differ from corresponding estimates shown in this table.

a) National accounts basis for OECD countries and balance-of-payments basis for the non-OECD regions.

b) Dynamic Asia includes Chinese Taipei; Hong Kong, China; Indonesia; Malaysia; Philippines; Singapore and Thailand.

c) Data prior to 1995 are OECD estimates.

d) Reflects statistical errors and asymmetries. Given the very large gross flows of world balance-of-payments transactions, statistical errors and asymmetries easily give rise to world totals (balances) that are significantly different from zero.

Source: OECD Economic Outlook 76 database.

Annex Table 53. **Export market growth in goods and services**

Percentage changes from previous year

	1987	1988	1989	1990	1991	1992	1993	1994	1995	1996	1997	1998	1999	2000	2001	2002	2003	2004	2005	2006
Australia	8.9	10.7	10.4	6.7	4.5	5.2	5.2	10.3	11.6	9.7	7.1	-2.8	7.9	12.8	-0.7	5.7	6.6	11.0	9.6	10.5
Austria	5.1	6.3	7.4	5.4	2.2	-1.9	-0.8	7.6	7.5	5.3	9.6	7.3	6.2	12.2	2.3	1.8	5.0	8.7	8.1	8.9
Belgium	6.1	7.5	7.8	5.5	3.9	2.1	-0.6	7.9	7.9	5.4	9.5	8.2	7.0	11.9	1.7	2.2	3.1	7.6	7.8	8.4
Canada	6.0	5.1	5.2	3.9	0.3	6.2	7.7	11.4	8.3	8.7	12.7	9.8	10.5	13.0	-2.1	3.4	4.6	10.1	8.0	7.8
Czech Republic	..	..	..	..	..	..	..	6.8	8.0	6.9	10.0	8.1	4.6	12.2	2.7	2.0	6.0	8.9	8.5	9.4
Denmark	5.6	6.4	7.4	4.3	1.5	1.4	0.3	8.8	7.8	6.2	10.3	8.1	6.2	11.3	0.6	1.5	3.9	7.6	7.7	7.9
Finland	4.8	7.2	7.2	2.3	-0.4	-4.4	1.8	8.1	8.3	6.5	9.7	5.3	5.1	12.5	2.0	3.4	5.8	9.5	9.3	9.5
France	6.3	7.6	7.8	5.4	4.0	2.7	0.1	7.5	7.8	6.1	9.7	7.0	7.0	10.7	1.6	2.3	3.9	7.6	8.3	9.0
Germany	6.2	7.8	7.6	4.3	0.6	1.5	1.4	8.4	8.6	6.6	9.9	7.0	6.1	12.1	1.6	3.1	4.3	8.7	8.8	8.9
Greece	5.0	6.4	6.7	3.2	0.6	-2.2	2.0	7.4	7.5	6.3	10.1	6.8	6.5	11.8	1.3	3.1	4.9	9.0	8.7	9.0
Hungary	..	..	..	..	..	..	..	7.8	7.6	5.1	8.9	6.9	5.7	12.0	2.6	1.6	4.8	8.3	7.9	8.7
Iceland	6.6	9.1	8.5	4.9	1.7	2.2	0.2	8.4	8.0	7.1	8.9	6.6	6.8	10.5	1.3	2.3	3.2	7.5	7.2	7.5
Ireland	6.9	8.4	7.9	5.0	2.4	3.6	1.0	8.3	7.9	6.6	9.5	6.8	7.4	11.3	1.0	2.7	3.3	7.5	7.7	8.1
Italy	5.5	7.6	7.6	4.4	3.1	-0.4	1.2	7.6	8.0	6.4	9.7	6.7	6.5	12.3	1.6	2.7	4.7	8.8	8.6	9.2
Japan	8.6	9.8	7.8	6.8	7.2	7.8	8.0	12.0	11.1	8.7	10.5	-0.2	9.0	14.8	-1.9	5.1	6.4	11.3	9.8	10.5
Korea	7.3	10.7	8.7	5.6	5.2	5.8	6.9	10.1	10.8	9.8	9.3	0.0	7.3	13.9	-0.6	5.1	7.4	11.5	10.0	10.8
Luxembourg	6.3	7.7	7.9	5.3	3.3	2.2	-0.7	8.3	7.5	4.8	9.1	8.6	6.5	11.4	1.5	1.5	2.7	7.0	7.2	7.8
Mexico	6.0	4.7	4.5	3.9	0.5	7.0	8.3	11.6	8.4	8.3	13.4	10.8	10.3	12.7	-2.4	2.8	4.4	10.1	7.9	7.5
Netherlands	6.4	8.0	8.2	6.0	4.1	2.0	-0.9	7.8	7.2	5.1	9.0	7.5	6.6	11.3	1.4	1.7	3.4	7.1	7.4	8.2
New Zealand	6.9	12.0	11.6	3.8	2.6	5.5	4.7	11.1	10.0	9.2	8.8	1.5	8.1	11.8	-1.4	6.0	6.6	10.9	8.8	9.6
Norway	6.3	8.5	7.5	3.6	1.1	2.9	1.0	8.8	7.7	6.2	10.1	8.2	7.0	11.5	1.1	2.3	2.9	7.1	7.6	7.7
Poland	..	..	..	..	..	..	..	7.3	7.7	5.1	8.6	5.6	4.6	12.6	4.0	2.7	5.7	9.5	8.9	9.5
Portugal	7.7	8.4	8.8	5.9	5.0	3.6	-1.5	8.2	7.7	5.5	10.1	9.3	7.7	10.8	2.1	2.0	3.1	7.0	7.6	8.1
Slovak Republic	..	..	..	..	..	..	..	8.0	9.5	6.6	9.1	7.3	5.0	13.3	4.7	2.6	6.0	10.6	9.3	9.4
Spain	7.0	7.9	7.2	6.3	3.9	3.6	-0.8	7.6	7.6	5.0	9.9	8.6	6.0	10.9	1.4	1.4	2.5	7.6	7.7	8.2
Sweden	4.0	7.0	7.1	4.2	2.0	1.5	1.5	8.3	8.0	6.8	10.2	6.7	5.7	11.4	1.3	3.1	3.9	8.1	7.8	8.3
Switzerland	6.5	7.8	8.1	6.4	4.7	2.7	0.1	8.3	8.3	6.0	9.5	6.0	6.9	11.8	0.7	2.2	4.1	8.4	8.2	8.8
Turkey	3.5	6.5	6.9	2.1	1.5	-5.6	0.5	6.5	6.9	5.7	8.5	4.5	5.8	11.7	3.4	3.8	5.3	8.8	9.8	10.5
United Kingdom	5.5	6.9	7.8	5.1	3.9	2.4	1.3	8.7	8.5	6.2	10.0	7.3	7.2	12.2	0.8	2.7	3.8	8.3	8.4	8.9
United States	6.9	12.5	8.6	6.1	6.0	6.1	4.6	10.4	7.4	8.6	11.2	3.1	6.4	12.4	-0.7	2.2	4.0	9.8	9.4	9.2
Total OECD	6.4	8.5	7.7	5.3	3.7	3.6	5.2	9.3	8.4	7.2	10.3	5.4	7.1	12.3	0.3	2.9	4.4	9.1	8.7	9.0
Memorandum items																				
China	9.4	11.2	9.7	7.2	5.1	4.0	5.2	10.5	11.2	8.6	8.2	-2.2	6.6	13.6	-1.6	4.1	5.1	10.3	9.4	9.9
Dynamic Asia[a]	8.5	11.9	9.4	6.4	6.1	7.2	7.5	11.4	11.8	10.1	9.0	-1.5	8.5	14.8	-1.0	6.1	7.9	11.9	10.0	11.0
Other Asia	6.1	8.7	8.3	4.8	3.9	4.0	4.1	9.2	9.4	8.4	9.0	2.5	7.8	12.5	-0.1	4.7	5.7	9.9	9.3	10.0
Latin America	5.9	7.1	5.1	4.6	4.6	6.5	6.6	10.5	9.7	7.4	12.5	7.2	4.9	11.2	-0.2	0.5	4.3	10.5	8.9	8.8
Africa & Middle-East	6.9	8.8	8.9	6.0	5.1	4.1	2.4	8.8	10.3	8.3	8.2	1.1	8.1	12.4	0.1	4.8	5.6	9.7	9.6	10.5
Central & East Europe	3.6	6.9	6.9	-0.0	-4.9	-14.5	3.2	6.1	8.9	7.0	8.8	2.3	2.7	14.6	4.5	5.7	8.9	11.8	11.2	11.3

Note: Regional aggregates are calculated *inclusive* of intra-regional trade. The calculation of export markets is based on a weighted average of import volumes in each exporting country's market, with weights based on goods and services trade flows in 2000.

a) Dynamic Asia includes Chinese Taipei; Hong Kong, China; Indonesia; Malaysia; Philippines; Singapore and Thailand.

Source: OECD Economic Outlook 76 database.

Annex Table 54. **Import penetration**

Goods and services import volume as a percentage of total final expenditure, constant prices

	1987	1988	1989	1990	1991	1992	1993	1994	1995	1996	1997	1998	1999	2000	2001	2002	2003	2004	2005	2006
Australia	10.6	11.8	13.4	12.8	12.5	13.0	13.1	14.2	14.7	15.2	16.1	16.2	16.8	17.5	16.5	17.5	18.6	20.1	20.7	21.5
Austria	23.2	24.0	24.9	25.4	25.7	25.6	24.6	26.1	26.9	27.4	28.5	28.9	29.3	30.6	31.5	31.2	32.2	33.3	34.6	35.8
Belgium	36.3	37.7	39.1	39.5	39.7	40.2	40.5	41.4	42.0	42.3	42.6	43.8	44.1	45.2	45.3	45.3	45.5	45.6	46.5	47.7
Canada	19.5	20.7	21.3	21.6	22.4	23.0	23.8	24.4	24.9	25.5	27.3	27.5	27.9	28.4	27.0	26.7	27.0	28.0	29.2	29.9
Czech Republic	..	..	..	..	..	..	31.5	32.4	35.4	37.4	39.1	41.4	42.3	45.2	47.7	48.7	50.0	53.4	55.3	56.7
Denmark	20.5	21.6	22.2	22.3	22.6	22.4	22.0	23.1	23.9	24.1	25.3	26.4	27.0	29.0	29.3	30.6	30.4	31.2	32.1	33.0
Finland	18.4	19.0	19.5	19.7	18.7	19.4	20.1	21.3	21.5	22.2	22.9	23.2	23.4	25.2	25.1	24.9	25.1	24.4	24.6	25.1
France	14.5	15.0	15.5	15.9	16.1	16.1	15.8	16.6	17.4	17.5	18.2	19.4	19.8	21.5	21.4	21.7	21.7	22.6	23.6	24.5
Germany	17.7	17.9	18.6	19.3	18.8	18.6	17.9	18.7	19.2	19.6	20.7	21.8	22.8	24.2	24.2	23.9	24.6	25.6	26.2	27.2
Greece	15.8	16.2	17.1	18.2	18.6	18.7	19.0	18.9	20.0	20.7	22.3	23.3	25.3	27.1	25.3	24.1	24.1	24.4	24.4	25.2
Hungary	..	..	..	..	..	..	29.3	30.5	30.0	31.0	34.9	38.5	40.3	43.8	44.1	44.7	46.4	48.9	50.8	52.5
Iceland	27.9	27.0	24.8	24.8	25.8	25.3	23.6	23.6	24.2	26.2	26.8	30.0	30.0	30.5	28.1	27.7	28.7	29.9	31.1	31.8
Ireland	32.7	33.0	34.6	33.9	34.0	35.1	36.1	38.1	39.3	40.2	41.4	45.1	45.2	47.7	47.8	47.2	45.7	45.9	46.7	47.2
Italy	15.2	15.4	16.2	17.4	17.5	18.5	16.9	17.7	18.7	18.5	19.6	20.7	21.4	22.0	21.8	21.7	21.5	22.0	23.0	23.8
Japan	5.3	5.8	6.4	6.6	6.3	6.2	6.1	6.5	7.2	7.8	7.7	7.3	7.5	8.0	7.9	8.1	8.3	8.7	9.1	9.5
Korea	16.6	17.2	18.6	18.6	20.2	20.4	20.2	22.6	24.7	25.9	25.8	22.6	25.3	27.3	25.8	27.3	28.6	30.2	32.0	33.9
Luxembourg	49.5	50.0	49.9	49.8	49.9	48.6	48.7	49.3	49.8	50.9	52.0	53.9	55.4	56.7	57.2	56.0	55.7	56.4	57.1	57.9
Mexico	8.0	10.4	11.7	13.1	14.3	16.1	16.1	18.2	16.8	19.1	21.3	23.1	24.9	27.4	27.1	27.2	26.8	27.9	28.9	29.8
Netherlands	29.3	30.1	30.7	30.6	31.2	31.2	31.1	32.4	34.0	34.3	35.5	36.4	36.8	38.3	38.5	38.6	39.0	39.9	41.0	42.3
New Zealand	17.8	17.3	19.0	19.5	19.0	20.1	20.2	21.2	22.0	22.7	22.6	22.8	23.9	23.3	23.2	23.8	24.8	26.6	27.2	28.1
Norway	21.3	20.9	21.0	20.9	20.4	20.2	20.5	20.5	20.7	21.2	22.3	23.3	22.6	22.5	22.3	22.4	22.7	23.3	23.4	23.5
Poland	..	..	..	..	..	..	14.2	15.0	17.0	19.9	21.9	24.1	23.6	25.6	24.4	24.6	25.5	26.4	27.6	29.0
Portugal	19.7	21.2	21.1	22.8	23.3	25.0	24.7	26.1	26.7	27.0	28.1	29.9	30.8	31.3	31.2	31.0	31.1	32.2	32.9	33.7
Slovak Republic	..	..	..	..	..	..	37.1	34.6	35.8	38.6	40.7	43.4	41.4	43.3	45.0	45.2	47.4	49.5	51.3	52.9
Spain	11.9	13.0	14.4	15.1	16.0	16.8	16.2	17.4	18.6	19.4	20.7	22.1	23.5	24.5	24.7	24.9	25.3	26.1	27.2	28.1
Sweden	21.1	21.4	22.2	22.2	21.4	21.9	21.8	23.2	23.7	24.2	25.9	27.3	27.4	28.7	27.9	27.2	27.8	28.5	29.6	30.4
Switzerland	23.4	23.7	24.0	23.3	23.1	22.4	22.4	23.6	24.3	24.8	25.9	26.8	27.4	28.6	29.0	28.3	28.7	29.3	30.1	30.9
Turkey	15.1	14.3	15.1	17.8	16.8	17.6	21.1	18.0	21.0	23.0	25.4	25.2	25.4	28.5	24.5	25.8	29.5	32.5	33.8	34.9
United Kingdom	15.4	16.4	17.0	17.0	16.5	17.4	17.6	17.8	18.2	19.2	20.1	21.1	21.9	22.7	23.2	23.6	23.4	23.6	24.3	25.0
United States	7.7	7.7	7.7	7.9	7.9	8.1	8.5	9.1	9.6	10.0	10.8	11.4	12.1	13.1	12.7	12.8	13.0	13.6	14.1	14.5
Total OECD	11.8	12.2	12.7	13.0	13.1	13.3	13.4	14.1	14.7	15.3	16.1	16.7	17.5	18.6	18.4	18.5	18.8	19.5	20.2	20.9

Note: Regional aggregate is calculated *inclusive* of intra-regional trade as the sum of import volumes expressed in 2000 $ divided by the sum of total final expenditure expressed in 2000 $.
Source: OECD Economic Outlook 76 database.

Annex Table 55. **Quarterly demand and output projections**

Percentage changes from previous period, seasonally adjusted at annual rates, volume

	2004	2005	2006	2005 Q2	Q3	Q4	2006 Q1	Q2	Q3	Q4	Fourth quarter[a] 2004	2005	2006
Private consumption													
Canada	3.3	3.2	2.9	3.3	3.2	3.1	2.8	2.7	2.7	2.7	3.6	3.2	2.7
France	2.3	2.2	2.2	2.0	2.2	2.2	2.2	2.3	2.4	2.4	2.5	2.1	2.3
Germany	-0.7	0.8	1.9	1.1	1.4	1.7	2.0	2.1	2.3	2.3	0.0	1.3	2.2
Italy	1.3	1.5	2.6	1.6	2.2	2.4	2.8	2.8	2.6	2.6	1.5	2.0	2.7
Japan	3.4	2.2	1.7	2.0	2.0	2.0	1.6	1.6	1.6	1.6	3.3	1.9	1.6
United Kingdom	3.0	1.8	1.7	1.8	1.8	1.8	1.6	1.6	1.6	1.6	2.6	1.8	1.6
United States	3.6	3.1	3.1	2.9	3.0	3.1	3.2	3.2	3.2	3.2	3.3	2.9	3.2
Euro area	1.2	1.6	2.4	1.8	2.1	2.2	2.5	2.5	2.6	2.6	1.5	1.9	2.5
Total OECD	2.9	2.5	2.7	2.7	2.8	2.8	2.7	2.7	2.7	2.8	2.8	2.7	2.7
Public consumption													
Canada	2.8	3.1	3.1	3.2	3.2	3.2	3.2	2.8	2.8	2.8	2.7	3.2	2.9
France	2.3	1.7	1.7	2.4	2.0	1.6	1.6	1.6	1.6	1.6	1.4	2.1	1.6
Germany	0.1	0.0	0.1	0.0	0.0	0.0	0.2	0.2	0.3	0.3	-0.1	0.2	0.2
Italy	0.7	0.6	0.3	1.2	0.7	0.2	-0.1	0.1	0.5	1.0	-0.4	0.9	0.4
Japan	1.9	2.1	2.0	2.0	2.0	2.0	2.0	2.0	2.0	2.0	2.2	2.0	2.0
United Kingdom	3.8	1.9	2.0	3.0	3.0	3.0	2.8	0.4	0.4	0.4	1.6	2.7	1.0
United States	1.8	1.6	1.2	1.5	1.3	1.1	1.2	1.2	1.2	1.2	1.8	1.4	1.2
Euro area	1.4	1.1	1.1	1.3	1.2	1.1	1.0	1.1	1.1	1.2	0.9	1.3	1.1
Total OECD	1.9	1.7	1.5	1.0	1.3	1.2	1.8	1.6	1.6	1.5	2.0	1.2	1.6
Business investment													
Canada	5.4	7.1	6.8	7.8	7.4	7.4	6.6	6.6	6.1	6.1	5.4	7.6	6.3
France	3.9	3.3	3.9	2.8	3.5	3.8	4.1	4.0	4.1	4.1	4.4	3.2	4.0
Germany	-1.0	1.8	5.6	1.7	4.5	5.2	5.8	6.8	6.7	6.8	-1.2	3.2	6.5
Italy	4.4	5.9	4.9	6.4	6.5	5.8	5.0	4.2	3.2	3.3	7.3	6.3	3.9
Japan	9.0	3.4	4.0	4.0	4.5	4.5	4.0	3.8	3.6	3.6	3.4	4.2	3.7
United Kingdom	6.0	3.8	3.3	3.6	3.2	3.2	3.2	3.2	3.2	3.2	5.4	3.3	3.2
United States	10.2	9.9	9.8	9.2	10.0	10.0	10.1	9.7	9.3	9.4	9.9	9.2	9.6
Euro area	2.4	3.7	4.9	4.0	5.0	4.9	5.1	5.0	4.7	4.8	2.3	4.4	4.9
Total OECD	6.9	6.4	6.7	6.4	6.9	6.9	6.8	6.6	6.3	6.3	6.1	6.5	6.5
Total investment													
Canada	6.2	5.3	4.5	5.4	5.0	4.9	4.3	4.3	4.1	4.1	5.4	5.2	4.2
France	3.5	3.1	3.3	2.8	3.2	3.3	3.5	3.5	3.3	3.3	3.9	3.0	3.4
Germany	-2.0	0.6	3.4	0.7	2.5	3.0	3.5	4.2	4.2	4.3	-2.9	1.7	4.0
Italy	3.8	4.9	4.2	5.1	5.2	4.8	4.3	3.7	3.0	3.0	6.2	5.1	3.5
Japan	2.8	1.2	2.2	2.3	2.6	2.5	2.2	1.9	1.8	1.9	-0.6	2.4	2.0
United Kingdom	6.5	5.3	3.5	5.9	5.1	4.0	2.8	2.8	2.7	2.7	6.2	5.1	2.8
United States	8.9	5.8	5.9	4.8	5.3	5.6	6.3	6.4	6.2	6.2	7.7	4.9	6.3
Euro area	1.9	2.9	3.8	3.2	3.9	3.9	4.0	3.8	3.6	3.7	1.7	3.6	3.8
Total OECD	6.0	4.5	4.7	4.6	4.8	4.8	4.7	4.6	4.5	4.6	4.8	4.7	4.6

Note: The adoption of new national account systems, SNA93 or ESA95, has been proceeding at an uneven pace among OECD member countries, both with respect to variables and the time period covered. As a consequence, there are breaks in many national series. Moreover, some countries are using chain-weighted price indices to calculate real GDP and expenditures components. See Table "National Account Reporting Systems and Base-years" at the beginning of the Statistical Annex and *OECD Economic Outlook* Sources and Methods *(http://www.oecd.org/eco/sources-and-methods).*

a) Year-on -year growth rates in per cent.

Source: OECD Economic Outlook 76 database.

Annex Table 55. **Quarterly demand and output projections** ***(cont'd)***

Percentage changes from previous period, seasonally adjusted at annual rates, volume

	2004	2005	2006	2005			2006				Fourth quarter[a]		
				Q2	Q3	Q4	Q1	Q2	Q3	Q4	2004	2005	2006
Total domestic demand													
Canada	3.0	3.9	3.2	3.7	3.5	3.4	3.1	3.0	2.9	2.9	3.1	3.7	3.0
France	3.2	2.5	2.3	2.2	2.3	2.3	2.3	2.3	2.4	2.4	3.4	2.3	2.4
Germany	0.3	0.9	1.8	0.7	1.3	1.6	1.9	2.1	2.2	2.2	0.3	1.0	2.1
Italy	1.2	2.1	2.5	2.5	2.6	2.5	2.6	2.5	2.3	2.4	1.6	2.5	2.5
Japan	3.2	1.9	1.9	2.2	2.2	2.1	1.8	1.8	1.7	1.7	2.3	2.1	1.8
United Kingdom	3.8	2.4	2.0	2.7	2.6	2.4	2.0	1.6	1.6	1.6	2.8	2.5	1.7
United States	4.7	3.4	3.5	3.1	3.3	3.4	3.6	3.6	3.6	3.6	4.3	3.2	3.6
Euro area	1.7	1.9	2.4	1.9	2.3	2.4	2.5	2.4	2.5	2.5	1.6	2.1	2.5
Total OECD	3.6	2.8	3.0	3.0	3.1	3.0	2.9	2.9	2.9	2.9	3.1	3.0	2.9
Export of goods and services													
Canada	7.7	6.8	5.6	5.7	5.5	5.5	5.7	5.7	5.7	5.7	10.0	5.6	5.7
France	3.4	6.0	7.5	6.9	7.3	7.4	7.6	7.6	7.6	7.8	3.9	6.9	7.7
Germany	8.1	5.7	8.1	6.8	7.9	8.0	8.1	8.3	8.3	8.3	7.8	7.4	8.2
Italy	4.5	6.1	5.4	3.6	6.4	5.3	5.2	5.3	5.5	5.7	7.8	4.5	5.4
Japan	14.4	7.4	8.0	8.0	8.0	8.0	8.0	8.0	8.0	8.0	10.4	8.0	8.0
United Kingdom	2.6	7.9	8.2	7.4	8.2	7.8	8.6	8.5	8.0	7.7	4.8	7.9	8.2
United States	8.9	9.2	10.0	10.0	10.0	10.0	10.0	10.0	10.0	10.0	7.4	10.0	10.0
Total OECD[b]	8.9	8.2	8.9	8.3	8.7	8.8	8.9	9.0	8.9	8.9	8.1	8.5	8.9
Import of goods and services													
Canada	8.4	9.1	6.3	8.2	7.0	6.1	6.1	5.9	5.9	5.7	9.3	7.7	5.9
France	7.7	7.7	7.5	7.3	7.5	7.4	7.6	7.5	7.5	7.5	8.6	7.4	7.5
Germany	6.4	4.9	7.5	5.0	6.0	7.0	8.0	8.3	8.3	8.4	6.0	5.7	8.2
Italy	4.3	7.5	6.7	6.1	8.2	6.9	6.8	6.6	6.1	5.9	7.4	6.9	6.3
Japan	9.9	7.1	6.9	7.0	7.0	7.0	7.0	7.0	6.5	6.5	9.8	6.7	6.7
United Kingdom	4.7	6.5	6.3	6.5	6.8	6.4	6.3	6.3	5.9	5.7	4.8	6.6	6.1
United States	10.1	7.7	7.3	7.0	7.0	7.0	7.5	7.5	7.5	7.5	9.8	7.0	7.5
Total OECD[b]	9.0	7.6	7.6	7.3	7.5	7.5	7.8	7.8	7.7	7.6	8.8	7.3	7.7
GDP													
Canada	3.0	3.3	3.1	3.0	3.2	3.3	3.2	3.1	3.0	3.1	3.6	3.1	3.1
France	2.1	2.0	2.3	2.1	2.2	2.2	2.2	2.3	2.4	2.4	2.1	2.1	2.3
Germany	1.2	1.4	2.3	1.6	2.3	2.3	2.3	2.4	2.6	2.6	1.2	1.9	2.5
Italy	1.3	1.7	2.1	1.7	2.0	2.1	2.1	2.1	2.1	2.3	1.7	1.8	2.2
Japan	4.0	2.1	2.3	2.5	2.5	2.5	2.2	2.1	2.1	2.2	2.6	2.4	2.1
United Kingdom	3.2	2.6	2.4	2.8	2.7	2.6	2.4	2.0	2.0	2.0	2.7	2.7	2.1
United States	4.4	3.3	3.6	3.2	3.4	3.5	3.6	3.7	3.6	3.6	3.8	3.3	3.6
Euro area	1.8	1.9	2.5	2.1	2.5	2.5	2.5	2.5	2.6	2.6	1.9	2.3	2.5
Total OECD	3.6	2.9	3.1	3.0	3.2	3.2	3.1	3.1	3.1	3.1	3.1	3.1	3.1

Note: The adoption of new national account systems, SNA93 or ESA95, has been proceeding at an uneven pace among OECD member countries, both with respect to variables and the time period covered. As a consequence, there are breaks in many national series. Moreover, some countries are using chain-weighted price indices to calculate real GDP and expenditures components. See Table "National Account Reporting Systems and Base-years" at the beginning of the Statistical Annex and *OECD Economic Outlook* Sources and Methods *(http://www.oecd.org/eco/sources-and-methods).*

a) Year-on -year growth rates in per cent.

b) Includes intra-regional trade.

Source: OECD Economic Outlook 76 database.

Annex Table 56. **Quarterly price, cost and unemployment projections**

Percentage changes from previous period, seasonally adjusted at annual rates, volume

	2004	2005	2006	2005 Q2	Q3	Q4	2006 Q1	Q2	Q3	Q4	Fourth quarter[a] 2004	2005	2006
Consumer price index[b]													
Canada	1.9	2.0	1.8	1.9	1.8	1.8	1.8	1.8	1.8	1.8	2.4	1.8	1.8
France	2.3	1.8	1.8	1.6	1.7	1.8	1.9	1.9	1.9	1.9	2.1	1.7	1.9
Germany	1.7	1.3	0.6	0.7	0.6	0.6	0.6	0.6	0.7	0.7	1.9	0.8	0.6
Italy	2.1	2.5	2.2	3.2	2.5	2.2	2.1	2.1	2.1	2.1	1.6	2.8	2.1
Japan	-0.1	0.1	0.6	0.3	0.5	0.5	0.6	0.6	0.7	0.8	0.0	0.3	0.7
United Kingdom	1.3	1.7	2.1	1.8	1.9	2.0	2.1	2.2	2.2	2.2	1.3	1.8	2.2
United States	2.6	2.4	2.1	2.1	2.1	2.1	2.1	2.1	2.1	2.1	3.2	2.1	2.1
Euro area	2.1	2.0	1.7	2.0	1.6	1.6	1.6	1.8	1.5	1.7	2.1	1.8	1.6
GDP deflator													
Canada	3.5	2.8	2.1	1.7	2.2	2.0	2.1	2.2	2.2	2.1	4.7	1.9	2.1
France	1.9	1.8	1.7	1.9	1.7	1.7	1.7	1.6	1.9	2.0	1.9	1.8	1.8
Germany	0.9	0.8	0.9	0.9	0.7	0.8	1.0	1.0	1.0	1.1	0.8	0.9	1.0
Italy	2.8	2.1	2.0	2.1	1.9	1.7	1.8	2.1	2.3	2.5	2.9	2.0	2.2
Japan	-2.3	-1.3	-0.3	-1.2	-1.0	-0.6	0.0	0.1	0.2	0.4	-1.6	-1.1	0.2
United Kingdom	2.1	2.2	2.3	2.3	2.4	2.4	2.4	2.3	2.2	2.1	1.9	2.3	2.3
United States	2.0	1.8	1.7	1.7	1.7	1.7	1.9	1.6	1.7	1.7	2.2	1.8	1.7
Euro area	1.9	1.7	1.8	1.9	1.7	1.7	1.8	1.8	1.8	1.8	1.7	1.8	1.8
Total OECD	1.8	1.7	1.7	1.5	1.7	1.8	1.8	1.6	1.7	1.8	1.9	1.7	1.7
Unit labour cost (total economy)													
Canada	1.3	1.6	1.5	1.5	1.8	1.6	1.4	1.4	1.5	1.4	1.5	1.6	1.4
France	0.5	1.1	1.3	1.1	1.6	1.2	1.1	1.5	1.3	1.2	0.4	1.4	1.3
Germany	-0.4	0.0	0.4	-1.2	-1.4	-1.0	1.5	1.4	1.3	1.0	0.9	-1.1	1.3
Italy	3.1	2.2	1.6	0.8	1.0	1.5	1.7	1.8	1.9	1.9	4.3	1.0	1.8
Japan	-3.9	-1.7	-1.3	-1.3	-1.1	-1.3	-1.5	-1.3	-1.2	-1.1	-2.7	-1.2	-1.3
United Kingdom	2.7	2.8	2.4	2.6	2.5	2.5	2.2	2.7	2.4	2.1	3.5	2.6	2.3
United States	0.7	2.2	2.0	2.2	2.0	1.9	2.5	1.7	1.8	1.8	1.3	2.3	1.9
Euro area	1.0	1.2	1.3	0.5	0.6	0.8	1.6	1.7	1.7	1.5	1.8	0.7	1.6
Total OECD	0.6	1.5	1.5	1.3	1.2	1.3	1.9	1.6	1.6	1.5	1.3	1.4	1.6
	Per cent of labour force												
Unemployment													
Canada	7.2	7.1	7.2	7.1	7.1	7.1	7.2	7.2	7.2	7.2	7.1	7.1	7.2
France	9.8	9.7	9.2	9.7	9.6	9.5	9.4	9.3	9.1	9.0	9.8	9.5	9.0
Germany	9.2	9.3	8.9	9.3	9.3	9.2	9.1	9.0	8.8	8.7	9.3	9.2	8.7
Italy	8.1	7.5	7.3	7.5	7.4	7.4	7.3	7.3	7.3	7.2	7.9	7.4	7.2
Japan	4.8	4.5	4.2	4.6	4.5	4.4	4.3	4.2	4.1	4.0	4.8	4.4	4.0
United Kingdom	4.7	4.7	5.0	4.7	4.7	4.8	4.9	5.0	5.1	5.2	4.7	4.8	5.2
United States	5.5	5.3	5.1	5.4	5.3	5.3	5.2	5.2	5.1	5.0	5.4	5.3	5.0
Euro area	8.8	8.6	8.3	8.7	8.6	8.6	8.4	8.4	8.2	8.2	8.8	8.6	8.2
Total OECD	6.6	6.5	6.3	6.5	6.5	6.4	6.4	6.3	6.3	6.2	6.5	6.4	6.2

Note: The adoption of new national account systems, SNA93 or ESA95, has been proceeding at an uneven pace among OECD member countries, both with respect to variables and the time period covered. As a consequence, there are breaks in many national series. Moreover, some countries are using chain-weighted price indices to calculate real GDP and expenditures components. See Table "National Account Reporting Systems and Base-years" at the beginning of the Statistical Annex and *OECD Economic Outlook* Sources and Methods *(http://www.oecd.org/eco/sources-and-methods)*.

a) Year-on -year growth rates in per cent.

b) For the United Kingdom, the euro area countries and the euro area aggregate, the Harmonised Index of Consumer Prices (HICP) is used.

Source: OECD Economic Outlook 76 database.

Annex Table 57. **Contributions to changes in real GDP in OECD countries**

As a per cent of real GDP in the previous period, seasonally adjusted at annual rates

	2003	2004	2005	2006
Australia				
Final domestic demand	5.1	5.3	3.9	3.8
Stockbuilding	1.1	-0.2	0.1	0.1
Net exports	-2.8	-1.9	-0.3	-0.4
GDP	3.3	3.6	3.8	3.6
Austria				
Final domestic demand	1.7	1.2	2.0	2.5
Stockbuilding	0.1	-0.2	0.0	0.0
Net exports	-1.5	0.7	0.2	0.1
GDP	0.8	1.8	2.3	2.6
Belgium				
Final domestic demand	1.6	1.9	2.1	2.6
Stockbuilding	-0.1	0.4	0.0	0.0
Net exports	-0.3	0.4	0.3	0.1
GDP	1.3	2.7	2.4	2.7
Canada				
Final domestic demand	3.4	3.6	3.5	3.2
Stockbuilding	0.9	-0.8	0.4	0.0
Net exports	-2.4	0.0	-0.7	-0.1
GDP	2.0	3.0	3.3	3.1
Czech Republic				
Final domestic demand	5.3	4.6	4.2	4.0
Stockbuilding	-0.4	0.6	0.0	0.0
Net exports	-2.2	-2.8	-0.9	-0.7
GDP	3.1	3.9	4.2	4.1
Denmark				
Final domestic demand	0.7	2.7	2.9	2.7
Stockbuilding	-0.4	0.2	0.1	0.0
Net exports	0.3	-0.5	-0.3	-0.1
GDP	0.5	2.4	2.7	2.6
Finland				
Final domestic demand	2.2	2.4	2.5	2.3
Stockbuilding	-0.2	1.0	-0.9	-0.1
Net exports	-0.5	0.9	1.2	0.8
GDP	2.1	3.1	2.8	3.1
France				
Final domestic demand	1.5	2.5	2.3	2.3
Stockbuilding	-0.2	0.7	0.3	0.0
Net exports	-0.8	-1.2	-0.5	-0.1
GDP	0.5	2.1	2.0	2.3
Germany				
Final domestic demand	-0.4	-0.8	0.5	1.7
Stockbuilding	0.9	1.0	0.3	-0.1
Net exports	-0.6	0.9	0.6	0.7
GDP	-0.1	1.2	1.4	2.3
Greece				
Final domestic demand	6.0	4.8	3.5	4.0
Stockbuilding	-0.1	-0.4	-0.1	0.0
Net exports	-1.3	-0.7	0.3	-0.5
GDP	4.5	3.8	3.2	3.5
Hungary				
Final domestic demand	5.4	4.5	3.5	3.4
Stockbuilding	0.3	0.4	0.3	0.0
Net exports	-2.8	-0.9	-0.2	0.2
GDP	2.9	3.9	3.6	3.5
Iceland				
Final domestic demand	8.0	8.4	7.7	5.9
Stockbuilding	-0.3	0.3	0.0	0.0
Net exports	-3.6	-2.6	-2.8	-1.1
GDP	4.1	5.9	5.2	4.8
Ireland				
Final domestic demand	2.3	3.1	3.6	3.2
Stockbuilding	0.5	0.0	0.0	0.0
Net exports	1.1	1.8	1.9	1.8
GDP	3.6	4.9	5.5	4.9
Italy				
Final domestic demand	0.7	1.7	2.1	2.5
Stockbuilding	0.6	-0.4	0.0	0.0
Net exports	-0.9	0.1	-0.4	-0.4
GDP	0.4	1.3	1.7	2.1
Japan				
Final domestic demand	1.4	2.9	1.8	1.8
Stockbuilding	0.3	0.2	0.0	0.0
Net exports	0.7	0.9	0.3	0.4
GDP	2.5	4.0	2.1	2.3
Korea				
Final domestic demand	0.7	1.2	2.7	3.1
Stockbuilding	-0.6	0.0	0.0	0.0
Net exports	2.8	4.0	1.5	1.9
GDP	3.1	5.0	4.5	5.0

Note: The adoption of new national account systems, SNA93 or ESA95, has been proceeding at an uneven pace among OECD member countries, both with respect to variables and the time period covered. As a consequence, there are breaks in many national series. Moreover, some countries are using chain-weighted price indices to calculate real GDP and expenditures components. See Table "National Account Reporting Systems and Base-years" at the beginning of the Statistical Annex and *OECD Economic Outlook* Sources and Methods *(http://www.oecd.org/eco/sources-and-methods)*. Totals may not add up due to rounding and/or statistical discrepancy.

Source: OECD Economic Outlook 76 database.

Annex Table 57. **Contributions to changes in real GDP in OECD countries *(cont'd)***

As a per cent of real GDP in the previous period

	2003	2004	2005	2006
Luxembourg				
Final domestic demand	0.1	2.9	3.2	2.8
Stockbuilding	2.0	0.0	0.0	0.0
Net exports	0.6	1.1	1.3	1.6
GDP	2.9	4.2	4.5	4.3
Mexico				
Final domestic demand	2.3	4.5	4.3	4.5
Stockbuilding	-1.7	-0.7	0.1	0.2
Net exports	0.7	0.4	-0.4	-0.4
GDP	1.3	4.2	3.9	4.2
Netherlands				
Final domestic demand	-0.7	0.2	0.3	1.6
Stockbuilding	0.2	0.1	0.1	0.2
Net exports	-0.4	1.1	0.9	0.5
GDP	-0.9	1.2	1.2	2.4
New Zealand				
Final domestic demand	6.0	7.6	2.4	2.7
Stockbuilding	-0.3	0.1	0.2	0.0
Net exports	-2.3	-2.8	-0.5	-0.2
GDP	3.2	4.8	2.1	2.6
Norway				
Final domestic demand	1.3	3.2	3.0	2.2
Stockbuilding	-0.8	0.9	0.2	0.0
Net exports	-0.1	-0.9	0.1	0.7
GDP	0.4	3.2	3.2	2.9
Poland				
Final domestic demand	1.9	3.7	4.1	4.3
Stockbuilding	0.6	1.3	0.1	0.2
Net exports	1.3	0.6	0.0	0.0
GDP	3.8	5.4	4.3	4.5
Portugal				
Final domestic demand	-3.0	2.0	2.5	3.5
Stockbuilding	0.0	0.0	-0.1	0.0
Net exports	1.8	-0.5	-0.2	-0.6
GDP	-1.2	1.5	2.2	2.8
Slovak Republic				
Final domestic demand	0.1	2.9	4.4	3.6
Stockbuilding	-2.3	1.3	0.5	-0.1
Net exports	6.4	0.8	-0.1	1.6
GDP	4.2	4.9	4.8	5.0
Spain				
Final domestic demand	3.2	3.5	3.3	3.6
Stockbuilding	0.1	0.0	0.0	0.0
Net exports	-0.8	-0.9	-0.5	-0.6
GDP	2.5	2.6	2.7	3.0
Sweden				
Final domestic demand	0.8	1.9	2.8	2.5
Stockbuilding	0.4	-0.8	0.4	0.0
Net exports	0.6	2.4	0.3	1.0
GDP	1.7	3.3	3.3	3.2
Switzerland				
Final domestic demand	0.4	2.3	2.0	2.1
Stockbuilding	-0.2	-0.4	0.1	-0.1
Net exports	-0.5	0.0	-0.2	0.1
GDP	-0.4	1.9	1.9	2.0
Turkey				
Final domestic demand	5.9	13.9	5.6	5.3
Stockbuilding	3.0	1.2	-0.1	0.1
Net exports	-3.1	-5.0	0.4	0.4
GDP	5.8	9.8	6.4	5.8
United Kingdom				
Final domestic demand	2.6	3.9	2.5	2.1
Stockbuilding	0.0	0.1	0.0	0.0
Net exports	-0.4	-0.7	0.1	0.2
GDP	2.2	3.2	2.6	2.4
United States				
Final domestic demand	3.6	4.5	3.5	3.5
Stockbuilding	-0.1	0.5	0.1	0.1
Net exports	-0.5	-0.6	-0.3	-0.1
GDP	3.0	4.4	3.3	3.6
Euro area				
Final domestic demand	0.9	1.3	1.7	2.3
Stockbuilding	0.3	0.3	0.1	0.0
Net exports	-0.6	0.1	0.1	0.1
GDP	0.6	1.8	1.9	2.5
Total OECD				
Final domestic demand	2.4	3.4	2.8	2.9
Stockbuilding	0.1	0.3	0.1	0.1
Net exports	-0.4	-0.1	0.0	0.1
GDP	2.2	3.6	2.9	3.1

Note: The adoption of new national account systems, SNA93 or ESA95, has been proceeding at an uneven pace among OECD member countries, both with respect to variables and the time period covered. As a consequence, there are breaks in many national series. Moreover, some countries are using chain-weighted price indices to calculate real GDP and expenditures components. See Table "National Account Reporting Systems and Base-years" at the beginning of the Statistical Annex and *OECD Economic Outlook* Sources and Methods *(http://www.oecd.org/eco/sources-and-methods).* Totals may not add up due to rounding and/or statistical discrepancy.

Source: OECD Economic Outlook 76 database.

Annex Table 58. **Household wealth and indebtedness**[a]

	1992	1993	1994	1995	1996	1997	1998	1999	2000	2001	2002	2003
Canada												
Net wealth	440.6	457.2	476.2	483.7	498.3	508.5	505.4	514.4	505.2	506.2	514.0	515.0
Net financial wealth	194.9	204.2	214.2	225.7	236.0	245.0	240.5	247.6	243.4	237.5	233.8	225.1
Non-financial assets	245.6	252.9	262.0	258.0	262.2	263.5	265.0	266.8	261.8	268.7	280.1	289.8
Financial assets	291.6	303.8	317.3	329.1	342.9	354.5	352.4	361.6	356.1	352.4	350.1	344.9
of which: Equities	52.2	58.4	63.6	66.3	74.8	84.9	92.0	92.5	94.1	98.4	95.4	94.5
Liabilities	96.7	99.5	103.1	103.4	106.8	109.6	112.0	114.0	112.7	114.9	116.2	119.8
of which: Mortgages	64.6	66.5	68.5	68.8	70.8	71.6	71.8	71.8	69.6	69.8	70.9	73.0
France												
Net wealth	510.4	516.0	494.8	507.7	533.7	557.6	578.0	643.9	630.2	616.1	606.6	..
Net financial wealth	173.1	188.9	166.5	195.0	220.2	241.6	262.2	310.5	282.6	255.2	226.5	240.5
Non-financial assets	337.3	327.1	328.4	312.7	313.5	316.0	315.8	333.4	347.6	361.0	380.1	..
Financial assets	253.4	271.4	251.1	262.9	288.9	310.8	336.1	385.8	359.2	336.8	302.5	319.1
of which: Equities	115.5	126.2	94.9	89.6	104.5	117.1	137.6	177.6	155.7	129.9	100.7	110.2
Liabilities	80.3	82.6	84.6	67.9	68.7	69.2	73.8	75.3	76.6	81.7	76.0	78.6
of which: Long-term loans	53.0	54.7	53.7	51.6	52.2	52.6	52.9	55.0	55.2	55.6	56.9	59.9
Germany												
Net wealth	465.6	481.8	486.4	496.0	502.8	512.8	515.6	522.7	511.8	501.5	499.5	508.9
Net financial wealth	124.1	134.4	130.3	135.4	140.5	152.0	155.2	167.3	162.2	162.9	160.0	170.6
Non-financial assets	341.4	347.4	356.2	360.6	362.3	360.8	360.3	355.4	349.6	338.6	339.5	338.3
Financial assets	209.9	225.4	227.3	236.0	245.2	259.5	266.2	281.5	276.2	274.2	271.8	282.2
of which: Equities	30.8	39.5	40.7	43.4	46.8	57.2	53.0	75.4	74.5	70.6	57.1	62.2
Liabilities	85.7	91.0	97.0	100.6	104.8	107.6	111.0	114.2	114.0	111.3	111.8	111.6
of which: Mortgages	50.3	53.8	58.0	61.0	64.5	67.1	68.5	71.9	72.2	72.0	73.5	76.5
Italy												
Net wealth	746.3	782.4	748.0	739.4	721.5	752.8	772.1	805.4	819.3	799.6	810.9	..
Net financial wealth	205.3	226.6	228.6	228.3	230.4	250.1	275.1	310.7	314.7	278.8	251.9	..
Non-financial assets	541.1	555.8	519.4	511.1	491.1	502.8	497.1	494.6	504.6	520.8	559.0	..
Financial assets	237.7	261.0	256.0	254.6	263.3	283.9	314.9	349.1	350.2	323.5	295.5	..
of which: Equities	47.9	54.4	49.3	46.5	50.9	76.5	114.9	162.9	156.5	121.1	87.9	..
Liabilities	30.6	31.8	31.9	30.6	32.0	29.9	32.2	36.0	37.5	37.5	39.3	..
of which: Medium and long-term loans	14.4	14.9	15.2	18.6	19.1	20.5	22.5	25.9	27.3	27.6	29.7	..
Japan												
Net wealth	789.6	772.3	768.7	757.0	767.0	758.7	740.4	768.9	764.2	764.3	753.1	..
Net financial wealth	253.5	263.1	280.3	288.9	302.4	306.8	303.3	339.2	343.0	354.4	361.4	..
Non-financial assets	536.1	509.2	488.4	468.1	464.6	451.9	437.1	429.8	421.2	410.0	391.7	..
Financial assets	380.8	395.2	412.2	426.1	436.3	441.1	437.1	473.2	478.5	491.9	497.2	..
of which: Equities	35.7	36.9	45.5	44.7	40.0	35.9	25.4	47.5	41.4	37.6	41.7	..
Liabilities	127.3	132.1	131.9	137.2	133.9	134.3	133.8	134.1	135.5	137.6	135.8	..
of which: Mortgages	51.6	53.8	56.0	58.6	60.2	54.3	55.0	57.8	59.5	62.1	61.7	..
United Kingdom												
Net wealth	546.6	582.9	543.9	555.8	569.3	617.0	665.3	748.9	733.4	669.2	674.9	724.5
Net financial wealth	234.1	278.7	257.1	285.6	291.0	336.2	352.8	407.5	370.2	305.8	249.9	269.1
Non-financial assets	312.5	304.2	286.8	270.2	278.3	280.8	312.5	341.3	363.2	363.4	425.1	455.4
Financial assets	343.5	385.2	364.7	392.2	395.6	440.8	461.1	519.1	483.5	423.0	378.7	412.7
of which: Equities	61.1	73.6	70.2	76.2	75.6	91.3	91.7	120.2	108.7	76.7	56.5	67.3
Liabilities	109.4	106.5	107.5	106.6	104.6	104.7	108.3	111.5	113.3	116.6	128.7	138.9
of which: Mortgages	79.0	78.3	79.5	78.1	77.2	76.1	78.5	80.8	81.8	84.2	92.7	102.0
United States												
Net wealth	479.9	489.6	479.1	509.3	529.2	565.7	584.5	632.4	584.7	551.5	506.4	545.2
Net financial wealth	274.0	284.0	276.9	305.6	327.3	362.9	379.0	420.1	368.8	327.7	274.3	302.2
Non-financial assets	205.8	205.5	202.2	203.8	201.9	202.8	205.6	212.4	215.9	223.8	232.1	243.0
Financial assets	361.2	373.8	368.9	399.3	422.8	459.5	476.6	521.9	471.7	434.6	385.4	420.4
of which: Equities	75.3	85.5	79.2	97.9	111.9	136.9	148.0	182.5	146.7	121.3	91.5	111.1
Liabilities	87.1	89.7	91.9	93.8	95.5	96.5	97.7	101.8	102.9	106.9	111.2	118.1
of which: Mortgages	62.3	63.6	63.8	63.5	64.2	64.7	65.6	68.3	68.9	72.9	78.0	83.9

a) Assets and liabilities are amounts outstanding at the end of the period, in per cent of nominal disposable income. Vertical lines between columns indicate breaks in the series due to changes in the definitions or accounting systems. Figures after the most recent breaks in the series are based on the UN System of National Accounts 1993 (SNA 93) and, more specifically, for European Union countries, on the corresponding European System of Accounts 1995 (ESA 95).
Households include non-profit institutions serving households. Net wealth is defined as non-financial and financial assets minus liabilities; net financial wealth is financial assets minus liabilities. Non-financial assets include stock of durable goods and dwellings, at replacement cost and at market value, respectively. Financial assets comprise currency and deposits, securities other than shares, loans, shares and other equity, insurance technical reserves; and other accounts receivable/payable. Not included are assets with regard to social security pension insurance schemes. Equities comprise shares and other equity, including quoted, unquoted and mutual fund shares. See also *OECD Economic Outlook* Sources and Methods *(http://www.oecd.org/eco/sources-and-methods).*

Sources: Canada: Statistics Canada, *National Balance Sheet Accounts.* France: INSEE, *Rapport sur les Comptes de la Nation* and *25 ans de Comptes de Patrimoine* (1969-1993) Banque de France, *Flow of Funds Accounts.* Germany: Deutsche Bundesbank, *Monthly Report* and *Financial accounts for Germany 1991 to 1999,* Special Statistical Publication, 2000. Italy: Banca d'Italia, *Supplements to the Statistical Bulletin*; Ando, A., L.Guiso, I.Visco (eds.), *Saving and the Accumulation of Wealth,* Cambridge University Press, 1994; OECD, *Financial Accounts of OECD countries*. Japan: Economic Planning Agency, Government of Japan, *Annual Report on National Accounts.* United Kingdom: Office for National Statistics, *United Kingdom National Accounts,* and *Financial Statistics.* United States: Federal Reserve Statistical Release, *Flow of Funds Accounts* of the United States.

Annex Table 59. **Central government financial balances**

Surplus (+) or deficit (-) as a percentage of nominal GDP

	1994	1995	1996	1997	1998	1999	2000	2001	2002	2003	2004	2005	2006
Canada	-4.6	-3.9	-2.0	0.7	0.8	0.9	1.9	1.3	0.8	0.4	0.3	0.3	0.2
France[a]	-4.9	-4.2	-3.7	-2.8	-2.9	-2.4	-2.1	-1.9	-3.2	-3.5	-2.8	-2.3	-2.3
Germany	-1.2	-1.4	-2.2	-1.6	-1.8	-1.6	1.4	-1.4	-1.7	-1.9	-1.7	-1.7	-1.2
Italy	-9.1	-7.7	-6.9	-2.7	-2.5	-1.5	-1.1	-2.7	-2.6	-2.4	-2.9	-3.1	-3.6
Japan[b]	-4.3	-4.4	-4.4	-3.9	-5.5	-7.7	-6.7	-6.2	-7.3	-7.1	-6.8	-6.7	-6.4
United Kingdom	-6.7	-5.5	-4.6	-2.2	0.3	1.2	4.1	0.8	-1.7	-3.7	-3.4	-3.4	-3.5
United States	-3.1	-2.7	-1.9	-0.6	0.5	1.1	1.9	0.4	-2.6	-3.7	-3.7	-3.5	-3.6
excluding social security	-4.0	-3.5	-2.8	-1.6	-0.7	-0.4	0.4	-1.2	-4.2	-5.1	-5.0	-5.0	-5.2
Total of above countries	-4.0	-3.6	-3.0	-1.6	-1.1	-1.0	0.1	-1.2	-3.1	-3.8	-3.7	-3.6	-3.5

Note: Central government financial balances include one-off revenues from the sale of mobile telephone licenses.

a) Data for 2005 include the payment by EDF in respect of the transfer of its pension liabilities to the government.

b) Data are only available for fiscal years beginning April 1 of the year shown. The 1998 deficit would rise by 5.3 percentage points of GDP if it included the central government's assumption of the debt of the Japan Railway Settlement Corporation and the National Forest Special Account.

Source: OECD Economic Outlook 76 database.

Annex Table 60. **Maastricht definition of general government gross public debt**

As a percentage of nominal GDP

	1994	1995	1996	1997	1998	1999	2000	2001	2002	2003	2004	2005	2006
Austria	63.4	67.9	67.6	63.8	64.2	66.5	65.8	66.1	65.7	64.5	64.3	64.6	65.0
Belgium	135.7	133.9	130.6	124.7	119.5	114.8	109.2	108.0	105.4	99.9	95.5	95.1	91.7
Czech Republic	..	..	..	12.2	12.9	13.4	18.2	25.3	28.8	37.8	39.1	41.1	42.5
Denmark	77.4	73.2	69.7	65.7	61.2	57.7	52.3	49.2	48.8	45.9	44.8	43.3	41.8
Finland	57.9	57.0	57.2	54.0	48.6	47.0	44.6	43.8	42.6	45.5	45.8	46.5	47.0
France	48.4	54.5	57.1	59.3	59.5	58.5	56.7	56.5	58.7	63.7	66.5	68.7	69.8
Germany	49.3	57.0	59.8	61.0	60.9	61.2	60.2	59.4	60.9	64.2	66.0	67.7	68.1
Greece[a]	107.9	108.7	111.3	108.2	105.8	105.2	114.0	114.7	112.5	109.9	112.1	111.4	107.2
Hungary	..	..	..	64.2	61.9	61.2	55.4	53.5	57.2	59.1	55.9	57.6	59.1
Ireland	89.5	81.9	73.4	64.6	53.7	48.7	38.3	35.9	32.7	32.1	29.3	26.9	25.3
Italy	124.8	124.2	123.2	120.5	116.8	115.5	111.1	110.6	107.9	106.1	105.1	104.7	104.4
Luxembourg	6.3	6.7	7.2	6.8	6.3	6.0	5.5	5.5	5.7	5.3	5.2	5.2	5.4
Netherlands	76.4	77.2	75.2	69.9	66.8	63.1	55.9	52.9	52.6	54.1	57.0	58.9	59.5
Poland	..	..	..	44.0	39.1	40.3	36.6	36.7	41.1	45.4	46.9	50.8	52.[illegible]
Portugal	62.1	64.3	62.9	59.1	55.0	54.3	53.3	55.8	58.4	60.3	60.5	61.7	63.[illegible]
Slovak Republic	..	..	30.6	33.1	34.0	47.2	49.9	48.7	43.4	42.8	40.1	38.9	37.7
Spain	61.1	63.9	68.1	66.6	64.6	63.1	61.1	57.5	54.4	50.7	49.7	47.6	45.6
Sweden	73.9	73.7	73.5	70.6	68.1	62.7	52.8	54.4	52.6	52.0	51.3	50.3	49.0
United Kingdom	48.6	51.8	52.3	50.8	47.7	45.1	42.0	38.8	38.3	39.8	41.2	42.7	44.3
Euro area	70.0	74.4	76.5	74.9	73.8	72.9	70.4	69.4	69.3	70.6	71.5	72.2	72.1

Note: For the period 1994-2003, gross debt figures are provided by Eurostat, the Statistical Office of the European Communities, unless more recent data are available, while GDP figures are provided by National Authorities. The 2004 to 2006 debt ratios are in line with the OECD projections for general government gross financial liabilities and GDP. See *OECD Economic Outlook* Sources and Methods *(http://www.oecd.org/eco/sources-and-methods).*

a) Recent revisions to Greek budgetary data suggest gross debt data of 114.0, 112.4 and 112.3 per cent of GDP in 1997-1999 respectively.

Source: OECD Economic Outlook 76 database.

Annex Table 61. **Monetary and credit aggregates: recent trends**

Annualised percentage change, seasonally adjusted

		Annual change (to 4th quarter)					Latest twelve months	
		1999	2000	2001	2002	2003		
Canada	M2	3.8	7.3	5.7	6.0	5.2	5.9	(Sep. 2004)
	BL[a]	5.9	7.3	5.2	5.1	4.8	7.4	(Aug. 2004)
Japan	M2+CD	3.1	2.0	3.1	2.9	1.5	2.0	(Sep. 2004)
	BL[a]	-0.6	2.5	-1.4	-3.1	-0.5	2.4	(Sep. 2004)
United Kingdom	M0	9.8	6.6	7.7	6.9	7.5	5.8	(Oct. 2004)
	M4	3.5	8.9	7.7	5.9	6.5	9.8	(Sep. 2004)
	BL[a]	8.1	12.8	8.4	9.3	8.6	11.7	(Sep. 2004)
United States	M2	6.2	6.1	10.2	6.7	5.3	4.5	(Oct. 2004)
	M3	7.7	9.3	12.7	6.4	4.6	4.9	(Oct. 2004)
	BL[a]	4.4	12.1	2.5	5.0	5.8	8.5	(Sep. 2004)
Euro area	M2	6.7	4.0	8.5	6.6	6.8	6.2	(Sep. 2004)
	M3	5.1	4.6	10.7	6.7	6.9	5.9	(Sep. 2004)
	BL[a]	6.6	5.9	7.2	3.8	5.6	5.9	(Sep. 2004)

a) Commercial bank lending.

Source: OECD Economic Outlook 76 database.

OECD ECONOMICS DEPARTMENT

A wide range of news and information about recent Economics Department studies and publications on a variety of topics is now regularly available via INTERNET on the OECD website at the following address: ***www.oecd.org/eco***. This includes links to the *Economics Department Working Papers* series (***www.oecd.org/eco/Working_Papers***), which can be downloaded free of charge, as well as summaries of recent editions in the *OECD Economic Surveys* (***www.oecd.org/eco/Country_Surveys***) series and the *OECD Economic Outlook* (***www.oecd.org/OECDEconomicOutlook***).

OECD ECONOMIC OUTLOOK

The *OECD Economic Outlook* Flashfile, containing a summary of the *Economic Outlook* forecasts is now available on INTERNET at the time of its preliminary publication (a month to six weeks before the final publication date) at the following address: ***www.oecd.org/eco/statistics***. This includes key macroeconomic variables for all OECD countries and regions in Excel format, which can be input directly into most statistical and analytical software. The *Economic Outlook* Flashfile is available free of charge.

Subscribers to the OECD Economic Outlook, in addition to the two print editions, also have access to an online (PDF) edition, published on internet six to eight weeks prior to the release of the print edition :

http://new.SourceOECD.org/periodical/oecdeconomicoutlook

The full set of historical time series data and projections underlying the *OECD Economic Outlook* is now available online as a **statistical database** via SourceOECD and on CD ROM. It contains approximately 4 000 macroeconomic time series for OECD countries and non OECD zones, beginning in 1960 and extending to the end of the published forecast horizon. Subscriptions to the database editions can be combined in sets with the subscriptions to the Print and PDF editions and can be made at any time of the year.

For more information, visit the OECD bookshop at ***www.oecd.org/bookshop***, or contact your nearest OECD supplier : ***www.oecd.org/publishing/distributors***.

OECD ECONOMIC SURVEYS

For more in-depth, country-by-country analysis, read the *OECD Economic Surveys*. By providing rich information on economic and policy developments, this series constitutes a must for financial institutions, multinational enterprises, consulting firms, universities and libraries. Each issue contains OECD assessments of:

- Recent macroeconomic performance and the short-term outlook, with policy focus on the appropriateness of monetary policy and the sustainability of fiscal policy.
- Structural policy and reforms in areas such as the labour markets, product markets, the financial system, taxation, health care and the environment.
- Specific structural themes, among which: tax reform, public expenditure, ageing populations, sustainable development, migration and competition.

Surveys are available for the following countries:

Australia
Austria
Belgium
Brazil
Canada
Chile
Czech Republic
Denmark
Finland
France
Germany
Greece
Hungary
Iceland
Ireland
Italy
Japan
Korea
Luxembourg
Mexico
Netherlands
New Zealand
Norway
Poland
Portugal
Romania
Russian Federation
Slovak Republic
Spain
Sweden
Switzerland
Turkey
United Kingdom
United States
and Euro Area

Available on subscription. You also create your own personalised collection by ordering just the books you need, for example, major seven OECD countries, European Union, Asia-Pacific, or Central and Eastern European countries, just a single country. For more information, register to the OECD newsletters at ***www.oecd.org/OECDdirect*** or visit the OECD bookshop at ***www.sourceoecd.org*** or send your order to:

For customers in Germany and Austria
OECD Sales Office
August-Bebel-Allee 6, D-53175 Bonn
Tel.: 49 228 959 1215
Fax: 49 228 959 1218
E-mail: bonn.contact@oecd.org
Internet: *www.oecd.org/deutschland*

For customers in North America
OECD Washington Center
2001 L Street N.W., Suite 650
Washington DC, 20036-4922 USA
Tel.: 1 202 785 6323
Fax: 1 202 785 0350
E-mail: washington.contact@oecd.org
Internet: *www.oecdwash.org*

For customers in Japan and Asia
OECD Tokyo Centre
3rd Floor, Nippon Press Center Building
2-2-1, Uchisaiwaicho
Chiyoda-ku, Tokyo 100-0011, Japan
Tel.: 81 3 5532 0021
Fax: 81 3 5532 0035
E-mail: center@oecdtokyo.org
Internet: *www.oecdtokyo.org*

For customers in Central and South America
OECD Mexico Centre
Av. Presidente Mazaryk 526
Colonia: Polanco
C.P. 11560, Mexico D.F.
Tel.: 52 555 281 3810
Fax: 52 555 280 0480
E-mail: mexico.contact@oecd.org
Internet: *rtn.net.mx/ocde*

For customers in the rest of the world
OECD Paris Centre
2, rue André-Pascal
75775 Paris Cedex 16, France
Tel.: 33 1 45 24 94 16
Fax: 33 1 45 24 94 53
E-mail: sourceoecd@oecd.org
Internet: *www.sourceoecd.org*

Online ordering: *www.oecd.org/publications*
(secure payment with credit card)

OECD PUBLICATIONS, 2, rue André-Pascal, 75775 PARIS CEDEX 16
PRINTED IN FRANCE
(12 2004 76 1 P) ISBN 92-64-00776-8 – No. 53793 2004
ISSN 0474-5574